Gardening
ALL-IN-ONE
FOR
DUMMIES®

**by the Editors at the National Gardening Association and
Bob Beckstrom, Karan Davis Cutler, Kathleen Fisher,
Phillip Giroux, Judy Glattstein, Mike MacCaskey,
Bill Marken, Charlie Nardozzi, Sally Roth,
Marcia Tatroe, Lance Walheim,
and Ann Whitman**

WILEY

Wiley Publishing, Inc.

Gardening All-in-One For Dummies®

Published by
Wiley Publishing, Inc.
909 Third Avenue
New York, NY 10022
www.wiley.com

Copyright © 2003 by Wiley Publishing, Inc., Indianapolis, Indiana

Published by Wiley Publishing, Inc., Indianapolis, Indiana

Published simultaneously in Canada

For general information on our other products and services or to obtain technical support, please contact our Customer Care Department within the U.S. at 800-762-2974, outside the U.S. at 317-572-3993, or fax 317-572-4002.

Wiley also publishes its books in a variety of electronic formats. Some content that appears in print may not be available in electronic books.

Library of Congress Control Number: 2002114772

ISBN: 0-7645-2555-7

1B/RX/QS/QT/IN

Manufactured in the United States of America

10 9 8 7 6 5 4 3 2

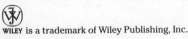

About the Authors

National Gardening Association: The National Gardening Association is the largest member-based, nonprofit organization of home gardeners in the United States. For more information about the National Gardening Association, write to 180 Flynn Ave., Burlington, VT 05401 USA; or visit its Web site at www.garden.org.

Bob Beckstrom, coauthor of *Landscaping For Dummies,* is a licensed general contractor. He lives in northern California and enjoys building things, spending time outdoors, and sharing what he's learned with other people. Bob has taught adult courses in house building and remodeling at The Owner Builder Center in Berkeley, California; and has written and edited extensively on home-improvement topics, including *Decks & Patios For Dummies.*

Karan Davis Cutler, coauthor of *Herb Gardening For Dummies,* is a former magazine editor and newspaper columnist and the author of seven other garden books. She publishes regularly in horticultural magazines and is an eight-time winner of the Quill & Trowel Award from the Garden Writers Association of America.

Kathleen Fisher, coauthor of *Herb Gardening For Dummies,* is former editor of *The American Gardener,* published by the American Horticultural Society. A longtime newspaper reporter, she now works as a freelance writer and editor.

Phillip Giroux, coauthor of *Landscaping For Dummies,* graduated from the University of Arizona with a degree in landscape architecture and ornamental horticulture. He established his landscape designing and building firm in 1978, and Philip is responsible for numerous large-scale projects, such as the Los Angles County Museum of Arts Sculpture and Japanese Pavilion Garden. Phillip has served as L.A. Chapter President for the California Landscape Contractors Association and is a member of the Royal Horticulture Society.

Judy Glattstein, author of *Flowering Bulbs For Dummies* as well several other gardening books, is a garden consultant. She lectures extensively across the United States and abroad, and has twice spoken for the Royal Horticultural Society at their Great Autumn Show in London.

Mike MacCaskey, coauthor of *Gardening For Dummies,* received a bachelor of science degree in ornamental horticulture from California State Polytechnic University, San Luis Obispo in 1976. He served as Editor-in-Chief of Vermont-based *National Gardening Magazine,* and his magazine writing has been honored by both the Western Magazine Publishers Association and the Garden Writers of America.

Bill Marken, author of *Annuals For Dummies, Container Gardening For Dummies,* and coauthor of *Gardening For Dummies,* is the editor of *Rebecca's Garden Magazine,* a publication from Hearst Magazines Enterprises based on a popular television show. Bill served as Editor-in-Chief of *Sunset, the Magazine of Western Living,* from 1981 to 1996. Earlier in his career, he wrote for the magazine's garden section, pitched in on several editions of the best-selling *Western Garden Book,* and generally nurtured his interests in subjects related to gardening, landscaping, travel, and other aspects of the good life in the West.

Charlie Nardozzi, author of *Vegetable Gardening For Dummies,* graduated from the University of Vermont in 1981 with a degree in plant and soil science. Charlie then spent three years in the Peace Corps in Thailand, helping farmers grow everything from rice to garlic, chili peppers, and mangoes. He returned to the United States and received a master's degree in education, again from the University of Vermont. After working as a landscaper, he served as a horticulturist at the National Gardening Association for more than 10 years.

Sally Roth, contributor to *Landscaping For Dummies,* is a lifelong naturalist, gardener, and writer. Her writing credits include books and magazine articles for several publishers. When she isn't digging in her garden or out walking in the woods looking at birds, Sally listens to blues and folk music, reads, and plays a mean game of Scrabble.

Marcia Tatroe, author of *Perennials For Dummies,* is a garden designer, lecturer, and writer who's been fortunate to have the opportunity to live and garden in areas as diverse as Highland, California; Tacoma, Washington; Lompoc, California; the Netherlands; and south-central England. Marcia, also a former Master Gardener of several years for Colorado State University's Cooperative Extension Program, says that tending the garden is one of her greatest passions, and she hopes that it's contagious.

Lance Walheim, author of *Roses For Dummies* and *Lawn Care For Dummies,* and coauthor of *Landscaping For Dummies,* graduated from the University of California, Berkeley, with a degree in botany. Shortly after, he started writing and researching books on gardening and since has authored or contributed to over 40 titles. He also has served as a writer for *Sunset* and *National Gardening* magazines.

Ann Whitman, author of *Organic Gardening For Dummies* and *Trees & Shrubs For Dummies,* earned a bachelor of science degree in plant and soil science at the University of Vermont and went on to complete a master of arts in landscape design in Massachusetts. She's been tending her own patches of soil for more than 25 years.

Publisher's Acknowledgments

We're proud of this book; please send us your comments through our Dummies online registration form located at www.dummies.com/register/.

Some of the people who helped bring this book to market include the following:

Acquisitions, Editorial, and Media Development

Compilation Editor: Tamara Castleman

Senior Project Editor: Alissa D. Schwipps

Acquisitions Editor: Pam Mourouzis

Copy Editor: Christina Guthrie

Acquisitions Coordinator: Holly Grimes

Technical Editor: Patricia Yuu Pan

Editorial Manager: Jennifer Ehrlich

Editorial Assistants: Melissa Bennett and Elizabeth Rea

Cartoons: Rich Tennant, www.the5thwave.com

Production

Project Coordinator: Maridee Ennis

Layout and Graphics: Amanda Carter, Carrie Foster, Joyce Haughey, Kristin McMullan, Jacque Schneider, Jeremey Unger, Erin Zeltner

Proofreaders: John Tyler Connoley, John Greenough, Betty Kish

Indexer: Sherry Massey

Publishing and Editorial for Consumer Dummies

    Diane Graves Steele, Vice President and Publisher, Consumer Dummies

    Joyce Pepple, Acquisitions Director, Consumer Dummies

    Kristin A. Cocks, Product Development Director, Consumer Dummies

    Michael Spring, Vice President and Publisher, Travel

    Brice Gosnell, Publishing Director, Travel

    Suzanne Jannetta, Editorial Director, Travel

Publishing for Technology Dummies

    Andy Cummings, Vice President and Publisher, Dummies Technology/General User

Composition Services

    Gerry Fahey, Vice President of Production Services

    Debbie Stailey, Director of Composition Services

Contents at a Glance

Table of Contents

Introduction

· ·

Gardening has moved out of the vegetable patch and the flower bed. Gardening now encompasses our lives — if you have a yard, even a very tiny one, you're a gardener. If you have a sunny windowsill, you're a gardener. National surveys show that gardening has become the most popular, least exclusive hobby of all. As you read these very words, hundreds of hard-core horticulturists may be laboring over their beloved specimens. But millions of other people are simply enjoying their time outdoors and striving to make their little corner of the world more peaceful and beautiful — a better place to live. And that's what this book is about.

About This Book

You have in your hands a gardening encyclopedia in miniature — all you need to know to get off to a good start. No matter what area of gardening interests you — growing roses or perennials or just cutting the grass — you'll find good advice here. In every chapter of every book, our basic goal is to give you the information you need to go out and plant or prune what you want. But novices aren't the only ones who can find this book useful. Gardening is such a huge topic that no one ever comes close to knowing everything about it. (That's one reason why gardening has become one of the most popular hobbies of all time.) This book offers lists of plants that you can choose from to create a beautiful garden. We list the plants by the common name first, followed by the botanical name. For international gardeners, we've added approximate metric equivalents for plant heights, planting depths, and other pertinent measurements.

Conventions Used in This Book

To help you pick out information from a page, we use the following conventions throughout the text to make elements consistent and easy to understand:

- Any Web addresses appear in `mono font`.

- New terms appear in *italics* and are closely followed by an easy-to-understand definition.

- **Bold** highlights the action parts of numbered steps or keywords in bulleted lists.

✔ Sidebars, which look like text enclosed in a shaded gray box, consist of information that's interesting to know but not necessarily critical to your understanding of the chapter or section's topic.

How to Use This Book

You can use this book in a few different ways:

✔ **Read from cover to cover.** You're certainly welcome to read this book from front to back. The plot isn't as sizzling as a summer beach read, but the book starts out broadly and then moves to more specific topics.

✔ **Skip all over the place.** Unlike a novel, you're not going to miss crucial information if you start on page 500 instead of page 1. Likewise, the book is designed to make perfect sense if you choose to read a patchwork of pages, moving from Book I to Book VI back to Book III. Anytime another book offers more information on a topic, we've provided a cross-reference so that you won't come up one spade short of a shovel.

✔ **Find what you need and move on.** The table of contents and index are good places to find the topic that most interests you. Feel free to bone up on one area and then put the book down. If you just bought a new home, landscaping (Book II) may be all you can handle for one gardening season. Or perhaps annuals (Book V) are your passion this year. When you suddenly get an urge to plant a few autumn bulbs (Book VI), this book will be happily waiting for you.

✔ **Use the book as a knee cushion while you plant.** You won't get much information that way, but you did buy the book so you could spend time outside, right? The bottom line is that this book is designed to be used in the way that is most useful to you!

Foolish Assumptions

In order to provide the most thorough information to the greatest number of readers, we've made one assumption about you: You're a gardener (or hope to become one) who wants a comprehensive book to answer your gardening questions and concerns. This book provides solid information for the beginning gardener whose total experience is looking longingly at seed packets. It also provides tidbits, tips, and tricks for experienced gardeners who are ready to take their gardens to the next level.

How This Book Is Organized

This reference is organized into seven books. Each book looks at a complete subject area. Because some areas of gardening are the same no matter where you live or what you grow, we've sprinkled cross references throughout the book. If you want the basics on improving your soil, for example, read Chapter 3 in Book I. Then if you want to understand soil issues specific to growing herbs, turn to Chapter 5 in Book VII. Every book discusses care and maintenance, and the books about specific types of plants each offer a listing of plants to consider for your own garden.

Book 1: Gardening Basics

This book takes an in-depth look at gardening without focusing on any specific kind of plant. Here, you'll find all you need to know about starting a garden — from understanding your microclimate to the tools you most need in your garden. We also cover pests and diseases common to any garden, along with recommendations for safe and effective cures.

Book 11: Garden Design

Mother Nature plants randomly, but most human gardeners find that they fare better if they begin with a plan. This book gives you guidelines for creating and building your landscape. Most landscapes incorporate containers and some sort of lawn, so you'll find chapters on those, as well.

Book 111: Roses

Most every gardener wants at least one or two rosebushes gracing the landscape, but growing roses can be an intimidating adventure. This book unmasks the mystery behind growing roses by providing all the information you need to select, plant, and maintain roses in your garden.

Book 1V: Perennials

Perennials are those plants that, like Labor Day telethons, return year after year. They're lovely, and they mix well with the other plants you may choose to grow. Gardeners often grow perennials in raised beds, so we show you how to build your own. This book gives you all you need for a yearly bounty of beautiful, healthy plants.

Book V: Annuals

Annuals are the one-hit wonders of the gardening world. They shine with magnificent, showy color throughout the summer, and then go to seed while the whole world watches. Annuals are perfect if you like to experiment, want to grow in containers, or enjoy being entertained by a new bevy of stars every season. This book shows you how to choose, grow, and maintain these sparkling plants.

Book VI: Bulbs

Bulbs are odd looking little creatures. Much like trolls in fairy tales, they're often shriveled and ugly and spend much of their life underground. The flowers they shoot forth, however, are all fairy princesses. This book helps you provide the happily ever after to the bulbs in your garden.

Book VII: Vegetables and Herbs

Growing your own food (and often medicine, in the case of herbs) is immensely satisfying. If you've ever stopped by a roadside stand or a farmer's market, you know how good fresh vegetables and herbs taste. Now, multiply the taste by the satisfaction that comes from knowing that you did the growing. This book points you in the right direction by offering everything you need to grow your dinner from planning to harvest.

Icons Used in This Book

All *For Dummies* books use icons to point out information that's particularly interesting or helpful. We use the following icons in this book:

Certain practices are particularly helpful — or particularly harmful to the environment. This icon alerts you to things you can do (or avoid doing) to protect the environment and its inhabitants.

Gardeners speak a language all their own. This icon points out terms that will make you sound like an old pro whether you chat with a neighbor across the fence or with a garden expert at your local nursery.

 Oddly enough, this icon points out things that you should remember as you work in your garden. Who'da thunk it?

 Paragraphs marked with this icon offer you some piece of advice that's guaranteed to make your gardening life easier or more enjoyable.

Things in the garden can hurt you, and you can introduce things to the garden that hurt the plants or other creatures who live there. This icon alerts you to some garden danger.

Where to Go from Here

To the garden, the nursery, or your favorite seed catalog! Get the info you need from this book and then get outside and start gardening. That's why you bought this book, right?

Book I
Gardening Basics

The 5th Wave   By Rich Tennant

In this book . . .

To paraphrase a song from the *Sound of Music,* starting at the beginning is a very good place to start. This book starts from the ground up to give you a sweeping overview of the gardening process. We tell you how to understand your climate, recognize the type of soil you have, and choose the appropriate fertilizers for your plot of land.

Pruning plants is essential to a healthy garden, but improper pruning can do a great deal of damage. You can find information here on the proper pruning process, which involves using the right tools for the job. Every gardener needs good tools, but the huge number of tools available in garden centers and discount stores can be intimidating — and expensive — for a new gardener. We save you time and money by listing all the must-have gardening tools, along with some that are just plain fun to have in your tool shed.

Finally, this book tells you how to keep your garden healthy and free from detrimental insects and disease. Like doctors, our motto is "first do no harm," so the tips and tricks you'll find here are environmentally friendly and designed to keep your family and pets safe and healthy as well.

Here are the Contents of Book I at a glance:

Chapter 1

Getting Your Garden Off the Ground

. . . .

In This Chapter

▶ Understanding what plants need from you

▶ Knowing what your garden can do for you

▶ Speaking garden-ese

. . . .

*W*e could begin a conversation about gardening by discussing some heavy-duty scientific terms, such as *cotyledon, cambium,* and the ever-popular *pith.* Or we could start talking about beautiful gardens like we're fine-art critics — employing words like *composition, energy, focal point,* and such. In fact, the chance to combine science and art is what draws many people to gardening in the first place — especially if you throw in a little farming and a few old wives' tales.

However, in this chapter, our only goal is to get you through a few basic principles of plant growth and garden planning, so that you can rush out into the yard when the weather's right for planting and the soil is ripe for digging.

Making Plants Grow, Not Die

Like other living things, plants have certain requirements for good health. For example, they require the right amounts of sunlight, moisture, and nutrients. Plants also need an equitable range of temperatures — neither too hot nor too cold.

When selecting plants, you can meet their requirements in one of two ways:

✔ **The backward approach:** Select your favorite plants and then do your best to alter the growing conditions at the planting site to meet their needs. (You can change the growing conditions by adding sprinkler irrigation, incorporating fertilizer, hauling in fresh topsoil, pruning some trees, or covering plants with blankets in winter.)

✔ **The better approach:** Study the conditions at the planting site first and then choose plants that grow under those conditions. The better you match plants to the planting site, the longer the plants will live, the better the plants will look, and the less work (watering, pruning, fertilizing, and controlling pests) you'll have to do to care for them.

Climate and microclimates

You need to match a plant to a planting site on both a large and a small scale. On a large scale, a plant needs to be adapted to the general climate of the area in which it lives. Can the plant withstand winter's low temperatures and summer's high temperatures? Is the annual rainfall enough to keep the plant alive, or will it need supplemental irrigation? Understanding your climate is a huge step toward successful gardening; in fact, Chapter 2 in Book I is devoted to climates.

On a smaller scale, can the plant grow well in the localized climate of your yard or the planting site? Smaller climates, called *microclimates,* can be quite a bit different from your area's overall climate. For example, your house may cast shadows that make the northern side of your house cooler and shadier than its southern side. Or, a planting site located beside a white, west-facing wall can be several degrees warmer than the rest of the yard because of the reflected heat from the wall.

Sun or shade

All plants need light to grow properly. However, the amount of light that plants need varies.

Many plants require full sun for at least six to eight hours per day. Plants that don't get enough sunlight become *leggy* (long, spindly stems), as if stretching out for more light. Plants that don't get enough sunlight also tend to flower poorly.

Note one obvious rule for gardening in the shade: Put shade-loving plants in the shade. Sun-worshipping plants just won't make it. Don't fret, though. You can choose from hundreds of incredible shade-loving plants (some with showy flowers and others with attractive foliage and form).

Some plants prefer shady conditions for the entire day (or for at least part of the day). Shade comes in more than one type, and each type of shade creates a different microclimate. For example, consider the area on the east side of your house. For at least half a day — in the morning — this area is sunny and warm. In the afternoon, the same area is shady.

The west side of the house is usually just the opposite — shady in the morning but hot and sunny in the afternoon. Heavy, all-day shade appears on the north side of the house, and you find filtered shade under trees. To further confuse the matter, shade can change with the seasons as trees lose their leaves and as the sun moves on the horizon. And in the hottest climates, some normally sun-loving plants prefer at least partial afternoon shade.

To complicate matters a little more, a plant's shade tolerance varies both by region and by specific garden conditions. For example, many plants that need full sun in cool northern climates (or in coastal areas) tolerate or require some afternoon shade when grown in warm southern climates.

Soil and water

The kind of soil in your garden — heavy clay or porous sand, for example — and soil moisture are closely related. Chapter 3 in Book I details the importance of these two factors and the ways in which they affect plant growth. Whether you see desert, snow, or palm trees when you look out your window, you can find plants that are well adapted to almost every situation. Wet, soggy clay soil is very difficult to correct, but certain plants can grow, and even thrive, under those conditions. Choosing plants to fit existing soil conditions is usually much easier than trying to alter the existing conditions to fit the plant.

Native plants

Nothing epitomizes the principle of choosing plants appropriate to the site more than growing *native plants*. Natives are plants that grow naturally in a specific region or locality. Over hundreds (probably thousands) of years, these plants have become superbly adapted to the exact conditions of the areas to which they're native. In those areas, or in similar areas, native plants grow with health and vigor and without the help of gardeners — abilities that make them very valuable as landscape plants.

Native plants are becoming very popular in many areas, particularly in arid regions of the western United States. Thirsty, nonnative plants are impractical in these areas because they use too much water — a precious resource out there. Local native plants can get by on what nature provides. And conserving natural resources always makes sense.

Using native plants also helps the native fauna — the birds, butterflies, squirrels, and other local animals — that depend on native plants for food and shelter. Many retail nurseries can help you select native plants. Some mail-order catalogs also specialize in native plants, especially wildflowers.

Exploring Uses for Your Garden

True, you can get some plants, stick them in the ground, and let them go at that. But many people want a "garden," which, by our definition, contains enough organization and space to allow room for growing plants, plus serve other purposes — playing, relaxing, outdoor dining, entertaining, and more.

A garden can make your life healthier, more comfortable, more colorful, and more convenient. A garden lets you expand your living area to the outdoors, harvest fresh food, and pick your own flowers. Take a look at the different ways that a garden can enhance your life:

- **A private getaway:** Imagine taking a vacation in your own backyard or relaxing in a shady spot, secluded from the hustle and bustle of daily living. This dream can be your reality, if you begin by creating a private area for your own pleasure.

- **A place for entertaining:** Whether you like large get-togethers with extended family or business associates or a quiet dinner with a few friends, your garden can provide an ideal atmosphere.

- **A playground for Junior . . . or Spot:** Remember, though, that children and pets have different garden interests than adults; you may want to take that into account when planning your garden.

- **A private flower shop:** Cutting an armful of flowers from your own garden and bringing them indoors is so satisfying. If you like freshly cut flowers, be sure to leave enough space to grow flowers for cutting and for displaying. (Several books in this reference deal specifically with flowers; just flip to the Table of Contents for more specifics.)

- **A personal grocery store:** One of your garden's most delicious aspects is its ability to produce wonderful vegetables, fruits, and herbs (see Book VII). You can grow gourmet produce and rare and special crops, and you can do so organically (see Chapter 3 in Book II).

- **A place to relax:** Anywhere that seems cozy and pleasant is a great place to put a sitting nook. Start with a comfortable bench or chair and position it in shade beneath a magnificent oak, at the end of your vegetable garden, or at the back of your yard near the swing set. If you put in all-weather footing (such as gravel or mulch), you can sit outside regardless of the soil conditions.

The possibilities for your garden are almost endless. Take some time to jot down everything you may possibly want in your yard, and then use this book to pull all your needs and wishes together in a garden plan.

Getting to Know Garden Speak

The language spoken in gardening circles can be quirky. For example, dirt isn't just *dirt*, it's *soil*. Dirt is what you make mud pies with; it's the stain on your shirt. Soil, on the other hand, is full of promise and good nutrients. And some gardenholics tend to go on and on about plant names. You may catch them at the nursery asking, "Which Latin name is *most* correct, the old one or the new one?" or "What is the proper pronunciation for that plant?" Real garden snobs even get into heated debates about how to spell a particular plant name. Don't be too hard on these people; they can't help themselves. Besides, you may find yourself behaving the same way someday.

Knowing something about plant names helps you appreciate gardening more — and helps you get through this book.

The fancy name

The proper (scientific) *botanical name* of a plant consists of two parts, much in the same way that people have a first and a last name. However, in plant language, the last name comes first.

The most important name is the *genus* — the "Smith" of Joe Smith, if you will. (The genus name always begins with a capital letter when used as part of a multipart name.) A genus is a group of closely related plants. Just as in your own family, some of the plant cousins look very much alike, while others don't bear much resemblance at all. Also like your family, some closely related individuals have very different comfort levels. One uncle lives in Phoenix, Arizona, and loves the heat, but his sister thinks that Oxford, England, is quite warm enough. Plants are the same way.

The second name, the "Joe" part of Joe Smith, is the *species* name. The species name usually describes some feature of the plant or its preferred habitat, or serves as a tribute to whoever discovered the plant. But the species name is disguised in pseudo-Latin, of course, just to keep things interesting. Consider, for example, *Hosta undulata*. *Hosta* is the genus name. The species name, *undulata*, describes the undulating shape of the leaf.

The plain, old-fashioned, natural species of some plants acquire new status in the face of prodigiously hybridized plants — tulips, for example. In those cases, the norm for the plant is some kind of hybrid of indeterminate botanical origin. That's why when gardeners finally have in their gardens an actual natural, nonhybridized type of tulip, they say something like, "And this is my species tulip." Gardeners are funny, aren't they? (**Note:** In this book, we use the abbreviation *sp.* for *species* and *spp.* for its plural.)

Occasionally, a third name follows the species name — the *variety*. Varieties are members of the same species but are distinctive enough to deserve their own name, which is preceded by the abbreviation "var." in roman type — for example, *Rosa gallica* var. *officinalis*.

Another part of a botanical name is the "cultivated variety," or *cultivar*. Whoever discovered or created the plant decided that it was special enough to have its own name. And the cultivar is also special enough to be maintained by cuttings, grafting, line-bred seed propagation, or tissue culture. The cultivar name, which appears after the species or variety name, is the only part of the botanical name that isn't in italics but is always enclosed with single quotation marks. For example, a very nice form of *Lychnis coronaria,* with a white flower and pink blush, is called *Lychnis coronaria* 'Angel's Blush'.

Common names

Of course, ordinary people don't go around using long Latin botanical names in everyday conversation. Instead, they use a sort of botanical nickname, called a *common name*. Common names are less formal and easier to pronounce than botanical names. They're also less precise. Just as your Aunt Norma calls you "Pumpkin" and Uncle Bob calls you "Big Guy," many plants have several nicknames.

Often, the common name describes some distinguishing characteristic of the plant. For example, the plant called blue star has starry blue flowers. Sometimes, the origin of the name is lost in the mythology of a former time. Does anyone have a clue just who was the Susan of black-eyed Susan fame?

Finding that several unrelated flowers share the same common name isn't unusual at all. Unfortunately, regular English flower names are often just as silly as their highfalutin Latin cousins, if for different reasons. For example, two distinct plants share the name "mock orange," and at least five different plants go by "dusty miller." At least three unrelated perennials are called coneflowers: *Echinacea purpurea,* the *Rudbeckia* genus, and the *Ratibida* genus. On the other hand, many plants have no common name! Go figure.

The long and short of it is that you need to pay some attention to plant names — if only to avoid buying and planting the wrong plant.

Chapter 2

Zoning Out in Your Climate

*P*ermanent plants — trees, shrubs, ground covers, herbaceous (non-woody) perennials, and vines — need to survive weather conditions that vary year-round in your garden: cool, wet weather, extreme heat or cold, and drought, for example. As a gardener, then, you need to understand plant hardiness and your USDA or heat zone. Year-round conditions aren't an issue for most vegetables and similar annuals — plants that complete their life cycle (from germination to flowering to seed formation to death) in one growing season. What's important for annuals and vegetables is the *length* of that growing season, the number of days between frosts. This chapter gives you the foundation for understanding your plants, your climate, and your growing season.

Understanding Plant Hardiness

Gardeners are keenly aware of the seasonal effects of temperature, particularly freezing temperatures, on the growth of landscape plants. Terms such as *cold hardy, frost hardy,* and *winter hardy* describe plants that can survive varying degrees of freezing temperatures without injury during winter dormancy. Some very large and substantial plants curl their toes and turn mushy if exposed long enough to low temperatures. Imagine a banana tree thriving all summer in Duluth, Minnesota, and then imagine what happens to it in September. On the other hand, some plants can survive freezing — even frigid — temperatures. Some escape the cold by hiding underground or under snow until spring.

These plants include the bulbs and many perennials. Others, such as hardy trees and shrubs, undergo metabolic changes between summer and winter.

A plant's genetic capacity to acclimate determines cold hardiness. When plants *acclimate,* they transform themselves from a nonhardy to hardy condition that allows them to withstand freezing temperatures. But temperature alone isn't the only criterion of hardiness. Many plants aren't injured by winter's minimum temperatures, but in spring and fall as they adjust to changing weather. At those times, while not growing at full tilt, plants aren't fully hardy, either. Consequently, determining where and when a plant is hardy can be complicated. Temperatures are crucial, but so are a region's climate patterns and how the plant responds.

Winter injury is easy to diagnose when you see lots of brown leaves on an evergreen plant, injury or death of flower buds, or splitting bark. But, sometimes, damage from winter temperatures is difficult to see, manifested only in delayed bud development or slightly reduced growth.

The safest course to ensure plant adaptability is to grow plants native to your particular region. Such plants most likely have the constitution to survive in your garden. And for the most part, local nurseries stock only plants that are known to survive in their region. Playing it safe isn't always fun, though. If you want to experiment a little, you need some way to compare the nursery gardens' climates with the climate where the plant grows well. Zone maps play a critical role here. Most often, when people refer to their growing zone they're talking about which USDA zone they live in.

Peering at the USDA Plant Hardiness Zone Map

The U.S. Department of Agriculture's Plant Hardiness Zone Map is the most widely used hardiness zone map. The map (shown in the color insert) has been so useful for gardeners in the United States that the system has been extended to Europe and other regions. The USDA zone map is the one that most gardeners in the United States use, and the one that most garden magazines, catalogs, and books currently use.

The USDA zone map divides North America into zones based on the average annual minimum temperature. Each zone is 10°F (–12°C) warmer (or colder) in an average winter than the adjacent zone. North America encompasses 20 zones, numbered 1 through 11. (Zones 2 through 10 are subdivided into *a* and *b* regions where average minimum temperatures differ by 5°F, or 15°C. We don't include the subzones in this book because these designations exist only for North America.) Western Europe has 10 zones (numbered 1 through 10).

The sun sets in the West

In the western United States (west of the 100th meridian, which runs roughly through the middle of North and South Dakota and down through Texas, west of Laredo), the USDA map is less useful than in other regions. The key problem is the map's absolute reliance on *average winter minimum temperature* — a system that can equate regions of climates that differ in every way but temperature, such as San Diego and Florida.

If you live in western North America, we suggest that you check out the zone maps featured

in the *Sunset Western Garden Book* (Sunset Publishing Corp.). This zone system is based on what plants grow where rather than on a single feature of climate, such as minimum temperature. Many garden experts have contributed to the Sunset zone maps over the years, so these zones reflect the plants that thrive there. You can also check out this zone system at Sunset's Web site, `www.sunset.com/sunset/Magazine/Sections/Garden/gardengateway.html`.

These zone maps link regions that share an average winter minimum temperature. For instance, typical winters in Colorado Springs, Colorado; Albany, New York; and Prague, Czechoslovakia, reach –20°F (–29°C), so each city is in USDA Zone 5. The climate in these distant cities isn't necessarily the same, and the same plants may not grow well in all three cities. But the average winter minimum temperatures are very similar, which is one of the key factors that determine plant survivability. All the plants in this book bear the code for a USDA hardiness zone. If you live in one of the plant's recommended zones, you have some assurance that the plant is hardy enough to survive winter.

Unfortunately, no zone map — including the USDA map — is perfect. In the eastern half of North America, the USDA map doesn't account for the beneficial effect of a snow cover over perennial plants; the regularity or absence of freeze-thaw cycles; or soil drainage during cold periods. Other factors that determine plant survival that this zone map can't accommodate include the amount and distribution of rainfall (or availability of irrigation water), and soil conditions.

Peeking at the AHS Plant Heat-Zone Map

The significance of winter's lowest temperatures decreases as we shift from places where winter freezes can kill many plants to areas where freezes merely mean frost on lawns and windshields. Obviously, winter lows above 20°F (–6.6°C), and especially lows in the high 20s, are much less damaging than lower temperatures. But on the other hand, areas with mild winter temperatures often have soaring summer temperatures. Gardeners have discovered that summer high temperatures can limit plant survival just as surely as winter low temperatures.

In 1997, the American Horticultural Society published a zone map that accounts for a plant's adaptability to heat. Called the *AHS Plant Heat-Zone Map* (or the *Heat Map*), this 12-zone map of the United States indicates the average number of days each year when given regions experience temperatures of 86°F (30°C) or higher. According to the AHS, 86°F is the temperature at which many common garden plants begin to suffer damage from heat. The zones range from summer cool zone 1 (one day or less at 86°F or warmer) through hot summer zone 12 (210 days or more per year). Full-color posters of the AHS Heat-Zone Map are available for $9.95 — call the American Horticultural Society at 1-800-777-7931 extension 110 or order online at `www.ahs.org/books/logo_wear.htm`.

Stretching Your Garden Season

You can grow most vegetables and annual flowers anywhere! Some of the largest, most beautiful vegetables we've ever seen were from avid gardeners in Alaska. If you can grow vegetables where the sun doesn't shine for six months of the year, you know they're easy to grow. Which USDA zone you live in isn't as critical for vegetable growing as it is for fruits, perennial flowers, trees, and shrubs. When it comes to vegetables and other annuals, the length of your growing season is much more important.

A *growing season* consists of the *average* number of days between frosts. Sometimes, you hear "growing season" referred to as "frost-free days." Some vegetables are very quick to grow and mature, so they require relatively little time. Others need a long growing season. Usually, seed packets or garden catalogs show a number along with the phrase "days to harvest" or something similar. This number is a rough guide to how long a season that particular vegetable needs to mature. Table 2-1 shows USDA zones and typical number of frost-free days.

Table 2-1	Typical Number of Frost-Free Days by USDA Zone (Northern Hemisphere)		
Zone	*Last Frost Date*	*First Frost Date*	*Typical Number of Frost-Free Days*
Zone 1*	June 15	July 15	30
Zone 2	May 15	August 15	90
Zone 3	May 15	September 15	120

Zone	Last Frost Date	First Frost Date	Typical Number of Frost-Free Days
Zone 4	May 10	September 15	125
Zone 5	April 30	October 15	165
Zone 6	April 15	October 15	180
Zone 7	April 15	October 15	180
Zone 8	March 10	November 15	245
Zone 9	February 15	December 15	265
Zone 10	January 20	December 20	335
Zone 11	Frost-free		365

Susceptible to frost all year

When you live in a northern climate, you deal with a short growing season. If you want to increase your garden bounty, you need to squeeze in a few extra weeks of plant growth earlier and later in the year. By using some of the techniques described in the following sections, you can enjoy the advantages that gardeners have in one or two zones milder.

Planting earlier in the year

Gardeners are master manipulators and have devised all sorts of ways to get a jump on spring. The first simply is to plant early. Cool-season plants, such as snapdragons or lettuce, tolerate light frosts. Fool Mother Nature by starting them indoors, timed so that they're ready for transplanting about three to four weeks before the average last frost date. You can start frost-tender plants — such as marigolds — early, too. Plan to transplant them under protective cover (described in this section) about two weeks before the average last frost date.

Cold framing

You may also want to consider using a *cold frame*, which speeds seed germination and shelters plants from frost. The frame is a bottomless box, usually constructed from wood. The structure has a slanting, tight-fitting top made of old windows or other transparent or translucent materials such as plastic or fiberglass. A typical frame is approximately 3 feet wide and 6 feet long (1 x 2 m) with an 18-inch-high (30 cm) back sloping down to 12 inches high (46 cm) in the front. (See Figure 2-1.)

Place the frame outdoors, over a garden bed or against the south wall of your home. Orient the frame so that it slopes to the south. The sun warms the air and soil inside, creating a cozy environment for plants. Sow seeds for transplants directly in the cold frame. (Or grow crops, such as radishes, spinach, beets, and lettuce to maturity in the frame.) Prop the top open during the day for ventilation and lower it at night to conserve heat. If you can't check the frame regularly, consider buying a thermostatically controlled vent opener as insurance against cooking or freezing your plants.

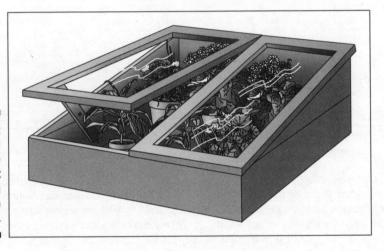

Figure 2-1:
Use a cold frame to protect young plants in early spring.

If you like the idea of a cold frame but want even greater temperature control, consider a *hot bed*. This device is essentially a cold frame with a heat source (commonly electric heating cable) to warm the soil. The cable usually includes a built-in soil thermostat preset for about 75°F (24°C), ideal for germinating most seeds. You can find cable with a thermostat and plug sold by wattage and length.

Frost guarding

When tender plants are ready for the garden, you need to protect them from frost. Here's a rundown of useful frost guards:

- ✔ **Use hot caps.** These devices are individual covers that work like miniature greenhouses. Hot caps can be homemade or store-bought. To make your own, cut the bottom out of a plastic gallon milk jug. Anchor it in the ground with a stake and leave the cap off so that your plant doesn't bake inside. Commercially produced hot caps are made of translucent wax paper, plastic, or fiberglass.

- ✔ **Set up a water-filled cloche.** A couple of different kinds are available, one with thin plastic, flexible walls and one with heavier, stiff walls. In both cases, you fill the walls with water. During the day, the water absorbs solar heat. As the water cools down at night, it releases heat slowly, protecting the plant inside from temperatures as low as 16°F (–9°C). Use cloches to protect seedlings from late spring frosts.

✔ **Use row covers.** Drape lightweight synthetic fabrics, called *floating row covers,* over the plants. The covers let light and water pass through while protecting plants from temperatures as low as 24°F (–4.5°C), depending on the fabric used. The fabrics are available in a variety of widths and lengths. (See Figure 2-2.)

Book I

Gardening Basics

Row covers of slit plastic are cheaper but usually require more work because they need support from hoops or a frame. You also have to pull the plastic aside to water. Plastic covers create higher daytime temperatures than fabric, which may be advantageous when you're trying to give heat-loving plants, such as peppers, a boost in cool weather.

✔ **Recycle junk from your house.** Every so often, an unexpected late spring frost catches you off guard. Usually, the frost prediction comes about the time green, tender, young plants dot the garden. To save plants, rummage around for anything that may protect them without crushing them. Cardboard boxes, old sheets, empty buckets, or even newspaper spread over the plants lend a few degrees of protection. Just remember to remove the stuff the following day, or the plants may bake.

In addition to providing frost protection, serious cold-climate gardeners often warm the soil in early spring before planting. They spread a soil-warming, plastic-type mulch over the soil surface and cut holes in it for the transplants. After planting, they protect plants with floating row covers.

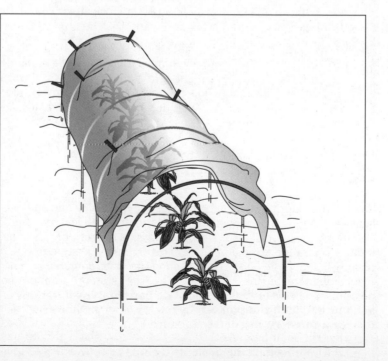

Figure 2-2:
Lay lightweight row covers directly over seedlings or support them with wire hoops. Plastic row covers develop more heat and must be vented.

Clear plastic traditionally has been the mulch of choice for heating the soil, but weeds really thrive under it. Now you can use a new high-tech option called *IRT mulching film*. This green film heats up the soil as well as clear plastic does, but blocks the portion of the light spectrum that supports weed growth. (Clear plastic is still the best to use if you want to *solarize* or heat the soil sufficiently to destroy insects, fungi, and weed seeds. This technique is most effective in hot summer regions that have many consecutive sunny days.)

Gardening beyond autumn

Now that you have a jump on spring, consider these tips on foiling the first frosts of autumn:

- **Cover up again.** You often face an occasional light frost before the first big killer. On those crisp, clear evenings when a light frost is forecast, throw a few bed sheets or floating row covers over tender crops. With a little effort, you can prolong the harvest of summer crops.

- **Spray on frost protection.** What if you forget — or are just too tired — to cover up crops on a chilly evening? Well, you have a second chance to save them (after you've rested, of course). Turn on your garden sprinkler during the late-night hours (as soon as the temperature drops below 33°F, or 0.5°C). Leave the water on until the sun has warmed the air up above freezing. A fine spray of water is more effective than large water droplets.

- **Plant again.** Cool-season plants tolerate frost. You can plant a second crop of many flowers and vegetables in mid-to-late-summer for a late autumn or winter. These plants grow quickly in the still-warm soil of summer and start maturing about the time tender crops are declining. Kale (both edible and ornamental), beets, chard, pansies, and turnips are among the stars of the post-frost harvest.

Gardening all year

Frost is the culprit that usually dictates the beginning and end of the gardening season. Planting dates revolve around the first and last average frost dates. If you don't know the dates for your area, ask a nursery professional or call your local cooperative extension office. The extension system phone number is usually listed in the phone book among the state university numbers or under *Extension* in the business section. (The extension program is a cooperative partnership between federal and state partners. Organizations in colleges and universities are authorized by the USDA to provide services that focus on research, education, and economics.)

In mild-winter regions, where an occasional light frost is as bad as it gets, the best way to stretch the season is to keep on gardening right through winter.

Winter gardening has many benefits: Pest and disease problems are fewer; you don't have to water much, if at all; and winter crops are varied, nutritious, and delicious. In addition to the cool-season vegetables, annual flowers such as pansies, calendula, stock, and primrose thrive in winter. (Book VII covers vegetables and Book V takes a look at annuals.) Autumn is prime planting time for winter gardening, although you can plant some crops, such as lettuce and beets, in succession through the winter.

Maximizing Winter Hardiness

Gardeners can, to some degree, help plants adapt to winter. For instance, reduce the amount of nitrogen fertilizer applied after mid-July and stop all fertilization by late summer. Also, do everything you can to ensure that your plants enter the autumn season healthy but not growing too fast.

Make sure the soil in which evergreens are growing is well-watered in mid to late autumn, before the soil freezes. If the landscape where evergreens are located is in a dry site, sandy soil, or under the overhang of a roof, also make sure that the soil is well watered in midwinter if the temperature is above freezing.

Here are some other steps you can take to decrease the likelihood of winter injury to plants:

- ✔ **Plant on the north side.** Choose a location for marginally hardy plants with a northern or eastern exposure rather than south or southwest. Plants facing the south are more exposed to the sun on warm winter days and thus experience greater daily temperature variation.

- ✔ **Mulch.** Apply a layer of mulch, 3 to 4 inches (7.5-10 cm) deep, after the soil freezes to keep the soil cold rather than protect the soil from becoming cold. This practice reduces injury from plant roots' *heaving* (coming out of the soil) because of alternate freezing and thawing. Plants that benefit from this practice include perennials, alpine, rock garden plants, strawberries, and other shallow-rooted plants. A mulch maintains a more even soil temperature and retains soil moisture.

- ✔ **Wrap with twine.** Plants such as arborvitae, juniper, and yew often suffer damage from the weight of snow or ice. Prevent plant breakage by fastening heavy twine at the base of the plant and winding it spirally around and upward to the top and back down in a reverse spiral. This technique is more necessary as plants become larger and begin to open at the top. Be certain to remove the twine during the growing season.

- ✔ **Use burlap screen.** Stretch a section of burlap around three stakes to protect young or not fully hardy plants from the south, west, and windward exposures. A burlap wrap with stakes protects plants from the drying winter sun and wind as well as drift from deicing salts applied to drives and streets. Wrap most of the plant, but leave some of the top of the plant exposed. Evergreen plants need light, even in winter.

✔ **Prevent drying.** Narrow and broadleaf evergreens lose moisture through their leaves in winter. Plant roots can't absorb moisture from the soil in winter because the soil may be frozen and therefore can't replace the moisture the leaves lose. The foliage desiccates, turns brown, and may drop, which can be serious with evergreen azalea, holly, boxwood, and rhododendron. Make sure that evergreens are properly watered throughout the growing season and into the fall. Decrease watering slightly in fall to encourage hardening off, and then water thoroughly in October and continue until soil freezes.

✔ **Prevent animal damage.** Some landscape plants, especially during a time of extended period of snow cover, become a food source for rabbits, mice, or voles. When their normal food supply is covered with ice or snow, rodents turn to the bark and young stems of apple, flowering crabapple, mountain ash, hawthorn, euonymus, and viburnum, among others. If the animals chew the bark completely around the plant and cause it to girdle, the plant may die. In *girdling,* the all-important living cells of woody plants are just under the bark. If these cells are damaged or destroyed, the water and nutrients flowing between the plant's roots and leaves become impeded or stop completely. Partial girdling creates wounds for borers and disease organisms to enter, and weakens the plant itself.

Chapter 3

Digging Up the Dirt on Your Soil

*P*reparing your soil is probably the most important step toward bringing your garden to life. Your goal, as you discover in this chapter, is to create an airy soil, rich in oxygen and nutrients that enable your plants to thrive.

Clearing the Site

Before testing and improving the soil, you first need to clear your site of existing vegetation. Follow these steps for clearing a site where you intend to place your garden:

1. **Outline the area where you'll go to work.**

   If you're developing a square or rectangular area, establish straightedge lines by stretching a string between two sticks. Leave the string in place or mark the line with a trickle of white ground limestone, spray paint, or flour. For curved portions of the garden, use a garden hose or rope to lay out the line. Adjust the hose position until the curve looks smooth.

2. **Use a flat spade to dig a small trench that establishes the outline of the garden plot.**

3. **Clear the surface by removing plants, brush, and rocks.**

4. **Mow the site to clear the rough ground.**

5. **Cut down woody plants and dig out the roots.**

6. **When the vegetation is down to a manageable level, you can remove the sod and other low vegetation.**

If the garden is currently lawn, you can strip off the turf, roots and all, by using a flat spade or sod cutter. This method is hard work but does a thorough job.

Stripping sod

Your site-clearing process may very well involve getting rid of natural sod. Here's how:

1. **A couple of days prior to digging, water the area that you want to clear to make stripping easier.**

2. **Starting at one side of the plot, slip your spade under the grass and slide it under the sod.**

   If you'd rather, you can precut the sod into square or rectangular sections and then loosen each section with the spade. Don't dig too deep; you want to remove merely the sod and an inch or two of roots.

3. **Pivot the tool up, letting the sod flip up over the spade, slice off the sod section, and toss it into a wheelbarrow for your compost pile.** If your lawn has been chemically treated, however, don't put the sod into the compost pile. Some herbicides don't break down during the composting process.

4. **Continue in this manner until the garden is free of sod.**

If you have a large area of sod to clear, consider renting a sod cutter. These machines are the size and weight of full-size rototillers, so you need a pick-up truck or trailer to get one home. (Some rental yards deliver and pick up heavy equipment for an extra charge.) After stripping the sod, stack the strips like bricks and let them become compost.

Other soil-clearing methods

You can clear a garden in other ways, as well:

- ✔ **Black plastic:** After a month under black plastic, existing plants die from lack of sunlight. Spread the plastic over the entire garden area, securing the edges with spare rocks, bricks, or boards. Overlap neighboring pieces of plastic by several inches so that no light can penetrate. Come back in a month, remove the plastic, and rototill the dead plant matter into the soil. Wait about ten days for any errant weeds to sprout and then cut or pull those that emerge.

- ✔ **Newspapers:** Recycle newspapers by spreading a five- to six-sheet layer over the entire area in the fall. Overlap the sheets about 5 inches (12.5

cm). Cover the newspaper with straw or other mulch and leave it alone for one season. After a few months, the newspaper will have decomposed enough to till under.

✔ **Repeat cultivation:** If you have plenty of time or if other site-clearing methods aren't practical, then consider the *repeated tilling method*. This process adds organic matter to the soil and kills existing weeds but takes much of the growing season to complete:

  • In spring, rototill the garden area and broadcast seeds of a cover crop such as buckwheat, Sudan grass, or black-eyed peas.

  • After the cover crop gets to be about 6 inches (15 cm) high, till again to work it into the soil.

  • Let the cover crop decay, which takes a couple of weeks during warm weather. Then till again and prepare to plant.

Meeting Your Soil

Armed with some basic knowledge and a few easy tests to determine your soil's characteristics, you can start improving your soil like an expert! To understand your soil, keep in mind what plants need from soil: moisture, air, and nutrients.

Soil texture

Soil comprises air spaces, organic matter, and, mostly, mineral particles. Soil minerals come in three types: sand, silt, and clay. Sand is the largest particle in most garden soils. Silt particles are smaller than fine sand and larger than clay. Clay is the smallest particle. The relative proportions of these particles in the soil determine its texture. The ideal soil texture is *loam,* which is composed of sand, silt, and clay. Loam soils have the properties of all three mineral types in roughly equal proportions — enough sand to allow good water drainage and air circulation, but enough clay to retain moisture and nutrients. (See Figure 3-1.) Most garden soils are best understood as either sandy, clay, or loam. (Silty soils occur but are not common.)

✔ **Sandy:** Water drains through sandy soils fast, so it dries quickly. Nutrients also pass through sandy soils quickly. Plants in sandy soils often need lighter, more frequent applications of water and fertilizer.

✔ **Clay:** Soils dominated by clay particles are heavy and tend to pack tightly. Clay soil sticks to your shoes and shovel when it's wet, and cracks when dry. Water enters and drains slowly from clay soils, which can make them difficult to manage. On the other hand, clay soil's ability to retain moisture and nutrients makes it very fertile.

▶ **Loam:** Loam soils come in many types, but all combine the properties of sand, silt, and clay. A "perfect" loam soil contains 40 percent sand, 40 percent silt, and 20 percent clay. Loam soils have such a good reputation because they're ideal for most plants.

A quick test for texture: Ribbons and bows

You can get a general idea of your soil's texture by using the *ribbons-and-bows method.* Take a handful of moist soil, squeeze it into a ball, and roll it into a ribbon between your thumb and your forefinger. Stand the ribbon straight up in the air.

▶ If you can't form a ribbon, the soil is at least 50 percent sand and has very little clay.

▶ If the ribbon is less than 2 inches (5 cm) long before breaking, your soil has roughly 25 percent clay in it.

▶ If the ribbon is 2—3½ inches (5—9 cm) long, it has about 40 percent clay.

▶ If the ribbon is greater than 3½ inches (9 cm) long and doesn't break when held up, it's at least 50 percent clay.

Figure 3-1:
The size of the mineral particles determines a soil's texture. Loam is the ideal soil for most plants.

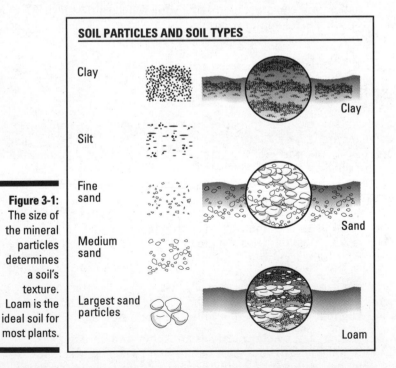

SOIL PARTICLES AND SOIL TYPES

Clay

Clay

Silt

Fine sand

Sand

Medium sand

Largest sand particles

Loam

A more accurate test for texture: The jar method

For most gardeners most of the time, knowing the exact texture of your soil is not so important. But when you do know, that information can help explain much of what goes on in your garden. You can then tailor your soil management for maximum effect. Allow several days to carry out the *jar method* test:

1. **Put 2 inches (5 cm) of dry, crushed garden soil in a tall quart (liter) jar.**

2. **Fill the jar ⅔ with water, add 1 teaspoon (5 mL) of a dispersing agent — such as liquid dish detergent or table salt — shake the jar thoroughly, and let the contents settle for three days.**

3. **Measure the depths of the different layers of soil.**

   When the sand settles to the bottom (in about a minute), measure the depth of that layer. Silt settles in four to five hours. Clay can take about three days and some of the smallest particles may remain permanently in suspension. You should see a color and size difference between the silt and sand layers; if not, subtract the sand depth from the total to determine the silt depth.

By measuring the depth of each layer, you can figure out the approximate percentages of sand, silt, and clay in your soil. For example, you have loam soil if the 2 inches (5 cm) of soil settles down as follows: The sand and silt layers are about ¾-inch (1.9 cm) each, and the clay layer is less than ½ inch (1.25 cm).

Soil structure

The way in which sand, silt, and clay particles combine or cluster is called the *soil structure*. Structure modifies texture's influence. Most often, gardeners use additions of organic matter — compost, peat moss, mulch, and so on — to improve soil structure.

No matter what kind of soil you have, adding organic matter improves the soil structure. Organic matter helps form *humus,* which enables small clay or silt particles to stick together to form larger aggregates; in sandy soils, humus acts like a sponge to catch and hold moisture and nutrients. For more details about humus, see the section "Exactly what do you add?" later in this chapter.

You can use either the *percolation method* or the *metal-rod method* to determine your soil structure.

A quick test for structure: Percolation

The percolation do-it-yourself test evaluates *water drainage* — the ability of water to move through the soil, which is called the *percolation rate*. To evaluate drainage, do the following:

1. **Dig several holes 1 foot deep and 2 feet wide (30 to 60 cm) in various places in your garden.**

2. **Cover the holes with sheets of plastic to let the soil dry out.**

3. **When the soil is dry, fill each hole to the top with water and record the time it takes for the water to completely drain.**

   The ideal time is between 10 and 30 minutes.

   • If the water drains in less than 10 minutes, the soil will tend to dry out too quickly in the summer. Amend the soil with moisture-retaining matter, such as peat moss and humus.

   • If the water takes 30 minutes to 4 hours to drain, you can still grow most plants, but you have to water it slowly to avoid runoff and to allow the water to soak in deeply.

   • If your soil takes longer than 4 hours to drain, you may have a drainage problem. In sandy soil, dig a foot or two (30–60 cm) deep to see whether a hard layer is blocking water movement. If so, break it up in the area you want plants to grow. You may have to dig down with a post-hole digger, though in some cases, the impermeable layer is too deep even for that. You can also use a nozzle on the end of a pipe to make a water jet bore through an impermeable layer.

If your soil is clay, create a raised bed and use purchased soil or a homemade soil mix for planting. The goal is to get plant roots up out of the soggy soil and into well-drained, elevated soil that's rich with organic matter.

Breathing space

Water, which carries soil nutrients used by plants, moves through pore spaces in the soil. When the soil contains very little pore space, the plants can't get enough water and dissolved nutrients. Roots and soil microorganisms, which decompose organic material and make nutrients available to plants, depend on air in the soil to do their work. Air and water lie in the spaces, called *pores,* between the solid soil particles. The ideal ratio is about 50 percent pore space and 50 percent solid particles, but the proportions of minerals, organic matter, air, and water in soil vary greatly depending on many factors, including the following:

✔ **Weather:** Flooded soil holds little air because the pore spaces fill with water.

✔ **Soil disturbance:** Driving, walking, digging, and other activities compress the soil particles together, squeezing out air.

✔ **Organic matter content:** Decomposing plant and animal material increases the amount of water and air that soil can hold.

✔ **Size and shape of soil particles:** Very small, flat particles pack together more tightly than larger, angular ones, which means less space for air and water. Large particles generally have large, air-filled pore spaces between them.

Another test for structure: The metal-rod method

In some regions, particularly ones that receive little rainfall, a concrete-like layer, known as *caliche,* lies just under the soil. This layer prevents normal water movement and root growth. Some soils also suffer from a layer of dense clay soil called *hardpan.* Though not as hard as caliche, this dense layer also prevents good plant growth. (See the section "Improving Your Soil," later in this chapter.) The simplest way to see whether your soil has a hardpan or compaction layer below the surface is to take a metal rod and walk around your property sticking it into the ground. If you can't easily push the rod into the soil at least 6 to 8 inches (15—20 cm) deep, you need to improve the structure of your soil. If you push it down and consistently meet resistance at a certain depth, you may be hitting a hardpan layer.

One more big thing: Soil pH

Soil pH represents the relative alkalinity (sweetness) or acidity (sourness) of your soil. The correct pH for your plants is important because certain nutrients are available only to plants within a specific pH range. Most soils in the world range between a pH of 5 and 9. Soil with a pH of 4.5 is strongly acidic and a pH of 9.5 is strongly alkaline. An absolutely neutral pH is 7.0. The ideal pH for most plants is from 6.0 to 7.0. A few plants (such as acid-loving rhododendrons and blueberries) prefer more extreme conditions. Usually, areas of high rainfall have a low pH, and areas of low rainfall have a high pH.

You can buy kits at many garden centers to test pH, or you can use a professional soil test. For a quick check of your soil's pH, try the following fizz tests. (They're not very accurate, but can be fun to watch!)

✔ To check whether your soil is severely alkaline, take a tablespoon (15 mL) of dried garden soil and add a few drops of vinegar. If the soil fizzes, the pH is above 7.5. (The "free carbonates" in the soil react with the acid at a pH of 7.5 and above.)

✔ To check for acidity in the soil, take a tablespoon (15 mL) of wet soil and add a pinch of baking soda. If the soil fizzes, the soil is probably very acidic (pH less than 5.0).

Consulting a professional soil tester

For the definitive word on your soil's chemistry and makeup, a professional test is the next step. Your local cooperative extension office may be able to test your soil or recommend a private lab. (The extension program is a cooperative partnership between federal and state partners. Organizations in colleges and universities are authorized by the USDA to provide services that focus on research, education, and economics.) The results of these tests can tell you about soil nutrient levels, soil structure, and pH. You also get suggestions on how to make your soil even better.

Keep in mind that the reliability of any soil test depends on the accuracy of the soil sample. Avoid contaminating soil samples with residue from tools, containers, or cigarette ash, for example. The small sample that you send to a lab must also be representative of your garden. Gather soil from several places and mix it together to form a composite picture of the plot. However, don't mix soil from different garden areas where you'll be growing plants with different needs or with soil near foundations or walls where construction residues may remain. Follow the directions from the soil lab or extension office for best results.

Improving Your Soil

If your soil is a nice, fertile blend — one that grows good grass — you may not need to do anything special to it to grow most garden plants. But beefing up the organic content never hurts, because organic matter is constantly being broken down. *Organic matter* — such as decaying leaves, hay, grass clippings, compost, and decomposed cow or horse manure — releases nutrients and other chemicals that make soil fertile and productive. Organic matter is especially valuable for adding richness to sand and lightness to clay. The organic material makes good gardens great and poor gardens better by making any soil more like the ideal loamy soil. Be careful not to use cat or dog droppings because this waste can contain parasites.

Before planting in reasonably good soil, dig in 1 or 2 inches (2.5 or 5 cm) of organic matter, such as compost, peat moss, decayed livestock manure, shredded leaves, or decayed lawn clippings. Then, each year, mulch planted areas with an inch or more of compost or organic mulch.

Amending your soil before planting isn't always necessary, especially if you're planting long-lived trees and shrubs and if your soil is reasonably good. If your soil is less than it needs to be for the kinds of plants you want to grow, try to correct the problem before you plant. Be prepared to amend the entire planting area, so that plant roots can grow freely without encountering a bewildering range of different soil blends. Dramatically different soil types can stop root growth cold. Apply a layer of organic matter, at least 2 to 4 inches (5 to 10 cm), and till it into the soil. Plan to maintain your improved soil by adding several inches of organic material each year — even more in warm climates or particularly difficult soils.

Here are some tips to improve tough soils:

✔ Add a 1- to 2-inch (5—10 cm) deep topdressing of compost to compacted soils in perennial beds annually. You don't need to rake it into the soil.

✔ Break up a compacted layer and build extra-deep top soil in annual gardens by double digging (see the section "Double digging" later in this chapter) or by deeply tilling the soil below the hardpan layer and mixing in generous amounts of organic matter.

✔ Build a raised bed (see the section "Simple raised beds" later in this chapter) if the thickness of the hardpan layer doesn't allow for planting: Build the bed about 8 inches (20 cm) high — or even higher if you install a retaining wall. Cover the existing soil with commercial topsoil that's preblended with about 20 percent compost.

Exactly what do you add?

Organic matter that you can add to your soil comes in so many forms and varieties that this book couldn't possibly list them all. Nursery and garden centers offer many kinds, often in 20- or 40-pound (10 or 20 kilogram) bags. But if you have really big plans, consider buying your organic amendment by the truckload. The following sections describe materials that can do wonders to improve the texture of garden soil.

Compost

When different kinds of dead plant material get piled together, dampened, and stirred or turned every week or so to keep air in the mixture, they become compost after a month (or two or three). Products labeled as compost can originate from all sorts of stuff, but enterprising people who have tapped into the yard-waste stream usually create them. Fallen leaves, shredded Christmas trees, and wood chips left from tree-trimming crews often find their way to compost-manufacturing facilities. Compost ingredients can also include sawdust from lumber mills, peanut hulls from peanut processing plants, and hundreds of other agricultural by-products.

One place to get lots of compost cheap is from your own city. Many municipalities offer free compost and mulch. Some charge a modest fee for it. The only caveat is quality. Some cities compost industrial by-products that you may not want to have in your garden. Check with your local Department of Public Works.

Expect to find little bits of sticks and other recognizable things in a bag of compost, but mostly judge quality by the texture of the material, which should be soft and springy. If you plan to buy a large quantity of compost, compare products packaged by different companies to find the best texture. A 3-inch (7.5 cm) layer of packaged compost, worked into the soil, is a liberal helping that should give instant results. To estimate how much you need, figure that a 40-pound bag (18 kg) covers a square yard (0.84 m²) of bed space.

Composted manure

In addition to its soil-improving properties, composted or "aged" manure also contains respectable amounts of nitrogen and other important plant nutrients. Nutrient content varies with the type of manure. Composted chicken manure is very potent, whereas steer manure is comparatively lightweight. Packaged sheep manure is quite popular among gardeners, and you may eventually encounter some truly exotic renditions based on the waste from zoo animals, bats, and even crickets.

The amount of manure you should use depends on your soil type. With bulky manure from large animals (cow, horse, goat, sheep, elephant), start with a 1-inch (2.5 cm) layer, or about 40 pounds (18 kg), per 3 square yards (2.5 m^2). Follow package application rates when using stronger manure from rabbits, chickens, and other birds.

Humus

Bags labeled as *humus* are the wild cards of the soil-amendment world. Anything that qualifies as organic matter for soil, or any soil-organic matter mixture, can be considered humus. Unlike compost, which is supposed to be "cultured" under controlled conditions, humus can come from more humble beginnings. For example, humus may be 2-year-old sawdust and wood chips from a lumber mill mixed with rotten leaves and dark topsoil. Or, it could be rotten hay mixed with soil and sand. You just don't know what to expect until you buy a bag and open it up. If the humus has a loose, spongy texture and dark color, and you like the way it feels and smells, go for it. A 2- to 3-inch (5 to 7.5 cm) layer (40 pounds per 2 square yards, or 18 kg per 1.7 m^2) is a good estimate.

Topsoil

Breaking into bags of topsoil to see what's inside is always interesting. Sometimes, the soil is exactly what you find in bags of humus or compost, and other times, it may look more like unbelievably black soil. Whatever the bag contents include, topsoil is almost always cheap. You can use bagged topsoil as a soil amendment, or use so much of it that your flower bed is filled with mostly imported topsoil and only a little of the native stuff.

Peat moss

Peat moss is a very spongy, acidic, brown material harvested from peat bogs in Canada, Michigan, and a few other places. On the plus side, peat moss absorbs and holds huge amounts of water and nutrients while frustrating soil-borne fungi that can cause plant diseases. Peat moss is more beneficial in sandy soil as opposed to clay soils. In sandy soils, the water-holding power of peat is put to good use. Clay soil retains water, so adding peat moss is overkill.

On the negative side, some gardeners are concerned about the sustainability of peat moss harvesting. Peat bogs damaged by overharvesting may require a thousand years to regenerate, so you may want to limit your use of peat moss to situations where it's most valuable, such as creating special soil mixtures for container-grown plants, or for planting shrubs that really like it, such as azaleas and rhododendrons. We think that most, but not all, of the peat moss in nurseries and garden centers is harvested responsibly and sustainably. Gardeners in some areas use shredded coconut husks as a substitute.

Book I

Gardening Basics

Changing pH

The pH scale shows the level of acidity or alkalinity of soil. A soil with a pH number below 7 is acidic, while one with a pH above 7 is alkaline. Most plants prefer a neutral pH level of 7 or slightly below. If you're growing pH-sensitive plants, or if you're dealing with very acidic or very alkaline soils, you can adjust pH with specific soil amendments. To make soil less acidic, add ground limestone. To decrease alkalinity, add soil sulfur. But rather than commit to the ongoing need to adjust pH, consider choosing landscape plants that grow well in your native soil with its existing pH. Amending soil with many kinds of organic matter gradually lowers pH. (Some animal manures tend to have an alkaline effect, so don't use them to acidify.) Likewise, most nitrogen-containing fertilizers, natural or manufactured, acidify soils — some a great deal, others only slightly. But if your soil pH is significantly too low or too high for the kinds of plants you want to grow, you need to add ground limestone or soil sulfur. To increase or decrease your soil pH, do the following:

- **Add limestone to raise your soil pH from 5.0 to 6.5.** To each 1,000 square feet (93 m^2) of sand, add 41 pounds (18.6 kg); to each 1,000 square feet of loam, add 78 pounds (35.4 kg); and to each 1,000 square feet of clay, add 152 pounds (69 kg).

- **Add sulfur to lower your soil pH from 8.5 to 6.5.** To each 1,000 square feet (93 m^2) of sand, add 46 pounds (20.8 kg); to each 1,000 square feet of loam, add 57 pounds (25.8 kg); and to each 1,000 square feet of clay, add 69 pounds (31.3 kg).

Adding nutrients

If your soil is low in nutrients, which you can determine by having the soil tested or by seeing that plants grow poorly, add extra nutrients. If your soil has been tested, add amendments and fertilizers according to the lab's recommendations. If you haven't tested the soil, add a *complete fertilizer* (one that contains nitrogen, phosphorus, and potassium, the major nutrients that all plants need) according to package directions.

Green manure crops and cover crops

One easy way for gardeners to add organic matter and nutrients to the soil is to grow *green manure crops*. These are plants grown to be chopped and tilled or spaded into the soil when they're still green (before they blossom and produce seeds). The succulent plant material breaks down quickly, adding nutrients and improving soil texture. You usually grow these crops during the main gardening season — between crops or just after harvesting a crop. In many climates, green manure crops remain standing over the winter and get plowed into the soil before spring planting.

The same plants used for green manure crops can be used for *cover crops*. However, the primary purposes of a cover crop are to prevent soil erosion and to choke out weeds, usually when the soil is bare of crops before and after the harvest.

You can divide green manure and cover crop plants into two broad categories: *legumes* and *nonlegumes*. Legumes have special nodules on their roots that house nitrogen-fixing bacteria of the genus *Rhizobium*. Examples of legumes are soybeans, vetches, cowpeas, and clovers. If you till the legumes back into the soil, succeeding crops benefit from the nitrogen that the legume and its *Rhizobium* absorbed from the air. Although nonlegumes don't add as much nitrogen to the soil as legumes do, many nonlegumes are very useful as green manure and cover crops simply for the organic matter that they add to the soil.

Loosening the Soil

The depth and techniques that you use to loosen the soil depend on which plants you intend to grow and the condition of your soil. For your average garden of annual flowers and vegetables, for example, you can use a process called *single digging* to break up the top 8 inches (20 cm) of soil by using a spade or rototiller. In existing gardens with light, fluffy soil, you may be able to turn the bed with a spade without too much difficulty and minimize organic matter loss. If you prepare the soil in autumn, let frost help break up the soil clumps. Then spade again in spring and finish up with a rake.

Begin the single-digging process by removing a section of soil the width of the bed and the depth of your spade. Soon, you'll have what looks like a shallow grave. Next, slice down into the adjacent portion of soil with the spade and roll that soil into the trench you just made. Continue this process until you have covered the garden width (or length). Finally, haul the soil excavated from the first trench and place it into the last space. After your first pass with the shovel, break up the clods and add the soil amendments and fertilizer. Then dig through the bed again, raking vigorously to break up clods and to mix in the amendments. Use a garden rake to comb through the soil and remove rocks, clods, and any vegetation or plant roots that you missed previously. Smooth the soil over the entire bed by raking, and you're ready to plant.

When to work the soil

Have you ever grown your own mouth-watering melon, checking it daily to see whether it's perfectly ripe? Preparing the soil is similar. You need to wait until the soil is in the right condition — lightly moist, but not wet. If too wet, clays can dry into brick. If too dry, soil can turn into dust and blow away, leaving beneficial soil life to perish. If your soil tends to be wet and clammy in spring when you're ready to plant annual flowers, you can avoid this frustration by preparing your beds in the fall, when dry conditions often prevail.

Fortunately, the right soil condition is easy to evaluate. Take a handful of soil and squeeze it in your fist. Tap the resulting ball with your finger. If it breaks up easily, the soil is ready. If it stays in a sodden clump, the soil needs to dry out more. If it doesn't cling at all, the soil is dry: Water the area, wait a day, and try again.

Time for a tiller

Digging a small flower bed is a good exercise program, but preparing a large one by hand in one day is almost impossible without the help of a tiller. If you need to cultivate more than 1,000 square feet ($93m^2$), consider renting, borrowing, or buying a tiller. Lightweight minitillers are sufficient for many tilling chores. For larger jobs, look to either front- or rear-tined tillers. Professional growers usually favor the latter.

You can also have someone else till your garden. No matter where you live, you can usually find someone in your community (through the classified ads or your local garden center) who does this sort of work in the spring. Before the person arrives to churn up your soil, have all the soil amendments that you intend to use on hand. After you till the area and rake out the weeds, spread out your soil amendments and fertilizer, and till it again.

Rototillers are a handy tool for occasional use. Beware, however, that repeated use of tillers can create a hardpan layer (known as *plow pan* or *pressure pan*). Tillers promote faster breakdown of soil organic matter because of how they stir and mix the soil; and tillers cultivate soil to only one depth, so the soil beneath the tilled layer becomes compacted from repeated pressure from the tiller.

Double digging

Double digging works the soil more deeply than single digging and is useful for deep-rooted plants or areas where drainage needs improvement. The effects of this labor-intensive process last for years.

1. **Mark out a bed 3 or 4 feet (1 or 1.2 m) wide and up to 25 feet (7.6 m long).**

2. **Across the width of the bed, remove a layer of the topsoil to create a trench 6 to 8 inches (15 to 20 cm) deep and 1 to 2 feet (30 to 60 cm) wide.**

   Place the soil in your wheelbarrow.

3. **With a digging fork, break up the subsoil at the bottom of the trench to the full depth of the tines — about 6 to 8 inches (15 to 20 cm).**

   Mix in plenty of soil amendments.

4. **Step down into the bed and dig the topsoil from the adjacent strip, moving it onto the exposed, loose subsoil of the first trench.**

5. **Break up the newly exposed subsoil with the garden fork, and add amendments.**

6. **Continue in this fashion until you break up upper and lower layers across the entire bed.**

   The soil from the first trench, held in the wheelbarrow, goes into the last trench.

7. **Spread soil amendments over the entire bed and rake it into the top 6 to 8 inches (15 to 20 cm) of soil.**

   After you finish, the earth is mounded up high in the bed. Walk on the adjacent ground rather than on the raised bed. When you prepare the bed in subsequent planting seasons, you'll be amazed at how little work it takes to loosen the ground.

Simple raised beds

Raised beds are an ideal way to loosen the garden's soil and define planting areas. To make a raised-bed garden, outline the beds with string. For vegetable gardens, a 3-foot (1 m) wide bed is best; for ornamental plantings, choose a size that best fits your design. After you define the beds, loosen the soil in the bed by using a shovel or a garden fork. Then shovel soil from an adjacent path onto the bed. Figure 3-2 shows a basic raised bed and one edged with wood.

Roses, carrots, parsnips, and other deep-rooted plants grow best when you loosen the soil 12 inches (30 cm) deep or deeper. This requirement calls for building a raised bed over the existing garden or for double digging.

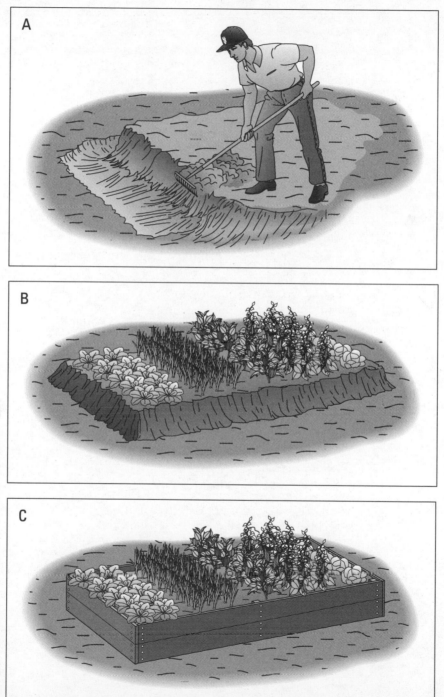

Figure 3-2:
Create raised beds by first (A) drawing soil from walkway areas onto loosened soil. Leave the edges as they are (B), or finish the edges with untreated wood or other materials (C).

Chapter 4

Balancing Your Garden's Diet

● ●

In This Chapter

▶ Bringing water to your garden

▶ Understanding plant nutrients

▶ Fertilizing and mulching your plants

▶ Using organic fertilizers

▶ Dabbling in the art and science of composting

● ●

*W*atering, feeding, and composting are the Big Three for creating and maintaining a healthy garden. But the amount of watering, feeding, and composting you do depends on where you live, what you grow, and all sorts of other local conditions. This chapter helps you understand your garden's particular health needs.

Watering Basics

How much water your plants need to stay healthy depends on several factors:

▸ **Climate and weather:** The average weather where you live on a season-to-season, year-to-year basis determines climate. Out-of-the ordinary weather can wreak havoc on your plants. Hot, dry winds can fry plants even when the soil is moist.

▸ **Soil types:** Sandy soil holds water about as effectively as a sieve, while the dense particles in clay cause the soil to crust over and deflect water drops. In both cases, adding organic matter helps alleviate the problems.

▸ **Location:** In general, shady gardens need less water than those receiving direct sun. However, in places where trees cast shadows, their roots may greedily hog all the water, leaving little for the flowers.

▸ **Genetic disposition:** Most plants need a consistent supply of moisture to remain healthy and free-blooming. Some types, however, can get by on less water than others.

Getting water to your garden

The best watering method often depends on how large your space is. In some areas, certain watering techniques become a matter of necessity instead of practicality. Where droughts are common or water supplies are unpredictable, conservation is the order of the day. And, where foliage diseases, such as powdery mildew are common, you want to keep water off the plant leaves and apply the water only to the roots. The following list describes several watering methods:

- **Hand watering:** Hose-end attachments soften the force of the spray and help apply the water over a larger area. You can control the amount of water each plant gets and even do some pest control at the same time — blast that blanket flower to wash away aphids!

- **Sprinklers:** The problem with sprinklers is that you have to drag the hose all around and move the sprinkler every so often, most hose-end sprinklers don't apply water very evenly, and you waste water if you forget to turn off the sprinkler.

- **Furrow irrigation:** *Furrows* are shallow trenches that run parallel to your rows. You typically dig the furrows with a hoe at planting time and then plant a row of flowers or vegetables on either side of the furrow. Ideally, the bed should slope just the tiniest bit so that water runs naturally from one end of the furrow to the other. (See Figure 4-1.) When you want to water, you just put a slowly running hose at the end of the furrow and wait for the water to reach the other end. Furrow irrigation keeps the foliage dry and doesn't promote disease, but you still have to move the hose around frequently, and it doesn't work well on fast-draining, sandy soil.

- **Drip irrigation:** Water slowly drips through tiny holes, or *emitters,* in black plastic pipe. The pipe connects to a water supply, filter, and, often, a pressure regulator. The pipes weave through the plants, applying water directly to the base of the plants. You can lay the pipe right on top of the soil and cover it with a mulch or bury it a few inches deep. Drip systems usually have to run for at least several hours to wet a large area, so watch the soil carefully the first few times you water. If you live in an area where the soil freezes, prevent your drip system from bursting in winter by draining the water, rolling up the tubing, and storing it in the garage.

  Drip emitters can wet an entire planting bed from one end to the other at each watering. (You can either snap the emitters into the pipe or buy the pipes with the emitters already installed.) Space the emitters 12 inches (30.5 cm) apart along the length of the pipe. Arrange the pipes so that you have no more than 18 inches (45 cm) between lengths or loops, as shown in Figure 4-2. The moisture radiates sideways and underground, and wets the soil between emitters.

- **Automated watering systems:** Automated watering systems work for both drip and sprinkler systems and can be real time-savers.

Figure 4-1:
Furrow
irrigation
uses gravity
to carry
water from
one end of
the furrow
to the other.

Figure 4-2:
Drip
irrigation is
an efficient
watering
solution.

You're starting to irrigate me

If you live in regions where irrigation is a fact of life, the local newspaper (usually on the page with the weather report) gives the recommended watering rate for lawns based on the evapotranspiration rate. If your local newspaper doesn't include such information, check with your local cooperative extension service.

To figure out how long you need to run the sprinklers to deliver a particular amount of water (usually expressed as inches of water), place containers with straight, vertical sides — juice cans work well — in important locations throughout your sprinkler's spray pattern. After running the sprinkler for a specific length of time, measure the depth of water in each can. Use the can with the least amount of water as the standard.

Now you can water by the newspaper's guideline. If, for example, the sprinkler test shows that your sprinkler puts out ¾ inch (2 cm) per hour and the paper says to apply 1½ inches (about 4 cm) of water this week, run your sprinkler for two hours. This same rate is a good starting point for trees, shrubs, annual flowers, and vegetables.

Conserving water

Water shortages are a reality in almost any climate or region. Following are some water conservation tips:

- **Use a timer.**

- **Install drip irrigation.** This frugal method applies water slowly without runoff.

- **Mulch.** Mulch cools the soil and reduces evaporation, thus saving water.

- **Pull weeds:** Weeds steal water meant for your plants.

- **Water deeply and infrequently:** Shallow sprinkling does very little good. Water to a depth of 8 to 10 inches (20—25 cm), then let the soil dry out partially before you water again.

- **Water early when temps are cooler and it's less windy:** That way, less water evaporates into the air and more reaches the roots.

- **Collect and use rainwater:** Measure rainfall at the same time. An inch is usually enough to let you skip a watering.

- **Plant at the right time:** Plant when your plants have the best chance of getting fully established before the onset of very hot or very cold weather.

Deciding when and how much to water

The best way to water is to replace the moisture that the plants use up by watering daily, three times per week, or weekly. Transpiration causes plants to lose moisture through their foliage. The soil also gives up water by evaporation. *Evapotranspiration,* the combination of evaporation and transpiration, is one way to figure how much water you need to apply. Hot, dry, and windy weather causes plants to use much more moisture than they do on a cool, overcast day. The *evapotranspiration rate,* measured as the total number of inches of water per week or month, tells how much water you can add to replace what the soil lost and what the plants used.

In some parts of North America where irrigation is a fact of life, you can find the evapotranspiration rates in the newspaper, along with recommended watering rates.

Note the condition of your plants. When plants start to dry out, the leaves get droopy and wilt. The plant may also lose its bright green color and start to look a little drab. Most plants need water when the top 2 to 3 inches (5 to 7.5 cm) of soil is dry. So take a small trowel or shovel and dig around a bit. If the top of the soil is dry, you need to water.

Providing a Balanced Diet

Sixteen elements are known to be essential for healthy plant growth. Plants particularly need carbon, hydrogen, and oxygen in large quantities. Plants also need energy from sunlight for *photosynthesis*, the process by which green plants take carbon dioxide from the air and water from the soil to produce sugars to fuel their growth. Apart from watering plants, gardeners can trust nature to supply these big basic requirements.

Plants also need nitrogen, phosphorus, and potassium in relatively large quantities. Plants take up these three elements, often called *macronutrients,* or *primary nutrients,* from the soil. If your soil doesn't have them, you can supply them by adding fertilizers. The percentages of these nutrients are the three prominent numbers on any bag or box of fertilizer, and the nutrients always appear in the same order.

- **Nitrogen (N):** This nutrient is responsible for your plants' healthy green color. It's a key part of proteins and *chlorophyll,* the plant pigment that plays a vital role in photosynthesis. Nitrogen-deficient plants show a yellowing of older leaves, along with a general slowdown in growth.

- **Phosphorus (P):** Phosphorus is associated with good root growth, increased disease resistance, and fruit and seed formation. Plants lacking in phosphorus are stunted, have dark green foliage, followed by reddening of the stems and leaves. As with nitrogen, the symptoms appear on the older leaves first.

- **Potassium (K):** This nutrient promotes vigorous growth and disease resistance. The first sign of a deficiency shows up as browning of the edges of leaves. Older leaves become affected first.

Plants need other nutrients as well, in addition to the three primary ones, but in smaller quantities.

- **Calcium, magnesium, and sulfur:** Plants need these three *secondary nutrients* in substantial quantities but not to the same extent as nitrogen, phosphorus, and potassium. Where the soil is acidic, adding calcium and magnesium is important to maintain a soil pH beneficial to plants and to supply the nutrients that the plants need. Where the soil is alkaline, adding sulfur to the soil is similarly beneficial. For more about pH, see Chapter 3 in Book I.

- **Iron, manganese, copper, boron, molybdenum, chlorine, and zinc:** These seven elements are the *micronutrients,* meaning that plants need only minute quantities for good health. Most soil contains these nutrients, but in soils with a pH too acidic or too alkaline, the nutrients may be unavailable to plant roots. Too much of any of these nutrients can be harmful, so in this case, adjust soil pH rather than add the nutrient.

Flowering by Fertilizer

When you buy a commercial fertilizer, its analysis appears on the label with three numbers. These three numbers are helpful because they let you know the amounts of nutrients (N-P-K) that are in a particular fertilizer. For example, a 100-pound (43 kg) bag of 5-10-10 fertilizer consists of 5 percent nitrogen (5 pounds, or 2.3 kg); 10 percent phosphorus (10 pounds, or 4.6 kg); and 10 percent potassium (10 pounds, or 4.6 kg). Altogether, the bag has 25 pounds of plant-usable nutrients. The remaining 75 pounds (34 kg) usually consists of only *carrier,* or filler. A small amount of the filler may contain some plant-usable material.

Any fertilizer that contains all three of the primary nutrients — N-P-K — is a *complete fertilizer.* The garden term *complete* has its basis in laws and regulations that apply to the fertilizer industry: It doesn't mean that the fertilizer literally contains everything that a plant may need.

Common fertilizer terms

You don't need a degree in botany to have a lovely garden. But you do need to understand some fertilizer terminology:

- **Chelated micronutrients:** These compounds bind to certain plant nutrients and essentially deliver them to the plant roots. Nutrients that plants require in minute quantities — such as iron, zinc, and manganese — are often available in a powder or liquid chelated form.

- **Foliar:** You apply these liquid fertilizers on a plant's leaves, and the leaves absorb the nutrients directly. Although a plant's roots also can absorb the nutrients in most foliar fertilizers, those absorbed via leaves have a quick effect.

  Don't apply foliar fertilizers in hot weather because leaves can become damaged.

- **Granular:** These fertilizers are the most common and most often sold in boxes or bags. Most granular fertilizers are partially soluble. For example, a 10-10-10 granular fertilizer is best applied to the soil about a month prior to planting in order for the nutrients to be available at planting time. You also can get special formulations, such as rose food or azalea food. These specialized fertilizers supply nutrients over a longer period of time than liquid or soluble fertilizers but not as long as slow-release kinds. (See Figure 4-3.)

- **Liquid:** Some fertilizers come as liquid in bottles and jugs. On a per-nutrient basis, liquid fertilizers are more expensive than most dry fertilizers. Most liquid fertilizers need further dilution in water, but a few are ready-to-use. Liquid fertilizers are easy to inject into irrigation systems, which is the reason many professional growers prefer them.

- **Organic:** These fertilizers are often made from dead or composted plants and animals. As a general rule, half the nutrients in organic fertilizers are available to plants the first season. (See more about organic fertilizers in the section "Organic fertilizers" later in this chapter.)

✔ **Slow-release:** These fertilizers release the nutrients that they contain at specific rates in specific conditions over an extended period, some as long as eight months. Slow-release fertilizers are very useful for container plants that otherwise need frequent fertilizing.

Figure 4-3: Use a spreader to apply granular fertilizer.

Kinds of fertilizers for various plants

Different kinds of plants need different kinds of fertilizers, and Table 4-1 lists our recommendations. Of course, the best advice before using any fertilizer is to have your soil tested, which we cover in Chapter 3 of Book I.

TIP

How about a nice cup of manure tea?

You can use animal manures and compost to make liquid fertilizers called *manure tea* or *compost tea*. The nutrients in these teas are readily available for plant use; the teas are gentle enough to use on young plants or spray on the plant foliage to give them a quick boost.

Follow these steps to make manure or compost tea:

1. **Place a shovelful of composted manure in a burlap or other porous cloth bag and secure the top.**

2. **Submerge the bag in about 10 to 15 gallons of water.**

3. **Let the liquid steep for one week or until the water takes on the color of brewed tea.**

   Pour off the manure tea as needed.

4. **Dilute the liquid with water until it resembles the color of weak brewed tea.**

5. **Use the diluted tea to water around plants.**

   Dilute it some more to half-strength tea for young seedlings and as a fertilizer spray.

Table 4-1		Fertilizing at a Glance
Plant	*Fertilizer*	*Comments*
Annuals	Granular	Apply before planting, supplemented by liquid soluble applications after planting.
Bulbs	Granular 8-8-8 or similar	Apply at planting time.
Fruit trees	Granular and/or organic	Apply as necessary in spring only.
Hanging baskets	Slow-release or liquid soluble	Apply every two weeks.
House plants	Slow-release or liquid soluble	Apply every two weeks in spring and summer.
Lawns	Granular and/or organic	Apply spring and fall in cool climates, and early and late summer in warm climates.
Perennials	Granular and/or organic	Apply in autumn; supplement with liquid soluble.
Roses	Granular and/or organic	Apply in spring and autumn for good growth.
Trees and shrubs	Granular and/or organic	Apply in autumn; supplement with complete granular (10-10-10 or similar) if spring growth is poor.
Vegetables	Organic	Apply in autumn or at least one month prior to planting. Continually enrich soil with organic fertilizers; supplement with granular 5-10-10 first two gardening seasons.

Organic fertilizers

Organic or natural fertilizers, such as manure and composts, are more cumbersome and possibly more expensive than synthetic fertilizers, but nothing quite takes their place. These fertilizers provide some nutrient value and, when you incorporate them into the soil, improve soil structure, which increases the soil's ability to hold air, nutrients, and water.

Plants take up nutrients in specific forms, regardless of whether the source is organic or synthetic. You can supply all the necessary nutrients by using only organic materials, but you need to use some care and effort to ensure that sufficient amounts of nitrogen, phosphorus, and potassium are available to the plants throughout the season. Usually, organic fertilizers contain significant amounts of only one of the major nutrients. Nutrients in organic fertilizers are made available to plant roots after soil microorganisms break down the nutrients, which happens fastest when soils are warm. Because the nutrients in organic materials are tied up in more complex molecules, these nutrients often take longer to become available to the plants, which can cause temporary nutrient deficiencies, especially in the spring.

Fresh manure can "burn" plants (damaging leaves and growth from excess application) just as surely as any chemical fertilizer, and woody materials (wood chips, sawdust, leaf piles, and so on) can cause a temporary nitrogen deficiency until they're sufficiently decomposed. The microorganisms that help the decay process may use up all the available nitrogen to break down the woody material. You can counteract this effect somewhat by applying a little extra nitrogen in the spring. Generally, the material is ready for the garden when it starts to resemble soil.

The following list provides information on the most common organic fertilizers:

✔ **Plant-based:** Fertilizers made from plants generally have low to moderate N-P-K values, but their nutrients quickly become available in the soil for your plants to use. Some of them even provide an extra dose of trace minerals and micronutrients. The most commonly available plant-based fertilizers include the following:

- Alfalfa meal
- Compost (We discuss composting later in this chapter.)
- Corn gluten meal
- Cottonseed meal
- Kelp/seaweed
- Soybean meal
- Humus

✔ **Animal-based:** Animals, fish, and birds all provide organic fertilizers that can help plants grow. Most animal-based fertilizers provide lots of nitrogen, which plants need for leafy growth. Following are some of the most commonly available ones:

- Manures
- Bat/seabird guano
- Blood meal
- Bone meal
- Fish products

✔ **Mineral-based:** Rocks decompose slowly into soil, releasing minerals gradually over a period of years. Some take months or years to fully break down into nutrient forms that plants can use, so one application may last a long time. Here are the ones commonly available:

- Chilean nitrate of soda

- Epsom salt

- Greensand

- Gypsum

- Hard-rock phosphate

- Soft-rock phosphate

- Limestone

- Rock dusts

- Sulfate of potash-magnesia (Sul-Po-Mag)

- Sulfur

Piling Onto the Compost Bandwagon

Composting is not only an easy, effective way to reduce solid waste at home, but it's also a valuable, natural soil amendment. Adding compost to garden beds and planting holes enhances nutrients and improves soil texture. Compost helps to loosen heavy clay soils, and it increases the water-holding capacity of sandy soils. (See Chapter 3 in Book I for more information.)

A *compost pile* is a collection of plant (and sometimes animal) materials, combined in a way to encourage quick decomposition. Soil microorganisms (bacteria and fungi) break down this organic material into a soil-like consistency. These organisms need oxygen and water to survive. Turning the pile over provides oxygen, and an occasional watering helps keep it moist. If the pile is well made and the organisms are thriving, it heats up quickly and doesn't emit any unpleasant odors. Finished compost that looks and feels like dark, crumbly soil can take as little as a month to produce.

From refuse to riches

Whether you make your compost in an elaborate store-bought bin (one that closes tightly) or simply in a freestanding pile, the essentials of good composting are the same. To get fast results, follow these steps:

1. **Collect equal parts, by volume, of dried, brown, carbon-rich material (like old leaves or straw) and fresh, green, nitrogen-rich material (fresh-cut grass, green vegetation, and vegetable kitchen wastes).**

Not every material belongs in an open compost pile. Farm animal manures are a safe source of nitrogen, but dog and cat waste can spread unhealthy organisms. Meat, fats, bones, and cooked foods decompose slowly, may be smelly, and may attract animal pests — only add these to compost bins that close tightly. Avoid chemically treated lawn clippings and diseased plant material. Finally, keep out tenacious weeds that spread by runners and roots, such as Bermuda grass, and weeds that are about to go to seed.

2. **Chop or shred the organic materials into small pieces, if possible.**

   Pieces that are ¾ inch (2 cm) or smaller are ideal because they break down quickly.

3. **Build the pile at least 3 feet x 3 feet x 3 feet (1 *cubic yard* or 1 *cubic meter*), alternating layers of the carbon-rich material with the green material.**

   Layer a thin covering of soil for every 18 inches of depth. The soil carries more microorganisms that aid in decomposition.

4. **Wet the pile as you build it.**

   Keep the material about as moist as a wrung-out sponge.

5. **After the temperature begins to decrease, turn the pile, wetting it as necessary to keep it moist.**

   A well-built pile heats up in approximately a week, peaking between 120°F and 160°F (49°C to 71°C). If you don't have a compost thermometer, use a garden fork to turn the pile every week or so the first month.

Bin there, done that!

You can use an enclosure, called a *compost bin,* to keep the pile neat and help retain moisture and heat. Depending on its design, a compost bin also keeps out animal pests. For these reasons, especially in urban settings, a bin is a good idea. (See Figure 4-4.)

Bins are available by mail order and, increasingly, through nurseries, garden centers, and even discount stores. You can spend as much as $400 or more for a commercial compost bin, or you can make your own with scrap materials.

A *wire bin* is perhaps the easiest type to make. You need an 11-foot (3.5 m) length of 36-inch-wide (1 m), welded reinforcing wire with a grid of about 2 x 4 inches (5 x 10 cm). Simply bend the wire to form a hoop and tie the ends together with strong wire. Lining the wire mesh with landscape fabric helps prevent the pile from drying out excessively. This bin holds about a cubic yard when full. To use the bin, fill it with the appropriate balance of organic material. When the pile is ready to turn, lift off the wire mesh and set it next to the pile; then, turn the material and fork it back into the enclosure.

Figure 4-4:
Compost
bins keep
the pile
neat.

Wire composter   High-rise composter   Tumbler composter

Another option is a *wooden compost bin,* made with wooden pallets, wooden scrap boards, and wire or — for the more elaborate model — 2 x 4 (5 x 10 cm) and 2 x 6 (5 x 15 cm) lumber. The Cadillac of the wooden compost bins uses three bins arranged side by side, as shown in Figure 4-5. Though this bin can be time-consuming to construct, some gardeners prefer the convenience of a three-box bin. Each bin is for compost at a different stage of maturity. For example, fresh material is added to the far-left bin, turned into the middle one after a few weeks, and then turned into the bin at the far right to finish.

Heapin' it on

So what else can you put in your compost pile besides the obvious? The following list describes several other materials found around the home and garden that make good additions to any compost pile:

- ✔ Ashes from the wood stove (sprinkle them lightly between layers; *don't* add them by the bucketful)

- ✔ Chicken or rabbit manure

- ✔ Coffee grounds and tea leaves

- ✔ Eggshells (crush them before adding)

- ✔ Flowers

- ✔ Fruit and vegetable peels, stalks, and foliage

- ✔ Fruit pulp from a juicer

- ✔ Grass clippings (mix them thoroughly to prevent clumping)

- ✔ Hedge clippings

- ✔ Shredded leaves (whole leaves tend to mat down and block air)

- ✔ Pine needles (use sparingly; they break down slowly)

- ✔ Sawdust

- ✔ Sod and soil

- ✔ Wood chips (chipped very small for faster decomposition)

Note: Just be sure not to use diseased material or grass/sod that has been treated with herbicides.

Figure 4-5:
A wooden
compost bin
with three
bins allows
for easy
turning.

Commercial bins come in four basic varieties:

- **Containers for hot compost:** Usually made out of recycled plastic, you use these bottomless boxes or cylinders in much the same way as the wire bin. You fill the bin with the right blend of materials and let the pile heat up. To turn the compost, when the bin is full, you lift off the top section of compost and place it on the ground (the section on top now becomes the section on the bottom). Then you reach in with a fork and lift some of the lower compost, making it the top section of compost, and so on. Some of these containers are stackable, which makes removing them and turning the compost easier. With sufficient turning, this type of bin delivers fast results.

- **Bins for a static pile:** With these plastic units (which usually have air vents along the sides), you make a compost pile by putting a balance of waste materials in the top of the bin and letting the mixture sit. As the waste decomposes, you remove the finished compost from the bottom of the bin and add more waste to the top. This type of bin is the most commonly available bin, although not necessarily the best. You don't need to do any turning, and you can add waste at any time; however, decomposition is slow, and you get only small amounts of compost at a time. Because the pile doesn't get very hot, weeds, seeds, and plant diseases may survive.

- **Tumblers:** With a tumbler, you place your compost inside the container and then turn the entire bin to toss the compost inside. Some tumblers have crank handles for turning. One tumbler system is designed to roll on the ground, tumbling the compost inside as it goes. With these units, you make a hot compost by balancing the waste materials and turning the bin frequently. Tumblers are generally the most expensive type of bin, but the ease of turning and the fast results may be worth the money. Choose one with at least a 1-cubic-yard (1 m³) capacity and test it for ease of loading and turning before you buy.

✔ **Anaerobic containers:** These sealed, closed-to-air compost bins require no turning or aerating. You simply fill the container with organic material, close the lid, and wait — sometimes up to six months. This type of bin requires no maintenance, but it often has insect and odor problems. The decomposed product is slimy and requires drying before use, and shoveling the compost out of the bin is difficult.

Composting aids

You don't need to have any store-bought gadgets to make compost. With or without accessories, you can create a perfect pile. A few supplies, however, do make composting faster, more exacting, and perhaps easier. Here's a rundown of these handy items for your consideration. All are available through mail-order garden supply catalogs.

✔ **Compost starters:** Manufacturers say that these products, sometimes called *inoculants* or *activators,* accelerate the composting process and improve the quality of the finished compost. We say that you don't really need them, and that adding a little garden soil for every 12- to 18-inch (30 to 46 cm) layer of yard waste will accomplish the same thing. At most, you may want to add a little cotton- or soybean meal, but only then if the materials are mostly brown (high in carbon).

As an alternative to buying a commercial starter, make a thin layer of rich garden soil when you first build your pile.

✔ **Compost thermometer:** This thermometer consists of a face dial and a steel probe (about 20 inches, or 50 cm, long). You use this tool to accurately monitor the temperature of compost. The instrument measures temperatures from 0°F to 220°F (–18°C to 104°C) and enables you to know when your pile is cooking and when it's cooling down and ready to turn. After you insert the steel probe into the pile, you can see the temperature reading on the face dial. If the compost gets hot, meaning up to 140°F to 160°F (60°C to 71°C), most of the bad players — weeds, diseases, and insect eggs — get killed.

✔ **Compost aerating tool:** You push a 36-inch (1 m), galvanized steel tool into the compost pile. As you pull the tool out, two paddles open, creating a churning action that enables oxygen to enter the pile.

✔ **Compost sifter:** Because different materials decompose at different rates, you may end up with some large chunks of not-yet-decomposed material in compost that is otherwise ready for the garden. The sifter separates out the large pieces, which you can then toss back into a new compost pile to further decompose.

You can save a few bucks by making your own sifter. To do so, use ¼-inch (0.5 cm) window screen stapled or nailed to a wooden frame made of lumber. Make the frame large enough so that you can position it over a wheelbarrow and sift compost through it.

✔ **Pitchfork:** This long-handled tool, with tines about 10 to 12 inches (25 to 30 cm) long, is the best instrument to use for turning compost.

A-Mulching We Will Go . . .

Mulch is any material, organic or not, placed over the surface of soil to conserve moisture, kill weed seedlings, modify soil temperatures, or make the garden look more attractive — or do all four at once. Mulch was traditionally thought to mean natural, organic materials, such as leaves, wood chips, and sand. Now, a multitude of plastic-based films or woven materials are available.

A common goal of mulching is to reduce weeding, so use inorganic mulches or seed-free organic mulches, such as the following:

✔ **Grass clippings:** Make sure that the clippings come from a weed- and pesticide-free lawn.

✔ **Leaves:** Make sure that they're shredded or composted.

✔ **Newspaper:** It can be either shredded or flat.

✔ **Pine needles:** Use for acid-loving crops.

✔ **Salt hay:** This generally weed-free plant is from oceanside meadows.

✔ **Shredded bark:** Use around trees or other prominent areas because this type of mulch is the most attractive.

✔ **Wood chips:** Use fresh chips from a local arborist, or better, composted wood chips from a soil or amendment supplier.

Inorganic mulch, such as gravel, landscape fabric, sand, and stone, holds in moisture and stops weeds but doesn't add fertility to the soil. Use this mulch around perennials, shrubs, or trees that are naturally adjusted to your soil and don't require additional fertilizer.

Double your gardening pleasure by using fertile mulch, which controls weeds *and* provides small amounts of nutrients. All organic mulches made of plant material fit this group. Some organic mulches quickly rot (decompose) and dissolve nutrients into the soil; these are green, fresh, and not too woody. The mulches that quickly decompose are useful in annual flower and vegetable beds. When sprinkled with water, or in rainy-summer areas, organic mulch that decomposes fairly quickly also leaches some nutrients while sitting on top of the soil.

A well-read mulch

Newspapers provide the ultimate organic "herbicide," a simple and cost-effective way to mulch out weeds. A thin layer of five to ten sheets of newspaper suppresses all sprouting weed seeds, stops some resprouting taproots, and makes life difficult for runner roots. Use newsprint that is plain black and white or that has colored pictures. The newspapers are best used around woody perennials, shrubs, and trees, but once you're familiar with the process, you can use them around flowers or vegetables.

To apply the newspaper, moisten the sheets so that they don't blow around as you lay them out among the plants. Cover the papers with a thin layer of a weed-free, attractive mulch. The mulch helps the newspaper last for 6 to 18 months, depending on whether you have wet or dry summers, respectively.

Cardboard works even better than newspaper for the really tough weeds.

Other organic mulches are slow to decompose and release few nutrients; these are usually dry, woody, and very low in nitrogen. Bark mulches are slowest to decompose because bark is naturally rot-resistant. Use these for pathways, or around trees and shrubs. Chips of tree sapwood may be fresh or composted. The latter is preferable, if available. Fresh wood chips can make an excellent mulch, but you should apply a little extra nitrogen fertilizer over the mulch so that it doesn't take all the nitrogen at your plants' expense.

Fertile mulches that quickly decompose but have weed seeds include cow, rabbit, goat, sheep, and horse manure; hay; some poultry bedding; sewage sludge; and straw. Fertile mulches that also quickly decompose but have no weed seeds include clean grass clippings, leaves, and salt hay. Newspaper, shredded bark, and wood chips add little fertility to the soil and decompose slowly because they are high in carbon; they have no weed seeds.

All the mulches we mention are just part of a nearly infinite selection of local specialties. Rice hulls, cocoa shells, sugar cane refuse, ground corncobs, peanut shells, and grape pomace are a few you may encounter, depending where you live.

Woven plastic materials (called *landscape fabric*) act as a seedling barrier as well, but these effective materials are not attractive enough for some situations. Also, sunlight deteriorates these mulches, so covering them with a weed-free organic mulch to block the sun's ultraviolet rays is a good idea. The fabric lasts longer and your garden looks better.

Chapter 5

Pruning from Limb to Limb

*Y*ou use both pruning and propagating to promote plant growth, but you use them for different purposes. *Pruning* refers to cutting plants to redirect the plant's growth to where you want it. *Propagating* (or taking cuttings) refers to cutting off a part of a plant and using the cutting to start a new plant. This chapter gives you the fundamentals that will have you happily snipping and cutting in no time.

Practical Pruning

One of the most misunderstood, and therefore neglected, gardening techniques, pruning is part maintenance, part preventative medicine, and part landscaping. Following are some common reasons for pruning plants:

- **Sculpting for decorative reasons:** Be aware that as soon as you embark on pruning a plant to a specific shape, it's hard to go back.

- **Shaping for strength and resistance to wind, snow, and ice damage:** Some fruit trees also need annual or semiannual pruning in order to continue bearing crops.

- **Keeping the plant healthy:** When you remove dead branches, the tree can more easily seal the remaining wound.

As a general rule, don't prune unless you must. Always consider whether the plant really needs to be pruned. (Table 5-1 shows the best time for pruning specific plants.) Many native or naturalized trees grow perfectly fine without pruning. But roses and fruit trees, among others, need thoughtful pruning for maximum production of flowers and fruit.

Table 5-1	When to Prune
Type of Plant	*When*
Shrubs that bloom in spring	Just after flowers fade
Shrubs that bloom in summer or fall	Early spring
Rhododendrons and azaleas	Just after flowers fade
Pine trees	Late spring
Formal hedges	Late spring and, if necessary, fall
Most trees, shrubs, and vines	Late winter or early spring

Pruning and how it affects plant growth

A mixture of hormones and food controls a tree's growth. Some of the tree's important hormones — growth stimulators or regulators — come from the bud at the tip of each leafy shoot or branch, which biologists call the *apical, leading,* or *tip* bud. The tip bud stimulates new, lengthy, vertical growth and stifles the growth of lower potential shoots — called *dormant buds.* When you clip out any tip bud, you take away the stifling tip hormones and their dominance. The dormant buds below the cut burst into growth and begin to produce the tip hormones themselves.

When a branch is positioned at a 45- to 60-degree angle, the flow of carbohydrates, hormones, and nutrients naturally favors the formation of flower buds. With many deciduous fruit trees, like apple, almond, and pear trees, the flower buds become long-term fruiting places, called *spurs*, in the following years.

Pruning the kind way

You prune plants by using the following techniques (see Figure 5-1 for examples of each):

- **Thinning cuts:** Whether you're pruning mature trees or tomato seedlings, *thinning cuts* remove an entire branch or limb all the way to its origin to create better air circulation or to reduce crowded conditions. Always make thinning cuts to just above a dormant bud. Cut at a slight angle and leave about ¼ inch (0.6 cm) of the shoot above the bud — not a long stub.

- **Heading cuts:** These cuts shorten a branch or stem but doesn't remove it entirely.

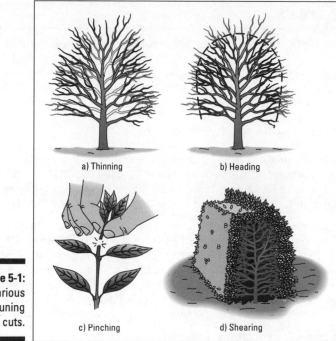

Figure 5-1:
Various
pruning
cuts.

a) Thinning

b) Heading

c) Pinching

d) Shearing

✔ **Pinching:** This action can be either a heading or thinning cut. Usually, you pinch soft growth between your thumb and forefinger. Pinching is handy with soft annuals and perennials, but also good for larger plants, if you do it early enough when their shoots are still young and soft. Any pruning done at this early stage is ideal because the plant suffers minimal harm and recovery is quick.

✔ **Shearing:** For this cut, use scissorlike pruning "shears" to keep hedge lines straight and neat. Boxwood and yews are commonly sheared.

Rules to prune trees and shrubs by

A few "rules of limb" apply when pruning all trees and shrubs:

✔ **Remove dead or diseased wood as soon as possible.** Be sure not to spread certain diseases, such as fireblight, with the pruning tools: Clean the blade with a 10 percent dilution of bleach after *every* cut.

✔ Cut out one or two branches or shoots if they rub against each other.

✔ Prune in the winter to encourage new shoots and leafy growth.

✔ Prune in the summer to remove unwanted shoots or limbs without stimulating too many new shoots.

Pruning trees

Use thinning cuts when pruning trees, but leave the *branch collar* intact. The branch collar is slightly wider than the shoot you're removing, is marked with many compact wrinkles, and is usually a slightly different tone or texture than the shoot. Natural chemicals within the branch collar encourage rapid healing and help prevent rot from entering the heart of the tree.

Consider these pruning tips before you take out your saw:

- ✔ **Sawing a medium-sized limb:** If the limb is small enough to hold so that it doesn't fall while cutting, you can use only one cut with a pruning handsaw. Leave the larger and more noticeable branch collar intact. Don't let the limb drop as you cut through it, or the bark will tear or rip.

- ✔ **Sawing a large limb:** You use three cuts to remove large, heavy limbs, as shown in Figure 5-2. First, a few inches (about 8 cm) outside of the branch collar, cut halfway through the limb from the underneath side. Then, a few inches outside of the first cut, make a second cut (from the top), this time going all the way through the limb. If any bark begins to tear, it will stop at the cut underneath. Trim off the remaining stub with a final cut just outside the branch collar.

- ✔ **Treating your tree's wounds:** Covering pruning wounds with tar or asphalt doesn't really help the tree much.

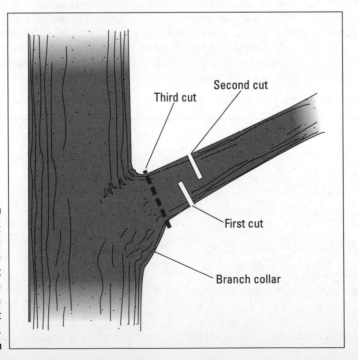

Figure 5-2: Removing a large limb without ripping the bark is a three-cut process.

Pruning in winter

The traditional season for pruning *deciduous* (leaf shedding) plants is while all the buds are dormant — in late winter or very early spring before flowers or leaves open. Such pruning stimulates new vegetative shoots — which are less fruitful with fruit trees. Cutting back a dormant branch causes two or more side shoots to emerge below the cut as a result of lost tip dominance. Winter pruning is especially helpful when you want to force new shoots to fill air space around the trunk with branches. The time to prune "bleeders," however, is during midsummer after new growth has hardened. *Bleeders* are trees that exude lots of sap, especially in late winter through spring. Maples, birches, and cherries are notable examples.

When you have many long, vertical shoots — called *suckers* or *watersprouts* — winter pruning only makes the problem worse. Thinning each vertical limb, even if cut to its base, usually multiplies the problem by causing two or more shoots to arise with the spring sap flow. You remedy this situation only with summer pruning.

Pruning in summer

Summer pruning can be extremely valuable. Careful summer pruning has the effect of mildly stunting or dwarfing trees. The partial removal of the foliage in summer means fewer leaves to convert sunlight into stored carbohydrates. Summer is the preferred time to begin a restoration program with neglected and overgrown trees. Summer pruning is also the best time for thinning cuts. The active photosynthesis allows the trees to begin forming a *callus* over the cut. The well-knit callus tissue that forms a ring around the cut resists the sprouting of new shoots the coming spring.

Pruning too early in the season, during spring's burst of vegetative growth, has a stimulating effect more like dormant pruning. Summer-prune after the initial flurry of spring growth, as the weekly growth rate slows down.

In cold-winter climates, summer-prune by the middle of summer because late summer pruning sometimes forces new, succulent shoots. These tender shoots don't harden off before freezing weather arrives and can die off.

Pruning tools

Poorly constructed tools can cripple or maim a gardener, so select a set of well-made, sturdy pruning tools. Here's a brief list of the essentials:

✔ **Hand pruner:** Reserve hand pruners for cuts up to ½ or 1 inch (1.3 to 2.5 cm) in diameter.

✔ **Lopper:** Loppers can cut limbs up to several inches in diameter. If you're restoring an abandoned tree or shrub, you need a lopper to remove older wood. (**Note:** You never need a lopping shear if your trees are well-trained from the start.)

✔ **Hand saw:** You definitely need a 12-inch (30 cm) bladed, folding saw. Make sure that you get one with a locking mechanism for the open position. If you're working on a disheveled or abandoned tree with large limbs slated for removal, you may want a large 24- to 36-inch long (61 to 91 cm) curved pruning saw with large 1- to 2-inch (2.5 to 5 cm) saw teeth. The bigger the saw's teeth and the wider the space between the teeth, the faster the saw cuts.

✔ **Ladder and pole pruner:** If you're caring for really large shade or fruit trees, you need a pruning ladder and/or a pole pruner. Buy a three-legged, aluminum (not wooden) orchard pruning and picking ladder. These ladders come in heights of 6 to 16 feet (2 to 5 meters) and cost from $75 to $200. The ladders aren't cheap, but they're the most comfortable way to prune a large tree with hand pruners and a lopper. If standing on a ladder makes you nervous, an extending pole pruner is your next best option. Buy one with fiberglass poles — they're lightweight and won't conduct electricity if you happen to touch a wire — that telescope from 6 to 12 feet (about 2 to 4 meters). A good pole pruner can set you back $125 to $180.

Down-to-Earth Propagating

When people speak of propagating, they usually mean *taking cuttings* — using pieces of stems, roots, and leaves to start new plants. (See Figure 5-3.)

Softwood stem cuttings, taken from spring until midsummer, root the quickest. During this time, plants are actively growing, and the stems are succulent and flexible. Here's how to take a softwood stem cutting:

1. **Use a sharp knife to cut a 4- to 5-inch-long (10 to 12 cm) stem (or side shoot) just below a leaf, and remove all but two or three leaves at the top.**

2. **Dip the cut end into rooting hormone.**

   Rooting hormone is a powder or liquid containing growth hormones that stimulate root growth on cuttings. Some also contain a fungicide to control root rot. Local nurseries or garden centers carry the product.

3. **Insert the cutting into a box or container (with drainage holes), filled with about 3 inches (8 cm) of moistened pure builder's sand, vermiculite, or perlite.**

4. **Slip the container into a self-sealing plastic bag.**

   Prop up the bag with something like toothpicks or short twigs so that the plastic doesn't touch the leaves. Seal the bag to minimize water loss, but open it occasionally to let in fresh air.

5. **Place the covered container in indirect light.**

6. **When the cuttings are well rooted (4 to 8 weeks, for most plants) and are putting on new growth, transplant them into individual containers of potting soil.**

   As they continue to grow, gradually expose them to more light. When the plants are well established in the pots and continue to put on top growth, *harden them off* (acclimate them to your weather conditions) and plant them in their permanent garden location.

   To harden off new plants, gradually move them to more extreme temperatures and sunlight. Moving them from the porch to outside in partial sun and finally to full sun over a week's time should do the trick.

Here are some easy-to-root plants to grow from stem cuttings:

✔ **Perennials:** Begonia, candytuft, chrysanthemum, carnations or pinks *(Dianthus)*, geraniums *(Pelargonium)*, penstemon, phlox, sage, sedum

✔ **Woody plants:** Bougainvillea, fuchsia, gardenia, heather, honeysuckle, ivy, pyracantha, star jasmine, willow

Figure 5-3:
Taking a
stem
cutting.

Divide and Plant-er

Sometimes, the best source for plant material for propagating is neighbors and friends. If your neighbor has a plant you want to grow, just ask to take cuttings. (Gardeners love to share.)

Another great way to get new plants is through *division,* the process of pulling apart clumps of plants to create new clumps. (See Figure 5-4.) As plants become established in a garden, most develop into larger and larger clumps made up of small plants. Dividing and then replanting these clumps is the easiest means of spreading and increasing them. Dividing works great with all but *tap-rooted* plants, namely plants with a main root that grows straight down, such as a carrot.

Use the following techniques to divide plants:

- Use a spade or digging fork to lift out a mature clump (usually 3 to 5 years old).

- Divide fine-rooted types, such as lamb's ears, by hand, gently teasing apart the clump into separate plants.

- Divide tough or fleshy-rooted types with a spade by cutting down through the roots, or use two garden forks back-to-back to pry the clumps apart.

Each new section for replanting should include several buds. Discard the older central section and replant the divisions as soon as possible.

The best season to divide plants varies by plant and climate. As a general guideline, divide spring-flowering plants in very late summer or early autumn, so that the new divisions can become established before winter. Divide summer- and autumn-flowering plants in early spring, while new top growth is just 2 or 3 inches (5 to 8 cm) high.

Figure 5-4:
Divide by
pulling apart
the root ball
or by using
a spade.

Chapter 6

Tooling Around the Garden

*H*aving the right tool for the job often makes the difference between a pleasurable experience and a frustrating chore. Luckily, gardening really doesn't require a shed full of tools. In fact, we recommend starting with just a few essential tools and then building your collection as specific jobs call for more-specialized tools. This chapter tells you which tools you need to have, and which ones you may want to put on your holiday wish list.

Hand Tools

To save money over the long haul, buy high-quality, durable tools. Generally, forged-steel tools hold up better than welded types. Relatively new on the market are tools with fiberglass handles, which are stronger than wood. Hardware stores and garden centers offer what you need to get started. Mail-order garden supply catalogs, such as A. M. Leonard, Inc., offer more-specialized tools.

Following is a list of the tools that you absolutely must have:

✔ **Garden hose:** Buy a top-quality hose with a lifetime guarantee. A good hose coils easily, resists kinking, and remains flexible even in cold weather. Choose one long enough to reach all corners of your garden.

✔ **Hand trowel:** A hand trowel is important for transplanting seedlings, scooping soil into containers, and doing close-up weeding jobs. Buy one that fits your hand and is light enough to be comfortable.

- ✔ **Lawn rake:** Nothing works better than a bamboo, polypropylene, or metal rake with long, flexible tines for gathering up lawn clippings, leaves, and even small rocks on both paved and natural surfaces. (See Figure 6-1.)

- ✔ **Pruners:** Most gardeners favor *by-pass pruners*, which cut like scissors. *Anvil pruners* that cut by pressing a blade into a soft metal anvil are less expensive. Use either type to cut soft and woody stems up to about ½ inch (1.3 cm) thick. Use this tool to clip flowers, harvest vegetables, groom shrubs, and prune trees.

- ✔ **Scuffle hoe:** This type of hoe is easier to use — instead of chopping (as you do with a conventional hoe), you push the hoe along the soil's surface. A scuffle hoe is indispensable for weeding on packed, level surfaces such as garden paths. Although scuffle hoes vary in design, all work with a push-pull motion. Some cut and scrape the tops off weeds on both strokes. Our favorite, the *oscillating* or *action* hoe, has a hinged blade that moves back and forth as it cuts.

- ✔ **Shovel:** A regular round-nose shovel, as shown in Figure 6-1, is the single most versatile tool you can own. You need it for digging, turning, scooping, and breaking up clods of earth. Choose a length and weight that's comfortable.

Figure 6-1: The lawn rake is effective for gathering leaves and lawn clippings. The round-nose shovel can dig, scoop, turn, and chop. A stiff-tined rake is useful for spreading and leveling soil.

✔ **Stiff-tined rake:** The first rake you should buy is a *stiff-tined* or *steel bow* rake, as shown in Figure 6-1. This rake is an important tool for spreading and leveling soil and for gathering organic materials. The rake also is a good tool for breaking up small clods of earth. Use both the *tines* (the thin, pointed prongs) and the back edge of the rake for building and smoothing raised garden beds: Keep the tines facing downward when breaking up lumps of soil or collecting stones, and keep the flat edge of the head downward when leveling.

After you invest in the seven essential tools — and if you still have space in your shed or garage — here's what to buy next. Though not as critical as the seven essential tools, these all-purpose tools are very useful to most gardeners:

✔ **Garden cart:** A lightweight, well-balanced cart that maneuvers easily allows a gardener to haul big, heavy loads of soil, compost, plants, containers, or wood with little effort.

✔ **Gardening gloves:** Gloves should fit well and be thick enough to protect your hands, yet not so clunky that you can't maneuver small objects. Cloth gloves with leather reinforcement hold up well to general garden tasks. Gloves with extra-long cuffs help protect your wrists from branches and thorns. Following are glove materials and their best uses:

  • **Cotton/polyester and leather:** General garden chores.

  • **Synthetics, such as Spectra and Kevlar:** Working with saws and knives.

  • **Latex or PVC:** Working with and around water.

  • **Chemical-resistant nitrile or neoprene:** Working with chemicals.

✔ **Lopping shears:** When you get serious about pruning trees and shrubs, loppers are a must. These tools cut easily through branches an inch or more in diameter. Figure 6-2 shows a pole lopper (also known as a pole pruner), which allows you to prune branches that are well above your head. (Read more about pole loppers in Chapter 5 of Book I.)

✔ **Tape measure:** A metal tape measure is essential for laying out garden beds and helpful in spacing plants. When staking out an entire landscape, a 100-foot (30 m) length helps you measure precisely.

✔ **Water wand:** This hose-end attachment is great for watering containers, garden seedlings, and seedbeds. Choose one with a shut-off valve. The wand should provide a full but gentle flow that doesn't wash away soil and seeds.

Take care of your hand tools — they'll last longer and work better. Try to clean and dry your tools each time you finish your gardening chores, but also know that primary maintenance consists of keeping wood handles smooth and sound, metal tool heads rust-free, and blades sharp.

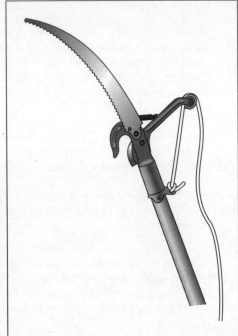

Figure 6-2:
A pole
lopper
allows you
to prune
branches
above your
head.

When wooden tool handles show wear, sand off the factory varnish and apply boiled linseed oil. Apply several coats, allowing the oil to soak in each time. Clean metal tool heads with a wire brush and sharpen edges with a file. Protect the metal by coating with rust-proof primer followed by a coat of rust-proof paint. Many by-pass pruners have replacement cutting blades that are easy to install. You can also sharpen pruners (the beveled side of the curved blade only) with a fine-grit diamond file.

Replace worn hand tool grips with a liquid plastic, sold in most hardware stores. The best tool lubricants are synthetic oils that lubricate, repel dust, protect against rust, and leave only a light film. Our favorite is Corona's CLP Shear Maintenance Oil, available from A. M. Leonard (`www.amleonard.com`).

Powering Up Your Tools

No matter whether you love or hate power tools, most gardeners use at least one of these tools from time to time.

Lawn mowers

One of the reasons that people get fed up with lawns (see Book IX for more about lawn care) is that lawns require this regular, monotonous maintenance called *cutting the grass,* which, for some of you, may conjure up memories of noisy, dirty, hard-to-start engines. We're here to tell you that times have changed! You have so many more choices now that you're more likely to find the mower that's right for you. New lawn mowers are quieter, better working, less polluting, and safer.

Choose a lawn mower according to the size of your lawn, the type of grass, your tolerance (or lack thereof) of noise, and your desire for exercise. Allow about an hour to mow 2,500 square feet (232 m²) of grass, using a 20-inch-wide (50 cm) rotary mower. The wider the mower or the faster it moves, the more quickly you can get the job done.

Push-reel mowers

Push-reel mowers are quiet and completely nonpolluting; they give your body a workout that equals a session (at the least) with a treadmill. If your lawn is 1,000 square feet (93 m²) or less and composed mostly of soft grasses, such as fescue, Kentucky bluegrass, or ryegrass, this type of mower is a serious option. Most cost around $100, but fancy ones can be twice that.

Power-reel mowers

The power-reel mower is the type of mower that professional gardeners and greenskeepers use. In all cases, the engine drives both the cutting blades and the wheels, but some types throw clippings to the front, and others throw to the rear. These mowers are much more expensive than rotary mowers ($300 and up), but they're unsurpassed at providing a close, even cut — even of dense, thick grasses such as Bermuda grass or zoysia.

Push rotary power mowers

Push rotary power is the type of mower that America uses to cut its grass. You provide the push power, but the engine and the spinning blade do the grass cutting. This type is relatively inexpensive ($200–$400, depending on features) and easy to operate. You need to choose between *side* or *rear bagging.* Side-baggers are cheaper and work just as well, but they're slightly less convenient because you can cut close only on one side of the mower.

Don't buy a push rotary power mower that doesn't include a blade break system, colorfully termed a *deadman switch.* This device makes the spinning blade stop within 3 seconds after the operator releases a lever on the handle. These mowers are more expensive, but they reduce mower-caused injuries.

Self-propelled and mulching rotary mowers

Self-propelled and mulching rotary mowers are basically the same as push rotary power mowers but with added features. Naturally, the price is steeper: $500–$700, usually. The *self-propelled* feature is plain enough: Pulleys and gears link the engine to the front wheels. The mulching concept is a bit more involved: The mower is basically the same, but the cutting blade and deck are redesigned to cut and recut the grass and leaves, resulting in pieces small enough that the grass filters back down into the lawn. As the cut blades decompose, they release nutrients to the growing lawn, and you don't have to bag and send clippings to the landfill. These mowers typically have no exit chute on the side or rear.

Electric rotary mowers

Electric rotary mowers are great, especially if you'd rather not deal with anything gasoline-powered. The machines are virtually silent and easy to start. Electric rotary mowers do have a downside, though. A long cord, usually of a maximum length, restricts your movements (and how much lawn you can cut); the umbilical-free, battery-powered kinds are a bit heavy and pricey. A variety of solar-powered mowers are available now, but these are expensive and not practical in many situations.

Lawn mowers that you can sit on

This category is broad:

- **Riding mowers:** These do nothing but cut grass. Typically, the engine is in the rear, the mowing deck out in front, and you sit somewhere in between. The mowing deck is 30 to 42 inches (76 to 106 cm) wide, and engines are 8 to 13 horsepower. Prices range from $700 to $1,000.

- **Lawn-and-garden tractors:** This mower is for a homeowner with a large property. Somewhat larger than sit-down lawn mowers, these look a bit more like real farm tractors. You sit and look out over a hood that covers the engine, and the mowing deck is right below your chair. Most have a channel steel frame and front axle and 12 to 18 horsepower. (Don't buy more horsepower than you need. Lawn-and-garden tractors with 14 horsepower are enough to cut several acres of grass and occasionally till the soil.) These mowers cut 38 to 48 inches (96 cm to 1.2 m) of grass in one swipe. Some models take attachments, such as tillers and snowthrowers. Expect to pay anywhere from $1,000 to $4,000.

- **Garden tractors:** These are actual, scaled-down versions of farm tractors. Equally heavy-duty as their full-size brethren, their frames are heavy, 10-gauge steel, and both front and rear axles are cast iron. These machines use anywhere from 12 to 20 horsepower and cut 38 to 60 inches (96 cm to 1.5 m) of grass at once. The benefit of a garden tractor over a lawn tractor is that the garden tractor can accept a variety of attachments, such as rototillers, chippers, and snowblowers. A garden tractor is a good tool for a weekend farmer who needs to do lots of chores. Expect to pay at least $3,000 and as much as $10,000.

Trimmers

After lawn mowers, the string trimmer is the most widely used power tool. Some are electric; others are gas powered. Most of the gas-powered kinds use two-stroke engines, which requires that you mix special oil into the gasoline. A few manufacturers now offer quieter and less polluting four-stroke engines on their trimmers. Gas-powered trimmers are louder than electric versions. Most trimmers cut soft grass and weeds with a spinning nylon cord. Some use a solid nylon disk, and some can accept other, heavy-duty cutting blades. For a basic string trimmer, look for one with an automatic or semiautomatic "feed" system for the nylon whip. Some trimmers force you to stop the engine and lengthen the string or whip by hand every time the string wears down.

Electric trimmers with power cords are the least expensive kind. These trimmers enable you to work 50 to 100 feet (15 to 30 m) from an outlet, they're lightweight, and they're quiet. Prices start at about $50. Models powered by batteries allow you to roam more freely, but they limit you to about 45 minutes of continuous trimming. They also cost a bit more — about $100.

Trimmers with gas power work roughly the same as the electric models, but they give you more power, need more maintenance, make more noise, and let you do more work in less time.

Even though the spinning whip of cord is safer than a whirling blade, it can damage the bark of young trees and shrubs (not to mention hands and feet). If you use this type of trimmer around trees, protect the lower trunk with a heavy plastic collar (available at garden centers). Or better yet, add a ring of mulch around the tree and eliminate the need for close trimming!

Tillers and grinders

Most tillers and grinders (also known as "chipper-shredders") are hefty machines. Weight begins at about 70 pounds (32 kg) and goes up to a few hundred pounds. Engine horsepower begins at 3, but some have 8 or more. The cost begins at around $500 and ranges upward to $1,600. As big and heavy as they are, both are big time-savers. If you regularly garden a quarter acre or more, both may be smart investments. If you need a tiller or chipper just once or twice a year, consider renting over buying your own.

A tiller consists of an engine that provides the power to a transmission that channels the power to the wheels and the tiller. Tillers with the tines in front don't have powered wheels, so the transmission has only to drive the tiller.

All rotary tillers are categorized as either *front tine* or *rear tine*. Front-tine rotary tillers are lighter in weight and cheaper; consider them medium-duty machines. If the soil you're tilling is relatively loose, these are very effective.

These tillers, however, aren't as efficient if the soil is compacted or rocky. The tines pull the tiller forward; so if the tines connect with a big stone or root, the machine lurches forward. The other downside of front-tine tillers is that you must walk directly behind them, through the freshly fluffed soil.

Heavy-duty tillers have the engine in front and the tines in the rear. Expert gardeners prefer rear-tine tillers because they're much easier and less jarring to operate (even though they're heavier). The tines dig down into the soil rather than force the machine to lurch forward, and the operator doesn't need to walk through freshly tilled soil.

As the tines turn

Most tines rotate in the direction of travel. The resistance of the soil on the blades causes the tiller to drive itself forward. You need to restrain this driving force to ensure even tilling of the soil.

Tillers offer several kinds of tines, with many different functions. By far, the most common kind of tine is the *bolo* tine, which is shaped like an *L* and is sharpened on the cutting edge. The bottom of the *L* is twisted slightly so that the soil lifts up and away as the tine turns. Some tines are further bent so that they can enter the soil more easily.

The higher the tine speed, the more easily and more finely you can prepare the seedbed. A higher tine speed is also necessary to adequately chop up crop residues or compost and incorporate them into the soil. The common tine speed for front-tine tillers is 100 to 175 rotations per minute. Commercial tillers often allow you to vary the tine speed for different uses. The throttle setting also affects tine speed.

Mini-tillers

Also referred to as *lightweight tiller/cultivators, hand-held tiller/cultivators,* and *power cultivators,* mini-tillers are 20- to 30-pound (9 to 13 kg), gasoline-powered (usually two-cycle) machines. In most designs, the horizontally mounted engine (1½ horsepower) sits directly above the tines. Connected to this engine and tine unit are handlebars with a lever for throttle control and an on/off switch. The cost of mini-tillers varies with the number of attachments you buy, but expect to pay around $300.

Mini-tiller tines are made of sharper-edged spring steel and spin faster than the heavier tines of large tillers. The patented Mantis tines are star-shaped, so they tend to slice into the soil. The others have conventional, L-shaped tines that dig like a hoe.

On small patches of ground that are in good condition, hand tools are probably just as quick and efficient and not as damaging to soil structure. Tillers of any kind may create a layer of packed and hardened soil at the bottom of their cultivating depth — the so-called *plow sole*. But on larger stretches of relatively stone-free ground, the mini-tillers can be worthwhile. They dig about twice as fast as a person skillful with a fork and spade and require much less bending than working the soil with hand tools does.

An automatic clutch activates the tines, which control forward motion. A lever on either the right or left handlebar controls engine speed. At idle, the tines don't move. As you squeeze the lever, the engine speeds up, and the tines engage. Tines work soil to a depth of 3 to 10 inches (7.5 to 25 cm). An average working depth after two passes through an average soil is probably about 6 inches, but by working the machine back and forth, you make it dig deeper.

Use a mini-tiller for the following tasks:

- Tilling loamy, stone-free soil
- Tilling soil in small or raised beds
- Cultivating compacted, weedy soil between rows of vegetables
- Cultivating soil in narrow, tight locations
- Weeding in compacted walkways
- Mixing compost and amendments into planting beds
- Digging planting holes for trees, shrubs, and perennials

Garden grinders

Most garden grinders available today are part chipper and part shredder. The former consists of a 3- to 4-inch (7.5 to 10 cm) hardened steel blade inserted into the main flywheel of the machine. You feed material — branches or corn stalks, for instance — to it via a narrow tube. The shredder part is a larger opening designed to accept armloads of preferably dry leaves. The opening leads to a chamber in which a number of 2-inch (5 cm) long flails spin and "shred" the material.

Electric motors, gasoline engines, or power-take-off (PTO) connections of garden tractors supply power to grinders. Electric grinders are suitable for chipping small prunings up to an inch or so in diameter. Gasoline-powered grinders have 3 to 12 horsepower engines and a manual or automatic clutch.

Garden grinders are among the most dangerous tools gardeners regularly use. Wear goggles or protective glasses at all times and avoid loose-fitting clothing. Follow all the safety precautions carefully, and always turn the engine off and wait for it to stop completely before reaching in to unclog.

Where to Shop for Garden Tools

All plants are not created equal, nor are tools, potting mixes, and most gardening implements. So to get what you want for your garden — the best quality, a true bargain, or something really strange (such as an electric bulb-planting drill) — you need to know where to shop:

- **Nurseries:** In addition to plants and information, larger nurseries offer seeds, bulbs, soil amendments, bark mulches, containers, fertilizers, pesticides, tools, irrigation supplies, and even garden ornaments.

- **Hardware stores and home-building centers:** Look to these places for garden tools and materials to build garden structures, such as lumber, nails, and twine for trellises.

- **Farm and feed stores:** These stores are a great source for seeds, tools, soil amendments, fertilizers, pesticides, fencing, and irrigation supplies.

- **Discount stores:** If you know a quality product by brand name or know how to judge the quality of a product, you may find a true bargain at a discount store. But just because something is inexpensive doesn't mean that it's a bargain. Heed this warning: Know what you're paying for.

- **Mail order:** Shopping by mail greatly broadens your choice of seeds, plants, tools, and supplies. However, besides having to wait for delivery, you can't see what you're buying. Make sure, then, that your sources — especially nurseries — are reliable.

Chapter 7

Avoiding Plague, Famine, and Pestilence in the Garden

*W*hen you venture into the gardening world, you face many foes, namely insects, weeds, and disease. This chapter details the dangers that face your garden and the best ways for you to protect your precious plants.

Going Buggy

The average square yard of garden contains over a thousand insects, and most of them help — not hurt — your plants. Only a small fraction cause much damage. This section looks at insects and helps you sort out the predators from the pests.

Gathering the usual suspects

When insect eggs hatch, they become *larva*, immature insects, which is often the most plant-destructive period of an insect's life. Many insects go through a stage between larva and adult when they form a cocoon or hard shell around themselves. They don't eat or cause damage at this stage, but they don't succumb easily to predators or pesticides, either. Adult insects usually have wings and are at their most mobile life stage. Some adult insects feed on plants by piercing or rasping holes and sucking or sponging up the plant juices. Others chew on plant parts.

Outwitting critters

While insect feeding is subtler and causes incremental damage over time, larger critters can eliminate an entire plant — or row of plants — almost right before your eyes. You can, however, keep damage to a minimum by getting to know their habits:

- **Birds:** Birds in the yard are a mixed blessing. You appreciate their appetite for insects, but when they nibble on the plants themselves, they cross the line into nuisance territory. Keep birds away from your plants by draping bird netting or row covers over them. You can startle birds with noise, fluttering objects, and, of course, anything resembling a predator. Birds catch on quickly though, so change your scare tactics regularly.

- **Deer:** You can try a few things to make your garden less appealing to deer. Install a fence so that it slants outward away from the garden, which can intimidate the deer by making the fence appear wider than it really is. In early spring, row covers can deter the deer long enough to give your plants a head start and allow time for wild food plants to become plentiful. You can also buy deer repellents, but avoid spraying fruits and vegetables, because you don't want to eat the stuff yourself.

- **Rabbits:** The best way to keep rabbits away from your plants is to fence them out. Because they burrow, a fence must also extend underground. We've had good luck repelling rabbits with mothballs or hair gathered from hair salons and dog groomers. Sprinkle it around the boundary of a garden and replenish it every few weeks. You can also purchase commercial repellents.

- **Groundhogs:** Groundhogs can climb up almost as well as they can dig down, so use a sturdy 4- or 5-foot fence and bury the bottom 18 inches underground. Bend the top of the fence outwards so the groundhog will fall over backwards if it attempts to climb over. You can also use repellents. Traps are available that capture a live groundhog, which you then release into the wild. Be sure to check with local and state ordinances about restrictions on live trapping and releasing of wild animals.

- **Gophers:** You can plant gopher spurge (*Euphorbia lathyrus*), a natural repellent, as a protective border around the garden or spray castor oil on your plants. Or, stick vibrating devices, such as large whirligigs, in the ground near tunnels to send them packing. If gophers are a serious problem, you may want to go to the trouble of lining the sides and bottom of your garden (at a depth of 2 feet) with hardware cloth to keep them out. Gopher-resistant wire baskets, which you place in planting holes prior to planting, are commercially available. For persistent problems, use traps.

- **Mice:** Mice cause the most damage to plants in the wintertime, when food is scarce and the bark of your favorite tree makes an easy meal. Even during the summer, if you have a thick layer of mulch surrounding the tree right up to the trunk, a mouse can hide in the mulch and feed undetected. Leave a space of several inches between the trunk and the mulch to deter feeding. During winter, the snow cover provides a similar hiding place, so wrapping the trunk with a tree guard made of wire or plastic provides the best protection.

✔ **Moles:** These critters are the innocent burrowers of the garden pest realm. They simply love to burrow in search of grubs, earthworms, and other insects. In the process, they inadvertently expose plant roots to air or push the plants out of the ground, both of which kill plants. Field mice or voles also use the mole tunnels to reach plant roots and flower bulbs, which they eat. The best strategy is to control the grubs.

✔ **Cats:** Roaming cats enjoy loose soil and mulch and frequently use gardens and landscaped areas as litter boxes. Laying rough-textured or chunky bark mulch or ornamental rocks on the soil may repel them. Or, you can lay chicken wire on the soil and cover it with mulch. Spreading dog hair, anise oil, or shredded lemon or grapefruit peels also deters cats.

Butterflies and moths don't damage plants as adults and actually help pollinate plants.

The following list includes the worst offenders of the insect world. (Many more insects cause damage, of course, and you can get more information about the ones to watch out for in your area from your local cooperative extension office.)

✔ **Aphids:** These tiny (up to ⅛ inch), pear-shaped pests come in many colors, including black, green, and red. They pierce holes in plant tissue and suck the juices, leaving behind sticky sap droppings, called _honeydew,_ which attract ants and may turn black if covered with sooty mold. Aphids can proliferate quickly on weakened plants and tend to congregate on the newest leaves and buds.

✔ **Bagworm:** Adults lay eggs in bags in the fall. After hatching in late spring, bagworm caterpillars feed on the leaves and twigs of many trees and shrubs, especially arborvitae and juniper.

✔ **Bean leaf beetles:** Adult beetles chew large holes in bean leaves and the larvae attack the roots.

✔ **Billbugs:** The adult beetles have a long snout and eat turf grass leaves, while the grubs consume the grass roots and lower stems.

✔ **Black Turfgrass Ataenius (_Ataenius spretulus_):** These 14-inch-long black beetles lay eggs in turf grass in the spring. The eggs hatch into small white grubs, which feed on grass roots until midsummer.

✔ **Borers:** Some beetle and moth larvae or grubs tunnel into the wood, canes, and stems of various trees and shrubs. The tunneling weakens the plant, makes it more disease-prone, and can cut off sap circulation, causing wilting and twig or cane death.

✔ **Cabbage loopers:** The 1-inch-long gray adult moths lay eggs on cabbages and similar types of crops in late spring to early summer.

- ✔ **Chinch bug:** Both the immature nymphs and the black-and-white, ⅙-inch-long winged adult bugs cause significant damage to lawns and grain crops by sucking the juice from grasses.

- ✔ **Colorado potato beetle:** The yellow and black-striped adults emerge and lay orange eggs on the underside of potato-family leaves, such as potato, eggplant, and tomato. The reddish grubs devour the plant leaves, mature, and lay a second generation of eggs later in the summer.

- ✔ **Cucumber beetles:** Striped and spotted cucumber beetle species — adult and larvae — cause significant damage by chewing large holes in leaves and vegetables, and eating their roots. They can also carry viral and bacterial wilt diseases, and spread them throughout your garden.

- ✔ **Cutworms and armyworms:** The 1- to 2-inch-long cutworm caterpillars chew through the stems of young plants at night, kill them, and then spend the day curled in the soil nearby. Armyworms also feed at night, usually in early summer, stripping the leaves from grasses, grains, and vegetable crops.

- ✔ **Flea beetles:** These highly mobile, shiny blackish beetles are only ⅒-inch long, but they tend to feed in large groups, skeletonizing leaves in a few days' time. Adults emerge in spring and do most of their damage by midsummer. Larvae eat plant roots until late summer.

- ✔ **Gypsy moth:** The adult moths lay masses of eggs under a fuzzy covering on trees and other surfaces in autumn, producing 2-inch-long caterpillars that are gray with brown hairs and distinctive red and blue spots. They emerge in spring to eat the foliage on a number of shade trees. This pest spreads across the country as caterpillars and egg clusters hitchhike on cars and trucks.

- ✔ **Imported cabbage moth:** The white moths have a distinctive black dot on each wing. They lay yellow eggs on the underside of cole crops in spring and early summer. The fuzzy green caterpillars feed on leaves and developing flower buds, leaving piles of green excrement.

- ✔ **Japanese beetles:** Found mostly east of the Mississippi River, the fat, white, C-shaped, ¾-inch-long larvae live in the soil, where they consume grass roots from early spring to early summer. The adults — ½-inch-long, metallic blue-green beetles with coppery backs — emerge from the soil in midsummer and attack plants with gusto, stripping leaves, buds, and flowers.

- ✔ **Lace bugs:** These ⅛-inch-long insects suck the sap out of the underside of foliage, giving the leaves a whitish or yellow blotchy appearance. Look under the leaves for their brown, sticky droppings.

- ✔ **Leaf miners:** The larvae of tiny sawflies, moths, beetles, and flies tunnel through the leaves of trees, shrubs, flowers, and vegetable plants, leaving discolored patches on the foliage.

- ✔ **Leafhoppers:** These small, wedge-shaped adults jump from plant to plant, especially when disturbed. The adults and immature nymphs suck plant juices, distorting plant growth and spreading plant diseases.

- **Nematodes:** Plant-damaging nematodes are microscopic, worm-like creatures that live in the soil. They usually attack plant roots, but some also attack stems and leaves.

- **Root maggots:** Small flies of several species lay eggs in the soil near host plants or on the base of the plant. When the maggots hatch, they burrow into the roots, killing or stunting the plant.

- **Scale:** Adult-scale insects may have a hard or soft, shell-like exterior that resemble bumps on plant stems and leaves. They suck plant sap and can weaken and even kill plants if present in large numbers. Many species secrete sticky honeydew that encourage fungus.

- **Snails and slugs:** These pests feed on the tender leaves of many ornamental, fruiting, and vegetable plants during the cool of night or in rainy weather. They proliferate in damp areas, hiding and breeding under rocks, mulch, and other garden debris.

- **Spruce budworm:** These caterpillars cause significant damage to spruce and fir forests throughout North America and can severely disfigure and kill landscape trees, too. In midsummer, moths lay eggs, which hatch into small, orange-yellow to brownish caterpillars. The caterpillars hibernate until the following spring when they emerge to eat the mature and newly developing needles.

- **Squash bugs:** These brown, green, or gray, ½-inch-long bugs and their nymphs attack the leaves of squash and pumpkins. They become a problem when their population swells in late summer.

- **Tarnished plant bug:** Very destructive plant bugs pierce plant tissues and suck the sap. Their feeding damages the plant, causing swelling, dead spots, bud drop, and distorted growth. The brownish, flattened oval bugs, shown in Figure 7-1, also spread plant diseases.

- **Thrips:** These tiny, slender-bodied flying insects damage all soft parts of ornamental and vegetable plants, including leaves, flowers, and roots. Infested flowers and young fruits look distorted. Leaves have silvery or white discolored patches on them, sometimes speckled with black.

Figure 7-1:
Tarnished
plant bugs
attack
vegetables,
flowers, and
fruits and
move
quickly
when
disturbed.

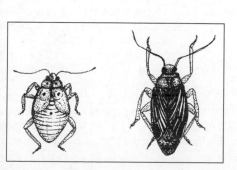

- **Webworms:** This group includes a number of moth species whose caterpillars spin webs or cocoons around themselves and their host leaf, which they devour. Fall webworms attack trees and shrubs in late summer, garden webworms prefer vegetables and strawberries, and turf webworms go after grass.

- **White grubs:** Many beetle species lay eggs in the soil, which hatch into root-eating grubs. Common grub species include June beetles, Japanese beetles, and rose chafers.

- **Whiteflies:** Resembling small, white moths, these insects suck plant sap and spread plant diseases. Infested plants may release clouds of them when disturbed.

Identifying the good guys

Each harmful insect has a predator or parasite that attacks it, called a *beneficial insect*. Whether you know it or not, you rely on these allies to help keep the insect balance from tipping too far in the destructive direction. If you familiarize yourself with these good guys, you can encourage their presence in the garden and avoid killing these innocent bystanders.

Encouraging other insect predators

Many creatures depend on insects for food, and you can enlist them in your pest control efforts:

- **Bats:** Their steady diet of insects — beetles, moths, and, of course, mosquitoes — makes them worth a gardener's tolerance. Some gardeners put up *bat houses,* structures which look like birdhouses with entrance slots in the bottom, to help keep bats nearby. Bat houses are available at many garden supply outlets.

- **Birds:** Birds consume huge numbers of insects. A house wren, for example, can gobble more than 500 beetles, grubs, and insect eggs in an afternoon. Welcome birds to your yard by providing food, water from bird baths, and shelter that includes a diversity of trees and shrubs, including evergreens. Put up birdhouses to encourage your favorite feathered friends to raise their families nearby.

- **Toads:** If you're lucky enough to have a resident toad in the garden, consider him an ally. He'll consume up to 100 insects — cutworms, grasshoppers, grubs, slugs — every night during the gardening season. He may even hang around for years if you make your yard hospitable. Toads lay their eggs in water, so a water garden or pond will ensure future generations. You can easily provide drinking water by setting a low dish or birdbath on the ground near some tall plants that offer shelter.

- **Beneficial nematodes:** These tiny, worm-like creatures live in the soil and prey on Japanese beetle grubs, as well as on armyworms, cutworms, onion maggots, raspberry cane borers, and sod webworms.

- **Big-eyed bug:** These fast-moving, ⅛- to ¼-inch bugs resemble the pesky tarnished plant bugs, which are a favorite food of the big-eyes. They also dine on aphids, leafhoppers, spider mites, and some small caterpillars.

- **Braconid wasps:** Several species of braconid wasps parasitize pest insects. Both the slender adults and tiny, cream-colored grubs feed on a range of pests, including aphids, cabbageworms, codling moths, and corn borers.

- **Centipedes:** Indoors and out, multilegged centipedes feed on many insect pests. Most species don't bother humans (unless you count the screech with which they're frequently greeted), and none are dangerous.

- **Damsel bugs:** These slender, ⅜- to ½-inch bugs have strong-looking front legs, and they prey upon aphids, caterpillars, leafhoppers, and thrips.

- **Ground beetles:** Many beetle species live in or on the soil where both their larval and adult stages capture and eat harmful insects. They vary in color — black, green, bronze — and in size. Most live close to the ground, feeding on aphids, caterpillars, fruit flies, mites, and slugs, but the 1-inch-long caterpillar hunter climbs trees to feed on gypsy moths and other tree-dwelling caterpillars.

  Ground beetles bear an unfortunate likeness to cockroaches, but the latter have longer antennae and a different overall shape. Most of the helpful ground beetles are large, dark, and fast moving. They often have nasty-looking mandibles and eyes on or near the fronts of their heads.

- **Hover flies:** The adults, resembling yellow jackets, are important pollinators, while the brownish or greenish caterpillar-like larvae have an appetite for aphids, beetles, caterpillars, sawflies, and thrips.

- **Ichneumonid wasps:** A valuable ally in controlling many caterpillars and other destructive larvae, the dark-colored adult wasps (see Figure 7-2) vary in size from less than 1 inch to 1½ inches. They have long antennae and long egg-laying appendages — called *ovipositors* — that are easy to mistake for stingers. The adults need a steady source of nectar-bearing flowers to survive.

- **Lacewings:** These ½- to ¾-inch insects have delicate green or brown bodies and transparent wings. The spindle-shaped, alligator-like, yellowish or brownish larvae feed on a wide variety of soft-bodied pests, such as aphids, scale, thrips, caterpillars, and spider mites. The distinctive, pale green oval eggs each sit at the end of its own long, thin stalk on the undersides of leaves.

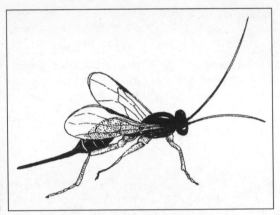

Figure 7-2: Ichneumonid wasps look threatening, but only spell danger for caterpillars and grubs.

- **Lady beetles (lady bugs):** Both adults and larvae prey on soft-bodied pests, including mealybugs and spider mites.

- **Minute pirate bug:** These bugs have a voracious appetite for soft-bodied insects, such as thrips, corn earworms, aphids, and spider mites. The adults are ¼-inch long, somewhat oval-shaped, and black with white wing patches. The fast-moving, immature nymphs are yellow-orange to brown in color and teardrop-shaped.

- **Rove beetles:** These beetles, which resemble earwigs without pincers, feed on soil-dwelling insects, such as root maggot eggs, larvae, and pupae. In mild, wet climates, they also eat slug and snail eggs.

- **Soldier beetles:** The favorite diet of both adults and larvae of these common beetles consists of aphids, caterpillars, corn rootworms, cucumber beetles, and grasshopper eggs. The adults are slender, flattened, ⅓- to ½-inch long. The larvae have the same shape and are covered with hairs.

- **Spiders:** All spiders rid the garden of many common pests.

- **Tachinid flies:** These housefly-sized flies have a bright orange abdomen, black head and thorax, and a fringe of short black hairs on the hind legs. They feed on tent caterpillars, armyworms, corn borers, cutworms, stinkbugs, and other pests.

- **Tiger beetles:** A variety of brightly colored and patterned ½- to ¾-inch beetles feed on a wide range of soil-dwelling larvae.

- **Trichogramma wasps:** Tiny as a pencil point, these parasitic wasps inject their eggs inside the eggs of more than 200 species of moths. Their developing larvae consume the host.

- **Yellow jackets:** These insects take home flies, caterpillars, grasshoppers, and many larvae from your garden to their young.

Attracting beneficial insects

You can take important steps to welcome beneficial insects to your yard and encourage those you purchase to stick around. (*Note:* You can buy beneficial insects that aren't already in your garden through mail-order garden suppliers.)

- **Wait to release beneficials until you've seen their favorite prey in the garden.** Beneficials won't stay where they don't find food. You can even purchase food for lady beetles (from the companies that sell the beetles) to encourage them to stay after aphid populations decline.

- **Grow some plants that attract beneficial insects.** With a constant supply of nectar, adult beneficial insects can live much longer than they would without it. Shallow-throated flowers are easier for many of the tiny beneficials to feed from than deep-throated flowers. Goldenrod is a favorite, attracting more than 75 different species of beneficial insects.

- **Include a diversity of plants in your yard to attract a diversity of insects.** Plant different species, including evergreens, and plants of different sizes and shapes. A mixture of trees, shrubs, perennials, and annuals in the yard provides lots of options for food and hiding places.

- **Avoid using broad-spectrum insecticides.** Even some organic insecticides, such as pyrethrin and rotenone, are toxic to beneficials. Often, beneficials are even more susceptible to the insecticide than pests because, as predators and parasites, they must move quickly over leaf surfaces and thus they come into contact with insecticides more readily.

- **Provide a water source for beneficial insects.** Fill a shallow birdbath or bowl with stones and water and place it near the garden. Change the water frequently to discourage breeding mosquitoes.

Setting Up Pesky Roadblocks

Pests can't damage your plants if they can't get to them. Block their access with simple, but effective barriers around your plants, such as the following:

- **Copper bands:** Copper has the unique ability to repel slugs and snails. Their slimy coatings react chemically with copper, generating a toxic reaction — similar to an electric current — that sends them elsewhere. Use copper sheet metal to fashion permanent edging around your garden beds or staple copper-backed paper (available from garden centers) to the sides of wooden planter beds.

- **Dust barriers:** You can repel some insects with a barrier of a sharp-particle dust, such as *diatomaceous earth* (DE), or wood ashes. Dusts work best when dry, and you have to reapply them after a rain.

✔ **Row covers:** Developed to raise the temperature around plants and extend the growing season, these lightweight air- and water-permeable fabrics can also keep plants relatively safe from insect pests. Cover your plants early in the season, or the insects will have a chance to set up housekeeping in the garden and thrive under the protective covering. Remove the covers from plants, such as squash, that depend on insects for pollination when the plants bloom.

✔ **Cutworm collars:** Make cutworm collars from empty toilet paper or paper towel rolls cut into 2-inch cylinders, or from strips of newspaper that encircle the stem completely, but not tightly, and extend 1 inch into the soil. Place the collars around transplants when you put them in the ground.

✔ **Sticky coatings:** Halt insects in their tracks by applying a sticky coating to traps that attract specific insects. Make your own by mixing equal parts mineral oil or petroleum jelly and liquid dish soap, or purchase sticky substances at local hardware stores or garden centers. To make cleanup easier, cover the lure with plastic wrap before applying the sticky coating.

Picking Your Poison

Organic pesticides, which we prefer, come from plants, animals, minerals, and microorganisms, such as bacteria and fungi. Each of these pesticide groups — and individual products — kills pests in different ways. To get the best result from any product, you have to know as much as you can about the pest you hope to control.

"Organic" doesn't necessarily mean "nontoxic." Some commonly accepted organic pesticides are just as toxic, if not more so, than some synthetic chemical pesticides. *Organic pesticides* are derived from plant, animal, and mineral sources. *Synthetic chemical pesticides* come from petroleum and other chemical sources. Organic pesticides generally have far fewer health side effects than synthetic pesticides, but not always. For example, nicotine — derived from a plant and used as an organic pesticide — is highly toxic to humans and many other species.

Dust to dust

Insects have a waxy cuticle that covers their bodies, holding in moisture. Dusts work by disrupting the waxy cuticle, which causes the insects to dry out and die. Unfortunately, these dusts harm beneficial insects, too. Although not toxic to humans, use them with caution to avoid harming the innocent "bugstanders."

✔ **Diatomaceous earth (DE):** DE resembles microscopic shards of broken glass, which pierce the soft bodies of insects, slugs, and snails. DE kills beneficial as well as harmful insects. Some DE products contain non-toxic bait that induces pests to eat the dust, which is also fatal. Apply the dust to damp foliage to control soft-bodied insects or sprinkle on the ground to target slugs, snails, ants, and earwigs. Reapply after a rain.

Although not toxic to animals, the dust can irritate your lungs — wear a dust mask to avoid breathing the dust. The DE that gardeners use as a pesticide is not the same as the DE used in swimming pool filters; the two kinds aren't interchangeable.

✔ **Iron phosphate:** This mineral product, when mixed with bait, attracts and kills slugs and snails.

✔ **Boric acid:** For cockroaches, ants, and silverfish, look for boric acid powder. If kept dry, the powder remains effective for years without harming animals, people, or the environment.

Soaps and other oily characters

Insects breathe through pores in the cuticle that surrounds their bodies. If you plug up the pores, the insects suffocate and die. Disrupt the cuticle with special soaps and oils and — poof! — the insects can't maintain their internal moisture. Soaps and oils kill a wide range of pest insects, but affect beneficial insects, too.

Oils do have several drawbacks. Don't use them when temperatures are likely to rise above 90°F, when plants are suffering from drought stress, or if you have applied or plan to apply sulfur fungicide within 30 days. It will also remove the bluish waxy coating from Colorado blue spruce, so avoid using it on that species. Read the label carefully for other precautions.

✔ **Horticultural oils:** Use horticultural oils in the winter to suffocate over-wintering pests, such as aphids, mites, and scales, on dormant fruit and ornamental trees and shrubs. During the growing season horticultural oils work against aphids, mites, lace bugs, corn earworms, mealybugs, leafminers, and many others, including tough-to-kill scale insects. Mix with water according to label instructions and then apply with a sprayer.

✔ **Citrus oils:** The oils from the skin of citrus fruits kill a broad range of insects on contact by poisoning them. The oils continue to repel pests, such as fleas, ants, and silverfish, for weeks and are safe around people and pets. The active ingredient d-Limonene. Look for it on the label.

✔ **Plant extracts:** Many herbs, spices, and plants contain chemicals that repel or kill insects. Garlic is one of the most well known and effective extracts against thrips and other leaf-eating insects.

✔ **Insecticidal soaps:** The active ingredient in insecticidal soap, called *potassium salts of fatty acids,* penetrates and disrupts the cuticle that holds moisture inside insects' bodies. When sprayed with soap, many soft-bodied insect pests, such as aphids, dry out and die. Some pests, however, especially beetles with hard bodies, remain unaffected. Insecticidal soap is nontoxic to humans and other animals and breaks down quickly in the environment. If you use a concentrated product, dilute it with soft water before using for the best effect. Hard or mineral-rich water decreases its effectiveness.

Insecticidal soap also disrupts the waxy cuticle on some plants, making it toxic to young and thin-leafed plants, especially tomatoes. If you aren't sure of the plant's sensitivity to the product, always test it on a leaf or two and allow a couple of days to pass before spraying a whole plant. Follow the label directions carefully.

Microbes

Even bugs get sick. You can use a variety of *microbes* — infectious microorganisms — that target specific pests. The beauty of these disease-causing microbes is that they're completely harmless to most beneficial insects, humans, and other animals. Microbes take time to work, but they often remain active in the environment long after you apply them. All bacteria-containing pesticides degrade when exposed to sunlight and high storage temperatures. Also, insects must eat the pesticide to become infected.

Understanding pesticide toxicity

All pesticides are toxic, but some are more toxic than others. Some, called *acute toxins,* poison immediately upon exposure. Others, called *chronic toxins,* may accumulate in body fat or other organs and reach a toxic level after repeated exposure.

Pesticides are categorized as follows:

- **Class I:** The most highly toxic pesticides, their labels always bear skull-and-cross-bones and the words "DANGER" and "POISON" on the label. A special license is required for their use.

- **Class II:** Moderately toxic pesticides. Their labels always say "WARNING."

- **Class III:** Slightly toxic pesticides. The labels say "CAUTION."

- **Class IV:** The least toxic pesticides; they may say "CAUTION" on the label.

Pesticide toxicity varies from one individual to the next and depends greatly on how you're exposed to the chemical. In some cases, such as sabadilla, the chemical may have low toxicity if ingested, but cause severe lung damage if inhaled. Some chemicals cause bodily harm other than acute poisoning. Treat all pesticides with respect and always read the label completely before using. Check the weather, too. Don't spray or apply dust in breezy conditions because the chemical may drift away from the target area and harm nearby plants or animals. If you expect rain, don't bother to apply pesticides that will wash off before doing their job.

Using integrated pest management (IPM)

Integrated pest management (IPM), is a system that combines biological, cultural, physical, and chemical strategies to control pests. IPM strategies are like a series of steps. The first steps are the least toxic and least harmful control methods. The most potentially toxic controls are last resort steps. Here's how the steps stack up:

✔ **Cultural control:** Give plants optimal growing conditions, use pest and disease-resistant varieties, and practice *crop rotation,* which means moving particular crops to new parts of the garden each year.

✔ **Crop sanitation:** Keep pests and diseases out of the garden in the first place by inspecting new plants, cleaning your tools, eliminating weeds, and using best watering practices.

✔ **Mechanical control:** Prevent pests from getting on your plants by covering them with special fabrics or by using hot water, air, fire, and the heat of the sun to kill them without poisons. Simply knocking pests into a can of soapy water does the trick, too.

✔ **Biological control:** Every pest has a natural control, whether it's predator or a disease. You can buy and release many of these control organisms or encourage the ones that already exist around your garden.

✔ **Chemical control:** As a last resort, apply the least toxic pesticides. The best ones target only the pest and don't affect the innocent bystanders, such as bees, spiders, and other beneficial insects.

✔ **Bacteria:** Several insect-infecting bacteria, or *Bacillus* species, that exist naturally in most soils have become important tools in the battle against damaging caterpillars, beetles, and other pesky bugs. Another very important group of bacteria, *Bacillus thuringiensis,* or *Bt,* infects many insect pests, especially their larval stages. Different strains or varieties of the bacteria affect different kinds of pests.

✔ **Fungi:** Many naturally occurring fungi infect and kill insect pests, and one of the most promising for garden use is *Beauveria bassiana,* commonly known as the white muscadine fungus, which lives in the soil and affects aphids, caterpillars, mites, grubs, whiteflies, and others. Mere exposure to the fungus can lead to infection, so avoid using it whenever bees and beneficial pollinators may be affected. The fungus may also be toxic to fish, so don't use it around fish-containing waters. To encourage the native *Beauveria* population in your garden, avoid using fungicides.

Botanically correct pest control

Insect and disease killers that come from plant extracts are called *botanical pesticides* or *botanicals.* Derived from natural sources, botanicals aren't necessarily safer or less toxic than synthetically derived pesticides. In fact, most botanicals are broad-spectrum insecticides, which kill both good and bad bugs indiscriminately. Some botanicals cause allergic reactions in people, others are highly toxic to fish and animals, and some may even cause cancer.

Use pesticides — including botanicals — only as a last resort after thoroughly reading the label on the package. The following pesticides are listed from least to most toxic to humans:

- **Hot pepper wax and powder:** The chemical *capsaicin* is the active ingredient in these useful botanical products. In low doses, hot pepper wax repels most common insect pests from vegetables and ornamental plants. It doesn't cause the fruit or vegetables to become spicy hot, but instead stays on the surface of the plant where it remains effective for up to three weeks. Stronger commercial formulations kill insects as well as repel them. Hot pepper wax is even reportedly effective in repelling rabbits and tree squirrels.

- **Neem:** This pesticide is made from the seeds of the tropical neem tree, *Azadirachta indica,* and it comes in two forms — azadirachtin solution and neem oil. When insects eat the active ingredient in neem, it interrupts their ability to develop and grow to their next life stage or lay eggs. It also deters insects from feeding. Amazingly, plants can absorb neem so that any insects that feed on them may be killed or deterred from feeding. Neem breaks down in the presence of sun and soil within a week or so. To discourage insects from eating your plants, spray neem before you see a large infestation.

- **Pyrethrins:** These insecticidal compounds occur naturally in the flowers of some species of chrysanthemum plants. The toxins penetrate the insects' nervous systems, quickly causing paralysis. In high enough doses or in combination with other pesticides, the insects die. Powerful synthetic compounds that imitate the natural chrysanthemum compounds are called *pyrethroids*.

  Although relatively harmless to humans, pyrethrins are highly toxic to fish and bees and moderately toxic to birds. Pyrethrins kill both beneficial and pest insects. To keep bees safe, spray pyrethrins in the evening after bees have returned to their hives for the night and avoid spraying blooming plants. The compound breaks down rapidly when exposed to sun and air and becomes less effective if stored for longer than one year. Many commercial products contain pyrethrins.

- **Ryania:** This pesticide, which comes from the tropical *Ryania speciosa* plant, is moderately toxic to humans, fish, and birds. It's very toxic to dogs. Seek other botanical pesticides before considering ryania.

- **Sabadilla:** Made from the seeds of a tropical plant, sabadilla is a powerful broad-spectrum insect killer. Some people have severe allergic reactions to the chemical. Use it only as a last resort.

Whacking Weeds Out of Sight

Getting weeds out of your garden takes perseverance and a variety of strategies, including the following:

✔ **Pull 'em out.** If they don't contain seeds, add them to your compost.

✔ **Eat them up.** Many weeds are edible and nutritious.

✔ **Mulch.** See Chapter 4 in Book I for a detailed discussion of mulch.

✔ **Change the environment.** Some weeds prefer certain soil and sun conditions and fail to thrive when deprived of their ideal situation.

✔ **Give them competition.** Plant more desirable plants that grow faster and stronger than the weeds do.

✔ **Burn them up.** Use clear plastic to heat up the soil and kill the seeds or use a weed flamer to shrivel the young plants.

✔ **Use chemical warfare.** As a last resort, use herbicides.

Many weeds are actually symptoms of another underlying problem with your soil or gardening practices. For example, some weeds show up in poorly drained soil; others in overly acidic or alkaline soil. For more on this topic, look for *Weeds and What They Tell* by Ehrenfried E. Pfeiffer (Biodynamic Farming and Gardening Association). Written nearly 50 years ago, some of its information is out of date, but the book remains unique and useful.

Solarization

One of the niftiest ways to beat the weeds in a new garden is to *solarize* them. The concept is simple: Capture the sun's heat under a sheet of clear plastic and literally bake the weeds and waiting seeds to death. This technique takes several weeks in warm, sunny climates. If you garden in a cool, cloudy climate, try it during the warmest or sunniest times of year and allow up to eight weeks for the process to work.

Here's how to solarize the weeds in your garden:

1. **Mow closely or till the ground to remove as much of the existing vegetation as you can.**

   Solarization works best on bare ground.

2. **Dampen the soil.**

   Moisture helps speed the process.

3. **Spread and tautly stretch a sheet of heavy-gauge clear plastic over the area, as shown in Figure 7-3, anchoring it with stones.**

4. **Seal the edge of the plastic to hold in the heat by covering it all the way around with soil or boards.**

Avoid tilling the soil after solarization or you may bring new seeds to the surface. If the soil gets hot enough, solarization also eliminates some soil-dwelling pests and diseases.

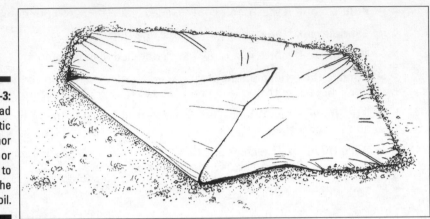

Figure 7-3:
Spread clear plastic and anchor with soil or boards to solarize the soil.

Flaming

Propane-fueled flamers (shown in Figure 7-4 and available at garden supply stores) make quick work of weeds. Instead of setting plants on fire, they have special nozzles that work by literally boiling the sap inside the plants and bursting their cells. Expect to pay from $30 to more than $100 for a flamer hose, fittings, nozzle, and valves. They attach to any standard propane tank, such as the kind used for barbecue grills. For the most effective control, use your flamer when weeds are small. Large weeds and tough perennials may need repeat treatments.

Avoid using flamers in windy or dry conditions, especially if you live in an arid region. Always keep a hose or other water source handy.

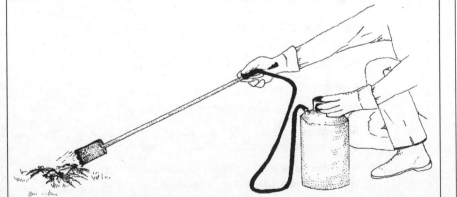

Figure 7-4:
Propane-powered flamers are especially effective against weeds.

When bad weeds grow good

Despite most people's preoccupation with ridding their gardens of weeds, some weeds may actually be beneficial. Some ways that weeds can help include the following:

✔ Provide habitat for desirable insects

✔ Bring up nutrients from deep in the soil

✔ Add nitrogen to the soil

✔ Break up hard-packed earth

✔ Protect soil from erosion

Cultivating

Good old-fashioned hand-pulling and hoeing aren't among gardeners' favorite garden chores, but they work, especially if you follow these two basic rules:

✔ **Disturb the soil as little as possible:** This first rule is really important because many weed seeds lie dormant in the darkness just under the soil surface. When you churn up the soil, you expose them to the light and air that they need in order to sprout and attain pest status.

✔ **Get them while they're small:** Little weeds with fragile roots and stems take little effort to destroy. Large weeds take more work, disrupt more soil, and potentially contribute to the seed population in your soil. Also, the longer the weeds live, the more water and nutrients they rob from your food and landscape plants.

Herbicides

When all else fails, gardeners can still turn to herbicides to kill the weeds. Herbicides work in different ways that depend on a particular plant life stage or characteristic to be effective:

✔ **Pre-emergent herbicides:** These herbicides kill tiny seedlings as they sprout and are especially useful on lawns and other places where mature weeds are difficult to remove. The timing of application is critical, however. If you put them on too early, they may wash away before they have a chance to work. Put them on too late and the seedlings will be too big to be affected.

✔ **Herbicidal soap:** Plants have a waxy coating on their leaves, which prevents moisture loss. Herbicidal soap damages the waxy layer, allowing the plant to dry out and die. This type of herbicide works best on young, tender, actively growing weeds in hot, dry weather.

Before you turn to chemical herbicides try this very effective, and organic, approach to wiping out weeds: Go to your kitchen pantry or cupboard and dig out that bottle of plain white vinegar (either 5 percent or 10 percent acidity). Dump some into a clean spray bottle and apply a uniform coat over the leaves of the weed. USDA research has proven that the vinegar can kill the top growth of even the most stubborn weeds, such as Canada thistle and burdock.

Deflecting Disease

Plant diseases are a concern in any garden. The following sections help you recognize — and hopefully, prevent — illness in your plants.

Biological diseases

Several different kinds of organisms cause plant diseases, just as they do in people. Viruses are the toughest ones because they're incurable — all you can do is try to prevent them. Bacteria are nearly impossible to eliminate, too, after the plant is infected. Fortunately, fungi cause most plant diseases and they do have effective control chemicals, although prevention is still the best course of action. The following list describes some of the most common diseases of trees, shrubs, vegetables, flowers, and fruits:

- **Anthracnose:** This group of fungi, spread easily by splashing water and walking through wet plants, can attack many plants and trees. Look for small, discolored leaf spots or dead twigs, especially on the youngest ones. The disease can spread to kill branches and eventually the whole plant. Many plant varieties are resistant to anthracnose fungi — choose them whenever you can.

- **Armillaria root rot:** This fungus infects and kills the roots and lower trunk of ornamental trees, especially oaks. Symptoms include smaller than normal leaves, honey-colored mushrooms growing near the base of the tree, and declining tree vigor. Trees may suddenly fall over when the roots weaken and decay. Keep trees growing vigorously and avoid damage to their roots and trunks.

- **Botrytis blight:** This fungus attacks a wide variety of plants, especially in wet weather. It causes watery-looking, discolored patches on foliage that eventually turn brown. Infected flowers, especially roses, geraniums, begonias, and chrysanthemums, get fuzzy white or gray patches that turn brown, destroying the bloom. Strawberry and raspberry fruits, in particular, develop light brown to gray moldy spots and the flesh becomes brownish and water-soaked. Discourage Botrytis by allowing air to circulate freely around susceptible plants and avoid working with wet plants. Remove and destroy any infected plant parts.

- ✔ **Club root:** This fungus mainly infects cole crops, such as cabbage, broccoli, and collards, and grows best in acidic soils. Symptoms include stunted growth, wilting, poor development, and swollen lumps on the roots. Some vegetable varieties are immune.

- ✔ **Cytospora canker:** Cankers appear as oozing, sunken, or swollen areas on tree bark. The new shoots turn yellow and wilt, then die back. The disease attacks woody stems on susceptible plants, such as fruit trees, spruces, and maples, forming cankers that can kill infected branches. Plant resistant or less-susceptible plants, keep them growing vigorously, and avoid bark injuries that provide an entrance for infecting fungus.

- ✔ **Damping off:** Mostly a problem in young plants and seedlings, this fungus rots stems off near the soil line, causing the plant to keel over and die. Avoid overwatering and provide good air circulation to help prevent the fungus. Clean your tools in isopropyl alcohol.

- ✔ **Fusarium wilt:** This fungus is fatal to many vegetable crops. The first symptoms are yellowing leaves and stunted growth, followed by wilting and plant death. In melons, the stems develop a yellow streak, which eventually turns brown. You can't cure infected plants, so choose Fusarium-resistant varieties.

- ✔ **Galls:** These appear as swollen bumps on leaves, stems, and branches. Bacteria, fungi, gall wasps, aphids, and mites can all be culprits. Usually the damage is only cosmetic.

- ✔ **Leaf spots and blights:** Several fungi show up first as circular spots on leaves of susceptible plants. The spots increase in size until the leaves die and fall off. The fungi spread easily in wet conditions. Remove all plant debris at the end of the gardening season, clean tools between uses, buy disease-resistant varieties, and avoid contact with wet plants.

- ✔ **Root rots:** A number of fungal root diseases cause susceptible plants to turn yellow, wilt, and sometimes die. Nearly all plants are susceptible under the right conditions. The fungi can survive in the soil for many years without a host. Build healthy, well-drained soil to prevent root rot.

- ✔ **Slime flux:** This bacterial rot inside infected trees, usually elms, maples, and poplars, causes oozing and often bad-smelling sap to run from old wounds or pruning cuts. There's no control after the symptoms appear.

- ✔ **Verticillium wilt:** This fungus affects many plants. Look for wilting and yellow leaves, especially older ones. In some plants, the leaves curl up before falling off. Prevent future infections by cleaning up garden debris, cleaning tools thoroughly, and choosing resistant varieties.

- ✔ **Viruses:** This group of diseases is incurable, so prevention is your only strategy. Usually the leaves develop mottled yellow, white, or light green patches and may pucker along the veins. Flowers may develop off-color patches, and fruit ripens unevenly. Viruses often live in wild bramble plants and weeds; aphids, leafhoppers, nematodes, and whiteflies spread the virus as they move from plant to plant.

Environmental diseases

Plants live intimately with their environment, which means that air, water, and soil quality, weather, and animals can take their toll. Look through the following list of probable causes before you start blaming innocent viruses, aphids, and fungi:

- **Air pollution, ozone:** Automobile exhaust and other pollutants contain gases that injure susceptible plant leaves. Ozone gives foliage a white speckled appearance. Another common pollutant in urban areas is peroxyacyl nitrate (PAN), which causes silvery damage to leaf undersides. Sulfur dioxide, an industrial air pollutant, turns leaves yellow, especially between the veins.

- **Lawn mower, string trimmer damage:** Mechanical damage to the bark and stems of trees and shrubs poses a serious threat to their health. Even small wounds open the plant to insect and disease invasion. Maintain a wide weed- and grass-free area around trees, shrubs, and gardens so that you don't have to mow or weed whip close to them.

- **Nutrient deficiency:** Although most natural soils contain enough nutrients to support healthy plants, disturbed soil around new homes and in improperly maintained gardens may have some nutrient shortages.

- **Salt damage:** Salt used to de-ice roads poses a serious threat to perennials, trees, and shrubs. Injury appears as stunted growth, brown needles on conifers, and wilting. Avoid planting within 20 feet of a frequently iced road and divert drainage water from the road away from plants.

Book II
Garden Design

In this book . . .

Because a garden always takes its place within a landscape, you need to plan your garden within the context of your landscape. This book shows you how to develop a landscape plan — including how to maximize use of your side yards — and then how to make that plan a reality.

Keep in mind that landscaping includes the ornamentation that you add to your yard. You may also want to add plants that don't grow well in your soil or need to come indoors part of the year. Container gardening, which we cover in Chapter 3, offers lovely and unique ornamentation while solving the problems of poor soil or temperamental plants.

No matter what size your yard or how large your garden, your landscaping will almost certainly include a lawn, trees, and shrubs. This book tells you how to plant and care for a lawn, and how to select, plant, and care for trees and shrubs. With the information we provide here, you'll soon be the envy of the cul-de-sac.

Here are the contents of Book II at a glance:

Chapter 1

Plotting Your Landscape Design

- -

In This Chapter

▶ Assessing your current landscape

▶ Using designer's techniques to design your dream landscape

▶ Getting the tools you need

▶ Calculating the final price tag

▶ Checking municipal regulations — before you start planting

- -

andscaping consists of two parts: the *hardscape* (the parts of your land-scape that are physically hard, such as a deck walkway, trellis, or fence), which creates an outdoor room for you and your family, and the plants, which can provide beauty, privacy, sunblock, and so on. This chapter gives you the tools you need to design the landscape that's perfect for you!

Assessing What You Already Have

Your first landscape project is to assess your property as it is now by per-forming a *site analysis*. You need to determine your current landscape's strengths and weaknesses, what you like or dislike about your yard, and what kind of problems you're trying to solve in your landscape. (Figure 1-1 shows a sample site analysis.) Follow these steps to begin your site analysis:

1. **Make a rough drawing of your property with paper and pencil.**

   Be sure to include your house with windows and doors, existing plants, and general north/south directions. Try to draw to scale, but don't worry about being too precise right now.

2. **Put the drawing on a clipboard and walk around your yard at differ-ent times of day, making notations of the following:**

- **Sun and shade:** Mark areas that are sunny or shady, and at what times of the day. When you're ready to purchase plants for your landscape, this notation helps you match plants with appropriate light conditions. Noting sunny and shady areas may also give you ideas about creating more comfortable outdoor living space. For example, in midsummer, the south and western sides of the house will be sunniest and warmest.

- **Views:** Note good and bad views — ones that you may want to preserve and ones you may want to block. Good views are easy to recognize. Bad views, on the other hand, take a little more eyeballing. Can the neighbors see in your yard or can you see in theirs? Do you have things on your own property that you'd rather not see? What will you see if you put in a raised deck? Does the view change when deciduous trees lose their leaves?

- **Prevailing winds:** You may be able to block regular winds with fencing or plants.

- **Slope and drainage:** Put in some arrows that give you a rough idea of your yard's contour. Sloping ground or uneven terrain can be an interesting part of a landscape, especially if you accentuate it with walls or plants combined with stone to simulate a dry stream bed. High points may also provide some good views. On the other hand, sloping ground can also mean erosion or drainage problems that can threaten your house or yard. Be sure that water drains away from all of the walls of your house. Mark down any areas that seem overly wet or where moss or algae is growing; go outside in a rainstorm and watch where excess water flows.

- **Existing plants:** Draw in large trees, shrubs, vines, and perennials that you may want to preserve.

- **Interesting natural features:** If you're lucky enough to have a small stream or handsome rocks protruding from the ground, they can become special landscape features.

- **Noise, smells, and lights:** Let your senses go and write down anything that you notice — lights at night, noise from next door, and even unpleasant odors. You may be able to fix them.

3. **Make notations of what you see from *inside* the house:**

- **Views:** Look out your windows and note the good and bad views. Who can see in the windows from the street or next door?

- **Sunlight:** Note whether the sun blazes through certain windows or casts pleasant light through others.

- **Lights:** Check to see whether car lights or signs shine through your windows at night.

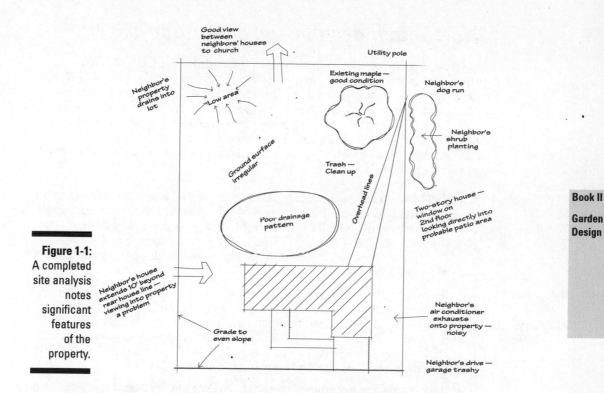

Good view
between
neighbors' houses
to church

Utility pole

Neighbor's
property
drains into
lot

Low area

Existing maple —
good condition

Neighbor's
dog run

Neighbor's
shrub
planting

Ground surface
irregular

Trash —
Clean up

Overhead lines

Two-story house —
window on
2nd floor
looking directly into
probable patio area

Poor drainage
pattern

Figure 1-1:
A completed
site analysis
notes
significant
features
of the
property.

Neighbor's house
extends 10' beyond
rear house line —
viewing into property
a problem

Grade to
even slope

Neighbor's
air conditioner
exhausts
onto property —
noisy

Neighbor's drive —
garage trashy

Envisioning Your Landscape — Realistically

A good landscape meets your needs. You can design and invest in an elaborate landscape, but if you can't find a comfortable place to set up the barbecue and you *love* to grill, your yard isn't much good to you. The following sections help you design a landscape that's perfect for you.

How long are you staying in your house?

How long you plan to live in your house influences your landscape planning. If you're only planning to live in your house a couple of years, concentrate on fast-growing trees and shrubs to give you a more powerful effect, sooner. Expensive projects, such as a deck or pool may add to your home's value, but you may not recoup those costs before you're ready to move. In general, the shorter your stay, the less complex your landscape plans should be.

How much of your yard can you use?

Most houses are plunked somewhere in the middle of the lot. Though the surrounding areas may vary in size, you almost always have a *four-sided landscape* — a front yard, a back yard, and two side yards. You may have difficulty overcoming the tradition that back yards are where you actually live, front yards are for show, and side yards are mostly ignored. Instead, make your entire landscape your living area. Using your entire yard allows you to take advantage of different times of the day when one part or another of your landscape is at its best:

✔ **Shield the front yard with walls of greenery or a privacy fence:** On weekend afternoons when the rest of the neighborhood is carousing in their back yards, you'll have the front all to yourself. If you think that's too bold of a step (and it may well be for your neighborhood), at least you can move some of your ornamental garden beds to the front instead of having a boring, look-good lawn.

Be aware that you may need to keep your front yard neat to avoid neighborhood resentment and comply with your local municipality's ordinances. If you're inspired to plant a prairie or a naturalistic woodland out front, talk to your neighbors first (and call your local government) so that they know what you're doing. Keep well-groomed paths so that the landscape looks guided instead of frighteningly wild.

✔ **Back yards are usually safest for children's play areas:** If you're a veggie grower with kids, put your garden near the play area, so that you can keep one eye on them while you weed the zukes.

You don't have to relegate vegetable patches to the back yard — put them wherever the light, soil, and convenience are best. A well-tended patch, planted in an interesting design of diagonals or squares with vegetables that are interspersed with flowers and herbs, has a lot of curb appeal. (Keep in mind that vegetable gardens definitely have an off-season that is less attractive.)

✔ **Give yourself reason to linger in your side yard:** Place a hammock or move a table and chair to the area. A sunny side yard can be the perfect place for a strawberry patch or a row of raspberries. You can also make your side yard a destination by adding surprises — a whimsical garden ornament, a small garden pool, or a dollhouse — to it.

How are you going to use your yard?

Customize your landscape to your life by developing a landscaping wish list. Following are a few suggestions for your personal list:

- ✔ **Cut fresh flowers.** Books IV, V, and VI cover different flowers.

- ✔ **Entertain guests, play sports, and watch kids play.**

- ✔ **Grow vegetables and herbs.** See Book VII for more on this topic.

- ✔ **Swim in a pool, soak in a spa, or watch fish in a small pond.**

- ✔ **Compost lawn clippings, raked leaves, and kitchen scraps.** Chapters 3 and 4 in Book I tell you how to create your own compost heap.

- ✔ **Grow prize-winning roses.** Book III tells you everything you need to know about growing roses.

- ✔ **View colorful container plants.** See Chapter 3 in Book II for more on container gardening.

Who is going to use your yard?

Before finalizing any wish list ideas into concrete plans, consider who's going to use the yard:

- ✔ **Children:** Safety is a big consideration with young children. You may also want to include a storage bench for their toys.

- ✔ **Cooks:** If you spend much time grilling in the summer, you may enjoy a built-in barbecue — as close to the kitchen door as possible — and an outdoor sink?

- ✔ **Pets:** You may want to fence in an area or put in a dog run.

Where do you need to walk?

As you begin to get an idea of where the best places are for all the things on your wish list, stroll around and figure out the routes that will get you and others from one area to the next.

As you begin fiddling with potential pathways, you may discover that they can make your garden seem bigger. Obscured by shrubs, ornamental grasses, or other tall plants, paths can double back, twist and turn, and run along in a limited space for much longer than you may think.

Consider the following when planning your paths:

- ✔ **Plan some direct routes:** Don't forget humdrum daily activities — getting to the mailbox or getting to your car in the morning.

- ✔ **Plan a wide, flat, solid path:** You need a way to trundle a wheelbarrow full of compost, manure, grass clippings, and other goodies from one place to another.

Finding ideas

Gathering new ideas for your landscape design is in many ways a treasure hunt. Try the following:

✔ **Plan weekend outings to nurseries for ideas on what plants flourish in your area.** Nurseries often display plants according to their needs for sun or shade. Many nurseries offer free lectures during weekends, which provide valuable information on plants.

✔ **Visit local botanical gardens and arboretums.** You'll see a great variety of plants, much of it unusual, but proven in your climate.

✔ **Join a garden club or plant society.** Your local nursery should be able to hook you up with garden clubs or societies dedicated to specific plants.

✔ **Ask your neighbors for a garden tour.** Investigating the level of landscape in your neighborhood gives you a benchmark on the level and quality of landscaping that the neighborhood warrants.

✔ **Subscribe to garden magazines.** Cut out the articles that interest you and make folders organized by plant type. We keep folders on bulbs, perennials, annuals, evergreen trees and shrubs, deciduous trees and shrubs, vines, tools, lawns and ground cover, bugs (both good and bad), plant diseases, decks and patios, garden paths, and garden furniture.

✔ **Try to make your pathways link up with each other:** You don't want your landscape to be full of dead ends.

✔ **Make paths the right width:** A path's width affects the speed at which people walk it. Narrow paths tend to make people unconsciously uncomfortable, feeling that they have to hurry along. The minimum width for two people to walk side-by-side is 48 inches.

✔ **Think outside the cement:** Paths don't have to be made of paving materials — they're just clear routes to get you from here to there.

✔ **Make sure that fenced areas don't block access to other parts of the yard:** Include gates or leave sections open for easier access.

If you're having trouble visualizing your paths, use oatmeal or flour to sprinkle a biodegradable path through your yard — you can see in a minute whether your path design works.

How much privacy do you want?

Privacy structures — tall hedges, fences, arbors, and walls — work wonders at making your yard your own space. Walls help to keep your noise in and other noise out, so that you don't have to keep shushing your kids or resent the neighbor kid's souped-up car. Privacy structures define the boundaries of your landscape. Imagine decorating your living room if it had no walls. A little tricky to make it feel cozy, isn't it? Outdoor living rooms work the same way. Walls — in this case, the plants and ornaments — make the furnishings look better by providing a backdrop.

When will you use your landscape?

When dreaming up your ideal landscape, think of the times of day and the times of year in which you plan to use your yard. If you plan to be outdoors in the late afternoon, locate the area where you'll be most comfortable at that time of day. Good outdoor lighting is a must if you like to spend time in the garden at night. A covered porch or patio keeps bugs at bay and lets you be outside during the rainy season. If you enjoy every minute of summer outdoors, choose trees, shrubs, and flowers that bloom all season.

Book II

Garden Design

How much maintenance is too much?

Landscape maintenance is an ongoing event. However, you can design low maintenance into a landscape. For example:

- **Plan a yard with hardscape and very few plants if you travel frequently.**

- **Avoid overplanting or using fast-growing plants that get too large for their space.** They'll need more pruning later on.

- **Plant perennials or flowering shrubs rather than higher-maintenance annuals.** Books IV and V cover perennials and annuals.

- **Consider ground cover.** If you plant a new lawn instead, plan on mowing it weekly during its growing season.

- **Use masonry (brick and concrete) for your hardscape.** If you build wooden landscape elements, such as decks and fences, plan on painting or applying preservatives every two to three years.

- **Invest in an automated irrigation system.** Without an irrigation system, you have to water everything by hand — unless you live in a climate where rain keeps the garden wet enough.

Thinking Like a Designer

In the language of landscaping, you want to achieve unity, use the appropriate proportions and a correct sense of scale, and balance color, texture, and form. Landscaping lingo may sound like mumbo-jumbo at first, but if you can dress yourself in the morning, you can understand the rules that help change your yard into something more satisfying.

Unify with unity

Unity is what keeps all the separate parts of your landscape tied together, so that the eyes and feet flow from one part of the yard to another. To achieve unity in your landscape, do the following:

- **Clearly define pathways.**

- **Link greenery.** Two shade trees and a forsythia bush stuck in your lawn do *not* create a unified landscape design. Plant ground cover at the feet of all three to visually link them together, continue the same ground cover along the fence and around the corner to the patio, stick a couple more forsythias at the corner, and presto! — unity.

- **Have a style.** Know what you want your garden to say about you:

  - If your tastes run to formal precision, for instance, you probably want clipped hedges, classic statues, brick or stone pathways, and symmetrical plantings that provide calming mirror images.

  - A cottage garden jumble of exuberant flowers with rustic fences, bent-twig benches, and a concrete frog along the path tells visitors that you're more of a free-spirit type.

  - Avoid the "collector garden," where you have just one of each kind of plant that catches your eye. Build a sense of rhythm by planting multiples of the same plant. The exception to this guideline is if the single plant is the focal point of your garden, such as a beautifully shaped Japanese maple in the center of your yard.

  Combining the two styles looks disjointed and has a disquieting effect on your landscape. But you can still have your formal rose garden and your wildflower meadow without sacrificing unity. Just don't put them side-by-side: separate them by a hedge, put them on opposite sides of the house, or link them by a transition zone that gradually makes the shift from control to wilderness.

- **Repeat color.** Repeating colors throughout the landscape makes it look like it's all one piece. Place clumps of yellow flowers in various beds, pots, or plantings across your back yard, and your eye will travel from one patch of yellow to the next in a seamless, satisfying way. You can combine plant colors with house or hardscape colors, too. For example, a cobalt blue lattice matched with big, blue-and-yellow flower pots gives you a two-tone color scheme to run throughout the garden.

Repeat after me

Repetition of hardscape materials — including brick, wood, stone, concrete, wood chips, and fencing — is a simple way to make your garden look like it's all one piece, even if the areas are distinctly different.

Manmade materials — basically, anything other than plants — carry great weight in the landscape, because they draw viewers' eyes like a magnet. Select your hardscape materials to match your garden style and repeat them throughout the landscape. For example, you can use a single section of diagonal, framed lattice to support a climbing rose along the wall of your house; an L-shaped couple of sections to shield the compost pile from view; or three or four linked sections to serve as a privacy screen along the patio, as shown in Figure 1-2. Depending how large your yard is, you may want to repeat the lattice theme in variation by installing solid, vertical-board privacy fence topped by a narrow strip of lattice.

Placing the same plants here and there is an easy trick. Simply repeat backbone plants that perform well most of the year, such as evergreens, ground covers, and shrubs to tie your garden areas to each other. Repeating shapes helps pull things together, too: curved outlines of beds, undulating paths, bosomy urns, and mounds of plants. Or, try no-nonsense point-A-to-point-B paths, yardstick-straight bed edges, spiky plant forms, clipped hedges, or vertical board fences.

Book II

Garden Design

Figure 1-2: Simple devices, such as these screens, help create repetition.

How many pink flamingos are enough?

Manmade objects carry much more weight in the garden than plants — our eyes are instantly drawn to them. That's why a single urn or birdbath draws the eye like a magnet, even in the midst of the most beautiful garden.

When it comes to adornment, less is more. You can still have your gazing globe, your collection of birdhouses, your gargoyles, and your angel fountain, but keep them separate visually with intervening shrubbery or bends in the path, so that they don't all burst on the scene at once. Place your *objets d'art,* then walk out of the garden. Do something else for a while, and then go back to the garden as though you're seeing it for the first time. If your gaze hops around from one outrageous, er, wonderful piece of lawn art to another, you have too much stuff.

Play with color

Hot colors — white, bright pink, yellow, orange, and orange-red — jump out at you, making distances seem shorter. Cool colors — blues, purples, deep reds, and pastels — recede, making spaces seem longer. If you want to make a small yard seem bigger, plant hot colors at the entryway and cool colors across the garden at the far end, where they'll look like a misty watercolor painting.

To make wide-open spaces seem smaller, plant bright, hot colors across the way, where they'll seem to jump forward. Just be sure to choose colors in the same palette. You can use vivid orange and golden yellow dahlias at a gate, for instance, then soften the hue into apricot and pale sulphur yellow as the plantings recede.

Get rhythm

Repeating elements create a rhythm in your landscape, a pacing that you can control by your plant choices, just like turning the dial to a different radio station. If you want slow, smooth-flowing music, choose quiet colors and wide stretches of greenery. To jazz it up, look to bright hues and vertical forms, such as sword-leaved irises, vertical clumps of ornamental grasses, and decorative posts and columns. Figure 1-3 shows this concept in action.

Figure 1-3:
Repeating
elements
create
rhythm.

When accompanied by neighboring plants of lower voltage, any eye-catchers in the garden work to create a lively rhythm. Anything bigger, brighter, taller, or otherwise strikingly different than its neighbors are all showoffs that grab attention and make your garden dance with a lively beat. On the other hand, stretches of greenery and cool-colored flowers in shades of blue, purple, or pastels are restful rhythm makers.

Pay attention to hardscape

The patio, deck, walkways, fences, trellises, and other hardscape elements of your landscape are just as important as the plants. Whether you're shopping for store-bought or creating your own, make your hardscape elements as attractive as your planting beds. Remember that you'll be looking at them unadorned in the off season, when leaves have fallen and plants are dormant. Soften them in all seasons by planting woody shrubs, vines, ornamental grasses, and trees nearby. A patio without softening plants may look fine in summer surrounded by lawn grass, but in winter, it can look pretty bleak without a few natural plant forms to anchor it to the earth.

Shopping for hardscape and for the materials to make it can be a rude intro-duction to sticker shock. Bricks, arbors, benches, fences, and all those other "extras" can be a much bigger investment than the plants. Considering how valuable they are in transforming an average garden into a great one, though, hardscape is well worth the investment. Search out the most beautiful arbor in the world, and you'll love your garden forever. Skimp on the deck, and you'll rue your miserly impulse for years.

Focus on the details

You may have some favorite plants that you want to include in your new land-scape. Look at the subtle details of these plants before they make the final cut and you make the first dig:

- ✔ **Look at the leaves with an eye toward design attributes.** Unless you're growing only annuals, your plants will be mostly leaves much of the time.

- ✔ **Notice the texture of foliage.** Broad and strappy, flat and wide, ferny and delicate, fuzzy, velvety, or shiny are just some of the textures you'll find.

- ✔ **Consider the form of the flower.** Is it simple and flat like a daisy, emphatically spiky like gayfeather, or soft and wide like yarrow? Also, consider that most perennials bloom for just a few short weeks. What will they add to your garden the rest of the time?

- ✔ **Study a plant's growing habits.** Cast a critical eye toward the mature shape of the plant, which may end up being upright, mounded, arching, single-stemmed, branching, swordlike. Find out whether it stays in a clump or travels to form a colony.

Contrast and combine plants, so that they make the most of one another. Put frilly ferns next to plain-leaved hostas, so they can both show off without competing with each other. Partner upright growers, such as iris, with mounders and sprawlers so that they stand like punctuation points. Echo colors, leaf shapes, and forms to create beds of delicious texture. Play with your plants! And don't worry if you don't get it picture-perfect on the first try. If you decide you don't like a combination, hey, there's the shovel.

Employ the Goldilocks theory

Select plants that are the right scale for your yard and the right proportions to each other. Fill a small yard with great big plants, and you create a feeling of being overwhelmed. Instead, use small-leafed plants of small stature to stay in scale and make the most of your limited space. If you must have that large plant or tree, make it a focal point by partnering it with low-key plants that don't compete in size and stature, as shown in Figure 1-4.

Figure 1-4:
Select components that are the proper scale for your yard.

Choosing the right trees for your yard is where you must follow the Goldilocks rule — not too big, not too small, but just right. Never overlook one of the most important lines on the nursery tag — the ultimate size of the tree. Choose trees that fit your yard. Big yard, big tree. Small yard, small tree.

Layer upon layer

Think of layers as you plan the general look of your landscape. Your pencil plan shows only a flat oval for a flower bed, but in your mind, that flat shape should be three-dimensional, with roses or other flowering shrubs rising above the perennials, and small trees or trellises adding even more height to the bed. Layering not only adds height to your landscape, which instantly makes it more interesting, but it lets you wedge in a lot more plants than a design that calls for side-by-side planting.

Layering your landscape with plants of different heights definitely improves the look of your landscape. Ground covers and grass form the lowest layer, followed by flowering perennials and annuals, then by shrubs, then small trees, then medium trees, and then venerable tall trees. You can substitute structures for any of the plants: a pedestal birdbath for a midheight shrub, for instance, or a vine-covered wall or fence for a small tree.

Big trees take a step down

Big, old shade trees are a great asset, but they can be frustrating to work into a landscape plan because their size makes them stick out. A little trick called *stepping down* anchors your big tree to the rest of the garden. Here's what you do: Plant smaller trees beside your giant — redbuds beneath a maple, perhaps — and shrubs beside the shorter trees, so that your gaze makes a transition to the tops of the trees in graduated steps instead of one giant leap. You can also use horizontal visual weight to balance height.

Drawing Out Your Ideas

Think of your landscape plan as a tool to help you get a handle on the price tag of your project, establish your priorities, and make sure that all the separate parts of your landscape — the barbecue pit, a meditation pool, the kid's area — are present and accounted for. Transferring dreams to paper requires more than a little imagination, but with some practice on perspective, you can tell whether your plan is an aesthetically-pleasing one.

In order to draw your plan, you may want to pick up a few of the drawing supplies shown in Figure 1-5, but you can get away with just some large-size paper, a pencil, and an eraser. More complicated drawing tools help you keep your lines straight and maintain consistent sizes for the elements of your landscape. (Alternatively, you may want to invest in a computer landscape design package.) Consider using graph paper, which has a printed grid of squares that makes transferring real-life elements to a flat piece of paper much easier. You can, for example, transfer your measurements to the graph paper using a 1-foot to ¼-inch ratio — a 1-foot-long line in real life covers ¼ inch on graph paper. If necessary, tape sheets of graph paper together, so that your plan fits.

Sketching the base plan

Before you can start adding your wonderful new landscape features, you have to map what's already there. Here's how:

1. **Measure the lengths of all edges of your property and draw the outline of your yard on paper.**

    Taking measurements is a pain in the neck, but you're far ahead of the game when you get estimates for what this new design is actually going to cost. Measurements eliminate guesswork and give you the confidence of knowing that your plan will work.

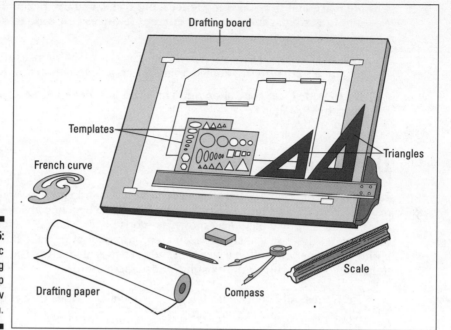

Drafting board

Templates

French curve

Triangles

Figure 1-5:
Basic
drafting
tools help
you draw
your plan.

Drafting paper

Compass

Scale

Book II

Garden
Design

Invest in a 100-foot tape measure to avoid the frustration of marking off 12-foot lengths and adding them up to get a reading on your 400-foot side boundary. Enlist a helper when you're ready to measure to make the job go quicker. If you have the original map of your property, skip the measuring and trace that. No need to reinvent the wheel.

2. **Measure and draw in the outline of your house.**

Be sure to place the house exactly where it sits on your lot.

3. **Measure and add any outbuildings that currently exist.**

After that, draw in other elements and show their locations in relation to known measurements.

4. **Measure and draw in whatever paving is already in place and that you want to keep.**

Don't assume that the right angles and parallel lines that are formed by walls, fences, driveways, and property lines are always perfect. Verify the distance between objects with as many measurements as you can.

5. **Measure and draw existing fences, big trees, hedges, perennials, vegetable gardens, and any other current features you want to keep right where they are.**

   Indicate the precise location of a tree trunk or plant by measuring the distance from it to two known points, such as two corners of the house.

6. **Go to your local copy shop and run off a half-dozen or so copies of your base plan.**

Dreaming on paper

Tape a piece of tracing paper over your base plan, and you're now ready to transfer your dreams into a plan. You don't need to be a fine artist — just draw circular or oval balloons (known as "goose eggs") and write inside the circles what they are ("shed" or "play area," for example). Make the balloons about the same proportional size that they are in real life. Add the following items to your drawing of the existing landscape features:

- ✔ **Activities:** Add goose eggs for all the special activities that you eventually want to enjoy in your yard.

- ✔ **Paths:** Draw any paths that you want to add, using your lines to indicate their shapes and widths.

- ✔ **Hardscape:** Sketch in fences, a spa, a patio, a deck, front porch improvements, and any other hardscape elements that you've chosen.

- ✔ **Plants:** Add goose eggs for flower beds, shrubs, vines, new trees, vegetable gardens, and so on.

After all the parts of your new design are in place, you should have something that looks like Figure 1-6.

Taking your design for a test drive

When you're satisfied with your paper sketch, you need to test your design. Now, you get to play with a bunch of weird objects to make your landscape look alive. Pull your garden hoses out of their perpetual nest-of-snakes tangle, collect a handful of tomato stakes or wire cages, get the rope from the garage, drag out the plastic lawn chairs and buckets, prepare a wheelbarrow load of leaves or a bale of straw, and get ready to play make-believe. Work on one section of the plan at a time:

✔ **Outline curving paths with hose or rope, or sprinkle a path of oatmeal or flour so that you can see the direction it takes.**

To make a straight line, invest in a *chalkline,* a chalk-filled device that looks like a tape measure. The chalk powders a pull-out string. Tie the chalked string between two uprights, clip the end, lift the taut string in the center with your fingers, and let it ping hard toward the ground. It snaps against the grass or soil, leaving a perfect straightedge. Use the chalkline to mark potential beds and paths when you're drawing your design, then use it again later when you start digging.

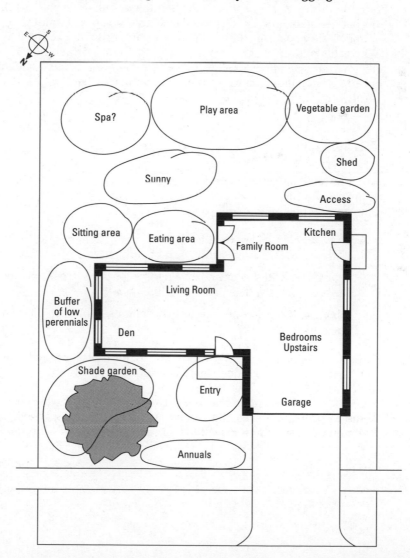

Figure 1-6:
Using tracing paper over your base plan, draw shapes to identify what you have and what you want.

✔ **Put lawn chairs where you plan to add shrubs or young trees.**

✔ **Pound in tomato stakes to show the future homes of roses or large perennials in your flower beds.**

✔ **Rake the leaves or straw into the outlines of your new beds.** If you have a bounty of fall leaves, grass clippings, or straw, you can spread them out to fill in the outlines to get a feel for your new beds.

✔ **Use a step ladder to represent an arbor.**

Squint your eyes, throw your imagination into full gear, and check the position of the elements you've placed from every vantage point that you can think of. Move your portable garden around until you like the way it looks. When this part of your yard is arranged to your satisfaction, mark your rough plan with revised lines to show bed edges, plant placement, and any other niceties. Then move on to the next section of yard and do it again. Repeat until your landscape plan is — gasp! — finished.

Creating the final plan

After you're comfortable with each section of your proposed landscape, transfer your ideas to paper in real form — not just goose eggs. Your final plan should include the following:

✔ **Hardscape:** Be sure to include deck, patio, benches, fences and gates, paths, spa, tool shed, arbor, gazebo, and so on.

✔ **Plantings:** Add flower beds, vegetable gardens, trees, shrubs, vines, lawns, perennial beds, and ground cover.

✔ **Dimensions:** Add dimensions for the house, for each element, and for the entire yard.

The example in Figure 1-7 may look a little more professional than your drawing, but it gives you an idea of what to shoot for.

Some hardscape features may require construction drawings. Have the more complex projects (decks, big arbors, and the like) professionally drawn, so that you can get construction bids, obtain permits, and order materials.

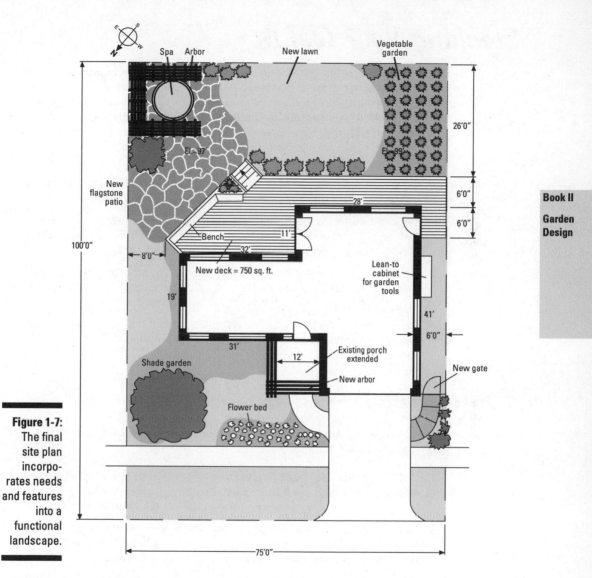

Spa   Arbor

New lawn

Vegetable garden

New flagstone patio

El. 97

El. 99

26'0"

6'0"

6'0"

100'0"

New deck = 750 sq. ft.

Bench

28'

11'

32'

8'0"

19'

Lean-to cabinet for garden tools

41'

6'0"

31'

12'

Existing porch extended

New arbor

New gate

Shade garden

Flower bed

75'0"

Figure 1-7:
The final site plan incorporates needs and features into a functional landscape.

Stocking Your Tool Box

Every job has its tools, and landscaping is no different. Depending on what projects you plan to tackle, consider investing in the following:

- ✔ **For planting perennials, annuals, and bulbs:** Shovel or spade, stiff-tined rake, hand trowel, hand pruner, and a hose and spray attachment. Optional equipment includes garden gloves, knee pads, plant labels, soaker hose or other irrigation system, bucket, and a bulb planter.

- ✔ **For planting trees, shrubs, and vines:** Square-nosed shovel or garden spade, hoe, stiff-tined rake, and a garden cart or wheelbarrow.

- ✔ **For hardscape:** Posthole digger, pick, digging bar, hammer, handsaw, square, nail set, chisel, plane, circular saw, power drill, power sander, power screwdriver, caulking gun, sawhorse, and stepladder.

- ✔ **For planting lawn seed or sod:** Sharp knife, roller, broadcast spreader, and soil preparation equipment, including a rotary tiller and heavy rake. (See Chapter 4 in Book II for more on basic lawn care.)

- ✔ **For maintenance:** Lawn mower, trimmer, hedge clippers, hand pruner, loppers, pruning saw, hoe, lawn rake, broom, and stiff-tined rake.

Going Green — as in, "Money"

Divide your landscaping project into logical sections according to your list of priorities, and start your tally:

1. **List the plants you want to use in each section of the project, and either collect your own prices by shopping nurseries and garden centers or ask a nursery to give you a quote on the whole shebang.**

2. **Use your plan to measure the areas where you want to install brick, pavers, concrete, or other hardscape materials, and take your measurements to a supplier to get estimates on materials.**

3. **Make a checklist of the costs of each section of the project, including hardscape items and the plants.**

4. **Consider what, if any, new tools you need to buy.**

Visit a building supply store, taking your lists of figures along with you. There, you find an expert who can calculate exactly what each part of your project will cost. Be sure to find out the delivery charge, and get an estimate on installation, too. Although you may want to do all the work yourself, having the installed price isn't a bad idea — just in case you run out of steam. Fill out a checklist like the one shown in Table 1-1 for each section of your landscape and then tally up a grand total.

Locating property lines

You don't find your property lines drawn on the ground. If you're lucky, though, you can find *monuments,* or markers, at the property corners. These markers may be conspicuous posts driven into the ground, but more likely, they're small pipes or brass medallions, often covered by several inches of accumulated soil. Property corners at the street are usually marked by small crosses inscribed in the concrete curb or gutter.

Keep in mind that your actual property line may be set back several feet from these markers; check your deed to see whether the street occupies an easement along the front of your property (an *easement* essentially means that your city, county, or neighbor can use the space if it ever needs it). Refer to your deed's legal description of your property. It may be a "metes and bounds" description based on known landmarks or a reference to a lot number on a subdivision map that's recorded with the appropriate agency, such as the county recorder's or tax assessor's office.

If you can't find your markers easily, ask your immediate neighbors or long-time residents living nearby. As a good-neighbor policy, you may want to conduct the search with your immediate neighbors anyway, especially to clarify the ownership of fences. If you can't verify the property lines, hire a surveyor, perhaps sharing the cost with neighbors. If your neighbors don't want to cooperate, you can still hire a surveyor yourself and seek his advice about any disputes.

Book II

Garden Design

Table 1-1		Pricing Checklist	
Element	*Price*	*Delivery Charge*	*Installation Charge*
Plants			
Topsoil			
Mulch			
Concrete			
Lumber			
Bricks			
Gravel			
Sand			
Stone			
Pavers			
Fence			
Lattice			

Table 1-1 *(continued)*			
Element	*Price*	*Delivery Charge*	*Installation Charge*
Trellises/arbors			
Outdoor furniture			
Lighting			
Irrigation system			
Tools			

The advantage to having separate price tags attached to the various sections of your plan is that you then have an idea of how big a bite each new step is going to take out of your budget. Keep in mind, though, that the estimates you start with may change — go up, that is — by the time you actually begin the next phase.

Breaking Ground, Not Rules

Before you begin your landscaping project, call your local governing body — town council, zoning board, or any other likely agency that you find in the commercial pages of your phone book — and ask what permits are necessary for the work you're planning. Tell them what kind of job you're undertaking; chances are, you have some red tape to get through. You may also want to let your neighbors know what you're planning — before the backhoe arrives. Also, before beginning your landscape project, consider which tasks may be too time-consuming — or require too much expertise — for you to tackle alone.

Landscape one clod of dirt at a time

Renovating your entire yard in one fell swoop can overwhelm even the most dedicated gardener, unless you have an unlimited budget or a staff of helpers on hand.

✔ **Establish your priorities.** Plan to work on the areas that you'll use — and enjoy — the most.

✔ **Have a long-term plan.** Redo your yard on a two-to-five-year plan. Weigh the plan against your budget to see which projects you can do this year.

✔ **Do a little at a time.** Rarely does one weekend of hard labor a landscape make. Avoid a disheveled yard by focusing on one small area at a time, and completing it before you move on to the next.

Call before you dig

Utility companies have a great deal going on under the ground, including gas and water mains, electric lines, fiber optic phone cables, and other related goodies. Follow the advice of those cautionary "call before you dig" signs and get the okay from those companies. If you think that the cost of bricks is high, wait'll you get the bill for slicing through a phone cable!

Dealing with City Hall

Book II

Garden Design

Local restrictions vary greatly from one place to the next. In many communities, for instance, the height of a fence is a matter of law. Better to find out ahead of time that 5 feet is the limit before you invest in 6-foot privacy walls. Ponds and pools, even small ones, may require a fence to keep neighborhood toddlers or the meter reader from falling in. You may need to have an inspector check your work. At the very least, you'll likely need permits for erecting any kind of permanent structure.

Setback is a popular term with zoning departments. The setback is the distance from an adjoining property line that a structure can be erected. Before you dig, make sure that you're putting it in the right place. Building a deck is hard work. Taking it down and moving it two feet inward is plain aggravation.

Keeping the neighbors happy

Keep peace in the neighborhood with a very simple action — talk to your neighbors. Let them know what kind of work you're planning, so that they don't panic about how it will affect their property. Neighbors are as territorial about their own places as pit bulls. Pay attention to how your changes may affect them. Before you plant a row of 12-foot evergreens or put up a privacy fence, consider whether you'll be blocking their view or creating a shade problem for them. Will your improvements be a positive thing for them, too, or will they be left staring at the ugly backside of your new fence or swatting mosquitoes attracted by your garden pool?

Deciding when to hire help

Before you tackle a new project, such as laying a patio, assess your physical strength, your skills, and how trainable you are. Read the helpful pamphlets at building supply stores, or read more in how-to books, then take a merciless look at your un-Schwartzeneggeresque biceps and your already jam-packed free time, and decide whether you and the task are compatible. You may want to get professional help on some of the following big jobs:

- ✔ Installing a fence and gate, pool, or irrigation system
- ✔ Building steps, stone or stacked-concrete walls, or large outdoor structures, such as a shed
- ✔ Planting large trees
- ✔ Doing electrical, plumbing, or gas-line work
- ✔ Pouring concrete, installing a patio, or building a deck

Practicing conservation — of your wallet!

You can shave hundreds off of your landscaping price tag with a few cost-cutting tricks:

- ✔ **Buy from the source.** Look for brickyards, paving makers, stone and slate quarries, gravel yards, and other nearby sources of raw materials. Such suppliers are probably listed in your phone book. Do some comparison shopping and know how much you need — before you ask for a price.

- ✔ **Find a friend with a pickup truck.** Don't strain the springs of your own or a friend's truck with stone or other ultra-heavy materials, but do haul your own lumber and anything else that you can safely carry. You save big on delivery charges.

- ✔ **Combine brick with concrete.** Instead of installing costly all-brick walks, combine brick with concrete. Use the brick as decorative strips in the walk.

- ✔ **Eliminate mortar between pavers or bricks.** Set the materials into a frame made of rot-resistant lumber or strips of concrete. Set bricks or pavers into a sand base between the edges of the frame and brush sand into

the cracks. The frame prevents the paving from shifting.

- ✔ **Salvage cool stuff.** Architectural salvage dealers offer real buys on fencing, arbors, ironwork, and decorative touches. No telling what you'll find, but we defy you to come away empty-handed. Check your phone book under "Architectural Salvage" or "Junk Dealers."

- ✔ **Make a faux stone wall out of free concrete.** Pieces of broken concrete sidewalk can look much like fieldstone when you stack them for a dry wall. Next time you see a sidewalk being ripped out, ask if you can have the broken pieces. Most contractors will gladly dump the stuff in your yard, so that they don't have to haul it to the landfill where they pay a fee for dumping.

- ✔ **Ask for wood chips from tree services and utility companies or road crews clearing roadside right-of-ways.** You can often get a truckload for zero cash. Use the chips for path surfaces and for long-lasting mulch.

Chapter 2

Building Your Landscape

In This Chapter

▶ Using and enjoying your entire yard

▶ Planting for privacy, water conservation, and other special circumstances

▶ Designing your landscape with a particular theme in mind

Most people want yards that look welcoming. And most lots come with challenges that make landscaping intimidating. This chapter offers several solutions for unique landscaping situations.

Using Every Bit of Your Yard

Too often, people forget that they can landscape — and enjoy — their entire yard. The following sections give you some ideas for landscaping all around the house.

A park-like front yard

What do you want from your front yard? You may want shade trees and a big lawn that merges with the neighbors'. Or maybe you want a courtyard — an approach that has worked in Spain for hundreds of years — that provides privacy from a busy street. Also consider the overall effect of the front yard in Figure 2-1: spacious and simple with a big lawn, shade trees, and evergreens creating a green, park-like effect. Guests have a pleasant walk to the front door any time of the year. Mixed perennials add bursts of seasonal color.

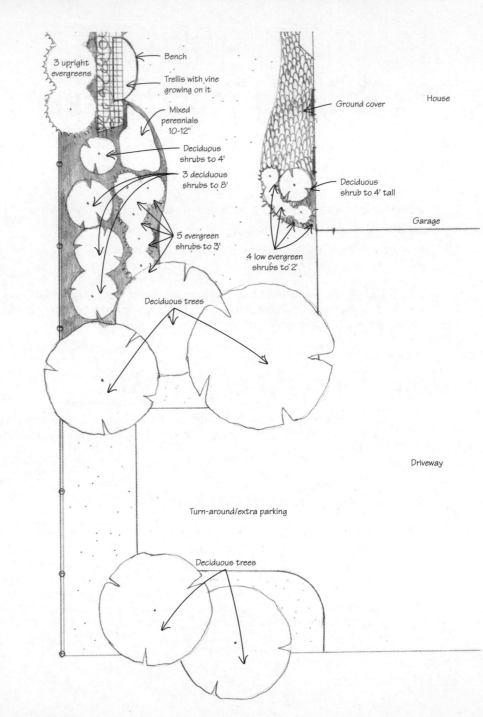

3 upright evergreens

Bench

Trellis with vine growing on it

Mixed perennials 10-12"

Deciduous shrubs to 4'

3 deciduous shrubs to 8'

5 evergreen shrubs to 3'

Ground cover

House

Deciduous shrub to 4' tall

Garage

4 low evergreen shrubs to 2'

Deciduous trees

Driveway

Turn-around/extra parking

Deciduous trees

Figure 2-1:
A gracious
front yard.

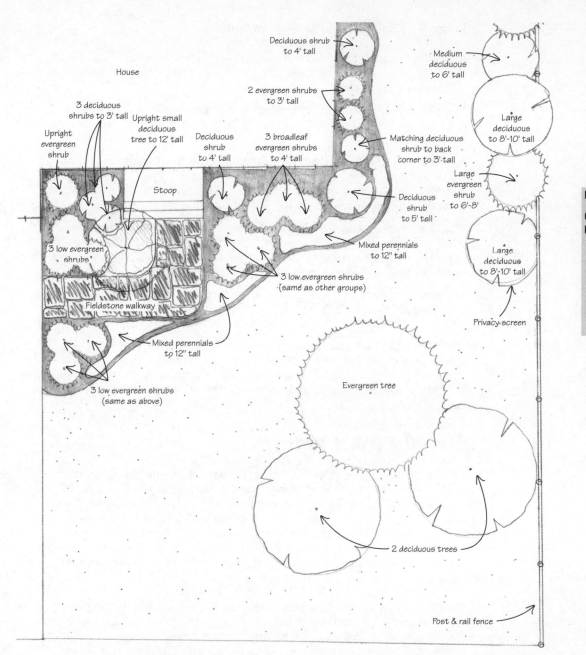

House

Deciduous shrub
to 4' tall

Medium
deciduous
to 6' tall

2 evergreen shrubs
to 3' tall

Large
deciduous
to 8'-10' tall

3 deciduous
shrubs to 3' tall

Upright small
deciduous
tree to 12' tall

Upright
evergreen
shrub

Deciduous
shrub
to 4' tall

3 broadleaf
evergreen shrubs
to 4' tall

Matching deciduous
shrub to back
corner to 3' tall

Large
evergreen
shrub
to 6'-8'

Stoop

Deciduous
shrub
to 5' tall

3 low evergreen
shrubs

Large
deciduous
to 8'-10' tall

Mixed perennials
to 12" tall

Fieldstone walkway

3 low evergreen shrubs
(same as other groups)

Privacy screen

Mixed perennials
to 12" tall

3 low evergreen shrubs
(same as above)

Evergreen tree

2 deciduous trees

Post & rail fence

This front-yard plan provides interesting features:

- ✔ **A gracious fieldstone walkway:** You can vary your walkway in size, shape, and the material you use. This walk leads from the driveway to a spacious front stoop.

- ✔ **A turnaround to allow for extra parking:** Deciduous trees help define the turnaround area, as well as create a little mystery and screening for the side yard planting.

- ✔ **A deciduous tree to add vertical interest to the front entry:** A tree that's so close to the house shouldn't exceed 12 to 15 feet in height. It should also have an upright growth habit, so that it won't block the view from the front door or jut into the walkway.

- ✔ **Mixed evergreen and deciduous shrubs:** These plants provide privacy where it's needed — on the property lines. Remember that deciduous plants won't provide much privacy during their leafless season, so don't use them where all-year screening is critical.

- ✔ **Foundation plants that are compact, for low maintenance:** Choose varieties that grow no taller than 4 feet (except for the plants at the corner, which can reach 6 feet, unless roof eaves don't allow room).

- ✔ **Repetition in plantings:** To provide continuity, the front entry planting has three groups of the same three low-growing masses of evergreens. And note that the same deciduous shrubs are used on both sides of the front door. Chapter 1 in Book II discusses repetition in more detail.

A friendly front entry

Think of a front entry garden as your personal way of greeting visitors. This part of your yard is a personal statement, and it can reflect *you* — your favorite plants, touches of outdoor decoration, a wreath on the door at the holidays. Of course, you also have to think of the mailman and others who use the entry for practical purposes — they should at least be able to find the front door. And speaking of the practical, you want something that's not unreasonable to maintain and keep tidy. Remember that this is the one part of your yard that you use every day of the year.

The front entry plan in Figure 2-2 falls in the category of a warm, but dignified greeting — sort of a friendly hug. It has an orderly, straight-ahead approach by way of the rectangular walk and the broad concrete stoop and steps. Skimping on the size of the front porch always seems like an unfriendly gesture — no place to stand comfortably while you're waiting. Fieldstone set into the walk lends a nice informal touch, but you can always substitute concrete, bricks, or gravel.

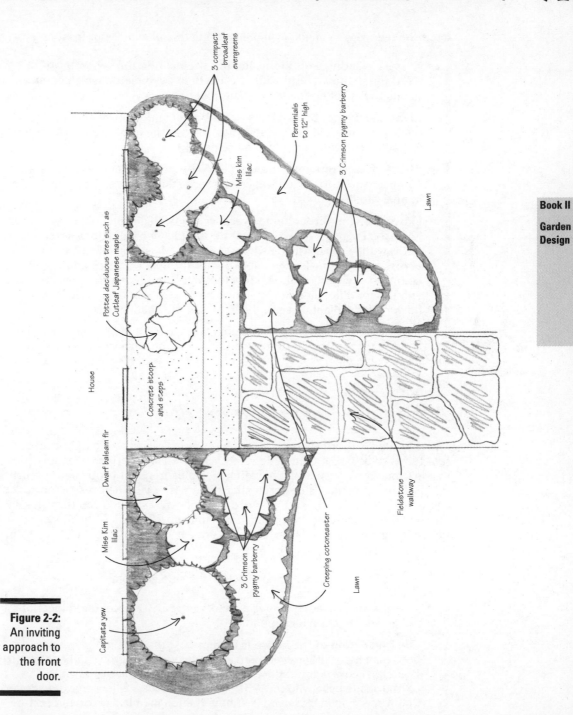

3 compact broadleaf evergreens

Miss Kim lilac

Perennials to 12" high

3 Crimson pygmy barberry

Lawn

Potted deciduous tree such as Cutleaf Japanese maple

House

Concrete stoop and steps

Dwarf balsam fir

Miss Kim lilac

Capitata yew

3 Crimson pygmy barberry

Creeping cotoneaster

Lawn

Fieldstone walkway

Figure 2-2:
An inviting
approach to
the front
door.

Book II

**Garden
Design**

Keep the following in mind when considering this plan for your front entry:

- ✔ **Curved planting beds alongside the walk soften the geometry of the front porch, house, and walk.** Notice their asymmetry, which complements the offset door and adds interest to the design.

- ✔ **Plants are layered.** Tall plants in back against the house, medium-sized ones are in the middle, and low plants are in the front border. (Chapter 1 in Book II explains layering in more detail.)

- ✔ **Plantings are low-maintenance.** All except the capitata yew are dwarf or compact varieties, which will call for less maintenance. (The yew needs annual pruning, though.)

- ✔ **Flowers bloom throughout several seasons.** Red-leafed plants, such as 'Crimson Pygmy' barberry repeat to provide color for a long season and to draw the eye across the whole planting. 'Miss Kim' lilac is repeated across the planting for the impact of its spring bloom. For additional color, use low perennials (up to a foot tall) throughout the season or add annuals for different color schemes every year. Choose shade-loving flowers if you plant close to the house where shade is deep.

Use the front porch to display a small tree in a container, such as red-leafed Japanese maple (to repeat the red of the barberries). For even more color, fill in around the base of the tree with blooming flowers.

A side yard getaway garden

Space in the side yard is often neglected, mainly because it's a tight space that tends to be out of sight. Side yards also often suffer from too much shade from your house or the neighbor's — plus frequent problems with privacy. At the same time, side yards offer great potential. Their restricted space can offer an intimacy that the rest of a yard doesn't, and you can turn shade into a blessing. The side yard plan shown in Figure 2-3 makes the most of a typical long narrow side yard shape. This one is designed to be admired from inside and out.

Keep the following in mind when viewing this side yard plan:

- ✔ **A trellis over a bench makes a shady getaway.** The centered location of the bench creates a focal point.

- ✔ **The foundation of the house is covered.** At the base of the house, pachysandra or other evergreen ground cover that grows tall enough (to 12 inches) covers the exposed foundation — and the plants enjoy the partial shade usually found at the base of a house. Select a ground cover that forms a solid mass and is subdued enough in leaf color and texture not to detract from the rest of the plantings. If the side of the house includes some bare wall panels, without windows, you may want to add shrubs along the house's foundation. The plants provide a cooling effect and reduce reflected heat, plus they offer a better view from the bench.

✔ **Plants provide privacy.** Plantings on the property line form a backdrop and privacy screen from the neighbors.

✔ **'Carol Mackie' daphne serves as bookends to planting.** This semievergreen has white- or gold-edged leaves, is attractive year-round, and doesn't drop all its leaves in the fall.

✔ **The area has close-up color.** Colorful flowering plants are intended to be appreciated at close range.

Book II

Garden Design

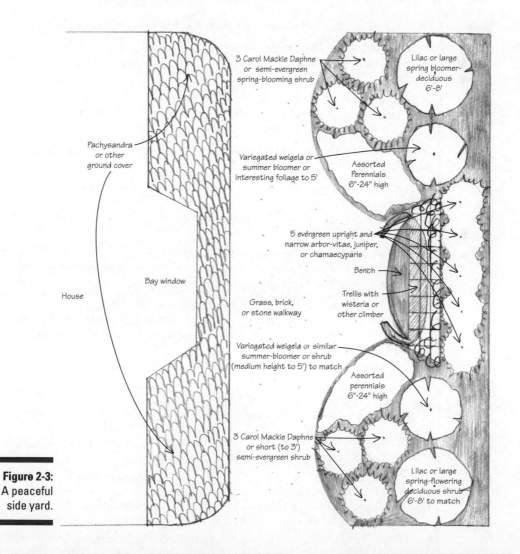

Figure 2-3:
A peaceful
side yard.

Labels in figure:
- 3 Carol Mackie Daphne or semi-evergreen spring-blooming shrub
- Lilac or large spring bloomer-deciduous 6'-8'
- Pachysandra or other ground cover
- Variegated weigela or summer bloomer or interesting foliage to 5'
- Assorted Perennials 6"-24" high
- 5 evergreen upright and narrow arbor-vitae, juniper, or chamaecyparis
- Bench
- House
- Bay window
- Grass, brick, or stone walkway
- Trellis with wisteria or other climber
- Variegated weigela or similar summer-bloomer or shrub (medium height to 5') to match
- Assorted perennials 6"-24" high
- 3 Carol Mackie Daphne or short (to 3') semi-evergreen shrub
- Lilac or large spring-flowering deciduous shrub 6'-8' to match

A multipurpose back yard

Out of sight of neighbors and passersby, the back yard is the place where every family member wants their own pet projects — flowers, vegetables, a swing set, croquet, horseshoes, horses — whatever. The backyard plan, shown in Figure 2-4, is for lucky homeowners with a big back yard, but you can choose to duplicate only a portion of this yard, if yours is smaller. Different activities are allotted their own, defined space, but without high dividing fences. The big, green lawn provides plenty of play space as well as visual relief for the more complex surroundings. Note the following about this back yard plan:

- **Divided patio:** The two-level patio makes the spaces seem more intimate.
- **Safe play area:** The children's play area doesn't need fencing (except for the backdrop of side yard fencing), and you can see playing children from the house and patio.
- **Shade trees:** A big tree near the patio provides shade at just the spot where you want to spend your summer days. More strategically located shade trees make the children's play area comfortable in hot weather.
- **Privacy shrubs:** Big evergreen and deciduous shrubs form privacy screens along the property lines.
- **Well-located vegetable garden:** The vegetable garden basks in the yard's sunniest spot — away from trees. The fence and raised beds add an element of structure that makes the garden more presentable during its off-seasons.
- **Seasonal color:** A border of perennials and shrubs provides seasonal color right where you can see it most — at the edge of the patio. Select plants that are low enough not to cut off the view.
- **Container flowers:** Annuals and perennials grow in containers to brighten corners of the patio. Choose pots that are 12 inches in diameter or larger, and cluster them in groups of at least three. See Chapter 3 in Book II for more on container gardens.

Planting for Special Situations

The following sections try to help you plan the parts of your landscape that demand special treatment.

Planting for privacy

The challenge in landscaping is to provide privacy while creating an enjoyable and useable space. For this plan, shown in Figure 2-5, we use both plants and fencing for privacy. When carefully selected and placed, plants can help screen neighbors, muffle noise, and create interest and beauty of their own. Remember, too, that plants eventually can grow much taller than a fence — if height is what you want. When reviewing this privacy planting, consider the following:

- **Use fencing for privacy.** Use solid stockade fencing for a high degree of privacy. Otherwise, use a more open type of fencing with vines.

- **Create a private patio.** A free-form surfaced patio with fieldstone, brick, concrete pavers, pea gravel, or mulch, gives an informal look.

- **Use a mix of plants for privacy.** Evergreens are mixed with deciduous plants for screening. Evergreens provide year-round privacy, but deciduous plants may work fine for you because their foliage blocks views during spring and summer when you're most apt to use the space. Keep in mind the eventual heights of the plants you choose. The taller plants in this plan generally reach 5 to 8 feet in height.

- **Pay attention to the shape of plants.** The rounded, enveloping shape of the planting creates a feeling of extra privacy.

- **Use deciduous and evergreen plants for screening and extra privacy.** Your local nursery can offer several good choices beyond what's shown in Figure 2-5.

Book II

Garden Design

Planting to conserve water

If you live in an area where water conservation is a priority, you may want at least part of your landscape to thrive without irrigation. (Keep in mind that almost anything you plant needs watering to get it started and for the first year.) The low-water plan, shown in Figure 2-6, works in most climates, with the plants that are hardy in Zones 3 to 8 or 9 (see Book I for more on plant zones). Special features of this low-water plan include:

- **Layered plants:** The design is a fairly typical border with the low plants up front, tall ones at the back. Low plants grow underneath the window so not to obstruct the view. Russian olives are the big guys. (Chapter 2 in Book II discusses layering in more detail.)

- **Plenty of colors:** A great deal of silver — from the artemisa and the Russian olive — goes nicely with the blue tones of the junipers, along with the spring flowers of the ceanothus. Seasonal flowers add their colorful punctuation — spiraea in early summer and bright yellow potentilla for a long season.

- **Trees and shrubs that require little water:** You can choose from several low-water trees and shrubs at your local nursery.

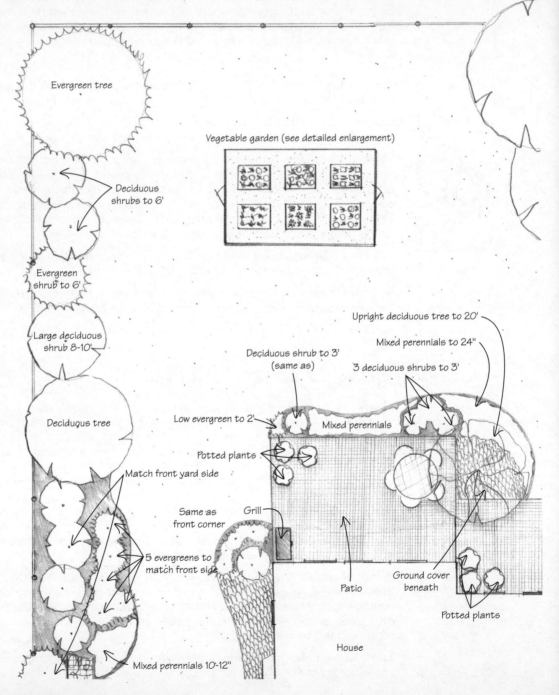

Evergreen tree

Vegetable garden (see detailed enlargement)

Deciduous shrubs to 6'

Evergreen shrub to 6'

Large deciduous shrub 8-10'

Upright deciduous tree to 20'

Mixed perennials to 24"

Deciduous shrub to 3' (same as)

3 deciduous shrubs to 3'

Low evergreen to 2'

Mixed perennials

Deciduous tree

Potted plants

Match front yard side

Same as front corner

Grill

5 evergreens to match front side

Ground cover beneath

Patio

Potted plants

House

Mixed perennials 10'-12"

Figure 2-4: This back yard has it all.

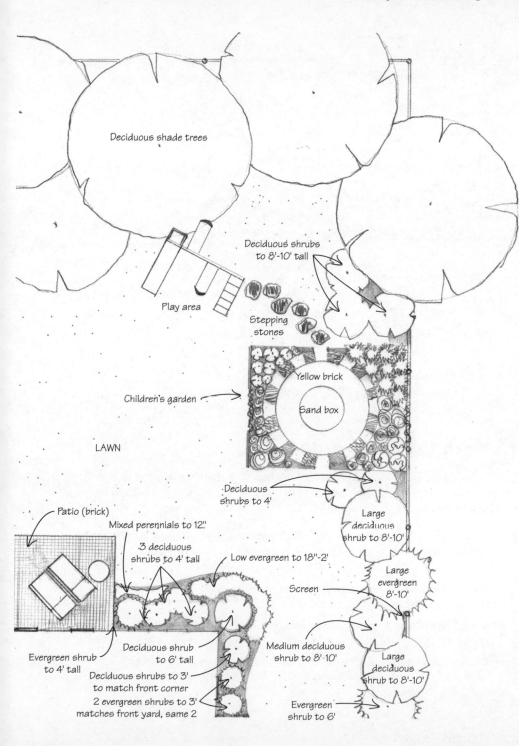

Deciduous shade trees

Deciduous shrubs
to 8'-10' tall

Play area

Stepping
stones

Children's garden

Yellow brick

Sand box

LAWN

Deciduous
shrubs to 4'

Large
deciduous
shrub to 8'-10'

Patio (brick)

Mixed perennials to 12"

3 deciduous
shrubs to 4' tall

Low evergreen to 18"-2'

Large
evergreen
8'-10'

Screen

Evergreen shrub
to 4' tall

Deciduous shrub
to 6' tall

Medium deciduous
shrub to 8'-10'

Large
deciduous
shrub to 8'-10'

Deciduous shrubs to 3'
to match front corner

2 evergreen shrubs to 3'
matches front yard, same 2

Evergreen
shrub to 6'

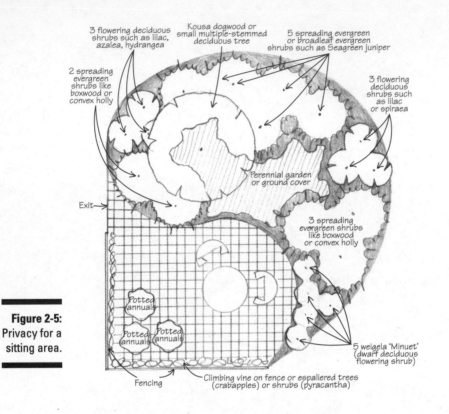

3 flowering deciduous shrubs such as lilac, azalea, hydrangea

Kousa dogwood or small multiple-stemmed deciduous tree

5 spreading evergreen or broadleaf evergreen shrubs such as Seagreen juniper

2 spreading evergreen shrubs like boxwood or convex holly

3 flowering deciduous shrubs such as lilac or spiraea

Perennial garden or ground cover

Exit

3 spreading evergreen shrubs like boxwood or convex holly

Potted annuals

Potted annuals

Potted annuals

5 weigela 'Minuet' (dwarf deciduous flowering shrub)

Fencing

Climbing vine on fence or espaliered trees (crabapples) or shrubs (pyracantha)

Figure 2-5:
Privacy for a
sitting area.

Planting around a pool

Landscaping around a pool first involves choosing the kind of look that you want — tropical, natural, sleek, and so on. Keep the following practical considerations in mind when making your plans and selecting your plants:

- **Don't create shade.** Plants shouldn't cast shade where you don't want it. Choose low-growing or dwarf-type plants. Palms are different — even big ones may not cast too much shade.

- **Stay away from mess-makers.** Avoid leaf, blossom, and berry shedders that drop debris into your pool.

- **Avoid bee-attracting blossoms.** Many summer annuals fall into this category.

- **Choose low-maintenance plantings.** You probably want to use your poolside areas for relaxing and not for heavy-duty gardening.

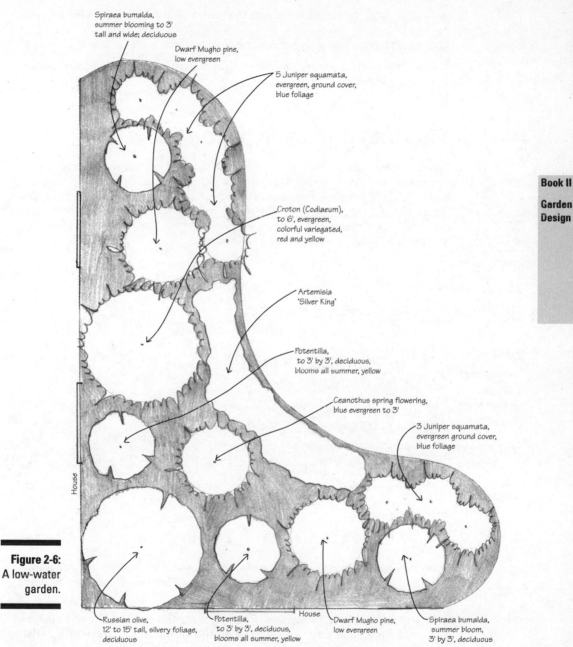

Spiraea bumalda,
summer blooming to 3'
tall and wide; deciduous

Dwarf Mugho pine,
low evergreen

5 Juniper squamata,
evergreen, ground cover,
blue foliage

Croton (Codiaeum),
to 6', evergreen,
colorful variegated,
red and yellow

Artemisia
'Silver King'

Potentilla,
to 3' by 3', deciduous,
blooms all summer, yellow

Ceanothus spring flowering,
blue evergreen to 3'

3 Juniper squamata,
evergreen ground cover,
blue foliage

House

House

Russian olive,
12' to 15' tall, silvery foliage,
deciduous

Potentilla,
to 3' by 3', deciduous,
blooms all summer, yellow

Dwarf Mugho pine,
low evergreen

Spiraea bumalda,
summer bloom,
3' by 3', deciduous

Figure 2-6:
A low-water
garden.

Book II

**Garden
Design**

Here are few suggestions for plants that work well around a pool:

- **Low shrubs and ground covers:** Agapanthus, juniper, moraea, rosemary
- **Medium-sized to large shrubs:** Holly, Japanese black pine, pittosporum, pyracantha

Planting a hillside rock garden

Instead of viewing a slope as a landscape liability, consider it a great opportunity — a place to display a rock garden. Rock garden plants are quite beautiful, and growing them on a slope near a walkway gives you the opportunity to view them up close. The rock garden plan shown in Figure 2-7 combines plants, steps, and boulders, and can work in the backyard at the edge of a lawn or in front, right off of a sidewalk.

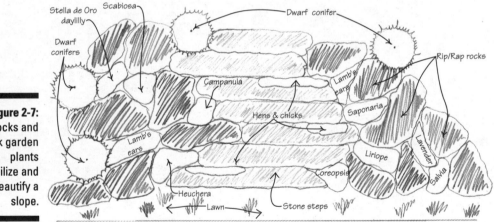

Figure 2-7: Rocks and rock garden plants stabilize and beautify a slope.

Keep the following in mind for creating this sort of rock garden:

- **The steps are stones.** Use stones of different lengths for a more natural look. Choose stones with a smooth, flat surface, and put them in place firmly. Create planting pockets on the steps.
- **Rip-rap rocks help the soil.** Randomly stacking rocks of varying size is an economical way to retain soil on the slope — the steeper the hillside, the closer together you want the rocks to stabilize the soil effectively. Add planting pockets between the rocks to soften harshness.
- **Boulders add a natural touch.** Keep them in scale, not too big or too small for the site.

- ✔ **Color and texture come alive.** Typical rock garden plants are small and slow growing, offering a variety of textures that are best viewed close up. For color, include blooming perennials, such as lavender, coreopsis, and salvia.

- ✔ **Small trees and shrubs add beauty.** Potential rock garden trees include dwarf arborvitae *(Thuja occidentalis)*, dwarf hemlock *(Tsuga canadensis)*, dwarf hinoki cypress *(Chamaecyparis obtusa)*, Japanese maple *(Acer palmatum)*, and Mugho pine *(Pinus mugo mugo)*. As for shrubs, try bog rosemary *(Andromeda polifolia* 'Nana'), dwarf heath *(Erica)*, dwarf Japanese holly *(Ilex crenata)*, dwarf junipers, and dwarf Scotch heather *(Calluna vulgaris)*.

- ✔ **Small perennials bring bursts of color.** Perennials that work well in a simple rock garden include bellflower *(Campanula)*, Cranesbill *(Geranium)*, Moonbeam coreopsis *(Coreopsis verticillata* 'Moonbeam'), primroses *(Primula)*, thrift *(Armeria)*, thyme *(Thymus)*, and Yarrow *(Achillea)*.

Planting a small balcony garden

A balcony offers a host of gardening challenges — no soil, perhaps too much shade or too much sun, and difficulty in bringing water to the garden. But with planning, a small balcony can offer some of the same amenities as a garden in the ground: lush green foliage, colorful flowers — even vegetables. And you have the garden right up close where you can appreciate it. Plants provide seasonal interest and a bit of privacy, and you still have room for outdoor dining and relaxing.

Keep the following in mind when planning a balcony garden:

- ✔ **Create a focal point.** The focal point in this plan is a small tree or *standard* (a shrub trained as a small, single-trunk tree). For extra color, underplant the tree with trailing spring or summer-blooming annual flowers (pansies, lobelias, marigolds, petunias, and so on).

- ✔ **Use window boxes.** Fasten window boxes to your balcony's railing, so that they're viewable from indoors or from outside. Use them to create more privacy or to frame a view. Change plantings in the window boxes seasonally by growing annuals in the summer and stuffing the boxes with greens and dried-berry plants for winter and the holidays.

- ✔ **Grow container plants.** Colorful pots of annuals provide surprising amounts of flower color at close range. Chapter 3 in Book II discusses container plants in greater detail.

Water draining from the containers can stain the balcony surface or drip on your neighbor below — keep saucers under the pots.

- **Don't forget veggies.** Squeeze herbs and vegetables into your balcony garden. To save space, train climbers, such as cucumbers and tomatoes, on teepees or in cages.

- **Install an outdoor faucet.** Consider installing an outdoor faucet to avoid the tedium of watering with a watering pot.

Size (not too tall or spreading) and maintenance (not too demanding) are your main considerations when making plans for a balcony garden. Also check on your sun and shade exposure throughout the day. The following small trees and shrubs need sun most of the day and could serve as a focal point on a balcony garden:

- Camellia (needs shade in hot climates)

- Crape myrtle (*Lagerstroemia indica*)

- Hibiscus (standard)

- Japanese black pine (*Pinus thunbergi*)

- Japanese maple (*Acer palmatum*)

- Palms (indoor/outdoor)

- Tree rose (*Rosa*)

Teeming with Themes

You can make landscaping even more delightful by creating a *theme garden* — one with a specific purpose, created for fun. Theme gardens make your yard more interesting and useful to you. This section offers suggestions for several theme gardens that you may want to consider adding to your landscape.

A landscape to attract wild creatures

Nothing brings a garden to life more than living things — *desirable* living things, that is. The sight and sound of birds is particularly appealing and easy to arrange. But you can also invite butterflies, chipmunks, and beneficial insects to your landscape. What brings creatures into a garden are plants — and certain plants bring certain creatures.

Following are a few general points to keep in mind when you want your garden to attract different types of life:

- **Strive for diversity in your plant selection.** This concept may conflict with a designer's approach to unity, but for this plan, a variety of plants means a greater chance of attracting a variety of wild creatures.

- ✔ **Provide a year-round supply of water, such as a pond or bird bath.**
- ✔ **Grow plants that are native to your region.** These should be most familiar and attractive to your local creatures.

A space for kids

Designed in the shape of a clock, (see Figure 2-8) this kids' play area appeals to the sense of fun, adventure, and taste buds of nearly all children.

WARNING!

Be extremely careful when selecting plants for your child's garden. If you have any questions, check lists of poisonous plants (which may be available from your county extension office) or consult your local nursery.

Book II

Garden
Design

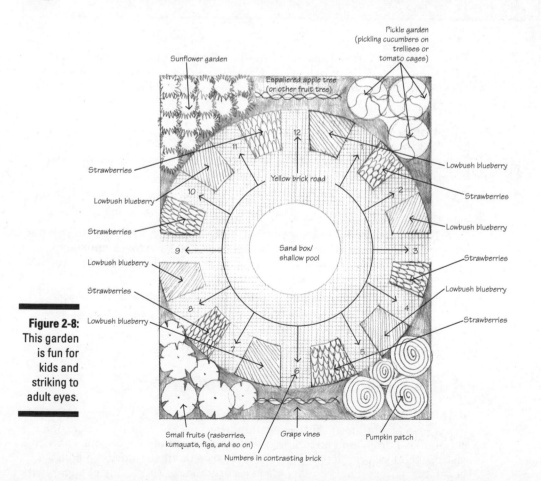

Figure 2-8: This garden is fun for kids and striking to adult eyes.

Fun plants

You can make a kids' play area more fun by including plants that have extra appeal for youngsters.

✔ **Gourds:** Harvest and dry the gourds — which are as easy to grow as squash — for crafts projects or decorations.

✔ **Popcorn:** Grow popcorn just like sweet corn, but don't plant it near sweet corn unless you want to demonstrate the bizarre effects of cross-pollination.

✔ **Pumpkins:** The draw is obvious, but pumpkins need a lot of room and water and a good three or four months to reach harvest stage.

✔ **Mickey Mouse plant:** Kids see a strong resemblance to Mickey Mouse in one stage of the black and red flowers on this little shrub. The plant's botanical name is *Ochna multiflora.*

This plan is meant mainly as inspiration. Feel free to change its scale (the minimum space is 10 by 10 feet) or, instead of a clock, make it into a sun, a daisy — whatever suits your needs. This plan contains the following fantastic features:

✔ **At the center of it all is a whimsical sculpture or sandbox.** Remember that the sandbox won't be fun for kids (or for you) if neighborhood or family cats have access to it. To block out sun, cover the sandbox with plywood or an outdoor awning cloth.

✔ **The brick clock garden is a real eye-catcher.** Strawberry and blueberry plants alternate in cutouts between numbers or spaces left blank.

✔ **The plants don't just sit there.** Various training devices get them off the ground and make them more interesting — trellises for cucumbers, cages for tomatoes, and so on. You can use a section of fence to train the apple tree into a flat *espalier* (plant that grows flat along a fence).

✔ **The plants are fun.** In addition to the berries, other edibles include pumpkins, figs, and grapes. Sunflowers are big and striking — and irresistible to kids.

A neat and tidy vegetable garden

A well-designed vegetable garden (Book VII discusses vegetable gardening in detail) can be both beautiful and an important part of your landscape, if it's situated in a prominent area. And, by making maximum use of your space, it's also much more productive. Figure 2-9 shows a tightly organized plan for a vegetable garden that is handsome in its orderliness and highly efficient in its use of space.

Gate

Fencing

Corn and head lettuce interplanted

Cages with cucumbers or squash, interplanted with onions

Spinach with carrots

Bell peppers with radishes

Mulch or stone or brick pathways

Tomatoes on cages with garlic

Pole beans on teepees with potatoes

Figure 2-9:
This vegetable garden is attractive as well as productive.

Book II

Garden Design

Keep the following in mind when designing your vegetable garden:

- ✔ **Divide the garden.** Dividing the area into square or rectangular beds allows for easy access to each planting section and makes the garden both ornamental and functional.

- ✔ **Build in walkways.** Pathways between the beds allow you to get around without muddying your feet. Surface paths with mulch, pea gravel, brick, stepping stones, or sawdust.

- ✔ **Interplant.** *Interplanting* (planting one kind of plant between another) is key for space efficiency. For example, you can interplant radishes with peppers. By the time the peppers have spread out, the fast-growing radishes have finished their season and are out of the way.

- ✔ **Go organic.** Interplant pungent plants, such as garlic, basil, and marigolds, with tomatoes to naturally ward off insects. Even if they didn't help with your pest control, they'd still be a nice addition to any vegetable garden. (Chapter 7 in Book I has more on organic pest control.)

- ✔ **Create shade.** Corn is a tall crop that's used to shade the ground for cool-season crops like lettuce.

- ✔ **Grow up.** By using teepees, trellises, and fences you can train vining crops (such as peas, beans, and cucumbers) up the structures to save ground space and make picking easier. Vertical structures also add visual interest to a vegetable garden. Tomato cages are another good way to introduce verticality into a vegetable garden. Near the base of vine teepees, underground crops like potatoes and onions work well because they take so little space.

A pretty, formal herb garden

Herbs fit somewhere in every garden. Many herbs and perennial flowers thrive under similar conditions. Some basic landscape plants, such as rosemary and lavender, are also herbs. You can grow them in containers and snip parsley right out your back door (see Chapter 3 in Book II for more on container gardening), or you can grow a traditional formal herb garden. Figure 2-10 shows a formal herb garden in the traditional circular plan. This garden takes careful planning and installation, as well as a good deal of maintenance, but it could easily be the high point of your garden.

Use the following tips when creating your own herb garden:

- ✔ **Establish a focal point.** Consider something man-made, such as a sundial, bird bath, or outdoor sculpture. Don't be afraid to improvise.

- ✔ **Establish pathways.** Use brick for traditional, formal pathways. More informal alternatives include stepping stones, bluestone, mulch, or *pea gravel* (small stones with smaller aggregate mixed in so you can pack it down).

✔ **Keep herbs separate.** Define and separate the herb plantings with buried edging of brick, metal, or wood to control the spreading tendencies of some herbs.

✔ **Create herb hedges.** For a formal look, prune lavender and rosemary around the outside into hedges.

✔ **Maintain the garden.** An herb garden needs regular maintenance — mostly pruning and trimming to keep plants confined to their spaces. For bushy growth, pinch and trim plants while they're small and tender-stemmed — don't wait until they get too tall and woody.

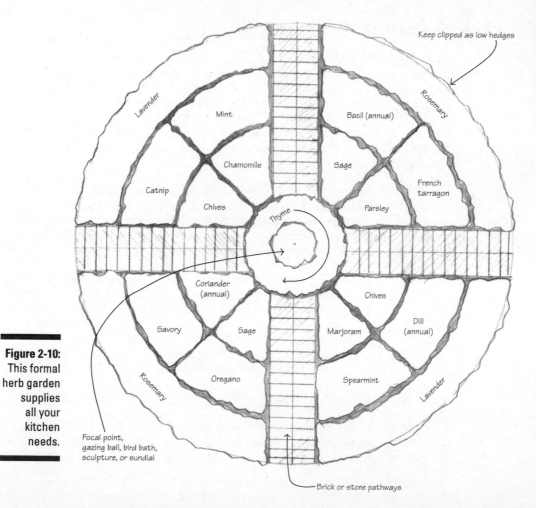

Figure 2-10: This formal herb garden supplies all your kitchen needs.

Keep clipped as low hedges

Lavender

Mint

Rosemary

Basil (annual)

Chamomile

Sage

Catnip

French tarragon

Chives

Parsley

Thyme

Coriander (annual)

Chives

Savory

Sage

Marjoram

Dill (annual)

Rosemary

Oregano

Spearmint

Lavender

Focal point, gazing ball, bird bath, sculpture, or sundial

Brick or stone pathways

As a rule, most herbs, particularly those in this plan, need similar care:

- ✔ **Provide a spot in full sun.**

- ✔ **Don't worry about soil.** Herbs don't need soil that's rich or high in organic matter.

- ✔ **Keep the soil well-drained and keep plants on the dry side.** A few herbs, such as parsley and chives, need more water than others, so keep an eye on them.

Winter performance depends on your climate. In mild climates, many herbs stay evergreen all year.

A lush water garden

As daunting as a water garden may sound, take heart in the fact that many products and kits are now available to help. To create a pond, most people use a flexible liner made of PVC or butyl-rubber. You can buy reassuringly reliable pumps in a wide range of sizes and power. Start with a trip to your garden center or hardware store, track down a knowledgeable salesperson, and pick up literature if you can. Many mail-order suppliers are also willing to send you water garden material; look for addresses in the back of gardening magazines.

Before you start planning, you need to keep some important factors in mind. Locate the pond in a wind-sheltered spot to avoid falling leaves. For pond health, water gardens need at least a half day of sun. You also need to cover more than half of the water surface with plants. Safety is critical; you may need a fence to keep out curious children.

You also face some tough design challenges. You have to make sure that the pond fits gracefully into the rest of the garden — you don't want it just sitting there looking like an abandoned bath tub. You also have to figure out what to do at the pond's edges. The water garden plan in Figure 2-11 is designed to look good and to blend naturally into the surrounding garden. It's based on a good-sized space, including several existing trees, but you can scale it up or down in size, depending on your available space.

When reviewing your water garden plan, consider the following:

- ✔ **Use rocks.** The pond is made with a liner, and rocks help to hold it down, look natural, and soften the transition from the pond to the planting and beyond.

✔ **Use small and large plants.** The small plants at the pool's edge all have hanging foliage to hide and soften the pond's edge. The larger, moisture-loving plants provide a transition to the rest of the garden.

✔ **Keep waterlilies in check.** Grow waterlilies in the pond in containers to keep them from running rampant, especially in small pools. (Chapter 3 in Book II has more on container gardening.) Waterlilies require quiet water, so don't grow them near a fountain.

✔ **Use containers.** Marsh marigolds and Japanese iris are best grown in containers to keep them from spreading, and so that they can be moved around for best placement. Use underwater shelves to keep them at the correct heights under water. You can also use stacked bricks — remove bricks one at a time as plants grow taller.

Book II

Garden Design

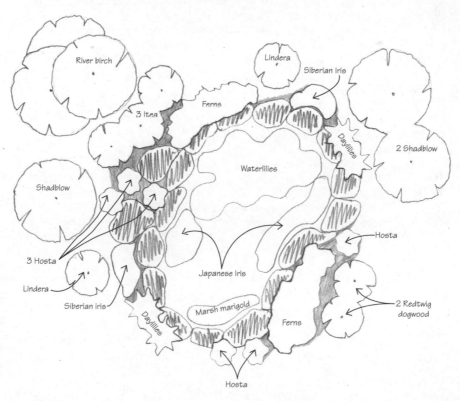

Figure 2-11:
A complete water garden plan.

Chapter 3

Containering Your Excitement

Containers can provide a healthy, happy home for an array of indoor and outdoor greenery. Growing plants in pots, baskets, tubs, barrels, or other containers up to and including discarded footwear can be fun in a garden of any size and shape. Growing plants in pots is easy, but you can make it as challenging as you like. This chapter tells you everything you need to know to make container plants part of your landscape.

Taking the Container Plunge

Here are four good reasons why you may choose to grow plants in containers:

✔ **You can grow plants in impossible places.** Container plants are portable; they can grow where you don't have a conventional garden.

✔ **You can make plants look good.** Highlighting a plant by growing it in a pot brings out qualities not noticeable in a garden bed or in a block of plants at the garden center.

✔ **You can grow plants that you think you can't grow.** Containers allow and encourage experimentation. You can give plants the exact conditions that they need, and you can grow plants with different soil and watering requirements side by side, which isn't possible in a garden.

✔ **You can do stupid container tricks.** Whatever the motivation, container gardeners can exercise spunk without polluting the atmosphere.

Before you take another step toward container gardening, make sure that you acknowledge and respect this concept: A container is not a natural place for a plant to grow. A container is confining, and without natural insulation, its contents dry out quickly. Nutrients wash out rapidly. The root system requires water and food in adequate doses. Roots run out of space and demand repotting. But think positively. With containers, you can provide exactly the right soil the plant needs, move the plant around when weather doesn't suit it, and protect the plant from pests. Plus, you get to know individual plants better as they respond to your care.

Designing with Container Plants

Containers can do all the things that a whole garden can: announce the seasons, flash bright color, and create miniature slices of nature. Your designs really depend on maintenance considerations — plan placement of plants, whether in the same container or in several containers grouped together, according to their shared requirements for care.

Thinking about style

Here are a few general-direction reminders to keep in mind when creating container plantings:

- **Use container plants to complement your home or existing garden.**
- **Think about color.** Using mostly green or white creates a cooling effect. Bright, hot colors (zinnias, for instance) heat things up.
- **Evaluate the plants you're choosing and use their shapes to complement and contrast with each other.**
- **Decide whether you want a formal or casual look.**
- **Remember the value of repetition and scale.** See Chapter 1 in Book II for information on using these and other factors as part of your design.

Grouping containers

Arranging groups of container plants is like hanging pictures or moving furniture — complete with possible backaches. Don't be afraid to experiment, to move plants around again and again. Remember the most important thing: You're satisfying *your* taste. Container groupings generally look best with at least three plants, but you can accommodate dozens.

Growing your imagination

Anything that offers room for root growth and provides drainage in some way can be made into a unique and interesting container. When you don't use run-of-the-mill containers, give your prize picks special consideration, so that you can show them off properly:

✔ **Avoid clustering too many different kinds of containers together.**

✔ **Put a single, outstanding container in a prominent place.**

✔ **Create a grouping for collections, such as antique cans or buckets.**

✔ **Consider how the container drains, and plan to drill drainage holes if necessary.** Keep in mind that small containers need water often.

✔ **Give your whimsical container a home that suits it.** A hollowed-out piece of tree trunk is perfect brimming with colorful impatiens in a shady glade near a deck.

A few basic rules apply for grouping container plants:

✔ **Use matching types of containers, such as terra-cotta, in different sizes.** Make one or two pots a lot larger than the others. If you want, throw in a maverick, like a glazed pot.

✔ **Use lots of pots and mix sizes, styles, and shapes for a big deck or expanse of paving.**

✔ **Mix plants of different textures, colors, and heights.**

✔ **Do just the opposite and group identical pots with identical plants.**

✔ **Raise some containers higher than others.** Doing so can add emphasis as well as put the plants at better viewing levels.

✔ **Be careful with small plants.** They tend to go unnoticed. Clumsy people trip on them (we know from personal experience).

✔ **Try to place containers where people gather.** A seating area, for instance, offers opportunity to view plants up close and appreciate their fragrance.

✔ **Place containers near the house where you can notice them.** Container plants scattered selectively along garden paths can provide a pleasant surprise. Another good placement is in the transition zone between a patio and lawn or between a lawn and wild garden.

Understanding Container Anatomy

Among the joys of gardening is the opportunity to combine aesthetic challenges and satisfactions with practical, "science-y" stuff. Whether you buy containers, make them yourself, or improvise, your attention to materials, colors, shapes, and cost can yield a great statement about your personal taste. Make sure that you approach the process with a horticultural-science frame of mind. Your chosen containers need to be good for the plant's health.

Container materials

Containers are available in a huge variety of materials — especially if you start making your own or finding unusual planter prospects. As you look, be sure to consider at least two key factors:

- ✔ **Porosity:** Some materials used for containers are more porous than others and allow moisture and air to penetrate more readily. Unglazed terra-cotta, wood, and paper pulp dry out faster but also allow soil to cool by evaporation and to "breathe" (roots need oxygen).

- ✔ **Drainage:** For healthy root development, soil must drain water properly and have enough space for air. Select containers with drain holes.

The following materials are used most often for containers these days:

- ✔ **Terra-cotta or unglazed clay:** Unglazed clay or terra-cotta is usually reddish-orange in color. Pots do come in other colors and in many shapes and sizes. Unglazed clay pots generally offer good value for the money; higher-quality pots, with thick walls fired in high heat, last longer.

  In cold climates, terra-cotta pot sides can split when moist soil freezes and expands inside the pot.

- ✔ **Glazed clay:** Usually inexpensive, these pots come in many more colors than unglazed pots — bright to dark, some with patterns. Many fit nicely in Japanese-style gardens. They're great in formal situations or to liven up a grouping of plain clay pots. Glazed pots are less porous than unglazed and can hold moisture better. They are breakable.

- ✔ **Wood:** You can buy many styles of square and rectangular boxes and round tubs, which are usually made of rot-resistant redwood and cedar. They're heavy, durable, and stand up well to cold weather. Wood containers provide good soil insulation, keeping roots cooler and providing less evaporation than in terra-cotta. Thicker lumber is better — at least $\frac{7}{8}$ inch. Bottoms may rot if they stay too moist; raise containers at least an inch off the ground with stands or saucers. To make wood last longer, treat the insides with wood preservative.

- ✔ **Plastic:** Many plastic pots are designed to imitate standard terra-cotta pots. Plastic is less expensive, easier to clean, and lighter than terra-cotta. It's also nonporous and doesn't dry out as quickly as terra-cotta, so be careful that you don't overwater. Watch for poor quality plastic pots, which can fade in the sun and become brittle.

TIP

The plastic look isn't for everyone. You can camouflage plastic pots in a group of more decorative pots. Or sink a plastic pot with a plant into a larger pot for an instant facelift without even transplanting.

✔ **Other materials:** You're less likely to encounter containers made of the following materials; but each has its own appeal and reason for being:

- **Cast concrete:** Durable, heavy, and cold-resistant.

- **Paper pulp:** Compressed recycled paper that degrades in several years. You actually can plant pot and all directly in the ground, and the roots grow through the sides as the pot decomposes. Inexpensive and lightweight, but not particularly handsome. Use them where looks don't matter.

- **Metal:** Look for metal containers at boutiques and antique shops. Check that drainage is provided.

✔ **Improvised containers:** Turning mundane items into plant containers is fun.

✔ **Raised beds:** Built-in garden planting beds — made with lumber, brick, or many other materials — are actually a form of container.

✔ **Containers of your own making:** You can make your own containers. Check with a local building supply store for plans and materials.

Window box basics

Window boxes are just easy-to-plant containers attached to the house. Here are some key points to keep in mind to help you choose, plant, and care for a window box:

✔ **Select a style that matches your house.** Boxes come in treated softwood or hardwood, plastic, metal, terra-cotta, or concrete boxes. Position the box below the window by a few inches. If you happen to have a window that opens outward, you have to lower the box.

✔ **Pay attention to size, too.** A window box looks best if its length is within a couple of inches of the window's size, although slight differences won't hurt. Boxes should be at least 8 inches wide to provide room for top

growth and 8 inches deep for the roots. Make your own box if your window is oddly sized. Use 1-inch boards and simple joinery with waterproof glue and galvanized or brass screws to secure the pieces. Drill drain holes on the bottom.

✔ **Go for a sunny exposure to please the most plants.** Remember that some window boxes are protected from rains, so you need to check regularly for dryness.

✔ **Choose one of three options for planting.** Plant directly in the container, drop in potted plants and fill around them with moss, bark, or another lightweight material, or place plants in a plastic or metal liner that fits inside the box.

Container size

A pot that's too small crowds roots, cutting off moisture, oxygen, and nutrients that are vital for healthy growth. If the pot is too big, the superfluous soil may stay too wet and can smother the roots. Rules for ideal container size differ a bit for permanent plants and seasonal plants:

- **Permanent plants:** For permanent plants, such as Japanese maple or conifers, think longer term and choose a pot that looks in scale with the plant when you buy it and allows room for a year or two of root growth. As a rule, when buying a nursery plant, transplant it to a container that is 2 inches deeper and wider than its nursery container.

- **Seasonals:** You can crowd seasonals, such as annuals and bulbs, together more closely than plants that you grow in the ground, providing much more impact quickly. Crowded conditions can't persist for long, but you can satisfy the tight-quarters demands for extra water and food over your plants' short seasons. As a rule, figure that if the recommended spacing for ground planting is 10 to 12 inches, container planting translates to 6 to 8 inches apart. As a general rule of scale, if the annuals normally grow 10 or 12 inches tall, provide a pot with a diameter of at least 8 inches.

Container shapes vary. Some are designed for practicality, and others, we can assume, look the way they do because someone likes their appearance:

- **Standard pots:** Most standard pots, which work for most plants, are taller than they are wide, allowing the roots to grow deep. Small containers, up to 8 inches in diameter, can hold a few annuals or perennials, and a single, young permanent plant. Standard pots up to 12 inches in diameter can hold half a dozen annuals or small perennials or medium-sized shrubs or vines. Use larger pots (at least 18 inches in diameter) for bigger shrubs, small trees, bamboo, and mixed plantings of annuals and perennials.

- **Low containers:** Sometimes called *azalea* or *fern pots,* these containers are wider than tall, typically sold in diameters from 4 to 14 inches, and usually terra-cotta. Use them for shallow-rooted plants.

- **Bulb pots:** Usually made of terra-cotta and sold in 6- to 12-inch diameters, these shallow containers aren't much deeper than saucers. You can get away with planting bulbs in such a small amount of soil. You can use shallow bowls for smaller annuals, but make sure that you provide enough soil for growth, and water and fertilize carefully.

- **Other shapes:** Many other styles are also available: bowls, tapered Spanish pots, and bonsai pots (which are shallow). With all of these, remember to check for drainage and space for roots.

Down-to-earth advice

Before you head off to the nursery, we offer a few nitty-gritty reminders:

✔ **Containers can be messy on a deck, patio, or balcony.** They may drip water and stain surfaces.

✔ **Container plants don't always maintain their good looks.** Patience is in order before annuals start blooming, when bulbs are drying out after bloom, and when deciduous shrubs are leafless.

✔ **Remember your climate and the limits it puts on all plants, especially container plants.** If you live in cold region, be prepared to move prized plants into protection when winter arrives.

Introducing Ms. Plant to Mr. Container

Before you consider sticking a plant in a container, try to digest a fair share of basic planting advice. (Book I provides preplanting information in detail.)

Follow these steps for most shrubs, trees, annuals, and perennials:

1. **Prepare the container.**

   Soak new terra-cotta pots in water for 10 or 15 minutes before planting to prevent clay from absorbing moisture from the soil mix. If you're using old pots, clean them to remove salt deposits and rinse with a 10 percent bleach solution to reduce chances of disease. Apply preservative to wood containers before you plant.

2. **Check the drain hole to make sure that it's the right size.**

   Most commercially made pots have drain holes to allow water to flow out of the container. Don't ask why, but these holes usually are too big, allowing too much water to escape. You need to partially cover the drain holes to keep soil mix from slipping through. Use a piece of fine-mesh metal screen large enough to cover the hole, or cover the drain holes with *pot shards* (pieces of broken pot). You can also use a rock with an uneven shape that doesn't completely block the hole.

   If your container lacks a drain hole, you need to make one. In the base of a wooden box, drill one ½-inch hole for a box up to 12 inches square; two to four ½-inch holes for larger boxes or a half barrel. For clay pots, use an electric drill with a masonry bit. Support the pot on a block of wood, and start drilling with a smaller bit, eventually reaching the final size of ½ inch; adding water to the drill hole may help.

3. **Make sure that the nursery plant's soil is moist enough to hold the roots together when you plant.**

   If the soil is dry, soak it thoroughly, and let it drain for at least an hour.

4. **Remove the plant from the nursery container; inspect the root ball.**

   Wet the soil and then tip plastic containers upside down, taking care not to break branches, and let the root ball slip out, catching it with one hand. Tap the rim of the container upside down on a hard surface if the root ball doesn't slip out easily. If your plants are in plastic cell-packs, turn the pack upside down and wiggle the base of each cell. Tug gently, taking care not to break the stem or loosen the root ball. For small, root-bound plants, gently loosen the mat of roots with your fingertips. For larger plants, such as 1-gallon or 5-gallon shrubs, use a knife to score some vertical scratches in a tight root ball.

5. **Incorporate a complete food into your soil if your soil doesn't include fertilizer.**

6. **Check to see whether the soil mix is moist.**

   If it's dry, wet while it's still in the bag by adding water and stirring or kneading the soil until it reaches the desired level of moisture.

   Do not use soil from your yard, because it tends to compact when in a container. Roots can't penetrate this soil, and drainage becomes a problem. Instead use a growing medium developed specifically for container gardening.

7. **Add soil mix to your container.**

   Fill to an inch below the rim of the container for small plants, 2 inches or more for large containers. The amount of soil you add depends on the type of plant:

   • **For small plants in packs or little pots:** Fill the pot to the level that you want to end up with. With your hands or trowel, scoop out a little hole for each plant, slip in the plant, and firm down around its edges with your fingers. If soil level starts to rise too high, remove some soil. Match the soil level to your plants' previous growing conditions — don't bury too deep or allow root balls to rise above the soil level. Figure 3-1 shows the ideal.

   • **For plants in gallon cans and larger:** Size up the root ball by placing it in the empty pot. Add enough soil mix to raise the top of the root ball to the desired level in the pot, from 2 to 4 inches below the rim. Set the root ball on top of the soil mix and then fill in around it and tamp it down with your hands, a trowel, or a shovel handle. Tamping down is important to establish firm contact between the root ball and new soil mix. Keep adding soil mix until it levels up with the top of the root ball.

- **For bare-root plants:** First trim off the root tips as recommended by your nursery or have it done for you (also ask about pruning the top growth back, especially for fruit trees). Mound the soil mix at the bottom of the container, spread roots over mound, and adjust level of mound until the plant's former soil line (usually indicated by a faint discolored ring around the trunk) matches up with the desired soil level in the container. Fill around the roots until the soil reaches the plant's former soil line.

- **For balled-and-burlapped plants:** Place the root ball on soil mix at the bottom of container as for plants grown in 1- or 5-gallon nursery cans. Cut away the twine holding burlap in place at the top of the root ball. Fold back and trim away the top several inches of burlap with heavy scissors or a knife — the lower, buried part gradually decomposes. Fill with soil mix around root ball as recommended for container-grown plants.

8. **Water the newly planted plant.**

WARNING!

Watering a just-planted container is trickier than you may imagine. Water tends to follow the path of least resistance and drains quickly through the loose soil mix, bypassing the denser root ball. You walk away thinking that your watering job is done. Days later, you realize that the root ball never really got wet and the plant is desiccated. Protect against this problem by watering thoroughly the first time. Use a watering can, a hose gently trickling, or a hose-end bubbler to provide a slow and gentle stream. Slowly fill the pot to the rim, and repeat several times. Probe with your fingers to find out whether the root ball has absorbed water — if it hasn't, try soaking it again.

Book II

Garden Design

Figure 3-1: This one's planted just right.

9. **Apply mulch to shrubs and trees with a great deal of exposed soil.**

   Mulching helps to conserve water. Use stone or bark chips, or other organic matter that is in scale with the container and the plants.

10. **Stake and tie trees or tall annuals or perennials.**

11. **Add a trellis to the container for vines that need support.**

Packing Plants in Containers

Containers may limit how much room you have, but they don't limit what you can plant in them. The following sections look at the various categories of plants and give you the information that you need to grow them in containers.

Announcing annuals

You may want to grow annuals (see Book V for more on annuals) in containers for a variety of reasons:

- ✔ **Annuals are fun to grow.** They have the brightest, most appealing flowers, which attract butterflies and almost anyone who wanders past.

- ✔ **Annuals are movers.** They grow fast, bloom when young, and give you the longest season of abundant bloom of any plants.

- ✔ **Annuals are relatively inexpensive — especially if you buy small plants — and responsive.** Provide them with good care and you see the results — lush leaves, lots of flowers, and a long bloom season.

Remember that annuals like to set a fast pace with no pit stops: Running out of water or food can set them back for weeks or abruptly end their seasons. Watering is much more critical with annuals grown in the confined spaces of containers. Never let the soil dry out. Feeding container-grown annuals is also more critical than nourishing the same plants grown in the ground. Start feeding a few weeks after planting. One proven method is to use liquid fertilizer at half the recommended rate and twice the frequency (every two weeks instead of monthly, for example).

Pinching and deadheading are important chores that keep new flowers coming for as long a season as possible. Start pinching back tip growth to encourage bushy growth as soon as you plant, or even right before.

Potting perennials

Here are some of the reasons gardeners love perennials in containers:

- **Time, money, and labor:** Many gardeners prefer to fill their pots with perennials simply because the plants can last a long time.

- **Size counts:** Perennial plants tend to grow larger than annuals and bulbs, so they can fill large spaces if that's what you want.

- **Custom environments:** If your garden beds are too sunny for hostas or your soil too cold and wet for lavender, try growing them in containers.

 Always consider the plant's size now *and* its size at maturity. A perennial in a pot may not get quite as big as a ground-grown plant, but it'll come close. Put that little plant into a 6-inch (or 10-inch) pot and repot it to larger size pots as it grows or put it in a pot that can accommodate its ultimate size, and add annuals to fill the empty space for now. Make sure that the pot you decide to use is large enough to accommodate the ongoing root growth while remaining topple-free as the plant matures.

If you buy perennials by mail order, they're likely to arrive as *bare-root plants*. The roots are exposed and devoid of any potting soil — a handy, lightweight way to ship perennials and a healthy way to start new plants. Here are the basic planting steps in that case:

1. **Remove the plastic wrapping.**

2. **Gently extricate the plant roots from the paper or wood shavings.**

   Alternatively, if the material is biodegradable, you can just leave it on the roots and plant it with your plant. The wrap protects the roots from any unnecessary disturbance.

3. **Soak the plant in tap water for an hour or so before you're ready to plant it.**

4. **Prepare your pot.**

   Be sure to moisten the potting mix thoroughly and let it drain to settle the soil until it feels about as damp as a wrung-out sponge.

5. **Dig out a hole an inch or so deeper and wider than the longest root on the plant in the potting mix for the plant.**

6. **Gently spread the roots so that they fan out in all directions from the base of the plant.**

   Separating the roots may be difficult if the plant has a particularly intertwined system. Just be sure that the roots aren't all clumped together beneath the plant.

Book II

Garden Design

7. Carefully fill in the hole with potting mix, covering the roots as you work your way toward the base of the plant.

Add potting mix until the base of the plant is just below the surface of the soil. Don't cover any of the green, growing parts with potting mix.

8. Firm the mix around the plant and water it well to eliminate any air pockets in the potting mix.

Label the plant with its name and the date that you planted it.

Perennials aren't terribly demanding, but the following list explains the care they do need:

- ✔ **Deadhead:** When you see a perennial whose flowers are fading, remember that you're seeing a natural process — after it flowers, the plant produces seeds. If the plant is still growing strong when the bloom fades, you can encourage a new flush of flowers by deadheading.

- ✔ **Fertilize:** Perennials need a longer-lasting fertilizer than annuals. A good strategy for proper nourishment is to mix slow-release fertilizers into potting soil before planting, and supplement weekly with fish emulsion and other natural products during the plant's major growing season; add more slow-release fertilizer as the old runs out. As a general rule, find out what the specific varieties need in your area, and feed just a bit more than you'd deliver to the same plants in the ground.

- ✔ **Provide winter care:** Gardeners in cold climates overwinter their plants (keep them in a protected spot) to shelter them until the milder temperatures of spring arrive. Here are two methods of overwintering:

  - Before cold weather strikes, place more tender perennials, in their pots, in an insulated garage or basement where they can lose their leaves and go into a dormant state. Continue to water once a month through winter to be sure that they don't wither and die. Move plant back into the garden in spring, after frost danger has passed.

  - For hardy perennials, wait until the first hard frost. Then cut foliage back to just a few inches above the soil. Bury each plant, still in its pot, in the middle of your compost or mulch pile, or place in your basement or an insulated garage. When the weather warms in spring, monitor the pots until you see signs of life from the stub of each plant. When plants start to grow, move them back to their spots in the garden.

Perennials look a little ratty when they're not blooming or when their leaves fall off, so plan on moving the containers out of prime view when the flowers are less than glorious.

Bulb strategy

Having a strategy ahead of time can make all the difference in transforming your ugly bulbs into beautiful flowers worthy of the finest containers!

✔ **To get the most for your money and effort, prominently display your containers of blooming bulbs.** Keep the containers out of sight until the plants are ready to bloom and, when they finish blooming, move them out of the way where adequate water and sunlight is available for the rest of the growth period.

✔ **Good timing is a must.** You have to shop at the right time, plant at the right time, and follow directions for depth of planting and spacing.

✔ **Planting just one bulb variety per pot ensures that all the bulbs in the pot will bloom at the same time.** Mixing varieties in a container, on the other hand, results in flowers coming at different times, which has much less impact. If you want different flower colors and bloom times, grow different varieties in *separate* containers. You can use the same tactic to extend your blooming season, which is short for most bulbs.

Book II

Garden Design

Brightening up with bulbs

Spring-blooming bulbs create a blaze of color just when it's most welcome — late winter and early spring. Nothing else announces spring more emphatically and lyrically. Planting bulbs in containers allows you freedom of movement to meet your needs. Place the containers nearby at bloom time for close-up viewing (and smelling, in some cases). Store the containers out-of-sight when your portable garden isn't very interesting — during the several months when nothing shows above ground and the several months after bloom, when foliage is growing and then dying back.

Bulbs look fine in a wide variety of container shapes and styles. Choose containers that allow at least 2 inches of soil beneath the bulbs. The traditional container in which to grow spring bulbs is a clay or plastic *bulb pan,* a shallow pot 10 inches or larger in diameter and only 5 or so inches deep. These pots don't hold much soil — which is perfectly okay for spring bulbs and their typical one-season stay in containers. For other kinds of bulbs, especially those that can live in containers for several years, make sure that roots have enough growing space. Pick containers at least 12 inches deep for lilies and other more permanent bulbs.

To brighten the dreariest winter days with sweet fragrance and spring colors, you can *force* (or trick) bulbs to bloom early indoors. Your best bets for forcing early blooms are crocuses, daffodils, hyacinths, and tulips. Because you have to move containers indoors when you force a bloom, you probably want smaller pots than for outdoor use. For example, try half a dozen tulips or daffodils in a 6- to 10-inch pot; one daffodil or tulip or three small bulbs (such as crocus) in a 4-inch pot.

Follow the steps for growing bulbs in containers in Chapter 1 of Book VI. Start checking for roots and sprouts after two or three months (usually after New Year's Day). When stored bulbs show 2- to 6-inch sprouts, bring them indoors to a cool room (60 degrees or so) to speed up the bloom season. A week or two later, when sprouts have buds that show a little color, move the bulbs into normal room temperature (a room that's too warm shortens the bloom period) in a spot that gets as much sunlight as possible. Flowers should appear within the next week or so. Continue to keep the soil moist. When the plant finishes blooming, move the container outdoors and make sure that soil is kept moist until the leaves are dry, as suggested for bulbs grown outdoors.

Toying with trees and shrubs

Grown in containers, shrubs and trees and vines are most appreciated when you have little or no ground space to grow them. These plants can perform big-time in containers. Here are just a few things they can do for you:

- ✔ **Create a sense of scale in a garden:** They can make a small terrace or balcony seem like a garden.

- ✔ **Produce seasonal displays:** Spring blossoms, fall color, winter berries.

- ✔ **Look handsome or dramatic in their own right, especially if pruned to emphasize structure:** A container plant that's attractive enough to stand alone and be admired is called a *specimen plant* or *accent*.

- ✔ **Work hard in a landscape:** They can create a privacy screen, a divider, or shade, as well as provide a dependable green background for seasonal container plants, such as annuals and bulbs.

- ✔ **Let you experiment:** Try plants that are dicey in your area because of cold weather or bad soil.

Permanent plants generally need less care and replacement than annuals or perennials, but they're not maintenance-free:

- ✔ **Planting:** Planting schedules are the same for shrubs and trees in the ground and in containers. Generally, you plant in spring in cold climates, and in spring or fall in mild areas.

- ✔ **Soil:** Use a good soil mix, possibly even a special mix recommended for specific plants.

- ✔ **Container:** Pay special attention to container selection because a permanent plant can live in the same container for a number of years. The basic rule applies: Start with a container that's 2 or 3 inches wider and deeper than the one in which the plant was grown.

- ✔ **Feeding:** Plan to feed at least several times during the growing season. For best results, incorporate slow-release fertilizer into the soil mix at planting time.

- ✔ **Watering:** Consider a drip irrigation system if you have several containers. (See Chapter 4 in Book I for more on watering methods.)

- ✔ **Pruning:** See Chapter 5 in Book I for basic pruning instructions and tips.

- ✔ **Repotting:** If you keep plants in the same containers for a few years, you can count on a round of repotting. Look for clues that it's time to replace your plant's happy home: when roots fill the pot or start to show at soil level. Another clue is that the plant always seems dry.

Book II

Garden Design

Visiting vegetables and herbs

With some care and a good deal of sun, you can eat your own container-grown produce all summer long. The convenience is tough to match: Just walk out on the deck and snip some lettuce for a salad or swipe a few peas for a stir-fry. And, the flexibility yields some fresh ideas: Combining ornamentals and edibles in the garden is a popular design concept these days. You can even move containers from deck to garden and back. (Chapter 1 in Book VII offers more on growing vegetables in containers.)

And don't overlook herbs for containers. Usually less demanding than vegetables, many perennial culinary herbs are of Mediterranean origin and like it on the hot and dry side. Brush by a pot of thyme, rosemary, or sage on the way to the door, and you may imagine you're in the south of France.

Providing the essentials to vegetables and herbs growing in containers can be more challenging because their growing space is limited. To ease the caretaking task, container plants can grow right outside your back door where you can dote on them:

- ✔ **The right container:** Use a container that has a diameter of 12 to 18 inches and a depth of 15 inches — the larger size accommodates the necessary volume of soil and water — and drain holes at the bottom.

- ✔ **Soil mix:** You can use commercial soil mixes straight from the bag, but many vegetables and herbs benefit from additional organic matter, such as bagged compost or ground bark. Add one part of organic matter to each three parts of soil mix.

- ✔ **Fertilizer:** In general, vegetables and herbs are heavy feeders — especially when grown in containers. As a rule, add an all-purpose dry fertilizer — organic or chemical — according to package directions when you plant. Fertilize regularly, following label directions.

- ✔ **Water, water, water:** Watering is crucial with container vegetables and herbs — let them wilt once and they may never really get back on track. Containers can dry out in a day or in a few hours depending on the planter's size and intensity of the summer heat. Check pots and planters often and don't allow the soil to dry out more than an inch or two below the surface.

- ✔ **Sunlight:** Most vegetables need a minimum of six hours of direct sunlight — that is, sun on the plant, not somewhere nearby. Exceptions are lettuce and spinach, which actually benefit from some shade in the heat of midsummer to keep them from *bolting* — sending up flower heads that end your salad-picking days.

Containing cactus and succulents

A *succulent* is a plant that has adapted to arid conditions by creating water storage units in leaves, stems, and roots. *Cactus* is a type of succulent, set apart from other of the fleshy-tissued plants by two features. One is that cactus has a structure called an *areole* at the plant's growing point, sometimes visible as small pads. New leaves, stems, and flowers spring up from this opening. The more significant difference between cactus and other succulents is that most cactuses have spines, which makes them interesting to look at, and especially amusing to handle. Both cactuses and succulents have many virtues when grown in containers:

- ✔ **Low maintenance:** These plants don't require much water or attention, so they're a great choice if you're busy (or forgetful).

- ✔ **Offer surprising contrasts:** Instead of flower color, these plants offer shapes that range from bulbous to stringy, and textures from smooth to spiny to hairy.

- ✔ **Grow slowly:** Slow growth means less time repotting plants that outgrow their containers.

- ✔ **Portability:** Containers offer the chance to move those precious plants indoors when the temperature starts to drop.

Light and temperature are the defining needs of many succulents. In general, most need a great deal of bright light, although some take part shade.

Most can't survive for more than a night with temperatures below 40°F, but some are hardy in all climates. The basic rules for growing succulents in containers are pretty simple:

- **Provide as much light as possible during the summer.** Occasionally, full sun in really warm places, including their desert homelands, can be too hot for many succulents in the confines of a container. Some types prefer part shade.

- **Protect succulents from cold weather in the winter.** Move them indoors to a sunny window where temperatures don't drop below 40°F.

Succulents lend themselves to terra-cotta pots, but any porous pot, such as stone and concrete, works well. Make sure that the container has drainage holes! Feel free to use a shallow container (just 4 to 6 inches deep) if it looks best for your plants — succulent roots don't go very deep. For a plant with a rounded shape, choose a container that's 2 inches wider than the plant. For an upright plant, choose a pot that's half the diameter of the plant's height.

Book II

Garden Design

Quick drainage is the most important quality of a soil mix designed for succulents. The standard mix consists of one-half organic matter (peat moss, leaf mold, or something like that) and one-half grit (crushed rock or sand). You can find many cactus and succulent mixes already bagged.

Water regularly during the growing season — which is winter for some species. Thorough watering is better than a sprinkle every day or two. Water when the soil is completely dry. One effective way to water smaller pots is to sit them in a tub of water nearly up to their rims, leaving them there until the top layer of soil is moist. During their dormant season and in cool temperatures (50°F), most cactus and succulents can go without water for weeks at a time. Don't become complacent and forget that the poor things are even alive. Resume regular watering just before the growing season begins.

When plants are in a growing stage, fertilize about once a month — or every other time you water, if you water every two weeks. Succulents need all the nutrients that other plants do — nitrogen, phosphorus, and potassium — plus trace elements. You can use just about any complete liquid fertilizer or a special fertilizer designed for cactus and succulents.

If you need to repot a cactus, use a piece of rolled-up cloth or paper to remove the plant from its original container, as shown in Figure 3-2.

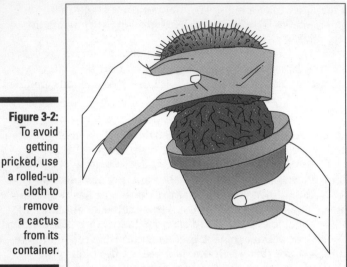

Figure 3-2:
To avoid getting pricked, use a rolled-up cloth to remove a cactus from its container.

Keeping Up with the Containseres

Not everything about container gardening is glamorous and exciting — you do have a few routine chores. This section takes you through the basics of various odd jobs because, in the long run, they help you grow better plants.

Replanting regimen

Repotting plants that have outgrown their container is no big deal. In some cases, you repot to allow room for growth; in others, you repot to reduce or slow growth.

Following are some tips to make repotting go smoothly:

- **Repot when roots show.** You need to replant if you notice poor flowering, soil drying out quickly, stunted leaves and stems, leaf drop and *die-back* (parts of the plant turn brown and die), lots of roots coming through the drain hole, or matted roots near the soil surface. Generally, you repot every few years with permanent plants, as often as every month or so with seasonal bedding plants and annuals.

- **Repot at the right time for the plant.** Repot spring blooming permanent plants in fall, evergreens in spring or fall, and spring-flowering bulbs in fall. For summer-flowering bulbs, repot in winter or spring. With bedding plants and annuals, repot as needed through the growing season before the full flush of flowering hits.

✔ **Choose the right-sized container.** If you want to increase growth, you need to give plants more room for roots by transplanting into larger pots. Move up in size to a new pot that's only a few inches larger. If you want to control growth and keep the plant from getting too big, you need to trim the roots and return the plant to a pot of the same size.

✔ **Replant and root prune.** Take the plant out of its current home and then plant just as you do for any other plant. Turn the container upside down, tap the rim, and slide the plant out. In some cases, you may have to trim off large roots poking through the drain hole. For plants going into larger containers, gently pull apart tangled roots, and then set the plant in its new or newly filled existing pot. For some permanent plants, you probably need to *root prune,* in which you use shears to cut away root growth. Root pruning controls growth and forces plants to grow new roots, which leads to limited but healthy new growth. To root-prune properly, remove about a quarter of the soil and untangle as much of the root mass as you can. Using shears, cut between one-half and one-third of the roots. For tightly balled roots, slice off one-half inch all around the outside and make vertical cuts top to bottom in several places.

✔ **Allow roots to dry out first before removing a plant from a large container.** Always let gravity help and pull by gripping the main stem or trunk. For stubborn root masses, use a rubber mallet to tap the sides or slide a knife down the sides and around the pot.

✔ **Wash any pots you reuse.** Before reusing the pot, remove bacteria by washing the pot with hot water and a 5 to 10 percent bleach solution.

✔ **Find a temporary solution, if necessary.** If you can't get to a complete repotting job, replenish the top few inches of potting soil with fresh potting material and a little added fertilizer.

✔ **Protect ceramic and clay pots from chipping or cracking.** Wrap an old towel around the outside before you tilt and tap the sides.

Book II

Garden Design

Making repairs (or Humpty-Dumpty duty)

If the pieces still fit tightly and you use the right adhesive, you can successfully mend your wounded containers:

✔ **Choose an epoxy glue.**

✔ **Fit the pieces together and tie the pot so that it's securely held in place.** Use cord or rope for large pots; try tape for small ones.

✔ **Wipe off any glue that spills out of the cracks when you fit the pieces together.** Use sandpaper after the glue is dry to remove any residue.

Here are a few things to look out for and a few ways to mend any wear and tear your wooden containers experience:

- ✔ **Prevent or at least reduce the chance of rot with wooden containers by raising them off the ground.** Raising the container allows the wood to dry between watering.

- ✔ **Watch for new or widening gaps where pieces join, and check for loose parts or rot if containers suddenly show signs of excessive drainage.** Check containers at least every couple of months and make repairs without delay.

- ✔ **Look for exposed nails, staples, or screws.** Small gaps only become larger under the weight and pressure of the soil and plants. Rejoin boards by using galvanized wood screws long enough to penetrate each piece by an inch or more.

- ✔ **Reinforce wooden sections that may be starting to rot by adding new pieces on the inside of the container.** Use redwood or cedar blocks on corner or end joints and insert screws through the original wood and well into the new piece.

- ✔ **Reposition and reattach any barrel staves that are beginning to slip.** Slide the stave up into its original spot and use small nails with large heads to secure it in several places around the container.

You can save work in the long run if you make sure that wooden containers are ready to hold up to the elements before you begin planting. Choose rot-resistant materials in the first place; redwood and cedar are your best bets. Prolong the life of wooden containers — especially those made of soft woods — with a wood preservative that's safe for plants. You can also paint or stain your containers. These surface treatments give wood longer life, and allow you other decorating angles as well.

Chapter 4

Lawn(ging) Around

*Y*our lawn is an important part of your landscape. This chapter tells you everything you need to know to start and maintain a healthy lawn without wasting your time or precious natural resources.

Taking Your Grass's Temperature

Think of cool-season and warm-season grasses as the yin and yang of the turf world. Or better yet, when you think of cool-season grasses, think of blue spruce. When you think of warm-season grasses, think of palm trees.

Where the cool grasses grow

Generally, cool-season grasses are best suited for moist, northern climates, where summers, although warm, are relatively short, and winters are cold. Such grasses also do well in high elevations with adequate rainfall and coastal areas where temperatures are moderate. If you live in a transitional zone between cool and warm-season climates (where the ground doesn't freeze in winter), cool-season grasses stay green all winter. But, in such areas, you should talk to your local nursery or extension office about the most appropriate grasses or go with native grasses.

Cool-season grasses grow actively in the cool weather of spring and fall at temperatures averaging 60°F to 75°F. As summers get warmer, cool-season grasses grow slower and are subject to more disease problems. These grasses also grow more slowly in summer and may turn brownish and go completely dormant when the weather is dry and hot for long periods of time. Proper watering keeps cool-season grasses green throughout the summer season. In hotter areas with severe water restrictions, you may have to get used to a brown summer lawn, but, never fear, fall rains usually bring dormant grasses back to lush, green life again.

The most commonly planted cool-season grasses include bent grass, Kentucky bluegrass, fescues, and ryegrass. Of those, Kentucky bluegrass has been the most commonly planted lawn for years. But new and improved varieties of tall fescue have recently increased in popularity due to its finer textures and improved qualities while maintaining greater vigor and resistance to harsh conditions, including drought and heat.

Where the warm grasses grow

Warm-season grasses are the grasses of southern climates, where summers are long and hot (consistently over 85°F), and winters are relatively mild. Warm-season grasses grow most vigorously during the warm months of summer and turn brown in winter. People commonly overseed these grasses with cool-season types to get a green lawn year-round. Plant warm-season grasses after the weather warms in mid- to late spring.

The six most commonly used warm-season grasses are Bahia grass, Bermuda grasses (which includes common Bermuda grass and hybrid Bermuda grass), Centipede grass (*Eremochloa ophiuroides*), St. Augustine grass, and zoysia grass.

ECO-SMART

Small is plenty in the big, bad West

By looking carefully at how people use lawns, water agencies in the West determine that many people need only about 600 to 800 square feet of grass. Unless you regularly use your lawn for rugby matches, 600 to 800 square feet — about the size of a large patio — is enough for a small play area or for just lounging around. If you want to play volleyball, badminton, or croquet, you can get by with a rectangle measuring 45 x 80 feet (3,600 square feet).

If you decide that a lawn isn't a great idea for your part of the country or neighborhood, you do have some wonderful alternatives. Consider using other plants besides grass. You can create a border around the outside of your yard and plant it with trees, shrubs, flowering perennials, or other blooming plants. A border may cost you a little more to get started, but you make it up in saved time and energy in the long run. And your yard will be so much more beautiful.

Going native

North America's native American grasses are growing in popularity among more environmentally conscious lawn lovers because of their lack of demands on precious resources and labor. Native grasses need little water once established, very little fertilizer, and a haircut only a few times a year. They're very tough once established, and although they turn brown during dormancy, they tolerate wide temperature fluctuations. They haven't been bred for uniformity, so they provide a wild-looking lawn cover:

✔ **Blue grama** *(Bouteloua gracilis):* Hardy, grayish-green, and fine-textured pasture grass with slightly fuzzy blades. Goes dormant, but tolerates extreme heat and cold fluctuations (down to –40°F!). Very drought-tolerant. Offers moderate wearability, but is slow to recover from wear damage.

✔ **Buffalo grass** *(Buchloe dactyloides):* Fine-textured, low-growing, and grayish-green. Where adapted, it can tolerate almost no maintenance. Drought-tolerant when established and becomes even more so if mowed infrequently and high. Thrives in areas that receive only 10 to 15 inches of rain a year, but will go brown if allowed to go completely dry. Heat- and sun-loving. Tolerates dry, compacted, clay soils. Doesn't do well in dense shade or in sandy, poorly drained soils. Goes brown with the first frost of winter and is slow to green up in spring. Fairly disease- and pest-resistant. Weeds can be a problem, though, if the grass is overfed, overcut, or overwatered. Very expensive to plant.

Book II

Garden Design

As a group, the warm-season grasses are mostly vigorous, spreading plants that can often become weedy. They also have the propensity to develop thatch, and most look best when mowed low with a reel mower. Warm-season grasses are more heat-tolerant and need less water than cool-season grasses.

Feeling a Little Seed-y

Starting a lawn from seed is probably the least expensive way to plant a new lawn, and it can be one of the most enjoyable. The following sections help you grow your lawn from seed.

You can start all cool-season grasses from seed. On the other hand, many warm-season grasses are best started, or can only be started, from stolons, sprigs, plugs, or sod, which we discuss later in this chapter. When we talk about *sowing* seed, we mean the process of spreading seed evenly over a seedbed. A *seedbed* is the area where you have prepared the soil and plan to plant your lawn.

The best time to start lawns from seed, or by any means, is just prior to the grass's season of most vigorous growth. For cool-season grasses (which grow best in fall, spring, and, in some areas, winter), the best time to plant is late summer to early fall. At that time of year, the ground is still warm enough for quick germination, and the young grass plants have the entire upcoming cool season to become established. Early spring is the second-best time to start a cool-season lawn from seed. The young grass has less time to become established before the onset of hot weather, but results are usually satisfactory as long as you start seeding early enough. Warm-season grasses are best planted in late spring. At that time, the weather is still mild enough to let you get the grass established, but the hot weather of summer and the most vigorous growth are just around the corner.

Tools of the seed-planting trade

Don't be doomed to scraggly lawn eternity. The following supplies can get you on the way to a head-turning lawn:

- **Grass seed:** Buy quality seed to avoid battling weeds and uneven turf for the rest of your lawn-loving days, and don't even think about using more seed than is recommended — using too much seed results in a weakened lawn.

- **Organic matter for topdressing (thin mulch):** Peat moss is the best topdressing because it spreads so nicely with a peat spreader. Put down a thin layer, about ¼-inch deep. If you put down too much topdressing, the seeds never reach the surface. One cubic foot of peat moss covers about 50 square feet.

- **Peat spreader:** This cylindrical wire cage throws down a thin topdressing of peat moss to protect your seed from hungry birds, drying out, or blowing away. Your local nursery may loan you a peat spreader, or you can rent one from a rental yard.

- **Seed spreader:** You usually use a *drop spreader* for applying fertilizers, but you can calibrate it for grass seed. *Handheld spreaders* are relatively inexpensive devices that you can also use for fertilizer. For larger areas, use a wheeled or handheld spinning *centrifugal spreader* (also known as a *broadcast* or *rotary spreader*). Your local nursery can usually lend you a larger spreader, or you can rent one at a rental yard.

- **Starter fertilizer:** After you know the size of the area to be seeded, you can determine the quantity of starter fertilizer that you need to buy. (We discuss fertilizer later in this chapter.)

- **Water-filled roller:** This piece of lawn gear presses the seed into the soil, ensuring good contact. (The roller also levels the planting surface after soil preparation.)

Ready, set, grow

When your soil is ready, the site is level, and the watering system is in place, follow these steps to plant the seed:

1. **Spread the seed.**

   Make sure that you properly set your spreader rate for sowing seed. Put half the grass seed in the spreader. To ensure even coverage, spread the first half of the seed by walking in one direction and then spread the second half crisscross to the first direction. Don't forget to use a starter fertilizer. Starter fertilizers are high in the nutrient phosphorous, which is essential to seedlings.

2. **Topdress the seed to hold moisture.**

   Open the door of the cage roller and fill it with peat moss or other fine-textured organic matter. You may end up spilling some, so don't do this on the lawn surface; otherwise, you have to clean up the mess, disturbing the seedbed as you do. Briskly push the cage roller back and forth over the lawn until you cover the entire area with a very thin layer.

3. **Roll the surface.**

   To ensure good contact between seed and soil, roll the entire area with a roller that you've filled only halfway with water. Roll the perimeter first and then finish the entire area.

4. **Water.**

   With the first watering, make sure that you apply enough water to wet the soil down to at least 6 to 8 inches. (We give you more details on watering later in this chapter.) Apply the water gently so that you don't wash the seed away or create puddles. You may have to water several times in short intervals until the bed is thoroughly wet. After that, water often enough to keep the top inch or so of the seedbed moist until the seed germinates. Sprinkle the seedbed lightly with a handheld hose several times a day — especially if it's hot or windy — to get even germination across the entire lawn.

5. **Protect the seedbed.**

   Encircle your newly seeded lawn with brightly colored string attached to small stakes or, for small lawns, surround the whole area with some roll-out metal fencing available at hardware stores.

As your new lawn becomes established, you can start easing up on the water, depending on the weather. When you have a pretty even ground cover of new seedlings, try skipping a day of watering and see what happens. Watch the grass carefully. If the color starts to go from bright green to dull gray green, the grass needs water. You may have to water some quick-to-dry areas with

Book II

Garden Design

a handheld hose. If the grass doesn't dry out, keep stretching the intervals between watering until you're on a schedule of once or twice a week, or as needed. When you do water, don't forget to water deeply, getting the moisture down 6 to 8 inches. Don't be a light-sprinkling fool — you end up with one lousy lawn.

Mow the new lawn when it reaches 3 to 4 inches high and the soil is on the dry side; otherwise, you may tear up the new turf. Make your first application of fertilizer about four to six weeks after germination. Young seedlings have a hefty appetite, so don't skip this important feeding.

Going Green Around the Sod

Having an attractive sod lawn is a little trickier than just laying down the stuff and starting the party. Although you get the look of an instant lawn, you still have to prepare the soil prior to planting. After the sod is down, you have to water and care for it diligently until the grass becomes established. And, starting a lawn from sod is more expensive than planting one from seed.

Starting a lawn from sod does have advantages. Because it's already growing, the sod isn't quite as susceptible to drying out as are the young seedlings, and sod does a good job of smothering weed seeds. Sod often is easier to start on slopes than seed, and it's often the best way to start a lawn in shady areas where seeds are difficult to establish. As long as the soil isn't frozen solid and you can till it about 6 inches deep, you can plant sod almost any time of year. In contrast, you usually need to plant seed in spring or fall.

The ideal time to plant sod is just prior to the period of optimum growth for that type of grass. Good weather makes a big difference in how easily you can successfully plant a lawn from sod. If the weather's too hot, you run around like a nut trying to keep the sod from drying out and dying. And don't forget: As easy as sod is to install, the work still involves some pretty hefty lifting. The cooler the weather, the better. Also, try to time your planting right before you expect some rain; Mother Nature can help you out with some of the watering chores.

To order the right amount of sod, you need to know pretty accurately how many square feet of planting area you want to cover and then add a little extra. Most importantly, you don't want to be short of sod on planting day. For an irregularly shaped lawn, order 15 or 20 percent more than your measurements. You can also order sod by the number of sections. In that situation, you need to know the size of the section the sod farmer cuts, as well as the size of your area. Sod can vary in size, but say that you're looking at pieces 2 feet wide by 6 feet long, or 12 square feet of sod (length × width). To cover the same 600 square feet — plus 10 percent extra — you need 55 pieces of sod (660 ÷ 12 = 55).

Be a discriminating sod buyer

Sod is very vulnerable stuff after it gets cut. With only a thin layer of roots, the grass dries out quickly. If you leave the pieces rolled up for too long, the grass suffers from a lack of light, and it also begins to heat up, which can get hot enough to kill the grass. (Sod begins to decompose slowly after it's cut, and that decomposition process produces heat.)

Look for these qualities to make sure that the sod is healthy:

- **The sod, especially the roots and soil, should be moist, but not dripping wet.** The edges shouldn't be dry, cracked, or starting to curl.

- **The grass should be evenly bright green and a consistent length.** If the grass is starting to turn yellow or brown, don't buy it. Blades that are uneven in length are another sign the sod may have been stored too long.

- **The sod should be thick enough that it doesn't tear easily when handled.** The total thickness of a piece of sod — grass blades, roots, and soil — can vary from 1 to 3 inches, but the roots have to be at least ½ inch long to hold everything together. Some sod is grown over plastic netting to help hold it together. However, this netting can become a problem in home lawns. In areas where people walk a lot, the sod may wear and the netting come to the surface. So you may want to avoid netted sod.

- **The sod should feel cool to the touch.** Heat is a sign of decomposition.

- **Be suspicious of sod that's rolled out on the ground.** When watered several times a day, sod can last a long time rolled out on plastic, asphalt, or concrete. If it looks the least bit parched, though, pass it by.

Get ready, get more ready, get sodding

Fresh sod should never sit around for more than a day in hot weather and three days in cool weather. If you can't plant the day the sod arrives, store the sod in the shade and keep it moist with a light spray from a hose until planting. If you really get stuck and can't plant for more than 24 hours in hot weather or three days in cool weather, unroll the sod, lay it out on a flat surface — but not your planting area — and keep it moist. Bare ground is ideal for the rerolling; a driveway or walkway can work, but gets pretty hot and dries out the sod quickly. Be careful if you use those areas. Don't cover the sod with anything like plastic. You're better off letting it breathe.

Here are a few more pointers before you lay the sod down:

- **Make sure that the planting area is moist, not soggy or dry.** Water thoroughly one or two days before the sod is delivered so that the top several inches of soil are wetted. Allow time for the soil to drain so that it's not muddy and is workable.

✔ **Make sure that the sod is cool and moist to the touch, but not dripping wet.** Sprinkle it quickly to keep cool, but don't soak it. As soon as you've laid down the sod, soak it with impunity.

✔ **Handle the sod with care so that it doesn't tear or fall apart as you move it.**

✔ **Fertilize with a starter fertilizer.** Apply fertilizer to the entire area after the final leveling, if not before. Lay the sod right on top of the fertilizer.

Follow these steps to lay the sod:

1. **Start laying sod along a straight edge.**

   If your lawn has an irregular shape, run a string across the center of the lawn area, with each end of the string attached to a stake. Lay sod on either side of the string. To avoid roughing up the planting surface or the new sod, kneel on a board or piece of plywood as you work.

2. **Unroll the first piece of sod.**

   Make sure that you place the edges of the sod tightly against any hard surfaces, such as cement edgings, walks, or driveways. Otherwise, you have empty gaps where the edges of the sod can dry out.

3. **Set the loose end of the second piece tightly against the end of the first piece and unroll it.**

4. **Cinch the edges as close as possible without overlapping or stretching the sod.**

   The edges of the sod are the first part to dry out. To avoid four corners from coming together in one spot — where they dry out even faster — stagger the ends as though you're laying brick (see Figure 4-1).

5. **Level the planting surface with a rake as you go.**

   If part of the planting surface gets roughed up, level it with a steel rake. Otherwise, you'll have a bumpy lawn. Occasionally, you may need to lift a piece of sod, rake level, and then replace the sod.

6. **When you come to the end of a row, roll the sod out over the edge and cut it to fit with a sharp knife.**

   If you have in-ground sprinklers, cut small holes in the sod to fit it around them.

7. **After you lay out all the sod, place soil in any open seams between pieces of sod.**

   You're bound to have a few narrow gaps where the sod may shrink and expand as it gets wetter or drier. Fill the seams with good soil — potting soil is ideal. Don't try to fill the spaces with small pieces of sod, which dry out too fast and are likely to die.

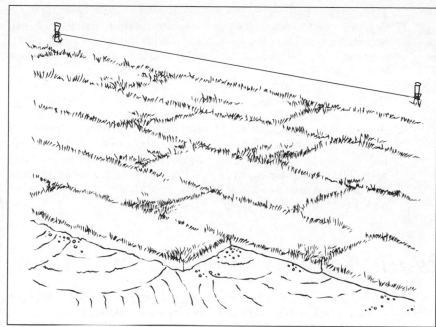

Book II

Garden Design

Figure 4-1:
Stagger
the ends
of the sod
as though
you're
laying brick.

8. **Roll the sod with a water-filled roller.**

   Use a roller that's half full of water. Roll perpendicular to the length of the sod to ensure good contact between roots and soil.

9. **Water the lawn thoroughly, applying enough to wet the soil 6 to 8 inches deep below the sod.**

Work while the grass knits

You need to watch your newly sodded lawn carefully until the roots grow into (or *knit* with) their new soil. The goal is to prevent the newly laid sod from drying out while not saturating the soil below. Water lightly every day for a week or so — maybe more often in hot weather. Apply enough water so that the sod, plus the top of the soil is moist. In a week or so, the roots start knitting with the soil. (Lift a corner of the sod to see whether the roots are growing into the soil.) At this point, you can get by with less watering, but still keep your eyes open for dry areas. Start by skipping a day or two and see how the lawn reacts. In a few weeks, you should be able to get by on twice weekly waterings in most areas.

The edges of the sod are the first to dry out. If the edges start to curl or look dry, you need to water. (Dry grass exhibits a dull, bluish-gray cast.) You may find that certain areas, such as near a driveway or a sloping part of the lawn, are first to dry out. Water these areas in between your regular waterings with a handheld hose.

Let the newly planted lawn grow a little taller than normal before you mow it. Mow only if the sod has knitted tightly with the soil. Mowing too early tears up the sod. When you mow, cut off only about a third of the height of the grass. Mowing too low slows root growth. If you have to let the lawn grow quite tall before you can mow it, bring the height back down to size slowly by cutting just a little more off each time. Fertilize six to eight weeks after planting. You can use your lawn when you can no longer lift the corners of the sod — usually about four to six weeks.

Planting Sprigs, Stolons, and Plugs

Sprigs, stolons, and plugs are a different way to vegetatively plant warm-season grasses that you can't plant by seed. (Skip this section if you're planting cool-season grasses.) Basically, pieces of warm-season sod are shredded, torn, or cut apart, and spaced evenly over the planting area. When properly cared for, the pieces gradually grow together to create a lawn.

Warm-season grasses spread by *stolons* that creep above-ground or by *rhizomes* that grow below-ground. Think of rhizomes and stolons as vigorous, horizontally growing, branch-root combinations. Even the smallest piece of one of these little stolons or rhizomes (we call these pieces *sprigs;* a *plug* is a small, 2- to 3-inch-wide, -square or -round piece of sod) has the capacity to root and spread into a much larger plant.

Sprigs and plugs can take a long time to fill in, sometimes more than a year; planting very densely can save you some time. While the lawn fills in, you have the labor-intensive task of keeping the weeds out between the spaces.

Planting at the right time

Late spring to early summer is the best time to plant sprigs and plugs. The earlier you plant, the sooner the grass fills in. Don't plant any later than two months prior to the average first frost date in fall. (Your nursery-grower can tell you that date.) Otherwise, the grass may not be established before the onset of cool weather.

You get sprigs by tearing some sod into little pieces. Each sprig should have two to four swollen nodes where the roots will grow. You can also order them from your nursery by the bushel. Your nursery-grower can tell you exactly how much you need. Keep sprigs in a cool place, out of direct sun, and lightly moist, so that they don't dry out and die. Before planting, the soil should already have a starter fertilizer and be lightly moist, but not so wet that it makes a mess when you walk on it. Spacing is really up to you. You can plant sprigs in three ways:

- ✔ **Row planting:** Use a hoe to create 1- to 2-inch-deep furrows, spaced 10 to 18 inches apart. Lay the sprigs in the furrow, with any tuft of foliage pointing up, spaced about 4 to 6 inches apart. Then go back and fill the furrow with soil. About a third of the sprig should be above ground. Work in sections so that the sprigs don't dry out. Smooth the whole planting area with a rake and then roll with a half-full water roller.

- ✔ **Stick planting:** Space the sprigs evenly over the planting area and gently push them into the ground with a small stick. Complete small sections at a time so that the sprigs don't dry out, and then roll the whole area with a half-full water-filled roller.

- ✔ **Broadcast sprigging (or stolonizing):** To *stolonize,* spread the sprigs evenly over the planting area. Use a cage roller (your nursery-grower can usually loan you one) to spread about ¼ to ½ inch of mulch on top. (You may also be able to rent a tool called a *stolon disc,* which pushes the stolons into the ground as it rolls over them.) After the mulch is in place, roll the entire planting with a half-filled water-filled roller.

Book II

Garden Design

Plugging it up

A plug has more roots and is easier to get established, so plugging is usually a more reliable method than sprigging. Plugged lawns, however, usually take longer to fill in because you usually use less material. However, if you want a quicker fill-in, plant the plugs very close — up to 3 inches apart (any closer, and you may as well plant sod). You can cut your own plugs from sod or buy them growing in small plastic trays. Sizes usually range from 2 to 4 inches in diameter. Plugs are usually planted in rows, with 6 to 12 inches between plants and between rows. Stretch out a long string or rope to keep your rows straight — the whole thing looks better as the plugs fill in.

Use some type of bulb planter to simplify digging all the holes. Then set the plug in the hole and firm the soil around the sides. Level the ground with a rake and then roll with a water-filled roller.

After planting, keep the soil moist until the grass pieces become established. Keeping the plugs, and especially the sprigs, moist is the secret to success. Let them dry out just a little and you may as well start over from scratch. Lightly sprinkle at least once a day for the first week or two. In hot weather, you may have to water several times a day. Four to six weeks after planting, apply a high-nitrogen fertilizer.

Watering or heavy rain may slowly erode some of the open soil between the pieces of grass. If this happens, add organic matter or good garden soil and level with a rake; otherwise, you end up with one bumpy lawn. You also need to eliminate weeds growing in the open areas. The best way to keep weeds under control is to use a hoe when the weeds are small, especially right after planting. After the pieces are growing and established (four to six weeks after planting), you may be able to use an herbicide. Ask your cooperative extension agent or nursery-grower for a recommendation. Just make sure that you tell them you need help with a newly planted lawn.

When the grass pieces become established and are growing (three to six weeks after planting), mowing helps them spread and fill in. Set the mower a little higher than normal so that you don't scalp the grass. Remember that the mower wheels may be traveling on bare ground and be lower than normal, which can lead to scalping. If the mower pulls any of the plugs or sprigs out of the ground, stop and wait another week or two before trying to mow again.

Drinking Up — Down to the Roots

Proper watering is the most important aspect of caring for your lawn. This section tells you everything you need to know about watering your lawn properly. You're about to become a turf-grass irrigation specialist.

Healthy roots are the key to a healthy lawn. Grass roots grow only in soil that is moist and *well aerated* (has plenty of oxygen). Root growth doesn't move from dry soil to wet soil in search of water. If you water your lawn deeply, then the roots grow deep. (Most grass roots are concentrated in the top 6 to 8 inches of soil, but some may go much deeper.) As the roots grow deeper, the soil reservoir of water they can draw from increases — and you need to water less frequently. However, if you water too often and keep the soil water-logged and void of air, roots don't grow deeply and can drown. At the other end of the spectrum, if you apply just enough water to wet the top few inches of soil, that's the only place the roots grow. Shallow roots translate to a lawn that dries out quickly and needs help. (See Figure 4-2 for examples of various root states.)

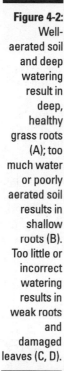

Figure 4-2: Well-aerated soil and deep watering result in deep, healthy grass roots (A); too much water or poorly aerated soil results in shallow roots (B). Too little or incorrect watering results in weak roots and damaged leaves (C, D).

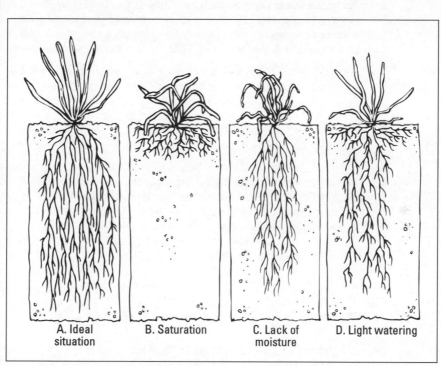

A. Ideal situation   B. Saturation   C. Lack of moisture   D. Light watering

Follow these tips when watering, and your lawn will shine:

- ✓ **Water to the proper depth.** Moisture should penetrate to about 6 to 8 inches deep. Watering less deeply results in a shallow-rooted lawn that dries out quickly; watering more is wasteful because most grass roots don't grow longer than that. Check how deep the water penetrates by probing the ground with a stiff metal rod or long screwdriver. The rod moves easily through wet soil and then stops, or becomes difficult to push, when it reaches dry soil. You can also buy a *soil probe* at a local nursery or irrigation supply store. The probe removes small cores of soil that you can feel to find out how wet they are.

- ✓ **Allow the lawn to partially dry out between waterings.** Doing so creates the good moisture-air relationship that is essential for healthy roots. The lawn shows you when it's getting dry and needs water: When you walk on the grass, you can look back and see your footprints.

- ✓ **Avoid runoff.** If you apply water faster than the lawn can absorb it, which happens with many types of sprinklers, the water runs off into street gutters and into oblivion. Instead, water in short intervals of about 10 to 15 minutes, turn off the water (or move the sprinkler) to let the water soak in, and then turn the sprinkler back on for another 10 to 15 minutes until you get the water down to about 6 to 8 inches deep.

✔ **Water in the morning.** Early morning is the best time to water because the weather is usually cool and calm, humidity is usually high, and water evaporates less. Morning watering also gives the lawn a chance to dry off before evening. Wet grass at night can be a disease organism's delight.

✔ **Apply 1 and 2 inches of water a week in midsummer.** You can apply the whole amount of water once a week, but most people get better results by splitting it into two applications. In sandy soils where the water penetrates quickly, splitting the water into three applications may work better. Don't water more frequently than three times a week, though — you'll be applying so little water each time that you'll get shallow roots, and you know how bad that is.

✔ **Watch your lawn and make appropriate adjustments.** If the lawn doesn't seem to dry out between waterings, stretch the intervals in between. If the water doesn't get deep enough, apply a little more at each watering, but water less often. If everything seems fine, try cutting back on the amount you apply anyway and see what happens. Don't forget to make adjustments with the season.

Applying an Apéritif — Fertilizer

You can apply dry lawn fertilizers with either *drop spreaders,* which apply the fertilizer to a narrow band of grass directly below the spreader, or *broadcast spreaders* — handheld or wheeled — which throw fertilizer over a wider area and are particularly useful for large lawns. (If you don't need this equipment often, both are available at rental yards, and many nurseries loan them.)

Applying dry fertilizers evenly by hand is very difficult. If you have no other option, apply the fertilizer very carefully and only on small lawns. Wear gloves and walk backwards across the lawn as you throw the fertilizer as evenly as possible with a sweeping motion. You can apply liquid or water-soluble fertilizers with handheld, hose-end applicators. Liquids are more difficult than dry fertilizers to apply evenly and the handheld sprayers require frequent refilling on large lawns. When using liquid fertilizers and handheld sprayers, follow the label instructions precisely.

The key to applying fertilizer evenly is to properly use the spreader. Uneven fertilizer application leads to uneven greening or burning of the grass. Take the following steps to achieve a well-nourished, attractive lawn:

1. **Set the spreader settings to correspond to the amount of fertilizer you want to apply.**

   The information you need is on the fertilizer label or spreader instructions. If not, you need to calibrate the spreader.

2. **Place the spreader over a hard surface (such as a driveway or walkway) and fill it with fertilizer.**

   Sweep up any fertilizer that spills.

3. **Start at the edges of the lawn first, as shown in Figure 4-3.**

   Move at your normal walking speed. Then move back and forth between the edges. To avoid missing strips when using a drop spreader, make sure to overlap the path of the wheels. Turn the spreader off when you reach the end strips, when you come to a stop, or when you're turning around to avoid uneven application.

Book II

Garden Design

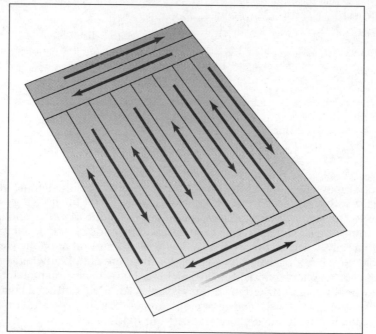

Figure 4-3:
Spread fertilizer at the edges of your lawn first.

4. **Water the lawn thoroughly after fertilizing.**

   Fertilizer can burn your lawn if it remains on the leaves. To avoid this, water in the fertilizer to wash the nutrients into the soil where lawn roots can use them and where heavy rains won't wash them away. When you finish, clean the empty spreader with a hose to avoid corrosion. Wash out the spreader on the lawn and let it dry before storing. If you have a spill, clean up the fertilizer as best as you can (you may want to try a vacuum cleaner) and flood the area with water to prevent the lawn from chemical burns.

To apply liquid fertilizers, start in a corner or edge of the lawn and walk backwards in a straight line as you spray. Turn the sprayer off at the end of each row.

Fertilizing without polluting

Fertilizers feed your lawn to make it look great and stay healthy, but they can pollute ground water, lakes, streams, and oceans if used improperly. Act responsibly and take the following steps:

✔ **Test your soil and choose a proper fertilizer.** When you know your soil contents, you don't apply unnecessary nutrients. Buy fertilizer that matches your lawn's nutritional needs.

✔ **Use slow-release forms of nitrogen.** They're less likely to leach through the soil into ground water.

✔ **Correctly time your fertilizer applications.** Don't apply fertilizers when grasses don't need them or can't use them.

✔ **Prevent misapplications of fertilizer.** Use buffer or mowing strips along the edges of the lawn, shut off spreaders when crossing driveways and sidewalks, and sweep up any spills.

✔ **Use a mulching mower or leave clippings on the lawn.** You can reduce your lawn's nitrogen needs by as much as 25 percent, maybe more.

Giving Your Lawn a Haircut

Proper mowing is one of the most important practices in keeping your lawn healthy. Grasses are like most plants — if you clip off the *growing points* (the tips of the stems where the new leaves develop), the plants branch out and become denser, which in this case, turns thousands of individual grass plants into a tightly woven turf or a lawn. If you didn't mow at all, your yard would look more like a prairie than a lawn. But the mere act of mowing isn't what makes a lawn look good. Mowing height and mowing frequency determine how healthy and attractive your lawn looks. After all, cutting a lawn is stressful for the grass. The leaves make the food for the roots — and how would you like it if someone kept cutting off your food?

Most grasses have a range of recommended mowing heights. Stay at the upper end of that range when the lawn is under stressful conditions, such as hot weather or drought, or if you have a shady lawn. In cooler weather, you can cut the grass a little lower. Follow the one-third rule. For a thriving lawn, never cut away more than one-third of the grass blade in any one mowing. If the grass "gets ahead of you" because of wet weather or your busy schedule, move up the cutting height of your mower to the highest possible setting and mow. If clippings are too long and heavy, even at that cutting height, catch them with the bagging unit or clean-up after mowing with a leaf rake. Then move the cutting height back to your normal range and cut the lawn again a few days after that first mowing. Table 4-1 shows suggested mowing heights for different grass types.

Table 4-1	Ideal Mowing Heights
Grass type	_Height_
Bahia grass; fescue, tall; blue grama; buffalo grass	2 to 3 inches
Bent grass	¼ to 1 inch
Bermuda grass, common	¾ to 1½ inches
Bermuda grass, hybrid	½ to 1 inch
Centipede grass; zoysia grass*	1 to 2 inches
Fescue, fine; St. Augustine grass	1½ to 2½ inches
Kentucky bluegrass	1¾ to 2½ inches
Ryegrass, annual and perennial	1½ to 2 inches

*You can mow some newer, dwarf varieties lower.

Book II

Garden Design

Cut your grass, not yourself

Every year, hundreds, maybe even thousands, of people get injured when using lawn mowers. Power lawn mowers can be dangerous even when used properly. Be proactive when it comes to safety and follow these tips to avoid injuries:

✔ **Know the equipment.** Read the owner's manual. Become familiar with all the safety features and don't disconnect any of them. Keep all nuts and bolts properly tightened. Never pull a walking mower.

✔ **Check the lawn before mowing and wear proper clothing.** Pick up any rocks or debris. Heavy shoes and long pants provide the best protection from flying debris. If you're using a reel mower, don't wear loose clothing.

✔ **Protect your hearing.** Doing yard work can get pretty noisy. In addition to the lawn mower, high-decibel noise comes from trimmers, edgers, and blowers. Use earplugs or earmuff-type hearing protection.

✔ **Keep pets and children away from the lawn as you mow.** Don't let children operate a lawn mower unless they're strong enough, responsible, and understand all the operating and safety features. Even then, supervise them. Never give a young child a ride on a ride-on mower. Sudden stops, flying objects, or an excited child can spell disaster.

✔ **Be careful when fueling.** Stop the mower and let the engine cool for 10 minutes before fueling. Never fill the tank with the mower on the lawn. Avoid spills by using a gas can with an adequate pouring spout. Clean up spills immediately and put the used rags in a covered metal can. (Gasoline-soaked rags are a fire hazard.)

✔ **Turn off the mower.** Never leave the mower running unattended, or work on a motor that is running. Turn off the power when you cross nongrass areas.

✔ **Be careful on hills.** Steep slopes are always dangerous because a mower can flip over or go out of control. Plant a ground cover other than turf in these areas. On gentle slopes, mow across the slope, not up and down. Use a walk-behind mower.

Lawn mowers — a tree's worst enemy

Repeatedly banging a mower against a tree trunk or whipping it senseless with a weed whip each week can seriously damage the bark and the sensitive tissues underneath. The damage can restrict the growth of young trees to the point where the base of the trunk is so weak and girdled that the tree just snaps off in the slightest wind.

To protect the tree, leave a ring of grassless soil at least 3 feet wide around the trunk. Put in a nice brick or stone edging around the outside. Better yet, cover the open soil with a thick layer (3 to 6 inches deep) of organic mulch, such as compost or bark. (Keep the mulch a few inches away from the base of the tree.)

You can also go to a garden center to buy *trunk protectors,* plastic sleeves that encircle the trunk, if you have to have the grass right up against the tree.

Edging and trimming are the finishing touches of mowing, kind of like getting a shave after you've had a haircut. Edging and trimming are pretty close to being the same thing. Some tools are called *edgers* because they're designed to trim the lawn along a hard surface like a driveway or sidewalk. Edgers cut a nice clean edge, but leave some dirt and grass debris that you need to clean up. On the other hand, you can use *trimmers* anywhere — along a hard surface, in tight spaces, next to planting beds, and so on. Trimmers also leave some clippings on paths and driveways that you need to sweep up.

Never put grass clippings in a plastic bag and send them off to the dump. (In some areas, sending grass clippings to the dump is illegal.) Grass clippings are valuable organic matter, chock-full of nitrogen and other nutrients. As long as you mow often enough to remove no more than one third of the grass blade, the easiest thing to do is just to leave clippings on the lawn. The pieces break down quickly and reduce the amount of fertilizer you have to use by as much as 25 percent. And research has proven that the clippings don't cause thatch to build up.

Breathing Room: Dethatching and Aerating

Excessive thatch is a common problem. *Thatch* is a layer of organic matter, consisting of tightly woven, living and dead grass stems, roots, and crowns, that forms between the grass blades and the soil line. These parts of the grass plants are high in *lignin,* an organic material that breaks down slowly.

In most healthy lawns, those parts do break down. Frequent, shallow watering; overfertilization; infrequent, high mowing; excessive use of pesticides; improper soil pH; soil compaction; or heavy clay soils can all cause thatch.

A little bit of thatch — less than ½ inch — isn't bad. The thin layer cushions the turf, reduces soil compaction, and helps conserve moisture. A thick layer of thatch between grass blades and soil blocks the movement of air, water, and nutrients to grass roots, resulting in either a shallow-rooted lawn or a spongy, bumpy lawn. Thatchy lawns are also more susceptible to insects and disease. If your lawn feels spongy when you walk on it, check for thatch by removing a small wedge of the lawn (go deep enough to get some soil) with a knife or shovel. You can see the thatch — the spongy layer of brownish, peat-moss-like stuff below the grass blades and above the soil — when you examine the turf. If your lawn's thatch is more than a ½-inch thick, you need to dethatch or aerate.

Dethatching involves actually cutting through the thatch with knife-like blades and then removing the debris. You can use a *thatching rake,* which has knifelike blades rather than normal tines to basically comb out the debris, but it's hard work and really only practical for small lawns. The more practical and effective method is to rent a gas-powered machine called a *dethatcher, vertical mower,* or *power rake.* Available for rent, a dethatcher easily cuts through the thatch with rotating blades or stiff wire tines, but the machines can be fairly heavy and a bit difficult to maneuver. For thick grasses, use a vertical mower with steel blades. Use the wire-tine type of dethatcher on Kentucky bluegrass or fescue lawns.

A dethatcher works best when the lawn is lightly moist — not too wet or too dry. Here's how to do it:

1. **Mow the lawn a little lower than normal right before you dethatch.**

2. **Make at least two passes — with the second pass at a 90-degree angle to the first — over the lawn with the dethatcher.**

3. **Rake up all the debris.**

   If you haven't used any pesticides on the lawn and it's not a weedy grass, such as Bermuda grass, you can compost the debris or use it for mulch.

4. **Water and fertilize the lawn.**

Dethatching is stressful on a lawn. The lawn ends up looking pretty ratty, but if you dethatch at the right time, the lawn recovers quickly and fills in. For a quicker fill-in, some people prefer to reseed the lawn right after dethatching. If you don't want to reseed but worry that weed seedlings may take over before the grass recovers, apply a *preemergent herbicide* (it prevents weed seeds from germinating) after dethatching.

Aerating is the process of punching small holes all over your lawn. The most effective type of aerating is with a gas-powered machine called a *core aerator* that pulls out small cores of grass and soil. Other aerators use short spikes to punch holes in the turf. Spiking isn't nearly as effective as core aerating, but it's better than nothing.

Aerating annually is one of the best things you can do for your lawn, thatch or no thatch, and it's particularly beneficial for heavily compacted clay soils and on sloping ground. Aerating your lawn breaks through a thatch layer, enables the roots to breathe, and improves water and nutrient penetration. Aerating also helps break down thatch and it isn't nearly as traumatic as dethatching. You end up with little cores of soil all over the lawn, but you can rake them up if they bother you. If you leave the cores alone, they break down into nothing in a few weeks. Signs that your lawn needs to be aerated include the following:

- Worn areas where people walk often
- Water puddles after irrigating
- Water runs off the lawn after only a few minutes of watering
- Parts of the lawn that just can't seem to keep moist

When you aerate, strive for an even 3- to 4-inch spacing between holes throughout the lawn. To do so, you must make two passes in different directions. Make sure that the soil is slightly moist. Set the aerator to pull out cores about 3 inches long. After aerating, water and fertilize the lawn.

Renovating Your Lawn

Renovating a lawn can be simple or complex, depending on the problems you have. Simple renovation may include just aerating and dethatching to solve thatch problems. More severe renovation may involve killing the entire lawn and then replanting. In that case, follow these steps:

1. **Plan ahead.**

   The last step in a complete renovation is replanting, but you need to plan everything and get the timing right so that you end up replanting at the ideal time — fall for cool-season grasses, summer for warm-season grasses. Killing the old lawn takes some time, maybe as long as a month if you have some really tough weeds. Removing the old lawn and replanting takes only a day or two, but it can be hard work. You may want to stretch out the process over a few weekends.

2. **Kill the old lawn and all its weeds.**

   Spray the entire lawn with a broad spectrum herbicide, preferably one containing glyphosate. (See Chapter 7 in Book I for more on herbicides.)

   The herbicides take a few weeks to kill the lawn, but they generally work faster in warmer weather and on vigorously growing plants. To make sure that the lawn is dead, or if you have some really tough plants like Bermuda grass, start watering the lawn three or four days after you spray. See what grows after everything else has died. Repeat the application if necessary.

3. **Remove the dead grass.**

   Here you have two choices. The easy way, which usually works fine, is to run a power rake or dethatcher over the dead lawn at least twice, aerate, and then rake up everything. (At least it sounds easy. Don't worry, you'll sweat.) If your thatch is more than 2 inches thick, if you're renovating an old lawn, or if your lawn has some serious soil problems, rent what's called a *sod cutter,* which strips off the old lawnlike pieces of sod. After you cut off the old sod, roll it up and dispose of it.

4. **Replant.**

   If you used a dethatcher to tear up the grass, level the ground with a rake, reseed, mulch, and keep moist. If you used a sod cutter, replant as though you're starting from scratch: add organic matter, till the soil, level, and replant.

Patching a dead patch

Small dead spots are a fact of life for most lawn owners, but fortunately, patching a dead spot is relatively easy. In fact, most nurseries and garden centers carry several lawn patch kits, which usually combine grass seed with a biodegradable paper-like material that acts like a mulch and helps keep the new seed moist until it's firmly rooted. You can also patch a lawn by just buying some seed or a piece of sod of the same type of grass. Here are the basic steps to patching a lawn:

1. **Dig out the dead spot.**

   Use a small shovel or spade to remove the dead grass. Remove everything right up to the edge of the healthy grass, taking an inch or two of soil.

2. **Water the spot.**

   Make sure that you've solved the cause of the dead spot first!

3. **Amend the soil.**

   Add a few inches of organic matter such as compost or leaf mold, and work it into the soil with the shovel.

4. **Level the soil.**

Smooth out the soil and level it with your hand or a rake. If you're going to reseed the spot, the soil should be level with the surrounding soil. If you use sod, the soil needs to be an inch or so lower, so the new sod will be level with the surrounding grass.

5. **Replant.**

Sprinkle seed over the spot, making sure not to overdo it. Cover the seed with organic matter and water. If you plant sod, cut a piece the size of the patch and lay it in. Put a little organic matter around the edges to prevent them from drying out and water. You need to treat the new patch just like a new lawn and that means watering at least once a day (more in hot weather) until the grass is established.

Overseeding: Turning brown grass green

If you live in a hot-summer, mild-winter area where warm-season grasses predominate, you don't have to put up with brown grass in winter. You can overseed the lawn with cool-season grasses, which keep the lawn green all winter. Because annual ryegrass fills in so quickly, it's usually used for overseeding, but you can also use perennial ryegrass or one of the fescues.

Here's an easier way to overseed:

1. **Scalp the lawn.**

In fall, use a heavy-duty reel-type mower (you can rent one, if necessary). Set the cutting height very low so that it is just above the soil line, and mow to scalp the lawn.

2. **Rake up the debris.**

Compost it by itself, because some warm-season grasses can be weedy.

3. **Sow cool-season seed.**

Put it down heavier than normal (up to 10 pounds per 1,000 square feet for annual ryegrass).

4. **Topdress, water, and fertilize.**

Apply a thin layer of organic matter and then fertilize and water as you would for a newly seeded lawn.

5. **When the cool-season grass becomes established, mow it at the proper height over the winter.**

As the weather warms up in spring, fertilize and start cutting the lawn at the lower height for the warm-season grass. Soon, the warm-season grass again predominates and the winter grass disappears.

Leveling and fixing uneven spots

If you have a high or low spot in your lawn that raises havoc with your mower, here's how to fix it:

1. **Strip off the grass.**

   Outline the uneven area by pushing a spade in a few inches around the perimeter. If the area is large, cut across the middle with the spade so that you create 18- to 24-inch wide strips of sod. Then push the spade about 2 inches underneath the sod and gently pry it up so that the roots separate from the soil.

2. **Roll up the sod and keep it moist.**

3. **Level the soil.**

   Turn the soil with the spade and add or remove enough soil to bring the area to the proper level. (Don't forget to consider the thickness of the sod.) Water the area to settle the soil.

4. **Replace the sod and then water.**

   Unroll the sod in the same order in which it was removed. Because the bottom of the sod probably won't be smooth, shave off a little or remove some soil, so that it sets evenly. Water the leveled area just as you would newly planted sod.

If you have a small low spot, you can often raise it simply by gradually spreading good soil (potting soil works well) over the area, no more than an inch at a time. Eventually, the grass grows through the soil, and the area will be higher.

Book II

Garden Design

Chapter 5

Tree-ting Yourself to Shrubbery

In This Chapter

▶ Appreciating the difference between trees and shrubs

▶ Assessing your current landscape

▶ Adding trees and shrubs to your landscape design

*T*rees and shrubs form the permanent elements that provide the structure around which you plan and plant everything else. Beyond providing aesthetic pleasure, these plants make several practical contributions to your home's landscape. They separate your yard from everyone else's, screen private areas of your yard from public view, and block unsightly service areas, such as dumpsters and gas tanks. Plants improve air quality, help prevent soil erosion and storm runoff, and help hold the snow and moisture on your property in arid climates. Trees and shrubs bring a natural element to urban landscapes, giving homes to welcome birds and wildlife and providing them with nuts and berries to eat. Trees and shrubs can also reduce your heating and cooling costs. Foliage deflects and absorbs the rays of the sun and, in return, gives off moisture that cools the air — a valuable resource in cities and around paved areas. Shade on your roof from nearby trees can reduce the temperature in your attic by as much as 40°. Shaded air-conditioning units operate two to four times more efficiently, too. Also, U.S. Forest Service studies show that attractively landscaped homes are worth 5 to 20 percent more than homes without trees and shrubs.

This chapter provides you with the information you need to effectively incorporate trees and shrubs into your landscape design.

Separating the Trees from the Shrubs

Trees and shrubs — often called *woody plants* — share several characteristics, as well as some anatomical features. For example, trees and shrubs have hardened *woody stems* and trunks that survive from year to year in favorable environments and increase in diameter as the plant grows. Some shrubs die to the ground each year if you plant them in unsuitable climates, but in their *natural range,* where they normally grow, their stems endure from one year to the next.

The difference between shrubs and trees can be confusing, but the following guidelines can help you distinguish trees from shrubs:

- ✔ **Trees:** These plants usually have a single main stem that gets thicker with age and develops large secondary branches and limbs. Some trees appear to have more than one trunk, but often, what you see are actually several trees growing close together in a clump. Trees that have been injured sometimes send up two or more trunks, too, but that isn't their usual habit.

- ✔ **Shrubs:** By nature, shrubs have lots of woody stems coming from a central growing point under or close to the ground. Shrubs often form a dense tangle of stems called *thickets*. The stems on a shrub usually don't grow large side branches — shrubs generally grow to less than 20 feet high. The line between trees and shrubs gets blurred when a tall shrub is pruned so that it has a single trunk.

Examining Current Conditions

Before you add trees and shrubs to your landscape, you first need to evaluate your yard's current state. Two areas that particularly affect trees and shrubs are slope and wind. (Refer to Chapter 1 in Book II for a detailed list of other conditions to assess.)

Slope

The most important aspect of slope in your landscape, as far as trees and shrubs are concerned, is its influence on how water moves across the soil's surface. On steep slopes, fast-moving water can wash the soil away from their roots. In flat landscapes, water sometimes puddles around them. People who work with soil often describe the steepness of a hill as *percent slope*. The following steps show you how to measure the percent of a slope. (See Figure 5-1 as well.)

1. **Assemble your tools — a carpenter's level, tape measure, a 10-foot straightedge, and a buddy.**

2. **Position the straightedge and level.**

   Set one end of the straightedge at the top of the slope and support the other end over the downhill slope. Place the carpenter's level in the middle of the straightedge. Adjust the downhill side of the straightedge up and down until the carpenter's level shows that the straightedge is level. The distance that the straightedge measures is called the length, or *horizontal run*.

3. **Measure the height of the straightedge.**

   Have your buddy measure the distance from the downhill end of the straightedge to the ground. The height of the slope at that point is called its *vertical rise*.

4. **Calculate the percent slope.**

   Use the following formula to calculate the percentage of your slope:

   (vertical rise ÷ horizontal run) × 100 = percent slope

   For example, if the rise or distance from the ground to the end of the straightedge is 2 feet and the run or length of the straightedge is 20 feet, your percent slope is 10 percent.

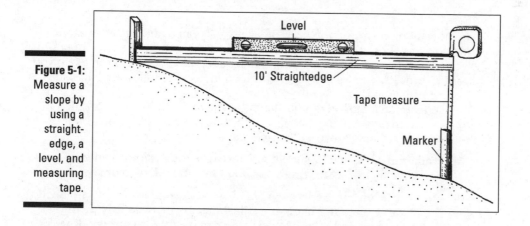

Figure 5-1:
Measure a slope by using a straight-edge, a level, and measuring tape.

Water moves very slowly and may puddle on grassy, 2 percent slopes. On steeper slopes, however, water moves more quickly and can wash away the soil. Plant roots hold the soil in place while their foliage decreases the impact of heavy rain on the soil surface. On slopes that measure greater than 20 percent, use shrubs or other low maintenance, ground-covering plants that don't require mowing.

Wind

If your site lacks protection from hills or trees or if you live near tall urban buildings, strong winds may blow through your yard. Wind contributes to soil erosion and plays a role in how well plants survive the winter in freezing climates. Gentle breezes cool hot summer days and help prevent some plant diseases, but gusty and stormy winds blow away your patio chairs and break tree limbs.

Speak up, I can't hear the trees for the cars

Trees and shrubs don't necessarily block sound if your home is near the highway. A hedge and several trees between you and the road won't keep out the sound of trucks, trains, and cars. According to engineers and landscape architects who study how to block sound, you have to install a planting of dense-foliaged evergreens at least 100 feet wide to begin to make a dent in the noise. Trees' and shrubs' greatest value is screening the source of the sound from view. Plants also soften the look of barriers, such as solid fences, walls, and earth mounds, which really do block sound.

If you want more protection from the wind, you can plant a *windbreak*. Windbreaks planted perpendicular to the prevailing wind offer the most protection, but they must be at the right height and distance from the place you want to protect. For the most wind protection, use the following guidelines:

- **Determine the direction of the prevailing winds.** Note from which direction the wind usually blows. If you aren't sure, ask a neighbor or call the National Weather Service bureau in your state.

- **Walk into the prevailing wind and measure the distance from the area you want to protect to where you want to plant a hedge or row of trees.**

- **Find the height of the trees or shrubs you must plant.** To do so, divide the distance by four. That is the tallest height you need. Divide the distance by ten to find the lowest effective height for your windbreak. The taller the windbreak and the closer it is to the protected area, the greater protection it provides.

- **Make sure that the windbreak extends far enough.** The windbreak should extend 50 to 100 feet beyond the area you're protecting for maximum effectiveness. If, for example, you want to protect your house from a prevailing northwesterly wind, plant a 10- to 25-foot-tall windbreak 100 feet from the northwest side of your house. Extend both ends of the windbreak at least 50 feet beyond the length of your house.

Designing with Trees and Shrubs

Consider the landscape changes that you want to make and how to match the right trees and shrubs to your needs and your site. Each plant offers its own unique contribution to your landscape. Knowing which ones to choose and deciding where to put them can be daunting. Familiarizing yourself with a few basic design rules and the characteristics of the trees and shrubs themselves helps you make good choices for you and your plants.

Making a site plan

Play time! Get out your *site analysis map,* a pencil and eraser, and a few sheets of tracing paper. (Refer to Chapter 1 in Book II for information on drawing a site analysis map.) Place a sheet of tracing paper over your map and start doodling. Draw ovals and circles on your dream map to represent ideas and where you want to put them. Label your ideas inside each circle and let your site's existing features guide your plans. Before you rush out to buy trees and shrubs to fill in your doodles, consider the following concepts and plant features that professional designers use to plan landscapes (Chapter 1 in Book II also covers design elements in-depth):

Book II

Garden Design

- ✔ **Public, private, and utility areas:** Think of your site as a series of outdoor rooms in which different activities take place, just as they do inside your home. Trees and shrubs form the walls that divide these spaces from each other.

- ✔ **Form and function:** Trees and shrubs, and all other plants for that matter, grow in specific shapes, called their form. A plant's form suggests its *function* in the landscape. For example, to fulfill the function of shade, you need a tree whose form is tall and leafy. To refine the form further, choose a *deciduous* tree — one that loses its leaves in the fall — to provide summer shade and let most of the winter sun shine through.

- ✔ **Scale and mass:** *Scale* — the relative size of a tree or shrub — and *mass* — the density of its foliage and branches — determine a plant's appropriate place in the landscape, too. A plant's mass or density can change your perception of the plant's scale. A tree with high branches and an open canopy dominates the landscape less than a dense, low-branching evergreen of the same height.

  When you choose plants, consider their ultimate size. As a general rule, trees appear in proportion to your house when they grow no taller than approximately ¼ to ⅓ taller than the roof (see Figure 5-2). Very large trees, especially ones with dense mass, overwhelm small houses and properties. Little trees quickly grow tall, possibly hanging over your roof or car or blocking your sidewalk. Their roots, too, can damage sidewalks and driveways and grow against building foundations.

- ✔ **Composition:** Planning a landscape is similar to, in some ways, painting a picture. Repetition, balance, and sequence lead the eye through the composition. Framing holds all the elements together, adding structure, mystery, and drama to your landscape just as it does to photographs and paintings. When you use plants to partially hide a space or view, you create a sense of mystery. Use trees to frame distant views or a gap in the hedge to highlight a focal point or frame an intimate space. (See Chapter 1 in Book II for more tips on creating an appealing composition.)

✔ **Color, texture, and year-round interest:** When you choose shrubs and trees, consider all their parts — branches, flowers, bark, fruit, and foliage — and what color and texture they bring to your design. Bark adds color and texture to your yard — an important feature in wintry landscapes. Many trees and shrubs also produce colorful fruit that remains attractive long after the petals have fallen. Foliage, however, offers the greatest opportunity for bringing color into your site. You can find a wide range of shrubs and trees with colorful foliage. Place shrubs and trees with complementary, but different colored foliage together to create depth and contrast. The most useful trees and shrubs combine several appealing features for year-round interest. A shrub that blooms for one week a year is less valuable than one that blooms and offers attractive foliage or bark, for example. If you have room on your site for only a few plants, choose those that offer decorative form, texture, and color in at least three seasons of the year.

Don't mix too many competing elements into a small space. Plants with brightly colored foliage, for example, stand out in the landscape — use them judiciously. Better to choose one shrub with flamboyant foliage or group several together as an accent than to scatter them around and create visual clutter.

Figure 5-2: Choose trees and shrubs that remain in scale with your home.

Girl trees, boy trees, and other oddities

Flowering trees and shrubs add color, fragrance, and drama to your landscape. If you plan to grow flowering trees and shrubs for their fruits or nuts, however, you need to know that some plants are male, some are female, and some are both. For those plants with separate male and female plants, you need at least one of each sex to produce fruits, but only the female bears fruit. Some plants, such as apple trees, have both male and female flower parts on the same tree, but they're incompatible and can't form fruit. They need the pollen of another tree of a different variety to set fruit. This is called *cross-pollination*. In other words, to get 'Red Delicious' apples on your tree, you need a 'Granny Smith' or some other kind of apple that blooms at the same time planted nearby.

The fruit or flowers of some plants are so messy or foul smelling that you may want to avoid the particular sex of plant that produces them. Plant breeders have been busy working on these problems, however, and they've produced many fine plants with better flowers and fruit and without the offending characteristics.

Book II

Garden Design

Matching trees and shrubs to your site

Knowing what you expect your trees and shrubs to do in your landscape and how much maintenance you're willing to accept helps you match the right plants to the right place. Think about how you want your plants to function. Also decide what you don't want from your plants — frequent pruning, watering, raking, or spraying, blocked views, or sparse lawn, for instance. Consider all the following aspects before making your choices:

- **Vigor:** How fast does the plant grow? Very vigorous trees and shrubs quickly fill their allotted space and provide shade and privacy in just a few years. These plants tend to require frequent pruning, however, and have brittle limbs and short life spans. Plants that grow slowly usually live longer and require little pruning.

- **Size:** How tall and wide will the tree or shrub get? Consider this aspect carefully if you have limited space or dislike pruning. All too often, shrubs that naturally grow to 8 feet high get planted under low windows, which the shrubs eventually cover. Final width matters, too, especially when choosing shrubs for hedges and groundcovers for which you need to calculate the planting distance between plants. To determine how much space a particular shrub will fill at maturity, take your tape measure with you to the garden center. Use it to do a "reality check" before you bring home a plant that will outgrow your space.

- **Culture:** Is the tree or shrub adapted to your climate as well as the sun, soil, and water conditions at the proposed planting site? Try to match as many of your site's conditions to your chosen plant's cultural needs as possible. (Book I provides details on garden culture.)

✔ **Bad habits:** Does the plant have any habits that may cause problems in your landscape? Find out whether the plant will have invasive roots that ruin your lawn or driveway; weak limbs that snap in the wind; messy fruit, leaves, or flowers; and particular pests or diseases that frequently shorten its life.

✔ **Ornamental interest:** Does the plant offer ornamental value for more than one season of the year? Look beyond the obvious flower and foliage colors and consider the texture and color of all the plant parts.

Avoiding inappropriate placement

More than just a matter of aesthetics, planting the right trees and shrubs in the right place promotes safety and prevents damage to the plants, nearby buildings and utilities, and relations with the people who live next door. Anticipate the consequences of poorly placed plants — dangerous limbs hanging over your roof or growing into electrical wires, roots clogging your sewer pipe or leach field, inaccessible utility service boxes, unhappy neighbors, and unsafe driving conditions. Pruning efforts to correct the problems after the trees and shrubs mature can damage the plants and leave them looking unnatural and more prone to pests and diseases. Consider the following situations before you plant:

✔ **Overhead power lines and utilities:** The best way to keep your overhead wires clear of tree limbs is to consider the mature height and spread of trees before you plant. The International Society of Arboriculture (www.ag.uiuc.edu/~isa/) recommends planting trees that grow no taller than 20 feet directly beneath utility wires. Taller trees should be planted so that their mature canopy grows no closer than 15 feet from the wires.

You can't safely prune your own trees if they grow too close to overhead wires — even if they grow on your property. Limbs that touch or fall across electrical wires can electrocute you. Climbing a ladder or the tree itself with a saw in hand also poses the hazard of falling from a dangerous height. If you already have trees growing into your overhead wires, call the utility company and ask that they send a pruning crew to your home. Be aware, however, that a utility company's primary concern are the wires, not the tree. They will be sure to remove limbs and branches that are too close to wires, but your tree may end up looking deformed afterwards. *Arborists* — professional people who preserve and care for trees — will also prune your trees for a fee.

✔ **Buried wires and gas lines:** Frequently, utility companies bury electric, telephone, and cable television wires underground, especially in new developments. That tactic makes choosing tree or shrub locations easier because you don't have to worry about overhead wire, but you still need to think about the underground cables. Don't assume that the wires are buried deeper than your planned planting hole — sometimes, they're buried just below the surface. Natural gas pipes pose another problem. Although pipes should be buried at least 3 feet below ground, gas companies prefer a tree-free corridor of 15 to 20 feet on either side of pipes to allow for safety and maintenance. Gas leaks within a plant's root zone can also damage or kill it. If you have a propane tank with copper tubing running underground to your house or another building, be aware that the pipe may be buried very close to the surface. Cutting through a buried wire or gas line can result in severe injury. The utility company also may charge you a fee for interrupting service and for necessary repairs to their damaged property.

To avoid disrupting underground utilities, many states have laws that require you to contact utility companies that may have wires or pipes on or close to your property before you dig. The companies send someone out to locate and mark the path of the wires or give you a toll-free phone number to a regional clearinghouse. The clearinghouse routinely marks underground wires and pipes for the utility companies. When you know the location of underground utility lines, avoid planting close to them because, when the cables or pipes need repair in the future, digging may harm your trees or shrubs.

Book II

Garden Design

✔ **Service boxes and wellheads:** You may want to disguise your wellhead and the unattractive metal box that the utility company planted in your front yard, but someone will need access to them someday. Plan your shrub plantings so that the mature shrubs won't touch the box or wellhead. Better yet, allow enough space for someone to actually work on the utilities located in the box without having to prune back your shrubs. And have a heart, avoid spiny plants in your planting plan.

✔ **Buildings:** Insurance companies take a dim view of large tree limbs hanging over their customers' homes and businesses — and with good reason. A strong wind can send branches crashing through your roof. Overhanging limbs also drop leaves that clog your gutters and sticky sap that can stain siding. Dense shrubs planted against your house may grow up to block the view from windows or provide a hiding place for unwelcome intruders. Keep shrubs at least several feet from your house and plant trees that grow to 60 feet or more at least 35 feet away.

✔ **Streets, sidewalks, and septic lines:** Think about roots when you consider where to plant trees. Some trees, such as poplar and willow, grow large roots close to or on the ground's surface where they heave paving and everything else out of their path. Shallow-rooted trees also compete with lawn grasses and other plants, and make for bumpy mowing. Roots cause other problems, as well. To tree and shrub roots seeking out sources of moisture and nourishment, your septic leach field looks like a Sunday buffet. Moisture-loving species cause the most trouble when their roots grow into the perforated drainpipes, clogging them and disrupting the leach field's function. Plant roots usually grow two to three times farther from the tree trunk than the aboveground branches do, so leave plenty of room between the planting hole and your driveway, sidewalk, or septic field for outward expansion.

✔ **Property boundaries and public rights of way:** Before you install a hedge along your property line or plant trees along the sidewalk out front, do a little homework. Your state and municipal governments own the land on either side of all public roads. The width of this *right-of-way* may vary from 50 feet to more than 120 feet, as measured from the road's center line. Many communities and highway departments prohibit planting in the public right-of-way or have regulations that you must follow. Contact your local government office for guidelines, or call the State Highway Department if your property borders a state or federal highway.

Homeowners commonly plant privacy hedges along their property boundary. If you plan to plant a hedge or row of shrubs or trees between you and the neighbors, avoid future disputes by hiring a professional surveyor to find the actual property lines. When you plant the shrubs, allow enough space so that mature shrubs won't encroach on the neighboring property. You'll also have room to maintain them from your own yard.

✔ **Merging traffic:** Sitting in the driver's seat of an average automobile, the driver's eye is about 45 inches from the ground. Shrubs and hedges near intersections, including the end of your driveway, must be lower than that height or planted far enough from the road to allow drivers to see oncoming motorists, bicyclists, and pedestrians. If your street is on a hill, adjust the hedge's position so that you have a clear view of traffic in both directions. For safety's sake and to avoid possible liability, keep signs and lines-of-sight clear.

My, how you've grown!

Calculating the height of a mature tree takes more than a tape measure. Here's a simple method of finding the ballpark height of a tall object:

1. **Position a person or other object of known height near the tree.**

2. **Hold a pencil or stick vertically in your outstretched hand and back away from the person until the pencil "covers" the person from head to toe.**

3. **Standing in the same spot, use the pencil as a ruler to measure the tree's height by eyeballing the number of pencil lengths it takes to cover the height of the tree.**

Multiply the tree's number of "pencil lengths" by the person's height. If your friend is 6 feet tall, for example, and it takes four pencil lengths to cover the tree height, the tree is 24 feet tall.

Book III
Roses

In this book . . .

Rare is the gardener who doesn't want at least a couple of rose bushes holding court over his or her landscape. Rarer is the gardener who doesn't initially find the prospect of growing roses downright scary. Never fear, Book III is here! Roses aren't that difficult to grow, so long as you have some basic knowledge — knowledge that this book provides. We explain everything from how roses grow to how to keep roses growing in your garden. Along the way, we examine rose scents, show you how to properly plant rose bushes, and provide the information you need to keep your rose plants pest and disease free. (If you're not sure which type of rose or which color will work best in your garden, make sure that you read Chapter 3 for suggestions.)

Here are the contents of Book III at a glance:

Chapter 1

Everything's Coming Up Roses

- -

In This Chapter

▶ Breaking the hard-to-grow myth

▶ Finding out where roses come from

▶ Knowing the definition of budding

▶ Knowing which roses to grow

▶ Understanding how roses are grouped

▶ Looking at where new rose varieties come from

- -

You can find no plant more beautiful and satisfying than roses. Roses are fun and easy to grow, particularly if you know a little about them before you start. If you want to go out and dig a hole this very minute, stop. Read this chapter first. But if you've already dug yourself into a hole by jumping in without knowing what you were doing, remember the old adage: *If at first you don't succeed, read the directions and try again.*

Are Roses That Hard to Grow?

The idea that roses are hard to grow is, plain and simple, a myth. But, like many stereotypes, it contains a grain of truth. We may be stretching the point, but we're using an analogy with cars anyway: Some cars are expensive, and some aren't. Some look great, and some don't. Some are easy to maintain, and some aren't. Yet they're all cars. If you're wary of working on cars, you wouldn't buy an antique Jaguar or Triumph. You probably wouldn't buy a new Lamborghini, either. If you want basic, care-free transportation, you buy a basic, easy-to-maintain vehicle.

The same holds for roses. If you don't want to fuss over your roses after you plant them, don't choose the fanciest, most beautiful, most fragrant long-stemmed hybrid tea. Look for something a bit more . . . well, practical. And please don't assume that an "easy" rose doesn't look good. Some groups of roses, such as the shrubs and floribundas, are almost all easy to grow. Out of the thousands of roses available, some are the easiest, most trouble-free plants you'll ever meet, and some thrive on the indulgent fussing that some gardeners love to provide.

Which Rose Should 1 Grow?

To decide which rose to grow, you have to become familiar with what's available, develop some preferences (for a color or fragrance, for example), and give some thought to the type of rose likely to thrive in your garden (and to how much care you're willing to provide).

Color is one good place to start, but you may also want to consider looks, fragrance, climate, and how you want the rose to function in your garden. There's a rose for every passion. You can gain a great deal of knowledge by consulting a local rose expert (a *rosarian*) and by visiting public gardens that offer substantial rose displays.

Where Do Roses Come From?

Botanists believe that roses in some form flourished long before humans inhabited the earth and that people have been cultivating roses for more than 5,000 years. Many of these early rose varieties, called *old garden roses* or *species roses* (you can read about them in Chapter 3 of Book III), are still around. But humans have been applying their genius to rose culture (growing) and rose breeding (hybridizing) for a long time. Now, gardeners can have the best of both worlds — species and old garden roses as well as modern hybrids.

Most of the rose plants you can buy today are grown by commercial rose growers in huge rose fields in fairly temperate climates. In the United States, nearly all rose plants are grown commercially in California's San Joaquin Valley, in Arizona, and in Texas. These plants are grown in fields for two years before they're harvested while dormant (during their normal winter rest period). The rose plants are stored *bareroot* (meaning that they have no soil on their roots) in huge, moist, refrigerated facilities to keep them from growing before being shipped to gardeners, nurseries, and garden centers nationwide in winter or early spring. You can find out more about shopping for roses in Chapter 4 of Book III.

You may wonder whether roses are ever grown from seed. Most of the roses that you buy are not. A rose grown from seed is usually not what you expect in terms of flower color and form. However, many of the varieties available may originate as seedlings. These are hybrids from crosses of two other roses. The seed from the original cross-breeding experiment grew into a beautiful rose, and so the hybrid was grown and offered to other rose growers.

What's in a rose?

For all their perceived mystery, roses are pretty simple plants, as Figure 1-1 shows. They consist of roots that take up water and nutrients from the soil, and *canes* (or stems) that grow from the crown of the plant (where the canes end and the roots begin). The canes usually have thorns (ouch), but some varieties have fewer than others, and a few (see the roses with "smooth" in their name in Chapter 3 of Book III) are thornless. The leaves and branching canes grow from *bud eyes,* small buds that sprout at intervals along the cane. The leaves are usually produced in five-leaf leaflets. As a plant thrives, new canes sprout both from the crown of the plant and from the junction of the cane and the leaflets.

The flowers of the rose plant are called roses, flowers, blooms, or blossoms. A rose flower stays on the plant and looks like a rose for a certain length of time, depending on the variety. When the flower fades, falls apart, or otherwise dies, it's called a *spent bloom,* and you should cut it off the plant to encourage repeat flowering. Cutting off dead flowers is called *deadheading,* which we discuss in Chapter 5 of Book III. If you don't cut off the dead flower, it forms a seed pod called a *hip.* The rate at which a rose plant can form a new flower is called *repeat.*

Book III

Roses

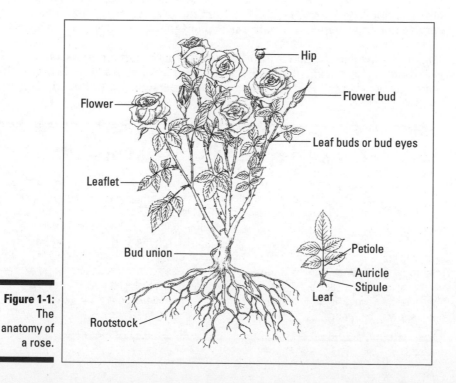

Figure 1-1:
The anatomy of a rose.

Most modern roses — those that have been bred since the late nineteenth century — are ever-blooming or free blooming, which means that they're repeat bloomers and flower almost continuously throughout the growing season. Many old roses, such as the damask variety 'Marie Louise', bloom only once a season. To find out more about rose flowers, see Chapter 2 of Book III.

How does budding make a rose?

Many types of roses are grafted, or, more correctly, budded, onto a rootstock, as opposed to growing on their own roots as most perennials do. Many commercial growers believe that certain varieties of roses perform better on vigorous rootstocks; with a good rootstock, new plants take less time to establish their root systems, and growers get a larger percentage of roses to thrive on rootstock than they do with roses on their own roots.

Commercial growers take canes from the rose varieties they want to propagate. They cut off the bud eye (a dormant bud that will eventually grow into a cane) at the junction of the cane and a leaflet, and insert it under the bark on the cane of a rootstock plant. When the canes and foliage above the bud are cut off the rootstock plant, all the plant's energy goes toward making the newly budded eye grow. The bud eye from the desired variety has all the genetic material needed to create a new plant that's identical to the original.

The point at which the bud is inserted into the bark of the rootstock plant is called the *bud union*. On mature plants, the bud union looks like a knob. As the plant grows in your garden, new, large canes grow from above the bud union.

In cold climates, the bud union is the part of the plant that's most important to protect in winter. Plant the bud union several inches below the ground in cold-winter climates, and protect it by covering it with a mound of soil during the winter months. (For more about growing roses in cold regions, see Chapter 5 in Book III.)

How Are Roses Grouped?

Rosaceae is the third largest plant family. This family includes many ornamental landscape plants, fruits, and berries, including apples, cherries, raspberries, and pyracantha, characterized by the shape of the *hypanthium* (the part of the flower where the seeds develop) and by petals in groups of five. Roses are members of the plant genus *Rosa*. Within that genus, roses are grouped into classifications based on the characteristics that each particular plant displays.

Your choice of rose depends on how you plan to use it and on your personal preferences. Some rose gardeners grow only one or two types of roses, and others grow many types. Try growing one or two in each class and see which rose types you prefer. The following list shows you the basic differences among the various types of roses, which we describe in more detail in Chapter 3 of Book III:

Book III

Roses

- **Hybrid teas:** These roses bear large flowers that commonly grow one to a long stem and bloom continually throughout the growing season. The bush can grow quite tall, with an upright *habit* (a term rosarians use to describe the shape or look of a plant). Hybrid tea roses are usually budded onto a vigorous rootstock, and are a great choice if you like large flowers with a pleasant rose form (see Chapter 2 of Book III) and if you like to make rose arrangements or have cut flowers in the house.

- **Grandifloras:** These are upright plants with hybrid tea-type flowers. The flowers often grow in clusters, but the stems on each flower within a cluster are long enough for cutting. Grandifloras normally grow to between 3 and 6 feet tall. They're almost always budded and are a good choice if you like lots of blooms for color in the garden and stems for cutting, all on the same plant.

- **Polyanthas:** A forerunner of modern floribundas, the plant itself can be quite large, covered with small flowers. Their usual habit is compact, hardy, and generous-blooming. The variety you see most often is 'The Fairy' — a wonderful variety, covered with small pink flowers on a plant that can spread to several feet in height and width.

- **Floribundas:** These plants have flowers that are smaller than hybrid teas and which grow in clusters on short stems. The bush is usually quite compact and blooms continually throughout the growing season. Most floribundas are budded, but commercial growers are beginning to grow them on their own roots. Choose floribundas if you need fairly low-growing plants that produce great numbers of colorful flowers.

- **Miniatures:** Extremely popular small plants, miniatures are usually between 6 and 36 inches in height, with their leaves and flowers in perfect proportion. They customarily grow on their own roots, and aren't budded, which makes them hardier in cold climates. Most mini varieties bloom profusely throughout the growing season and are a great choice for lots of color in a small space. You also can grow miniatures indoors in pots under a full-spectrum fluorescent light or grow light. Merely putting them on a windowsill won't work — they won't get enough light to thrive and blossom.

  Recently, the American Rose Society classified roses thought to be too large to be miniatures and too small to be floribundas as "mini-floras." The name hasn't yet been completely accepted by nursery workers, so we continue to group these varieties as miniatures.

- **Climbers:** These plants don't really climb like clematis or other true vines that wrap around or attach themselves to supports. They do, however, produce really long canes that need to be anchored to a fence, trellis, or other support. Otherwise, the plants sprawl on the ground. Flowers bloom along the whole length of the cane, especially if the cane is tied horizontally, such as along a fence. Some climbers bloom only once in the spring, but many modern climbers produce flowers throughout the growing season.

- **Shrubs:** Because most are quite hardy and easy to grow, and great for landscaping, shrubs have become very popular in recent years. They're generally large plants, and most, particularly the modern shrubs, bloom profusely throughout the season. If you want to fill a large space with color, the shrub category offers a great many choices.

- **Old garden roses:** Often referred to as Antique roses, these roses were discovered or hybridized before 1867. The classification "old garden roses" is made up of many subclasses of roses, including alba, bourbon, China, hybrid perpetual, damask, and the species roses. Many old garden roses bloom only once during the growing season. Old garden rose aficionados enjoy the history and study of these lovely and often fragrant plants.

- **Tree roses, or standards:** These aren't included among the basic categories because nearly any rose that is grafted (or budded) onto a tall trunk is a tree rose. Most often, hybrid teas, floribundas, and miniatures are used as tree roses. These plants really aren't even trees. Most just have that lollipop tree look, as shown in Figure 1-2, but are only 2 to 6 feet high. They're wonderful either in the ground or in containers but are very susceptible to winter damage, and in cold climates, you must either bury the entire plant in the ground or bring it into a cool garage.

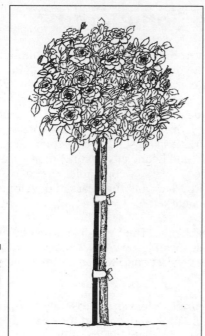

Figure 1-2:
A tree rose trained to grow as a tree.

When you go to a garden center to choose your rosebushes, knowing which classification of rose you want is important. The classification gives you hints about how you can use it in your garden. The variety you choose (see the following section) depends on your personal preference as to color, hardiness, and so on. You don't want to plant a once-blooming old garden rose in a spot where having season-long color is important.

Where Do Rose Varieties Fit In?

Within each classification of roses are *varieties*. If you're talking to a bona fide rose snob, however, be sure to say *cultivar* (a combination of cultivated and variety), not variety, even though the two terms mean the same thing. Either word indicates a particular plant within a classification (which is much less complicated than it sounds). Each variety is a distinct individual and every plant so named is identical.

For example, the variety 'Olympiad' is classified as a hybrid tea rose. So if you're looking for a lovely red rose with a classic rose form that grows on long stems, suitable for cutting, you may want to consider the hybrid tea 'Olympiad'. If instead you want a fragrant, orange-yellow hybrid tea, you may want to go with 'Sutter's Gold'.

Where Do New Roses Come From?

Many new varieties of roses are introduced to the gardening public each year. Some of them are so fabulous that you can't resist buying them for the pleasure of seeing them grow in your own garden. But who invents new rose varieties? Well, rose breeders, more correctly called *rose hybridizers,* are unique people. Some are amateurs — usually rosarians — who take their hobby a step further and try their hand at hybridizing. Some are independent hybridizers, who develop new varieties and sell them to commercial rose growers. But the most successful (and financially secure) rose hybridizers are employed by commercial rose growers — companies that can afford to support large-scale hybridizing programs and the years of development needed to bring a new rose to the market.

Roses are cross-bred by pollen exchange. The hybridizer must be an expert in rose genetics in order to choose existing varieties whose desirable characteristics will be passed on to a new variety and whose undesirable characteristics will not.

After pollen is exchanged, the hybridizer leaves the rose hip to ripen. At harvest, the hip is cut off the plant and broken open, and the seeds are stored for a few weeks before they're planted in flats in a carefully controlled greenhouse. In one hybridizing season, hundreds of thousands, perhaps half a million, seeds are planted. From the seedlings, eventually only three or four are deemed worthy of selling to gardeners.

New seedlings are tested for several years to ensure that the new variety grows well in all climates, isn't a haven for every pest and disease that comes along, and has pleasing flowers and a desirable growth habit. It's not unusual for a new rose variety to be tested for ten years or more before it comes to market.

How does a rose get its name?

The American Rose Society oversees international rose registration to ensure that names and descriptions of rose varieties are original and correct. But most of the time, the people who bred the rose think up some of these wild names. Sometimes, roses are named after a favorite person, relative, or celebrity, such as 'Princesse de Monaco'. Of course, in such cases, you have to get permission from the owner of the name. Many old roses have French names, for which you can probably thank Empress Josephine, wife of Napoleon I. Her collection of roses from all over the world really launched rose growing to new heights.

Chapter 2

Flowers That Smell Sweet as a Rose

In This Chapter

▶ Examining rose anatomy

▶ Following roses from bud to bloom

▶ Blooming in good time — ever-blooming, once-flowering, and remontant roses

▶ Sniffing out what makes a rose fragrant

▶ Making the most of rose "scentsations"

▶ Recognizing James Alexander Gamble Fragrance Medal winners

Flowers — the color, the shape, the substance, the fragrance, the size, and the overall appeal — are why people grow roses. No matter what kind of roses you like, the flowers are endlessly fascinating. Rose flowers come in almost every color and in many shapes. Some plants flower once; some all season long. And, like preferences for blond or brunet, blue eyes or brown, tall or petite, what's perfection to you may not be perfection to someone else. This chapter examines rose flowers and fragrance, so that you can make sure that the rose you buy has the color, shape, size, fragrance, and blooming schedule that suits your yard, your climate, and your expectations.

Anatomy of a Rose

Roses have both male and female organs in one lovely flower, and a rose's petals surround all the plant's sexual parts. Figure 2-1 shows a cross section of a rose flower. The *stamens,* so lovely in many varieties of roses, are the male parts of the rose. The *anthers,* at the top of the stamens, produce the pollen that fertilizes the *ovules,* or eggs, located at the bottom of the *pistil,* the female part of the flower, inside the flower's hypanthium. Rose flowers can self-pollinate, but the resulting plant is rarely as good as the original.

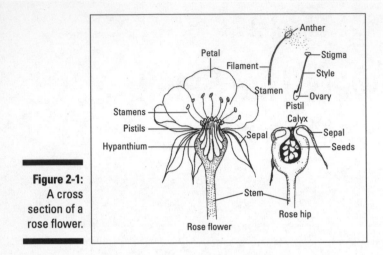

Figure 2-1:
A cross
section of a
rose flower.

The *sepals* are leaf-like structures that cover the rose buds before they open, protecting them. Sepals slowly separate to reveal the color of the developing flower and finally pull away entirely, allowing the petals of the bud to unfurl. The sepals are often a very attractive part of the flower, particularly if their feathery ends extend above the top of the bud. When they drop, allowing the petals to open, they're often a very decorative underpinning to a beautiful flower.

How many petals make a rose?

A rose may have no petals at all, like the famous green rose, *Rosa chinensis* 'Viridiflora', of the China family of old garden roses. (See Chapter 3 in Book III for more about old garden roses.) What appear to be the petals of the flower are actually lots of sepals. A rose can also have so many petals that it won't open in anything but the hottest weather. Sometimes, these many-petalled roses are so fabulous that they're worth growing, even if you see only a few blooms a year during a heat wave. The most notorious rose for having so many petals that many of the flowers end up as squishy rotten balls at the top of a strong cane is the red hybrid tea 'Uncle Joe'.

The most common petal formations fall into three categories:

- ✔ **Single:** Many beautiful roses have only a single row of petals (usually 5), as shown in Figure 2-2. Like the wonderful 'Dainty Bess' (featured in the color insert), a single hybrid tea with five large, pale pink petals sur-rounding bright red stamens, single-petaled roses can be very lovely. 'Eyepaint' is another beautiful single rose.

✔ **Semi-double:** Roses considered semi-double may have only two or three rows of 12 to 16 petals, as shown in Figure 2-3. The pink floribunda 'Simplicity', which Jackson & Perkins (www.jacksonandperkins.com) sells as a hedge rose, has semi-double flowers.

✔ **Double or fully double:** A rose is considered double if it has more than 17 petals (see Figure 2-4). Sometimes, roses with 26 to 40 petals are called *fully double,* and those with more than 40 petals are called *very double.* Double roses are generally larger and showier than singles or semi-doubles. The red hybrid tea 'Mister Lincoln' (featured in the color insert) has double flowers and is a fragrant favorite.

Figure 2-2:
A single rose has a single row of petals.

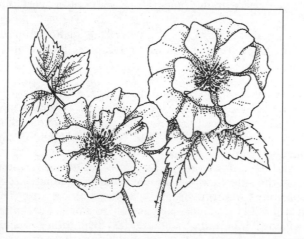

Figure 2-3:
A semi-double rose has two or three rows of petals.

Book III

Roses

Figure 2-4:
A double
rose has
many petals.

Whether you choose roses with single, semi-double, or double flowers makes no difference. If you like them, they're perfect.

Roses with form and substance

The way a flower's petals unfurl is called *form*. Whether a rose is considered to have good form depends on the kind of rose you're looking at, as well as your own idea of what's attractive. Many people think that the quartered form (in which the center petals are folded into quarters) often found in old garden roses is very attractive. Other people prefer the complete lack of form found in other old garden roses, with floppy petals that jut out in every direction.

But really, when you talk about rose form, you're talking about modern roses. Modern roses, including hybrid teas, floribundas, grandifloras, and miniatures, can have two types of form:

- ✔ **Exhibition or formal:** Many-petalled rose flowers with great (or formal) form are often called *exhibition roses*. The flowers are gracefully shaped, with the petals symmetrically arranged in an attractive circular outline coming to rest in a high, pointed center. The arrangement of the unfurling petals should be symmetrical and evenly spaced, with no evident gaps. The center of the bloom should be perfect — well-defined, high, and pointed. From the side view, you should notice a symmetry of structure as the petals unfurl uniformly from the high, pointed center. The outer row of petals should be as close as possible to a horizontal plane. Each variety has its own inherent characteristics. Exhibition roses are at their perfect phase of bloom when they are one-half to three-quarters open.

- ✔ **Garden decorative or informal:** Decorative (or informal) form is evident when a rose doesn't have a well-defined, high, pointed center. A decorative rose may be *ruffled* (wavy) or *cupped* (curved inward) and can have a low center. Decorative roses usually have fewer petals. These roses are often referred to as garden roses, as opposed to exhibition roses.

Climate conditions, culture, and weather can affect rose form. As you get involved in the rose hobby, you may find that form becomes more important to you. If so, buy varieties known as exhibition varieties. If a rose has exhibition form, the catalog description generally says so. Not quite as many roses with exhibition form are available as roses with decorative form, but you still have plenty to choose from.

Following is a list of hybrid teas that we think are top-notch in the exhibition form department:

- **'Crystalline':** White hybrid tea
- **'Keepsake':** Pink hybrid tea
- **'Moonstone':** White and pink hybrid tea
- **'Signature':** Deep pink hybrid tea
- **'St. Patrick':** Yellow hybrid tea
- **'Stainless Steel':** Silvery lavender hybrid tea
- **'Touch of Class':** Pink hybrid tea

Miniature rose form is judged like hybrid tea form. Here's our list of top exhibition minis:

- **'Figurine':** Light pink miniature
- **'Jean Kenneally':** Apricot miniature
- **'Kristin':** Red and white miniature (featured in the color insert)
- **'Minnie Pearl':** Pink miniature
- **'Rainbow's End':** Yellow and red miniature
- **'Snow Bride':** White miniature

Unless you're planning to exhibit your roses at a rose show, however, form really doesn't matter much, as long as it's pleasing to you.

Substance is a quality in a rose that's extremely important to the stability and durability of its form and to its keeping quality, or vase life. Substance is the amount of moisture in the petals, and it's manifested in the texture, firmness, crispness, thickness, and toughness of the petals. You can determine the presence of substance in rose petals by feeling the thickness of the petals and seeing an opalescent sparkle and sheen in pastel-colored roses or a velvety appearance in red roses.

Book III

Roses

Color me pink (and white, and red, and . . .)

With so many colors of roses, we hardly know where to begin! Well, we can start by talking about the elements that contribute to a rose's color:

- ✔ **Brightness:** This term refers to the clarity and vividness of the color, and the absence of cloudiness or muddiness.

- ✔ **Hue:** This component gives visual impact to the eye and distinguishes one color from another.

- ✔ **Chroma:** The purity and intensity of the hue is called the chroma. Ideal chroma has virtually no gray or white in the hue.

Ideal hue is a combination of ideal brightness and ideal chroma.

The American Rose Society (www.ars.org), keeper of the world's rose knowledge, divides rose colors into 18 color classes. Every rose fits into one of these categories, and when anyone registers a new rose with the International Registration Authority — Roses (IRAR), she must specify one of these 18 color classes. Mail-order rose companies may describe colors of roses in terms that are more accurate or whimsical, such as "candy apple red" or "salmon orange," but the official color class is one of the 18 listed here:

White (includes near-white and white blend)

Light yellow

Medium yellow

Deep yellow

Yellow blend

Apricot (includes apricot blend)

Orange (includes orange blend)

Orange-pink

Orange-red

Light pink

Medium pink

Deep pink

Pink blend

Medium red

Dark red

Red blend

Mauve (includes mauve blend)

Russet

For the record, a *blend* is a rose with different shades of one color, or two or more different colors on the same flower, and they're most often grouped by the most dominant color. If a rose has several colors, it's a "multicolored rose" in this book.

The search for a black or blue rose

When someone develops a blue rose or a black rose, the American Rose Society will have to add new categories. But you probably won't see those colors during your lifetime. Hybridizers have just about given up on black because the dark tissue of the petals absorbs so much heat that the flower dies before it opens.

As for blue, well, a couple of research groups send out media releases every year or so saying that they almost have a blue rose. Then their funding gets a shot in the arm. The appearance of a blue rose in the foreseeable future is pretty unlikely, though. The problem is that roses have no natural blue pigment. The pigment that makes mauve roses mauve is really a red pigment which is altered by the pH in the rose's cells. An interesting note: The red pigment in mauve roses doesn't photograph well, showing up as pink on film. That's why the color of many mauve roses isn't quite accurate in most catalog photos unless, of course, the photo is doctored.

Making a blue rose will require some big-time gene splicing, and because biologists haven't even identified most of a rose's genes, splicing 'em will be pretty hard. Also, the chemical response to the pH in the cell, once altered, would have to react favorably with the process of photosynthesis and with the plant's metabolism. A plant scientist could make this project his life's work. But if the scientist were successful, he'd be rich beyond anyone's dreams!

Although these 18 color categories are the official colors of roses, we group them into seven color groups in this book: red, pink, orange, yellow, white, lavender, and multicolored or blends. Rose color can change slightly when a rose is grown in different climates. That's why our "official" color descriptions sometimes vary from the color of the rose in your own garden.

Book III

Roses

Becoming Flower-Full

You know what makes a good rose a good rose — all that stuff about form and substance and colorful petals — but how do those naked-looking sticks you plant in the spring get to the flower stage? The process is nothing short of miraculous.

With the chemical element phosphorus working with elements in the soil that plants need to promote *photosynthesis* (you remember from high school science: light and carbon dioxide go into the leaf, water and oxygen come out), your rose plant develops new canes from two places:

- From the crown of the plant (the bud union on budded roses)
- From the bud eyes located at intervals along the canes

Rose flowers form at the top of a new cane. You can watch the tiny bud as it forms and grows.

Hybrid tea roses

Hybrid teas usually form flowers one to a stem in early spring, but subsequent blooming during the summer often produces two or more buds to the sides of the large main bud. The energy that the plant must expend to make the side buds grow takes vitality away from the larger central bud, so all the flowers will be small.

If you want your hybrid tea flower to reach its full size and potential, you must *disbud* it when the tiny side buds are forming. You can disbud easily by snapping off the side buds when they're very small. Doing so allows the main bud to reach its maximum size. If you like more flowers per plant and don't care about their size, don't bother to disbud.

Floribunda roses

Floribundas usually form flowers in clusters, often called sprays. A cluster forms at the top of a cane, just like a single flower, but instead of only one bud, you have several.

 As the buds grow, the center, or *terminal,* bud grows faster than the others in the cluster and opens several days sooner than the others. If you want all the flowers to open at the same time, you must nip out the center bud. From that point on, all the buds in the cluster mature at the same time. Having all the flowers in a cluster open at the same time is important only if you're going to exhibit the spray in a rose show.

So When Do They Bloom, Anyway?

Few flowering plants are truly *ever-blooming,* producing new flowers from spring to late fall. But roses do bloom on and off throughout the season (from midspring to fall), making them among the most desirable garden plants. Most modern hybrid teas, floribundas, grandifloras, miniatures, and modern shrubs are called *ever-blooming, repeat blooming,* or *free-flowering (remontant),* while many old garden roses flower either once a year or once in the spring and again in the fall.

You can expect your roses to bloom for the first time about six to eight weeks after growth starts in the spring. The flower needs that long to form and mature. The first bloom in the spring, when all your roses are in full bloom, is always the most spectacular, making that time of year — whenever it may be in your area — a favorite time for everyone who loves roses. Modern roses continue to produce flowers throughout the season, and the process for repeat flower development takes the same six weeks or so. But the plants almost always have flowers at different stages of growth, making for a continuous display.

Roses That Bloom Once a Season

Roses that bloom once a season are called *once-flowering*. These are usually old garden roses or antique roses — those discovered or hybridized before 1867. Some antique roses, namely the hybrid musks, hybrid perpetuals, noisettes, Chinas, teas, and about 60 percent of the rugosas, are ever-blooming. But all the others — like albas, centifolias, damasks, and gallicas — bloom only once. However, the display they put on when they do bloom is worth the wait. As if they're saving up all their energy for a whole year and then throwing it all away in an explosion of bloom, old garden roses that bloom only once can produce as many as 50 times more total flowers than ever-blooming roses.

These great roses bloom only once a year in spring: You can read more about them, and others like them in Chapter 3 of Book III:

Book III

Roses

- ✔ **'Empress Josephine':** This old garden rose has rich pink, semi-double flowers, loosely shaped with large, wavy petals and well-branched growth.

- ✔ **'Harison's Yellow',** *Rosa harisonii*: This flower has cupped, soft yellow blooms with golden stamens.

- ✔ **'Ispahan':** This damask rose has bright pink flowers, which are loosely double and very fragrant. Though it blooms only once, its bloom season is long.

- ✔ **'Königin von Dänemark':** This alba rose grows vigorously and produces very full, medium-sized, fragrant blooms of pale pink flowers with a darker center.

- ✔ **'Mme. Hardy':** A damask rose whose flowers are pure white, occasionally tinged pale pink, with a green center. The plant grows vigorously, producing very fragrant, cupped, large blooms.

- ✔ **'Mme. Plantier':** The flowers of this hybrid alba rose are creamy white changing to pure white, with very fully double, flat blooms in clusters. The plant is fragrant, vigorous, and bushy.

Fragrance

Fragrance isn't the main reason most people grow roses, but it sure is a nice benefit. At one time, scent wasn't as desirable an attribute as it is now, and roses were bred for other characteristics, so many of the world's most beautiful modern roses have little or no fragrance. More and more people think that fragrance is an important characteristic in a rose, however, and are now seeking out only fragrant varieties.

An estimated 25 percent of all roses have no fragrance or only a small amount, 20 percent are intensely fragrant, and the remainder lie somewhere in the middle. So if you shop only for fragrant roses, you may miss out on some of the world's most beautiful varieties.

Rosarians have been asking rose hybridizers to try to breed fragrance into new varieties, especially hybrid teas, which, as a group, have long been bred for flower form and are often scentless. But breeding for fragrance isn't as easy as it sounds. A single gene isn't responsible for fragrance — a series of genes is. And that series is elusive. You may think that if you cross one fragrant rose with another, you'll get a fragrant rose. Not so. In fact, when you cross two fragrant varieties, you're just about guaranteed to get no fragrance at all! So when a hybridizer does come up with a new fragrant rose, it's cause for great excitement throughout the rose world.

Nearly every part of a rose can emit fragrance — even the thorns. On moss roses (see Chapter 3 of Book III for more information about them), the fragrance is concentrated in the moss, or the hairs on the sepals and stem. But most often, fragrance, or at least the highest concentration of it, is in the petals of a rose.

What Makes the Fragrance

The fragrance of a rose is, like everything else in the living world, the product of a series of chemical reactions — both within the rose, and with the atmosphere around the rose. Several chemical groups are responsible for floral fragrance, including aromatic alcohols, aldehydes, carbonic acid, essential oils and resins, fatty acids, and phenols. Certain other chemicals, such as citronellol and phenylethyl, have been identified as being responsible for certain scents, but this chemical stuff is complicated (and you probably don't care, anyway). Better to know how your nose interprets those chemicals in everyday terms.

What the nose knows

There are just about as many rose fragrances as there are noses. Certainly, everyone gets something different when they bury their nose in a rose. But several individual scents have been more or less definitively identified. Many experts think that a connection exists between fragrance and other rose characteristics:

- Darker roses are generally more fragrant than lighter colored ones.
- Heavily petalled roses have a stronger or more intense scent than those with fewer petals.
- Red and pink varieties are more closely associated with the classic rose scent.
- The aromas of yellow and white roses are often compared with the fragrance of orrisroot, nasturtiums, and violets, along with other flowery and lemony scents.
- Orange roses are often associated with a fruity scent.

You can, however, count on exceptions to all these "rules."

The following list includes the most commonly identified scents, and at least one rose considered representative of that fragrance:

- **Apple:** 'New Dawn', 'Honorable Lady Lindsay'
- **Apple and clove:** 'Souvenir de la Malmaison'
- **Apple, clove, parsley, and lemon:** 'Eden Rose'
- **Apple, rose, and clove:** 'Zéphirine Drouhin'
- **Bay:** 'Radiance'
- **Classic rose:** 'Scentsational', 'Seattle Scentsation'
- **Clove:** 'Dainty Bess'
- **Fern and moss:** 'Queen Elizabeth'
- **Fruit:** 'Fragrant Plum'
- **Lemon:** 'Confidence'
- **Lily of the valley:** 'Madame Louis Lévêque'
- **Linseed oil:** 'Persian Yellow'
- **Nasturtium:** 'Buccaneer'

Book III

Roses

- **Orrisroot:** 'Golden Masterpiece'
- **Orrisroot and raspberry:** 'Kordes' Perfecta'
- **Orrisroot and violet:** 'Golden Dawn'
- **Quince:** 'Sutter's Gold'
- **Raspberry:** 'Angels Mateu'
- **Rose and clove:** 'Chrysler Imperial', 'Dolly Parton', 'Fragrant Cloud'
- **Rose and lemon:** 'La France', 'Mirandy', 'Tiffany' (featured in the color insert)
- **Rose and nasturtium:** 'Sarah Van Fleet'
- **Rose and parsley:** 'American Beauty'
- **Spice:** 'Soleil d'Or', 'Scentimental', 'Ain't She Sweet', 'Secret'
- **Violet:** 'Margaret McGredy'
- **Wine:** 'Vandael'

Not all these roses are widely available, but the next time you go to one of the public rose gardens (or to visit your rose-growing Uncle Floyd), try comparing the fragrances of different roses. Doing so is kind of fun, especially for kids.

Enhancing your sniffing pleasure

Although fragrance is a genetic characteristic present in some roses and not in others, other factors affect the strength of the fragrance within a fragrant variety. Excellent *culture,* including planting in good soil with correct pH and watering and fertilizing, is vital to ensuring that a rose's fragrance reaches its full potential. (See Chapter 5 of Book III.) Even more important is the amount of moisture in the soil. Rose fragrance is sweetest when plants have adequate water.

Temperature, humidity, wind conditions, and time of day also affect fragrance strength. Roses emit more fragrance later in the day than they do in the morning. Scent is more pronounced on warm, sunny days, is significantly reduced on cloudy days, and is hard to detect when the weather is overcast and cold. After a rose is cut, its fragrance stays with the petals, but the scent is strongest when the room is warm and the air is more humid than dry.

Choosing Fragrant Varieties

Because fragrance is a great selling point, mail-order rose catalog descriptions never keep fragrant varieties a secret. To further narrow your choices, you can always look for those that have been awarded the American Rose Society's James Alexander Gamble Rose Fragrance Award. Not only must a nominee be fragrant, it must also possess a number of other attributes, including vigor, pest- and disease-resistance, form, substance, color, and extreme popularity for more than five years. These qualities, of course, make any rose wonderful, which is why all the Gamble Award winners, even though they have a little age on 'em, should still be readily available at your local garden center.

The following list includes all the roses ever to have won the prestigious Gamble Fragrance Award:

- **1961:** 'Crimson Glory', red hybrid tea
- **1962:** 'Tiffany', pink and yellow blend hybrid tea
- **1965:** 'Chrysler Imperial', red hybrid tea
- **1966:** 'Sutter's Gold', orange-yellow hybrid tea
- **1968:** 'Granada', red multicolored hybrid tea
- **1970:** 'Fragrant Cloud', orange-red hybrid tea
- **1974:** 'Papa Meilland', red hybrid tea
- **1979:** 'Sunsprite', yellow floribunda
- **1986:** 'Double Delight', red and white bicolored hybrid tea
- **1997:** 'Fragrant Hour', orange-pink hybrid tea

You may have noticed that most of these roses are hybrid teas. As we said earlier, many hybrid teas don't have strong fragrance, which is true. But isn't it also interesting that some of the most fragrant roses are hybrid teas? What a wacky world.

Some of our favorite fragrant old garden roses are the following:

- **'Alfred de Dalmas':** Light pink moss
- **'Ispahan':** Medium pink damask
- **'Mme. Hardy':** White damask
- ***Rosa gallica officinalis:*** Light crimson gallica
- **'Sombreuil':** White tea

But don't for one moment believe that a whole bunch of newer roses aren't fragrant and great plants, too. The following varieties are readily available and wonderfully fragrant:

- ✔ **'Melody Parfumée':** Plum grandiflora
- ✔ **'Fragrant Plum':** Mauve grandiflora
- ✔ **'Scentimental':** Red-and-white-striped floribunda
- ✔ **'Scentsational':** Pink and mauve miniature
- ✔ **'Secret':** Pink and white hybrid tea

And don't forget the David Austins, Generosas, and Romanticas (check out Chapter 3 in Book III for more). Most have great fragrance.

Chapter 3

A Rose by Any Other Name

In the big, wonderful world of roses, you have more to choose from than you can imagine. This chapter tells you about the best varieties, organizing them by type and flower color. Just about everything you need to know about each bloom and plant is here. Fasten your seatbelts — it's going to be a colorful ride!

Hunting Down Hybrid Teas

Hybrid teas are by far the most popular type of rose, and probably the most popular flower in the world, period. The blossoms are exquisite, slowly rolling open petal by petal from beautifully formed buds. Each flower may have as many as 60 or more petals and is often more than 5 inches wide. Supported by long, strong stems, hybrid teas are unmatched as cut flowers. And the fragrance, oh the fragrance — not always powerful but, in some varieties, strong enough to carry you away.

Recognizing a hybrid tea

The way in which hybrid teas grow distinguish them from other roses. As shown in Figure 3-1, hybrid teas produce their flowers mostly one bloom to a long stem instead of in clusters. Most hybrid tea plants grow about 3 to 6 feet high and tend to be open rather than bushy, with long, straight, upright canes.

Virtually all hybrid teas are repeat bloomers, producing flowers throughout the growing season.

The hybrid tea rose plants available for purchase are always budded onto hardy rootstock. The *bud union* (the point at which the plants are budded) grows to almost the size of a fist as the plant matures. The bud union is the magic place at the base of the plant where new canes sprout and grow, but it's also the most vulnerable part. If grown without winter protection where winter temperatures reach 10°F (–12°C) or lower, the bud union is the first part of the plant to be damaged or killed by cold and wind.

Hybrid tea roses may require a little extra work, especially in cold climates, but they're no more or less pest- or disease-resistant than any other classification of roses. Hybrid teas are available in almost every color except true green and blue. Some red varieties are so dark that they're almost black. And the mauves are the closest any rose gets to blue. Many of the loveliest hybrid teas are bicolors or blends. See the section, "A Spot of Color: Hybrid Tea Types," later in this chapter for a color-by-color breakdown of the different varieties of hybrid tea roses.

Figure 3-1:
Hybrid tea flowers are typically borne one to a stem and have more than 25 petals. The buds are pointed and the petals unfurl in a spiral around a high center.

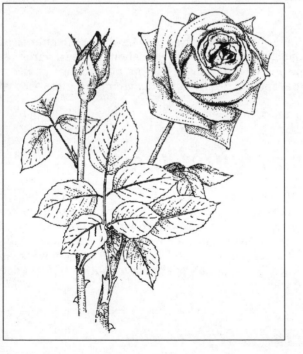

Filling out the form

Hybrid tea flowers with excellent form have long, pointed buds that unfurl in a perfect spiral around a high, pointed center. When viewed from the side, the flowers have a triangular shape, with the outside, or lowest petals, remaining horizontal rather than falling below the horizontal plane. Because great form is always associated with the hybrid teas, other classifications of roses that have really good form are often described as having hybrid tea form.

Planting hybrid teas

Although you can nicely integrate hybrid teas into a perennial border and in landscape plantings, they're easier to care for when they're in beds by themselves. Plant them 18 to 36 inches apart. (You can plant upright varieties a little closer than spreading ones.) Because hybrid teas have little foliage near the base of the plants, and spindly growth in that area should be removed, they may look a little more naked than other types of roses when used in the landscape. However, if you plant low-growing perennials or herbs at their base, hybrid teas can be attractive in flower beds. Hybrid teas also combine beautifully with other plants in large containers. (Book II covers container gardening.)

Growing hybrid teas takes little more effort on your part than growing most other kinds of roses. They need water, fertilizer, and possibly an occasional spray with a good fungicide. They are, however, usually pruned more severely (see Chapter 5 of Book III for pruning information) in late winter or spring than are other classifications of roses. Pruning hybrid teas involves cutting out spindly canes and leaving only the strongest canes to grow. Ideally, prune the strong canes to about 12 to 24 inches in height, but the plant will still do well if winter damage dictates lower pruning. Drastic pruning encourages the plant to produce larger flowers and longer, stronger stems, while less severe spring pruning results in more but smaller flowers often on weak stems.

Book III

Roses

Taking a spot of color: Hybrid tea types

You can choose among hundreds of hybrid tea roses. You can go for color, fragrance, cut flowers, thornless (look for "smooth" in the name), or even a wacky name. Most people choose by color, so that's how we break them down.

Red hybrid teas

Red roses are by far the most popular, but no single variety is considered the "perfect" red rose. Here is a list of a few of our favorite red roses:

- ✔ **'Dublin':** Large, smoky red, double blooms (35 to 40 petals) have a unique raspberry fragrance.

- ✔ **'Mister Lincoln':** Easy-to-grow with deep red buds that open into large, velvety red, double blossoms (30 to 35 petals) with a heady rose fragrance. (This rose is featured in the color insert.)

- ✔ **'Old Smoothie':** Large, deep red, lightly fragrant double blooms (45 to 50 petals) on long, straight, thornless stems.

- ✔ **'Traviata':** Bright red, many petalled (up to 100) flower with old-fashioned fragrance and modern disease resistance.

- ✔ **'Veterans' Honor':** Dark red blooms with a light raspberry fragrance. Portions of the proceeds from sales of this rose are earmarked for the Department of Veterans Affairs.

Pink hybrid teas

You need pink roses, if for no other reason than they go so well with red roses in a garden and in a vase. Following are a few of many popular pink roses:

- ✔ **'Brides Dream':** Slightly fragrant, creamy pastel pink, double (25 to 35 petals) flowers.

- ✔ **'Color Magic':** Apricot-pink buds open into large, salmon-pink, double blooms (25 to 30 petals) that gradually fade to deep pink. Fruity fragrance.

- ✔ **'Dainty Bess':** Free-blooming rose with clusters of single (5-petalled) pink blossoms centered with maroon stamens. The lightly fragrant flowers resemble the blooms of a dogwood. (This rose is featured in the color insert.)

- ✔ **'Elizabeth Taylor':** Elegant, large, dark pink, double (30 to 35 petals) blooms with even deeper pink edges that put out a slight, spicy fragrance.

- ✔ **'Pink Peace':** Deep pink, double rose (50 to 60 petals) with a strong rose fragrance.

Orange hybrid teas

Orange is a strong color; if you're not careful, it can really mess up the visual impact of other colors you choose for your garden. Feel free to mix orange with reds, whites, and yellows or use it by itself, but watch out if orange gets around pink or lavender. Those color combinations are jarring to the eye.

Here are orange (or almost orange) hybrid teas available at the nursery or in catalogs:

- ✔ **'Brandy':** Beautifully formed, double blossoms (25 to 30 petals) bloom in rich shades of light apricot-orange. Mildly sweet fragrance.

- ✔ **'Dolly Parton':** Bright, coppery, reddish orange, double blossoms (35 to 40 petals) have an alluring, strong, spicy clove fragrance.

- ✔ **'Just Joey':** Rich apricot, double flowers (25 to 30 petals) emit a strong, fruity fragrance. Free-blooming and easy to grow.

- ✔ **'Spice Twice':** Bright coral-orange, double blossoms (about 30 petals) with a lighter cream-orange on the back side of the petals have a slight fragrance.

- ✔ **'Voodoo':** A blend of orange and yellow with a touch of scarlet, these large, double flowers (30 to 35 petals) have a strong, fruity fragrance.

Yellow hybrid teas

Yellow roses are about as sunny as you can get — and they look so good with green-foliaged plants. Here are a few of our favorites:

- ✔ **'Elina':** Soft pastel yellow, double flower (30 to 35 petals). Light fragrance.

- ✔ **'Golden Masterpiece':** Huge, golden yellow, double flowers (30 to 35 petals) with a strong licorice-like fragrance.

- ✔ **'Houston':** Large, intense yellow, double blooms (35 to 40 petals). Nice, fruity fragrance.

- ✔ **'Midas Touch':** Easy-to-grow, bright yellow, double flowers (25 to 30 petals) are produced in abundance. Moderate, fruity fragrance.

- ✔ **'Oregold':** Large, deep golden yellow, double flowers with a slightly fruity fragrance.

White hybrid teas

White hybrid teas light up the garden or a bouquet, making every other color look brighter. All the varieties in the following list are good choices:

- ✔ **'Garden Party':** Creamy white, double blooms (25 to 30 petals) with a touch of pink on the outside petals boast a light fragrance.

- ✔ **'Honor':** Large, clear white, double flowers have exquisite form and substance. Lightly fragrant.

- ✔ **'John F. Kennedy':** Double rose (40 to 45 petals) that starts out greenish white in the bud and gradually turns clean white as the flower opens. Moderate-to-strong fragrance.

- ✔ **'Pascali':** White, well-formed, double flowers (30 to 35 petals) with a light fragrance. Easy to grow.

- ✔ **'Sheer Bliss':** Soft, creamy white with a blush of pink, the double flowers (about 35 petals) have a strong, sweet fragrance.

Lavender hybrid teas

As much as people want to call these roses blue, they're really lavender or purple. Each rose in the following list can add a delicate color accent to your garden:

Book III

Roses

- ✔ **'Barbra Streisand':** Large, mauve-pink, double blossoms (more than 35 petals) blushing darker around edges, with a rich rose-citrus fragrance.

- ✔ **'Blue Nile':** Large, dark purplish lavender, double flowers (25 to 30 petals) with a fruity fragrance.

- ✔ **'Heirloom':** Deep lilac, double blooms (30 to 35 petals) are darker purple on the edges of the petals and have a strong, sweet fragrance.

- ✔ **'Moon Shadow':** Strongly fragrant, nicely formed, deep lavender, double blooms (30 to 35 petals) borne in clusters.

- ✔ **'Purple Passion':** Dark purple, double flowers (about 30 petals) with strong lemony fragrance make a unique cut flower.

- ✔ **'Stainless Steel':** Pale silvery lavender, double blooms (25 to 30 petals). Strongly fragrant and easy to grow. Improved version of 'Sterling Silver'.

Multicolored hybrid teas

These whirlwinds of color change complexion on a daily basis. How distinct their colors are usually depends on where they're grown. Before you buy a variety, check it out at a local rose garden to make sure that you're getting what you want. Any selection from the following list will make a splash in your garden:

- ✔ **'Broadway':** Large orange-yellow, double blossoms (30 to 35 petals) edged with red emit a strong, spicy fragrance.

- ✔ **'Diana, Princess of Wales':** Creamy white petals gracefully touched with a clear pink blush. Large, double flowers (30 to 35 petals). Sweet fragrance. A portion of the proceeds from the sales is donated to the Princess of Wales Memorial Fund.

- ✔ **'Granada':** Swirling, ever-changing shades of gold, yellow, pink, and red adorn these double blossoms (18 to 25 petals) with a strong, spicy fragrance.

- ✔ **'Monet':** Huge, double rose (30 to 35 petals) in blended shades of pink, yellow, peach, and apricot. Moderately fragrant.

- ✔ **'Peace':** Large, perfectly formed, double blossoms (40 to 45 petals) are bright yellow edged with pink and emit a light, fruity fragrance.

- ✔ **'Secret':** Lovely, creamy white, double flowers (30 to 35 petals) are edged with soft pink and carry a strong, spicy fragrance.

Going Gangbusters with Grandifloras

Grandiflora roses always seem to be having some type of identity crisis. The class was created around 1954 to accommodate 'Queen Elizabeth', a tall, vigorous hybrid that has large flowers — like a hybrid tea — but long stems that grow in clusters — like a floribunda. The 'Queen' is still very popular, but grandifloras as a class haven't really made the big time in the rose world yet. In fact, England doesn't even recognize grandifloras as a true class of roses. Instead, they call them clustered-flowered and include them with floribundas. Still, with the introduction of some great new varieties, the future is starting to look good for grandifloras.

As a class, grandifloras bear large, long-stemmed, hybrid tea-like flowers (see Figure 3-2), either in clusters or one to a stem. Generally, grandiflora plants are tall, hardy, and vigorous, but plant habits can vary a bit. Some of the newer varieties are smaller, more compact plants.

Figure 3-2:
Grandiflora flowers resemble hybrid teas, but more often are born in clusters.

Caring for grandifloras

Care for grandifloras as you would hybrid teas — watering, fertilizing, winter protection, pruning practices, and so on are pretty much the same. (You may want to prune 'Queen Elizabeth' a touch higher — don't cut it as far back — in winter, especially if you're using her for a tall hedge.) Gardeners often use grandifloras like hybrid teas, planting them in rows for cut flowers. However, they tend to put on a better show of color than many hybrid teas do, so don't hesitate to use them in the landscape (see Book II for more on landscaping).

Tall varieties make useful hedges or background plants. You can mix lower-growing types, such as 'Crimson Bouquet', with other flowers in perennial borders.

Coloring with grandifloras

The following sections list some of our favorite grandifloras.

Red and pink grandifloras

Here are some beautiful red and pink grandifloras to consider for your garden:

- ✔ **'Candy Apple':** Lustrous apple-red blossoms with a slight fragrance and lots of petals bloom in a cupped form.

- ✔ **'Fame!':** Large, beautifully formed, deep pink, lightly scented double blossoms (30 to 35 petals).

- ✔ **'Love':** Bright red flowers with a silvery reverse and 35 petals. Slight, spicy fragrance.

- ✔ **'Prima Donna':** Deep, fuschia-pink flowers have 27 petals. Light fragrance.

- ✔ **'Queen Elizabeth':** The first grandiflora, and still the finest. Clear pink, ruffled blooms adorn the stately, tall bush in long-stemmed clusters. The abundant blooms are high-centered or cup-shaped, moderately fragrant, and vigorous.

Orange grandifloras

Choosing a favorite orange grandiflora is tough, but any of these are contenders:

- ✔ **'Candelabra':** Glowing coral orange, double flowers (about 25 petals) have exceptional form and a slight fragrance.

- ✔ **'Montezuma':** Produces loads of long-stemmed, reddened coral-orange flowers with 30 to 35 petals and a light scent.

- ✔ **'Olé':** Long-lived, ruffled flowers with brilliant orange-red tones that don't fade. The blooms have 40 to 45 petals and a slight fragrance.

- ✔ **'Reba McEntire':** Bright orange-red, double blooms with about 30 petals are borne in clusters and have a slight fragrance.

- ✔ **'Solitude':** Brilliant bright orange blooms with hints of yellow and gold and 30 to 35 petals show their best color with heat. Mild, spicy fragrance.

Yellow and white grandifloras

We like the following grandiflora roses. Of these two white grandifloras, only 'White Lightnin' has stood the test of time:

- ✔ **'Gold Medal':** Nearly constant supply of dark gold buds and richly fragrant, golden-yellow flowers have a flirtation of red at the tips and 30 to 35 petals. (This rose is featured in the color insert.)

- ✔ **'Mt. Hood':** Masses of full and fleshy ivory-white flowers with 40 to 45 petals on a bushy plant. Light fragrance.

- ✔ **'Shining Hour':** Deep yellow, cup-shaped flowers grow singly and in clusters or sprays with 33 petals and have a moderate fragrance.

- ✔ **'White Lightnin':** Small, white clusters of cupped, very fragrant flowers with 26 to 32 petals burst forth all season on the low growing, robust bush.

Lavender grandifloras

The rose world contains several great lavender (or mauve) grandifloras. Take your pick of these beautifully fragrant varieties:

- ✔ **'Cologne':** Light lavender, intensely fragrant double flowers with 17 to 25 petals.

- ✔ **'Fragrant Plum':** The buds are long and pointed; elegant, deep plum flowers have good form and a strong, fruity fragrance. Color brightens in heat.

- ✔ **'Lagerfeld':** Light silvery lavender, double flowers (30 to 35 petals) have a strong fragrance.

- ✔ **'Melody Parfumée':** Deep purple buds open into lavender double blooms (about 30 petals) gradually fading with a silvery sheen. Sweet, spicy fragrance.

- ✔ **'Spellcaster':** Deep mauve and lavender blooms with 26 to 40 petals and intense fragrance.

Book III

Roses

Multicolored grandifloras

All these are good, but 'Octoberfest' really shines:

- ✔ **'Arizona':** High-centered blooms with 35 to 40 petals are blended tones of bronzy orange and mellow pink that don't fade. Powerful fragrance.

- ✔ **'Heart O' Gold':** Deep golden-yellow blooms edged with soft pink. Flowers have 30 to 35 petals and a strong, fruity fragrance.

- ✔ **'Octoberfest':** Autumn shades of red, orange, and yellow bloom in large clusters of double blooms with about 17 to 25 petals. Pleasing, fruity fragrance.

- ✔ **'Quaker Star':** The double flowers with 35 to 40 petals are dark pink with orange tips and orange reverse. Free-blooming but has no fragrance.

Peeking at Polyanthas and Floribundas

Polyanthas and floribundas are the workhorses of the rose garden. Of all the different kinds of roses, they're the most prolific bloomers, plus they're useful in the landscape, in perennial borders, and in large group or mass plantings. Most varieties need winter protection in areas where temperatures fall below 10°F (−12°C), but the springtime bloom makes it all worth it.

Pretty polyanthas

Polyanthas originated in France in the late 1800s, and only a few varieties are still widely grown. But polyanthas are important, not only as excellent roses, but also as the forerunners to the very popular and useful floribundas. Polyanthas are compact plants that usually grow about 2 to 3 feet high. And do they ever bloom! They virtually cover themselves in large, flat clusters of small flowers (usually about an inch wide) in shades of white, pink, red, orange, and yellow. (See Figure 3-3.) Plus, they bloom and bloom again, all season long.

Figure 3-3:
Polyanthas
bear small
flowers
in large
clusters.

Polyantha leaves are small and narrow, and the plants are fairly hardy, at least more so than hybrid teas. The most common polyantha, 'The Fairy', is one of the hardiest and most reliable, thriving without winter protection even to −25°F (−31°C).

Fancy floribundas

Early in the twentieth century, someone got the bright idea to cross the generous-blooming polyanthas with the larger-flowering hybrid teas. The results are what we now call the floribundas, which, as their name suggests, offer flowers in abundance. Today, floribundas are one of the most useful types of roses. The flowers emerge in large clusters like polyanthas, but the individual blooms are bigger, often with that beautiful hybrid tea form, and most are great cutting flowers. They really shine in the landscape, where they can brighten a dreary corner of the yard, highlight a garden ornament, or keep a perennial border wonderfully colorful all season long.

Floribundas come in all the hybrid tea colors, which is probably almost any flower color you can think of except blue and true green. The plants grow from 3 to 5 feet high and may be upright or low and spreading — or anything in between. Their range in plant shape makes them versatile landscape plants. (See Book II for more on landscaping.) Some floribunda varieties have compact growth habits and are easy to tuck into small areas of the garden. Others grow tall and wide and exhibit many of the characteristics of modern shrubs. "Grow as shrub" is a common description in rose catalogs. Choose varieties that suit the area in which you want to plant them.

Book III

Roses

All this and easy to grow, too

Floribundas and polyanthas are among the easiest roses to grow. Most have good disease resistance and need little care other than water and fertilizer. Removing spent flowers during the growing season is important if you want a bush to keep producing flowers. You can just get out your hedge shears to cut off faded flowers. In warm climates, you may need to whack off a cane or two during the season to keep the plant within bounds, and then cut back the whole plant 25 to 50 percent in winter. But in cold climates, floribundas need pruning only in early spring. Cut off any part of the plant that was damaged over the winter.

Today's rose hybridizers are working very hard to breed disease resistance into new varieties of roses. Therefore, many of the newer floribunda varieties are naturally resistant to the diseases that attack our favorite flower. Rose culture, especially for the new floribundas, is getting simpler every year. If a floribunda variety excels in the disease resistance department, you can bet that the rose catalogs will say so. So if you don't care much for spraying for black spot and powdery mildew, choose disease-resistant varieties. On the other hand, as is always the case, many of the most distinctive and desirable varieties are susceptible to disease but respond nicely to disease-control measures. It just goes to show you: If it's not one thing . . .

Even though these plants tend to be slightly hardier than hybrid teas, you may still need to provide winter protection if you live where winter temperatures fall to 10°F (−12°C) or lower.

A few of our favorites

The following sections list our favorite floribunda and polyantha varieties.

Red roses

Here are four great red floribundas. You can't lose with any of them:

- ✔ **'Europeana':** Large clusters of dark crimson, long-lasting blossoms with 15 to 20 petals. Slightly fragrant flowers bloom abundantly throughout the season.

- ✔ **'Frensham':** A glorious red rose with a light scent that bursts open to reveal feathery, golden stamens. An excellent midseason and repeat bloomer.

- ✔ **'Lavaglut':** Deep, velvety red, ruffled blossoms are double (25 to 30 petals) with light fragrance and borne in never-ending clusters.

- ✔ **'Showbiz':** An orange-red workhorse whose 29 to 30 petals are rarely out of bloom. Excellent ever-blooming mass of color on dark green, glossy leaves.

Pink roses

All the roses in this batch of pink floribundas and polyanthas are good choices:

- ✔ **'Columbus':** Egg-shaped, pointed buds unfurl into deep, rose-pink blooms with 28 petals carried singly or in sprays of three to five.

- ✔ **'Fashion':** Small, red-tipped buds unfold into lustrous coral-pink flowers with 21 to 24 petals. Sweet and fruity fragrance. Spreading shrub, always in bloom.

- ✔ **'Johann Strauss':** Large, candy-pink, very double blooms (up to 100 petals) with a strong lemon verbena fragrance.

- ✔ **'Nearly Wild':** The bright pink, single (5 petals) flowers have a sweet, fruity fragrance. Very hardy.

- ✔ **'Playgirl':** Flowers almost continuously with showy, large clusters of hot magenta-pink with five to seven petals and a slight fragrance.
- ✔ **'Sea Pearl':** Stylish, long, pointed buds unfurl with free-blooming intensity, revealing pink blooms with creamy yellow reverses and 24 petals. Blooms tend to occur early to midseason in clusters and have a light fragrance.

GARDEN JARGON

The *reverse* is the underside of a petal. A different color on the reverse makes for visual interest both coming and going.

Orange roses

These floribundas make a stunning statement in bright orange and apricot:

- ✔ **'Brass Band':** Large blooms of 25 to 30 petals mix bright shades of melon with subtle apricot and lemon reverses. Moderately fragrant.
- ✔ **'Gingersnap':** Long, pointed buds open into highly ruffled, pure bright orange blossoms. Large (30 to 35 petals), lightly scented flowers singly or in clusters.
- ✔ **'Livin' Easy':** Large apricot-orange blooms with 25 to 30 petals come and come and come and keep coming. Moderately fruity scent.
- ✔ **'Sarabande':** Spectacular orange-red flowers with 10 to 15 petals open to reveal bright yellow stamens. Blooms continuously in flashy clusters.
- ✔ **'Trumpeter':** Produces abundant and continuous brilliant orange-red flowers with 35 to 40 wavy petals. Slightly fragrant plant is disease resistant.

Book III

Roses

Yellow roses

These yellow floribundas are as clear and bright as a sunny day:

- ✔ **'Amber Queen':** A combination of amber yellow color, sweet scent, and glossy green foliage with 25 to 30 petals. High degree of disease resistance.
- ✔ **'Brite Lites':** Provides never-ending clusters of colorful, vivid yellow ruffled blooms (28 to 32 petals) that don't fade. Moderate fragrance.
- ✔ **'Sun Flare':** Bright lemon-yellow blossoms of 25 to 30 petals in large clusters. Lightly fragrant flowers bloom all season. Highly disease resistant.
- ✔ **'Sunsprite':** The best of the yellow floribundas has every quality you could ask for — nonstop bloom, fragrance, vigor, and disease resistance. Flowers are a glowing lemon-yellow with 25 to 30 petals and glossy, dark green leaves.

White roses

Two of our all-time favorite roses, 'French Lace' and 'Iceberg', are among these white floribundas. Both are top-of-the-line landscape plants.

✔ **'Class Act':** Produces continuous clusters of pure white semidouble flowers that open flat and bloom continuously. Mild fragrance.

✔ **'French Lace':** Large, full blossoms with 35 creamy white petals bloom on cutting-length stems. Mild, fruity scent. Disease resistant but not winter hardy.

✔ **'Iceberg':** One of the best white roses for landscape planting, and probably the best-known rose in the world. Not only is it robust, beautiful, and delightful to smell, but it also flowers freely and profusely with little care.

✔ **'Margaret Merril':** Large, soft white blossoms with a hybrid tea-type shape and 28 petals. Extremely fragrant.

Lavender roses

Here are all six of the great lavender floribundas:

✔ **'Angel Face':** Unusual, deep mauve flowers, with 35 to 40 ruffled petals, send out an ambrosial fragrance that permeates the air throughout the summer.

✔ **'Blueberry Hill':** Clear lilac, sweetly fragrant flowers (8 to 15 petals), grow in clusters on long stems perfect for cutting. Displays all summer long.

✔ **'Cotillion':** Light lavender purple blooms are doubles with at least 40 petals and an English rose look. Pleasantly fragrant.

✔ **'Intrigue':** Red-purple buds give way to velvety, plum flowers with an intense perfume and 25 to 30 petals. Blooms midseason with good repeat blooms. Disease resistant but not winter hardy without protection.

✔ **'Love Potion':** Deep lavender flowers, with 20 to 25 petals. Strong fragrance.

✔ **'Shocking Blue':** Clear lavender with a powerful fragrance, and 25 to 30 petals on medium-to-tall, upright bushes.

Multicolored roses

Here's a dazzling collection of multicolored floribundas:

✔ **'Betty Boop':** Semidouble ivory yellow flowers (6 to 12 petals) edged in bright red. Moderately fruity fragrance. Free-blooming even without regular *deadheading* (regularly removing faded flowers). This rose is featured in the color insert.

✔ **'Eyepaint':** Buds open into lightly scented scarlet flowers of five to six petals with white centers and golden stamens. Flowers continuously.

✔ **'Judy Garland':** Strongly perfumed blossoms with 30 to 35 petals blush from yellow to hot orange to scarlet. Blooms abundantly in clusters.

  ✔ **'Purple Tiger':** Deep purple color with stripes and flecks of white and
  pink. Large flowers (26 to 40 petals) bloom in small clusters. Nice
  fragrance.

  ✔ **'Sweet Vivien':** Pink, lightly scented flowers (17 petals) with soft yellow
  centers. Bloom in clusters. Large, pear-shaped hips are colorful in the fall.

Managing Miniature Roses

Miniatures, shown in Figure 3-4, are perfectly scaled, smaller versions of
larger roses, with all the colors, forms, substance, and often, fragrance of full-
sized roses. Like other types of roses, each variety of miniature rose has different characteristics, with plant size ranging between 6 inches and 4 feet or
more and plant shapes that include bushy, compact, climbing, and cascading.
But no matter what the shape or growth habit, a good miniature rose has
flowers and leaves in perfect proportion. Smaller definitely doesn't mean less
attractive, and in most cases, smaller does mean easier to grow. Their smaller
habit makes miniatures ideal for growing in containers (see Book II for more
on container gardening). The flowers provide bright and constant spots of
color throughout the growing season, and you can cut their flowers for mini-
bouquets and arrangements. The selection of varieties is awesome, and hundreds of new ones are introduced each year.

Book III

Roses

Figure 3-4:
A miniature
flower looks
quite similar
to a flower
on a full-size
plant.

Miniatures are wonderful landscape plants. (See Book II for more on landscaping.) Because the plants are so small when you buy them, it seems as if they'll take forever to grow and put on a good show. But don't let that small size fool you. Miniature roses reach full size quickly, and they flower big-time all season long. Miniatures make beautiful up-front plants. Use them to edge a flower border or walkway, or plant them at the base of taller-growing plants.

Tiny but tough: Protecting and pruning

Miniature roses are actually pretty tough plants. They're almost always propagated and grown on their own roots, which gives them greater hardiness in cold weather than many other types of roses. Like most plants, however, they're not real thrilled with harsh winter winds and the nasty freeze-and-thaw cycles that some winters bring. Even though your miniature roses will most likely live and do fine the next season no matter what you do or don't do, if you live where temperatures regularly fall below 10°F (–12°C), they'll suffer less damage and thrive more readily if you mulch the base of the plant with leaves for winter protection.

Smaller plants mean smaller roots, and smaller roots don't grow very deep in the soil. So, if Mother Nature doesn't provide rain, your mini-rose needs more frequent watering. Also, smaller plants require smaller doses of fertilizer. Generally, plan to fertilize a third as much, twice as often.

As with full-sized roses, deadheading is pretty much all the pruning you need to do during the growing season. You don't need to cut back minis in the fall, and in spring you need only prune away the dead parts. If you have lots of minis to prune, a hedge trimmer does a great job. Shear plants back about halfway, meaning that a 12-inch-high plant should be about 6 inches tall after pruning. For fewer — but bigger — flowers, you can prune minis just as you would hybrid teas.

Don't believe people who try to convince you that growing miniature roses indoors on a windowsill is easy. A miniature may stay in bloom for a week or two inside, but eventually the plant needs to go outside where light is sufficient and conditions are better for healthy growth. Those who do have success growing miniatures indoors usually have a greenhouse or provide some type of supplemental lighting.

The lowdown on miniature varieties

You don't have to look far to find miniature roses, which seem to show up in places where you don't usually see rose plants for sale, such as supermarkets and florist shops. But if you want varieties that really have proven themselves in garden situations, you're better off buying from a local nursery or a mail-order catalog that specializes in roses. The following sections list some of our favorites — a nice mix of the new and the tried and true.

Red miniatures

Here are some of our favorite red miniatures:

- ✔ **'Black Jade':** Pointed, near-black buds open to chocolatey red blossoms on long stems. The blooms have 30 petals and a slight fragrance.

- ✔ **'Cherry Hi':** Dark red double blooms with little fragrance are held generously above a compact plant. Free-blooming even in hot climates.

- ✔ **'Jingle Bells':** Large, bright red blooms have a lighter reverse.

- ✔ **'Miss Flippins':** Beautifully formed double blooms are bright red with pink reverse and make great cut flowers.

- ✔ **'Old Glory':** Large, lightly fragrant, red blossoms of 23 to 25 petals grow alone or in small sprays.

Pink miniatures

You have many pink miniatures to choose from:

- ✔ **'Angelica Renae':** Free-blooming, medium pink blooms with a splash of orange at the base form a nice, rounded, 2-foot-high bush.

- ✔ **'Cuddles':** Deep coral-pink petals unfurl evenly into slightly fragrant, long-lasting blossoms with 55 to 60 petals. Disease resistant and winter hardy.

- ✔ **'Judy Fischer':** Rose pink flowers last for weeks and don't fade, even in hot weather. The hybrid tea-shaped flower carries 24 to 30 slightly fragrant petals.

- ✔ **'Minnie Pearl':** Perfectly formed, double pink blooms have a touch of yellow at the base. Nicely shaped, slightly spreading bush grows 18 to 24 inches high.

- ✔ **'Renny':** Wonderful pink flowers with 25 pointed petals have a moderate fragrance and a generous bloom. Bushy, thornless plant.

Orange miniatures

You can't miss with any of these eight great orange miniatures:

- ✔ **'Dee Bennett':** Nicely formed flowers in blended shades of orange and yellow are borne singly and in clusters; they have 25 petals and a light fruity fragrance.

- ✔ **'Little Flame':** The bright orange, double (25 petals) blooms fade to burnt orange and have a slight fragrance.

Book III

Roses

- ✔ **'Mary Marshall':** Deep coral flowers with a yellow base blossom all season. Hybrid tea-type blooms have a slight fragrance.

- ✔ **'Orange Honey':** Bright orange-yellow, double (23 to 25 petals) with a fruity fragrance, this rose is perfect for pots or hanging baskets.

- ✔ **'Playgold':** Bright orange, single blooms with little fragrance take on shades of pink as they fade. Excellent disease resistance.

Yellow miniatures

These are all excellent yellow miniatures:

- ✔ **'Behold':** Produces abundance of nicely formed, bright yellow flowers.

- ✔ **'Golden Halo':** Bright yellow blooms sometimes have a touch of red. The flowers have a slight fragrance and 24 to 26 petals.

- ✔ **'Rise 'n' Shine':** Abundant and continuous blooms of brilliant yellow flowers with 30 to 40 petals set against dark green foliage.

- ✔ **'Little Tommy Tucker':** Buttery yellow, double flowers with a slight fragrance. Free-blooming, bushy plant. Excellent disease resistance.

- ✔ **'Yellow Doll':** Free-blooming, the large, light yellow flowers have 24 to 30 petals and a slight fragrance. Disease resistant and winter hardy.

White miniatures

These are all top-notch white miniatures:

- ✔ **'Fairhope':** Perfectly formed white to light yellow blooms. Slight fragrance.

- ✔ **'Gourmet Popcorn':** Cascading clusters of small, flat, bright white blooms (15 to 20 petals) explode all over this vigorous plant. Extremely fragrant.

- ✔ **'Little Eskimo':** Fluffy white, double blossoms (55 petals). Little fragrance.

- ✔ **'Snow Bride':** Formal, creamy white buds open to large, full blossoms with 20 to 25 petals and a mild scent. Forms the best flowers in moderate climates.

Lavender miniatures

Here are five of our favorite lavender-flowered miniature roses:

- ✔ **'Incognito':** Unusually colored flowers of dusty light mauve with a yellow reverse. Bush is always covered with flowers and grows to 30 inches tall.

- ✔ **'Lavender Delight':** Free-blooming, showy, semidouble to double (10 to 20 petals) lavender flowers have little fragrance.

- ✔ **'Lavender Jewel':** The mauve color of the open, cup-shaped flowers (12 to 20 petals) stays true. Little fragrance, but blooms throughout the season.

✔ **'Scentsational':** Nicely fragrant flowers are pink, edged with mauve, and have a creamy pink reverse. Easy to grow, 24- to 30-inch plant.

✔ **'Winsome':** Big, pointed buds and large, shapely, magenta blooms with 35 to 40 petals appear freely all season. Little fragrance but easy to grow.

Multicolored miniatures

These are all popular miniatures — choose your favorite color combination:

✔ **'Child's Play':** Pink and white blossoms have a classic hybrid tea shape. Easy to grow and sweet smelling. Foliage is dark green and very disease resistant.

✔ **'Dreamglo':** Long-lasting, double flowers are red, blended with white at the base. The 50 petals have a slight fragrance. Blooms with abandon midseason.

✔ **'Hot Tamale':** Beautifully formed, double blooms start out yellow then turn hot shades of pink, orange, and red.

✔ **'Magic Carrousel':** Open or cup-shaped, white blooms with a fine, red edge. Mild fragrance and 30 to 35 petals. Blooms continuously and is easy to grow.

✔ **'Splish Splash':** Double blooms in ever-changing shades of yellow and pink put out a nice fragrance.

✔ **'Tropical Twist':** Slightly fragrant double bloom (20 to 25 petals) in tropical sunset shades of orange and pink.

Collecting Climbing Roses

Climbing roses represent a diverse group of plants, producing long, supple canes that, in some varieties, can reach over 20 feet long. The plants aren't true vines in that they don't cling to, climb on, or in any way attach themselves to an upright support. Left on their own, they tend to be large, sprawling shrubs. But most climbing roses aren't left on their own. You usually tie them in an upright fashion to some type of vertical support, such as a fence, arbor, trellis, or wall. But you don't just train them straight up to the sky. Grown like that, they would only bloom at the very tip-top of the canes. So that you can benefit from climbing roses, you develop more *floriferous* (gotta love that word, which means blooms a lot) horizontal side shoots.

So many climbers, so little time

Climbers come in many different types, but most climbing roses fall into one of the following categories:

✔ **Large-flowered climbers**: The most popular and widely used climbing roses produce clusters of flowers (see Figure 3-5) on stiff, arching canes that generally reach 8 to 15 feet. They produce flowers throughout the growing season, but they bloom most heavily in spring. Large-flowered climbers are generally hardy to 15° to 20°F (–10° to –7°C) and need winter protection wherever temperatures regularly drop lower. They are, nonetheless, your best bet for a climbing rose if you live in an area with cold winters.

✔ **Climbing sports:** These climbers — generally named after their original variety, such as 'Climbing Queen Elizabeth' from the famous, pink grandiflora — result from unusually vigorous canes that grow from popular hybrid teas, grandifloras, shrubs, and floribundas. They produce the beautiful flowers of their shrubby parent on a more sprawling plant. Climbing sports don't usually bloom as heavily as large-flowered climbers, but do produce flowers with excellent size and character throughout the growing season. Generally hardy to 10° to 20°F (–12° to –7°C), these plants need protection in regions with colder winters.

✔ **Ramblers:** Because they bloom only once a year, in spring, ramblers are less popular than other types of climbing roses. These very vigorous plants can grow up to 20 feet tall. They're hardy to about 10°F (or about –12°C).

✔ **Climbing miniatures:** Some are sports of popular miniature varieties. Others were created by crossing miniatures with more vigorous roses.

Figure 3-5:
Some climbers produce clusters of flowers.

Tending to climbers

Climbing roses need a little different care than most other roses, particularly when it comes to pruning, training, and winter protection. You can find more information about those subjects in Chapter 5 of Book III. Otherwise, watering, fertilizing, and controlling pests on climbers is similar to doing all those things to other types of roses.

Climbers in every color of the rainbow

Climbers can grow up and over whatever you can tie them to and produce flowers in all the rose colors, as proven by the following lists of climbers by color.

Red climbers

All these red varieties are large-flowered climbers:

- **'Altissimo':** Large, lipstick red, saucer-like flowers (seven petals) display showy golden stamens, in clusters of about a dozen blooms. Mildly fragrant blooms last for days. Repeat blooming quickly throughout the growing season.

- **'Don Juan':** Deep red flowers, with an intense fragrance and 35 petals, bloom profusely from midseason on. Disease resistant. Not dependably winter hardy.

- **'Dynamite':** Dark red, clustered flowers with 40 petals. Slight fragrance.

- **'Tempo':** Deep red and full flowers, with 35 to 45 petals. Slight fragrance.

Pink climbers

'America' is always a favorite from these pink climbers:

- **'America':** Large, well-formed, cup-shaped flowers of coral pink have 40 to 45 petals and a spicy fragrance. Flowers bloom on old and new wood.

- **'Dr. J. H. Nicolas':** Heavily fragrant, large, round, rose-pink flowers, with 45 to 50 petals. Blooms profusely. Disease resistant and winter hardy.

- **'Dream Weaver':** Slightly fragrant, coral-pink blooms in large clusters. Easy to grow and train.

- **'New Dawn':** Large, pale pink flowers with 35 to 40 petals. Sweet perfume. Blooms continuously throughout the season. Very hardy.

- **'William Baffin':** Unscented, deep pink flowers in clusters containing as many as 30 blossoms with 20 petals each. Winter hardy.

Book III

Roses

Orange and yellow climbers

Orange is a rare color among climbers, but the following list offers the best of what's available, along with two great yellow climbers:

- ✔ **'Autumn Sunset':** Climbing shrub, with rich, apricot-gold, double flowers (20 to 25 petals) in large clusters. Strong, fruity fragrance.
- ✔ **'High Noon':** Climbing hybrid tea. Large, light yellow, loosely cupped flowers, with 25 to 30 petals, have a spicy fragrance and bloom all season.
- ✔ **'Rocketeer':** Climbing miniature. Small, coral-orange blooms have 15 to 20 petals and a slight fragrance.
- ✔ **'Westerland':** Reblooming climbing shrub, with Beautiful apricot-orange, double (18 to 25 petals), borne in large clusters. Strong fragrance.

White climbers

You have two good ones to choose from, both large-flowered climbers:

- ✔ **'Lace Cascade':** Fragrant, full, white flowers with 26 to 40 petals grow in small and large clusters amidst large, dark green leaves.
- ✔ **'White Dawn':** Free-flowering and vigorous, this rose delivers loads of bright white, ruffled flowers, with 30 to 35 petals, and a sweet perfume.

Lavender climbers

Few lavender large-flowered climbers exist, but you can get the 'Climbing Blue Girl,' a sport of the hybrid tea rose described earlier in this chapter.

Multicolored climbers

Following are four of our favorite multicolored climbers:

- ✔ **'Dortmund':** Climbing shrub. Nail-polish red blossoms, which have a small, white eye, bloom in clusters. The rose has five to eight petals. Moderate scent.
- ✔ **'Fourth of July':** Large, open faced, semidouble blooms (12 to 15 petals), borne in clusters, are bright red, striped with white. Sweet apple fragrance. (This rose is featured in the color insert.)

- ✔ **'Joseph's Coat':** Large-flowered climber. Kaleidoscopic colors — shades of red, pink, orange, and yellow — dance on the petals of this very popular rose, often in the same cluster. The lightly scented roses have 23 to 28 petals. The plant is somewhat tender and susceptible to mildew.
- ✔ **'Shadow Dancer':** Large-flowered climber. Ruffled, double blooms (15 to 20 petals), in swirling shades of light and dark pink. Mild fragrance.

Shimmying after Shrub Roses

Shrub roses are a diverse group of plants that don't neatly fit into any of the other rose categories. Shrubs, especially the modern ones, are popular because of their long season of bloom, pest and disease resistance, and versatility in the landscape.

A shrub by any other name . . .

When we say that shrubs are a diverse group of plants, we really mean it. Many of these rose plants are more different than they are alike. Some are neat, compact little plants that stay about 3 feet high. Others are upright giants that you'd swear would reach the clouds if you didn't whack them back once in a while. Still others are low-growing, sprawling plants that can grow to 10 to 12 feet wide. To further complicate things, many roses that really don't need to be called shrubs, such as floribundas and climbers — often are. And then some rose growers call their shrubs *landscape roses*. In fact, some mail order catalogs group shrubs by landscape use, such as shrubs for ground covers, tall shrubs for hedges, and so on. Shrubs are great roses with great flowers, as shown in Figure 3-6. Their diversity translates into versatility in the landscape.

Figure 3-6:
Shrub roses
produce
beautiful
flowers in
addition
to being
versatile
in the
landscape.

Even though shrub roses are diverse, some that resulted from the same breeding programs have similarities:

- **Hardy shrubs:** Several breeding programs have concentrated on creating hardy shrubs for cold climates. These shrubs include Buck hybrids, such as 'Prairie Princess' and 'Applejack', which were bred by Dr. Griffith J. Buck at Iowa State University, and the Morden and Explorer (which are made up of varieties named after famous explorers) shrub roses from Canada. Most of these hardy shrubs can withstand temperatures down to −15° to −25°F (−26° to −32°C) and lower and have excellent disease resistance.

- **Meidiland roses:** These roses originate in France, from the renowned Meilland hybridizers. Most are sprawling plants that are useful as ground covers or hedges. They're good repeat bloomers, have excellent disease resistance, and are generally hardy to about −10°F (−23°C).

- **David Austin English roses:** These shrubs are meant to combine the ever-blooming characteristic and disease-resistance of modern roses with the flower form and fragrance of old roses. They've been selected by the famous rose hybridizer, David Austin. The problem is that they don't always keep that promise. Although many are beautiful roses, some varieties do not rebloom and are prone to disease, especially black spot. Also, many Austin roses are very vigorous plants that get huge, especially in mild-winter climates. So choose carefully. Most varieties are hardy to about 0°F (−18°C).

- **Generosa roses:** These are sort of a French version of David Austin's English roses. Developed by one of France's oldest nurseries, Roseraie Guillot, plants tend to be smaller than the Austins, have equal or stronger fragrance, and have good disease resistance (although black spot can be a problem where summers are hot and humid). Most varieties are hardy to about 0°F (−18°C).

- **Flower Carpet:** These well-behaved, spreading plants make especially good ground covers. They're easy to care for, very free-blooming, and disease resistant. Flower Carpet roses are generally hardy to −10°F (−23°C).

Shrubs in the landscape

Most shrub roses are easy-to-grow roses that can get by on little care, other than regular watering and occasional fertilizer. Shrub roses can get along fine without much pruning, but you still want to deadhead them (remove the faded flowers) to keep them blooming over the entire season. A light shearing in late winter or early spring (earlier in mild climates, later in cold climates) keeps them compact. Otherwise, prune to keep some of the large varieties in bounds.

Many shrub roses are grown on their own roots and are pretty hardy, if not extremely so. But you still want to mound soil over their base in cold winter climates to protect them from freezing and thawing and to ensure that not all the above-ground parts are killed if the temperature gets really cold.

Shrub roses really come into their own as landscape plants. (See Book II for more on landscaping.) If you're thinking about planting any flowering shrubs, think hard before you overlook shrub roses. You can use sprawling types as ground covers and upright ones as hedges, and the smaller ones are ideal for pots, perennial borders, and low hedges.

Shrub roses by color

The following sections list the best of the most widely available shrub roses.

Red shrubs

These useful shrub roses have red flowers:

- **'Flower Carpet Red':** Large clusters of deep red, ruffled blossoms (25 to 30 petals) and bright yellow stamens bloom generously. Little fragrance.

- **'John Franklin':** Medium red, fragrant flowers with 25 petals bloom in clusters. Excellent disease resistance. Very hardy.

- **'Knock Out':** Produces nonstop deep cherry-red flowers with 5 to 7 petals and a light fragrance. Exceptionally resistant to black spot.

- **'Red Ribbons':** Dark red, semidouble flowers appear in huge quantities. Good bloomer. Grows well in difficult spots.

- **'Tradescant':** David Austin English rose. Many-petalled deep crimson rose has an intense, sweet fragrance and is an excellent landscape rose.

Pink shrubs

So many pink shrubs to choose from; here are just a few:

- **'English Sachet':** Light pink blooms have an old-fashioned, cupped and quartered form with 40 to 50 petals and a strong, sweet fragrance.

- **'First Light':** Very free-flowering, light pink, single blossoms with dark red stamens have a mild, spicy fragrance. Excellent disease resistance.

- **'Morden Centennial':** Clusters of clear pink, lightly perfumed blossoms with 50 petals and dark red hips. Rarely out of bloom. Very winter tolerant.

- **'Prairie Dawn':** Bright pink, double flowers with a good repeat bloom.

- **'Queen Margrethe':** Large flowers with over 50 petals of pure pink exude a delightful fragrance and is always in bloom.

Book III

Roses

- ✔ **'Royal Bonica':** Meidiland rose. Always in bloom, producing clusters of small, long-lasting, rosy-pink double blossoms with a light fragrance.

- ✔ **'Watermelon Ice':** Large clusters of pink to lavender-pink blooms have 15 petals and a slight fragrance. Hardy and disease resistance.

Orange and yellow shrubs

Here are the best shrubs that have orange or yellow flowers:

- ✔ **'All That Jazz':** Luminous, poppy-orange flowers with five to ten petals and a light scent. Almost impervious to disease and winter weather.

- ✔ **'Baby Love':** Bright yellow, single flowers (5 petals) with a light licorice scent. Very free-flowering plant is exceptionally disease resistant.

- ✔ **'Graham Thomas':** David Austin English rose. Large, cupped, deep yellow, double (50 to 100 petals) blooms are richly fragrant. The first bloom in late spring is abundant. Subsequent blooms tend to be fewer in number and sit on top of tall stems that can reach over 8 feet in climates with a long season. Ruthless pruning helps to keep the flowers lower.

- ✔ **'Perdita':** David Austin English rose. Blushing, billowy apricot blooms grow in small clusters. Continual blooms have at least 40 petals.

- ✔ **'Sunny June':** Daffodil-yellow, single-petalled blooms blanket this shrub all season long. The lightly scented flowers have five to seven petals.

- ✔ **'Tamora':** David Austin English rose. Small clusters of medium-sized, apricot-yellow, cup-shaped blossoms have more than 40 petals and are very fragrant.

White shrubs

Here's an extremely diverse and useful group of white-flowering shrub roses:

- ✔ **'Alba Meidiland':** Large clusters of pure white flowers loaded with over 40 lightly scented, ruffled petals blooms profusely throughout the summer. The old petals drop off completely, making deadheading unnecessary.

- ✔ **'Fair Bianca':** David Austin English rose. Large, cupped, fully double blooms of pure white, satiny petals open into a saucer shape. Extremely fragrant and repeat bloomer.

- ✔ **'Pearl Meidiland':** Small, double flowers begin as soft pink blooms and then fade to a pearly white. They grow profusely and continuously in large clusters.

- ✔ **'Sea Foam':** Produces lightly scented, double, creamy white flowers abundantly and continuously. Disease resistant and vigorous.

- ✔ **'White Flower Carpet':** White, double flowers have a light, sweet fragrance. Free-blooming plant that gets by on a minimum of care.

Lavender shrubs

Many of Shakespeare's characters congregate in the lavender shrubs:

- ✔ **'Lavender Dream':** Dainty, lilac-pink flowers with no fragrance are produced continuously in clusters on smooth, thornless stems with small, shiny leaves.

- ✔ **'Othello':** David Austin English rose. Large, cupped, fully double blooms begin as crimson and then fade to purple. Extremely fragrant repeat bloomer.

- ✔ **'The Prince':** David Austin English rose. Velvety, rich, royal purple flowers have a heady perfume. Fully double blooms have a cupped, rosette form.

- ✔ **'Wise Portia':** David Austin English rose. Heavy-textured , 40-petalled blooms display lovely shades of purple and mauve with golden centers. Repeat, abundant bloomer that emits a rich fragrance.

Multicolored shrubs

Color preference should guide your choices among the kaleidoscope of shrub roses:

- ✔ **'Carefree Wonder':** Large bright pink flowers with a white eye and a creamy reverse. Lightly scented with 25 to 30 petals. Amazingly care-free with superb disease resistance and hardiness.

- ✔ **'Kaleidoscope':** Unusual shades of tan, lavender, and pink adorn this medium-size, double (25 to 30 petals) with a lightly sweet fragrance.

- ✔ **'Rockin' Robin':** Lively blend of pink-, red-, and white-striped flowers with 45 to 50 ruffled petals. Free-blooming with mild, apple fragrance.

Book III

Roses

Assessing Antique Roses

Species roses and *old garden roses* — both sometimes referred to as *antique roses* — are the roses that preceded modern varieties. These roses are an incredibly diverse group of plants, with great variety in plant habit (the size and shape), flower form, and fragrance. Some have historical importance; others were useful to hybridizers as breeding stock to create modern rose varieties. Still others, such as the rugosas, are still used in breeding today to create new and better hybrids.

Species and old garden roses have always been popular because of their ruggedness, beauty, and intense fragrance. With these qualities come some drawbacks, however. For example, some species and old garden roses are very vigorous plants that literally can take over a small garden. Others are shy bloomers. In fact, many bloom only once a season. And some are extremely prone to disease. So, choose your species and old garden roses with care, especially if you're just getting into roses.

Antiques in the garden

The size and habit of species and old garden roses dictate how you can use them in the landscape. You can train vigorous types to a fence or arbor like a climbing rose, or leave them to sprawl over a slope as a ground cover. Shrubbier rose types make excellent hedges, or you can mix them in with perennial borders. (See Book III for more on perennials.) Even though many bloom only once, in the spring, old roses often make up for it by producing colorful hips that last long into winter. Others have attractive foliage that looks good throughout the growing season. Most antique roses have very interesting flowers. They're usually flat-topped, rounded, and rather cup-shaped, with many petals. If you like cut flowers, antique roses are tops. Although most don't have the strong, straight stems of modern hybrid teas, their beautiful flower form makes for a unique bouquet. And oh, the fragrance! It's not always there, but when it is, it can be overpowering.

Just remember one thing about many species and old garden roses: They usually grow on their own roots, so they often spread like crazy, forming dense thickets. Make sure that you plant these roses where they have plenty of room to grow.

Many species and old garden roses need less care than modern roses do. In fact, many seem to thrive on neglect. However, where summers are dry, regular watering is necessary to keep the plants healthy. And almost anywhere, applying fertilizer regularly keeps the plants growing vigorously. Prune your plants to keep them within bounds and remove dead branches. But, other than that, less pruning is probably better than more. Prune roses that bloom just once in spring after they bloom, if at all. If you prune in winter or late spring, prior to blooming, you remove branches that would otherwise produce flowers. You can prune repeat bloomers in winter to early spring as with other types of roses.

Few nurseries and garden centers carry a wide selection of species and old garden roses. For the best selection, you have to order plants from a catalog that specializes in antique roses.

Old families of rosedom

The following sections list the main types of old garden roses. We describe our favorite varieties of each type. To be honest, some people may consider some of the varieties modern roses, but, you know what, who cares?

Making a difference

To make the distinction between species roses and old garden roses clear (or at least somewhat more so): A species rose is a rose just as nature made it. You can still find many species roses growing naturally in various parts of the world. Each species rose has a specific botanical name, for example, *Rosa rugosa*. If you cross a species rose with itself, the roses that grow from the seed are identical, or nearly so, to the parents and to each other. Variants do occur, and if the variation is positive, a nursery or rose lover may propagate it and give it a variety name.

Exactly what makes an old garden rose an old garden rose is fairly precise. Any class of roses known to be in existence in 1867 is an old garden rose. So, many species roses are also old garden roses. Old garden roses are most often descended from a mixed background of natural or created hybrids, and when you plant their seeds, the resulting plants are different from each other and from the parents, although there may be some family resemblance.

Alba roses

These roses are thought to be hybrids between *Rosa damascena* or *Rosa gallica* and a white-flowering form of the dog rose, *Rosa canina*. Though once popular in Europe, few varieties are widely available today. Flowers generally range from white to pink, and are very fragrant, blooming primarily in spring. Plants grow upright to about 6 feet and are generally very hardy.

Book III

Roses

- ✔ **'Königin von Dänemark':** Clear pink flowers, with up to 200 petals, have a deeper pink center that resembles a button. This extremely weather-tolerant rose has an intense perfume and flowers once annually.

- ✔ **'Mme. Plantier':** Large, dense, arching bush that you can train as a climber. Once a year, early in the summer, it sends out clusters of extremely fragrant, white, pompon-like blooms with over 200 petals.

- ✔ **'Félicité Parmentier':** Ivory buds, tinged green, open into fluffy, very double, pink-and-cream flowers. Exceptional fragrance. Blooms abundantly in spring.

Bourbon roses

Useful as hedges, these roses are generally vigorous plants with a compact, shrubby, or slightly climbing habit. The blooms are pink to red, cupped, and nicely fragrant. The plants are hardy to about 5°F (–15°C) without protection. Unfortunately, they're very susceptible to black spot.

- ✔ **'Boule de Neige':** Outer petals (about 100 petals total) curl inward, resembling a big snowball. Fragrant repeat bloomer. Disease resistant and winter hardy.

✔ **'Honorine de Brabant':** Richly fragrant, full, double, pale lilac blossoms striped in crimson and violet grow abundantly in spring and autumn. Disease resistant and winter hardy.

✔ **'La Reine Victoria':** Cupped, double, intensely fragrant flowers are rosy pink, shading to a deep pink on the outer petals. Blooms abundantly early to midsummer and then again in the fall. Tolerates heat well; disease resistant and winter hardy.

✔ **'Souvenir de la Malmaison':** This extremely popular rose is a difficult one to establish in a garden. Immense, fragrant blooms start out cupped and then open flat. Pale, cream blush-pink flowers (65 to 75 petals) with rose shading at the center. Repeats blooming throughout the season. Doesn't like wet weather.

✔ **'Zéphirine Drouhin':** Produces peppermint-pink, loosely cupped blossoms with 20 to 24 petals all season. Almost thornless and very fragrant. A climber.

Centifolia (Cabbage roses)

The true cabbage rose (see Figure 3-7) is *Rosa centifolia,* whose flowers have very thin, overlapping petals, making each one look somewhat like a small head of cabbage. The flowers have a spicy fragrance. The plants bloom once in spring in pink to purple shades. Plant habit varies from shrublike to spreading. Most are hardy to –15°F (–26°C) without protection.

Figure 3-7:
A cabbage rose.

- ✔ **'Fantin-Latour':** Loads of petals (maybe 200) range from pale to deep pink. One profuse, annual flowering produces blooms with an intense fragrance.

- ✔ **'Tour de Malakoff':** Intensely fragrant double flowers (about 55 petals) that begin as pink but age to mauve. Blooms only once in a season.

China roses

China roses, descendants of *R. chinensis,* contributed many of their good characteristics, including repeat bloom, disease resistance, and a compact habit, to various modern roses. Typically, petal color intensifies with age. The variety 'Minima', with its dainty leaves and small flowers, is the forerunner of modern miniature roses. Chinas are excellent in pots, and as edgings. However, they lack hardiness and are tough to grow without winter protection if you live where temperatures drop below –15°F (–26°C).

- ✔ **'Archduke Charles':** Rosy pink, double blooms with 35 to 40 petals become deep, marbled red. Intensely fragrant. Blooms all season. Not winter hardy.

- ✔ **'Hermosa':** Clear pink, double flowers (35 petals) in clusters from spring until frost. Flowers age to darker crimson tones. Moderately disease resistant.

- ✔ **'Parsons' Pink China' (also known as 'Old Blush'):** Fragrance-free, cupped, pink flowers (24 to 30 petals) bloom continuously in loose clusters. Moderately disease resistant; winter hardy with protection.

- ✔ **'Eugène de Beauharnais':** Produces large, wonderfully fragrant, purple, double flowers all season. Very disease resistant. Not winter hardy below 10°F (–12°C) without protection.

Damask roses

The clustered flowers of these roses are intensely fragrant and come in shades of white, pink, and red. The plants are very hardy and don't need winter protection until temperatures drop below –20°F (–29°C). They have thorny stems and usually bloom only once a year.

- ✔ **'Autumn Damask' (also known as the 'Rose of Castile', 'Four Seasons Rose', and 'Quatra Saisons'):** Medium pink, double flowers bloom in clusters in the spring and then again in autumn. Rich fragrance. Winter hardy.

- ✔ **'Ispahan' (also known as 'Pompon des Princes'):** Bright pink, double flowers have an intense fragrance and bloom over a long period.

- ✔ **'Marie Louise':** Large, very double, mauve-pink with many petals and an intense fragrance. Blooms only once a year, in spring.

- ✔ **'Léda':** Soft, fragrant flowers with 200 petals are white, edged in red, and bloom once in the summer. Disease resistant and winter hardy.

Gallica roses

Various forms of *Rosa gallica* have been grown for centuries. The red, pink, or purple flowers are intensely fragrant, have showy yellow stamens, and are followed by bright red hips. The foliage turns red in the fall. Plants are stiffly upright but have a neat, shrub-like habit. They're very hardy to at least –20°F (–29°C).

- ✔ *Rosa gallica officinalis*: Intensely fragrant, light crimson flowers with 12 to 18 petals. Blooms once, in late spring. Has a tendency to *sport* (create shoots that mutate naturally and produce a different rose, so that the same bush may have one or more variations). Disease resistant and winter hardy.

- ✔ **'Empress Josephine':** Luminous pink, with deeper pink tones toward the center. Ruffled blooms have a papery quality and 24 to 30 petals. Slightly fragrant. Blooms once per year. Winter hardy and disease resistant.

- ✔ **'Charles de Mills':** Flowers in many variations of purple and red: maroon, crimson, grape, wine, and violet. The fully opened, fragrant blossoms have about 200 swirling petals and a flat-topped appearance because the petals are so evenly spaced. Blooms once, in midseason. Disease resistant. Winter hardy.

Hybrid musks

Most hybrid musks can be traced to the musk rose, *Rosa moschata*. The flowers have that strong, musky fragrance that most people call old rose fragrance. Most hybrid musks are vigorous, spreading plants that are best treated as climbers, but some are more like shrubs. They can be considered modern roses and bloom most heavily in spring and fall. Most varieties bloom in shades of pink, and many produce bright orange hips. Hybrid musks tolerate more shade than many other roses and need winter protection where temperatures drop below –15°F (–26°C).

- ✔ **'Felicia':** Large clusters of very fragrant, pink, double flowers grow repeatedly on long, arching canes. Tolerates filtered light well.

- ✔ **'Nymphenburg':** Fragrant, salmon-colored flowers (18 to 24 petals), shaded yellow at the base. Borne in clusters all summer.

Hybrid perpetuals

The fragrant flowers come in shades of pink, purple, red, and sometimes white. They bloom best in spring, but you often get some flowers throughout the summer — hence the name perpetuals. Plants are vigorous with arching canes and need protection where winter temperatures drop below –20°F (–29°C).

- ✔ **'Frau Karl Druschki':** Very large, pure white, full flowers (30 to 35 petals) bloom in early summer and again in the fall. Slightly fragrant.

- ✔ **'Henry Nevard':** Rugged, hardy bush produces loads of dark red, aromatic flowers with 30 petals all season. Winter hardy and disease resistant.

- ✔ **'Hugh Dickson':** Fragrant, deep crimson, double blossoms (38 petals). Continuous bloom until hard frost. Easy to grow and disease resistant.

- ✔ **'Paul Neyron':** Fragrant, tightly packed, deep pink petals (65 to 75) bloom lavishly in late spring and then again in autumn. Winter hardy. Prone to mildew.

Moss roses

In their true form, moss roses (see Figure 3-8) are naturally occurring sports of *Rosa centifolia* and damask roses. They get their name from the small hairs on their stems and the bottoms of their flowers. The flowers are double, come in shades of white, pink, and red, and are very fragrant. Early moss roses bloom only in spring, but newer hybrids are good repeat bloomers; hardiness varies.

Figure 3-8:
A moss rose.

- ✔ **'Alfred de Dalmas' (also known as 'Mousseline'):** Light blush pink, strongly fragrant, cupped blooms (55 to 65 petals) fade to white. Blooms repeatedly in clusters. Brownish moss on stems.

- ✔ **'Maréchal Davoust':** Wonderfully fragrant, deep pink flowers (100 petals), with a lighter pink reverse. Blooms once in early summer. Bears sparse moss.

Noisette roses

These roses contributed orange and yellow shades to many modern climbing roses. You're usually better off treating these plants as climbers, supporting them with a trellis or fence. They're not hardy plants and, if you don't protect them, they suffer damage in temperatures below freezing. Flowers are fragrant and come in shades of white, cream, yellow, orange, and sometimes red.

- ✔ **'Alister Stella Gray':** Dark orange-yellow buds, the color of egg yolks, open to honey yellow, fading to cream. Richly perfumed and almost perpetually in bloom. Disease resistant. Not winter hardy below 10°F (–12°C).

- ✔ **'Fellenberg':** Bright crimson flowers with 35 petals in a cupped form.

- ✔ **'Jeanne d'Arc':** Countless white, dainty-looking, semidouble blossoms in clusters, with an especially fine bloom in the fall. Red hips often appear along with the flowers. Intense fragrance. Needs a warm climate.

- ✔ **'Mme. Alfred Carrière':** Pearly pink, gardenia-shaped blossoms (35 petals) age to cream. Very fragrant. Borne continuously in clusters.

Rugosa roses

Rugosas (derived from *Rosa rugosa*) and their many hybrids are tough, extremely useful shrub roses valued for their spicy scent, attractive crinkled foliage, disease resistance, and hardiness. (They're among the hardiest roses, able to withstand temperatures down to –35°F [–37°C] with little protection.) These compact plants, 4 to 8 feet high, bloom in spring and fall in shades of white, pink, red, purple, and yellow. Many varieties produce colorful hips. (See Figure 3-9.)

- ✔ **'Henry Hudson':** Large, very fragrant, white flowers (25 petals) with showy yellow stamens. Repeat bloomer. Very hardy and disease resistant.

- ✔ **'Pink Grootendorst':** Small, lightly scented, rose-pink flowers with 25 lightly toothed, or serrated, petals resemble carnations. Bright green, crinkled foliage.

- ✔ **'Sarah Van Fleet':** Extremely fragrant pink blossoms, with 18 to 24 petals and showy yellow stamens, bloom repeatedly all summer.

- ✔ **'Sir Thomas Lipton':** Double, cupped, white blooms grow abundantly and repeatedly throughout the season on a vigorous, bushy plant.

- ✔ **'Thérèse Bugnet':** Produces abundant large, rose-red, double blossoms with 35 to 40 petals. Outstandingly fragrant repeat bloomer. Quilted gray-blue-green leaves. Exceedingly disease-resistant and winter hardy.

Figure 3-9:
A rugosa
rose.

Scotch roses

Scotch roses (sometimes referred to as *hybrid spinosissimas*) are attractive shrubs with white, pink, or yellow, mostly single, blooms. Many varieties have handsome, finely cut, or crinkled foliage and colorful hips. These plants require winter protection in areas that get colder than –15°F (–26°C).

- ✔ **'Frühlingsgold':** Large, fragrant, saucer-shaped, pale yellow flowers with a lemon glow at the center. The five-petal blooms show themselves only once — in late spring. Disease resistant and winter hardy.

- ✔ **'Frühlingsmorgen':** Fragrant, pink, saucer-shaped blossoms (5 to 7 petals) with amber centers reveal startling maroon stamens. One profuse bloom in late spring. Disease resistant and winter hardy.

- ✔ **'Stanwell Perpetual':** Light pink, fading-to-white flowers (45 to 55 petals) bloom singly on very short stems. Fragrant flowers bloom repeatedly after the plant is well established in the garden. Disease resistant and winter hardy.

Species roses

Various species of rose (a *species* is a plant that, when crossed with itself, produces seedlings that are identical to the parent and to each other) are native throughout most of the northern hemisphere and don't fall into the neat rose classes described here. This diverse group of plants has contributed many valuable characteristics to modern roses through natural and planned selection.

- ✔ *Rosa banksiae lutea*: Also known as a Lady Banks' rose. Large clusters of small, double, yellow, fragrant flowers cover the sprawling, thornless bush in late spring. Disease resistant, but not winter hardy below 15°F (–9°C).

- ✔ *Rosa harisonii* **'Harison's Yellow':** Tough, hardy, disease-resistant, and drought-tolerant. Fragrant, deep yellow, semidouble flowers bloom in spring. Can grow in poor conditions, including shade, and is fairly hardy.

- ✔ *Rosa hugonis* **'Father Hugo Rose':** Produces sprays of pale yellow, single flowers with five petals in spring. Little or no fragrance. Disease resistant and extremely hardy.

- ✔ *Rosa soulieana*: Bears small, single, white flowers in clusters. Blooms have orange-red hips and little fragrance. Can tolerate partial shade.

Tea roses

Tea roses are fragrant flowers that come in shades of creamy white, pink, and yellow. The bushy plants are best adapted to milder climates, where winter temperatures stay mostly above 15°F (–9°C), because they lack hardiness. They do have good disease resistance, however.

- ✔ **'Catherine Mermet':** Unusually elongated buds. Big, light pink, double flowers have a stiff-fabric. Blooms on long, drooping stems with a strong perfume. Flowers repeatedly. Thrives in summer heat.

- ✔ **'Lady Hillingdon':** Masses of cup-shaped, fragrant deep apricot blossoms (18 to 24 petals) fade to cream with sun exposure. Blooms all season. Bronze-green leaves. New foliage is dark plum-purple. Slow-growing but healthy.

- ✔ **'Sombreuil':** Fragrant, creamy white blossoms that open flat, displaying about 100 petals, cover this climbing tea throughout the summer.

Chapter 4

Rose, Rose, Come to Stay; Plant You in the Garden Today

In This Chapter

▶ Recognizing the difference between rootstock and own-root roses

▶ Going bareroot or picking potted

▶ Working with your soil

▶ Planting your roses, whether bareroot, potted, or miniature

So this rose deal sounds pretty good to you, and you're ready to get a couple of plants and give it a try. Of course, as soon as you get your roses home, you're going to want to get them in the ground, so that they start growing and, better yet, blooming! The way you plant your roses is the most important step in growing roses. Because they may be living in the place you plant them for many years, you really have only one chance to start them off right. This chapter tells you how to choose the perfect plants and how to plant them, so that they stay healthy and beautiful for many growing seasons to come.

Discovering Your Roots

Most rose plants have two parts: the top part that produces the nice flowers, called the *scion,* and the bottom of the plant that produces the roots, called the *rootstock* (see Figure 4-1). These parts are joined at the bud union. During winter, if you slip a small bud from the scion variety, say a 'Mister Lincoln' rose, into the bark of a rootstock, in a few months, the two fuse together and become one plant.

We know why growers want the top of the plant to be 'Mister Lincoln' — it's a great rose. But why do they need the roots of another rose? A rootstock can provide a number of advantages that wouldn't exist if a 'Mister Lincoln' were grown on its own roots, including the following:

- ✔ Greater vigor than its own roots can provide
- ✔ Resistance to certain soil-borne insects and diseases
- ✔ Adaptation to certain soil types

Commercial rose growers choose which rootstock to use (they may have 10 or 15 to choose from), but they don't label them on the plant you buy. That's all you really need to know about rootstocks, except for one other thing: The rootstock roses always live within the plant and may sprout again, except you won't know what variety they are.

Some commercial rose growers propagate rose varieties on their own roots (especially shrub and old garden roses), calling them *own-root roses*. These roses are grown as rooted cuttings and take less time to grow to salable size. Own-root roses can be an advantage in some areas, particularly where winters are very cold. Here's why: Suppose that the weather gets really cold — so cold that the temperature kills the top of your rose plant. The roots, insulated by the soil, live to resprout in the spring. But, if the rose was budded on a rootstock, the new sprouts may come from the rootstock, and you have no idea what variety that is. So instead of the 'Mister Lincoln' roses you had last summer, you get who-knows-what. If, on the other hand, the rose was grown on its own roots, you still have the rose you want.

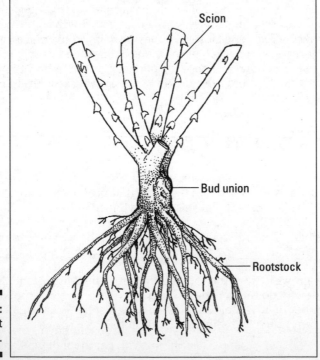

Figure 4-1:
A bareroot
rose plant.

The way an own-root rose sprouts *true to type* (meaning that it produces the type of flower you expect it to) is also an advantage when you grow shrub or landscape roses that need to be sheared. Pruning often causes the plants to sprout at the base, and if they're on their own roots — you guessed it — the sprouts are the type of rose you want.

The same venues that offer own-root modern shrubs also offer budded roses (the ones with rootstocks). Without careful inspection, you don't know whether a plant is own-root or budded, which really doesn't matter as long as the plant thrives. Own-root roses have a potential downside, especially when you're dealing with a very vigorous shrub or old garden roses. On their own roots, these plants often spread by root *suckers* — sprouts that come from the roots, as shown in Figure 4-2 — and spread is the key word. These sprouts can literally take over a garden. Rootstock roses usually don't produce root suckers, so the plants are easier to manage.

Figure 4-2: A downside to own-root roses is that root suckers can spread all over your garden.

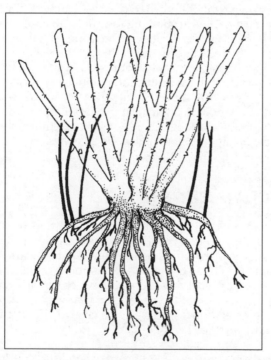

Rooting Around Your Roses

How your roses come to you dictates how you plant them, so knowing what you're getting into before you buy is important. You can buy roses in three ways: bareroot, potted, or in packages. How you get them depends on where you buy them.

✔ Some nurseries offer *bareroot roses* (dormant roses with no soil on their roots) early in the season.

✔ Many garden centers offer potted rosebushes grown in containers.

Barerooting it all

Come late fall to winter, when all the roses growing in the commercial fields are going *dormant* (resting) and losing their leaves, the growers prune them and dig them out of the ground, leaving all the soil in the ground, and none on the roses' roots. These roses are called — surprise — bareroot roses. Removing all the soil from the roots doesn't hurt the plant. As long as the rose plant is dormant and the roots are kept moist, the plant is in great shape. Plus, without soil, the plant weighs next to nothing — perfect for shipping.

The bareroot roses are then either bundled or packaged individually in plastic, usually with moist sawdust packed around the roots in both cases. Next, the roses are shipped off to retail nurseries all over the world, although they can be put in boxes and shipped directly to gardeners. (Not all the roses are shipped at the same time. In mild-winter climates, bareroot roses are shipped as early as December. In colder climates, the plants are stored until early spring and then shipped.) Upon arrival, the folks at the retail nurseries unpack the bundled bareroot roses and display them for sale, often in large bins with their roots packed in moist sawdust. Actually, the packing can be any lightweight organic matter that holds moisture, including peat moss and wood shavings.

Potting before planting

In many cold-winter and some mild-winter climates, bareroot roses are planted in pots immediately upon arrival. Bareroot roses are fine as long as the weather is cold and the plants are dormant, but if spring warms up and the plants start growing, you have to plant them — and fast. So, in late winter or early spring, that's exactly what most retail nurseries do. Any remaining bareroot plants are potted and sold the rest of the year with their roots growing in black plastic containers filled with soil. You can transfer them to more attractive pots on your own. (See Figure 4-3.)

Some roses, particularly miniatures and old roses spend their entire lives in containers. The vast majority of miniature roses are propagated and grown on their own roots in greenhouses and offered for sale in leaf or even in bloom. They usually come in 2½-inch or 4-inch pots, ready for transplanting into a garden or into containers for outdoor or indoor culture. Larger mail-order rose companies may send you field-grown bareroot miniatures that arrive looking more like big roses than minis. Treat them the same way you do other bareroot roses.

Tiptoe through the rose fields

Commercial growers plant and grow roses in huge rose fields for two years. Most of these large fields are in Arizona, Texas, or California. If you visit Wasco, California, just north of Bakersfield in California's San Joaquin Valley, you can see thousands of acres of rose plants — literally millions of plants. Make your visit in September when the plants are in full bloom, and you'll see and smell one of the most staggering and colorful displays of flowers imaginable.

For the most part, roses go from bareroot to you, or they go from bareroot to pot to you. Some nurseries pot the roses before others, but the process is basically the same. A few wholesale growers even take bareroot roses, plant them in *peat pots,* and enclose them in plastic or cardboard for shipping. A peat pot is a lightweight pot made of pressed peat. You can plant the rose, pot and all, and the peat pot eventually breaks down, allowing the roots to grow out into the surrounding soil. (Just make sure that none of the peat pot sticks up above the ground — otherwise, it acts as a wick, pulling moisture away from the roots.) However, the breakdown process takes too long for us. We remove the rose from the peat pot and plant it like any other container plant.

Book III

Roses

Figure 4-3: The roots of container roses grow in potting soil. Plant them any time of year.

Choosing Bareroot or Potted

Okay, so how do you decide between bareroot or potted? Read on for a discussion of when each works best.

Buying the best of the bareroot

Bareroot roses are generally less expensive than those sold in containers. Bareroot roses are also easier to handle, especially if you buy several plants. So, if you're going to plant several roses, you're better off buying bareroot roses during the dormant season. Bareroot roses are available during winter and early spring. You can buy them at retail nurseries or garden centers, or, for greater variety, you can purchase from a mail-order catalog.

Most mail-order nurseries send you top-quality bareroot plants, and the plants arrive in good condition. If they don't, you're entitled to a replacement. But when you shop in a nursery or garden center, examine the plants closely before you buy. Not that stores are trying to rip you off, but you want to be able to tell what's really a bargain and what isn't. You also need to be able to recognize a plant that's been hanging around too long or has been neglected. Small, shriveled stems and dried roots are sure signs of neglect.

The American Association of Nurserymen set the standards for grading roses. The grades — #1, #1½, and #2 — are based on the size and number of *canes* (branches) on the plant. More and thicker canes means a higher grade.

- ✔ A #1 is the highest-grade rose and represents a more vigorous, sturdy plant that should grow faster and make more blooms the first year after planting.
- ✔ The #1½ and #2 are usually the roses you find on sale at discount prices.

Although you often find good deals among the #1½ and #2 roses, if you want to get off to the best start, pay a little extra for a #1. Most roses have the grade listed on the package.

Other things to look for when buying bareroot roses include the following:

- ✔ Make sure that the packaging and the roots haven't dried out — a sure sign of trouble ahead.
- ✔ If you can examine the roots (they may be securely wrapped in plastic and not easy to get at) choose a plant that has a moist, well-developed root system. Avoid those with dry, broken, or mushy roots.
- ✔ Look for plants with thick, dark green canes — the more the better. Avoid plants that look dry, brownish, or shriveled.

Picking perfect potted roses

Buying roses in containers has its advantages — the main one being that you can get them almost anytime. But you can also buy growing, even blooming plants. These babies are ready to go in the ground immediately and give you instant beauty. Truth be told, in some climates, such as hot-summer areas of the American Southwest, you really shouldn't plant when it's blazing hot. The heat is just too tough on a newly planted rose. But if your climate is right, potted plants can give you a great-looking rose garden instantly.

When buying potted roses, keep these points in mind:

- ✔ **Buy as early in the season as possible.** The optimal time to buy potted roses is when new growth is minimal. If you do buy potted roses later in the season, choose plants with healthy, deep green foliage that's free of insects and disease. Look for vigorous new growth — deep red in many varieties.

- ✔ **Don't buy late in the season if you live in a cold-winter climate.** Resist the urge to buy, even if they're really, really cheap. The plants will go into shock, perhaps irrevocably, when you transplant them into your garden. And they won't have enough time to get established in the garden before winter comes. Buying an expensive rose in the spring that will live is better than buying a cheap one in the fall that will die.

- ✔ **Check the soil in the top of the pot:** A pot full of twisting, circling roots is a sign that the plant has been in the pot too long. Skip this plant — it probably won't grow well in the ground.

- ✔ **Look for flower buds:** Buds mean that the plant has been well kept. Choose plants with buds over those that have just finished blooming.

Book III

Roses

Bringing Home Baby

Planting your roses as soon as you get them seems like a good idea, but may not always be practical. What if your bareroot roses arrive in the dead of winter and the ground is frozen solid? Or what if it rains for 40 days and nights? Then what?

Storing bareroot roses

Unless you're lucky and have perfect weather and soft ground, you'll probably have to store bareroot roses for some time before you can plant them, particularly if you purchase them through the mail. The key is to keep the plants cool so that they don't start growing and the roots moist so that they don't dry out. Inspect bareroot roses, as soon as they arrive or you get them home. As long as plenty of moist packing surrounds the roots, you can store the plants in a cool (not freezing) place, such as a garage or basement, for a week to ten days (even longer if you have some empty refrigerator space). Keep the top of the plastic wraps open, the roots moist, and don't store the roses in direct sunlight.

If you have to store the plants longer, your best bet is to completely unpack them and heel them in. *Heeling in* is a way to store bareroot roses by packing their roots in moist (not soggy) soil until planting time. Where and how you heel in your roses depends on how many roses you have and on the soil conditions outdoors.

✔ If you have just a few roses, place them in a bucket or box and pack the roots and top third of the plant with moist sawdust, compost, peat moss, or soil. Store the whole thing in a cool (35° to 40°F or 1° to 4°C) place and check the packing often to make sure that it's moist. Unpack the roses at planting time, being very careful not to do too much harm to the tiny root hairs that may have grown along the main roots.

✔ If you have to store multiple roses and can work the ground outdoors, dig a shallow trench (about a foot deep), as shown in Figure 4-4, slightly slanted on one side, in a shady area of the garden (such as the north side of the house). Lay the roses on a 45-degree angle and pack the roots and the bottom third of the plant with moist soil or compost. Check the packing often to make sure that it's moist. Add water if necessary. Gently remove the roses from the trench at planting time.

Figure 4-4:
If you can't plant bareroot roses immediately when you get them, lay them in a shallow trench and cover their roots with organic matter to heel them in.

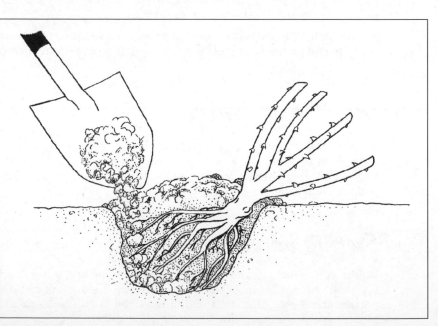

Don't keep roses heeled in much past the earliest planting time in your area because the plants start to develop fragile new roots and fragile new top growth, both of which you can damage when you start handling the plants.

Storing potted roses

Potted roses are easier to store until planting time. Just keep the soil moist, so that the plants don't dry out. If you store growing roses for more than a week or two, you may want to fertilize them with a diluted liquid fertilizer, following the label instructions.

Of course, you may want to grow your roses in pots or other containers. In this case, you can rest assured that you'll need a bigger pot than the one in which you bought your rose. (See Chapter 3 of Book II for more about container gardening.)

Getting in Touch with Your Inner Soil

Every gardener should have an intimate relationship with soil. You need to grab it, squeeze it, smell it — you need to love it so much that you know everything about it: the good, the bad, and the ugly. Why? Healthy soil means healthy roots, healthy roots mean healthy plants, and healthy plants mean fabulous flowers. (Refer to Chapter 3 in Book I for a comprehensive look at soil in your garden.) Provided that drainage is good, roses grow well in most soils. But if you wait until after you plant to find out that your soil has problems, you'll find those problems difficult or impossible to correct.

Book III

Roses

Checking drainage

Check your soil drainage by digging a 12- to 18-inch hole where you want to plant. Fill the hole with water, let it drain, and then fill it again. If the hole takes longer than two hours to drain after the second filling, you have a problem.

If you find you have bad drainage, plant somewhere else or plant in containers or raised beds. In certain areas, such as the southeastern United States, where abundant summer rainfall, clay soils, and hardpan make gardeners' lives difficult, planting in containers or raised beds may be the only way to grow roses.

Adding the big O

The big O is organic matter — stuff that is or once was alive, such as leaf mold, shredded bark, compost, peat moss, manure, and the like. You can incorporate organic matter into your soil when you plant — it helps to loosen and aerate clay soils, and improves the water- and nutrient-holding capacity of sandy soils. (You can also use organic matter as a mulch to protect your roses at ground level.)

If you're planting just a few roses, mix in the organic matter with the *backfill soil* — the soil you take out of the hole while you're digging it — and use this mixture to fill in the hole after you plant. Combine this backfill soil with about 25 percent volume (or more) organic matter to get your roses off to a better start.

If you have good loamy soil and no problems with excess clay or sand, you don't have to add any organic material; we always add as much as we can, no matter what the soil looks like, though. It can never hurt, and it always helps.

Balancing soil pH

A soil pH that's too high or too low interferes with or prevents the chemical reactions that make nutrients available to plants. (Refer to Chapter 3 in Book I for a detailed discussion of pH.) You can adjust acidic soils by adding dolomitic limestone. Correct alkaline soils by adding soil sulfur. Your local nursery or cooperative extension office can help you determine what and how much to add.

Roses prefer a slightly acidic soil pH. Ideal soil pH for most roses is between 6 and 6.5 but they grow pretty well in range from 5.6 to 7.2. If your soil is overly acidic (as is most often the case) or too alkaline (as it naturally is in some areas), adjusting the pH with one of several soil amendments is vital. If you have fairly acidic soil, avoid using acidifying mulches, such as pine needles. If you have alkaline soil, acidic mulches and soil additives slowly lower the pH, but getting it in the right range may take years. Check your soil pH every few years, especially if you have trouble keeping your roses green and healthy.

Returning Roots to Their Rightful Home

This section presents the basic procedure for planting bareroot roses. The key idea to remember: Don't plant a $10 — or more — rosebush in a 50-cent hole! Dig a hole at least 2 feet deep and 2 feet wide. Put the backfill into a wheelbarrow where you can mix it with fertilizers or amendments to adjust soil pH or add nutrients that are in short supply.

Soil polymers

Some rose growers dip their new roses in a *soil polymer* slurry instead of muddy water. *Soil polymers* are powdery materials that turn to a gelatinous substance when mixed with water. You usually add them to soil to increase its water-holding capacity, but when you dip roots in a slurry, the coating keeps extra moisture right where the plant needs it. Ask your local nursery person about soil polymers.

Preparing bareroot roses for planting

Before planting bareroot roses, soak the roots in a bucket of muddy water overnight. The water moistens the roots and the mud lightly coats them to slow drying out during planting.

If your bareroot roses look really dried out, with buds all shriveled and shrunken looking, the poor plants need special treatment — sweat them. Here's how:

1. **Soak the entire plant in water for 24 hours.**

2. **Enclose the whole thing in a clear plastic bag and keep it at room temperature (but out of sunlight) for 24 hours.**

   Boy, that plumps everything up!

Book III

Roses

Planting bareroot roses

To plant bareroot roses, follow these steps:

1. **Prune all the canes to about half their length and cut off any broken or mushy roots.**

   Most bareroot roses start with 10- to 16-inch canes. Shortening them to between 5 and 8 inches reduces the stress on the canes and roots while the new roots become established.

2. **Prune an inch or so off the roots to stimulate new growth.**

3. **Add a small amount of backfill to the hole and form it into a cone of soil; fit the bareroot neatly over this cone (see Figure 4-5).**

   Planting at the proper depth is very important:

   • **In mild-winter climates:** Position rootstock plants so that the bud union (the swollen part of the main stem where the rootstock joins the scion variety) is at the same level or just above the level of the surface soil.

- **In cold-winter climates:** Plant so that the bud union is 3 to 4 inches below the soil surface. Some rose growers prefer to plant deeper, covering the bud union with several inches of soil. Doing so should protect the bud union from cold, and it may also allow the top part of the plant to develop roots of its own, which, in turn, enables the plant to support itself if the rootstock is damaged.

- **For own-root roses:** Plant so that the point where the roots join the branches is just below the soil surface.

If, after planting, the rose settles in too deeply, grab the main stem near the bud union and gently pull upward. When you let go, the plant should settle slightly higher. If the plant settles too deep (or too high), pull it out and start over.

4. **After planting, create a soil basin around the plant and add lots and lots of water to the filled hole (as shown in Figure 4-6).**

   Adding water to the filled hole settles the soil and eliminates air pockets. After the water drains away, the soil and rose may settle lower than you want. If so, add more backfill and water again.

5. **Mound the soil over the top of the plant so all but the last few inches of the cane tops are covered, as shown in Figure 4-7.**

   Mounding the soil helps keep the plant from drying out before the roots have time to develop. When you see new growth, carefully remove the soil from around the canes.

Covering a newly planted rose with a brown paper bag (like you get from the supermarket) can also provide protection. Place the bag over the rose, cut a few holes in the top for air circulation, and seal the bottom with soil. We've also seen people protect new roses with Styrofoam caps usually used for winter protection.

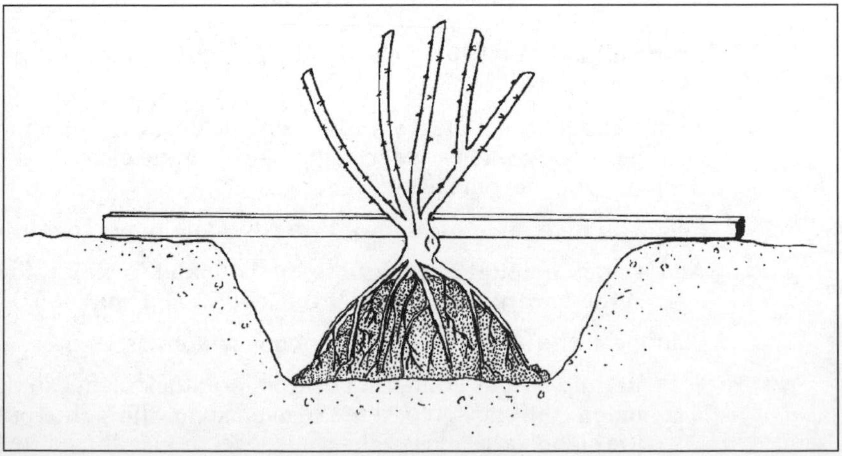

Figure 4-5: Place the rose bush in the hole at the proper level. Laying a stick across the hole helps you judge planting depth.

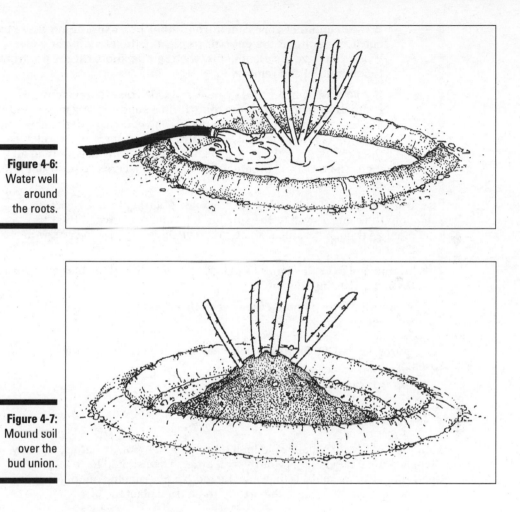

Figure 4-6:
Water well
around
the roots.

Figure 4-7:
Mound soil
over the
bud union.

Planting potted roses

Here are some tips for planting roses that come in containers:

- ✔ **Water plants thoroughly the day before planting.**

- ✔ **Dig a hole and add soil amendments to the backfill just as for a bare-root rose, but leave the bottom of the hole flat.**

- ✔ **Place your new rose into the hole, pot and all, so that you can estimate proper planting depth.** Again, the bud union should be at or slightly above the soil surface in mild-winter areas, or up to several inches below the soil in cold-winter areas.

- ✔ **Remove the container.** Because you want to disturb growing roots as little as possible during planting:

- **If your container rose is in a wood fiber pot, use a heavy knife to cut the bottom off the pot before placing the plant in the hole.** When you have the plant in just the right position, slit the pot from top to bottom and remove it.

- **If your rose is in a metal or heavy plastic container, remove the rootball from the pot.** If the roots form a solid, circling mass, gently loosen or cut them, or the rose will be slow to adapt to the new soil. If the roots are really tight, make three or four vertical cuts along the sides of the rootball with a knife. Don't go any deeper than an inch. The roots will eventually branch at the cuts and grow out into the surrounding soil.

✔ **Don't let the new plant dry out if you're planting in hot weather.** Until the roots grow into the surrounding soil, you have to treat the plant as though it's still in a pot. You may have to water every few days, if not more.

✔ **Mound soil over the canes as previously mentioned for bareroot roses if you're planting in winter.**

✔ **Water all newly planted roses every three days — more often in hot weather.**

See Figures 4-8 and 4-9 for the basic procedures for planting container-grown roses.

Planting miniature roses

Miniature roses are usually sold in 2½-inch or 4-inch pots, whether you buy them at a local retail nursery or by mail order. They should have fully developed root systems. In fact, they may be *rootbound* (running out of room for new root growth) and more than ready to be transplanted.

Remember that these little plants were grown in a comfy greenhouse, so they may need time to adjust to natural, outdoor conditions. This adjusting process is called *hardening off.* Help potted plants adjust to your weather conditions by gradually moving them to more extreme temperatures and sunlight. From the porch to outside in partial sun and finally to full sun over a week's time should do the trick. You can encourage the roots to grow sooner by transplanting the mini into a larger pot before you harden-off.

In cold climates, you can plant potted miniatures from the time the forsythias bloom in early spring well into midsummer. In warm climates, you can plant them just about anytime.

Digging a hole for a potted mini is somewhat easier than digging a hole for a big rose. You can dig the hole with a trowel, although removing a couple of spadefuls of soil ensures that the roots have a generous area in which they can spread. In any case, prepare the hole much as you would for a big rose.

Because your plant is smaller, the hole should be smaller — about 1 foot wide and 1 foot deep. Add smaller amounts of the same soil amendments that you use for big roses. Make a small cone of soil in the bottom of the hole.

Your mini rose should come out of its pot quite easily. Notice how all those roots have grown round and round inside the pot? To encourage the roots to spread out and grow into the new soil in your rose bed (or container), insert both of your thumbs into the bottom of the rootball and tear apart the bottom third, then place the entire torn rootball over the cone in the bottom of the hole. Next, backfill and water exactly as described in "Planting your bareroot rose," earlier in this chapter.

REMEMBER

Miniature roses always have shallower root systems than big roses and, therefore, need more frequent watering.

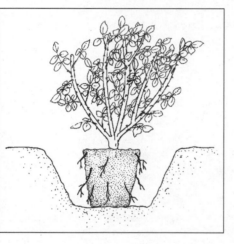

Figure 4-8:
Disturb the roots as little as possible when setting the container rose into a planting hole.

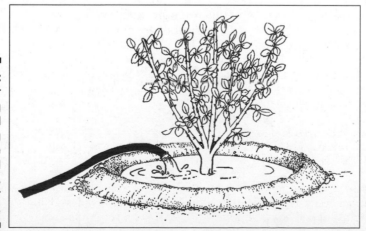

Figure 4-9:
After correcting the soil level and adding the amended backfill, water thoroughly.

Chapter 5

We Beg Your Pardon, We Do Promise You a Rose Garden

*G*etting your roses in the ground is just the beginning of the cycle of care that results in gorgeous blooms for faithful gardeners. This chapter tells you all you need to know to care for your roses with beautiful — and healthy — results.

Getting Down and Dirty with Water

Just like people, roses need water to be healthy and bloom beautifully. No water? No rose bush. You just end up with a dried-up dead stick poking through parched soil. Roses need more water more often in hot weather than in cool weather, and even steady rain may not provide enough water to keep your roses healthy. Also, roses growing in sandy soil need more frequent watering than roses growing in clay soils. (See Chapter 3 in Book I for more information about the different types of soils.) Following are some watering rules to keep in mind:

✔ **Water deeply, so that you wet the entire root zone.** Light sprinkling does little good.

✔ **Get down and dig in the dirt.** If the top 2 to 3 inches of soil are dry, you need to water.

✔ **Reduce disease problems by watering the soil, not the leaves.** Roses can benefit from overhead watering once in a while, especially in dry summer climates where black spot isn't usually a problem; however, make sure that you water early enough (in the morning on a sunny day is ideal), so that the foliage can dry before nightfall.

✔ **Mulch! Mulch! Mulch!** We cover mulching later in this chapter.

In the following sections, we get down to the nitty-gritty and answer the tough questions about how often and how much your roses need water.

Deciding how often to water

Theoretically, you can't overwater a rose. Of course, if you have no sun and steady rains for ten days, your roses won't be thrilled. But if drainage is good, the extra water usually won't hurt them, either. However, in some parts of the southeastern United States, where clay soils and heavy rain are a fact of life, drainage is a problem, and roses can suffer in overly wet soils. There you often have to create good drainage by planting in raised beds. (Chapter 5 in Book IV shows you how to build raised beds.)

Start with a watering schedule: Water once every five or six days, for example. If you live in a hot, dry climate, make it every two or three days. Watch the plant carefully and check the soil often, especially when you get to the end of the period. If the soil is bone dry about 2 to 3 inches below the surface at the end of your test period, you need to water. If the soil is still moist, wait a few days and check again. If the rose's foliage ever starts to look dull or droopy, you've definitely waited too long. Get those babies some water now and water more frequently. Over time, you'll get to know your soil and how quickly it dries out, no matter whether the weather is warm or cool, rainy or dry.

Figuring out how much water to apply

Water deeply, so that the entire root zone gets wet — for roses, that means to a depth of at least 18 inches. How far a given amount of water can penetrate into the soil depends on the soil type. (See Chapter 3 in Book I for more on soil.) If your soil is already lightly moist (never let it go bone dry), water will penetrate farther.

We consider different types of irrigation systems and how fast they apply water later in this chapter. For now, assume that your watering system is in place. Run your system for ten minutes or fill up your *water basin* (the 3- to 6-inch-high circle of soil you make around your rose when you plant it) once.

Let the water soak in and then probe the soil with a stiff rod or stick. The rod or stick should move smoothly through wet soil and then be hard to push when it reaches dry soil. Digging with a spade at a test spot away from your roses also lets you see exactly how deep the water has gone. From there, calculating how long to water is easy. For example, if the soil is wet to a depth of 6 inches after 10 minutes of watering, you need to water for a total of 30 minutes to get the water down 18 inches.

You may want to water a little longer than it takes to get the water down 18 inches, just to make sure that you're doing a good job and watering your roses thoroughly. But don't overdo it. If you water too long, the water will penetrate far below the roots and be wasted.

Watering your roses

Two tools can help you fine-tune your watering schedule. The first is a *soil probe* — an approximately 3-foot-long hollow metal tube about an inch in diameter that removes a small core of soil from the ground. By examining the soil core, you can tell how deeply you're watering or how dry the soil is. The second useful tool is a *rain gauge*. It can tell you exactly how much rain has fallen, and you can adjust your watering schedule accordingly. You can purchase soil probes and rain gauges through the irrigation supply stores listed in your local telephone directory.

You can use a number of methods to water roses. The key is to apply the water only over the soil where the roots are at a slow and steady pace:

✔ **Build a basin.** Build a 3- to 6-inch-high basin of soil around the plant and fill it using a handheld hose. Make sure that the basin is wide enough to hold the amount of water your rose needs. The basin should be at least 18 inches wide for new plants, and at least 36 inches wide for really big roses. You may have to fill the basin twice to get the water deep enough.

✔ **Use sprinklers.** Many types of sprinklers are available.

✔ **Use drip irrigation.** *Drip irrigation* (see Figure 5-1) is a particularly useful watering system for areas that are dry in summer, for areas where water shortages are common, or for busy gardeners who don't have time to water as often as they should. Most drip irrigation systems are built around ⅜- to 1-inch black tubing and specifically designed emitters. The emitters drip or spray water slowly — no faster than the soil can absorb it — and only wet the root area. Less wet ground means fewer weeds.

Book III

Roses

Watering to minimize disease

Many rose diseases, including black spot, rust, and downy mildew, thrive on wet foliage. If you live in areas where such diseases are problems, you may want to water in a way that keeps the leaves dry. Drip systems or bubbler-type sprinkler heads apply water at the base of the plant and do a good job of keeping the leaves from getting wet.

To complicate matters, some diseases, such as powdery mildew, spread more rapidly on dry foliage. And insect pests, like mites, thrive on dirty, dusty leaves (you can find out more about rose insects and diseases later in this chapter). In both cases, drenching the entire plant cleans the foliage of disease spores and dust, reducing pest problems. Remember, if you're going to water with overhead sprinklers, be sure to do it early in the morning on a sunny day so that the leaves have a chance to dry before nightfall. And whether or not you water overhead, keeping debris and dead leaves out of the garden really pays off.

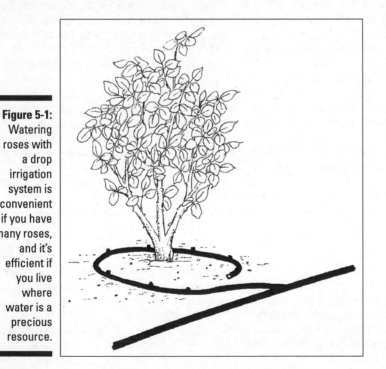

Figure 5-1: Watering roses with a drop irrigation system is convenient if you have many roses, and it's efficient if you live where water is a precious resource.

Mulching on Matter

Mulches really are a waterer's best friend. By reducing soil temperatures and evaporation, and by smothering greedy weeds (the seeds won't germinate if they're covered by several inches of mulch) that compete with roses for moisture, mulches not only conserve water but also even out rapid changes in soil moisture that can spell disaster in hot weather. (See Book I for a detailed discussion of mulch.) The best time to apply mulch is in early spring, about the same time you remove winter protection. In areas with warmer winters, apply mulch just before your roses start to leaf out and before weeds start to sprout. You can apply mulch anytime, and you usually need to replenish it every two to three months.

Using organic mulches

We recommend organic mulch (grass, compost, wood chips, and so on) for roses because, as the mulch breaks down, it adds organic matter to the soil, improving its texture and sometimes adding nutrients. Note that if you use grass clippings, mix it with another type of organic mulch for aeration because the clippings tend to pack down and decay into slime.

Mulch also gives the ground in your garden a cleaner, more orderly appearance. Many organic mulches break down fairly rapidly, so you need to replenish them often. For effective mulching, apply a good, thick layer (at least 3 to 4 inches) of mulch in spring before the weeds start to grow. Spread it evenly under the roses, over an area slightly wider than the diameter of the plant. Or spread it over the entire rose bed. Add a fresh layer whenever the first one starts to deteriorate. Figure 5-2 shows a properly mulched rosebush.

Composted manures make particularly good mulches, looking neat while adding nutrients to the soil as they break down. Just make sure that the manure is fully composted (it's sometimes hard to tell if you buy by the bag) and that you don't add too much. You can buy bags of composted manure in most nurseries and garden centers. Fresh manures contain salts that damage the plant and make its leaves look as if they've been burned by a blow torch. Different types of manure — that is, from different animals like horses, cows, or chickens — have varying amounts of nitrogen. Horse manure is generally safest and chicken manure the most dangerous. Mix manure 50/50 with some other organic mulch. That way, you won't burn your roses, but they still get some nitrogen.

Figure 5-2:
Use a layer of organic mulch to improve root growth.

Organic mulch has some downsides, so think about the materials you use and what they may do to your garden:

- ✔ **Keep a close eye on soil pH and correct it accordingly if you use bark mulches, such as pine, which are quite acidic.** See Chapter 3 in Book I for more information about soil pH.

- ✔ **Make sure that you haven't used weed killer on your lawn if you intend to use grass clippings.** The residue of weed killer can damage or kill your roses.

- ✔ **Add supplemental nitrogen if you use the organic mulches.** Fresh sawdust, for example, needs extra nitrogen to break down properly.

- ✔ **Avoid peat moss.** It can get hard and crusty when exposed to weather. Water may not penetrate it, so the water runs off instead of soaking through to the roots. At the very least, mix it with something else, such as compost.

- ✔ **Avoid lightweight mulches, such as straw, if you live in a windy area.** They can blow around, making a mess and leaving your roses unmulched.

Considering inorganic mulches

Inorganic mulches include plastic, gravel, stone, and sand. If you live in a cool-summer climate, a layer of gravel or rock beneath a rose can reflect heat and light up onto the plant. The extra heat may improve the quality of bloom for varieties that normally prefer warmer climates, and it may also cause water to evaporate off the foliage more quickly, reducing disease problems.

Generally, though, inorganic mulches, particularly plastic, are hard to handle, especially on roses, where you need continual access to the soil for fertilizing, watering, and so on. So unless you need to heat up your garden, or like the look of plastic, steer clear of these mulches.

There's one exception: Landscape fabrics are water-permeable, plastic or woven materials sold in rolls in most nurseries and garden centers. You lay them over the planting area, cut x-shaped holes in the fabric, and plant the roses through it. Landscape fabrics do a good job suppressing weeds, but water and nutrients pass right through. Add a thin layer of organic mulch on top and they even look good.

Fertilizing Fixation

But before we launch into all the whys and wherefores, keep in mind that no fertilizer on earth will help your roses if the pH of your soil is too high or too low. When the pH is off, important nutrients already in the soil are unavailable to plants. (See Chapter 4 in Book III for more on correct pH for roses.)

Fertilizers (see Book I for a more detailed discussion) come in three basic forms:

- ✔ **Granular:** Spread over the soil at the base of the plant and water it in.
- ✔ **Water soluble:** Dissolve either the powdered or liquid variety in water to feed the soil or foliage.
- ✔ **Timed-release:** Either spread this fertilizer on the soil or mix it with the soil for a constant release of nutrients over a long period of time.

As long as you apply it often enough, you can use any type of fertilizer. The granular form is easy to use and doesn't need mixing. Water soluble fertilizers get to roots quickly and are easy to use on container plants, but you usually have to apply them more often. Timed-release fertilizers are convenient, but alone they often don't supply enough nutrients to keep roses growing well over a long time; you usually have to supplement with granular fertilizers.

The following list explains the major and minor nutrients your rose plants may need:

- **Nitrogen:** Nitrogen fuels a rosebush's growth, and you must add it to the soil regularly — the nitrogen already present in the air and soil isn't enough. This element stimulates dark green, healthy foliage growth; because a plant's energy to make flowers is manufactured in its leaves, healthy leaves mean more flowers. Most rose foods have several times more nitrogen than phosphorous and potassium. Don't worry about the numbers too much. Just don't buy one of those "bloom" foods that has no nitrogen at all.

- **Phosphorus and potassium:** Along with nitrogen, phosphorus and potassium are called *macronutrients* because roses need them in larger supplies than other nutrients. Some soils already contain enough phosphorus and potassium for healthy rose growth; adding more to them does little good. Besides, phosphorus doesn't move easily through the soil like nitrogen and potassium — it gets "tied up" (you don't want to know the reasons why) and has to stay put. If your soil is short on phosphorus, add some directly to the planting hole when you put in your roses, so that it gets where it needs to go.

Only a soil test can tell you for sure whether your soil needs either of these nutrients. But if you use a complete fertilizer — one with a lot of nitrogen and a little phosphorous and potassium — on a regular basis, you should be okay.

- **Iron:** In areas where the soil is on the alkaline side, a rose plant may need applications of fertilizers containing iron. You know your roses need iron when their leaves turn yellow with green veins.

- **Magnesium:** Many rose growers swear by magnesium applications, but only when the soil is deficient in magnesium. *Magnesium sulphate —* called Epsom salts in drugstores — is the form that's usually applied. This chemical helps intensify flower color and increases production of new flowering canes. Water in ¼ to ½ cup per plant once or twice a year.

Micronutrients

Iron, zinc, and manganese are called *micronutrients,* meaning that the plant needs them only in small quantities. You may need to add these micronutrients to problem soils, especially if nitrogen isn't greening-up your roses. The fastest way to correct these deficiencies is to apply a liquid fertilizer containing *chelated* micronutrients (forget about all the terminology — it just means that they work better) to both the foliage and the soil. That's right, just spray the fertilizer over the whole plant. But look for cautions on the fertilizer label. Most manufacturers recommend that you not spray plants when they need water or when the temperature is above 85°F (29°C).

Determining your fertilizing program

Fertilizing is kind of a personal thing. Of course, you want to keep your plants healthy, but how you do so really depends on the type of gardener you are. Take your pick from the successful fertilizer programs in the following list:

- **Lazy and cheap formula:** *Complete fertilizers* contain all three macronutrients and are usually packaged as "rose foods." If your soil already contains sufficient amounts of phosphorus and potassium, you can use a fertilizer, such as ammonium sulfate or urea, that contains only nitrogen. These fertilizers are dramatically cheaper than complete fertilizers. You can also usually find bargain bags of *high-nitrogen, low phosphorus and potassium* fertilizers in most nurseries. One rose grower we know saves money and time by giving each rose one handful of ammonium sulfate (he wears gloves) every six weeks. He spreads the fertilizer evenly under each plant and then waters thoroughly to dissolve the granules and wash the nutrients into the soil. Simple, cheap, and his roses look great.

  Ammonium sulfate, an acidifying fertilizer that gradually lowers soil pH, works well on alkaline soils but makes acidic soils even more acidic.

- **Just plain lazy formula:** You can apply a timed-release fertilizer once or twice a year, which provides enough nutrients for an entire season, but you pay more for the convenience. Follow the label instructions carefully and watch your roses closely. If they slow down and stop blooming, the fertilizer may have run out early. Most rose growers who use time-released fertilizers supplement their use with one or two applications of a regular fertilizer in spring and late summer, just to make sure that the plants have enough nitrogen.

- **Tree-hugger's formula:** Many gardeners prefer to use organic fertilizers — ones that occur naturally — over chemical-based fertilizers. (See Chapter 4 in Book I for details on organic fertilizers.) One successful organic formula we've seen mixes equal amounts of alfalfa meal and cottonseed meal. Spread ten cups of the formula at the base of each plant every ten weeks and then cover them with a thick mulch of compost. Try it; your worms will love it.

- **Water and spray formula:** One friend of ours uses a hose-end sprayer to apply liquid fertilizers to the leaves, called *foliar feeding,* and soil. Leaves can absorb nutrients, too, and they do so much faster than roots do. Just make sure that the label says that you can apply the fertilizer to the foliage and follow instructions carefully. Our friend follows this routine at least every two weeks, but sometimes, she mixes the fertilizer at half strength and applies it weekly.

- **Gung-ho fertilizing formula:** A former president of the American Rose Society has a particularly high-powered fertilizer program. About a week after his plants leaf out in spring, he applies a water-soluble 20-20-20 fertilizer, diluting 2 tablespoons of fertilizer in 2 gallons of water and giving

Book III

Roses

each plant the whole 2 gallons. A week later, he puts ½ cup of Epsom salts (magnesium sulfate) around each bush. The third week, he applies fish emulsion at the same dilution as he applied the 20-20-20 fertilizer two weeks earlier. During week four, he applies a liquid fertilizer (16-4-2), which includes chelated micronutrients, at 1 tablespoon per gallon, 2 gallons per bush. In week five, he starts all over again. Whew, a lot of work — but, he says, twice the blooms and bigger flowers.

You can now buy a simplified version of the fertilizer program, packaged as one product called Magnum Grow. If you can't find it in local nurseries, you can buy it through the mail from Primary Products (`www.primaryproducts.com`).

Feeding frequently without overdoing

To keep roses blooming again and again, you should fertilize them about every four to six weeks, although the type of fertilizer you use may alter this rule a bit. Always follow label instructions when determining how much fertilizer to use. You don't need to fertilize roses that bloom only once in spring as often as repeat bloomers. Fertilizing once in early spring may be enough, but increase the number of applications if your plants aren't green and healthy-looking or aren't blooming up to your expectations.

Here are some general fertilizing guidelines:

- **Water before and after fertilizing.** A plant stressed from lack of water is more likely to be burned by nitrogen fertilizers, so make sure that the soil around the plant is wet before you add fertilizer. Watering after fertilizing helps to move nutrients into the root zone.

- **Start fertilizing in early spring and stop in late summer or fall.** Make your first application about four to six weeks before growth begins in spring or, in areas where winters are cold, about the time you take off your winter protection. Continue through summer until about six weeks before the average date of your first frost. Employees at your nursery can tell you exactly when that date is, but for most cold-winter climates, it's sometime in late August or September. Later fertilization may encourage growth that will be damaged by frosts and can result in roses that aren't fully cold resistant.

Going to the Rose Barber: Pruning

You prune to remove parts of a plant that you don't want in order to leave room for growth and circulation in the parts of the plant that you do want. When you prune, you cut the *canes* (think upright branches) of a rosebush. You may cut the canes near the top of the plant, at the base of the plant, or somewhere in the middle, depending on the result you're trying to achieve. Here's the skinny on why you really do want to prune your roses:

- ✔ **To improve flowering:** Proper pruning results in more or bigger blooms. Especially with hybrid teas grown for cut flowers, good pruning practices give you huge flowers atop long, strong stems. In general, the further back you cut a rose, the fewer but bigger flowers you'll get. Prune less, and you get smaller flowers but more of them.

- ✔ **To keep plants healthy:** Pruning removes diseased or damaged parts of the plant. It also keeps the plant more open in the center, increasing air circulation and reducing pest problems.

- ✔ **To keep plants in bounds:** Without pruning, many rose plants get huge. Pruning keeps them where they're supposed to be, and it also keeps the flowers at eye level, where you can enjoy them up close.

- ✔ **To direct growth:** Pruning can direct growth (and flowers) to a spot you pick. For example, you may prune a climbing rose to direct growth on a trellis.

Whenever you take a pruner to a rose cane, ask yourself why. If you don't stop to question your pruning, you may not get the effect you want.

Deciding when to prune

Plan to prune yearly, and during the proper season for pruning. The best season for big pruning is just before growth begins in late winter or early spring — exact timing depends upon your climate. If you do a good job then, you shouldn't have much to do throughout the rest of the season beyond *deadheading* (cutting off spent roses) and cutting great roses. If you wait too long to do your heavy pruning — say, after the plant's new growth is really in full swing — removing all that foliage weakens the plant, delays blooming, and makes your roses unhappy.

Where winter temperatures predictably reach 10°F (–12°C) and lower, wait until after the coldest weather has passed and any winter damage to the plant has already occurred. That's usually about a month before the average date of the last spring frost — March or April for most people — and coincides nicely with when you remove your winter protection. Your local nursery or cooperative extension office can give you exact frost dates for your area.

In climates where winters are cold or pretty cold (15°F or –9°C and lower), avoid pruning in fall. Any pruning after the first frost but before really cold weather sets in usually signals the plant to grow. New canes or shoots are very tender and cold weather will kill them. The only reason to cut anything off a rose plant in late fall is if really long canes would whip around in winter's wind and damage the plant — or anyone walking by.

If you live where winters are mild and temperatures rarely dip below 15°F (–9°C), you have to do your pruning earlier because plants start growing earlier. January or February is usually the best time. In areas with very mild winters, rose plants never really go completely dormant or drop all their leaves, so you have to prune with some foliage still on the plant — late December to February are usual times. In such cases, pick off as many of the leaves as possible, but be careful not to damage the bark, which may lead to disease. Removing leaves helps force the plant into dormancy (even roses need a rest now and then) and removes any disease organisms that may be waiting out the winter on the foliage.

Gathering proper pruning tools

Before you can start pruning your roses, you need the proper equipment. Quality, well-maintained pruning tools make pruning much easier. They're also better for your roses, giving you nice, clean cuts rather than crushed stems and torn branches. If you're serious about roses, be serious about your pruning tools. Buy a good set and take care of them. Store them indoors, oil blades and moving parts (even a few drops of oil on a saw blade makes it cut more easily), and keep the blades sharp.

Your basic rose-tending toolbox should include the following:

- **Heavy gloves:** Choose gloves that are flexible but not easily punctured. We like gloves coated in *nitrile* (a strong plastic-like stuff). Your nursery can recommend some other types designed especially for roses.

- **Hand pruners:** By-pass pruners — the type with a curved blade and cutting arm, as shown in Figure 5-3, provide the cleanest cut and are less likely to crush the cane below the cut, which often happens with anvil-type shears.

- **Loppers:** These are similar to hand pruners but have long handles to give you better leverage when cutting thicker canes. (See Figure 5-4.)

- **Pruning saw:** This saw is necessary for cutting really old, woody canes or dead wood. The folding type with a slightly curved blade fits neatly, if slightly uncomfortably, in your back pocket. (Folding the saw covers the blade, so you don't have to worry about injuring yourself.)

- **Sharpener:** You need a sharpening stone or small file (we like those diamond-coated fingernail files) to keep your pruners sharp. Sharp blades do less damage to the plant. Move the stone or file down the beveled edge of the blade, starting from the base and ending at the tip. Wear gloves when sharpening your pruners and apply gentle pressure. Sharpen before you prune — every time. If you're pruning ten or more bushes, carry your sharpener with you and sharpen when you notice that your cuts are getting harder to make, or that the cuts are crushing or tearing the canes.

✔ **Hedge clippers or hedge shears:** If you grow landscape roses as hedges, groundcover, or in flower borders, you may also need these long-bladed, scissor-like pruners that let you whack back plants in quick and easy fashion.

Figure 5-3:
By-pass pruners work better than anvil-type shears.

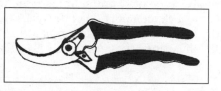

Figure 5-4:
Use loppers on thicker canes.

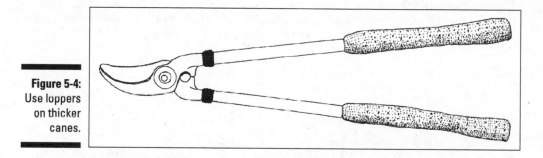

Book III

Roses

One thing you don't need is any kind of pruning paint or black goop to seal your pruning cuts. But if cane borers (we discuss rose pests later in this chapter) are causing serious problems in your garden, you may want to treat the surface of your cuts with a dab of standard white glue or a little green florist clay to prevent pests from entering the canes.

Perusing a pruning primer

You use three types of pruning cuts when pruning roses. Each one generates a very predictable response from the plant. As your pruning prowess grows, you'll find yourself using a combination of all three types of cuts:

✔ **Thinning removes a branch at its origin — that is, it cuts a branch back to another branch or to the base of the plant.** Usually, thinning doesn't result in vigorous growth below the cut. The result of thinning is that the plant is more open and less densely branched. Air circulation improves, which helps prevent disease.

✔ **Cutting back a dormant bud stimulates that bud to grow.** If you're pruning during the dormant season — when the rose is resting and leafless in winter — the bud won't grow until spring, but this type of cut focuses the plant's energy into that one bud and maybe one or two buds below it. Pruning back to a bud is the best way to direct plant growth and to channel energy into specific canes that you want to bloom.

✔ **Shearing is a more aggressive type of pruning but is sometimes effective.** Use hedge clippers to whack off a portion of the plant. The result is vigorous growth below the cuts and a denser, fuller plant. Shearing is particularly effective with landscape roses, especially if you plant them as hedges.

Pruning hybrid teas and grandifloras for bigger flowers

Because you usually grow hybrid teas and grandiflora roses for large, long-stemmed flowers, you prune them more severely than other types of roses. Taking off more of the plant channels the plant's energy into fewer canes, which produce bigger and better flowers. (See Figure 5-5.)

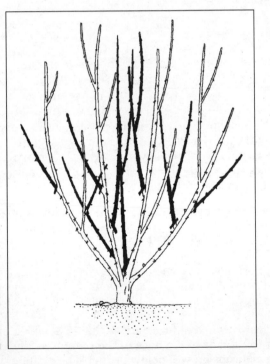

Figure 5-5: A typical hybrid tea bush before pruning. The darker canes are the best ones to remove.

Follow these steps to prune hybrid tea and grandiflora roses. (Figure 5-6 shows the before and after picture.)

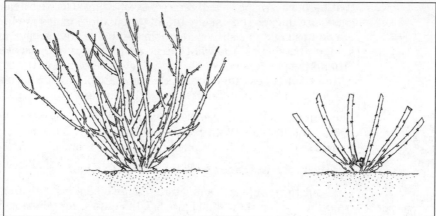

Figure 5-6: The bush on the left is before pruning; you can see the good job done in the after drawing.

1. **Remove dead or damaged canes.**

   Cold temperatures, insects, and disease are likely to have done their fair share of damage to your plants since the last time you pruned them. So first, look over the plant and remove the dead canes by using thinning cuts, cutting back at least far enough so that the insides of the canes are white again. You may have to use loppers or a saw to cut thick canes. After a really cold winter, you may have to prune all the way to the ground. If the plant looks dead, don't despair; wait a few weeks, and the plant may still put out new shoots. If it doesn't, you may have to practice *shovel pruning* — removing the dead bush and replacing it with it with something hardier.

   Dead canes are brownish or shriveled instead of bright green, but don't confuse these with older canes that are just thicker with rough bark. You can tell for sure by cutting off a piece. A dead cane is brown inside; a healthy one is whitish.

2. **Remove *suckers* — vigorous canes that arise from the rootstock below the bud union — if you're pruning budded plants.**

   You may have to dig around at the base of the plant to fully expose the bottom of a sucker. Cut it flush to the rootstock. But be careful: Don't mistake desirable new canes for suckers. If you suspect that a new cane is a sucker, let it grow awhile. If its leaves are distinctly different from other leaves on the plant, go ahead and cut it away. (If you're growing own-root roses, or roses that haven't been grafted but have their original roots, don't worry about suckers.)

3. **Select flowering canes.**

   Stop thinking about what you want to remove and decide what you want to save. You want to save the healthiest canes — the flowering canes

Book III

Roses

that bloom in spring — and remove everything else. The healthiest canes are thicker and usually bright green; older canes are brown or gray and sometimes shriveled looking. Remove any twiggy (small and scraggly) branches. You want the flowering canes to be as evenly spaced around the plant as possible. Try to leave the center of the plant open, without any canes. After you finish, the plant should be sort of cup-shaped with flowering canes around the outside.

The number of flowering canes you choose to save depends on the vigor and age of the plant. With recently planted roses, leave about three to five flowering canes. Older plants can support more.

4. **Cut the flowering canes back by a third to a half.**

Cut back to an outward-facing bud (called a *heading cut*), about ¼ inch from the bud, as shown in Figure 5-7. In cold-winter climates, you may have to prune back a little farther to remove all the damaged wood — possibly leaving just 3 to 4 inches of cane.

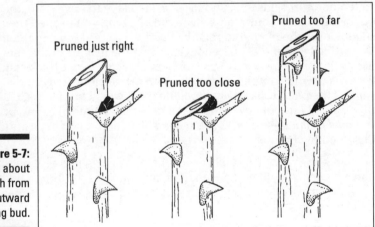

Figure 5-7: Prune about ¼ inch from an outward facing bud.

After your plants are in the ground for a few years, some of your flowering canes may get pretty thick and woody and lose some of their vigor and flower-power. Thin these canes by removing them with a saw or loppers. Allow a nearby *basal break* (a healthy new shoot from above the bud union at the base of the plant) to grow and replace it.

Pruning floribundas and polyanthas for shear pleasure

You can prune floribunda and polyantha roses much like hybrid tea roses, but because floribundas and polyanthas have a more twiggy growth habit (more, but smaller, stems and canes), you need to leave more flowering canes. Because most produce clusters of small flowers instead of those long-stemmed single beauties of the hybrid teas, and because floribundas and polyanthas are more often used en masse as landscape plants, you can prune in a much easier way — simply whack 'em back with hedge clippers.

Remove all canes that were damaged by winter. Then remove about one-third to one-half of the growth, shaping the plant into a nice, rounded dome. Then do a quick pass with a hand pruner, removing dead or very crowded branches and opening the center of the plant a bit. The result is a denser plant covered with blooms.

Pruning a mixed bag of shrubs

Shrub roses represent a real mishmash of different kinds of plants. Consequently, we don't have hard-and-fast rules about how to prune them. Still, you basically remove dead and diseased branches, open the centers a bit, and whack back whatever gets out of bounds. With most of these plants, the amount of pruning you have to do depends on your climate. Where summers are long and winters are mild, plants grow more and need more pruning. In short-summer/cold-winter climates, the opposite is true; you have to cut off less. Many rose growers take a less-is-more approach to pruning shrubs and often just leave the plants alone, which usually results in fewer blooms and wild-looking plants.

Pruning miniatures

You can shear miniature roses the same way that you prune floribundas and polyanthas, which is especially timesaving if you have several plants on landscape duty.

But because miniatures are so diminutive and often admired up close, many gardeners prefer to handle them more carefully. If you're one of those gardeners, treat minis like hybrid teas, opening the center, removing dead or twiggy branches, and selecting healthy flowering canes. To keep the plants compact, shorten the flowering canes a little more than usual — by as much as three-quarters of their height.

Pruning antiquity

Old garden roses are a greatly varied group of plants. We believe in a less-is-more approach to pruning. Take out the damaged and dead branches, shear back a bit — but not by over a third, or you may reduce bloom — and remove anything that's out of bounds. Prune old roses — remember, go lightly — that bloom only once in spring after they flower. Pruning them during their dormant season reduces next season's blooms. Hybrid perpetuals are one exception to the go lightly rule. They like to be pruned hard, just like their close cousins, the hybrid teas.

Pruning to new heights

Pruning climbing roses is a bit different from pruning other roses. Climbing roses don't climb like true vines. They don't twist around or attach to whatever they come in contact with like ivy or grapes. Instead, they put out long, longer, and longer yet, vigorous, arching canes. If you just leave them alone, they form a huge, sprawling shrub. Consequently, to get them to climb, you have to tie them to some kind of a support, such as a fence, arbor, or trellis. The most common types of climbers are the climbing offshoots, or sports, of hybrid teas and large-flowered climbers, which bloom repeatedly throughout the growing season. After planting, keep them within bounds and remove any dead or damaged growth, but otherwise leave these climbers alone for two to three years so that they can develop long, sturdy canes. Tie them to the support if you need to keep them out of the way.

The fun begins after the second or third year of waiting. Think of your climbing rose as having two parts: the flowering shoots and the main structural canes on which they grow. Your goal in pruning is to select the sturdiest canes and tie them to the support in some evenly spaced manner, ideally in an angled or nearly horizontal fashion. The pattern doesn't have to be fancy. The number of canes you choose depends on the size of your support and the age of the plant. As the rose gets older, you can select more canes to fill up, say, a large fence. These main canes form the basic structure of the plant. Remove other canes. After you bend these structural canes and tie them to the support, new growth sprouts along their length. These are the flowering shoots (sometimes called *laterals*) that — surprise! — flower. During dormancy, you should cut back these shoots to about two to three buds above the structural canes.

Occasionally, one of your structural canes may become too old and woody and not bloom as well as it used to. So get rid of it. New canes that you can train as replacements arise every year from the base of the plant. When you need these new canes, simply let them grow rather than pruning them as you've been doing since you selected your structural canes after the first two or three growing years.

The rules change a bit with climbing roses that bloom only once in spring. Wait until after they bloom to prune and then remove more of the older structural canes and replace them with the new ones. These new canes produce most of the next season's bloom.

Deadheading for grateful roses

You do need to prune a bit during the growing season. Most important, you have to deadhead, removing spent flowers — those that have withered and died — so that the plant can channel its energy into producing more flowers instead of seeds. As with other types of pruning, you can deadhead the hard way or the easy way:

- **Take the hard way for hybrid teas and grandifloras.** Cut back each spent flower shoot down to at least the first leaf with five leaflets. When you deadhead this way, the plants maintain a neater appearance, rebloom sooner, and produce sturdier stems that are less likely to result in droopy flowers.

Buds arising from thicker parts of a cane grow into sturdier canes themselves. Therefore, in order to get the largest possible new cane to grow from a bud eye, you have to cut down to where the main cane is fairly substantial. However, avoid weakening the plant by never removing more than a third of the plant at one time during the growing season.

✔ **Try the fast-track for multiple-flowered plants.** Get out your trusty old shears or hedge clippers and whack off the faded flower clusters. The disadvantage of the whack method is that the plants take a little longer to rebloom. Still, the plants are much better off than if you don't whack at all.

There is one time and place you may not want to deadhead. Some rose growers believe that letting the hips develop in fall increases rose hardiness, so you may not want to deadhead then, especially if you live in a cold winter climate. One side benefit: The hips provide some winter interest in the garden — pretty to look at against a snowy backdrop!

Other than deadheading, prune during the summer as you see fit.

Cleaning up after pruning

After pruning, cleaning up and discarding or destroying the plant debris is important. Many insects and diseases live on dormant leaves and branches, and they can find their way back to the bush if you leave the prunings hanging around.

Start by removing any leaves left on the rose plant during dormancy. Then, rake up all the plant debris and either discard or burn it. You can run the stuff through a shredder and add the debris to a compost pile, but you still risk harboring some pest organisms. To avoid future problems, keep the compost pile far away from your roses. Right after dormant pruning is the ideal time to apply a dormant spray to your plants that smothers insect eggs and kills disease organisms; you can apply the spray as long as the plants are still dormant and leafless and haven't started to grow.

Guarding Against Old Man Winter

Most plants' *hardiness* is judged by the minimum low temperatures that they can withstand in winter without being killed or damaged. Unfortunately, rose-hardiness isn't a cut-and-dried matter because conditions other than cold temperatures can devastate a rose plant. And these conditions vary from winter to winter. For example, if you get a foot of insulating snow in late November, and a thick snow cover stays around all winter long, your roses

Book III

Roses

will be safe and cozy, even if you haven't spent a lot of time protecting them. But the following winter, you may get very little snow, devastatingly cold temperatures, and a strong, dry wind that sucks the moisture from everything. In this case, the same rose, without proper protection, will most certainly be severely damaged or dead at winter's end. Also, if your yard is protected from winter winds, or if you plant your roses close to your house, your roses are safer than if your yard is very open.

Generally, though, if you live in an area where winter temperatures predictably reach 10°F (–12°C), many of the most popular roses — such as hybrid teas, floribundas, grandifloras, and climbers — need some kind of protection to survive the winter. Miniature roses and shrubs are generally somewhat hardier, with many shrub and species roses being hardier still. Luckily, protecting roses isn't a difficult task. You can do it by covering the base of the plant with soil.

Bundling up for a cold winter

A rose properly prepared for cold weather is said to be *hardened off*. Most roses harden off by themselves during the gradual onset of fall and winter. During this time, the plant's cell walls thicken as they prepare for dormancy. In many rose varieties, this process manifests itself by the canes taking on a purplish cast. Unfortunately, purple canes indicate the onset of dormancy only and don't give much of an indication as to whether the variety is hardier than varieties that harden off without turning purple. The key to hardening off a rose is to make sure that the plant stops growing and becomes fully dormant before the onset of the coldest weather. You can encourage full dormancy in two ways:

- **Stop fertilizing six weeks before the first frost.** Cutting back on watering may also help, but don't ever let your roses go into winter completely dry.

- **Let hips develop.** Instead of deadheading the spent flowers from late fall bloom, let the spent flowers go to seed. That is, let the hips — or the seed pods — develop fully. Not everyone believes that this increases dormancy, but roses slow down their vegetative growth while their seeds mature, and this slowing should combine with other factors to increase dormancy.

The better care your roses receive throughout the growing season, the better chance they have of getting through the winter unscathed, or at least with minimal damage.

Keeping roses cold

Whether or not a rose plant is damaged by cold is more than a matter of how low the temperatures get. Strong winter winds can dry out canes, and because the ground is frozen, the plant has no way to resupply the canes with water. And fluctuating temperatures, which can cause plants to freeze and thaw, refreeze, and thaw again can kill a cane in a snap or rip a miniature rose right out of the ground. When you winter-protect a rose, you want to insulate the plant not only from the coldest temperatures but also from unusually warm weather that may cause the plant to thaw prematurely. And you also want to protect the rose from drying winds.

Follow these steps for the easiest way to winter-protect roses:

1. **Make sure that your plants are well watered.**

   Fall rains usually do the job, but if the weather has been dry, water deeply (to a depth of at least 18 inches) after the first frost but before the ground freezes.

2. **In early to midfall, when the nights are getting regularly frosty, mound several spadefuls of soil over the base of the plant, extending the soil up at least a foot above the bud union.**

   To make things easier, cut the canes back to 3 or 4 feet high and tie them together with string. Don't worry about the part of the canes above the mound; you're going to prune them off in the spring, anyway. Get the soil from somewhere other than your rose bed; you don't want to have to dig around your roses' tender roots.

3. **When the ground is thoroughly frozen, cover the mound with at least a foot of mulch.**

   Doing so ensures that the ground stays frozen and all the plant is protected. If any leaves are left on the plant, pull them off. Besides harboring disease, leaves can increase drying. To keep the protective material in place in windy areas, enclose the rose with a cylinder of wire mesh and fill it with mulch or soil, as shown in Figure 5-8.

4. **When the ground begins to thaw in the spring, gently start removing the soil from the base of the plant.**

   Don't get started too early; a sudden cold snap can be brutal. Watch for the yellow blooms of the forsythia. When they're in bloom, removing the mound of soil is usually safe. Remove the soil carefully, because you may find that growth is beginning — look for buds that are swollen and beginning to stretch. Those new buds are very easy to break off. Applying a gentle stream of water to wash away the soil is often better than using your hands.

Book III

Roses

Figure 5-8:
Mulched
and
wrapped
roses ready
for winter.

Protecting climbers and tree roses

Because climbing roses and tree roses are more upright and thus more
exposed to cold and wind, they need special protection. If the rose is tied to a
trellis or fence and the canes aren't very flexible, untie the canes and wrap
them with insulating material (like you'd wrap pipes to keep them from freezing). Then retie them to the trellis. If you need to cut the canes back a bit to
make the job easier, go ahead. Also, cover the base of the plant with at least a
foot of soil. You may also be able to detach the canes from the trellis, lay the
whole plant down (staking the canes in place if necessary), and cover it with
soil and/or mulch (see Figure 5-9). When the weather warms in spring, gently
remove the covering and retie the rose to the trellis.

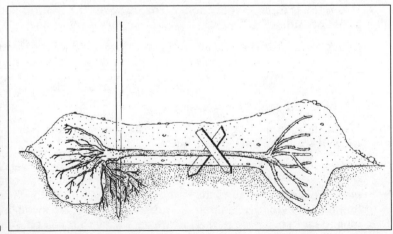

Figure 5-9:
Protect a
tree rose
through the
winter by
uprooting
one side of
the plant, so
that you can
lean it over
and bury it.

Dig up tree roses and store them for winter in a cool garage or basement. Or
dig only one side of the tree roses' roots so that it can lie on its side. Then
secure it in place with stakes and cover the whole thing with soil and mulch.

Preventing Problems

You can do several things to prevent insects and diseases from becoming problems for your roses:

- **Grow healthy plants.**

- **Plant problem-free varieties.** Many rose varieties, especially the newer ones, have natural disease resistance bred into them.

- **Encourage and use beneficial insects.** Beneficial insects are the insects that feed on the bugs that bother your roses. You probably have a bunch of different kinds of helpful insects in your garden already, but you can also purchase them and release them into your garden.

- **Keep your garden clean.** Rake around the base of your plants occasionally to clean up fallen leaves, and always discard or burn your prunings.

- **Know the enemy.** The more you know about specific pests and diseases common to your area — when they occur and how they spread — the more easily you can avoid them.

- **Apply a dormant spray.** Usually a combination of fairly benign horticultural oil and a fungicide like lime sulfur or fixed copper, a dormant spray smothers insect eggs and kills some disease organisms before they become a problem. Apply the spray right after you prune in late fall or winter.

Book III

Roses

Encouraging garden good guys

Following are some things you can do to encourage beneficial insects (see Chapter 7 in Book I for more on this subject) to populate your garden and reduce the number of rose pests:

- **Avoid indiscriminate use of broad-spectrum pesticides.** They kill everything — the good guys and the bad. If you do spray, use a spray that specifically targets the pest you want to eliminate.

- **Have a diverse garden with many different kinds and sizes of plants.** Doing so gives the beneficials places to hide and reproduce. Variety can also provide an alternate food source because many beneficials like to eat pollen or flower nectar, too. Plants that attract beneficials include Queen Anne's lace, parsley (especially if you let the flowers develop), dill, clover, fennel, and yarrow. You can find many of these plants described throughout this book.

If beneficial insects aren't numerous in your garden, you can buy them from mail-order garden suppliers. If you know that a particularly difficult pest is likely to appear, order in advance and release the beneficials in time to prevent problems. Following are some of the good insects that you can buy for your roses:

- **Lady beetles:** Both the adult and the Gila monster-like larvae of the basic ladybug are especially good at feeding on small insects, such as aphids and thrips. Releasing adults isn't always very effective because Mother Nature has preprogrammed them to migrate, and they leave your garden quickly. Try preconditioned lady beetles, which have been programmed (you don't want to know how) to be more likely to stick around, and release them just before sundown. That way, they'll at least spend the night. Release a few thousand of them in your garden in spring as soon as you notice aphids.

- **Green lacewings:** Their voracious larvae feed on aphids, thrips, mites, and various insect eggs. These insects occur naturally in most gardens and are one of the most effective beneficials at controlling garden pests.

- **Parasitic nematodes:** These microscopic worms parasitize many types of soil-dwelling and burrowing insects, including the grubs of Japanese beetles, June beetles, and rose chafers. Apply these worms to the soil around the base of your plants, as well as in your lawn where grubs tend to live, once a year in the spring.

- **Predatory mites:** This type of mite feeds on spider mites and thrips. Add them to your garden in spring as soon as frost danger has passed.

- **Trichogramma wasps:** Harmless to people, these wasps attack moth and butterfly eggs, reducing the number of eventual caterpillars. Release these garden good guys when the temperature is above 72°F (22°C).

Our stand on pesticides

We've included both traditional chemical controls and less toxic alternatives, such as botanical insecticides and beneficial insects in this chapter. However, we prefer to use alternatives first and turn to toxic materials only if a plant's survival is threatened. We *do not* believe in using combination products (fertilizer, insecticide, and fungicide). They're a shotgun approach to pest control that, although convenient, often results in excessive use of unneeded and often harsh chemicals that can harm the environment.

Aphid hors d'oeuvres

Good bugs hang out in gardens that offer the most diverse and reliable menu. So, eliminating every last insect pest from your garden makes no sense. Having some "bad" bugs around all the time is important. Aphids are like an hors d'oeuvre for so many helpful insects, so you always hope to have a few in your garden. Otherwise, what will the good bugs eat? But accepting the bugs also means that you have to accept a little pest damage once in a while. You're really just trying to manage the pests, not nuke them off the face of the earth. You want to keep them at acceptable levels, without letting them get out of control. Spend time in your garden, poking around, turning leaves upside down. Investigate, and get to know all the critters in your garden.

Preparing your first line of defense

To manage insects and diseases successfully, check your roses frequently for developing problems. If an insect or disease does get out of hand, you want to treat it effectively without disrupting all the life in the garden. (Chapter 7 in Book I offers a detailed discussion of managing pests and disease.) Start with pesticides that are very effective against a certain pest, pretty safe to use, and have a mild impact on the rest of the garden's life forms. In general, these products are short-lived after you use them in the garden — that's what makes them so good. However, in order to get effective control, you have to use them more frequently than you do stronger chemicals. Here are our favorites:

Book III

Roses

- ✔ **Biological controls:** This method involves pitting one living thing against another. Releasing beneficial insects is one example of biological control, but you can also use bacteria that, while harmless to humans, make rose pests very sick and eventually very dead. The most common and useful to rose growers are forms of *Bacillus thuringiensis,* or *Bt,* which kills caterpillars. Some strains of Bt control other types of pests. For example, one type (sold as milky spore) kills the larvae of Japanese beetles.

- ✔ **Botanical insecticides:** The following two plant-derived insecticides are especially useful against rose pests:

  - • **Neem:** It kills young feeding insects and deters adult insects but is harmless to people and most beneficials. Neem works slowly and is most effective against aphids and thrips, but it also repels Japanese beetles. We prefer neem oil over neem extract (check the product label) because the oil is also effective against all three common rose diseases: black spot, powdery mildew, and rust. Neem oil gets thick at cooler temperatures, so you need to warm it up a bit before trying to mix it with water. Just let the whole container sit in warm water a while before mixing. Use either kind of neem before you have a major pest problem. Neem is most effective when applied in early morning or late evening when humidity is highest. It can harm beneficials like lady beetles, so spray when they're not active. Reapply once a week or after rain.

- **Pyrethrins:** This broad-spectrum insecticide kills a wide range of insects, both good (spray late in the evening to avoid killing bees) and bad. That it kills beneficials as well as pests is the downside. The upside is that this insecticide kills pests like thrips and beetles quickly, breaks down rapidly in sunlight, and has low toxicity to mammals, which means that it's essentially harmless to people, pets, and the environment.

Avoid pyrethroids for home garden use. The terminology can be confusing. *Pyrethrum* is the ground-up flower of the daisy. *Pyrethrins* are the insecticide components of the flower. *Pyrethroids*, such as permethrin and resmethrin, are synthetic compounds that resemble pyrethrins but are more toxic and persistent.

✔ **Horticultural oils:** When sprayed on a plant, these highly refined oils smother pest insects and their eggs. The words *highly refined* mean that sulfur and other components of the oil that damage plants are removed. The two available oils are relatively nontoxic and short-lived:

- **Dormant oils:** Sprayed on roses when they're leafless in winter, these oils are often combined with a fungicide, such as lime sulfur or fixed copper, to help kill wintering disease spores.

- **Summer oils:** Usually more highly refined (or further diluted, or thinner) than dormant oils, these can be used on roses during the growing season, as long as the plants have been well watered and temperatures aren't above 85°F (29°C).

Avoid using oil sprays when temperatures are likely to reach above 85°F (29°C). When it's that hot, the oil can damage plant leaves.

✔ **Insecticidal soaps:** Derived from the salts of fatty acids, insecticidal soaps kill mostly soft-bodied pests, such as aphids, spider mites, and whiteflies. They can also be effective against Japanese beetles. They work fast, break down quickly, and are nontoxic to humans. Insecticidal soaps are most effective when mixed with soft water. Soaps sometimes burn tender foliage.

✔ **Baking soda (sodium bicarbonate):** Baking soda has been a popular powdery mildew remedy (partially effective against black spot) for the past few years. Mix 1 rounded tablespoon of baking soda with 1 tablespoon of summer oil in a gallon of water. Apply weekly to well-watered plants. Avoid damaging leaves by applying in the early morning, and don't spray if the temperature is above 85°F (29°C). Ongoing research shows that potassium bicarbonate may work a little better and be less prone to damaging leaves.

✔ **Antitranspirants:** When sprayed on plant foliage, antitranspirants form a thin, waxy layer that can prevent fungal disease like powdery mildew from invading the leaves. Antitranspirants don't kill disease, but they may prevent a disease from getting worse.

Rose problems: Knowledge before action

Before you wrestle with any insect or disease problem, make sure that you know what the problem is. For a start, consult our list of common insects and diseases that follows, and also take a look at the information we give about the best products and materials to use. If you need further help, contact a local nursery — the folks there should be familiar with the common problems in your area. Nearby botanical gardens and your local cooperative extension office also may be able to help.

You can also contact the American Rose Society (www.ars.org) and ask about their

Consulting Rosarian Program. Consulting Rosarians are recognized rose experts, and the ARS can put you in touch with the one nearest you. You can usually find several in any good-sized city, and nothing is better than asking a local expert for help. Plus, the advice is free!

If you prefer to look things up for yourself, ask your local nursery or library for the *Ortho Problem Solver* (published by Ortho Books). It's a 1,000-page encyclopedia of garden pest problems, with a color picture of each one.

Coping with insects that prey on roses

Book III

Roses

Following is a list of the most common insect pests you're likely to find infesting your roses (Chapter 7 in Book I deals with common pests in-depth), and the best ways to control them:

- **Aphids:** You can knock aphids off a plant with a strong jet of water from a hose, or you can spray them with an insecticidal soap. Malathion and acephate are traditional chemical controls for aphids.

  If you just wait a week or two, the aphid population boom is followed by a buildup in beneficial insects, especially lady beetles, and these beneficials take matters into their own hands (er, mouths) before serious damage occurs.

- **Cucumber beetles:** Control is difficult. Try spraying spray with pyrethrum, neem, or insecticidal soap. Parasitic nematodes prey on the soil-borne larvae. Carbaryl is a traditional chemical control.

- **Japanese beetles:** Treating your lawn and garden soil with parasitic nematodes or milky spore may reduce the larvae, but more adults will probably fly in from your neighbors' yards. Milky spore takes years to spread throughout your lawn. Turning the soil in the open areas of the rest of your yard to expose the grubs to birds may also help. Floral-scented traps that attract adult beetles are available, but the traps may bring in more beetles than you had before. If you try traps, keep them at least 100 feet away from your roses. Neem, insecticidal soap, and pyrethrum are effective alternative sprays for controlling adult beetles. Traditional chemicals that may help include carbaryl and acephate. You can also just pick them off your roses (late evening is the best time) and drop them into a can of soapy water.

✔ **Caterpillars:** Control them with *Bt* or by releasing trichogramma wasps. Acephate and carbaryl are traditional chemical controls that may be effective.

✔ **Rose midges:** If your rose plants look healthy but don't produce flowers, suspect rose midges. Insecticidal soaps sometimes work. For better control, attack the soil-borne larvae with Diazinon or chloropyrifos.

✔ **Rose chafers:** Control for these long-legged, tan-colored beetles is the same as for Japanese beetles, but milky spore isn't effective against the grubs.

✔ **Rose stem borers:** Cut off the wilted stem well back into healthy tissue. (You may be able to see a small hole where the borer entered the stem. Cut back below that.) If the tissue inside the cane is damaged, cut lower still until the inside of the cane is normal. If the borer has bored into the bud union, you may lose the plant. Few sprays of any kind are effective, although you may get some of the larvae as they drop to the ground after feeding by using parasitic nematodes near the base of the plant. To foil borers that enter through pruning cuts, put a drop of white glue on the top of the cane after you cut a flower or prune.

✔ **Spider mites:** A daily bath, working hardest on the undersides of the leaves, with a strong spray from a hose should keep infestations down. You can control spider mites by using insecticidal soaps, summer oil, or by releasing predatory mites. If the pests get completely out of control, you may have to use a miticide, such as Avid.

✔ **Thrips:** This almost-invisible troublemaker feeds on flower petals, causing them to become discolored and the buds to be deformed as they open. Thrips like all roses but are particularly fond of light-colored varieties. Many beneficial insects feed on thrips, especially lacewings. Insecticidal soaps are also effective, as are several other insecticides, including acephate.

Troubleshooting troublesome diseases

The following list discusses five of the most common rose diseases and suggests some techniques for controlling them. (*Note:* Most fungicides work only as preventives. They're ineffective after the disease is established, so apply them regularly before a disease becomes a problem.)

✔ **Black spot:** This fungus causes small black spots on rose leaves and stems, as shown in Figure 5-10. The edges of the spots are fringed, and the tissue around the spots often turns yellow. In bad infections, the plant may drop all its leaves. This disease is most common in warm, humid climates with frequent summer rain. To prevent black spot, plant disease-resistant varieties, clean up your winter prunings — the most common source of reinfection — and use a dormant spray that includes lime sulfur. Avoid overhead watering, or water early in the morning so that the leaves can dry out quickly. The baking soda-summer oil spray mentioned later in this chapter provides some control, as does neem oil. Effective traditional fungicides include triforine and chlorothalonil.

✔ **Downy mildew:** Often confused with powdery mildew and black spot, but much more serious, downy mildew has the capability to defoliate a plant in 24 hours. Round, purple blotches with yellow edges form on the tops of leaves, usually around the leaf veins. They may also occur on the stems. Grayish white fuzz sometimes forms on the bottoms of the leaves, which often turn brittle and drop off. Less common than other rose diseases, downy mildew usually shows up after long periods of cool, wet weather and then clears itself up when the weather warms. The disease needs moist conditions to spread, so avoid overhead watering and water early in the morning. Prune to increase air circulation, and clean up plant debris. A dormant spray may help.

✔ **Powdery mildew:** This grayish white, powdery fungus infects new leaves and flower buds, causing them to become distorted and crinkled-looking. Unlike most other fungal diseases, powdery mildew spreads on dry foliage. Many rose growers prevent the spread of powdery mildew by watering overhead or sprinkling down each day late in the afternoon, thus washing the spores off the leaves before they can establish themselves. Other preventive measures include planting resistant varieties, planting in full sun, and pruning to encourage air circulation. Effective preventive sprays include antitranspirants, the baking soda-summer oil mentioned later in this chapter, and neem oil. Triforine is one of several traditional chemical fungicides used to control powdery mildew.

✔ **Rust:** Small, orange pustules form on the undersides of the leaves and yellow spots appear on the tops. If the rust is severe enough, the plant can lose all its leaves. This disease is most troublesome when days are warm but nights are cool; prolonged hot, dry weather usually stops its development. Prevention is similar to black spot — winter cleanup and dormant spray. Make sure that you also strip off infected leaves. Neem oil provides some control, as do traditional fungicides like triforine.

✔ **Rose mosaic viruses:** Rose mosaic viruses cause yellow mottling on the leaves and deformed new growth. Some plants affected by one of the viruses grow poorly. You can't do much about it. Most of the time, it shows up on a few leaves and doesn't do much harm to anything. It can't spread from plant to plant, but you should definitely avoid taking cuttings from or hybridizing with infected plants because the virus is passed on to offspring. All reputable rose nurseries will replace a plant that has a virus. Destroy severely infected plants.

Pesticide safety

No matter which pesticides you decide to use, you must use them safely. Even pesticides that have a relatively low impact on your garden environment — including several commonly used botanical insecticides — can be dangerous to use and toxic to humans. After all, you're using these things to kill stuff! Here are some good guidelines to follow:

- **Always follow instructions** on the product label exactly: Doing otherwise is against the law, as well as a violation of common sense. Make sure that both the pest you're trying to control and the plant you're spraying are listed on the label. (Sometimes plants are listed in groups, such as *ornamental shrubs* or *flowering vines*.)

- **Wear plastic gloves** when mixing and spraying pesticides.

- **Spray when winds are calm.**

- **Wear eye protection,** a long-sleeved shirt, and long pants: Wash everything after spraying.

- **Store chemicals in the original** manufacturer's labeled containers well out of the reach of children: A locked cabinet is best.

- **Dispose of empty pesticide** containers as described on the label, or contact your local waste disposal company for appropriate disposal sites.

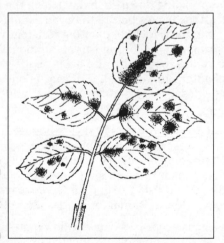

Figure 5-10:
Black spot
disease.

Book IV
Perennials

The 5th Wave — By Rich Tennant

"The seeds fell out of Walt's pocket six years ago and since then every August we just sit somewhere else."

In this book . . .

Much like that little rabbit from the battery commercials, perennials just keep, er, growing and growing and growing. Well, they do when provided with the right conditions. This book shows you how to make perennials work in your garden. You'll find chapters on selecting, planting, and caring for your perennials. Additionally, we help you decide whether (and which) to grow perennials from seed, start them from division, or buy them from a nursery. The last chapter in this book looks at special features for your flower bed — features that make your garden more accessible and uniquely yours. Just turn the page to get growing!

Here are the contents of Book IV at a glance:

Chapter 1

Perennials Nonstop

A perennial is any plant that lives for three or more years *when it's grown in conditions to its liking*. Book IV is really just about one type of perennial plant — the *herbaceous flowering perennial*. Technically, the term "perennial" includes such giants as the majestic, centuries-old redwood and the oak tree in the city park. Unlike trees and shrubs (which have woody stems forming their twigs, branches, and trunks) *herbaceous* perennials have soft, fleshy stems.

Perennials that hail from cold climates usually indulge in a winter nap, called a period of *dormancy*. (A few herbaceous perennials go dormant in summer, instead, playing a convincing game of opossum for their uninitiated gardeners.) During the period of dormancy, the perennial *dies back to the ground* — that is, allows its stems and foliage to die. The above-ground parts of a dormant plant are truly dead, but the roots are alive and well. In fact, the roots may be actively growing even when the top is resting. In more moderate climates, most herbaceous perennials are *evergreen* (meaning that their above-ground parts are alive and kicking all year long) because they don't need a coping mechanism, such as dormancy, to escape extreme temperatures.

Boning Up on Perennial Anatomy

Growing perennials is much easier if you have a basic understanding of how the flowers are put together. In spite of their significant variations, all the plants in this large group do share a few characteristics, as shown in Figure 1-1.

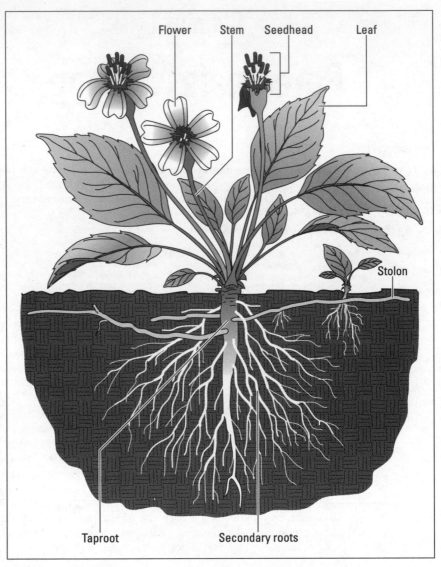

Flower Stem Seedhead Leaf

Stolon

Figure 1-1:
The basic
parts of a
perennial
plant are the
roots, stem,
leaves,
flowers, and
seedheads.

Taproot Secondary roots

The following list examines each of a perennial's basic parts:

✔ **Roots:** Roots pull water and nutrients from the soil and carry these
essentials to the stems. The roots even store extra water and nutrients
in case times get tough. The two main types of roots are *fibrous roots* and
taproots. Fibrous-rooted perennials have a network of branching roots.
Taprooted perennials have a fleshy central root (like a carrot), with
smaller secondary roots growing off the main root. Taproots can reach
quite deeply into the ground, but fibrous roots generally occur primarily
in the top 12 inches (30 cm) of soil.

✔ **Stems:** Stems transport water and nutrients from the roots to the leaves and flowers, and vice versa. Stems can be squared or rounded, upright or low and spreading, and single or branched. Stem tissue is sometimes specialized to create thickened underground repositories, where the plant can stash extra food and water. Perennials may also spread by modified stems called *stolons* (or *runners*) that travel just beneath the surface of the ground. The stolons often send up new shoots along their length, either close by or quite some distance from the original clump, varying by the type of perennial.

✔ **Leaves:** Although stems *can* manufacture food for the plant, this function is primarily the role of the leaves. Leaves also help the plant regulate its moisture content and internal temperature by allowing water to evaporate from their surfaces or by wilting, when necessary, to reduce their exposure to sun and air. Leaves come in a huge variety of shapes, sizes, and textures and can occur singly or as one of several leaves attached in a group on a single stalk. A cluster of leaves at the base of the plant is called a *basal rosette.* Stems and flower stalks rise from this clump of leaves and often die back to the basal rosette at the end of the growing season. Primroses are a good example.

✔ **Flowers:** Flowers are a perennial's reproductive structure. The bright, sweet-smelling flower blossom is meant to attract pollinators, such as bees and butterflies. Very small flowers are often wind-pollinated, producing prodigious amounts of pollen in a hit-or-miss system that greatly affects allergy sufferers. However, most garden flowers are chosen for their very showy blossoms, which don't cause allergies. Flowers can be held on a single stem or in multiples on spikes; in flattened clusters or loosely branched. What appears to be a single flower may actually be a cluster of many tiny flowers, forming a *flowerhead.* One example is the daisy, which is called a *composite* because it's composed of two kinds of flowers: the tiny tubular flowers forming the center button and the frill of petals around the outside edge.

✔ **Seedheads:** After a flower is pollinated, it forms seed. The flower deteriorates — first fading and wilting and then turning brown and dropping petals. If you don't cut off the dead bloom at this point, most flowers go to seed — that is, form seedpods or capsules. Some seedheads are as attractive as the flowers themselves. Flowers that develop seeds and germinate in your garden are said to *self-sow* or *volunteer.* The baby plants that come up are called seedlings. Some perennials are sterile and don't make viable seed. You can't grow more of these plants from seed, but you can chop the plants up and grow each part into a new plant that's identical to the parent.

Book IV

Perennials

Making the Argument for Perennials

Why grow perennials and not annuals? For two very good reasons: Perennials offer more visual interest than annuals, and (despite what you may think) perennials are actually easier to manage than annuals in the long run. (However, if you want to try both, Book V is all about annuals.) Perennial flower beds celebrate and, to some extent, choreograph the passing seasons. The institutional annual-flower displays, ever popular in municipal plantings, look exactly the same from the day they're planted until the first blackening frost. In sharp contrast, perennials reflect the passing seasons and are constantly changing and evolving. Tulips and daffodils give way to summer's bounty, and asters and chrysanthemums announce Indian summer.

Most perennials are endlessly forgiving as long as you plant their roots downward and point their leaves toward the light. In fact, perennials are such versatile plants that a few misconceptions about them have inevitably taken root. The novice gardener who chooses perennials to avoid having to replant annually is going to be disappointed to discover that many perennials don't survive the three years that, by definition, classify them as perennials. Many perennials are short-lived under any circumstances, and even the long-lived ones only endure when conditions are to their liking. Still, as long as expectations are realistic, perennials promise to bring even the most casual gardener endless hours of delight (peppered with occasional moments of frustration as a reality check). Wherever you live and whatever the conditions you have to offer, you can find perennial flowers that can oblige.

Caught in a perennial Web

The World Wide Web has a treasure trove of sites to help you plan and maintain your garden. Following are good sites to get you started:

✔ **The Perennial Plant Association** (www.perennialplant.org): This organization serves landscapers, nurseries, designers, educators, and the general public. If you join the association, you have access to an annual symposium, a membership directory for networking, and guides to regional meetings and gardens.

✔ **The National Gardening Association** (www.garden.org): This Web site provides a bounty of gardening information.

✔ **GardenNet** (www.gardennet.com): This site provides links to other gardening associations.

✔ **University of South Carolina Telegarden** (www.usc.edu/dept/garden/): Here, you visit a patch of virtual land entirely managed by members via the Internet. As a guest, you can move a mechanical arm around the garden to look at its various parts; as a member, you can plant seeds and tend to the garden! Telegardening is a fascinating way to experiment with different gardening designs and plans — and without pulling a single muscle!

✔ **National Wildflower Research Center** (www.wildflower.org/): This organization in Austin, Texas, grows a variety of interesting display gardens, which can give you ideas for your own patch of soil.

Making a Style Statement

Unless you're an old hand at creating gardens, you probably find the very suggestion of flower-bed design intimidating. Just remember that flower-bed design is simply a process that encourages you to take the time to thoroughly think through what you plan to do before you actually start. Good design happens automatically when you arrange all the various building blocks (which we provide here) into a satisfying layout.

There's no one right way to design your garden. Don't let anyone (not even us!) impose his or her own views and prejudices on you. Your garden should be uniquely your own, reflecting your personal taste. The design advice that we provide is meant to serve only as a guide, not as a set of rules for you to follow. (For more on landscape design, see Book II.)

Designing for success

Forget everything you've ever read about design theory. You have a built-in sense of what feels right to you — which is all that really matters. Mistakes are inevitable, but flower-garden foul-ups are among the easiest and least costly landscape disasters to remedy. To get an idea of how you want your flower garden to look, do the following:

✔ **Make a file or a notebook to keep track of your observations.** Note what about each garden appeals or doesn't appeal to you.

✔ **Visit public gardens, take a critical look around your neighborhood, sign up for garden tours, or watch garden shows on television.**

✔ **Write down any particular flowers that catch your fancy, noting what you like and dislike about the flower.** If you don't know what a particular flower is, knock on the gardener's door and ask. Gardeners are generally flattered and pleased to discuss their gardens.

✔ **Keep visual records.** Take some snapshots of the best ideas you find to study at your leisure. Look through magazines and cut out inspiring illustrations or make color copies from books. Remember that plagiarism doesn't apply to garden design. You can copy whatever you like!

After you compile all this information, you're likely to notice trends emerging:

✔ **Formal:** Neat and orderly, the formal garden relies on strong visual lines. Formal gardens are frequently based on geometric patterns and often divided into parts, with each part a mirror image of its opposite. Color and form are usually repeated regularly within the formal design. A rigidly formal design can be quite labor-intensive — every dead or stunted plant leaves an obvious gap, interrupting the line or grid pattern.

✔ **Informal:** The popular cottage garden style embodies the rustic, unaffected, informal garden. If you like to color outside the lines, you're probably more comfortable with an informal garden design. The informal design feels refreshingly free from rules and order, but it works best when you thoughtfully arrange it to create a subtle balance between the various colors and forms of the flowers. The informal gardening style is much like natural make-up. The goal is to appear less studied and fussy, but not to let nature have its way unrestricted. You can get a taste for what happens when nature is allowed to go its own way by visiting an overgrown vacant lot.

Skirting the issue: Beds and borders

Whether planning beds or borders, keep the shapes fairly simple for ease of maintenance and to prevent the viewer from feeling the motion sickness that squiggly lines can cause. Curves should undulate softly, not sharply zig and zag — especially when bordering the lawn. Flowers along sharp edges inevitably lose their heads to the errant lawnmower — no matter how careful you are.

Whether arranged formally or informally, flower beds come in two basic configurations — the border or the island bed:

✔ **Border:** The term *border* refers to any flower bed located alongside a wall, fence, hedge, or pavement. A border garden is usually long and narrow, with straight or curved edges, as it follows the contours of the backdrop. You may hear the term *mixed border* tossed about. The *traditional* or *herbaceous border* excludes any type of plant except herbaceous perennial flowers. The mixed border, on the other hand, contains a medley of flowering plants, including small trees, well-behaved shrubs, bulbs, annual flowers, herbs, vines, and perhaps even vegetables. Much of the mixed border's popularity today is due to the limited size of the modern lot. These days, garden space must do double or even triple duty.

✔ **Island bed:** The *island bed* is a free-standing flower bed surrounded on all sides by lawn, gravel, or pavement. Island beds can be any shape or size. Like border gardens, island beds can be mixed, but for some unknown reason, you never see the term "mixed island beds." The main advantage of the island style is that you can place the bed wherever conditions are ideal for the flowers that you want to grow. Island beds also counter the tendency to confine all the landscaping to the perimeter of the property, although these beds usually work best when you place them off to one side. Unlike flower beds grown against a barrier, island beds encourage you to walk around them and view their splendor from a variety of angles.

Interacting with various design elements

An interesting and attractive flower bed involves a complex interplay of many separate parts. Putting together such a garden can be a delicate balancing act. Too much sameness can easily become dull and boring; too much variety can slip into chaos. On the other hand, continually remind yourself that no garden design is wrong. Most gardeners are constantly playing around with their compositions, moving flowers to try new and better combinations (part of the appeal of gardening with perennials is their cheerful acceptance of such treatment). As you tinker with your flower beds pay special attention to the three most important design elements: color, texture, and form.

Color

Color fashion is always arbitrary. After a few decades of having the pastel garden represent good taste in garden design, stronger colors have recently begun to enjoy a surge in popularity. Avoid the myth of clashing colors. No natural law governs color compatibility — in nature, anything goes. You need to determine what colors you like together, regardless of convention. You can plan a garden around your favorite color, repeat the colors you use inside your home, or find some other creative approach. You also need to decide whether to stick with a single color, to use two or three colors, or to go wild and embrace the whole spectrum of the rainbow.

Try various color combinations by cutting out pictures from garden catalogs and putting them together until the arrangement pleases you. Or go to a nursery, pick up your favorite perennial in bloom, and carry it around, placing it next to other flowers until you discover attractive associations (matching the water, sunlight, and soil needs of the plants to each other and to your garden site is equally important). In fact, an easy way to choose perennials for your garden is to buy one-third of the flowers that you need to fill your garden while they're in bloom in the spring, buy another one-third in bloom in the summer, and one-third while in bloom in the fall. This way, you can be absolutely certain that they go together.

Look closely at a variety of flowers, and you notice that very few of them are solid colors. Most have shadings, and nearly all have contrasting centers. An effective design trick is to pick up these shades or center colors in neighboring flowers. For example, placing a white daisy with a yellow center next to a yellow lily visually ties the two together. You can also use intermediate colors to soften hard companions. If you have crayon reds and yellows fighting for your attention, adding either orange or pale yellow calms both of them down.

Looking beyond the blooms

When selecting flower colors, give some thought to the background. White flowers against a white wall don't make much of a statement and may even blend in so well that they become invisible at 20 paces. Light colors stand out better against dark surfaces, and the reverse is also true. Pale pastel colors, such as pink, lavender, and soft yellow, look best in soft light — either early or late in the day, in shade, or in overcast climates. Strong reds, purples, oranges, and yellows are more dynamic and stand up better to intense sunlight. White becomes luminescent at dusk or by moonlight.

And don't overlook foliage when considering flower color. Leaves of silver, gray, blue, purple, or red, as well countless shades of green, add another dimension to the flower bed.

Texture

Texture in the garden may be actual or perceived. You can touch the soft fuzz of lamb's ear or the waxy smoothness of 'Autumn Joy' sedum. Perceived texture is created by the varying shapes and sizes of flowers and foliage, the interplay of light and shadow, and background materials, whether hard surfaces or mulch. A brick wall has an entirely different tactile quality than a wooden fence. A smooth, painted fence has a different nature than one constructed of rough, unpainted cedar.

Fine texture generally feels more elegant and formal; coarse is more casual or rustic. Complete uniformity of either texture is almost always too dull. Generally, you want to aim for some contrast — varying the proportion of coarse to fine to suit your taste. Using one-third large foliage and flowers, one-third medium-sized, and one-third small is always safe. Traditional hedge plants have fine foliage; they don't call attention to themselves, so they form a somewhat neutral backdrop. Bold, large-leafed perennials have the opposite effect. They're attention-grabbing and bring drama and excitement to the mix.

Shape, size, and form

Other variables that merit your attention are size, shape, and form. Stimulating and intriguing gardens always depend on some diversity among all three of these elements, as shown in Figure 1-2. Perennials occur in countless different forms. Interesting arrangements play these characteristics against one another.

As important as contrasting form is varying flower and foliage size and shape. Flowers can be borne singly or in multiples. They can be spikes or spires, flattened or rounded, clusters, balls, daisies, stars, bell-, cup-, or saucer-shaped, clouds of tiny blossoms, or asymmetrical. Size varies just as widely — from ¼ inch (0.5 cm) to dinner plate proportions. Foliage is equally diverse in size, shape, and arrangement. Repeating size, shape, and form has a calming effect. Using a variety livens things up.

Figure 1-2:
Add dimension to your flower beds by choosing flowers with varying heights.

Accent

To further spice things up, consider using an accent or two in the flower bed. An accent can be anything that stands out or calls attention to itself — such as a strategically placed piece of sculpture; a bird bath; a large, bold plant; or a bright spot of contrasting color. For accents to be effective, they must be used sparingly. A single specimen of blue oat grass is conspicuous, but a grouping of the same grass blends together and doesn't have the same emphasis.

Succession of bloom

A flower garden can be planned so that instead of one brief moment of splendor, its beauty can span the whole year, with something happening at every season. Planning for a succession of bloom gives you the opportunity to pack a great deal into a small space. Generally, the aim is to have a third of the garden in bloom in the spring, a third in the summer, and a third in the fall. Figure out approximately how many plants fit into your allotted space, divide this number by three, and then purchase that number of flowers for each season. You can extend the color by choosing a few long-blooming flowers or flowers that have attractive seedheads. To further maximize your space, plant scads of bulbs. You can mix them right into the root zones of the other perennials without causing competition problems for either. (See Book VI for more information on bulbs.)

You can also choose to completely switch your color scheme from one season to the next. You may have pastels for spring, passionate jewel tones for summer, and hot colors to complement the pumpkins in autumn. Because

Book IV

Perennials

most perennials only bloom for a few weeks at a time, making such changes within the flower bed isn't difficult. If any flower blooms at the wrong season and causes a color catastrophe with its unintended neighbors, simply cut the offending blossoms and enjoy them in a vase inside the house.

Winter interest

For gardeners who live in cold climates, winter brings a well-needed respite from gardening. But that doesn't mean that the garden must be absolutely bare during this quiet season. Seedheads and the stark silhouettes of grasses stand in dramatic contrast to a blanket of snow. Many perennials are at least partly evergreen. Winter may never have the same exuberance as the rest of the year, but the trade-off is the possibility of a peaceful stroll that is uninterrupted by the nagging of myriad unfinished garden tasks.

Fascinating Foliage Follies

Because perennials generally bloom for only a few weeks at a stretch, foliage is all you have to look at for the rest of the growing season. But, if you remember the 1960's terrarium craze, you know how pretty a garden composed completely of foliage can be. A garden of flowers and no foliage isn't a pleasant thought. Imagine a musical score consisting only of the melody. When you add harmony, you get a rich blend of tones. Leaves can be the bass notes, the accents, or the whole supporting orchestra behind the soloist flowers. The perennials in this section give you the best of both worlds — beautiful flowers *and* better than average foliage.

The grass menagerie

Flowers and grass are natural partners, occurring together wherever ample sunlight is available. No other foliage plant surpasses grasses for the texture and beauty they bring to the flower garden. Still, if you've ever battled either weedy grasses or lawn grasses (see Chapter 4 in Book II for more on lawns) growing where they aren't wanted, you may question the sanity of intentionally introducing grass into the flower bed.

Granted, a few of the ornamental grasses, such as Ribbon grass, are every bit as tenacious and aggressive as crabgrass or quackgrass. These invasive grasses do have landscape applications for extremely difficult sites, and you can use them as ground covers for interesting alternatives to traditional lawn grasses. But for the flower garden, you want to seek out the better-behaved members of this large and diverse group of plants. Look for clump-forming grass varieties or slow-spreading *rhizomatous* types (those with creeping roots).

If you want the best of both worlds in your flower bed (the invasive ornamental grasses without the invasions), bury a large pot or a section of sewer pipe and plant the "attractive nuisance" inside the barrier, where you can confine its traveling ways. Vigilance is still prudent — check for escape attempts every so often. Some rhizomes inevitably try to go over the wall. Be sure to pull these run-away grasses out before they attempt to take over your flower bed.

Not all grasses are what most people think of as grass. Reeds, rushes, sedges, cereal grains, and bamboo are all lumped together in the same extended family with ornamental grasses. All grasses do share a few distinguishing physical traits. The most obvious is the foliage — long, narrow blades with parallel veins running the vertical length of each leaf. Their understated blooms aren't flowers in any traditional sense. Grass flowers are feathery or spiked affairs.

Big and bold herbaceous perennials

When you come across a perennial listed at 10 feet (3 m) tall, you're looking at the Incredible Hulks of the flower bed — herbaceous perennials who die back to the ground in winter to return each spring and quickly grow to the proportions of a large shrub. These plants can work magic on even the smallest garden. Large perennials are real attention-grabbers.

Many garden designers caution against including really massive perennials in the small garden. They fear that small spaces are too easily overwhelmed and dominated by such an imposing presence. But whether or not you include these big beauties in your little flower bed depends entirely on the look you're after. Large foliage makes a good accent and provides contrast to the fine texture. If all the flowers are shorter than waist high and have refined, subtle forms, your garden can easily become awfully dull. A few big and bold perennials are guaranteed to break up the monotony.

If you want a tropical, luxuriant air to your garden, use a large percentage of perennials with big blooms and dramatically oversized foliage. For more of a cottage garden ambiance, use only a few as accents, either standing alone or arranged in small groups of two or three. Keep in mind that the more large foliage you include, the less of an impact it has.

Book IV

Perennials

Gardeners traditionally place large-scale perennials at the back of the flower border or along the spine in the center of an island bed. This arrangement is logical enough — you don't want anything bulky blocking the view to all the flowers behind it. But you can make things more interesting by bringing some large plants forward to the mid-range or, in some cases, to the front row. Silver sage, for example, has a large, low rosette of magnificent silvery foliage. Place this plant at the front or in a corner of the flower bed where it has space to spread out completely unobstructed. The flower spikes are 4 to 5 feet (1.2 to 1.5 m) tall, but they're open-branched and candelabra-like, creating an attractive veil that enhances without upstaging the shorter neighbors standing behind them.

Following are some big and bold perennials to consider for your garden:

- ✔ **Monkshood (*Aconitum napellus*):** All parts of this plant are extremely toxic if eaten, even in small quantities.

- ✔ **Columbine (*Aquilegia* hybrids):** The hybrids capture every color but orange.

- ✔ **Tree mallow (*Lavatera thuringiaca*):** Little used, tree mallow ought to be in every garden within its hardiness range.

- ✔ **Plume poppy (*Macleaya cordata*):** The seedheads are as ornamental as the flowers; leave them uncut until the first frost.

- ✔ **Sticky Jerusalem sage (*Phlomis russeliana*):** This plant has good drought tolerance.

- ✔ **New Zealand flax (*Phormium tenax*):** Hardy to 10°F (–12°C), this tender perennial is invaluable where it's winter hardy.

- ✔ **Silver sage (*Salvia argentea*).**

- ✔ **Mullein (*Verbascum chaixii*).**

- ✔ **Culver's root (*Veronicastrum virginicum*):** This plant extends the blooming season in late summer.

A foliage rainbow

Foliage colors are as varied as the paint chip selections in your hardware store. The following list shows only a few of the best in each color category:

- ✔ **Blues:** Blue foliage tones never clash with stronger colors and actually have a neutralizing, calming effect. Planting blue foliage is a safe means to expand the foliage color palette; most of the blues lean toward bluish green, so the transition is usually a gentle one. Some good blues include red valerian (*Centranthus ruber*), baby's breath (*Gypsophila paniculata*), and shade lily (*Hosta sieboldiana* 'Elegans').

- ✔ **Purples and reds:** This foliage has a moody, sultry quality. It emboldens pastel color schemes or dampens the flames of red and orange companions to an exquisite smolder. Good perennials with this color foliage include Black mondo grass (*Ophiopogon planiscapus* 'Niger'), 'Husker Red' beardtongue (*Penstemon digitalis* 'Husker Red'), and Purple stonecrop (*Sedum telephium maximum* 'Atropurpureum').

✔ **Silvers and grays:** Many garden designers consider silvers and grays good mediators to calm harsh, jarring factions. Instead of creating neutral tones, these shimmering beauties call your attention to themselves and away from any warring colors nearby. With only a few exceptions, silver or gray foliage indicates at least a degree of drought tolerance and a need for full sun. Some to consider include 'Moonshine' yarrow (*Achillea* 'Moonshine'), Wormwood (*Artemisia absinthium* 'Lambrook Silver'), and English lavender *(Lavandula angustifolia).*

✔ **Variegated:** Usually, *variegation* (having multiple colors) is a natural mutation, showing up as mottling on an otherwise solid-colored leaf. The variegation may be dots, freckles, stripes, or blotches of contrasting color. Some foliage has more than two colors, while others have only a slight brushing of white on the leaf edges. These oddities are especially valuable for lightening and brightening shady gardens. Combine variegated foliage cautiously; too many patterns arranged too closely together can easily become clownish. Interesting variegated plants include Bugleweed (*Ajuga reptans* 'Burgundy Glow'), Yellow archangel (*Lamiastrum galeobdolon* 'Florentinum'), and Spotted dead nettle *(Lamium maculatum).*

✔ **Yellows:** These rare and unusual yellow, chartreuse, and golden-leafed perennials have become exceedingly popular. They're particularly desirable for bringing a luminescent glow to the shaded flower garden. The following plants are good choices: Creeping Jenny (*Lysimachia nummularia* 'Aurea'), Golden sage (*Salvia officinalis* 'Aurea'), and Lemon thyme (*Thymus citriodorus* 'Aureus').

Book IV

Perennials

Chapter 2

Perennials in Any Kind of Weather

· ·

In This Chapter

▶ Determining your climate and the perennials that thrive in it

▶ Soaking up the rays — sun-loving perennials

▶ Choosing perennials for shady spots

· ·

*E*very gardener sincerely believes that his own climate is the worst on the face of the planet. The cold-climate gardener who has to shovel snow from early fall until late spring isn't likely to feel compassion for the tropical gardener who experiences a few flakes once in five years. Yet that rare snow-fall is just what causes the worst damage to gardens. This chapter offers suggestions for perennials that do well in various climate conditions. (For a discussion of climate in general, turn to Chapter 2 in Book I.)

Cultivating Cold-Climate Perennials

Winter hardiness depends on a number of elements beyond low tempera-tures, although a record-breaking cold spell can damage even the hardiest plants. In addition, rainfall is often unpredictable in cold climates, and sum-mers may be either prone to drought or wet and humid, depending on where you live. The frost-free growing season is often unreasonably short in these climates — lasting only three to four months — and temperatures jump all over the thermometer.

Winter sun and thaw also pose a significant threat to plants. Many plants that don't survive winter die because they warmed slightly on a sunny day and then couldn't readjust quickly enough when frigid temperatures returned. From a plant's point of view, once frozen, better to stay frozen. Snow serves as the down comforter of mulches. A thick layer of snow keeps the ground solidly frozen and unaffected by constantly fluctuating air temperatures. Flowers tucked cozily under this insulating blanket aren't tempted to break dormancy prematurely. If a winter warm spell lasts long enough to melt the snow cover, vulnerable new growth gets zapped by the next passing storm. In regions where snow cover is reliable and durable, such weather fluctuations aren't as harmful.

Perennials that are only marginally hardy in your region may survive winter if you plant them on the north side of a building. In this normally shady location, plants are least likely to thaw on sunny winter days. Gardens in cold-winter climates tend to be high summer gardens. Because the gardening season is short, plants rush to bloom, with most peaking at about the same time. Instead of bemoaning the short season, plan a garden party for mid-to-late summer and amaze your friends from more temperate climes.

Dressing Up the Drylands

In cold-winter/dry-summer climates, summers are devilishly hot, except at higher elevations. Low winter temperatures average –20° F (–29° C) and erratic temperature fluctuations can wreak havoc on the garden and affect plant hardiness. Some common challenges of this climate include the following:

Xeriscape to Xanadu

Water is scarce and precious in arid regions. Coping with inevitable shortages has given rise to the *xeriscape movement* — combining good horticulture with water conservation to create flower gardens every bit as lush, full, and vibrant as those in more temperate climates. *"Xeriscape"* combines *xeric* (a dry habitat or a plant from such a place) with *landscape* to create xeriscape — literally, a dry landscape. Xeriscape is a system, not a style. A xeriscape can be as formal as Versailles or as casual as a cottage garden. You can't drive up and down the street and pick out the xeriscapes; only the water bill tells the story. Xeriscaping relies on choosing perennials with low water needs, and then fixing poor soils, grouping plants with similar needs, mulching, and practicing efficient irrigation.

Most drought-tolerant plants employ one or more of the following adaptations:

- **Succulent leaves:** Fat, fleshy leaves and stems act as water storage tanks.

- **Large roots:** Roots are an underground water storage system.

- **Silver or gray hairy leaves:** Light colored, fuzzy leaves reflect intense sunlight and shade the leaf surface.

- **Small leaves:** The smaller the leaf, the less surface area exposed to drying winds and sunlight.

✓ **Generally poor soils:** The dirt in this climate is usually stony, sandy, or highly alkaline clay. Humus content is very low. (See Chapter 3 in Book I for more information about soils.)

✓ **Notoriously low humidity:** The entire region is exceedingly dry.

✓ **Unreliable snow cover:** Because of the low humidity, snow usually evaporates before it has a chance to soak in.

✓ **Very little rain:** Lack of rain makes watering necessary, but water conservation usually limits the amount of watering allowed.

Managing Mild and Moist Year-Round

Some areas have mild weather year-round, even though the changing seasons are also clearly defined. A genuine Shangri-La for perennial gardening, this moderate, marine climate has the following characteristics:

✓ **Cool summers:** Summers are cool and overcast, punctuated by an occasional spell of bright, sunlit days.

✓ **Mild winters:** Snow does fall, but not often enough to make a nuisance of itself. Killing frosts occasionally sneak down from the arctic, but even then, the temperatures rarely plummet below 0° F (–18° C).

✓ **Moderate, steady rainfall:** Rainfall is moderate and conveniently spaced throughout the seasons. Even so, periods of extended drought aren't uncommon.

One advantage of living in an overcast climate is that you can safely use even the quietest pastel tones without fearing that the harsh sunlight will wash out the colors.

Sailing Along in Warm, Dry Maritime Climates

If a flower-gardening paradise exists, mild maritime climates approach it. Moderated by the ocean's influence, these regions suffer no extremes of heat or cold to test a plant's endurance. Much as in a greenhouse environment, cool and misty conditions prevail at all seasons. Frosts are infrequent in most maritime regions and almost unheard of in some. Even the occasional frosts aren't of the killer arctic nature. The temperature rarely dips much below 30° F (–1° C).

Book IV

Perennials

Summers are equally mild, dominated by foggy mornings and humid sea breezes. A few heat lovers don't get adequate sunshine, but most perennials thrive in this benevolent climate — as long as they get enough water.

Ah, water — the one shortcoming in maritime regions. Water shortages and periodic rationing are increasingly common in all arid and semiarid regions around the world. The wise maritime gardener plans for water shortages by choosing from the large number of perennials that need little or no irrigation to prosper.

Shaping Steamy Subtropical Gardens

Subtropical regions experience mild, wet winters and hot, humid summers. Most hot and humid regions experience just enough cold to make growing truly tropical plants a risky proposition. Even gardens in the warmest parts of these areas routinely experience a hard freeze once every 15 or 20 years, sometimes with an occasional snowfall. Periods of very heavy rainfall alternate with prolonged dry spells in these regions, so plants must be able to contend with both extremes. Soil types range from nearly perfect, fertile, well-drained loam to sticky, heavy clay and pockets of pure sand, and from overly acidic to highly alkaline.

The subtropical garden's riotous spring display also has few rivals. Camellias, dogwoods, magnolias, azaleas, and flowering vines all bloom together with reckless and colorful abandon. In general, the same perennials bloom earlier in the year and are shorter-lived when they are grown in warmer climates. Perennials also tend to be taller and less sturdy in the subtropical garden than their counterparts grown in cold-weather climates. Whenever one is available, choose a dwarf variety, because it's less likely to flop over without staking. Frequent division — as often as once a year — helps many types maintain their vigor.

Scraping by in the Scorching Desert

Mild winters distinguish the warm deserts from the cold drylands. Snow isn't unheard of in these regions, but temperatures rarely stay below freezing for long. Warm deserts share one universal characteristic: Soil and air temperatures are high. Although generally perceived as barren and desolate places, warm deserts actually have some of the richest and most diverse floras anywhere on earth. And you can't help but admire the fortitude and endurance of the plants that have evolved in such a seemingly forbidding climate. Adapt to the demands of desert gardening, and you can capture all the excitement and awe of the desert's natural beauty.

Desert soils range from pockets of wonderfully fertile soil to nearly pure gravel or heavy clay. Most soils are highly alkaline and some are also quite salty; they tend to be deficient in decaying organic matter — typically containing only 0.5 to 1 percent. Caliche (see Chapter 3 in Book I) is a problem, so you either have to break up the hardpan enough to enable plant roots and water to penetrate and drain through the soil, or build raised beds.

Rainfall is scarce and irregular throughout the warm desert regions. None of these areas receive more than 10 inches (25 cm) annually. Moisture evaporates from the soil faster than rain falls. The key to perennial gardening in this arid climate is to shelter the flower bed from the harsh elements so that it doesn't dry out so quickly. Rain often comes all at once, with one violent storm quickly dumping several inches. In such deluges, most of the water is wasted because it runs off before it has a chance to soak into the parched soil. Strong winds, sandstorms, and intense sunlight all routinely batter unadapted plants, challenging your patience and your sense of humor.

Exposing Sunny Dispositions

Flowers and sunshine are natural friends, and the majority of common perennials love to bask in the sun. This section shows you some easy-to-find, easy-to-grow perennials that you may choose to adorn your garden.

Perennials that are considered to need "full sun" exposure don't necessarily require sunshine all day long. An average of five to six hours of sun a day keeps the perennials in the following list fit and healthy, although most will settle for less sunlight without making too much of a fuss. Look for the term *partial shade* to find perennials that may need a bit more protection from intense afternoon sun.

- **Common yarrow** *(Achillea millefolium):* This perennial is absolutely easy-care, except for its wandering tendencies. The flowerheads are large, flat clusters of tiny daisies on long, straight stems — excellent for cutting or drying. Cut the stems down to within a few inches of the ground after blooming is finished. No winter protection is necessary. It enjoys hot daytime temperatures but prefers cool nights.

- **Blue star flower** *(Amsonia tabernaemontana):* This bushy plant has upright, arching stems and long, narrow, willowlike leaves. In the spring, each stem bears a cluster of steely blue, star-shaped flowers, and blue star turns a glowing yellow around the same time the pumpkins are ripening.

Book IV

Perennials

- **Japanese windflower** *(Anemone hybrida):* Japanese windflowers prefer partial shade, except in cool climates, where they can withstand full sun. In autumn, sprays of delicate pink, deep rose, or sparkling white flowers dance above light- to dark-green grapelike foliage.

- **Common thrift** *(Armeria maritima):* This plant looks like a cluster of drumsticks. In the springtime, tubular blossoms are packed into tight balls and held upright on stiff, straight stems above a tussock of grassy foliage. Diverse varieties are available. This plant's only requirement is fast drainage; common thrift is otherwise tough as nails. It tolerates salt, pure sand, and drought.

- **Butterfly flower** *(Asclepias tuberosa):* This flower adapts anywhere without complaint. Although unfashionably orange, butterfly flower (also called butterfly weed) is so pretty that the antiorange crowd overlooks this so-called flaw.

- **Frikart's aster** *(Aster frikartii):* An international celebrity, this aster produces masses of blue daisies from midsummer until frost. Individual plants are long-lived and carefree.

- **Peachleaf bellflower** *(Campanula persicifolia):* The bellflower family is a huge one with at least a dozen good garden perennials readily available. Most are easy and charming.

- **Tickseed** *(Coreopsis grandiflora):* Tickseed is the perfect choice for anyone who can't get enough daisies. This one blooms its head off if regularly deadheaded. The flowers have a casual air. Each petal is ragged-edged and arranged around a golden center.

- **Summer daisies** *(Dendranthema):* Summer daisies used to be called chrysanthemums until the botanists decided to change their names. All varieties have grayish green, strongly aromatic foliage. Touching the leaves can cause a skin rash in sensitive individuals. Summer daisies spread like wildfire in fertile soil and need dividing annually to stop them from taking over the whole flower bed.

- **Purple coneflower** *(Echinacea purpurea):* Large, purplish pink daisies with bristly orange centers contradict the old adage that pink and orange always clash. Foliage is large, coarse, and dark green. Purple coneflower is a good cut flower, and butterflies find it irresistible. It blooms for a very long period, from early summer to frost. After the petals fall, the cone is attractive in dried arrangements.

- **Queen-of-the-prairie** *(Filipendula rubra):* Masses of pink, cotton-candy plumes are an impressive sight when this regal perennial is in bloom, but it usually doesn't bloom until the second season after transplanting. It's tall and sturdy, forming large clumps of dark green, jagged leaves.

- **Blanket flower** *(Gaillardia aristata):* Blanket flowers bloom from spring to fall in loud, concentric circles of red and yellow, but the flowers tend to be short-lived. They strew their seeds around, but their progeny are usually quite changed in appearance from mom and dad. Handling the leaves of this plant may cause skin rashes in sensitive individuals, so wear gloves as a precaution. Blanket flowers grow anywhere — on sand dunes in Florida to almost the Canadian tundra.

- ✔ **Appleblossom grass** *(Gaura lindheimeri):* This delicate and airy plant has a really rugged constitution. Appleblossom-like flowers dangle on long, willowy stems. The flowers are white with shrimp-pink anthers, lower petals, and stems, which from a distance, looks like a pink cloud.

- ✔ **Bloody cranesbill** *(Geranium sanguineum):* Very long-blooming and adaptable, bloody cranesbill grows in a loosely mounded form and sports attractive leaves that turn crimson in fall. The simple, open-faced flowers are a strident magenta, held several inches above the foliage. It can spread far too rapidly in fertile, moist soil and is generally better behaved when kept a little stressed.

- ✔ **Transvaal daisy** *(Gerbera jamesonii):* Tender daisies grown as annuals outside their hardiness range, Transvaal daisies perform best in hot, humid regions where rainfall is high. They come in a rainbow of colors in single and double forms. Each flower is held singly on a strong stem, poised elegantly above low foliage rosettes. Buy the small seedling size for transplanting into the garden. The large, lush florists' pots don't have a good survival rate.

- ✔ **Common sneezeweed** *(Helenium autumnale):* Featuring pretty daisies on upright tidy plants, common sneezeweed is also tough and adaptable. It starts blooming during the midsummer slump when most of the garden is taking a siesta. The flowers resemble badminton shuttlecocks with a raised center knob and a frill of notched petals. *Pinch* in spring, removing the top few inches of each stem to create a bushier plant and delay blooming. Cut the stems back to within a few inches of the ground after flowering wanes. Divide every two to three years to renew vigor.

- ✔ **Daylily** *(Hemerocallis* hybrids): The daylily's dazzling trumpets are open for only one day, but are indispensable for the midsummer garden. Daylilies send up new flowers every day for two to three weeks. Hundreds of varieties are available. The foliage is green and grasslike, and the flowers are sometimes fragrant. Daylilies face the sun, so always place them where you can see their faces.

- ✔ **Shasta daisy** *(Leucanthemum maximum):* Shasta daisies are impressive, large white daisies with golden yellow centers. Many forms are available, from simple, rather formal daisies to shaggy doubles. Tall varieties flop over if they aren't staked. Cut stems back to within a few inches of the ground when blooming stops. Divide annually in hot, humid climates and pinch stems early in the season.

- ✔ **Gayfeather** *(Liatris spicata):* When in bloom, this attention-grabber looks like a bouquet of rosy purple exclamation points. Each individual flower is tiny, but the flowers are densely clustered on upright spikes. The foliage is dark green and grassy. Cut spikes to the ground when they're finished flowering to promote additional blooming. Gayfeather has tuberous roots that don't mind being treated like bulbs and shipped through the mail, making them a real bargain.

Book IV

Perennials

- **Sea lavender** *(Limonium latifolium):* A delicate haze of tiny lavender flowers fills the air above substantial, dark green foliage on this extremely hardy plant. The flowers dry on their stems and hold up almost indefinitely. It's equally happy with regular water or very little. Full sun is best in cold climates; afternoon shade is better in hot, humid regions. Cut it to the ground in spring.

- **Lupine** *(Lupinus* hybrids): Reliable and easy in cool climates, lupine is unfortunately finicky elsewhere. This perennial comes in a wide array of colors and two-tones. The substantial flower stalks are 1 to 2 feet (30 to 60 cm) tall over bushy clumps of dark green palm-shaped leaves. It blooms for eight to ten weeks if you cut the spent flower stalks back to the basal rosette.

- **Maltese cross** *(Lychnis chalcedonica):* Maltese cross has brilliant scarlet flowerheads. The individual flowers are cross-shaped and carried in rounded clusters at the top of tall, stately stems. It's easy to grow but is usually short-lived. Maltese cross scatters its seeds around, and some of the seeds do grow into new plants. The lower leaves may become brown during dry spells. Hide these "bare legs" behind other flowers. Deadhead routinely to promote continuous blooming and divide clumps every two to three years to maintain vigor.

- **Monkey flower** *(Mimulus* hybrids): Often grown as annuals in cold climates, these showy flowers come in a wide variety of colors. They're good choices for mild-winter climates. The dry varieties must have well-drained soil and occasional watering during the summer months.

- **Bee balm** *(Monarda didyma):* Available in varieties of pink, white, blue, violet, purple, and scarlet, bee balm's flowers look something like raggedy, mop-head daisies. All parts of the plant are deliciously aromatic, with a scent reminiscent of Earl Grey tea. The green foliage is mintlike, slightly toothed, narrow, and pointed. Clumps can spread invasively, but the runners are shallow and easy to pull out. Bee balm always comes down with powdery mildew late in the growing season. When the mildew becomes more than you can bear to look at, cut the plants down to the ground.

- **Ozark sundrop** *(Oenothera macrocarpa):* The huge-but-delicate, clear yellow, four-petalled blossoms of Ozark sundrop appear to be twisted from tissue paper. They fairly glow in both harsh and soft light. The plant has a relaxed spreading form, red stems, and waxy, long, narrow leaves. It flowers for most of the summer. The four-winged papery seedpods are also interesting and are so huge that they don't appear to come from the same plant. Cut it back to the ground annually in winter, and this plant asks for nothing more.

- **African daisy** *(Osteospermum barberae):* The flowers (lavender with pink and blue shadings and dark blue centers) on these rugged plants bloom fall through spring, and on and off throughout the summer in coastal or Mediterranean climates. The flowers close on cloudy days. Pinch back the tips several times a season to create fuller, bushier plants. These make good container plants outside of their hardiness range, which is to 20° F (–7° C). (See Chapter 3 in Book II for more on container gardening.)

✔ **Common beardtongue** *(Penstemon barbatus):* With scarlet tubular flowers on tall, graceful spikes over basal rosettes of shiny green, lance-shaped leaves, common beardtongue is a true hummingbird magnet. The seedheads are stiff, reddish brown teardrops and are attractive in winter or cut for dried arrangements. Common beardtongue and its hybrids are more tolerant of a wider range of conditions than most penstemon kin. All penstemons are short-lived, even in the best of circumstances

✔ **Wild sweet William** *(Phlox carolina):* Wild sweet William phlox (or spotted phlox) is more adaptable and mildew-resistant than its cousin, garden phlox. It produces plump clusters of delicate, five-petalled blooms for many weeks. Strong, upright stems support whorls of glossy, narrow leaves. They're highly fragrant and make good cut flowers. Deadhead finished flowers for reblooming.

Plant wild sweet William in well-drained, moist, humus-amended soil. Spotted phlox is the best tall phlox for hot, humid climates, but it's also very cold-hardy. Deadhead finished flowers for reblooming and fertilize and water regularly. Seedlings that pop up here and there usually revert to the mauve pink of the unimproved form. Phlox likes afternoon shade in hot, dry climates and full sun elsewhere. It's hardy to –40°F (–40°C).

✔ **Obedient plant** *(Physostegia virginiana):* This plant is generally easy to grow, forming expanding colonies of upright stems and lance-shaped fresh green leaves. Its tubular flowers are tightly arranged in rows at sharp right angles to one another. Obedient plant can spread very quickly in rich soil, so you may need to divide it annually to control its expansion. The blooms persist for several weeks and are an outstanding cut flower. The seedheads are attractive in winter.

✔ **Strawberry cinquefoil** *(Potentilla nepalensis* 'Miss Willmott'): The dark green, heavily textured, five-part leaflets of strawberry cinquefoil are arranged in a casually sprawling form. Cheerful pink flowers with dark centers are borne in loose clusters at the ends of arching stems for most of the summer. Strawberry cinquefoil likes cool nights and dislikes heat combined with humidity. It's intolerant of wet soil in winter and may be short-lived. In really hot climates, provide afternoon shade.

✔ **European pasque flower** *(Pulsatilla vulgaris):* This plant often appears well before tulips and daffodils are up. Large, chalice-shaped purple blossoms open while the foliage is still furry little tufts. The leaves are soft, silky, and finely divided. The seedheads, which look like silvery feather dusters, are as charming as the flowers. Many colors are available. Pasque flower may cause skin irritation and blistering, so use gloves when handling it. The plant goes dormant and its leaves disappear in midsummer. Where it's really happy, pasque flower provides abundant seedlings.

Book IV

Perennials

✔ **Orange coneflower** *(Rudbeckia fulgida sullivantii):* Easy, cheerful, uncomplaining, and long-blooming from midsummer through the first frost, coneflowers grow happily almost anywhere. Their large golden daisies are accented with flat, dark brown center disks. Standing straight and upright, they form dense colonies 2 feet (60 cm) tall and feature handsome dark green foliage. Deadhead the spent blooms until late in the season and leave the last wave of flowers to dry on the stalks for winter interest. The flowers are good for cutting.

✔ **Violet sage** *(Salvia nemorosa): Salvia* is a large family of garden perennials that are popular for their showy flowers, attractive and usually aromatic foliage, and ease of care. Violet sage is a very long-blooming hybrid with spikes of deep purple flowers and wrinkled, grayish green foliage. Sages like any well-drained soil. They aren't a good choice for hot, humid regions. Very drought tolerant, they require only an infrequent deep soaking to perform well. Cut back spent flower spikes to keep the form compact and to encourage continued bloom.

✔ **Pincushion flower** *(Scabiosa caucasica):* With pincushion flowers, a fluffy center tuft is surrounded by a lacy, ruffled row of petals. The flowerheads are held gracefully on long stems and come in many shades of blue, lavender, pink, and white. The leaves are long, narrow, and pointed. The plants bloom for months if you regularly deadhead them. They prefer climates with cool summer nights. Winter wet can be fatal; use a loose winter mulch to protect crowns in really cold regions.

✔ **Goldenrod** *(Solidago rugosa* 'Fireworks'): The attention-grabbing, golden yellow starburst flowers of goldenrod look very much like exploding sky rockets. The individual flowers are small, but their numbers make up for their size, forming graceful plumes over compact clumps of red-tinged foliage. The flowers are good for cutting or drying and are attractive to butterflies. They bloom for several weeks. In spite of the rumors you may have heard, goldenrod does *not* cause hay fever.

✔ **Lamb's ears** *(Stachys byzantina):* Few people can resist feeling this plant's soft-as-flannel leaves. Lamb's ears grows in loose rosettes that expand outward into mats. The flower stalks are as heavily felted as the leaves. The flowers, a delicate purplish pink, are a good choice for cut flowers — fresh or dried. If the plants die out in the center, dig up the whole mat and replant a few pieces. It spreads quickly.

✔ **Stokes' aster** *(Stokesia laevis):* The starry flowerheads resemble huge pink, blue, or white shaggy dandelions over narrow, long, dark green leaves. Butterflies love them, and they're a good cut flower. Stokes' asters demand well-drained soil, especially in winter. They bloom most of the summer if you routinely deadhead the spent flowers. In cold climates, cover the plants with a thick, loose mulch to protect the crowns over the winter.

- ✔ **Rose verbena** *(Verbena canadensis):* A vigorous and freely-blooming plant, rose verbena forms relaxed, spreading clumps that are attractive to butterflies. Its stems root wherever they touch the ground. The flowers, which come in many color variations, form rounded clusters that last all summer; the foliage is crisp and evergreen. Plant it in any well-drained soil; rose verbena rots if it's kept too wet, but it's quite drought tolerant.

- ✔ **Spiked speedwell** *(Veronica spicata):* Speedwell comes into its own when most of the perennial garden is having a heat-induced snooze. For nearly two months, speedwell produces dense spires of deep blue flowers over tight mats of shiny green or soft gray leaves, depending on variety. To keep the plants compact, don't over-fertilize. Remove the spent flowers for continued blossoming.

- ✔ **Prairie zinnia** *(Zinnia grandiflora):* The prairie zinnia brings a splash of bright yellow to the dry-climate garden. Low mounds of tiny, narrow foliage spread to create solid colonies. The flowers are golden yellow, sometimes with red centers, and dry to a papery texture. Prairie zinnia can be difficult to transplant. You must water it whenever the soil dries out until the plants are growing strongly. Give it well-drained, infertile soil in arid and semiarid regions. Individual plants are long-lived and slow to spread, and they're late to break dormancy in spring.

Shading in Color

If you garden in shade, you may be disappointed on your first trip to your local garden center to find that the number of shade-loving plants is considerably smaller than the selection of perennials for sunny gardens. But don't despair. Most of the sun-loving flowers we list in the preceding section can also handle at least partial or dappled shade. These plants may not flower as freely in the shade as they would in full sunlight, but the large majority of them can cope with some shade.

If you're dealing with extremes — for example, very dense shade with either soggy wet or very dry soils — the number of adapted perennials you can choose from is quite limited. If at all possible, give serious thought to moving your flower bed to a more suitable place. Alternatively, you may choose to thin out a few trees to bring in more light or to install drainage tiles or a watering system. If none of these solutions appeals to you, just enjoy the selection of perennials that *can* tolerate such extremes — and be sure to give them lots of encouragement and praise for their adaptability.

You can easily measure whether a particular perennial is adapting to its shady environment by watching its performance. When a flower fails to

Book IV

Perennials

bloom or starts to look pretty darn pathetic — with anemic, yellowing leaves on spindly, weak, and sprawling stems — it's time to admit defeat. Find the poor thing a sunnier home and try another plant. On the other hand, when a shade plant is getting too much sunlight, the leaves generally bleach out and become papery thin; they may actually sunburn and develop scorched patches and brown margins.

Getting more blooms with less sun

Designing a shade garden is no more complicated than designing any other. As always, the key is choosing plants that are compatible with your site or modifying the site enough to accommodate the flowers that you're bound and determined to grow. In some respects, designing for shade is simpler and more satisfying than designing for sun, because the focus on flowers is automatically diminished. Flower color is only one part of putting together an outstanding garden. Foliage shape, color, and texture are all equally essential elements (see Chapter 1 in Book IV for more on highlighting these aspects in your design). Shady perennials win hands-down over their sunny counterparts in this respect. Where light is low, catching sunlight becomes more important than conserving moisture loss through evaporation. The result is plants with massive leaves.

The shaded garden doesn't flower as freely as the full-sun flower bed. Most of the shade-loving perennials bloom in spring and then are unobtrusive for the rest of the year. To add flower appeal to your shady garden, leave space among the perennials for a few annuals — see Book V for more on annuals — to keep the flowering season going longer. Where tree roots interfere with planting annuals, grow them in pots and set them beneath the tree. Or hang baskets of annuals from lower limbs for another splash of color. (See Chapter 3 in Book II for more on container gardening.)

Back to the forest

A recurring theme among shade-loving perennials is a woodland origin. Most perennials that do well in the shade appreciate the typical conditions found in the forest.

✔ Give them a loose, porous soil, deeply dug, with plenty of added humus to get them off to a strong start.

✔ After planting, re-create the leaf litter found on the forest floor by spreading 2 to 3 inches (5 to 8 cm) of a light, airy, organic mulch, such as pine needles, between the plants.

✔ When experimenting with flowers that normally fancy more abundant sunlight, give each plant plenty of elbow room, so that it can take full advantage of whatever light reaches it. Spacing plants more widely in shade also creates better air circulation, which helps prevent foliage diseases.

Many bulbs (see Book VI) have woodland ancestors and do well in the shade, giving you the opportunity to add more color. If your garden is shaded by deciduous trees and has unobstructed sunlight during the winter months, you can likely grow any of the early sun-loving spring bulbs, such as tulips, daffodils, and crocuses. These flowers bloom before the trees don their spring leaves.

Locating shade-loving perennials

The following list makes up just a handful of the hundreds of true shade-loving perennials in circulation. Some of these plants absolutely *insist* on shade. Others don't mind direct sunlight in varying degrees, depending on your climate and light intensity. You can plant many of them in full sun if you live in a region where summers are generally cool and overcast. Some of the plants in this list can grow in *partial shade* — dappled, intermittent, or open shade with either a brief period of uninterrupted sunlight each day or plenty of bright light reflected from light-colored walls or sidewalks. Other plants can adapt to a greater degree of shadow. Use these recommendations as guidelines, not hard and fast rules. You need to experiment a bit to discover what works in your garden.

- **Lady's mantle** (*Alchemilla mollis*): Lady's mantle is perfectly content in full sun in cloudy, overcast climates, but intense sunlight badly scorches its leaves. This luxuriant plant's foliage resembles a pleated cape and is every bit as attractive as the flowers. The flowers, a froth of chartreuse yellow, bloom from spring through most of the summer and are outstanding when cut. Lady's mantle thrives in woodland conditions with moist but not sopping wet soil. It's more tolerant of dry soil in shade than in sun. This plant can be quite invasive, spreading into large patches and also seeding some distance away. Remove spent flowers to slow down spreading. Lady's mantle does best in regions with cool overnight temperatures and can withstand extreme winter cold, but it isn't tolerant of heat combined with humidity in subtropical regions.

- **Japanese painted fern** (*Athyrium niponicum* 'Pictum'): This fern's fronds are grayish green overlaid with silver. To add more complexity, the mid-ribs are burgundy red. The foliage is heavily cut and filigreed for a delicate and graceful texture. More rugged than its appearance suggests, this fern grows easily in well-drained, humus-enriched soil in either shade or partial shade. Early to emerge in spring, the Japanese painted fern goes dormant if you allow it to get too dry during the growing season. Protect and preserve moisture with several inches of light organic mulch. It sends up new fronds throughout the summer, but its deciduous fronds die back to the ground in winter.

Book IV

Perennials

✔ **Pigsqueak** *(Bergenia cordifolia):* Usually called by its botanical name, *bergenia,* pigsqueak is a more memorable name and certainly more descriptive. Pinching a leaf in your moistened fingertips produces a very pig-like squeal (and livens up those dull parties). Pigsqueak has large, thick, glossy leaves in open rosettes and pink flower spikes very early in the spring. This plant's evergreen foliage turns red during wintertime in mild climates. In climates with colder winters, pigsqueak is deciduous — or ratty enough that you wish the foliage would take a winter vacation. Although pigsqueak tolerates a full sun position in cloudy, cool regions, it prefers shade everywhere else. It's fairly drought tolerant in dry shade. Slugs can do a great deal of damage to this plant (see Chapter 7 in Book I for tips on dealing with these slimy critters).

✔ **Heartleaf brunnera** *(Brunnera macrophylla):* In early spring, dainty clusters of tiny blue forget-me-not flowers make their appearance above small, emerging leaves. The leaves — somewhat heart-shaped, rough to the touch, and heavily veined — quickly expand into their full size of 6 to 8 inches (15 to 20 cm) across. This plant prefers moist, fertile woodland conditions. It withstands full sun in overcast climates and is somewhat drought tolerant in shade, especially in heavy clay soils. This plant self-sows but doesn't make a pest of itself. To preserve moisture and keep the soil cool, use several inches of an organic mulch around the plants. Protect it from slugs.

✔ **Bleeding heart** *(Dicentra* hybrids): The hybrid bleeding hearts are unbeatable. They bloom for six months, possess beautiful foliage, and are long-lived, adaptable, and easy to grow. Clusters of charming, locket-shaped flowers hang over deeply cut, ferny foliage. All parts of bleeding hearts, if eaten, are toxic to both you and your pets. The roots contain the largest concentration of poison, so be especially careful when these plants are out of the ground. You can place bleeding hearts in full sun in cool climates, but they prefer shade anywhere else.

✔ **Lenten rose** *(Helleborus orientalis):* Dramatic and elegant, they're among the first nonbulb flowers to bloom in the spring. The foliage is handsome, glossy, and evergreen except in the coldest winters. The flowers are open bells of cream to soft rose, often with purple freckles and a touch of the palest green. Lenten roses are long-lived and easy to grow in any climate with wintertime lows above –30° F (–34° C). The clumps mature and increase very slowly, so buy large plants, or you may wait several years to see these lovely flowers for the first time. Some years the foliage and first flowers are zapped by cold temperatures. Cut them off, and the plants readily bounce back. Mulch plants heavily to preserve soil moisture.

✔ **Coral bells** *(Heuchera sanguinea):* Amazing things are happening to your grandmother's coral bells. Currently undergoing extensive selection and hybridization, a few more of these beauties hit the market every year. Varieties with attractive flowers come in shades of red, pink, coral, and white. The types chosen for outstanding foliage — evergreen in mild climates — usually don't offer much in the flower department, but what an amazing array of leaf colors! Speckled and splashed, washed in silver, deep purples, and subtle reds — each more fetching than the last. Full sun works in cloudy climates, but not where sunlight is truly intense. This plant is intolerant of wet soil in winter. Use an organic mulch year round and cover with pine boughs or other lightweight winter protection in bitterly cold regions.

✔ **Plantain lily** *(Hosta* hybrids): The plantain lily (also called *shade lily)* has hundreds of varieties to suit every taste. Tough and reliable, it's the ultimate shade perennial. Some forms have impressively immense foliage rosettes; other types are only a few inches tall. They come in every shade of green, steely blues, and translucent yellows; in solid colors; and every conceivable pattern of variegation in cream, white, or chartreuse. The purple or white flowers are often deliciously fragrant. Although some varieties can withstand full sun (especially in cool, overcast regions), most scorch and burn when either exposed to strong sunlight or allowed to dry. Protect these late-spring emergers from slugs and snails unless you like the "cut-work" look.

✔ **Virginia bluebells** *(Mertensia virginica):* Virginia bluebells are easy-care, long-lived wildflowers that put up with neglect and mistreatment without complaint. The leaves, green with purple tints, emerge in late winter or early spring. The flowers are nodding clusters of tubular bells, opening pink and aging to lavender blue. Bluebells go dormant with the beginning of hot weather, so always place them where other perennials hide their death throes. After the yellowing foliage starts to brown, cut it off — the only care these low-maintenance flowers ever need. The plants slowly spread to fill all the empty spaces in the shade garden.

✔ **Jacob's ladder** *(Polemonium caeruleum):* This plant features loose clusters of five-petalled, soft blue flowers on spikes above ladder-shaped leaflets. The blossoms are ornamented with prominent yellow stamens. Jacob's ladder is long-blooming, especially if you remove faded flower spikes. It's also available in white, lavender, and bright blue. This plant is not adapted to hot, humid climates, but where nights are cool and dry, it's dependable and easy to grow. It does well in full sun only in cooler, cloudy climates. For best results, water regularly.

Book IV

Perennials

✔ **Auricula primrose** *(Primula auricula):* This neat and tidy plant is extremely cold-hardy and more drought-enduring more than most of its moisture-loving clan. The species is yellow, but just about every color imaginable has been developed from it. The flowers often have contrasting eyes, and some have a coating of *farina* (a dense white fuzz), although they generally lose this coating when grown outdoors. This primrose grows in full sun in cool summer climates, but needs afternoon shade elsewhere. It's not well adapted to hot, humid subtropical climates.

✔ **Foam flower** *(Tiarella cordifolia):* A relative unknown, foam flower has suddenly become increasingly popular as hybridizers play around with leaf shape and color and flower color. The original plant has toothed, heart-shaped leaves with burgundy veining and attractive, bronze red fall color. The flowers are delicate and starry. New varieties feature deeply cut, ruffled, and brightly-colored foliage and fragrant pink, coral, or white flowers. The foliage is evergreen in mild areas. These flowers are best in cool shade, but they can stand heat as long as you keep them well watered. Use an organic mulch to keep the soil cool and moist. Water before the soil dries out completely. It's fast-growing and quickly forms good-sized colonies everywhere but the muggiest subtropical regions.

Chapter 3

Perennials to Buy, Grow, and Plant

- -

In This Chapter

▶ Buying perennials by mail

▶ Making a trip to the nursery

▶ Planting the perennials you purchase

▶ Starting perennials from seed

- -

The really fun part of a perennial garden is choosing and planting your plants. At some point, you may even decide to play Mother Nature, and start your garden from seed. This chapter shows you how to do all three.

Sending Away for Mail-Order Miracles

You may already receive several garden catalogs in the mail each winter and spring. Some catalogs specialize in only one type of perennial; others present a vast array for every climate. The best ones are packed with information describing each plant, detailed cultural information, and design advice. No nursery has the space to stock even a fraction of the thousands of perennials in cultivation. Mail-order sources are often the only way to locate the rare, the unusual, and the avant-garde of gardening. Nearly every garden magazine advertises dozens of mail-order nurseries. Most mail-order nurseries require a small fee to send you their catalogs, but they usually refund the amount after you make your first purchase.

Exercise prudence and caution when deciding which plants to order from a catalog. A few catalogs make exaggerated claims of performance, desirability, or hardiness. Before you buy, find out whether each perennial you want to order works in your climate.

Shipping plants has some inherent problems. The cost is high, and most nurseries try to keep the weight down by sending their plants either *bare root* or in small containers filled with lightweight, soil-less mix. Bare-root plants are just that — plants whose roots have been unearthed and are completely exposed. Mailed with their roots packed in moistened moss or wood shavings and wrapped in newspaper or plastic, these plants are very fragile and perishable. You mustn't allow them to dry out, but leaving them in their damp shipping material for very long encourages rotting. The time of year that your plants are shipped and the shape they're in when you get them depend on what type of plants you order:

✔ **Bare-root plants arrive in a dormant or semidormant state, usually in late winter or early spring.**

✔ **Bulbs and fleshy-rooted perennials are also shipped in summer and hardly seem to notice that they're out of the ground.** Peonies, bearded iris, daylilies, hostas, and liatris don't object to this treatment in the least. (See Book VI for more about bulbs.)

In some cases, your perennials can arrive quite unhappy and indignant (no matter what time of year they're sent) and may require pampering for a full year to recover their former health and vigor. Arrange for your plants to be shipped by the quickest option, especially during hot months when the plants can easily cook or dry out in transit. Ask that your order be sent at the proper planting time for your area and at a time when you can be at home to receive the package. Even plants that survive the initial journey don't last long if you leave them unattended on a hot porch.

When your plants finally arrive, unpack the box immediately in a cool, shaded location. Keep each label with its plant — green and brown lumps tend to look alike at this stage. You can store plants shipped in pots for several days in a shady spot with plenty of indirect light. Be sure to water the pots whenever they dry out, but don't overwater them.

If their bed isn't ready, you must find a temporary home for them. Many garden guides recommend *heeling in* bare-root plants. This process involves digging a trench, laying plants in it at a 30-degree angle, and covering the roots with soil. Heeling in works fine for shrubs but isn't a good practice for perennials. Flowers prefer you to plant them properly in their interim location — a vegetable garden is an ideal holding area for new perennials — and then transplant them later, after they establish strong new growth.

Most mail-order nurseries send instructions with your order. File away these instructions, along with your receipt and invoice, for future reference. Many companies guarantee their plants, and you need the paperwork to request a refund or replacement if the original plant fails. Keep the catalogs, too, as a source of information and to cut up to make garden records. Notify the nursery right away of any problems.

Taking the Nursery Safari

Whenever you have a choice between buying a plant by mail or from a local nursery, always go with the nursery. A plant purchased locally is almost always cheaper, and it's usually healthier because it hasn't been subjected to the trauma of traveling. Most nurseries bring in some of their stock bare root in the winter and grow it in containers before offering it up for sale. This way, the nursery takes the risk, and you buy only those plants that survived and prospered. Also, at a nursery, you can actually see the plant you buy and can pick out the best of the batch.

Many good nurseries offer gardening classes and employ a master gardener to answer your questions. They may also group plants by their cultural needs to help you decide what goes where. Shade plants are generally protected under some sort of structure. When you purchase plants, ask about a guarantee and save your receipts. Many reputable nurseries don't warranty the plants, however, because what you do to the plant after you leave the store is out of their control.

When purchasing a perennial, look for one with a compact form and proportioned-to-the-pot size. Pass on any plants that are tall and leggy or flopping over to one side. You want lean and mean, not overly lush. Check the foliage for any signs of disease. Don't buy plants that are wilted, yellowed, or mottled. Avoid plants that have orange, brown, or black spots or that have distorted or curled leaves. Flip a few leaves over to see whether tiny mites, aphids, or whiteflies reside there (see Chapter 7 in Book I for more on these critters). Look along the stems for scale insects. Don't be put off by a few holes made by chewing insects — these culprits are either long gone or large enough to remove easily.

Discounting perennials

Many home improvement centers, supermarkets, and discount stores carry a wide variety of perennials. You can find some real bargains at nonnursery stores, but you're usually more or less on your own to determine which plants are the healthiest or what cultural conditions they require. Plants may be selected for a national market and can be entirely inappropriate for the regions where they end up. Before you buy, make sure that the plants you buy have a ghost of a chance in your garden. Also, buy them as soon as they've been unloaded from the truck — hopefully before they've been mishandled or mistreated.

You can also find some great deals on nursery plants by watching for end-of-season clearance sales. Some of the plants are looking shop-worn by this time, but we figure that only the really strong-willed can survive several months on the sales bench. So these last plants, the rejected and overlooked, are usually worth the risk.

Healthy roots mean healthy perennials

Healthy roots are just as important as the above-ground parts of the plant, but they're more difficult to assess. Judging roots involves a bit of detective work. A top-quality container plant has a vigorous root system that fills but doesn't outgrow its pot. Ideally, the volume of roots and soil is about 50/50. You can get some idea of what condition a potted plant's roots are in by checking the surface of the soil. If you can see roots circling or trying to climb out, ask the clerk to remove the pot, so that you can get a better look. Nurseries routinely turn their pots upside down to monitor root status, so this request won't seem odd to the clerk.

Excess roots can displace most of the soil in a container, making the plant root-bound, a condition that causes a couple of problems. First, without enough soil to retain water or fertilizer, the plants quickly start to suffer from drought stress. More importantly, the roots don't have anywhere to go, so they start to circle and grow into a tight ball. Too few roots is just as bad a sign as too many. Reputable nurseries don't routinely sell perennials that are too recently transplanted, but occasionally a few slip through quality control. Roots should expand out at least to the edges of the container. If they don't, you're paying for a small plant and some very expensive potting soil. When you look at the bottom of the pot, a few small roots should be visible at the drainage holes.

Perennials come in many pot sizes. Occasionally, first-year seedlings are available in six-packs, the standard container for bedding annuals. These packages can be real money-savers when they contain varieties that mature quickly and bloom the first year from seed. Otherwise, you may have to wait a year or two to see the flowers. Perennials are more customarily sold in 2¼-, 4-, and 6-inch containers. The larger plants are more expensive because they cost more to produce. Most nurseries start their perennials in small pots and move them up to larger ones as they outgrow each size. Some perennials have large, fleshy roots and are only available in 6-inch pots because they just don't fit in anything else. Small plants are much easier to transplant — they require smaller holes, after all. But the trade-off is that the little ones need more care initially. They dry out faster and may need watering as often as twice a day until they're established and growing well.

Planting Purchased Perennials

In theory, you can plant container-grown perennials at any time of the year when the ground isn't frozen. But in reality, survival rates improve when you take your climate into consideration and schedule your planting accordingly. Newly transplanted perennials need a period of intensive care while they settle in and adjust to their new home. Strong sunshine, drying winds, and intense heat can stress any plant. These conditions are especially damaging to plants that have been recently disturbed and are busy repairing torn roots and coping with the inevitable trauma that transplanting causes.

Timing is critical

By planting at a time of year when you can count on the weather to be mild for a while, you give the garden a head start. In cold-winter regions, planting in early spring gives perennials a couple of months to get used to the climate before hot weather sets in. Only bulbs, bearded iris, peonies, and oriental poppies are safe to plant during the fall in the coldest winter regions. But in areas where winter temperatures don't fall below –20°F (–29°C), early fall is another excellent time to plant the flower bed. Even though the days are shorter and cooler, root growth continues unimpeded after frost has blackened the top of the plant, not stopping until the ground freezes solidly. Gardeners in mild coastal climates can plant their flower beds at any time of the year, whenever planting is convenient. In hot, humid, mild-winter regions, fall planting is preferable. Planting in fall enables perennials to grow strong root systems before they're subjected to the heat of summer.

Whatever time of year you decide to plant your flower bed, make sure that you can give it your full attention for several weeks afterward. A new garden needs vigilance — it's as needy as a new puppy. Check the flowers for wilting or other signs of distress at least twice a day until they start to put on new growth.

Hardening off

Hardening off is a way of increasing your plant's stamina before planting — similar to slowly acquiring a base tan before taking that outdoor, tropical vacation. Plants that have been growing outside at the nursery can go right into the ground, but greenhouse-grown plants are lush and soft and have never known a single day of sunshine in their lifetimes. You have to introduce them slowly to the harsh, real world.

Leave the plants in their containers and put them in a shaded area with some indirect light for a few days. A north-facing, covered porch is ideal. Whenever a freeze is predicted, bring the plants inside overnight. If these are shade plants, you can leave them in this protected site for a few more days and then put them in the garden. For sunny-spot plants, give them a few days in the shaded area and then place the plants in a sunny location for an hour one day. (Chapter 2 tells you all about sun- and shade-loving perennials.) Give them a couple of hours of sun the next day, and so on, increasing their exposure each day. At the end of a week, the plants are thoroughly accustomed to sunlight and wind and are ready to go into their new home.

Book IV

Perennials

Picking the perfect day to plant

To get your plants off to a vigorous start, you need to choose your planting day carefully. You're looking for a cool, overcast day, preferably the first of many with no record-breaking heat predicted for the near future. An imminent threat of a rainstorm is better yet, if you can get your bed finished before the storm strikes. If cooperative weather is not in the forecast, plant early in the morning or in the evening.

Distribute container plants, following your plan — if you've made one. (If you haven't yet made a plan but want to, see Books I and II.) Mark spots for bulbs and bare-root perennials with empty pots or stakes. Make certain that you've allowed adequate spacing for each plant to spread to its mature size; the nursery tag often has this information. Take note of where you need to add annuals for temporary fill until the perennials actually use their allotted space (see Book V for information on annuals).

If your flower bed is wider than you can easily reach across, lay some old boards or some stepping stones throughout the area. Standing on these additions keeps you off the fluffy soil.

Planting potted perennials

Planting a potted perennial is easy with a little practice. Plant the largest pots first; the smaller ones are easier to tuck in afterwards. Finish planting each perennial before going on to the next.

1. **Dig a hole that's at least double the pot's diameter, as shown in Figure 3-1.**

Figure 3-1:
Dig a hole large enough to fit in the plant's roots without crowding.

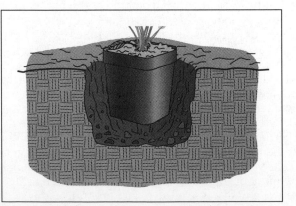

2. Remove the plant from the pot.

This step isn't always as simple as it sounds. When things are going well, you cradle the top of the plant between the fingers of one hand, tip the pot upside down, and slip the plant out to rest snugly against the palm of the opposite hand. If the plant refuses to budge, as often happens, try rapping the bottom of the pot smartly with your unoccupied hand. If that attempt fails, lay the plastic pot on its side on the ground and gently step on and compress the pot just a little. Next, give the pot a quarter turn and step on it again.

Whatever you do, don't try to pull the plant out by its top — instead of liberating the plant, you'll more likely kill it!

You can usually coax small pots into releasing their contents by pinching and poking through the bottom of the pot. You can also tear off a small pot. As a last resort, cut the pot off with heavy-duty shears.

3. Place the plant gently into the hole.

You want the plant's *crown* — where the top of the plant meets the roots — at ground level, so you need to adjust the soil level until the root ball sits at about the right height. Don't bury the crown or lower leaves. Break off any layer of moss or crud on the surface of the soil surrounding the plant. (You can drop whatever you break off into the hole for extra soil nutrients.)

Check for and remove weeds. Also look for slug eggs — masses of tiny clear balls — and dispose of them. Tease a few roots away from the root ball. Try to straighten out any large, fibrous roots. If the hole isn't large enough for a relaxed fit for the roots, remove the plant, enlarge the hole, and try again.

4. Fill the hole back up with dirt.

Fan out the plant's roots in the hole. Hold the plant with the crown at the proper height with one hand and start refilling the hole with the other hand. Add a handful of dirt at a time, breaking up large chunks as you go. You don't want to leave huge holes underground because the roots need to be in direct contact with the soil. Pat the soil around the plant carefully — no stamping of feet allowed, especially on clay soils. (See Chapter 3 in Book I for more on soil.) Check to make sure that all the roots are underground, and all the leaves are above the surface.

5. Water the plant.

With a watering can or a hose turned on very low, saturate the newly planted area with water. Some of the soil always collapses inward at this point, so add more as necessary. If the whole plant sinks, carefully pull it back up again and push some more soil underneath the root ball.

Book IV

Perennials

Breaking up root balls

Occasionally, you bring home a root-bound plant despite your best efforts to avoid them. If you plant the root ball intact, you may find it in the same shape and size when you dig up the carcass two years later. You can succeed with root-bound plants, but you need to treat them very roughly before you plant them.

Break apart the root ball as much as you can, untangling the largest roots as you go. Sometimes, your only option is to *butterfly* the root ball. Lay it on the ground and cut the root ball in two, approximately two-thirds of the way toward the crown. Spread the two sides apart and plant with the roots in this position.

6. **Label the plant.**

   Use the plastic nursery label or make one yourself. Push the label about two-thirds of the way into the soil near the crown of each plant, so that you can find it when necessary.

7. **Feed the plant.**

   Pour a weak solution of manure tea or liquid fertilizer (see Chapter 4 in Book I) mixed at one-fourth the usual strength recommended on the label. Use just enough of the solution to reach the soil at the base of the plant. This first feeding helps to improve the plant's chances of survival.

8. **Move on to the next plant, repeating Steps 1 through 7.**

9. **Spread mulch last, after you've watered, labeled, and fed all the perennials.**

   If you plan to use a mulch (as described in Book I, Chapter 4), apply it immediately after planting, so that weeds don't get a running start in the bare soil.

Planting "exceptional" perennials

A few varieties of perennials require special planting techniques. They may have special kinds of roots or prefer to be planted with their crowns deeper than ground level. Here are some specifics on a few common perennials that need a little special treatment:

✔ **Bearded iris:** Iris plants have a swollen, fleshy root called a *rhizome*. Green leaves, called a *fan,* protrude from the bottom. To plant an iris, dig a large shallow hole and build up a center cone of soil. Place the rhizome against the cone with the fan facing outward and the roots spread out and downward. If you're planting several rhizomes of the same iris, place the fans in a circle around the soil cone. Press soil over the roots and the rhizomes to keep the fans from falling down. Barely cover the rhizome with soil in cold climates. Leave the rhizomes partially exposed in warm, wet regions to improve the drainage.

✔ **Peonies:** Peonies prefer to be planted with their *eyes,* the buds emerging from the crown, 1 to 2 inches (2.5 to 3 cm) below the surface of the soil. If you plant them any deeper, peonies often fail to bloom.

✔ **Oriental poppies:** Oriental poppies like to be planted deeply with their crown buried 3 inches (8 cm) deep (measured from the top of the crown to the surface of the soil).

Planting bare-root perennials

The first time that you unwrap a package of bare-root perennials, you're probably in for a bit of a shock. Often, the whole shipment appears to be dead. Both the roots and the tops are brown when the plants are in a dormant state, and sometimes, you can hardly tell what side goes up. You may find swollen buds or remnants of dead leaves at the crown of the plant, or fleshy roots may look more alive than the top. If you really can't tell the top from the bottom, call the nursery that you ordered from for advice.

To plant bare-root perennials, follow these steps:

1. **Carefully unwrap and remove the packing material.**

2. **Soak the roots — just the roots, not the whole plant — in a bucket of water for a few hours or overnight.**

3. **Dig a roomy hole, building a cone of soil in the center of the hole.**

4. **Spread the roots over the cone.**

5. **Refill the hole.**

   Hold the crown of the plant at the soil level and form the soil around the roots with your fingers.

6. **Water the plant evenly and fill any sinkholes with additional garden soil.**

Protecting new transplants

Sometimes, the weather forecaster turns out to be wrong, and the promised cloud cover burns off. Your new garden is now faced with full sun and rapidly rising temperatures, and you must create temporary shelter quickly.

Placing evergreen boughs in a tent around the plant, stems poked into the ground and tips facing inward, does an effective job of protecting individual plants. You can overlap boughs to cover a whole flower bed if the plants aren't tall enough to be smashed down by the boughs. Alternatively, use a

Book IV

Perennials

lightweight, spun-bonded landscape fabric to provide temporary protection from the sun. Simply spread this fabric over the flower bed and anchor down the corners with stones or other heavy objects. These materials are porous, so you can leave them in place for as long as you need — water and air pass through readily.

No matter how careful you are, you may very well lose a few of your newly planted perennials. *Transplant shock* kills most newly planted perennials. Its symptoms are leafs and flowers that drop and wilt — even when the soil is damp. Don't water a plant exhibiting signs of transplant shock without first checking the root ball to see whether it's dry. Overwatering usually hastens the demise of a plant in this situation. Shelter the plant for a few days, cross your fingers, and hope for the best. Burning candles at the altar or repeating a mantra may not hurt, either. Most plants recover — even plants that appear to be dead can come back the following spring from live roots.

Growing Your Garden from Scratch

If you're limited by a tight budget but have plenty of time and patience, you can cut costs by growing your own new perennials. But thrift isn't the only motivation for bringing new perennials into the world. After you fill your own garden to capacity, you can share your bounty with friends and neighbors. Most perennials multiply as rapidly and as easily as field mice.

Multiplying perennials by division

A young perennial starts out with only one tuft of leaves and one set of roots. Many perennials reproduce themselves by sending out a length of root or stem from which a whole new plant grows. Eventually, a cluster of loosely connected but separate plants forms. The process of pulling clumps of perennials apart to create new ones is called *dividing.* Each piece then grows into a new clump that you can divide, and so on.

Reasons to divide

Producing more plants is the main reason to divide your perennials, but it's not the only reason. Some types of perennials reproduce themselves so quickly that they can overrun the whole flower bed if you don't intervene. Whenever you feel the need to restore order, dig up these miscreants, put a piece of them back where you originally planted them, and give the remaining pieces away.

A few perennials die out in the center of their clumps as they spread, creating a noticeable bald spot. Instead of contemplating some sort of a floral toupee, you can easily correct the problem by digging up the whole plant and dividing it.

Perennials that don't tolerate division

Division works best on perennials that grow into *colonies* — groups where each new plant develops its own set of roots and leaves. Similarly, most bulbs reproduce by forming clusters of new bulbs (Book VI covers bulbs), which you can divide in exactly the same way that you divide colony-forming perennials. Perennials with a single, large taproot and those with multiple stems arising from a single crown don't like to be divided. The following perennials don't tolerate division well:

- Monkshood *(Aconitum napellus)*
- Butterfly flower *(Asclepias tuberosa)*
- Basket-of-gold *(Aurinia saxatilis)*
- Blue wild indigo *(Baptisia australis)*
- Pinks *(Dianthus)*
- Bleeding heart *(Dicentra spectabilis)*
- Gas plant *(Dictamnus albus)*
- Globe thistle *(Echinops exaltatus)*
- Baby's breath *(Gypsophila paniculata)*
- Candytuft *(Iberis sempervirens)*
- Sea lavender *(Limonium latifolium)*
- Blue flax *(Linum perenne)*
- Lupine *(Lupinus)*
- Oriental poppy *(Papaver orientale)*
- Balloon flower *(Platycodon grandiflorus)*
- False lupine *(Thermopsis carolinian)*

A lesson in division

You can divide perennials whenever the ground isn't frozen, but the best time of year for division is a couple of months before severely cold or hot weather sets in. You want to give newly planted sections a chance to settle in and get a strong start before they have to cope with weather extremes. If you live in a cold climate, divide your perennials either in spring, when the newly emerging foliage is up several inches, or in late summer, six to eight weeks before temperatures are expected to drop below freezing. In warm-winter regions, divide your perennials in the fall.

Book IV

Perennials

To divide perennials, follow these steps:

1. **Soak the ground a few days before you plan to work, if the soil is hard and dry.**

   Ideally, the soil should be soft enough that you can dig into it easily with a shovel or spading fork, but not so muddy that it sticks to you or your tools.

2. **Cut all the stems down to 4 to 6 inches (10 to 15 cm) from the ground.**

3. **Dig up the whole clump.**

   Cut a circle a few inches outside the edge of the clump you're planning to divide. Don't worry if you cut roots — they grow back.

4. **Place the whole clump on a tarp or an old sheet and look it over.**

   Some plants come apart as easily as pull-apart cinnamon rolls. Others are impossibly dense and tangled. Tug at the crowns and see what happens. If the plant doesn't come apart easily, you have two options:

   • Soak the whole plant in a large bucket for a few hours to soften the soil and then rinse it off with a hose. Now, you can untangle the exposed roots by using your fingers to separate the individual crowns (see Figure 3-2).

   • Use a shovel or a sharp knife to slice the root mass into as many chunks as you need (as shown in Figure 3-3). For really tough roots, you may need to use an ax.

Figure 3-2:
Pulling apart
rooted
divisions by
hand.

Figure 3-3:
Cutting a plant into multiple rooted sections with a shovel.

5. **Pull off and discard all the dead stuff and any tough, woody parts.**

   Make certain that each plant has both roots and leaves. Keep the biggest, healthiest chunks and compost the rest.

6. **Replant according to the instructions earlier in this chapter.**

Growing perennials from cuttings

Growing perennials from cuttings involves creating a new plant from a stem that starts out with no roots at all. If you've ever stuck a stem of ivy in a glass of water and watched it grow roots, you already have some idea how this technique works. Not all perennials can grow from cuttings. Use the cutting method for perennials that don't tolerate division.

Book IV

Perennials

Follow these steps to coax your cuttings into growing roots:

1. **Punch a few pencil-sized holes in the side and bottom of any clean, flat, shallow container to provide drainage for excess water.**

   For a large number of cuttings, a plastic kitty litter tray is a good size. A plastic container of any sort works well if you're rooting only a few cuttings (recycled food containers are perfect).

2. **Fill the container with a moist, not soggy wet, mixture of 50 percent fine peat and 50 percent washed coarse sand.**

   Alternatively, you can use vermiculite or any potting medium labeled for starting cuttings. All these materials are available at your local nursery.

3. **Using a clean, sharp knife or scissors, cut the top 4 to 6 inches (10 to 15 cm) of the stem, just below a leaf or cluster of leaves.**

   Take your cuttings when the plant is growing vigorously but not blooming.

4. **With a knife or scissors, remove all the leaves from the bottom 2 inches (5 cm) of the stem.**

5. **Use a pencil or screwdriver to make a hole (2 inches [5 cm] deep and a little wider than the stem) in the sand or potting mix.**

   Make additional holes several inches apart if you're starting more than one cutting.

6. **Use a rooting hormone (available in powder or liquid) to stimulate root growth on the cutting.**

   You can purchase rooting hormone at a local nursery or most garden centers. Be sure to follow the instructions on the product you buy.

7. **Stick the stem into the hole and gently press the potting mixture against the stem, so that no air holes remain.**

8. **Cover the container with plastic wrap or a clear plastic bag to prevent moisture loss.**

9. **Place the container in a brightly lit location (out of direct sunlight) or under a grow light.**

10. **Water with a misting spray bottle as necessary.**

    Keep the potting mixture moist, but not soaking wet, at all times.

When the stems start to grow new leaves, they're ready for transplanting. Most cuttings are well rooted in about a month.

Sprouting perennials from seed

Starting perennials from seed gives you the chance to grow literally hundreds of plants from one package of seeds. The problem is that you probably don't want hundreds of identical plants. Even more frustrating is the fact that, unlike most vegetables and annuals grown from seed, most perennials you grow from seed take several years to bloom for the first time. Some types are also extremely fussy and require very exacting conditions to germinate. But sometimes, the only way to get your hands on a certain perennial is to grow it yourself.

The first thing you need to do with a packet of seeds is carefully read the directions and suggestions. Seeds of most annuals germinate just fine when you plant them directly in the garden. (See Book V for more on annuals.) However, most perennial seeds don't germinate very successfully when planted outside. By growing your seeds indoors, you can create an artificial environment to meet their needs. You can grow perennials indoors any time of the year. But if you start them in late winter or early spring, the seedlings are usually large enough to go into the garden by early summer. For best results, plant seeds outside at the time of year recommended on the seed packet. Some seeds need cool weather to sprout, and some need hot.

Here's a list of items you need to start seeds inside:

- **A light stand.** You can buy a stand like the one in Figure 3-4, or you can construct one yourself by using grow lamps or fluorescent shop lights. Rig the lamps so that you can adjust their height up and down. You can also place seed trays on window sills, although you'll have a more difficult time regulating temperature and light.

- **A sterile potting mix labeled for seed-starting.** Don't buy regular potting mix or use outdoor soil, because neither is free of disease organisms. You can buy sterile potting mix at any garden center.

- **Suitable containers.** "Suitable" translates into anything that potting soil and seed can fit into. Run your containers through the dishwasher or wash them in a weak solution of household chlorine bleach. Poke holes in the bottom and sides so that excess water can drain away.

- **A misting spray bottle filled with water.** Pick up a plastic, glass, or metal spray bottle at any nursery or discount store.

   Don't use a bottle that has previously held chemicals. The chemical residue may burn your seedlings.

- **Liquid or powder fertilizer.**

- **Plastic trays to hold several containers.**

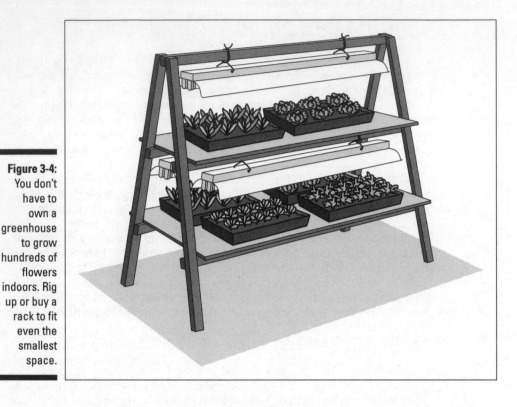

Figure 3-4:
You don't have to own a greenhouse to grow hundreds of flowers indoors. Rig up or buy a rack to fit even the smallest space.

Use the following instructions to start your seeds the first time. As you gain experience, you can customize the process and find your own shortcuts. The following directions work equally well for starting annuals (Book V) or vegetables (Book VII) from seed, too.

1. **Put the potting mix in a pan or bucket and gradually add warm water, stirring the mix until it's evenly moist but not sopping wet.**

    The mixture is wet enough if you can form a handful of it into a ball, but too wet if it drips. If you get the mixture too wet, add more potting mix or let the mixture dry out overnight.

2. **Fill your containers with potting mix to within ½ inch (1 cm) of the top; pat the mix down lightly to press out air pockets.**

3. **Using your forefinger and thumb, sprinkle the seeds over the surface of the potting mix.**

    As a general rule, use twice the number of seeds as the number of plants you hope to grow.

4. **Cover the seeds with dry potting mix according to the packet instructions.**

   You don't need to cover seeds smaller than grains of table salt; instead, use your fingertips to lightly press them into the soil.

5. **Label the container.**

   Write the name of the plant, the date you planted it, and any other information that you think may be useful.

6. **Cover the container with a lid, plastic wrap, or glass.**

   If the instructions tell you to exclude light, cover the container with aluminum foil instead of plastic wrap or glass.

7. **Place the seed containers on trays and set them on the stand under grow lights.**

   For those seeds that require heat, you can buy special heating cables to keep the trays warm if your location isn't warm enough.

8. **Open the container and check the seeds every day.**

   If the potting soil starts to dry out, wet it with a couple of squirts from your misting spray bottle.

9. **The moment that you see little green specks emerging from the soil, remove the lid and lower the grow light until it's positioned a couple of inches above the seedlings.**

   Raise the light as your plants grow taller.

10. **Continue to water with the misting spray bottle until your seedlings start to form real leaves; then water from the bottom by placing the container in a sink filled with a couple of inches of lukewarm water.**

    The first pair of leaves that appear are *seed leaves,* not true leaves. Seed leaves feed the young plant until it can grow the real thing. When your seedlings grow four true leaves, transplant them to larger, individual containers.

11. **When the time comes to transplant your seedlings, fill the new pots with damp potting mix and use a pencil to make a hole in the potting mix in each pot.**

    Recycled 2¼-inch (6 cm) and 4-inch (10 cm) nursery pots are handy for this purpose.

12. **Dump the seedling container gently onto your fingertips and then place the seeding clump upright on a tray.**

13. **Pull a seedling away from the clump, holding it by a leaf, and use a pencil to guide the roots into the hole you made in the potting soil.**

    Press the potting mix gently around the roots, so that the stem is at the same level it was in the seedling pot.

Book IV

Perennials

14. **Water the plant with a weak solution of liquid fertilizer (mixed at about a tenth of the normal label recommendation for perennials).**

    Fertilize once a week, gradually increasing the strength to the rate on the label for seedlings.

15. **Water from the bottom until the seedlings double in size; after that, you can use a watering can.**

Grow newly transplanted seedlings under grow lights or in a brightly lit location out of direct sunlight. When the plants are several inches tall, harden them off and plant them in the garden.

You can also grow perennials outside by following the preceding steps. But instead of placing your pots on a light stand, put the pots outside where they can remain undisturbed until they germinate. You can build a frame or a low box to house the pots. Some perennials may take years to germinate, so don't give up on them too hastily.

Chapter 4

Perennial Care and Cleaning

After devoting many, many hours to choosing and planting your perennials, you need to devote many, many more hours to maintaining them. What a great excuse to spend time among your flowers! This chapter gives you all the information you need to keep your plants happy and healthy.

Quenching Your Garden's Thirst

Figuring out how to water effectively and efficiently is the trickiest part of the whole gardening maintenance routine. How much water each perennial requires to stay fit and healthy depends on a number of factors:

✔ **Climate:** In climates where rainfall is regular and reliable, watering isn't a pressing need, except during occasional prolonged dry spells or drought. (Refer to Chapter 3 in Book IV for more on perennials and climate.) Every climate undergoes a dry spell periodically. In arid regions, irrigation is often an all-consuming activity, becoming the garden's artificial life-support system. Ironically, the same perennial that insists on frequent irrigation to survive in a hot, dry environment may rot in a wet climate.

✔ **Weather:** *Climate* is determined by average prevailing weather conditions; *weather* is what's happening outside as you read this. Out-of-the-ordinary weather can wreak havoc on your plants. Windstorms and high temperatures can dry out a garden very quickly.

✔ **Soil types:** Different soil types also affect how often the garden needs water. (See Book I for tips on watering particular types of soil.)

✔ **Location:** In general, shaded gardens need less water than gardens in the full blast of the midday sun. However, in places where trees are responsible for casting the shadow, their roots may greedily grab water, outcompeting the flowers.

✔ **Genetic disposition:** Some plants are splendidly adaptable, enduring swamp or desert with equal aplomb. But most plants prefer some approximation of their natural habitat.

Getting water to the garden

The three primary methods for irrigating flower beds are the following:

✔ **The portable system:** You probably already know the old hose-and-sprinkler routine all too well. This low-cost method has multiple drawbacks, however. Sprinklers work best when every flower is the same height. Most sprinklers spray in uneven patterns, so don't place them in the same spot each time. Sprinklers wet the foliage, which may spread diseases in the flower bed, making them a bad choice in hot, humid climates. But in hot, dry climates, wetting the foliage rinses dust off the leaves and helps prevent spider mite infestations.

✔ **Drip irrigation:** Two main types of drip irrigation are available: leaky hoses and individual emitters. Leaky hoses are either porous tubes manufactured from old tires or flat tapes with slits cut at intervals. You can lay either kind directly on top of the soil under the mulch (as shown in Figure 4-1), or bury them a few inches deep. In another type of drip irrigation system, you wind rigid plastic tubing through the flower bed. You place the individual emitters that are attached to the line directly on the root ball of each perennial. This system is highly efficient at delivering water.

✔ **The automated system:** Both sprinklers and drip irrigation can be fully automated. You can even purchase built-in timers or moisture sensors, so that the system comes on only when needed.

Figure 4-1:
Snake leaky hoses back and forth between the plants in the flower bed.

Grouping plants according to their needs

The one most important factor in creating a successful garden is grouping plants that have the same cultural needs, so that you can tend to them as a group, rather than individually. Build separate flower beds for flowers with dissimilar needs, and each bed can have its own personalized schedule for watering and other maintenance tasks.

Deciding when to water

Most perennials require water only after the top few inches of soil dry out, but before the plant starts to show symptoms of drought stress. Perennials from arid habitats benefit when the dry interval between waterings is longer. Plants from wet places prefer to never completely dry out. Problems occur when the soil is either too wet or too dry for too long. To complicate matters, overwatered and underwatered perennials exhibit nearly identical symptoms. Both conditions cause plants to wilt and droop miserably, to develop yellowed leaves with brown edges, and to experience stunted growth. Flowers and leaves start to drop off, and eventually, the plant dies.

You need to feel the soil to be certain whether the soil is too wet or too dry. When your perennials first start to show signs of stress, dig a small hole several inches deep and feel the soil. If the soil's wet, you know that you need to cut back on water. If the soil is dry, water more frequently. Clay is more difficult to judge than sand. The tiny clay particles can grab hold of moisture so tightly that the soil can feel cool and somewhat moist, and yet the plants can't get the water. Amending clay soil with plenty of organic matter alleviates this problem.

Accounting for seasonal variations

Adequate and even moisture is essential for most perennials during their spring growth spurt. But many regions have special watering needs:

- Mediterranean flowers and others from coastal regions often require a summer dormancy period and must be kept fairly dry during their nap. During the summer, give them only an infrequent deep soaking when the soil is completely dry.

- In regions with cold winters, always start lengthening the intervals between waterings in late summer to toughen your plants for winter.

- Where winters are cold and dry, the garden benefits from a drink once a month, whenever it hasn't rained or snowed for a few weeks. Water your garden on a day when temperatures are above freezing and the surface of the soil is thawed, so that the water doesn't simply run off.

Book IV

Perennials

Considering the time of day

Don't water in the hottest part of the day. Much of the water from a midday watering evaporates before it has a chance to soak in. The same goes for watering when a wind is blowing. Watering in the evening or early morning is preferable wherever you live, but keep in mind the following tips:

- **Water whenever the soil is dry and plants are wilting or showing signs of imminent death.** Most perennials wilt on a hot day, regardless of whether or not they need water. Water only when the soil is dry and the plants don't recover from their "faint" overnight.

- **Choose morning watering over evening watering.** Mornings aren't as windy as evenings, so less water gets blown away. Also, the moisture from a morning watering recharges your plants for the day. In tropical regions, wet foliage may help spread some diseases. If you live in a steamy, damp climate, it's especially important to water early in the morning, so that leaves dry off quickly as the day heats up.

- **Water in the evening if you live in a dry region.** That way, plants have ample time to absorb the water overnight.

Tending new transplants

Newly transplanted perennials are especially vulnerable in the first few weeks. Extra pampering gets them off to a good, strong start. Little root balls can dry out very quickly. During really hot spells, you may need to water more than once a day. Water new transplants every time their roots dry out, whether the surrounding soil is still damp or not. The only way you can tell whether the root ball is dry is to push your fingers into the soil at the base of each plant and feel for yourself.

A process called *wicking* can cause a newly planted root ball to remain absolutely dry, even while standing in a puddle of mud. Wicking can occur whenever two different types of soil meet. The soil in the prepared flower bed is almost always heavier and denser than the potting mix surrounding the root ball. Moisture is pulled out of the light soil, leaving the new plant high and dry. After a few weeks, the roots travel out into the new soil, and the problem is solved. But in the meantime, you must make certain that the root ball is actually getting wet.

Here's a good, low-tech, temporary, and free method you can use to water new transplants. This process creates an all-day, automatic drip system.

1. **Rinse out a 1-gallon (2-liter) plastic bottle or jug.**

2. **Using a needle, poke a small hole in the bottom near a corner.**

   You want a very slow drip, so that it takes several days for all the water to drain out of the container.

3. **Fill the container with water.**

4. **Set the container next to a newly transplanted perennial.**

5. **Refill the container as needed.**

   Leave the container in place until the plant puts on several inches of new growth.

Watering cans are another easy way to take care of your transplants' watering needs. Choose a can with a soft spray attachment. A hard splash can wash away soil and expose the tender roots.

Deciphering the proper amount of water

Perennials generally spread most of their roots in the top 12 inches (30 cm) of the soil, although roots may grow deeper in sandy, fast-draining soils and more shallowly in clay. Watering a few inches deeper than this root zone encourages roots to dive deeper, where they're protected from fluctuating surface temperatures. Roots grow best at constant, cool temperatures, and shallow-rooted perennials dry out too quickly and must be watered more frequently.

You can't tell how deeply the water is penetrating by looking at the surface of the soil. The only way to tell whether the water is soaking down deeper than the roots is to dig a few test holes and check. The best method for determining how long to water your garden is to follow these steps:

1. **Wait until your soil is fairly dry at least 6 inches (15 cm) deep.**

2. **Set up whatever system you plan to use and water the flower bed for a set period of time — say 30 minutes.**

3. **Dig a hole the next day to check how deep the soil is wet.**

   Use a narrow-bladed trowel to dig a small hole only 2 to 3 inches (5 to 7 cm) wide. Make the hole 1 foot (30 cm) away from the base of a plant. Don't worry if you cut into the roots — they grow back.

4. **If 30 minutes wasn't long enough to wet the soil 10 to 12 inches (26 to 30 cm) deep, let the soil dry out for a few days and water again — longer this time, say 45 minutes — and dig another hole.**

5. **Repeat this exercise until you discover just how long you need to run the water to get the soil wet to a depth of 1 foot (30 cm).**

   Different irrigation systems deliver water at varying rates, so retest whenever you change to a new sprinkler, hose, or system.

Book IV

Perennials

Cutting down on water waste

Watering too shallowly is wasteful because most of the water evaporates quickly, before the plants get a chance to quench their thirst. Watering too deeply is also wasteful because roots can only go so far down. Water shortages are a reality in any climate and region, and bans on watering aren't uncommon. The following list outlines a few things that you can do when water is scarce or limited, when you want to reduce your water bill, or when you just want to conserve the precious resource of fresh water:

- **Turn off the water.** Leaving a sprinkler running and then forgetting to turn it off is easy. Set an egg timer to remind you or buy a faucet timer that automatically shuts off the water.

- **Choose a drip-irrigation method.** Sprinklers waste a great deal of water, throwing much of it into the air where it either evaporates or is blown away.

- **Collect and use rainwater.** Use a rain gauge to keep track of rainfall. If you have a fixed watering schedule, skip a watering whenever you record ½ inch (1 cm) or more of rain.

- **Divert rainwater.** Divert the rainwater from downspouts to flower beds by using *French drains* and pits filled with gravel. A French drain is simply an underground plastic pipe, sometimes with holes along the sides, that directs the water flow from the drainspout to the garden.

- **Mulch the garden.**

- **Xeriscape.** Plant a water-conserving garden by choosing flowers that can get by on the average rainfall in your area. Then you can skip the chore of watering entirely, except while getting the perennials adjusted to their new flower bed and during occasional dry periods. (See Chapter 2 in Book IV for details on this type of gardening.)

Grooming and Primping Your Flowers

Some maintenance tasks require devotion to a regular routine during the blooming season to keep your flowers looking good. Other chores — such as getting the flower bed ready for winter — are seasonal. If you've ever had the burden of caring for a lawn, you'll be pleasantly surprised to find that flowers require much less attention than grass. Flower-garden maintenance can almost always wait until you have time for it.

Collecting the tools you need

Here's a list of the basic tools you need in order to work in your perennial garden:

- ✔ **Buckets:** Buy several.

- ✔ **Hand trowel:** A *hand trowel* looks like a very small shovel. It's the tool you use the most in gardening, so buy a good one. A high-quality hand trowel costs as much as a shovel, but don't skimp. You use it to transplant small flowers and bulbs, to enlarge holes you've dug with a shovel, and to weed. You may want to buy two sizes — one with a wide blade for digging and one with a narrow blade for weeding. If you only buy one, get the wider size.

- ✔ **Pruning shears:** Try out shears before you buy them to get a comfortable fit. When you hold the handles open in your hand, they shouldn't extend past the reach of your fingertips. Good pruning shears are very expensive, but they stay sharp longer than a cheap pair and have parts that are replaceable if they wear out. (Chapter 5 in Book I is all about pruning.)

- ✔ **Scissors:** A pair of lightweight aluminum household scissors are really slick for cutting foliage and lightweight stems (much larger handfuls than you can manage with pruning shears) and for all-around snipping.

- ✔ **Shovel or spade:** You need a shovel or spade for digging holes and for mixing amendments into the soil. We prefer a round-nose shovel, but many other gardeners swear by a short-handled, flat-bladed spade.

- ✔ **Stiff-tined rake:** A stiff-tined rake is helpful for smoothing out the surface of the soil and for spreading mulch. Use it with the tines up for spreading fine materials, tines down for coarse materials.

- ✔ **Wheelbarrow or garden cart:** A wheelbarrow or garden cart is a real time- and back-saver. Buy one that you can handle easily.

Buying the right tools

Always buy the best quality tools that you can afford; they last a lifetime if you take care of them. (Always quit gardening for the day while you still have enough energy and daylight to clean your tools and put them away.) Cheap tools break too readily to be a true bargain. Don't order tools through the mail without first trying them out. One size doesn't fit all. You actually need to heft a tool to see whether you can use it comfortably. A bad fit guarantees backaches and blisters. After you know which tools suit your grip, go ahead and order them from a catalog, especially if you can save some money by doing so.

Small tools have a way of getting lost in the nooks and crannies of a flower bed. To make your tools easy to locate, paint a band of bright color or wrap a strip of colored tape on the part of the handle that you don't hold. Some tools have a hole at one end so that you can hang them on a nail; tie a piece of brightly colored yarn through the hole to make your tool stand out against the garden's neutral backdrop. In this case, garish is good.

Renting the really big puppies

Large, gasoline-powered machines are a real help with large projects, but they're expensive to buy and take up a great deal of storage space. Renting

Book IV

Perennials

or borrowing these machines when you need them is more practical. Usually, these machines are rented out by the hour or the day. Unless you have a hitch on your vehicle and a small trailer, expect to pay a delivery charge as well. Rental costs vary but are usually about the same as a moderately priced dinner. The two most useful large machines are power tillers and chipper-shredders.

Developing a maintenance routine

A 100- to 200-square-foot (9- to 18-square-meter) flower garden shouldn't take more than a few minutes a week of tending, with a couple of hours of major cleanup several times a year. This section covers the housekeeping aspects of gardening, such as trimming, staking, and preparing your flower bed for winter.

Deadheading

Flowers in a vase eventually start to wither and die, and so do flowers in the garden as they age. Removing these crumpled corpses — called *deadheading* — serves several purposes:

- **Deadheading improves the look of the garden.**

- **Most dead flowers form seeds.** Some plants replace flowers with really attractive seedheads. But others scatter their seeds all over the garden, much like a dandelion does. You often wind up with dozens of baby flowers that you have to pull out to avoid ending up with a hundred daisies in one square foot of garden soil. Cutting off flowers before they form seeds prevents this maintenance headache.

- **Many perennials stop blooming after they form seeds.** Removing the fading flowers before they can complete the process encourages the plant to continue blooming.

To deadhead, simply cut the dead flower off — using scissors for lightweight stems or pruning shears for heavy and thick ones. Cut the stem below the flower at the first leaves or flower bud you come to.

Disbudding

If you like your flowers really big, you may want to indulge in the practice of *disbudding*. Before the buds start to open, remove all but one or two flower buds on each stem. The plant then directs all its energy to the remaining buds, resulting in large flowers. Gardeners commonly disbud dahlias, chrysanthemums, peonies, and carnations.

Nipping and tucking with scissors and shears

Here are more things you can do with your pruning shears and scissors:

✔ **Pinching:** To keep perennials denser and shorter, you may want to pinch or shear them, as shown in Figure 4-2, a couple of times early in the season. This process is called *pinching* because you can actually pinch off the top of each stem between your thumb and forefinger — but using scissors or pruning shears is quicker and easier.

Simply snip (or pinch) off the top few inches (8 cm or so) of the plant when it grows to a foot tall (30 cm) in spring and again in the middle of summer. Every stem you cut grows several new stems. The result is stocky sprays of more, but smaller, flowers. Chrysanthemums and asters are two perennials that are routinely pinched. Otherwise, they tend to get floppy.

✔ **Shearing:** For a quicker alternative to pinching, use scissors or pruning shears to cut the top 6 inches (15 cm) off your plants a couple of times before midsummer.

✔ **Cutting back hard:** When the directions for a plant tell you to *cut it back hard,* that means reduce the height of the plant by approximately one-third to one-half, using either scissors or pruning shears. Sometimes, hard pruning is recommended solely to improve the plant's appearance, but it may also be necessary to renew a plant's vigor.

Figure 4-2:
To keep late-flowering perennials more compact, shear or pinch a couple of times early in the season.

Book IV

Perennials

Staking perennials with bad posture

Some perennials slouch and sprawl as badly as a group of teenage boys in the neighborhood park. If slumping perennials were simply a problem of aesthetics, you could just ignore them, depending on your inclination toward discipline in the garden. But when a large perennial leans over on top of smaller, weaker companions, the bully may steal all the sunlight or actually crush the little ones. During fall cleanup, you often find that plants subjected to this treatment didn't survive the season.

Fortunately, you have many ways to prop up unruly (or just plain lazy) plants. Here are a few popular methods and devices for staking perennials:

- **Bamboo stakes:** Bamboo makes good support for flowers with tall, single spikes — such as delphiniums and lilies. Wait until the stems are several feet tall and starting to form flower buds. Pound the stake several inches into the ground at the base of the plant and tie the stem loosely to the stake. You can also encircle wide multistemmed perennials with bamboo-type stakes and run twine around the circumference and back and forth across the center a few times to make sort of a net — this way, the stems can grow through the twine and be supported.

- **Branches:** When you prune shrubs, save any trimmings that are 2 to 3 feet (60 cm to 1 m) long and brushy at one end, resembling brooms. When a perennial reaches about a foot tall, poke several of these branches — bushy side up and leaning slightly inward — into the ground around the plant. As the stems grow up through this circle of branches, the supporting mechanism is hidden by the perennial's foliage.

- **Commercial supports:** You can buy artistic metal supports from garden centers and nursery catalogs.

Creating a schedule of chores

The easiest way to see that necessary chores get done in a somewhat timely fashion is to set up some sort of schedule. Don't fret if you're out of town for a couple of weeks; the flower garden can wait until you get back without getting too impatient.

Weekly work

Take a few minutes each day to walk outside and have a look at your flower bed. At least once a week, take along a bucket with a hand trowel, scissors, and pruning shears and spend a few minutes tidying up. These are some of the things you should do:

- Cut off dead or dying flowers or leaves.
- Pull any weeds you find.
- Toss straying mulch back into the flower bed.

✔ Squash any bad bugs you can catch (to recognize the good, the bad, and the ugly bugs, turn to Chapter 7 in Book I), and treat plagues of bugs or diseases that have appeared during the past week.

✔ Stake any flowers that look as though they may topple over.

✔ Water as necessary.

Monthly maintenance

In addition to your weekly gardening chores, other jobs need attention about once a month. You can work these tasks into your weekly routine, allowing yourself a little extra time once a month.

✔ **Adjust your watering as the weather changes.** Give your flower bed more water during hot weather, less during cool weather.

✔ **Cut each perennial back by about a third when it stops blooming.** Or, if you want, you can cut the old stalks to the ground *after* new leaves start to sprout from the base of the plant.

✔ **Make notes in your garden journal of both artistic and practical successes and failures.**

Springtime strategy

Spring is the busiest time in the garden in most regions. As the weather starts to warm up, funnel some of your spring-fever energy into garden chores:

✔ In cold-winter and cool-summer climates, spring is the best time to plant perennials in your flower bed (see Chapter 2 in Book IV).

✔ Renew your mulch by adding a few inches of fresh material, if the old material is getting thin.

✔ Plant summer bulbs (see Book VI).

✔ In cold-winter climates, plant annuals (see Book V).

✔ Fertilize the flower bed (see Chapter 4 in Book I).

Autumn action

Fall is the second-busiest season in the garden. You need to devote a short burst of activity to your garden before winter sets in:

✔ In hot-summer, warm-winter climates, plant perennials in the fall.

✔ Plant spring bulbs.

✔ Prepare flower beds for planting the following spring.

✔ Build other structures — such as trellises, walls, paths, and so on — in the fall, while the weather is cool (see Book II).

✔ In warm-winter climates, plant annuals.

Book IV

Perennials

Winter preparation

If you live in a warm-winter climate, you can skip this section. All you need to do is clean up year-round, whenever your flowers show signs of wear — cutting off dead flowers, leaves, and stems as they materialize.

However, if frosts and snows are an annual feature of your backyard, the onset of winter is the time to do a few things to protect your plants:

- **Water less frequently.** Cutting down on water helps signal to the plants that they need to toughen up and hunker down for winter.

- **Dig and store tender bulbs (see Book VI) after the first frost has blackened the foliage.**

- **Replace mulch from under any perennials that were besieged by insects during the growing season.** Getting rid of the mulch also gets rid of any eggs. Compost the old mulch.

- **Place a 4- to 6-inch (10- to 15-cm) layer of organic mulch around perennials that you planted in late summer and fall, if you haven't done so already.** Let leaves that fall into the flower bed stay where they land to add to the mulch layer.

- **Cut back the stems on perennials (at least the ones that don't have pretty seedheads) to within 8 to 10 inches (20 to 26 cm) of the ground.** In really severe winter climates — where the temperature is often below 0° F (–18° C), don't cut back your perennials until late winter or early spring. The debris helps protect them from the cold.

- **Cover your whole flower bed with a loose mulch of hay, straw, or evergreen boughs after the ground freezes (or in midwinter if the ground doesn't freeze).** This extra layer protects your fragile perennials from severe cold. Leave this mulch in place until early spring and then remove it *gradually* as the weather starts to warm up.

- **Water the flower bed once a month in dry-winter climates, whenever snow or rain hasn't fallen in recent memory.** Water on a warm, sunny day, so that the water can soak into the ground.

Whenever an unseasonable frost is forecast, you can save your flowers by covering them with old sheets or special frost blankets, as shown in Figure 4-3. (Don't cover your flowers with plastic; it conducts cold too readily.) Leave the sheets or frost blankets in place until the cold snap is over. Cold-weather gardeners always need a few lengths of frost blanket, which is available from garden centers. This magical material is fairly expensive, but it lasts many years if dried between uses and stored out of direct sunlight.

If you live in a cold-winter climate, don't fertilize your plants after midsummer. Fertilizer encourages plants to put on soft new growth, which is really vulnerable to frost damage.

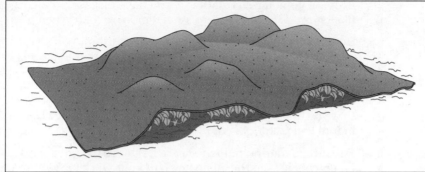

Figure 4-3:
For temporary protection from severe cold, cover your perennials with frost blankets.

Troubling Problems in Paradise

We're going to let you in on one of gardening's dirty little secrets: You can ignore most of the bugs that visit your garden. Folks that make and sell bug-killing products may try to convince you otherwise, but don't believe them. Doing nothing at all about bugs is often the best policy. Ninety-five percent of the bugs that visit your garden are either beneficial or neutral — neither good nor bad. But ignoring even the genuine pests gives nature's own controls the time they need to kick in. In most cases, nature's way is a much better remedy than anything you can buy. (See Chapter 7 in Book I for a complete discussion of garden pests and other problems.)

Staving off garden woes

Preventing a problem is easier than treating its results. Here are some things you can do to head off disasters before they strike:

- **Keep your flowers healthy and strong.** Opportunistic bugs and diseases move in for the kill when flowers are weakened by improper growing conditions.

- **Practice good housekeeping habits in your garden.** Remove dead and diseased leaves and stems promptly to get diseases out of the garden before they spread. Keep the flower bed clear of weeds, which may play host to diseases or insects. Clean and disinfect pruning shears and scissors (dip them in a solution of household bleach and water) after cutting diseased plants. If you smoke, wash your hands before gardening — tobacco can contain viruses that infect flowers.

- **Shower your flowers.** If you use drip-type irrigation, occasionally wash the dust and small insects off your flowers by using a spray attachment on the end of a hose. Get up underneath the leaves to knock off bugs that are clinging there.

Book IV

Perennials

✔ **Provide good air circulation.** If you have disease problems, give the plants more space. Diseases spread more quickly when plants touch.

✔ **Don't bring bugs or diseases into your garden.** When you buy new plants, check them over carefully to make sure that insects or their eggs aren't lurking on the undersides of the leaves. Don't buy plants with mottled, discolored, or spotted foliage. Look for pearly clumps of snail or slug eggs when you remove your flower from its pot, and destroy any that you find. Pull off any weeds that are hitchhiking with your flower before you plant it in your garden.

✔ **Encourage natural helpers.** Learn to ignore the good guys (even the creepy ones), and they'll do much of your work for you. Snakes eat slugs and mice. Bats, spiders, toads, and lizards all eat huge quantities of bugs, if you let them.

✔ **Get rid of problem plants.** Be hard-hearted and replace any flower that's a perennial problem.

Identifying the culprits

Spotting damage on the perennials that you're working so hard to grow can be frustrating, but don't overreact. Perennials are a tough bunch. A few holes in their leaves doesn't damage their vigor and probably aren't noticeable at ten paces, anyway.

If you're using insecticide to control bug damage, you may actually be aggravating the problem. Before you get involved in chemical warfare, find out exactly what's causing the problem. Environmental damage often creates symptoms that look very much like disease or insect mischief. Ask yourself whether any of the following conditions may be responsible for your flowers' ill health:

✔ **Air pollution:** Some flowers are sensitive to smog. Their leaves may appear bleached or distorted. If air pollution is your problem, select resistant perennials. If you live in an area where smog is a problem, ask a local nursery person to recommend resistant varieties.

✔ **Chemical damage:** An herbicide is anything that kills plants, although it's usually intended to kill only weeds. Use herbicides on cool, still days to prevent spray from accidentally drifting or descending as a vapor cloud onto your flower beds. Swimming pool chemicals can also damage plants. Mix all chemicals away from the flower bed and immediately put the lid back on the container to limit vapors from escaping. Symptoms of chemical damage include distorted and twisted stems and foliage, browning in an even pattern over the whole plant, or irregularly-shaped brown spots.

✔ **Drought:** Too little water causes plants to become warped-looking, stop growing, and develop brown tips or yellowing leaves.

✔ **Fertilizer burn or fertilizer deficiency:** Applying fertilizer improperly can scorch plant leaves. Too much can actually kill the plant. Shortages of any of the essential plant nutrients can cause stunting and leaf discoloration.

✔ **Freeze damage:** Frost can either blacken the most exposed parts of the plant or kill the plant to the ground. Hardy perennials usually grow back after freeze damage, but, just to be safe, protect plants from unseasonable cold spells by temporarily covering them with old sheets or blankets. Don't use plastic — frost goes right through plastic.

✔ **Inadequate sunlight:** When a flower isn't getting enough light, it turns sickly pale and its stems become long and spindly. If you plant in a shady area, choose shade-tolerant flowers. (See Chapter 2 in Book IV for a list of shade-tolerant perennials.)

✔ **Poor drainage:** Flowers that are too wet become yellowish or brown, wilt, and eventually die. Plant flowers that are tolerant of wet conditions or improve the drainage in your flower bed. (See Chapter 2 in Book IV for a list of plants that enjoy wet conditions.)

✔ **Salts:** Salt can either occur naturally in the soil or get carried to your garden on salt-ridden breezes, if you live near the ocean. Cars can also splash salt onto your garden when roads are salted in the winter. When salt concentrations build up, your flowers can become stunted and brown. The cure is to rinse the soil with plenty of fresh water.

✔ **Sunscald:** When shade-loving flowers are getting too much sunshine, they first become pale all over and then may develop papery patches or dark, irregular burns. Move the plant to a shadier location.

✔ **Transplant shock:** A recently moved flower can go into a real sulk and wilt badly. Provide temporary shelter from the sun and wind until the plant recovers and has settled into its new home. (See Chapter 3 for guidance on protecting new plantings.)

If you think that insects are eating your flowers, you first you need to identify the suspects. Don't panic when you look over the following list. Most insect infestations are localized — you aren't likely to ever get to know all these pests, unless you move around quite a bit. Insects also have good and bad seasons. You may be thoroughly plagued by leafhoppers one year but not find a single one the next. The following list describes the most common insect pests of perennial gardens; Chapter 7 in Book I tells you how to get rid of them:

✔ **Aphids:** Often, the first indication of aphid infestation is an odd twisting and distortion of the foliage.

✔ **Beetles:** Many types of beetles eat perennials; many other types eat bugs. If you catch them in the act, you can tell the difference.

Book IV

Perennials

✔ **Caterpillars:** Usually, butterfly caterpillars are big, brightly colored, and travel alone. You may decide to look the other way when one of these critters inches by. Other types run in packs and do a great deal of damage munching on leaves and flower buds. Still another type of caterpillar, called *borers,* tunnel destructively through stems or roots. *Cutworms* are soil-dwelling caterpillars who cut off whole young plants at ground level.

✔ **Leafhoppers:** These insect Typhoid Marys carry a disease called *aster yellows,* which does particularly nasty things to flowers.

✔ **Leaf miners:** Leaf miners are tiny fly maggots that tunnel in leaves, resulting in tell-tale trails.

✔ **Mealybugs:** Furry little white, oval-shaped critters, mealybugs (shown in Figure 4-4) would be cute if they didn't do so much damage and multiply so rapidly.

✔ **Spider mites:** As their name implies, spider mites are actually tiny arachnids, not true insects. Usually, the first hint of a spider mite invasion is a mottled bronze tint to the foliage. A closer look reveals traveling dots about the size of the period at the end of this sentence.

✔ **Thrips:** If your flowers turn brown and are distorted and streaked with silver, tiny thrips are the culprit.

✔ **Weevils:** Beetles with long snouts, weevils often drill holes in flower buds, so the flowers don't open properly, if at all.

✔ **Whiteflies:** Small, snow-white whiteflies (shown in Figure 4-5) suck plant juices and reproduce at lightning speed. Symptoms of whitefly attack are mottled and yellowed leaves.

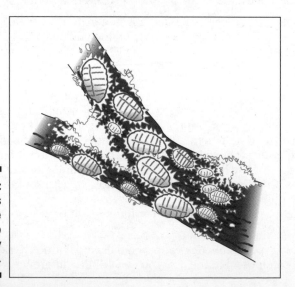

Figure 4-4: Mealybugs don't move much, so they're easy to spot.

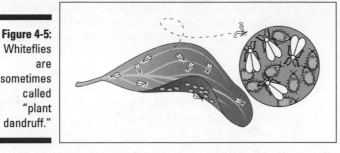

Figure 4-5:
Whiteflies
are
sometimes
called
"plant
dandruff."

Diagnosing plant diseases

You may be surprised to find out that plants can get sick by their own versions of the same organisms that attack you and me — fungi, bacteria, viruses, and microplasma. (Chapter 7 in Book I offers a complete discussion of plant diseases.) Plant diseases are primarily water-borne. Don't overwater, and let the soil dry out between waterings to slow down their spread. Following is a list of the diseases that are most likely to attack your perennials:

- **Aster yellows:** Plants infected with this disease become bizarrely deformed and distorted — the flowers may start to grow strange protrusions and the leaves curl and twist.

- **Gray molds:** Fuzzy brown or gray mold can form on leaves and flowers, and stems may become soft and rotten. Cool temperatures and humidity encourage their growth. Where this disease is a problem, water in the morning, so that plants dry quickly. Remove damaged leaves and flowers and destroy badly affected plants. To prevent mold, space flowers in the garden widely enough that they don't touch and clean up dead plant debris promptly.

- **Leafspots:** Both viral and bacterial infections can cause brown or black irregular blotches or circular spots.

- **Nematodes:** Nematodes are actually microscopic worms that can damage plant roots or foliage.

- **Powdery mildew:** Plants infected with powdery mildew look as though they've been dusted with talcum powder. This disease requires heat and a brief period of high humidity to form; the attack often occurs after the flowers have finished blooming. Some perennials are highly susceptible to powdery mildew, so plant resistant varieties.

- **Rust:** Rust fungi causes yellow, orange, or brown bumps to appear on stems or leaves. Keep plant foliage dry and pick out infected leaves.

Book IV

Perennials

✔ **Viruses:** Insects transmit viruses. Infected leaves may be mottled in irregular or sometimes circular patterns or may be yellowed overall. Destroy infected plants and practice good sanitation (wash hands and tools thoroughly).

✔ **Wilts:** When the whole plant wilts and dies, sometimes overnight, fungal or bacterial root rots may be responsible. Nematodes or gophers can cause the same symptoms. If root rots are the cause, continually wet soil encourages their growth. Improve the drainage and don't replant the same flower in affected soil.

Nudging out other garden nuisances

Bugs and diseases are not the only pests interested in eating your flowers. King-sized pests can damage more than a few leaves:

✔ **Snails and slugs:** If large patches of foliage disappear overnight, suspect snails and slugs. These heavy feeders come out at night, so it isn't always obvious who's causing the mischief. Look for telltale silvery slime trails, or go outside with a flashlight after dark. You can often find the guilty parties in action.

✔ **Wildlife vandals:** You have several options for declaring your flowers off-limits to the local wildlife:

- **Physical barriers:** Electric fences discourage deer. Buried hardware cloth — a type of heavy-duty metal mesh sold at building supply stores — prevents burrowing animals from entering the garden underground. Where all else fails, build raised beds and line them with hardware cloth.

- **Repellents:** Available at garden centers, repellents are supposed to offend the animal's taste or smell enough to drive it away. The effectiveness of repellents varies. Some animals actually seem to develop a fondness for noxious substances.

- **Scare tactics:** If you've ever seen crows sitting on the scarecrow, you already have some idea of how well scare tactics work. The effect is usually temporary. A hungry animal can get used to loud noises and flashing lights. Most garden-invading creatures aren't particularly nervous by nature, anyway.

- **Trapping:** Live traps are available to capture small animals. After you catch the little critters, you can release them in an unpopulated area. Be sure to check the trap daily, so that the little fellers don't have to go without water for very long.

- **Plant something different or enclose the garden:** You may have to learn to live with pests (perhaps by gradually switching over to plants that they don't like to eat), or enclose your garden by building a fence or draping netting over plants.

✔ **Human damage:** One immutable fact that you — like all gardeners — must accept is that when you put flowers within reach of pedestrians, you have to expect a few flowers to "walk away." No child can resist picking the occasional daisy. When adults yield to temptation, they sometimes dig up the whole plant. Here are some tips to cut your losses:

- The best defense is to plant rugged and heavy-blooming perennials, so that you don't miss the flowers that grow legs.

- Save your most expensive treasures for less public flower beds.

- Leave bunches of cut flowers in your front yard with a note that says, "Free." This unusual tactic may help you meet new friends.

Pulling weeds without pulling your hair

When perennial weeds pop up in an established flower border, getting the herbicide on the weed but not the flowers is difficult. Use a plastic bag to isolate the weed. Here's how:

1. **Cut a hole large enough to fit the weed through in the bottom of a plastic bag.**

2. **Pull the entire weed through the hole in the bottom of the bag.**

3. **Place a stone in the bottom of the bag to hold it in place.**

4. **Carefully spray herbicide into the top of the bag.**

   If you accidentally spray or spill some herbicide on adjoining flowers, immediately rinse them off with water.

5. **Seal the top of the bag with a twist-tie and leave the bag in place until the weed is dead.**

If your soil is loose and crumbly, a light tug is probably all you need to yank out the most stubborn weed. But in dense soil, what usually happens is that you tug at the weed and the top comes off neatly in your hand. The roots happily grow a new top, and the next time you look, the weed is back, looking refreshed and smug! To kill most weeds, you must get the root. Here's the simplest technique to do so:

1. **Slip the blade of your hand trowel into the ground straight down, next to the main root of the weed.**

2. **Push the trowel blade firmly against the root to loosen it.**

3. **Grab hold of the base of the leaves and pull.**

   Most of the time, this action gets you the whole weed — roots and all.

Book IV

Perennials

WARNING!

Defensive gardening

Gardens are full of critters. Unfortunately, rather than appreciating your hard work in their Eden, most of these fellows view you as a threat to their well-being. Whenever you work in the garden, dress defensively. Wear shoes, long sleeves, and long pants to cover your skin. If ants are a problem, pull your socks over the bottoms of your pant legs to keep the little armies from biting your exposed ankles. Gloves protect your hands from slivers and thorns. And don't forget to put on sunscreen and a hat to prevent a painful sunburn when you inevitably lose track of time.

Eulogizing dead perennials

New gardeners view the death of each plant as a real tragedy, but experienced gardeners kill many flowers and develop a fairly callous attitude about doing so. New gardeners who are still conducting memorial services for their dead flowers find it hard to be grateful when space opens up for something new and different, but owners of mature gardens spend more time attempting to find room for a new perennial than planting it. You may not believe it now, but you'll eventually come to view the death of each plant as an opportunity to try something new.

What killed my plant?

Sometimes, the cause of death is splendidly obvious — you did the deed, and you know exactly what you did. Those lessons are the easy ones. You hit yourself in the forehead, buy new plants, and vow never to do it again. In some cases, though, you never, ever discover what killed a particular plant. Unless the problem is really widespread or severe, save yourself the expense of calling in an expert. Flowers are mercifully inexpensive and easy to replace.

Is my plant playing possum?

Before you pull out a plant, make sure that it's really dead.

The first time that you grow a bleeding heart or an oriental poppy can be unnerving. The plant does magnificently until summer, and then it suddenly flops over like an actor in a spectacular Shakespearean death scene. Both of these flowers go dormant after blooming. Dormant, in this case, translates to "looks dead." (The nursery label probably didn't mention this habit because "looks dead in July" doesn't sell very many plants.) Many perennials that are evergreen in mild climates go dormant where winters are frigid.

Weed whacking

Like flowers, weeds come in two main groups — annuals and perennials:

- ✔ **The annuals form staggering quantities of seed; some produce up to 500,000 per plant.** Pull annuals out of your garden before they form seed.

- ✔ **Perennial weeds are harder to control.** They seem to live forever and expand by sending out roots or running stems for several feet in every direction. These weeds want to conquer the world. Pulling and digging at them appears to make them mad; they seem to spread even faster in response. Perennial weeds also form seeds, so don't ever let them get to this stage. Unfortunately, mulch doesn't stop their roots or runners. The most effective way to dispatch perennial weeds is with an herbicide.

Late-sleeping plants may also lead you to pronounce death prematurely. Late emergers are the adolescents of the plant world — they sleep until noon. For example, butterfly flowers and balloon flowers don't venture even a peek out of the ground until early summer. Mark these late emergers, so that you know where they are and don't inadvertently chop them up.

Book IV

Perennials

Chapter 5

Perennially Digging — Special Features for Your Flower Bed

*W*elcome to the sweat-making, blister-producing, muscle-building phase of gardening. The projects in this chapter are all within the scope of the typical do-it-yourselfer. (Check out Book II for more on garden design.) However, if you're a bit DIY-challenged, you can hire a landscape contractor to do the whole enchilada or any part of it. When choosing a contractor, get at least three estimates — prices can vary widely. Ask for references and then check with them to make sure that those people were satisfied and that the work was completed in a timely manner. Request a written proposal that clearly spells out the project, materials, and dates for beginning and ending the project.

Before You Build

When remodeling or starting from scratch, make sure that you don't paint yourself into a corner. The front yard may seem to be in more urgent need of cosmetic repair than the back. But don't block access to the rear, so that you end up driving heavy equipment over your newly installed landscape to get to other parts of your yard.

Save yourself a great deal of hauling labor by having deliveries of heavy materials dropped off close to the work site. A rear alleyway or adjoining vacant lot provides convenient access. But be aware that vacant lots have a habit of sprouting up new houses when your back is turned, so keep a vigilant watch for grading equipment.

Call before you dig

Before you start working on any really ambitious garden plans (beyond flower beds), call your city's public works department (in the phone book under government listings) to see whether your city requires permits for any of the structural work you plan to do. Usually, permits are necessary only for walls over 3 feet tall (90 cm) or for concrete or electrical wiring installation.

Call your utility companies to find out the location of underground water, sewer, electrical, gas, phone, or cable lines on your property. If you damage these lines, you're responsible for the cost of repairs. If you live in a covenant-controlled neighborhood, submit plans to the architectural control committee or the homeowner's association to ensure that you comply with its rules.

If you plan to build anything, even a small flower bed, along the property line, let your neighbors know what you have in mind. Keeping open communication with your neighbors can head off annoying grievances partway through your construction venture — and may even get your neighbors excited enough to pitch in and help.

Be sure to kill any perennial weeds or grasses before starting construction. Some weeds are persistent enough to eventually work their way to the surface of the new soil and renew their enthusiastic terrorism of the flower beds. For the specifics on getting rid of weeds, see Chapter 7 in Book I. Keep in mind that hand pulling usually just makes perennial weeds more resilient and determined. Every piece of root left in the ground can — and usually does — grow into a new weed.

The Magic of Raised Beds

Some soils and sites are so challenging for perennial gardening that your best option is to elevate the bed above ground level. When you're faced with a shallow soil over bedrock, put aside your crate of Acme dynamite and compromise by raising the bed.

A *raised bed* is any planting area in which soil is "raised" above the existing grade a few inches or more. Such beds may have sides of sloping soil, or they may be contained in planter boxes made of wooden frames or low stone walls. Raising a flower bed enables you to deal with salt-affected soils without the time-consuming and often unsuccessful battle of getting the salts out of the soil. In addition, good drainage is absolutely assured in a raised bed, even over *hardpan* (see Chapter 3 in Book I) or wet, soggy sites.

Controlling soil quality is simplified in a raised bed. You can choose exactly the right soil for the flowers you plan to grow. Use a good soil mix and fill the planter to within a few inches of the top to keep the soil from washing out. Fewer weed seeds find their way to an elevated surface, and those that do are conveniently within reach.

Raised beds offer many advantages beyond coping with bad soils:

- ✔ **Providing access for people with disabilities:** You can build raised beds to accommodate the needs of the wheelchair-bound or otherwise disabled gardener. The ability to reach the soil surface without having to bend or stoop is also a real help for anyone with back trouble. For even greater comfort, build benches right into the wall surrounding the raised bed, so that you can garden from a seated position. Built-in benches also provide convenient extra seating for guests.

- ✔ **Correcting property flaws:** You can use raised flower beds to break up uninteresting, flat pieces of property. Or terrace steep hillsides with a series of beds defined by short retaining walls and stairs to create more useful and eye-catching spaces.

- ✔ **Creating barriers:** Raised beds make effective barriers, directing traffic patterns around the bed and making it very clear that foot traffic is off limits there. Anywhere that a hedge seems an obvious choice, a raised bed provides a colorful, more solid alternative. Raised beds also add a decorative touch at the edge of walks, driveways, decks, and patios.

- ✔ **Extending the season:** Perennials benefit from raised beds even where soils aren't a problem. In climates with very short growing seasons, soil in a bed constructed from stone or brick thaws out and warms up faster in spring than soil at ground level. Stone and brick also collect and store heat during the day and slowly release it back into the bed when temperatures fall at night. Plants are thus protected from sudden cold snaps, and the growing season is extended. An extra few weeks can make all the difference in determining whether fall flowers have a long enough season to gather energy for their late show.

- ✔ **Protecting plants:** If you have small children or pets, putting the flowers in a raised planter keeps the flowers safe from casual assault. A single landscape timber is usually high enough to discourage drivers from running over and smashing flowers alongside a driveway, street, or alleyway. For a softening effect, plant flowers with a trailing habit at the edge of the bed so that they can spill out and flow down the sides. Some gardens are completely overrun by gophers, moles, or other burrowing rodents. These furry gourmets enjoy nothing better than a meal of your perennials' roots. Line the bottom of the planter box with wire mesh to prevent these pests from getting into the soil.

Book IV

Perennials

Boxes and berms

The simplest raised bed is a freestanding square or rectangular box, but you can build the bed in any shape at all. Design the bed to follow the contours of any feature in the landscape, or tuck a planter box against stairs or in front of an existing retaining wall to highlight or de-emphasize its structural character. For example, build a planter box at the foot of a tall, severe retaining wall to tone down that "Great Wall of China in the backyard" look. If you construct the planter box from the same materials as the retaining wall, the whole structure appears to be a single unit.

A *berm* is a mound of earth with sloping sides (see Figure 5-1). Berms are often less obtrusive than boxes are because they're completely free-form in shape and are the most flexible style of raised bed. Just be careful that the berm you build isn't too square, or it can look more like a bunker than a flower bed. Pattern berms after rolling hills — without obvious symmetry and sloped gently enough that gravity doesn't cause mini-landslides.

Figure 5-1:
A berm is
just a raised
bed without
a wall to
contain it.

Berms must be stable, so that they don't collapse when you stand on them to weed or care for the flowers. A few well-placed flat rocks give you a level surface to stand on and, at the same time, protect the soil from becoming compacted. Bury at least two-thirds of each rock into the hillside for stability and a more natural look.

Berms can be as simple as a dump truck load of topsoil or as complex as a formal rock garden. A foot of topsoil can also be layered over a core of tree trimmings, dead sod, or rock rubble. Whatever materials you use to construct a berm, allow for a great deal of shrinkage. Berms can settle as much as 50 percent the first couple of years.

Making the beds

Build a bed at least 12 to 18 inches (30 to 46 cm) high to create a deep space for plant roots to grow when your main objective is to raise the plants above bad soil or to improve inadequate drainage. A height of 6 inches (15 cm) is plenty when your only concern is deflecting foot or automobile traffic. If you plan to build benches into the garden wall, 14 to 18 inches (35 to 46 cm) is a comfortable height. Make the bed no wider than you can easily reach across — 3 to 4 feet (90 cm to 1.2 m) when the bed is accessible from only one side, not much wider than 6 feet (1.8 m) when you can get to either side. In hot, dry climates, raised beds tend to dry out very rapidly. Wherever irrigation water is in short supply, keep the bed wide and low to slow evaporation and moisture loss.

Mortared brick, stone, or cinder blocks make elegant and durable planters. Stucco and patterned concrete are also strong, long-lasting materials. You must install drainage holes in any of these solid walls, so that water can freely escape. Dry laid stone, recycled concrete chunks, and interlocking concrete modular systems are easy for the do-it-yourselfer with a strong back.

Stacking pressure-treated wood timbers, peeled logs, or railroad ties brings back memories of playing with Lincoln Logs, albeit very large ones. Cedar and redwood wear better than other wood products, but all wood deteriorates eventually from moisture, ultraviolet light, and attack from insects and microorganisms. In some climates, wood needs to be replaced frequently, perhaps in less than ten years. Wood may also attract termites. Where termites are a problem, don't build wooden beds close to the house or other structures.

To build a raised bed, follow these steps:

1. **Mark off the dimensions of the project (see Book II for advice).**

2. **Kill any weeds by following the tips in Book I, Chapter 7.**

3. **Build the planter's walls.**

   Of course, if you're building a berm, you can skip this step.

4. **Place several inches of gravel (available at most garden centers) in the bottom of the planter if salty soils are the reason you're raising the bed.**

   To counter salty soil, you must construct a barrier to keep the salt out of the new bed.

5. **Where the underlying soil is acceptable, use a spade or a shovel to loosen the top 6 inches (15 cm) of the soil.**

Dig up one shovelful at a time, turning the soil and breaking up large clods with the shovel blade, to create a place for the plant roots to go deeper.

6. **Fill the planter with good soil.**

If it's available, you can import good soil from other parts of your property. Otherwise, purchase soil from your local garden center.

Walks and Paths

Walks through the perennial garden serve a number of practical functions. They enable you to get up-close and personal with your garden. The viewer who can sit or stand inside the flower bed, surrounded by the flowers, feels less like a spectator than a person standing at the edge of a bed looking in to the flowers. You can also use paths to divide large areas into several smaller and more easily managed sections, creating the illusion of a larger space. The total area of the garden is expanded while reducing the size of the flower beds themselves — meaning more floral impact and less work for you.

Planning walks

Walks must always appear to have a logical destination (see Book II for more information on designing landscapes). They can either pass completely through the garden, loop back on themselves, or lead to an objective. A bench, sundial, or piece of art placed at the end of a path gives a sensible reason for stopping at that place, whereas dead ends are unnerving. If you use curves, make them gentle and meandering, not twisting and turning. You can vary the width of the walk and create wide spots for standing or sitting to make the walk more interesting.

Paths are seldom wide enough to be practical or comfortable. Don't be skimpy. A 30-inch (75 cm) walk is adequate for a wheelbarrow or a lawn-mower, but forces visitors to walk single file. Two people strolling side by side need a minimum of 4 feet (1.2 m). Keep an eye on your paths; they have a tendency to shrink through the seasons. Flowers that are content to sit primly along the edges in spring have often thrown themselves out onto the path with careless abandon by midsummer. They lie in wait to tangle and trip the unwary. After a rainstorm, every passerby is slapped and soaked by overhanging or path-encroaching wet foliage. Put a stop to this horticultural version of running the gauntlet with wider walks and timely pruning.

Choose a material and a style that reflect the mood and nature of your garden as a whole. Straight lines and rigid brick or cut stone have a more formal air than curves and gravel. Consider coordinating with existing structural elements — for example, build a red flagstone walk to echo the rusty tones of a used-brick house.

Working paths

Narrow paths do have their uses, especially as secondary trails that lead into the heart of the flower beds. Their purpose is to let you get close enough to weed and do other chores without stepping on and compacting the soil. Any bed wider than you can easily reach across needs working paths to prevent you from tumbling into the flowers as you try to get hold of a belligerent thistle just beyond your grasp. Make these working paths as unobtrusive as possible to discourage casual use by anyone but yourself — children and pets love these hidden passageways. Extra bricks or pieces of flagstone provide solid footing for you to hop from one to the next as you work.

Equally handy behind flower beds that border a fence or house wall are narrow catwalks. A 30-inch (75-cm) stretch of mulch gives you access for painting and other maintenance without smashing the soil or the plants.

Choosing materials

For safety and practicality, select materials for walks that are stable and fairly even. Nothing is more disconcerting than a surface that wobbles underfoot. Visitors should be free to enjoy the flowers, not subjected to an impromptu agility test. Avoid slippery or highly irregular textures that can cause tripping or injury. A level or only slightly sloping grade is best; anything steeper needs to be broken up with steps.

An almost infinite variety of materials is available for building walks:

- ✔ **Brick or stone:** Mortar these onto a concrete base when permanence and ease of care are your first priorities. Utilitarian concrete also offers great durability and flexibility. You can disguise its stark commercial appearance with textures, colors, stains, pebble aggregates, or a brick border. In fact, you can make patterned concrete look like just about any material imaginable. Modular concrete and crushed stone bricks and pavers are available in a vast selection of sizes, colors, and shapes.

  Laying bricks, stones, or pavers over a base of sand or gravel is within the scope of the do-it-yourself weekend project. For installation in a concrete base, you may want to hire a brick mason.

- ✔ **Sod:** A sod path seems natural in flower gardens, but remember that a lawn demands regular care. You can't leave lawn paths for more than a week without mowing and edging them.

- ✔ **Gravel:** If you don't like the crunch of gravel underfoot, place the gravel on top of finely crushed stone to provide a firmer surface.

- ✔ **Mulch:** A rustic path can be simply a mulch of pine needles, wood chips, or shredded bark.

Book IV

Perennials

You can combine mulch or gravel with paving stones or cut rounds of wood. Underlay loose materials with plastic or weed barrier to prevent weed growth. Alternatively, plant the spaces between stepping stones with low, spreading perennials, such as woolly thyme (*Thymus praecox* 'Pseudolanuginosus') or pussy toes (*Antennaria dioica*). Just be aware that these low growers aren't very good at weed suppression.

Edging — Keeping the Garden Put

The key to easy maintenance in the flower garden is preventing different materials in the landscape from commingling. You've got to keep soil, mulch, and flowers in the bed, and keep the adjoining lawn out. Edging can solve this problem as well as provide a decorative finish to the flower bed.

Edging types

Whether you prefer sharply or softly defined edges is mostly a question of personal taste, and fortunately, you have many different types of edging from which to choose. After you decide on the look you want, consider the practical side of edging. When a flower bed borders surfaces, such as patios or driveways, your goal is to stop the garden's contents from spilling out onto the pavement. By amending the soil, you've probably raised the flower bed's original elevation. So, unless you're very fond of sweeping, you're going to have to install some kind of barrier. You have two choices — up or down:

- Edge the bed with a landscape timber, a row of small rocks, or any other barrier that's slightly taller than the bed itself.

- Dig a trench 6 to 8 inches (15 to 20 cm) deep and 1 foot (30 cm) wide the whole length of the bed to trap falling mulch and soil.

For effective edging that doesn't obstruct regular lawn maintenance, bury a row of bricks at ground level around your flower bed. This type of ground-level edging gives your garden a border that you can mow right over.

Holding back an invading lawn

Ask any gardener — lawn grasses are among the worst weeds. The same quality that you want in grasses — the capability to spread and fill in gaps quickly — makes them bad neighbors for a flower bed. Lawn grasses can invade and smother flowers with lightning speed. They become so thoroughly entwined into the crown of plants that picking out the grass is often impossible without digging up the whole clump and physically separating them root by root. Even the products that are marketed to kill grass but not flowers sometimes damage the perennials, too.

The only way to keep lawn and flower bed separate is to build a line and then stay vigilant. A trench works if you routinely clear grass out of it. Many inconspicuous metal and plastic barriers are also available. Because grass roots go down at least 6 to 8 inches (15 to 20 cm), choose the deepest barrier you can find.

Sharp edges can be dangerous to bare feet and pets' paws. You can buy plastic capping strips that are designed to cover the exposed edges on metal barriers. Some metal edging has a turned-down top for safety.

A hose pulled across a flower bed can chop the flowers out of the ground as effectively as a hoe. You can find a variety of decorative and utilitarian hose guides. When strategically placed at the corners of the flower bed, these devices catch the hose, preventing plant mutilation. As an inexpensive alternative, blocks of wood or turned posts perform the same function.

Going Vertical

For the gardener who never seems to have enough room in the flower bed, a trellis is the shoehorn that lets you squeeze in just one more plant. You can trellis beds along fences and walls to within an inch of their lives with a continuous expanse of lattice-work, individual trellises spaced along the span, or unobtrusive wires stretched between hooks, screws, or other attachment devices.

Fanciful, free-standing supports of diverse materials and design are plentiful — you can find them in garden catalogs and nurseries. Anything that can support a vine is fair game. Use your imagination. Prop up an old, rusting garden gate or discarded chair to add a touch of whimsy. Search junkyards for interesting items and give them a new home. You can also encourage a few stems of each vine to escape the trellis and travel along the ground, weaving through and scrambling over taller flowers.

Using tropical vines as annuals where they aren't hardy is also popular. These vines bloom the first year from seed. A few of them get too large to fit in a flower bed when grown in their native tropical or subtropical climates, but you can cut them back to the ground when necessary to keep them in bounds. Most of the better-known landscape vines are far too vigorous for the small garden bed. Many of these reach 50 feet (15 m) or more and can obscure entire buildings. Table 5-1 lists a few of the dozens of smaller vines that are compatible with the smaller-scale flower garden.

Book IV

Perennials

Table 5-1	Small Vines for Flower Beds	
Common Name	*Botanical Name*	*Exposure*
Chickbuddy	Asarina scandens	Sun
Pagoda flower	Clerodendrum speciosum	Partial shade
Glory bower	Clerodendrum thomsoniae	Partial shade
Violet trumpet vine	Clytostoma callistegioides	Partial shade
Cathedral bells	Cobaea scandens	Sun
Bonnet bellflower	Codonopsis clematidea	Partial shade
Dwarf morning glory	Convovulus tricolor	Sun
Yellow bleeding heart	Dicentra scandens	Partial shade
Annual bleeding heart	Dicentra torulosa	Sun
Morning glory	Ipomoea purpurea	Sun
Dusky coral pea	Kennedia rubicunda	Sun
Perennial sweet pea	Lathyrus latifolius	Sun
Sweet pea	Lathyrus odoratus	Sun
Annual passion vine	*Passiflora gracilis*	Partial shade/sun
Scarlet runner bean	*Phaseolus coccineus*	Sun
Cape plumbago	*Plumbago auriculata*	Partial shade/sun
Black-eyed Susan vine	*Thunbergia alata*	Sun
Nasturtium	*Tropaeolum majus*	Sun
Canary creeper	*Tropaeolum peregrinum*	Light shade
Flame flower	*Tropaeolum speciosum*	Roots in shade

Book V
Annuals

The 5th Wave®   By Rich Tennant

"Well, no, they aren't pretty. But look on the bright side—with your luck growing flowers, they won't live long."

In this book . . .

Most of the time when something is "annual," it happens every year. In the flower world, however, annual means just the opposite — these flowers put on a magnificent and gloriously colorful show for one summer. After that, they fade away like a teenage romance, leaving sweet memories for your gardening yearbook. This book discusses the pros and cons of choosing annuals for your garden. Then, we tell you how to choose, plant, and care for those annuals. Finally, we take an alphabetical look at a number of commonly available plants to consider for your garden.

Here's to soon finding yourself basking in a summer of sunny, annual color!

Here are the contents of Book V at a glance:

Chapter 1

Shining the Sunlight on Annuals

· ·

In This Chapter

▶ Distinguishing annuals from other garden plants

▶ Discerning annuals' special needs based on your climate and soil

▶ Deciphering how climate impacts your annual garden

▶ Deciding when to tackle various annual gardening tasks

· ·

*B*rilliantly colorful, yet short-lived, annuals are especially rewarding plants to grow because they're fun, versatile, easy, and they respond well to good care. Annuals don't mess around. They grow fast and bloom young, even while they're still in little nursery packs. And, as a group, annuals give you more color for your money than any other plants. This chapter explores the fundamentals of the annual world.

Separating the Annuals from the Chaff

An *annual* is defined as a plant that undergoes its entire life cycle within one growing season, as illustrated in Figure 1-1. You plant a marigold seed in May, the seedling sprouts quickly, it starts blooming in July, frost kills it in October, seeds scatter and (with luck) sprout the next spring to start the process again. The good news is that nature typically blesses annuals with bright flowers to attract insects that will ensure pollination for seeds to sprout the next season.

Compare an annual with a *perennial.* By definition, a perennial is a plant that can live for several years, sprouting new growth and making new blooms year after year. (Book IV covers perennials.) Also compare an annual to a *biennial,* which takes two years to bloom and complete its life cycle. In general, biennials grow only foliage for the first year and then bloom the second. Some biennials can bloom in their first year if you plant the seeds early enough, or if they happen to be one of the biennials bred for speed. As you may expect, these general rules do come with a couple of qualifications:

> ✔ **Some plants that appear to be annuals, such as violas (Johnny-jump-ups) are actually fast-growing biennials that can complete their two-year cycle in one year.** For simplicity's sake, we refer to such plants as annuals.

✓ **Some perennials act like annuals when you grow them in cold climates.** Ivy geraniums *(Pelargonium peltatum),* for example, may not survive the month of June in a climate with late frosts but will live longer than you do if planted in a mild climate. We refer to such fair-weather perennials as annuals, as well.

At nurseries and in seed catalogs, certain kinds of flowers have specific names. Some examples appear in Figure 1-2 and in the following list:

✓ **Single:** A single flower, which is the type most typical in nature, has a single layer of petals.

✓ **Double:** A double flower has additional layers of petals, usually the result of breeding that has transformed some of the flower's other parts, such as sepals or stamens, into showy petals.

✓ **Bicolor:** A bicolor flower has two prominent colors in its petals. This flower type is similar to, but not the same as, the *picotee.*

✓ **Star:** A star flower has a star-shape — what a surprise!

✓ **Picotee:** The tips of a picotee flower have a different color than the rest of the flower petals.

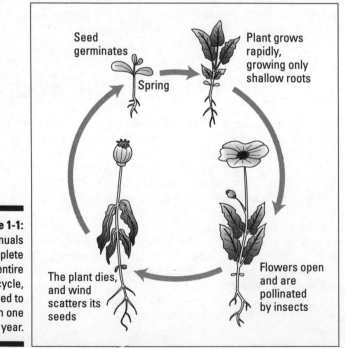

Figure 1-1:
Annuals complete their entire life cycle, from seed to seed, in one year.

There they go, the All-Americas

What do the words *All-America Selections* (AAS) mean when they appear on a nursery label or alongside an annual described in a seed catalog?

In 1932, seed growers developed the All-America Selections program to recognize and promote outstanding new flower and vegetable creations. (Fleuroselect is the European equivalent of All-America Selections.) Each year, plant breeders enter new plant variations in the AAS competition, where they're grown at test gardens across North America. Judges look for improved qualities, such as early bloom, disease or pest tolerance, new colors, novel flower forms, and longer bloom periods. The AAS logo on a plant indicates that it's a winner.

Over the years, more than 300 flowers have won AAS honors. Many are great; others have fallen by the wayside. Anytime you see the AAS symbol, you can feel pretty confident that the annual is well worth a try in your garden.

The rest of the annual, as well as its flowers, comes in a wide range of improvements. Most of the breeding efforts have been directed at smaller, more compact plants *(dwarfs),* but you can also find many varieties developed to trail from hanging baskets *(trailers).* Annuals that plant breeders have worked with for a long time (more than 100 years with marigolds) show the widest range of plant forms. Marigolds have many, many varieties classified as tall, intermediate, and dwarf.

Figure 1-2: Flowers come in a range of shapes, sizes, and colors, including these favorites.

GARDEN JARGON

Hybrids: The pinnacle of the breeder's art

Today's flashy and dependable annuals owe a great deal to the hybridization efforts of plant breeders. A *hybrid* is the result of crossing two specific parent plants, such as a petunia with red and white flowers that results from crossing a red petunia with a white one.

An *F1 hybrid* is the result of crossing two carefully controlled parents to create seed that will grow into very predictable offspring. When you plant F1 hybrid seeds, you know exactly what they'll grow into (a red and white petunia, for example). However, this second generation of plants won't produce seeds that grow into plants with the same predictability. The predictable F1

hybrid qualities only last one generation. So the bottom line when you come across F1 hybrids is this: They cost more to develop and are priced higher at the nursery, but they offer benefits, such as new flower colors, longer bloom season, bigger plants, or greater resistance to disease.

Hybrids are usually created in greenhouses where pollination can be carefully controlled. *Open pollination,* which occurs when annuals are grown in fields and allowed to be pollinated naturally by insects, yields far less predictable results than with hybridization.

Beautifying Your Neck of the Woods

Plant annuals at the right season and in the right spot, and you can easily have months of glorious blooms. But, start a marigold too early, place a zinnia in a spot that's too shady, or stick a begonia where it's too dry, and you'll get a quick lesson in the importance of understanding your garden's climate patterns and other conditions. (Chapter 2 in Book I discusses climate in detail.) This section looks at annual-specific climate issues.

To grow annuals, you don't need to worry about your precise climate zone and temperature extremes as much as you do with permanent plants, such as perennials, trees, and shrubs. Annuals are more straightforward. You simply have to wait until after the last killing frost to plant.

Cooling down, warming up

The first thing you need to know about any annual that you want to add to your garden is whether it's a warm-season or a cool-season annual. The difference is vital to planting annuals at the right time of year in your area.

Cool season and *warm season* are, of course, relative terms. Where summers are cool, such as along the foggy California coast or other overcast climates, you can grow cool-season annuals all summer. Where winters are warm and nearly frost-free, such as in low-elevation Arizona, fall through spring is an ideal time to grow cool-season annuals, such as Iceland poppies and stock, and even some warm-season annuals, such as petunias. In fact, winter and early spring make up the main flower-growing season in Arizona — summer there is too hot to grow any annuals except the most heat-tolerant warm-season varieties.

TIP

Projects for gardeners at any level

Even if you've never grown anything before, you can create some wonderful effects with annuals. Here are a just a few fairly easy, always impressive things you can do with annuals:

✔ Grow a sunflower taller than your rain gutter.

✔ Create a sophisticated color combination.

✔ Grow flowers for dinner.

✔ Plant a flower bed in one step by sowing packs of seeds directly in the ground.

✔ Bring in some instant color.

✔ Grow bouquets of cut flowers.

✔ Become a container maestro (see Chapter 3 in Book II for more on container gardening).

If you're not sure what to plant, go to the nursery and buy what looks good from this list of good-looking, foolproof annual flowers: cosmos, impatiens, lobelia, marigolds, nasturtium, petunias, portulaca, sweet alyssum, sweet William, and zinnias.

With hundreds and hundreds of annuals available, you have plenty of opportunities to try something new, different, and a little more challenging. More seasoned gardeners may want to try some of the following:

✔ **Grow beautiful, old-fashioned bouquets.**

✔ **Grow a colorful annual border with no flowers.** Not all annuals use blooms to get their color. Coleus, for example, is an annual that's prized for its big, colorful leaves. Such nonflowering annuals are great for shady spots where flowers may not bloom well.

✔ **Create a 365-day border.** If you live in a mild-winter climate, you can have annuals in bloom every day of the year. The secret is to overlap plantings and be brutal about rotating plants.

✔ **Grow a hanging basket as big as your car.** See Chapter 3 in Book II for more on container gardening.

✔ **Pamper a prima donna.** Some annuals require perfect drainage, perfect weather, and perfect snail control. Are you up to the task?

✔ **Take pride in your petunias.** Petunias are easy to grow from transplants, but really difficult to grow from seed. The seeds are about the size of dust, for one thing, and they demand a surprising amount of painstaking care. However, you get a much bigger selection when you buy seeds instead of nursery transplants.

✔ **Coax a miracle from a patio crack.** Expert gardeners sometimes try duplicating nature by planting lobelia or African daisy seedlings in a situation that resembles a natural occurrence. With luck, the plants will adapt and reseed. Here's our advice: Take what nature gives you. Give those little sproutlings a chance — they're obviously comfortable in the spot they've chosen and may do better than anything you intentionally plant there. Tolerate a little disorder and plant improvisation among your annuals.

Do you live in an all-year climate for annuals?

In some places, you can grow annuals all year. Winter temperatures rarely drop much below freezing in these regions, which include California (except for higher elevations), low elevations of the Southwest, and milder sections of the South, such as the Gulf Coast.

In mild-climate regions, you can plant cool-season annuals in late summer or early fall (after summer cools off). Blooms may appear before Christmas and peak in late winter and early spring. After growth and flowering slow down in spring, replace the cool-season annuals with

warm-season annuals. In mild climates, you can also plant cool-season annuals through the winter and early spring. They miss out on fall's warm weather to push them into growth, but they surge as soon as temperatures start to warm in late winter and early spring.

Truly tropical climates, such as those found in Hawaii and southern Florida, are in a separate category and have their own special guidelines for growing annuals. If you live in a tropical climate, check with local nurseries for advice.

If you live where summer gets hot, which is most of the U.S., plant cool-season annuals as early as possible (even before the last spring frost), and replace them after they fade in hot weather. If you live where summers are hot and winters are *relatively* mild (not dropping too far below freezing), you can plant these cool-season annuals in the fall, leave them over the winter, and they'll bloom in early spring.

The cool cats

Cool-season annuals are those that perform best when temperatures are mild — about 70°F (21°C) — days are short, and soil is cool. In most parts of the United States and Canada, these conditions are typical in early spring and early fall. Temperatures may be similarly mild all season in mountain regions or in regions to the far north (or the far south, in the Southern Hemisphere). In some coastal regions, temperatures stay mild year-round. Cool-season annuals can stand varying amounts of frost; some types, in fact, are quite hardy and are actually perennials that live through the winter in many areas. The enemies are hot weather and long days, which cause cool-season annuals to produce fewer blooms and ultimately die. Examples of cool-season favorites are calendulas, pansies, and snapdragons.

You're usually safe planting cool-season annuals a few weeks before the average date of the last spring frost in your area. If you live where weather is cool year-round or during the growing season, plant mostly cool-season annuals. If you live where summer days are hot and winters are mild, plant cool-season annuals in the fall for a winter garden.

In the typical cold-winter/hot-summer climate, the time to plant cool-season annuals is early spring — from four to eight weeks before the typical last frost or as soon as you can *work* the ground (dig and turn over the soil).

Their season ends with the arrival of hot weather, when you can replace them with warm-season annuals. Where summers rarely heat up, many cool-season annuals can thrive all summer right alongside warm-season annuals that don't demand hot weather.

Some like it hot

Warm-season annuals are those that thrive in hot summer weather. Most are tender, and freezing temperatures damage — or destroy — them. Examples are celosias, marigolds, vinca rosea (also called Madagascar periwinkle), and zinnias. Plant these heat-seekers after soil and air temperatures begin to warm up and expect them to reach their peak in midsummer.

The magic date for planting warm-season annuals depends on your climate. Suppose, for example, that you live in the most typical climate, the one that predominates over most of the northern United States, Canada, and northern Europe. This climate typically has cold winters (usually with snow) and warm, often humid summers. In this climate, you can generally grow warm-season annuals from late spring through late summer or early fall. The basic rule for planting is to wait until the danger of frost has passed and the weather has warmed up a bit. Note that some warm-season annuals need more heat than others.

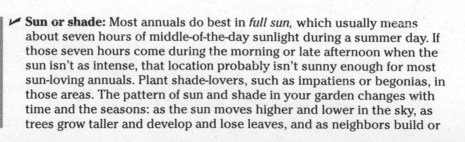

The *growing season* is the typical number of days between spring's last frost and fall's first frost. Generally, the farther north, the shorter the growing season. Growing-season length can be a factor when you're choosing annuals, especially from seed catalogs, which list the number of days to bloom. *Days to bloom* is an important number for annuals. It's usually listed right on the seed packet or in the seed catalog, sometimes right after the plant name. Specifically, this figure refers to the average number of days a plant requires after you plant its seed for the flower to bloom. Your goal is to determine whether a plant's days-to-bloom average fits comfortably within your growing season.

Reining in your garden's climate

Before you plant, observe the conditions in your garden. Keep the following factors in mind when considering which annuals to plant and where to plant them:

- **Sun or shade:** Most annuals do best in *full sun,* which usually means about seven hours of middle-of-the-day sunlight during a summer day. If those seven hours come during the morning or late afternoon when the sun isn't as intense, that location probably isn't sunny enough for most sun-loving annuals. Plant shade-lovers, such as impatiens or begonias, in those areas. The pattern of sun and shade in your garden changes with time and the seasons: as the sun moves higher and lower in the sky, as trees grow taller and develop and lose leaves, and as neighbors build or tear down buildings. Definitions of sun and shade also depend on your climate. For example, near a coast, where it's cool and often overcast, plants generally need more sun than do plants in inland regions. In these cool, cloudy regions, sun-loving plants may have trouble growing even in direct sun, and plants that prefer shade can come out from the shadows to flourish in full sun. The following terms may help you determine what kind of sunlight your garden has:

- **Full shade:** A northern exposure, for example, is probably blocked from the sun all day.

- **Part shade:** The east side of your house, unless it's blocked by trees or buildings, probably gets sun in the morning and shade for the rest of the day.

- **Full sun:** A southern exposure gets the most hours of sun. A western exposure may get shade in the morning and full sun in the afternoon — this usually should be considered a sunny location because of the intensity of the light. (Shade plants will probably cook there.)

Pay attention to the sun/shade requirements recommended by your local nursery, and watch the flowers that you plant to see how they respond. Signs of too much sun include brown, burned spots on the leaves. Too much shade can result in spindly foliage growth and weak blooming.

✔ **Wind:** Wind can dry out the soil quickly and rob plants of moisture. Stiff breezes can topple tall plants and break brittle ones. Although you can't do much about the wind, you *can* make sure that you water carefully. Planting shrubs or trees to provide a windbreak also may help. Alternatively, find a more protected spot for your annuals.

✔ **Soil:** You may be stuck with soil that drains poorly or that otherwise makes life tough for annuals. Chapter 3 in Book I gives you the lowdown on soil.

✔ **Slope:** Gardening on a hillside presents some special challenges — watering is more difficult, for one thing. Terracing and drip irrigation (see Chapter 4 in Book I) are ways to ensure that enough moisture gets to plant roots. Hilly terrain also can affect weather conditions. A sunny, south-facing slope can provide a milder situation for annuals because cold air drains away. You may find a hillside garden to be several degrees warmer and several weeks ahead of the neighbor's garden at the bottom of the hill.

✔ **Reflected heat:** Pavement, house walls, and other heat-reflective surfaces can warm up a garden. Although these surfaces can be positive factors under certain conditions, reflected heat usually causes plants to burn up. Before you plant, be aware of too-bright conditions, such as the pavement around a swimming pool. Unless your plants can take intense heat, plant them somewhere with a little more shade.

Gardening Month by Month

The calendars in this section can help you do all the right things for your annuals at the right time. Because annuals are fairly easy to grow, these calendars of advice are on the simple side. We divide the United States and much of Canada into big annual-growing regions. You can use this simplified system rather than the complicated 11-climate USDA zone map, discussed in Chapter 2 in Book I, because annuals don't need to survive cold winters year after year the way permanent plants must. You only need to know information, such as when to plant what annuals, when insect and disease problems may strike in your area, and how to care for your flowers. If you live in a country other than the United States or Canada, follow the advice of a climate region that comes close to yours.

By nature, climates are complex, and weather varies from year to year. Weather is also local, with big swings in cold, heat, rain, snow, and almost everything else occurring over just a few miles. So use the calendars here as a guideline, but continue looking to the skies, checking the thermometer, and talking to the friendly folks at your local nursery to make sure that you're on the right track.

We're not covering tropical climates in this section because, frankly, we don't need to. The tropics tend to have wet and dry seasons, not so much cold and warm seasons. You can grow annuals year-round in tropical regions as long as you have water. We also don't cover interior Alaska, which is a climate unto itself. If you live in these regions, you must rely on local advice.

The North: Warm summers, cold winters

The most important concern for growing annuals is not how cold the winter gets, but rather, when the first and last frosts of the growing season are likely to occur. The frost dates determine seeding schedules, planting times, duration of garden chores, and the ability to grow fall-blooming annuals. The hallmark of these regions are warm summers and cold winters. The main season for annuals begins with planting time in early or midspring and ends when serious frosts hit in the fall.

- ✔ **January:** Settle next to the fire with a stack of new seed catalogs. As you order seeds, think about where you want to plant your annuals and what color combinations you find appealing.

- ✔ **February:** Prepare a space for starting seeds if you haven't already done so. Clear an area in a sunny window or set up fluorescent lights for seedlings to sprout and grow. Buy seed-starting trays or use old trays that you've cleaned with a dilute bleach solution and rinsed well. Consider providing bottom heat, which maintains an even, warm soil temperature and improves germination; many mail-order catalogs offer heating mats specifically for seed starting. Use a commercial potting mix for starting seeds: a fine germinating mix for tiny seeds, and a coarser, peat-based mix for larger seeds and for growing your seedlings on to maturity.

✔ **March:** March through mid-April is seed-starting time in cold climates. Plan a seeding schedule — essential in short-season climates where you want to make every day count. Start by figuring when you want to transplant annuals into the ground in the weeks and months ahead, and work backward to calculate the best time to sow the seeds indoors — four to eight weeks ahead of transplanting time, in most cases.

✔ **April:** You still have time to sow seeds indoors for transplanting next month — especially in colder climates where winters are most severe and the growing season is shortest. If your last-frost date falls around Memorial Day, sow seeds for all annuals, except fast-growing, tender plants (cosmos and zinnias, for example), by mid-April. If you live in warmer areas with milder winters, you can start sowing seeds of hardy annuals directly into the ground a couple weeks before the last frost date in their region. If it's still cold in April where you live, wait until next month to direct-sow seeds. If you plant nothing else, sow sweet pea seeds as soon as the ground can be dug. They appreciate the early start — especially if they can bloom before hot weather. Depending on your region, late April or May is the time to lay out beds and prepare the soil. Adjust the soil pH based on soil tests done in the fall (see Chapter 3 in Book I for more). Amend the soil with a 2- or 3-inch layer of organic matter and a complete fertilizer (refer to Chapter 4 in Book I).

Watch indoor seedlings for pests and diseases. *Damping off* is a common disease that affects new seedlings; sprouts rot near soil level and collapse. Prevent this disease by using a sterile soil mix and not overwatering. (See Chapter 7 in Book I for more information on pests and diseases.)

Here's a good test to determine that your ground is dry enough for planting: Form some garden soil into a ball and drop it from waist-high distance. If it doesn't easily crumble apart when it hits the ground, the soil is still too wet to plant, and seeds are likely to rot if sown directly into the ground.

✔ **May:** Early May is generally the best time to plant hardy annuals (seeds or transplants) in most areas — 10 to 14 days before the last frost is usually safe. Check local garden centers for ready-to-plant, cool-season annuals. Look for stocky, green plants when shopping at garden centers. Avoid plants with dead lower leaves and brown, overcrowded roots, as well as plants that are already flowering. Start transplanting tender annuals, such as impatiens, lobelia, and petunias, into the ground when frost danger has passed, the soil and air have warmed up, and the nights are no longer cold. Memorial Day is considered optimum timing for planting tender annuals in many places.

Tender plants set out too early may not be damaged by frost, but they don't grow during cold weather. If you start seeds indoors, be sure to harden off transplants before planting them in the garden. (Books III and IV tell you how to harden off your plants.) Beware of rogue frosts, and be ready to cover young transplants if necessary. Also watch for cutworm damage to direct-seeded crops and young transplants (see Chapter 7 in Book I for more on cutworms and other garden pests).

✔ **June:** Continue planting tender annuals, and remember that newly planted seeds and transplants are vulnerable. Gardeners in cold, mountainous areas often wait until June 10 to plant the most tender plants, such as impatiens, because cold nights early in the month stress heat-lovers. Water if June is dry. Weeds compete for nutrients and water; hoe or pull them while they're young and easy to remove. Watch for cutworms, slugs, and aphids that can stunt plants. Mulch to conserve water and slow weed growth. Pull off or pinch back fading blooms of cool-season annuals to extend their season of color.

✔ **July:** Plants require extra water and nutrients to keep them at their peak in hot, dry weather. Container-bound plants, particularly, suffer from heat stress and usually need daily watering if they're located in the sun. Container gardens quickly deplete soil nutrients; feed window boxes and pots with a liquid fertilizer every couple weeks. (Chapter 3 in Book II has more on container gardening.) Continue feeding annuals to promote steady growth for the remainder of the summer. Stake taller annuals. Deadhead flowers regularly. Japanese beetles make an appearance toward the end of the month. Hand-pick bugs and drop them into a container of soapy water. In hot climates, cool-season annuals probably have peaked, so pull them out.

✔ **August:** In northern regions where the growing season is 90 to 110 days long, late July through early August is the garden's peak. It's called *high summer* because so many kinds of plants are blooming all at once. Continue to deadhead, water, and weed. Containers, especially, still need to be fertilized. Tidy beds and containers by pulling out plants that have been crowded out or have passed their peak. Harvest flowers for drying and enjoy fresh-cut bouquets. Keep picking Japanese beetles.

✔ **September:** Be ready with row covers or blankets if an early frost is predicted and you still have tender plants in bloom. Use pots of asters, calendulas, and flowering kale to replace frosted or dying annuals. Collect seed pods, dried flowers, and grasses to make arrangements.

You can pot some annuals — begonias, coleus, impatiens, and geraniums — and bring them indoors. If plants are lanky by summer's end, cut stems back by about a third. Place pots in a sunny window or under grow-lights. Water and fertilize less frequently than you did when the plants were in the ground. Plants seem to need a resting phase after a summer of blooming.

✔ **October:** Pull out dead plants and add them to your compost pile. (Chapter 4 in Book I covers composting.) Take soil samples in the fall to know how to amend soil next spring. Use the results of the soil tests to gauge any adjustments that you need to make in soil pH and fertility. (Refer to Chapter 3 in Book I for more information.)

✔ **November through December:** Sharpen, clean, and oil your tools. Keep a record of any extra seed you have. Store the extra seed in an airtight container in a cool location; add packets of silica gel to absorb any moisture in the container. Build your own window boxes or trellises for next year. Build a cold frame (see Chapter 2 in Book I) for growing and hardening off your transplants. Seek inspiration for next year's garden in books and magazines.

The South: Hot summers, mild winters

This calendar's timing aims for the middle south in the middle of each month. For the lower south, the tasks will fall toward the beginning of the month. For the upper south, wait until month's end.

Tropical Florida (Dade County south to the Keys) has its own rules for planting annuals, which are unlike the guidelines for any other gardening region in the continental United States. If you live in tropical Florida, check with local experts for recommended varieties and planting times.

✔ **January:** Keep pansy blossoms plucked to get more buds and blooms. Remember that winter annuals grow while all else lies dormant, so fertilize garden beds and containers of annuals when you're watering this month. Start any indoor plants now. Make the most of a wet, warm day to get rid of winter weeds. Pulling even tiny oak trees is a no-sweat job in this type of weather. Take advantage of breaking weather to work the soil for spring planting. Add organic matter and a complete fertilizer, and then let it mellow till March.

✔ **February:** As soon as possible, plant early spring annuals, including petunias and geraniums. Start a garden journal to record what and when you plant, and how it fared. Knowledge is (flower) power. Put up a trellis ahead of time to support vigorous vines for summer shade. (See Chapter 2 in Book II.)

✔ **March:** Transplant indoor plants outside. Water transplants well and feed them with fish emulsion or root-stimulator fertilizer (refer to Chapter 4 in Book I), following the directions on the label. Make sure that young poppies and larkspur don't dry out; as they put on flower buds, water and mulch around the base of the plants. Gently pull the mulch away from pansies and other transplants tucked in last fall. Slugs and snails destroy tender transplants. (See Chapter 7 in Book I for tips on combating these pests.)

If you've had trouble starting seeds in the garden, try topping your garden soil with an inch of potting soil or compost. Seeds planted in this way still may dry out before sprouting, however, so lay a board on top to hold in the moisture until they sprout.

✔ **April:** Add mulch around spring annuals and don't forget to apply fertilizer and thoroughly water the flowers you transplanted last month. Deadhead spring flowers for a second round of flowers; if you allow the seeds to set, the plant's done for the year.

✔ **May:** Water regularly with a sprinkler to discourage spider mites and aphids. Make composts of pansies and violas, which respond with smaller flowers and skinnier stems when night temperatures rise. Don't plant vinca rosea (sold as annual periwinkle in many Southern nurseries) until this month at the earliest.

✔ **June:** Start watching your garden for signs of trouble. One common warning flag is yellow leaves on young plants, an indication that plants need nitrogen. Yellow leaves at the growing point signal a root problem or that the flower was planted too deep. To fertilize beds in dry spells, water them first and then use a fertilizer mixed with more water. Make sure that the water soaks through thick mulches; rake back a bit of mulch if you must or, better yet, use soaker hoses.

✔ **July:** Plant the second round of heat-loving summer annuals: balsam, celosia, cockscombs, marigolds, and zinnias. Include some dwarf sunflowers, Mexican sunflower, portulaca, scaevola, and vinca rosea, "bounce-back" flowers that recover quickly after thunderstorms. Cut back impatiens and all sorts of hanging-basket plants that have become leggy with the heat. Rejuvenated, these plants will bloom again for months. Choose a spot with late afternoon shade to grow flowers for cutting. Irrigate slowly to soak the bed deeply for best rooting, and finish watering in time for the leaves to dry before darkness falls.

✔ **August:** Replenish mulch around annual plantings. Adding another inch of pine straw or ground bark suppresses weeds and moderates the most stressful months of the growing season. Plant small chrysanthemum plants during this month. Save the seeds of celosia, cosmos, four o'clock, the morning glory family, spider flower, and zinnias. Let plants mature as much as possible before gently crushing the flower heads to collect the seeds. Separate the seeds from other materials.

✔ **September:** Use a complete fertilizer on fall-blooming and other flowers planted in July. Get to know *overwintering annuals,* such as pansies and violas, which perform best when planted in the fall for early spring blooms. Transplant the garden chrysanthemum right away. Planting them close together provides a carpet of flowers. Keep mums moist, so that flowers open as expected. Deadhead first blooms so that side buds can open. Sow seeds of the following flowers in flats for transplanting next month: calendula, candytuft, pinks, sweet alyssum, and sweet William. Grow outdoors in late-day shade in a mix of half potting soil and half compost. Keep moist; add fertilizer at half-strength every other week.

✔ **October:** After five consecutive nights with temperatures in the 60s (15 to 20°C), transplant pansies, ornamental cabbage, and flowering kale. Transplant the other annuals you started last month after they develop three sets of true leaves and you've had two weeks of night temperatures in the 60s. Sow poppy and larkspur seed with sand for better spacing.

✔ **November:** Don't mulch patches of fall-seeded annuals, such as candytuft, larkspur, and poppies. Watch for seedlings and keep the beds weeded. Fertilize once before the end of the year.

✔ **December:** Wild temperature swings can be deadly to dry plants. Prevent drought damage by watering before plants wilt. For warmer water that's gentler on the plants, set timers for midday, lay your hose out in the sun, or capture rainwater in dark-colored containers before using the water to irrigate. Watch for caterpillars. Pile the mulch on transplanted annuals. Make excellent, free mulch from leaves chopped up into coin-sized pieces. Rake away fallen leaves, spent flowers, and frosted plants, including weeds. Compost this debris, adding kitchen waste and the first cutting of your overseeded rye lawn. Tidying up now can mean fewer weeds, pests, and diseases next season.

The West: Dry summers, wet winters

The West exhibits some of the most complex climates in the United States. In the states west of the Mississippi, annual flowers encounter some of the shortest growing seasons (in the Rocky Mountain region) and the longest (in Southern California). The Pacific Northwest has a long but cool growing season. Arizona's garden-growing season is the opposite of most other climates: Fall, winter, and spring are the seasons to enjoy annuals because summer is too hot for them.

This section divides the West into four subregions for growing annuals: the bulk of California, the high-altitude regions, the low-altitude deserts, and the Pacific Northwest. Each subregion has different seasons, starting times, opportunities, and challenges.

Growing annuals in most of California

The seasonal advice in this section works for the majority of California, with two notable exceptions: the mountains, where the growing season is much shorter, and the low-elevation desert, where the main growing season for annuals is fall through early spring.

✔ **January:** Select annual seeds for sowing soon (cool-season types) or in several months (warm-season annuals). Start seeds of cool-season annuals indoors to set out in four to six weeks. Brighten your garden with already blooming annuals sold in 4-inch pots and larger sizes at garden centers. Pansies and primroses offer maximum color now — especially if they're planted in containers. Limit your planting to large annuals that are already in bloom. Save smaller-sized plants for warmer weather next month.

✔ **February:** As the weather starts to warm up, and if the soil is dry enough, set out seedlings of cool-season annuals. This month or next, start seeds indoors of warm-season annuals. Wait until next month to sow seeds if you live in a cooler climate. Sow seeds of low-growing annuals to fill in between emerging spring bulbs. Fertilize cool-season annuals. Try to feed regularly — either monthly or twice a month. Watch for snails and slugs around young plantings, especially if the weather is on the wet and mild side. Try to eliminate insect hideouts by cleaning up piles of leaves and other garden debris. Hoe or pull out weeds fostered by winter rains before they overtake planting beds.

✔ **March:** Cool-season annuals should be at their peak bloom now. Maintain top performance by monthly feeding and pinching off dead blooms. Be especially vigilant in cutting off faded pansy flowers. Except in the hottest climates, you can still plant cool-season annuals. In warmer climates, such as southern California and inland valleys, this month begins the planting time for warm-season annuals — make sure that frost danger is past and weather is heating up. Prepare flower beds for major spring planting this month or next month.

✔ **April:** April is the main planting month for warm-season annuals. Wait a month to plant warm-season annuals in cooler coastal climates, where you can still set out most cool-season annuals. Soon after planting, pinch back warm-season annuals to encourage bushy growth. Begin a regular fertilizer program several weeks after planting warm-season annuals. Mulch with a layer of organic matter around young annuals to conserve moisture and curtail weeds.

✔ **May:** Plant seedlings of heat-loving annuals. You also can plant the warm-season annuals recommended for April. Cosmos, marigolds, and zinnias sprout quickly if sown directly in the ground now. If the weather has started to warm up, sow sunflower seeds directly into the ground. If a hot spell strikes, protect newly planted annuals with temporary shading with shade cloth or floating row covers draped over the plants. In cool coastal climates, you can still plant cool-season annuals (pansies and violas, especially), as well as many warm-season annuals. Continue grooming and fertilizing.

Earwigs emerge as a major threat to annuals. Earwigs love dark, wet places. To create an environment that's unappealing to these pests, don't mulch between plants, cultivate the soil regularly to keep it dry, and in severe cases, spray the plants with an insecticide, such as pyrethrum.

✔ **June:** Continue planting warm-season annuals. For faster results, select 4-inch pot sizes. Plant shady spots; warm weather encourages rapid growth of shade-lovers. In all but the mildest climates, cool-season annuals are probably over the hill. Pull them out, clean up planting beds, and refresh them with a layer of organic matter dug in to a depth of 10 or 12 inches. Put in replacement warm-season annuals as soon as possible. Never let your annuals dry out. Thin and pinch back seedlings of annuals. As weather warms, watch for signs of budworm damage (hollowed out buds and tiny black droppings) on petunias and annual geraniums (*Pelargonium*).

✔ **July:** For quick color, look for warm-season annuals in 4-inch pots or larger sizes. Transplant these flowers into pots, but make sure that you add enough soil mix to encourage continued root growth; pots should have a diameter at least 2 or 3 inches larger than the nursery container. In hotter climates, plant in the cool of evening and provide temporary shade on hot days. Mulch to conserve soil moisture and keep your plants well watered. Watch for budworms. Fertilize regularly.

✔ **August:** Start seeds of cool-season annuals in flats or pots to set out in late summer or early fall. Watch for spider mites and whiteflies. Continue to feed and pinch. If lobelia and impatiens look too lanky, cut them back by as much as a third; they'll respond with a burst of late-summer growth.

✔ **September:** Plant cool-season annuals now; they'll bloom by the December holidays and continue blooming through spring. During hot weather, plant in the evening and provide temporary shade. Extend plantings of warm-season annuals by continuing to water thoroughly, feed, and remove faded flowers. Pull out summer flowers when their beauty fades to avoid delaying your fall planting. Mildew on summer flowers is a sign that their season is over. Start seeds of cool-season annuals in flats or pots for transplanting next month.

✔ **October:** If you plant spring-flowering bulbs, follow up with annuals on top. Pansies and violas are classic bulb covers for tulips and daffodils. Continue to plant all cool-season annuals. Watch for snails and slugs given new life by cooling weather. Start to regularly fertilize fall annuals two or three weeks after planting.

✔ **November:** Early November is the last chance for planting cool-season annuals with expectation of midwinter flowers. You can still plant bulb covers. Snails and slugs are almost inevitable. Continue regular watering until winter rains keep the soil constantly moist. Watch for a new crop of winter weeds; pull them while the soil is wet and soft.

✔ **December:** Keep watering if winter rains arrive late. Plant cool-season annuals if you haven't already. You missed the warm fall weather that pushes annuals into midwinter bloom, but you still can expect a strong spring show from annuals planted now. If rains soak the soil, let it dry out a bit before planting.

Growing annuals at high altitudes

The high-altitude western United States — from California to Colorado, north to Montana, south to mountainous Arizona and New Mexico — offers terrific, albeit abbreviated, growing conditions for annuals. Frosts can hit late in the spring and strike early in the fall, but the cool nights and bright, dry summer weather bring out the best in many annuals. If you live in a temperate, high-altitude climate, follow the calendar for the North, earlier in this chapter. Start seeds indoors and set out seedlings as recommended for colder sections in the northern part of the United States. Consult your local extension service, the Department of Agriculture, or the nursery for specific recommendations.

Growing annuals in lowland deserts

The Southwest deserts encompass mild-winter climates of the low-elevation deserts of Arizona and California. (The mountains of Arizona and New Mexico, as well as west Texas, have a more typical cold-winter, summer-only season for growing annuals.) Glory time for annuals is late winter and early spring in low-desert Arizona, primarily around Phoenix and Tucson, and California's Coachella Valley. This calendar starts in September to reflect the true beginning of the planting season:

- **September:** Prepare planting beds. Midmonth or later, set out nursery transplants for winter and spring bloom — maybe even by Christmas. Provide temporary shade during the hottest weather. Early in the month, you still have time to start annual flower seeds in flats or pots to transplant into the ground later in the fall. If summer annuals are still going strong, keep them watered thoroughly and fertilize every two or four weeks.

- **October:** Continue to set out annuals for blooms before the end of the year. Water thoroughly after planting and provide temporary shade during extra-hot spells. Sow seeds of low-spreading annuals to cover bare spots in bulb beds. If your timing is good, everything will bloom all at once. Start regular feeding a few weeks after planting annuals.

- **November:** You still have time to plant for winter and spring bloom. Cooler weather encourages a new crop of aphids, plus slugs and snails.

- **December:** You still have time to plant seedlings. Watch your soil for signs of dryness, and water as needed.

- **January:** After the holidays, nurseries stock up with blooming annuals in small pots. Shop for color that you can use right away in pots or in gaps in planting beds. Watch for aphids and take steps to control them. Pull or hoe seasonal weeds, or mulch beds with a layer of organic matter to smother weeds and weed seeds.

- **February:** Cool-season annuals are peaking this month in the low desert. Maintain top performance by removing dead flowers, watering thoroughly, and feeding regularly. Start seeds of warm-season annuals indoors to transplant into the garden in four to six weeks. Prepare beds for spring planting.

- **March:** In the low desert, transplant warm-season annuals. Pinch back at planting time and snip off flowers to encourage bushier growth. A few weeks after planting, fertilize young annuals and begin a regular (bi-weekly or monthly) fertilizing schedule.

- ✔ **April:** Plant heat-loving annuals, such as marigolds and zinnias. Adjust the frequency of sprinkler systems as the weather heats up.

- ✔ **May:** Spring flowers are winding down. Pull them out and replace them with heat-lovers. Pinch tips of young annuals for bushier growth.

- ✔ **June:** This is your last chance to plant for summer blooms. Make sure that you choose from among the true heat-lovers: globe amaranth, salvia, and the most reliable of all, vinca rosea.

- ✔ **July and August:** Water and mulch. You don't do any planting at this time of year. Feed summer annuals regularly. Remove faded flowers.

Growing annuals in the Pacific Northwest

Compared with California, the Pacific Northwest, including the milder parts of British Columbia, has a much more straightforward pattern for growing annuals — a long season from spring through fall. West of the Cascade Range, the lingering cool spring tends to favor cool-season annuals, and the relatively cool summers encourage spectacular displays of annuals. East of the Cascades, where winters are longer and much colder, the annual season is shorter, but the heat and the dry climate are terrific for sun-loving annuals.

- ✔ **January:** Order seeds for starting indoors in a few weeks or outdoors in a few months. Prepare an indoor area for starting seeds.

- ✔ **February:** Start seeds of annuals indoors for transplanting in spring. If the ground isn't too wet, you can start seeding the following hardy annuals directly in the ground late this month: calendula, clarkia, cornflower, dwarf pink, English daisy *(Bellis perennis)*, pansy, stock, and sweet alyssum. Transplanting hardy annuals, such as pansies and primroses, if nurseries offer them and the soil is dry enough, or plant them in containers.

- ✔ **March:** Prepare beds for major spring planting as long as the soil isn't too wet. Sow sweet peas seeds before midmonth; sow seeds of other hardy annuals. Continue indoor seeding of annuals. Begin sowing warm-season annuals, such as marigolds and zinnias, for transplanting when the weather warms up in May.

- ✔ **April:** Set out transplants of cool-season annuals, such as calendulas, pansies, and snapdragons. Begin transplanting warm-season annuals if the weather and soil have warmed up. Watch for snails and slugs to begin their most damaging season around young annuals.

- ✔ **May:** This is the Northwest's prime time for planting annuals. Almost anything will grow if planted now. Start feeding annuals two or three weeks after planting. Protect young annuals from snails and slugs. Sow asters, cosmos, marigolds, and zinnias from seed directly in the ground.

✔ **June:** Planting season continues, but try to finish soon to get the longest season. Continue to sow seeds of heat-loving annuals, such as marigolds and zinnias. Soon after planting annuals, pinch them back to encourage bushy growth. Continue regular feeding and grooming, and never let them dry out.

✔ **July:** Keep annuals going strong by feeding them regularly. If planting beds need extra watering, run a soaker hose between the plants. You can still plant annual seeds for later summer bloom.

✔ **August:** Watch for late summer invaders, such as spider mites. If impatiens and lobelia get a bit straggly, cut them back by about a third to encourage a late summer burst of growth.

✔ **September:** Extend the summer bloom season by removing dead flowers and watering as needed. For color until frost strikes, set out dwarf pinks, Johnny-jump-ups, pansies, stocks, and kale.

✔ **October:** Remove over-the-hill summer annuals. Clean up beds and turn over the soil for fall or spring planting. Keep hardy annuals, such as pansies, going for another few weeks by continuing to feed, water, and groom them. Sow wildflowers and other annuals that get off to an early start in spring. Scatter the seeds, cover them with a thin layer of organic matter, and then water thoroughly.

✔ **November:** You still have time to sow seeds of hardy annuals and wildflowers for blooms next spring. Clean up all annual planting beds.

Chapter 2

Pickin' Out Annuals, Puttin' 'Em in Your Garden

....

....

*1*f you want to experiment with flowers, annuals are perfect — inexpensive, fast-growing, and long-blooming. Try out wild color combinations, carpet an entire bed, or fill pots to overflowing with these varied and rewarding plants. If you do make a hideous mistake, you may have time to replant during the same growing season. If not, you can design a new scheme for next year. (Book II has loads of information on designing your flowerbeds and landscape, as well as container gardening.) This chapter offers suggestions for designing and planting a garden full of annuals.

Eyeing Your Design

Before you can plant, you have to plan. The following sections look at various design elements as they pertain to annuals.

Playing with color

Color is the first thing that people notice in a garden, and like music, it goes a long way toward creating a mood. Consider the tone that you want for each garden area and choose colors accordingly. Base your choices on your own feelings about the color, not on what so-called experts of design say that the colors should make you feel.

You need to consider more than just flower color when selecting annuals. The colors of the annual's foliage, the colors of the foliage and flowers of nearby trees and shrubs, the colors and textures of paving materials like walkways and driveways, and even the color and style of your house are also important factors to consider when choosing an annual. The most important way to decide on the colors of your annual garden is to experiment with different combinations of color to find what you enjoy most. Try mixing colors and trust your own eyes. One gardener's favorite combination, such as purple petunias with scarlet geraniums, may be another gardener's worst color-clash nightmare.

An easy way to select garden colors is to think of all colors as falling within the ranges of *hot* or *cool*. Hot colors are bright and bold, lively, cheerful, and energizing: lemon yellow, hot pink, fire-engine red. Most cool colors — pale pink, sky blue, and lavender — blend well together, creating a feeling of harmony and serenity. The distinction between hot and cool isn't absolute (pink, for example, can range from a deep, vibrant "hot" pink to a soft, pastel "cool" pink), but generally, red, orange, and yellow are considered hot; green, blue, and purple are considered cool. Don't be afraid to mix and match the two; cool accent colors can really bring out the vibrancy of hot colors. Mixing in a little white can spark any color scheme, bringing out the best in the other flower colors. You can also use white exclusively to create a cool and restful garden that looks its best at dusk and in cloudy, damp weather.

Too often, gardeners forget that green is a color, too, and forms the backdrop for all the other colors in the garden. Foliage on annuals varies from a dark forest green to bright emerald to palest chartreuse. Some annuals even have green flowers.

Many plants now come with *variegated* (multicolored) foliage, which creates a tapestry of color and pattern even when the plant isn't in bloom. Yellow-foliaged plants or those with leaves splotched in cream or white can brighten a dark corner as effectively as white flowers, giving the effect of sunshine lingering on the leaves. Leaves make a rich pattern to accent flower color, and variegation can add its showy speckles and stripes to any color scheme.

Perceiving shape, height, and texture

A plant's form is often every bit as important as its color. Like color, the shape, height, and texture of a garden's plants affect the mood it evokes. Annuals vary in form as they develop. Some flowers grow tall; sunflowers, for example, reach heights of 8 to 10 feet. Other annuals, such as sweet alyssum and lobelia, prefer to hug the ground, making them perfect for trimming edges of beds and borders.

Spinning your color wheels

The color wheel that you studied in grade school comes in handy when planning your garden. You may recall that the color wheel is divided into the same colors and in the same order as a rainbow. Keep these color combinations in mind when designing your annual garden:

✔ **Primary colors:** These three colors — red, blue, and yellow — are equidistant on the wheel. All other colors result from mixing these three.

✔ **Complementary colors:** These pairs of colors are opposite each other on the wheel — orange and blue, yellow and violet, or red and green, for example. Complementary colors can be jarring if overused in mass plantings. Rather than alternating yellow marigolds and purple petunias in a large bed, consider intermixing yellow and orange marigolds, using purple sparingly as a bold accent color.

✔ **Harmonious colors:** These colors blend gradually between two primary colors, such as red to orange to yellow. Harmonious colors unify a landscape without creating the monotony of using a single flower or color. A garden that moves like a sunset from yellow to orange to red or various shades of blue like the clear sky creates softer impressions on the viewer.

✔ **Shades of color:** Shades refer to lighter and darker variations of the same color.

You can create a very effective, charming, and easy planting by using just one color — an especially effective technique in container plantings (see Chapter 3 in Book II). Choose one or a few flowers in similar colors and mix them with attractive foliage plants. Single-colored beds are also popular for creating a pleasing, impressive, and formal look.

REMEMBER

Contrary to what you may think, no rule specifically states that you *must* plant the shortest flowers in front and the tallest flowers in back. Annuals can quickly add height to a garden, with towering sunflowers or foxgloves creating screening or providing color at the back of the border. As you hike in the woods, notice how nature layers plants: tall trees, understory trees, large shrubs, ferns, and then ground cover plants carpeting the forest floor. Such complexity pleases the eye, and you can mimic that pattern by planting low-growing annuals in front and taller ones in the rear. You can blend annuals in with other plants to create this same effect in your garden beds.

Texture adds another element to the garden. For example, the droopy, chenillelike softness of love-lies-bleeding *(Amaranthus caudatus)* adds a striking note to a planting scheme; the feathery foliage of love-in-a-mist *(Nigella damascena)* knits together varied plantings in the front of a border.

Perfuming the air

The fragrance of annual flowers can add another dimension to your garden. Floral fragrances are a matter of personal preference, so take the time to choose the flowers that most please your sense of smell. Then mix those flowers in throughout the garden. Plant generously so that you have plenty of flowers to pick for bouquets. As a rule, choose the old-fashioned varieties of flowers, which usually tend to be the more fragrant. (You may need to order seeds by mail to find the older, most strongly scented varieties.)

Remember to add a few fragrant blooms to every pot, window box, or hanging basket. Concentrate sweet-smelling flowers near walkways, entries, patios, and decks, so that you and your guests can enjoy them often. Some plants don't waste their scent on the daylight hours because they're pollinated by night-flying moths. Flowering tobacco (*Nicotiana*) and the moonflower vine (*Ipomoea alba*) release their sweet scents in the evening air and so are ideal additions to planting beds or pots near bedroom windows or patios used after dark.

Here are some favorite easy-care annuals that add fragrance to the garden:

- **Heliotrope:** Vanilla-scented purple or dusky white flowers.
- **Mignonette:** Easy to grow from seed with a strong, sweet fragrance.
- **Flowering tobacco:** White flowers with a nearly tropical scent.
- **Night-scented stock:** Old-fashioned favorite with a clove scent.
- **Scented geraniums:** The leaves come in a variety of scents.
- **Sweet alyssum:** Masses of tiny scented flowers.
- **Sweet peas:** Older varieties retain the sweetest of scents all day long.

Branching out with lesser-known annuals

We have nothing against such familiar fixtures as geraniums and petunias, but keep in mind that a vast array of lesser-known plants is available. Consider the following ideas for putting unusual annuals to work for you:

- **Create a summer-long tactile treat.** Put a large pot in your shady doorway and fill it with fragrant lavender verbena and the felted chartreuse leaves of the licorice plant (*Helichrysum petiolare* 'Limelight').

- **Create a thing of beauty out of an unsightly shed or utility area.** Tack a piece of lattice to it to provide support for a fast-growing annual vine, such as moonflower (*Ipomoea alba),* with its large, heart-shaped leaves and sweetly scented white flowers.

- **Create a hedge for a border or tall backdrop for flowers.** Plant several packages of cosmos seeds in early spring, and you can enjoy a hedge that grows 6 to 8 feet tall with feathery foliage and daisylike flowers in elegant shades of pink, lavender, rose, crimson, and white from June to October.

Hundreds of different kinds of annuals are available, so search out unusual or particularly fragrant varieties from the hundreds of annuals available in seed catalogs or specialty nurseries.

Bordering on Getting Bedder

The beginning of this chapter focuses on design principles. This section takes a pragmatic approach, giving you suggestions of exactly what to plant where to achieve the effect that you want for particular areas in your yard.

In just about all cultures and styles of gardening since garden-making began, beds and borders (Chapter 5 in Book IV and much of Book II offer some specifics on creating a flower bed) have been the major elements used to organize landscape design. (See Chapter 1 in Book II for more on landscape design.) Appealing beds and borders typically combine plants of varying heights and textures in a pleasing color scheme. They include fragrant annuals as well as annuals that bloom when bulbs fade away in the spring, they produce flowers that you can cut for indoor bouquets, and they provide color contrasts or accents when planted between or in front of trees, shrubs, and perennials in existing borders.

The big guys

Tall-growing annuals, reaching a height of 3 to 4 feet or taller, function in three major ways in beds and borders:

- They form a backdrop to show off the flowers in the front of the bed when planted along the back edge of borders.
- They provide height down the middle of the bed in a planting bed meant to be viewed from all sides.
- They're useful for quick-growing screening — to hide a utility area or cover the wall of a garage, for example.

The following annuals grow to 3 to 4 feet or taller:

- Basket flower *(Centaurea americana)*
- Castor bean *(Ricinus communis)*
- Cosmos *(Cosmos bipinnatus)*
- Flowering tobacco *(Nicotiana sylvestris)*
- Love-lies-bleeding *(Amaranthus caudatus)*
- Spider flower *(Cleome)*
- Sunflower *(Helianthus annus)*
- Verbena *(Verbena bonariensis)*

Middle of the pack

Ranging from 1 to 3 feet, these plants are the ones that you use most frequently in all your planting schemes. They're ideal for the middle of beds and borders, and they're also the right scale for most containers:

- African daisy *(Arctotis)*
- Ageratum
- Calendula
- Dwarf dahlia
- Geranium, zonal *(Pelargonium hortorum)*
- Gloriosa daisy, or black-eyed Susan *(Rudbeckia hirta)*
- Heliotrope
- Larkspur *(Consolida ambigua)*
- Marigolds *(Tagetes)*
- Phlox, annual *(Phlox drummondii)*
- Snapdragon *(Antirrhinium majus)*
- Zinnia *(Zinnia angustifolia)*

Short stuff

Short annuals (usually less than 8 inches tall) play two of the most important roles in beds and borders: They fill in spaces between larger annuals, and they spill over or trim the edge of a bed, softening the other, more distinct flower shapes. Be sure to choose dwarf varieties when an annual comes in a wide range of sizes. The following dependable annuals stay under 6 to 8 inches tall:

- Bedding or wax begonias *(Begonia semperflorens)*
- Impatiens
- Lobelia *(Lobelia erinus)*
- Mignonette *(Reseda odorata)*
- Nasturtium
- Pansy *(Viola wittrockiana)*
- Petunia
- Sweet alyssum *(Lobularia)*
- Verbena

Six designs for beds and borders

Before you put in your beds and borders, reflect on how the location of your garden can give you viewing pleasure throughout the season. Plant annuals where you can most enjoy their color and fragrance during their relatively brief life. Almost everyone's yard has some features that are ready-made for planting beds and borders. Find the situation that most closely matches your yard and discover how to re-create a design or adapt it for your own garden:

✔ **Sunny patio bed:** Many homeowners have a backyard patio that they use for various summer activities. Creating a flower bed between the patio and the lawn is easy — and a perfect way to show off annuals during the warm months. Plant the tallest flowers in the interior of the bed so that your bed looks nice from both the patio and the lawn. If the bed is so large that you can't reach the middle to weed or water, create a meandering path of a few stepping stones through the bed. When choosing your own annuals for a border around your sunny backyard patio, you can use the following criteria to limit your search. (Because nurseries and garden centers can offer such an overwhelming number of plants to select from, you may want to narrow down the possibilities even more by picking a color scheme.)

   • **Choose annuals that flourish in the sun and have a long bloom season.** Start with healthy transplants in nursery six-packs or 4-inch pots, both of which bloom more quickly than annuals started from seeds.

   • **Look for sturdy, stocky plants — anything too tall or leggy will probably block the patio from the lawn or be damaged.** Plant low, carpeting-type annuals for areas of the bed that get the most traffic.

✔ **Shady bed around a large tree:** Trees are usually the largest and often the most distinctive element in a garden. One way to show them off is to plant a circular flower bed around their trunks. A mix of pastel colors looks great in the shade, particularly with the addition of plenty of white and an accent of green lawn. A nicely pruned specimen tree, encircled by a flower bed, can serve as the main element in creating a stunning front garden. Make the bed large enough to really accent the tree and to allow for a pleasing complexity of plants. A circular bed 10 feet in diameter serves nicely in this situation.

Remember that flowers may have difficulty thriving in a tree's shade because they're competing with the tree roots for water. As you plan such a bed, select less-thirsty annuals that flower well in dappled shade. One simple planting scheme includes annuals that perform under those conditions and, at the same time, add a cool splash of color and a large dose of drama to any garden.

✔ **Border for a formal walkway:** Annuals can brighten up the skinniest of spaces providing bright color and a sweet scent you can appreciate as you pass by. A 20-foot-long brick walkway between your entry gate and your front door may have only a 2-foot-wide border along each side. In such restricted spaces, consider a simple color scheme with a minimum of different kinds of plants. Typically, formal walkways are in full sun.

✔ **Border for an informal walkway:** When you're edging a curved walkway made of irregularly shaped paving or stepping stones, you're likely to want different styles and colors of plants than you'd choose to line a straight brick pathway. The most appropriate planting choices for curving walkways are a loose variety of annuals that duplicate the appearance of a cottage garden border — even within such a confined space as a 3-foot-wide walkway border.

✔ **Border for a modern-style walkway:** Front pathways leading to ranch-style houses, or more modern-style houses, often stretch from the driveway along the front of the house to the porch and doorway. Such pathways are usually made of poured aggregate or smoothly laid stone. The border running alongside this pathway is best planted in just one kind of flower. Your goal here is to completely fill the border. This simplicity of single-variety planting suits both the sleekness of the path and the style of house. Even within such a simple scheme, you have plenty of choices. Consider planting zinnias in cool colors or gloriosa daisies, also called black-eyed Susans, in warm colors. Space transplants 6 to 8 inches apart, staggering them to avoid the look of soldiers lined up at attention. Deadhead and water the plants throughout the growing season, and they'll provide a dramatic, colorful walkway border that belies the simplicity and ease of your planting scheme.

✔ **Border against a backyard fence:** Large borders consisting mainly of trees and shrubs usually form a backdrop in most gardens. You can call on annual flowers to fill in bare spaces between the permanent plants and to brighten the view across the garden. A border that radiates outward from a fenced-corner and is curved in front is likely to include a variety of shrubs and maybe a small tree or two. Annual plantings between the shady bays formed by the trees and shrubs, and along the front edge of the border, add color and interest to this border during the summer months, when you spend the most time in your backyard.

Getting Ready for Bed

"Dig a ten-dollar hole for a ten-cent plant." That old gardening expression is a great way to look at soil preparation for annual flowers. You can spend loads of money on fine geraniums or the newest petunias, but they'll grow like ragamuffins if the soil is shabby. The opposite is also true: Plain-Jane annuals can blossom into real knockouts when grown in truly superior soil.

More bed and border annuals

Tons of annuals perform beautifully in both beds and borders. You can use the following annuals to fill different roles, such as providing long bloom, pleasant fragrance, or bright foliage. Some are especially easy to grow or have the ability to flourish in less-than-ideal situations.

Easy annuals for beginning gardeners

Forget-me-not (These also reseed themselves.)

Impatiens (These also have a long bloom season.)

Lobelia (These also have a long bloom season.)

Pansy

Sweet pea (This annual vine is also fragrant.)

Annuals that reseed themselves

California poppy (These are also drought resistant.)

Cornflower, or bachelor's button

Nasturtium (Those with variegated leaves also have colorful foliage.)

Shirley poppy

Spider flower (These are also drought tolerant.)

Annuals with a long bloom season

Bedding begonia, or wax begonia

Cosmos

Flowering tobacco (These are also fragrant.)

Gazania

Marigold, African and French

Zinnia

Annuals with colorful foliage

Coleus

Flowering kale and flowering cabbage

Licorice plant

Love-lies-bleeding

New Guinea impatiens

Snow-on-the-mountain

Drought-tolerant annuals

Baby's breath

Gloriosa daisy (black-eyed Susan)

Sweet alyssum (These are also fragrant.)

Strawflower

Verbena

Fragrant annuals

Heliotrope

Mignonette

Pink

Stock

Sweet sultan

Annual vines

Black-eyed Susan vine *(Thunbergia)*

Cup-and-saucer vine *(Cobaea scandens)*

Love-in-a-puff *(Cardiospermum halicacabum)*

Moonflower

Morning glory

Dealing with delinquent drainage

If you go to dig your flower bed and find that the soil is damp and swampy even though the rest of the yard seems dry, you may have a drainage problem Sometimes, you can correct a drainage problem by aerating the soil and adding organic matter, but you probably should look elsewhere for a place to grow flowers. Bad drainage means that the roots of any plants that do grow there are deprived of air and exposed to excessive amounts of water, instead. Very few annual flowers are willing to put up with this kind of abuse. One notable exception is the cardinal flower *(Lobelia cardinalis)*. It grows naturally in and around bogs and similar wet spots and requires constant moisture.

The best solution for wet or poorly drained soil is a raised bed. Raised beds can be as simple as mounds of soil that are 6 to 8 inches above the surrounding soil level, or they can be more complex affairs, utilizing boards, stones, or similar materials to make a soil-retaining border. (See Chapter 5 in Book IV for more on creating raised beds.)

Making the bed your flowers will lie in

Before you dig in to your gardening project, get all your materials together — soil amendments, fertilizer, digging tools (shovel, digging fork, and a dirt rake or hoe), work gloves, a garden hose, and perhaps a wheelbarrow or garden cart, if you plan to do some really serious digging.

1. **Mark off the area you want to dig, as shown in Figure 2-1.**

2. **Start at the edge of your bed with a flat-tipped spade and skim an inch or two below the surface, stripping off the sod as shown in Figure 2-2.**

3. **Use a shovel or digging fork to turn the soil.**

   Lift up a spadeful of soil and drop it back onto the ground upside-down. Pull out weeds that come loose and toss them into a pile. If your soil changes color and becomes very hard just a few inches below the surface, you have *hardpan*. (Chapter 3 in Book I offers advice on dealing with hardpan.)

4. **Using a hoe or rake, hack away at the big clods to break them up, pulling out weeds as you work.**

Figure 2-1:
Marking off the area you plan to make into a flower bed keeps you from getting carried away with your digging.

Figure 2-2:
Skimming off the sod and setting it aside helps keep grass and weed roots from resprouting and taking over your garden.

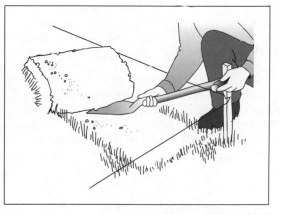

5. **Pour on your soil amendments and fertilizer.**

6. **Dig through the bed again with your shovel, working in the amendments and fertilizer.**

7. **Rake over the bed vigorously with a stiff-tined rake to break up clods.**

   Rake the bed, so that it has a level top and slightly sloped sides. If you like, you can make a little lip around the top inside edge to help hold water, at least until the lip washes away.

If you have a dog or cat who's been watching from the sidelines and is poised to continue cultivating your bed as soon as you go inside, sprinkle the surface lightly with cayenne pepper. One sniff is all it should take to make them change their minds.

If growing flowers sounds like more work than you expected, don't switch to raising tropical fish as a hobby just yet. Bear in mind that you have to do the really hard digging, or *sodbusting,* only once. In subsequent seasons, as you work your soil and add more organic matter, your garden soil will become so well behaved that digging it will be a pleasure. If you really don't want to dig, you can plant your annuals in containers (see Chapter 3 in Book II) or in raised beds.

Going Seed-y

Planting a seed and nurturing it into a beautiful flower is an experience that satisfies the primitive, soulful side of gardeners' personalities. Plus, starting with seeds can save you a great deal of money. But the most compelling reason to grow at least some of your annuals from seeds is the opportunity to have unusual flowers that are impossible to find as bedding plants. The variety of choices in terms of color, size, and species is nothing short of mind-boggling when you start with seeds.

Flower seeds come in all shapes and sizes, from begonia seeds the size of salt grains to pea-sized nasturtium and sweet-pea seeds. Larger seeds tend to be easier to handle, and they also grow into comparatively large seedlings. But don't be afraid to try growing small seeds. Just be forewarned that tiny seeds take longer to grow into big plants.

Smart seed shopping

In the spring, every garden center and home supply store installs big seed racks right on your way to the checkout line. The seeds are usually good quality. However, just to be sure, look beyond the picture on the front of the packet to find the following information (also shown in Figure 2-3):

- Species and/or variety name
- Mature height
- Packing date (don't buy seeds that are more than a year old)
- Special planting instructions

Seeds by mail

Mail-order seed companies are able to maintain huge selections, and they also tend to be meticulous about storage conditions. However, because mail-order companies display and guarantee their seeds in their catalogs, the actual packets often give little information beyond variety name and the approximate number of seeds inside. As soon as your mail-order seeds arrive, read over the packets and write the year on the packet (if it isn't already stamped there), thus creating a reminder not to plant the seeds two years from now.

Figure 2-3:
To verify that you're starting with fresh seeds, look for the words "packed for . . ." followed by the year of the next gardening season.

$1.39

Lobelia
'Crystal Palace'

Lobelia erinus

Annual
Blooms spring to fall frost
Spreads 12"
2" tall
Sun
Low growing ground cover with intensely rich, deep blue flowers, massed over the top of the plant

net weight
125 mg

To open: Peel this flap back.
Peel back side and bottom flaps
to find additional information
on inside packet!

'Crystal Palace' Lobelia catches your eye with dazzling, vibrant, dark blue flowers.

When to plant outside: Spring after average last day of frost. In mild winter areas, sow late summer for winter color.

When to start inside: 8-10 weeks before last frost. This is the recommended method since Lobelia takes a long time to germinate.

Important! Read inside of packet for more specific information. See top flap for directions.

Packed for 1998

7 36210 00011 9

Some seed packets also include the expected *germination rate,* which is the percentage of seeds in the packet that you can realistically expect to sprout. The rate always should be above 65 percent. If no germination rate is given, you can usually assume that the seeds meet or exceed the germination standards for that species. All the reputable seed companies trash bad seeds rather than sell them. Because the seed business is tremendously competitive, seed quality tends to be very high.

Some retailers sell seeds left over from the previous year. Although many flower seeds do remain viable for several years when stored in a cool, dry place, a retailer who sells old seeds is obviously trying to cut corners.

Seed needs

The process of growing flowers from seeds is pretty straightforward. Plant them in a soft soil, add water, and keep them constantly moist until they sprout. The moisture triggers the germination process and softens the hard outer covering of the seed, called the *seed coat,* so that the sprout can emerge. How quickly this miracle occurs also depends on the temperature. For most seeds, the warm side of 70°F (21°C) is just dandy. From the moment the sprout breaks through the soil, seedlings need light.

Starting seeds indoors

If you plant your annuals too early in the spring, frost may damage them. On the other hand, annuals like to do most of their growing before the weather turns too hot. Starting seeds indoors is the perfect solution to the weather challenges facing annuals. Giving your plants a head start indoors also allows you to control the temperature and moisture, so that seeds have no excuses not to sprout. Plus, having little green things growing under lights is a reason to start celebrating spring while winter still rages.

Every seed catalog sells equipment, such as various trays, domes, and other paraphernalia for starting seeds. These set-ups help take some of the guesswork out of seed starting, but they aren't required equipment. See Chapter 3 in Book IV for a list of equipment you need to start seeds indoors.

To sow annual seeds in containers, follow these steps:

1. **Fill containers to the top with seed-starting mix and then level the top by sweeping across it with your hand or a table knife.**

   For seeds that are very tiny, use a tamper or piece of wood to down the starting mix until it's just ¼ inch below the rim. Water the soil and let it drain. Sprinkle the fine seed over the mix and then *gently* tamp again. That's it — no need to cover with mix. When it's time to water, don't do it from above. Rather, set the container over a shallow tray of water and let the soil soak up from the bottom as in Step 4. Continue by going to Step 5.

2. **Use your fingertip or a pencil to make small depressions for seeds.**

   The depth of the holes doesn't have to be exact, but try to plant the seeds about three times as deep as the seeds are wide.

3. **Drop one or two seeds into each depression and cover them with pinches of seed-starting mixture.**

   Seed-starting mixture is a lightweight soil mix, usually containing peat moss, vermiculite, and perlite. Compared to potting soils, the particles in a seed-starting mix are smaller, which make controlling sowing depth more precise. Garden centers carry seed-starting mixes.

Book V

Annuals

4. **Dampen the soil thoroughly.**

   To keep from flooding out the planted seeds, use a pump spray bottle to mist the containers repeatedly, or place the containers in small pans or trays and fill the pans with 1 inch of water. After about an hour, the containers will absorb the water from the pans.

5. **To keep the surface of the planted containers from drying out, cover them lightly with plastic wrap or enclose the whole tray in a large plastic bag.**

6. **Keep the containers in a warm place and start checking for germination after three days.**

   Typical warm locations around the home include on top of the refrigerator, near a baseboard heater, or near the furnace in the basement.

7. **As soon as the first sprouts emerge, remove the plastic and move the seedlings to good light.**

   Unless you have a greenhouse, it's best to use some sort of supplemental light to grow stocky seedlings indoors. Tabletop fluorescent fixtures are perfect for this job. Arrange your indoor garden so that the seedlings are always about 2 inches away from the light, and leave the lights on for 12 to 16 hours per day.

8. **Thin out the seedlings.**

   Most of the time, you end up with way too many seedlings. If left alone, the plants will become so crowded that they won't grow well. You must thin your plants so that they're spaced at least 2 inches apart in all directions. Do this by pulling out the weakest sprouts with your fingers or tweezers. It's painful to pull up your precious seedlings, but the remaining ones will grow much better if you do! Try to thin your seedlings when they're just an inch or two tall, before the roots become entangled. That way, you'll be less likely to disturb the roots of the remaining plants.

   To thin your seedlings without wasting any plants, dump out the container on its side, tap the mass of roots to make them fall apart, and gingerly transplant the tiny seedlings to individual containers filled with sterile soil-less mix. As long as you handle young seedlings by their leaves, and never, ever touch their tender stems, they transplant very easily.

9. **Fertilize the seedlings about two weeks after they emerge.**

   When the time comes to treat the seedlings to their first meal, use a fertilizer that you can dilute with water, and mix it at half the strength recommended on the package. (See Chapter 4 in Book I for information on fertilizers.) Fertilize seedlings about once a week, or every other time you water them.

10. **Prepare your seedlings for outdoor life.**

   After four to six weeks, your seedlings will be big enough to move outside. To help the seedlings get ready for the big move, spend a little time letting them *harden off* (gradually become accustomed to outdoor sun and wind). Set seedlings outside for a few hours the first day and then gradually increase their time outdoors over a one- to two-week period, until they're staying out all day. Be prepared to bring the seedlings indoors if the temperature drops below 50°F (10°C). Eventually, you can leave the seedlings out for several days and nights before you transplant them to flower beds or outdoor containers.

Sowing seeds directly in the ground

All seedlings grow roots as rapidly as they grow leaves, and some annual flowers put an awesome amount of energy into roots right off the bat. Flowers that spend their infancy developing long, brittle, carrotlike taproots are often difficult or impossible to transplant, so they're best sown right where you plan to grow them.

When everything goes exactly right, *direct-sowing* (which means sowing seeds right where you want them to grow) is great. Follow these guidelines to make direct-sowing a pleasant and rewarding experience:

- ✔ **Give special attention to plants that *must* be grown from direct-seeding, such as poppies and larkspur.**

- ✔ **Plant seeds of plants that you will recognize or that have a distinctive appearance.** For example, nasturtium leaves look like no other plants, and mistaking a bean or pea seedling for a weed isn't easy.

- ✔ **Soak large seeds in water overnight before planting them.** This step really speeds things along when you're sowing hard seeds, such as sweet peas and morning glories. Before soaking, break the hard seed coat by scratching or nicking the coat with a file. Doing so does a great deal in helping the seed take in moisture.

- ✔ **Sow seeds in the right season.** Some direct-seeded annuals are best planted in the fall or first thing in the spring; others do best when they're planted in warmer soil in early summer.

- ✔ **Prepare the planting bed thoroughly.** Take extra care to rake smoothly — lumpy soil and clods interfere with germination.

- ✔ **Sow seeds in a definite pattern.** When you see a pattern of little sprouts in your soil, you'll know that those growths are flowers, not weeds. Some seeds are best sown in rows, but you can scatter others.

- ✓ **Sow large seeds by hand directly where you want them to grow.** If seeds are too small for your fingers, gently tap them out directly from the packet. Mix seeds with sand to help you broadcast them more evenly, if you like.

- ✓ **Pay attention to the seed-packet directions for best planting depth.** For many seeds, a light layer of sifted compost is sufficient coverage. At other times, you simply press seeds into the soil with the back of a hoe.

- ✓ **Water gently and with care.** Keep the soil damp until seeds sprout.

- ✓ **Cover seeds with something for a few days after you plant them.** Old blankets and cardboard boxes make an excellent seed cover. The coverings keep the soil constantly moist while the seeds are germinating. Remove the covering as soon as you see the first sprout.

- ✓ **Weed early and often.** If you have trouble weeding around small seedlings, use a table fork to gently pull out awkward little weeds.

- ✓ **After seedlings develop two sets of true leaves, thin out those that stand too close together.** Gently pull extra seedlings without disturbing the ones you want to keep.

Putting Seedlings in the Ground

The quickest way to paint your yard with color is to add some ready-grown annuals to your landscape. Generations of nursery professionals and home gardeners have called these flowers *bedding plants* — a name that suggests their most typical use in the garden. Some of the flowers commonly offered as bedding plants are simple to start from seed, so you have to decide whether you want to take the time and effort to raise your own seedlings or purchase them. You can't beat the convenience of purchasing your bedding plants already sprouted. In one afternoon, you can transform a patch of soil into a lush and colorful garden. Visiting local gardening centers and stocking up on flower seedlings is a springtime ritual in many cold-winter regions.

Shopping for seedlings

The bedding plant industry takes some of the guesswork out of shopping for seedlings by shipping plants to nurseries and garden centers at the best time to plant them. Early in the spring and again in the fall, expect to find annuals that grow best in cool conditions. Annuals that require warmer weather generally arrive later in the spring and keep coming as long as customers keep buying. Remember, however, that nurseries can't predict the weather. You need to be prepared to protect tender seedlings from any late frosts.

Babes in bloom

Statistics show that consumers are much more likely to buy plants that are already in flower. As a result, plant breeders have tinkered with genes to develop flowers that pop a blossom or two at an early age and then devote a few more weeks to vegetative growth before they start blooming again.

If you buy plants already in flower, pinch off the blossom when you set out the plants — unless you're having guests for dinner, in which case you can wait until the next day. This preemptive pinching encourages the plants to get on with the business of growing buds and branches.

To make sure that you get a healthy plant, check the way the store displays its annuals: Are all the flowers simply lined up in the blazing sun, or have shade-lovers, such as coleus and impatiens, been protected from the sun? Most bedding plants, including those that grow best when they're planted in full sun, do better when kept in partial shade until they're planted.

Be sure to protect your plants as you tote them home in your car. You wouldn't leave the family dog locked up in a hot car with the windows rolled up, so don't treat your plants that way, either.

Nurseries sell annuals in containers of all sizes. If you're looking for immediate impact in a flower bed or container, you may want to purchase annuals grown in 4- to 6-inch (or larger) pots. Plants grown in smaller containers take longer to fill their allotted space; however, they cost significantly less than those in larger pots, so if you can be patient, they may be a better choice.

As you shop, look for bedding annuals that are a good green color, appear to have been watered regularly, and are relatively short and stocky. Although picking out the largest plants with the most flowers is tempting, these plants may have grown too large for their containers and will suffer during transplanting. You're better off choosing a healthy, compact plant with few or no flowers. These youngsters transplant better and quickly catch up to larger plants.

Avoid large plants growing in small pots — if a plant's roots entirely fill its container and are poking out of the drainage holes, it may be *rootbound,* meaning that the roots have begun to grow in a tight spiral around the perimeter of the pot and may refuse to spread outward after transplanting, stunting the plant's growth. At the nursery, don't be shy about tipping the plant out of its pot or pack and inspecting its roots.

Seedlings that you purchase directly from a greenhouse benefit from a short period of hardening off. If your new seedlings have already spent some time outdoors at the nursery or garden center, they can skip the hardening off and go straight into your garden. Ask the garden center staff whether the seedlings have been hardened off and are ready for transplanting.

Spacing leaf to leaf

Gardeners tend to have very tight plant spacing in window boxes and containers, but in open beds, the best strategy is to space seedlings so that they'll barely touch each other when they reach full maturity. Because different annual flowers grow to different sizes, the amount of space they require varies. The plant tags tucked into the containers of bedding plants often suggest the best spacing.

Instead of setting your annuals in straight lines, try staggering them in a concentrated zigzag pattern so that you have two or more offset rows of plants. This planting design fills a large space more uniformly and looks less rigid than plants lined up in rows. Better yet, plant groups of similar annuals in teardrop-shaped clumps (called *drifts*); this design often looks more natural and helps create focal points in the design. The clump approach also allows you to more easily care for many flowers. When planning your planting arrangement, you can estimate the plant spacing and simply make little holes in the prepared bed where you intend to set the plants. Or you can mark the planting spots with craft sticks or lightly dust each spot with plain all-purpose flour. If you already purchased plants in individual containers, simply place the plants where you intend to plant them, and move them around as needed until you're happy with the arrangement.

Extras and understudies

Frequently, after planting your garden, you end up with a few extra bedding plants. Don't throw them away. If your garden follows a formal design, where even one additional plant would stand out, transplant the extras to slightly larger individual pots. This way, if a few plants spontaneously expire or get dug up by your neighbor's dog, you can quickly plug in a replacement that's an exact match. Another way to use annual orphans is to plant them together in large containers. Place the tallest, most upright flowers in the middle and surround them with smaller plants. In a few weeks, you'll have a remarkably pretty container bouquet that looks like you spent hours designing it.

Digging up some dirt

Whether you buy your seedlings or grow them from seeds, follow these steps to ensure that your plants get off to a good start in your garden:

1. **The day before transplanting, water the planting bed so that it will be lightly moist when you set out your plants.**

   Transplant during cloudy weather or late in the day. Hot sun during transplanting causes unnecessary stress to the little plants.

2. **Water your seedlings thoroughly a few hours before transplanting, and then carefully remove the seedling from the container.**

   If small roots are knotted around the outside of the drainage holes, pinch off the roots and discard them before trying to remove the plants. Then push and squeeze on the bottom of the container to make the entire root ball slip out intact. If it won't come out easily, use a table knife to gently pry it out, the same way you might remove a sticky cake from a pan. Pull on the top of the plant only as a last resort.

3. **Gently tease roots apart.**

   Use your fingers or a table fork to loosen the tangle of roots at the bottom of the root ball, which encourages the roots to spread out into the surrounding soil.

4. **Make final spacing decisions and dig planting holes slightly larger than the root balls of the plants.**

   Set the plants in the holes at the same depth they grew in their containers.

5. **Lightly firm soil around the roots with your hands to remove any air pockets around the plant's roots.**

   Firm soil just enough so that the plant can remain upright.

6. **Gently water the entire bed until it's evenly moist but not muddy.**

   Take care not to wash away surface soil, leaving roots exposed. After a few days, check to make sure that soil hasn't washed away from the top of the plants' roots. If it has, use a rake or small trowel to level the soil around the plants.

7. **Mulch around plants as soon as new growth shows.**

Yielding Year-Round Beds

In climates with very long growing seasons, annual beds are often *turned over* two or three times a year. For example, if you live in a warm region where winters don't freeze at all, or where they freeze only slightly, you can plant pansies in the fall and enjoy them all the way until May. By then, the pansies are pooped, and you need to replace them with something new. You can complete such a garden renovation very quickly by following these steps:

1. **Dampen the soil to make the old plants easy to pull out.**

2. **Grab the plants close to the soil and pull to get as many of the roots as you can.**

    Throw out the roots or toss them into a compost heap, if you have one.

3. **Spread a 2-inch layer of compost or composted manure, along with a light dusting of a balanced time-release or organic fertilizer, over the empty section of your bed.**

4. **Dig or till the bed as needed to mix in the compost and fertilizer, and rake the soil smooth.**

    You're now ready to install a new crop of annuals.

Seasonal and day-to-day changes make every walk through your garden an adventure. Here, brilliant azaleas, rhododendrons, and other spring-blooming shrubs signal the beginning of a new gardening season in USDA Zone 8. See the climate zone map in this insert to discover which zone you garden in.

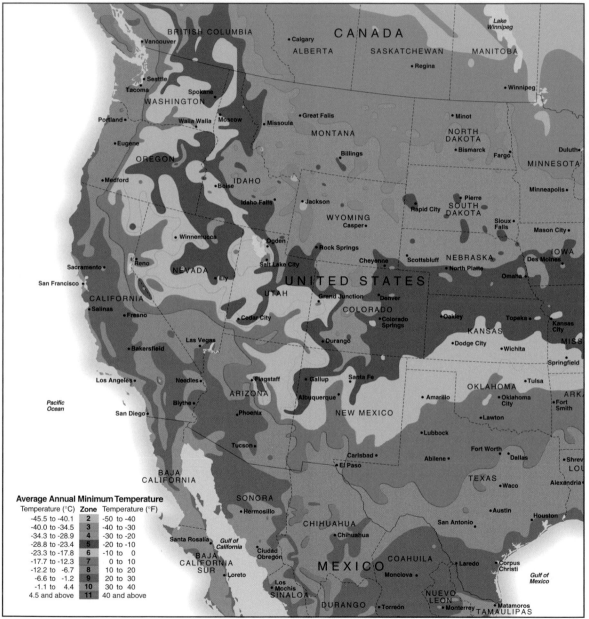

Average Annual Minimum Temperature

Temperature (°C)	Zone	Temperature (°F)
-45.5 to -40.1	2	-50 to -40
-40.0 to -34.5	3	-40 to -30
-34.3 to -28.9	4	-30 to -20
-28.8 to -23.4	5	-20 to -10
-23.3 to -17.8	6	-10 to 0
-17.7 to -12.3	7	0 to 10
-12.2 to -6.7	8	10 to 20
-6.6 to -1.2	9	20 to 30
-1.1 to 4.4	10	30 to 40
4.5 and above	11	40 and above

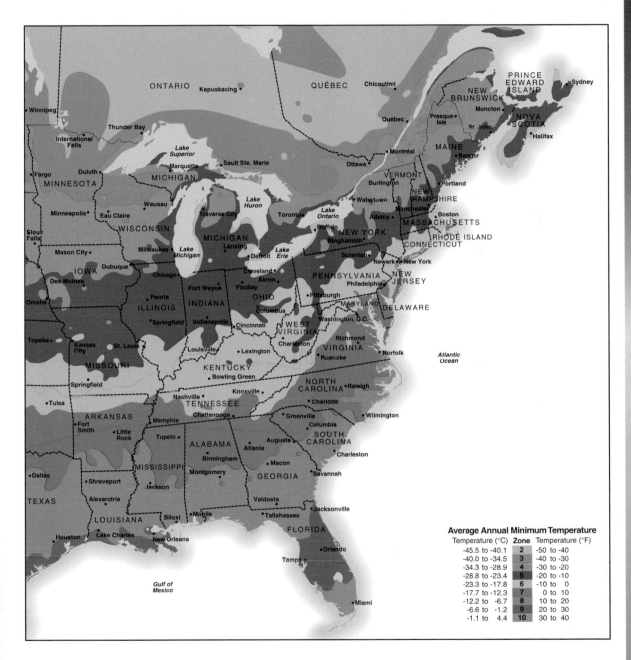

Average Annual Minimum Temperature

Temperature (°C)	Zone	Temperature (°F)
-45.5 to -40.1	2	-50 to -40
-40.0 to -34.5	3	-40 to -30
-34.3 to -28.9	4	-30 to -20
-28.8 to -23.4	5	-20 to -10
-23.3 to -17.8	6	-10 to 0
-17.7 to -12.3	7	0 to 10
-12.2 to -6.7	8	10 to 20
-6.6 to -1.2	9	20 to 30
-1.1 to 4.4	10	30 to 40

© Michael Landis

Experiment with container gardening to add variety to your garden design. (See Chapter 3 in Book II for more on container gardening.)

© John Glover

A festival of flowers, this border garden of perennials and bulbs features tulips 'Mrs. John T. Scheepers' and 'West Point', with wallflower, cloth of gold, and 'Purple Queen' forget-me-nots.

Design your garden around a small mowing strip for low-maintenance landscapes. (See Chapter 4 in Book II for more lawn-care tips.)

Do your back a favor: Add raised beds with fertile soil to your garden design to increase crop yields and make gardening more convenient. (Chapter 5 in Book IV shows you how to build a raised bed.)

A plant collector's garden in containers is staged for height on stone blocks.

A garden of specimen cactus is safely exhibited in some interesting pots.

Grow fresh vegetables in minimal space. For example, this patio-type tomato variety takes up little space but provides a delicious harvest.

An otherwise abandoned corner of the house is a good place for container plants, such as these impatiens, pansies, and daises.

Flowering shrub spirea (*Spirea japonica* 'Magic Carpet') with Colorado blue spruce (*Picea pungens* 'Glauca').

Oleander *(Nerium oleander),* here in white and pink, is an evergreen shrub.

White flowering dogwood (*Cornus florida*), a flowering tree.

Spirea (S. 'Limemound') with smokebush (Cotinus coggygria 'Royal Purple') are both deciduous shrubs.

Deciduous Tricolor European beech (*Fagus sylvatica* 'Tricolor') with reddish foliage.

© Saxton Holt Photography

'Tiffany'; hybrid tea, fragrant, multicolored.

© Saxton Holt Photography

'Flower Carpet'; shrub.

© Saxton Holt Photography

'Mister Lincoln'; hybrid tea.

© Saxton Holt Photography

'Fourth of July'; fragrant, climber.

© Saxton Holt Photography

'Kristin'; miniature.

© Saxton Holt Photography

'Blanc Double de Coubert'; hybrid rugosa.

© Saxton Holt Photography

'Betty Boop'; floribunda.

© Saxton Holt Photography

'Gold Medal'; fragrant, grandiflora.

© Saxton Holt Photography

'Dainty Bess'; hybrid tea.

These perennials show off the colors and textures of spring, including variegated hosta, leaves of plume poppy, and late-blooming red tulips. The blue flowers are Spanish hyacinths. (See Book IV for more on perennials.)

Hot yellows and golds of tickseed (*Coreopsis grandiflora* 'Early Sunrise'), gloriosa daisy *(Rudbeckia),* and blanket flower *(Gaillardia aristata)* combine here to make a river of daisies.

A colorful sea of cheerfully bright cosmos can fill any landscape *(Cosmos bipinnatus)*.

Purple alyssum and salmon-colored geraniums can spice up your herb garden with a dash of annual color. (See Book V for more on annuals and Chapters 4, 5, and 6 in Book VII for more on herbs.)

Annuals give you the power to create a large, lush garden in just one year. This all-annual flower bed — now filled with tall, pink lavatera, a mixture of zinnias, pink geraniums, sweet white alyssum, and petite marigolds — was bare in early spring.

This annual border provides privacy. Sunflowers do the heavy lifting, but tall zinnias and marigolds fill in thickly enough to turn the strip of soil into a wall of color.

© Michael S. Thompson

Want to add punch to your garden? Plant marigolds! Marigolds and celosia, along with white-and-blue petunias and red-and-pink dianthus, add the spice to this sunny garden.

With long and late bloomers like marigolds (edging the path) and zinnias (in the background), this late-summer garden gives you color right up to the first hard frost.

© Jerry Pavia

Although most annuals love the sun, you can bring color to shady spots by combining impatiens (in the foreground) and coleus (the variegated foliage at the base of the tree).

© Michael S. Thompson

Certain annuals can meet the challenge of nearly any patch of soil. In this narrow, shady strip, for example, coleus and impatiens team up with the yellow flowers of tuberous begonia (another shade-lover) and pink ageratum, an annual that needs partial sun.

Tazetta narcissus 'Geranium'.

Canna, flowering in the summer.

© John Glover

Snowdrops *Galanthus nivalis* **(common snowdrop) with** *Crocus tommasinianus;* **flowering in the late winter.**

Lords and Ladies *Arum italicum;* **flowering in the fall.**

© John Glover

Tulips 'Apricot Beauty' and 'Alabaster Carrara' with *Cytisus x kewensis.*

Lavender *(Lavandula Munstead)*.

Oregano *(Origanum vulgare)*.

Rosemary *(Rosmarinus officinalis)*.

Nasturtium *(Tropaeolum majus)*.

© R. Todd Davis Photography, Inc.

© R. Todd Davis Photography, Inc.

© Crandall & Crandall Photography

© Crandall & Crandall Photography

The pink 'Dainty Bess' rose makes a charming addition to this lovely garden. Climbing up the wall in the background is the old-fashioned noisette 'Mme. Alfred Carrière'.

Chapter 3

Raising Your Annuals Right

After selecting and planting annuals, you spend the rest of your gardening time caring for them. This chapter tells you all you need to know to give your annuals the best care possible. (Book I gives general information for caring for your garden, and you can find tips and hints on caring for other types of plants throughout this book.)

Punching the Garden's Water Clock

Watering may be one of the trickiest aspects of growing annual flowers. Like many plants, annuals need consistent moisture in the soil in order to grow and bloom beautifully. Annuals aren't very forgiving if they don't get the water they want, when they want it. If you let some of these finicky plants dry out, they'll stop growing and quit blooming for good. (Drowning your plants has that same effect.) If they don't die, most under- or overwatered annuals at least shut down for a while. For a more permanent plant, a temporary halt in growth may not be the end of the world. But with annuals, fast, consistent growth is critical. If the plant stalls, you may lose a good part, if not all, of the blooming season.

The amount of water that annuals need to stay healthy and full of blooms depends on a number of factors:

✔ **Climate:** Climate encompasses a wide range of factors, such as the amount of average rainfall, the high and low temperatures, the relative humidity, and the amount of wind. (Book I, Chapter 2 discusses climate in detail.) If you live in an area where rainfall is regular and reliable watering isn't a constant chore, except during prolonged dry spells or periods of drought. In drier areas, you must water almost every day. You have to water container-grown annuals even more frequently than your plants in the ground. In fact, daily watering of annuals in containers is essential in almost all climates during certain times of the year. (Book II, Chapter 3 covers container gardening.)

✔ **Weather:** *Climate* is determined by the average weather where you live on a season-to-season, year-to-year basis. *Weather* is what's happening outside at any given moment. Out-of-the-ordinary weather can wreak havoc on your plants. Adjust your watering as follows:

   • **Water less:** Cooler temperatures, cloudy or overcast conditions, low wind, high humidity, and rain

   • **Water more:** Warmer temperatures, bright sunshine, high wind, low humidity, and no rain

✔ **Soil type:** Different soil types affect how often a garden needs water. (Chapter 3 in Book I shows you how to determine what type of soil you have.) Luckily, when you grow annuals, you can amend the soil with organic matter on a yearly, if not seasonal, basis. Adding organic matter, such as compost, leaf mold, or ground bark, helps sandy soils to retain moisture and helps break up clay soils to improve aeration and drainage.

✔ **Garden location:** In general, shady gardens need less water than those planted in direct sunlight. By blocking the sun's heat, shade cuts down on the amount of water that evaporates from the soil. However, in places where trees are responsible for casting the shadow, the tree roots may be greedily hogging all the water, leaving little for the flowers. Maples in particular have roots so close to the surface that it's almost impossible to apply enough water to satisfy the tree and the flowers. The farther from the trunk of the tree you place your flowers, the more room they have to spread their roots, and the less they have to compete with the tree for water and nutrients.

If you plan to plant in a shady area, choose annuals that don't need direct sunlight to thrive. Impatiens, forget-me-nots, and browallia are good choices for the dark corners of your yard.

✔ **Type of annuals you're using:** Although most annual flowers need a consistent supply of moisture to remain healthy and free-blooming, some annuals can get by on less water than others. Read up on the water requirements of the plants you like and then decide whether you can modify your soil or site to accommodate them. Aside from amending your soil, group plants according to their water needs. If you garden in containers (as described in Chapter 3 of Book II), you have much more control because you can move the pots around if your plants begin to complain about their present location.

The water needs of your annuals vary with the weather and the seasons, and you must make adjustments accordingly. The roots of most annuals grow in the top 8 to 10 inches of soil, where the soil is well-aerated, and conditions suit root growth. When you water, therefore, you must make sure that the moisture reaches a depth of 8 to 10 inches. If you water any shallower, the roots won't be able to grow deeply because they just won't penetrate the dry soil. On the other hand, very few roots are growing deeper than 8 to 10 inches, so to water deeper than that is just wasting water.

Here are two easy ways to tell when your plants need water:

✔ **Look at your plants.** When an annual starts to dry out, the leaves get droopy and wilt. The plant may also lose its bright green color and start to look a little drab. Your goal is to water before a plant reaches that point, but the plant will tell you when it needs water more often.

✔ **Dig in the ground.** Most annuals need water when the top two to three inches of soil are dry, so take a small trowel or shovel and dig around a bit. If the top of the soil is dry, you need to water.

Eventually, through observation and digging, you start to develop a watering schedule, and you can eliminate some of the guesswork from this part of your gardening routine.

Feeding Those Hungry Annuals

If annuals are flowering powerhouses (and they are), fertilizer is the coal that fuels the powerhouse. Proper fertilization, especially when annuals are young, is very important to the quality of bloom. Even though young transplants or seedlings may not be blooming much, their growth during the first six to eight weeks after planting has a huge impact on how well they bloom later. Keeping annuals growing vigorously, never letting them stall, and building healthy foliage early on results in spectacular power when they're ready to bloom. And after annuals have started blooming, proper fertilization keeps them blooming as long as possible. (Chapter 4 in Book I offers more information on fertilizing your garden.)

Hungering for nutrients

Plants need 16 different elements for healthy growth. Carbon, hydrogen, and oxygen — the foundation blocks for photosynthesis — are required in large quantities, but nature or your watering hose automatically provides these elements.

Plants also need relatively large amounts of nitrogen, phosphorus, and potassium, which are called *macronutrients*. Plants require *secondary nutrients* (calcium, magnesium, and sulfur) in smaller quantities and need the *micronutrients* (iron, manganese, copper, boron, molybdenum, chlorine, and zinc) in even smaller amounts. Plant roots typically absorb macronutrients, secondary nutrients, and micronutrients from the soil. If any nutrient isn't present in the soil in sufficient quantities, or is present in a form that the plant can't absorb, you must add it as fertilizer or correct the conditions that are prohibiting nutrient absorption.

Luckily, most soils already contain enough nutrients for healthy growth. In fact, when growing annual flowers, many gardeners may find that nitrogen is the only element that they need to apply via fertilizers. But how do you know for sure? You can look for a yellowing of the lower leaves (a sure sign of nitrogen deficiency), but to be absolutely sure that the problem is lack of nitrogen, you can have your soil tested. A soil test, discussed in detail in Chapter 3 in Book I, reveals which nutrients are or aren't present in your soil so that you can know the type and quantity of fertilizer to apply.

A soil test doesn't provide *all* the answers; it only tells you what to work into your soil *before* planting. You still have to apply nitrogen, and maybe other nutrients, later on.

Thirsting for nitrogen

If your annuals aren't producing their quota of blooms, the reason is probably that the soil doesn't contain enough nitrogen. Luckily, plants usually respond quickly to nitrogen application, so nitrogen deficiency is easy to correct by simply adding fertilizer. Nitrogen is often the only nutrient that you need to apply as a fertilizer. Soil tends to be nitrogen deficient because plants use more nitrogen than any other nutrient, quickly depleting nitrogen supplies. Nitrogen is also less stationary in the soil; you can wash it out of the soil when you water. Phosphorus and potassium are less mobile — so once they're there, they stay put for quite a while.

Keeping other nutrients in check

In addition to nitrogen, phosphorus and potassium (the other two macronutrients) also play important roles in plant growth. Phosphorus is associated with good root growth and with flower, fruit, and seed production. Potassium is necessary for healthy roots, disease resistance, and fruiting. Only a soil test can positively identify deficiencies in either of these nutrients. Because phosphorus and potassium are less mobile than nitrogen, you have to work those nutrients into the soil at planting time. That way, they're located right where the roots can absorb them.

Determining the secondary nutrients and the micronutrients that your plants need is also hard, if not impossible, without a soil test. Some of the nutrients may be present, but the soil's pH prevents the plants from being able to absorb them. In such a case, the soil test tells you how to adjust your soil pH so that the nutrients can be absorbed. (You can find more on soil pH in Chapter 3 in Book I.)

More bang for your fertilizing buck

Fertilizers sell for a range of prices. Some are very expensive considering the amount of nutrients they contain. For example, premixed liquid fertilizers include a large amount of water, which makes them heavy and more expensive to ship. When you know how to decipher the information on fertilizer product labels, you can become a better, more price-conscious shopper.

If a 10-pound bag of fertilizer contains 10 percent nitrogen, it includes 1 pound of what's called *actual nitrogen* (determined by multiplying the weight of the package by the percentage of nitrogen). By calculating the actual nitrogen in different fertilizers, you can compare the price of nutrients. For example, suppose that the

10-pound bag of fertilizer with 10 percent nitrogen costs $5. The price of the 1 pound of actual nitrogen is $5 (the price divided by the pounds of actual nitrogen). Compare it to a 20-pound bag with 20 percent nitrogen, or 4 pounds of actual nitrogen, costing $10; the cost of the actual nitrogen is $2.50. The larger bag is a better deal, and your plants don't know the difference between more expensive fertilizer and bargain brands.

The amount of actual nitrogen in a package of fertilizer also influences application rates. The more actual nitrogen, the less you use with each application. But don't try to calculate the correct amount of fertilizer yourself; recommended application rates are listed on the package.

Applying fertilizer to your flower bed

The best time to start fertilizing your flower bed is before you start planting. Giving your annuals a nutrient-rich home from the get-go ensures healthy development during their most formative period. For the best results, add your fertilizer no more than a day or so before planting. You can add organic matter at any time. Some gardeners prefer to start cutting back on nitrogen after their annuals reach full bloom, thinking that the nitrogen may force leaf growth at the expense of flowers. If you're tending annual flowers properly, by removing spent blooms, consistent applications of nitrogen throughout the life of the plant result in more blooms.

Don't fertilize dry plants. Plants need water to move fertilizer nutrients to the roots and help them take these fertilizers up into the plant. Without adequate water, the plant roots that do contact the fertilizers may be burned, causing the roots to die and the plant to suffer. Always water your plants well before and after fertilizing to get the most benefit from the fertilizer. Overfertilizing can be much worse than not applying enough fertilizer. Excess nitrogen, for example, can burn the edges of leaves and even kill a plant. Besides that, if you apply too much fertilizer, it can leach into ground water, and then you're a nasty polluter. So always follow instructions on the fertilizer label and apply only nutrients that you're sure are deficient in your soil (have your soil tested if you aren't sure); too much of any nutrient can cause problems with plants and the environment.

Fertilizing annuals in containers

Annuals growing in containers need more water than those growing in the ground. The more you water, the more you flush nutrients from the soil, and the more often you have to fertilize. You can offset some of this constant loss of nutrients by mixing slow-release fertilizers into the soil before planting.

The best pots of annuals we've seen are on a constant feeding program. Give your flowers a little liquid fertilizer every time, or every other time, you water them. Cut the recommended rates on the bottle of fertilizer in half or into quarters, so you're applying only about a teaspoon or so of fertilizer per watering. Wait until you see the results — bloom city! If fertilizing every time you water is too much hassle for you, use a liquid fertilizer once every week or two. Follow the rates recommended on the label, and your annuals will still do great.

Chopping Away at Garden Chores

Gardening chores may not always be fun, but the payoff is worth your time and effort. Conscientious gardeners are rewarded with prettier, healthier plants that last longer and provide a most impressive display.

Garden maintenance involves four simple tasks (all of which we discuss in greater detail in Book I):

- Deadheading
- Staking
- Pinching and pruning
- Mulching

Timing is important to help you keep the tasks small and manageable. Here are some key strategies for garden maintenance:

- **Observe a regular maintenance schedule.** That way, no chore gets too far out of hand. Start the jobs early, before the situation gets out of hand, and do jobs as you notice that they need to be done.

- **Be a bucket gardener.** Take a bucket with you into the garden so that you have an easy and convenient place to toss your garden waste until you can take it to the compost pile or recycling bin. For large areas, consider keeping a plastic garbage container (the kind with wheels is great) or a wheelbarrow nearby. Handy equipment means that you're more likely to spend a few minutes doing chores each time you visit the garden rather than waiting until you have a large chunk of time to lug all your equipment from a distant spot.

✔ **Make regular tours of the garden.** Think of these tours as minivacations. Don't get your hands dirty on these garden strolls, but do make a mental note of what jobs you need to tackle next. When the time comes to do some work in the garden, you already know what tools you need and what chores are most pressing, so you can work smarter.

✔ **Have the materials and tools you need to do the job.** Store tools in a set location where you can always find them, and keep them clean. Keep track of supplies and restock as amounts get low.

✔ **Evaluate how much maintenance you're doing.** If you feel that you're spending too much time and effort on your garden, try to find ways to do your chores more efficiently or consider scaling down the garden to a more manageable size.

Deadheading: Out with the old . . .

Deadheading is the act of cutting or pinching off a faded flower. By removing the spent flower, you stimulate the plant to produce a new bud in its exhaustive quest to make seeds to reproduce. Deadheading not only keeps plants looking tidy, but it also prolongs the bloom period and gives you significantly more flowers. Start deadheading as soon as you see the flowers fade and the petals begin to fall. Remove part of the stem as well as the faded flower, so that you're sure to get the seed pod, too. With some flowers, such as petunias, you can pull off the petal part and think you've done the job, but the seed pod remains. Use your fingers to pinch off flowers with fleshy stems. Use pruners for stiffer or more stubborn flowers.

Watch for flower-producing side shoots a bit down on the stem. When removing spent flowers, cut the stem *above* this point to save the new buds coming on. Cosmos, zinnia, and gloriosa daisy are famous for producing these lower buds. If you don't see any side shoots, cut the stem just above a set of leaves.

Holding a stake-out

Staking is a simple but important job — especially for plants more than 3 feet tall and for plants with large, heavy flowers or slender stems. Staking keeps plants steady in the wind and ensures that blossoms stay healthy and upright. It gives the garden a neat and tidy look and helps plants produce the maximum number of flowers. Keep an eye on all your annuals as they develop to see whether flowers seem to be giving in to gravity, thus requiring you to stake them.

Stake early! By staking early when you set out transplants or after seedlings reach a few inches tall, you can direct the stems to grow upward right from the start and tie them at intervals along the stake as they grow. After a mass of flowers falls over, bringing them back to a vertical position without damaging them is difficult. Don't worry about the aesthetics of the stake; the stake may look stark at first, but the stems and leaves will quickly surround and hide the stake from view.

Tie stems to slender bamboo sticks, wooden stakes, or even straight and sturdy woody branches that you saved from your pruning chores. For light plants with sturdy stems, such as cosmos and cornflower, you can use twine or twist ties. For large-flowered plants, such as sunflowers, use plastic garden tape or strips of fabric — under the weight of those heavy flowers, twine can cut into stem tissue, as can the newer type of hook-and-loop plant ties. For the largest plants, insert a single stake a few inches from the stem at planting time and loosely tie the seedling to the stake. As the plant grows, continue to tie the stem at intervals along the stake, as shown on the left plant in Figure 3-1.

You can also corral smaller plants by setting stakes in the ground around the circumference and winding ties or twine horizontally to enclose the area. Or you can buy wire stakes with a loop that encircles individual stems (shown on the right-hand plant in Figure 3-1). Also available are mini-fences that hook together in sections to support many plants at once.

Figure 3-1:
Staking a
single large
plant or
corralling
many stems.

Don't forget to stake your container plants. Stake these flowers when they're little by using either one slender stake per plant (pushed several inches down), or three or four stakes around the edge of pot with twine wrapped around the them. Try green wire stakes in containers — they blend in and disappear among the flowers. (See Chapter 3 in Book II for more on container gardening.)

If you're growing annual climbers, be sure to plant seeds where the flowers will have serious support nearby. Good choices are planting areas near a fence, lattice, post, pillar, or arbor. Many of these climbers twine themselves around the support, but you may need to give some stems guidance by using soft ties. Run the ties through U-shaped staples in posts, pillars, or fence boards.

Pruning and pinching

Pinching and pruning annuals are far simpler tasks than similar care for more permanent plants, such as perennials and shrubs. Still, the jobs clearly have their rewards. *Pinching* refers to removal of soft tip growth, usually with the thumb and forefinger. It encourages plants to become bushy and full rather than rangy and tall. A side effect of pinching is that plants develop uniform growth and plenty of buds — although pinching tends to postpone the flowers a bit if you remove their buds.

Pinch plants when they're young — before they develop long stems. Remove the tip growth by pinching above a set of leaves. To promote good overall shape, pinch both upright and side stems (as shown in Figure 3-2). When you have a mass of plants in the bed, pinch back the tallest ones so that they don't shoot up past their neighbors. Good candidates for pinching include petunias, snapdragons, impatiens, chrysanthemums, marguerites, and geraniums. Avoid pinching plants that send up strong central shoots with flowers at the tip, such as stock and celosia. These flowers don't branch well anyway, so you don't want to pinch off all the flower buds.

Pruning is the process of cutting back plants to keep them within the boundaries that you've set and to promote bushier growth. Annuals rarely need the heavy-duty pruning that perennials and shrubs demand. Trim rangy, floppy, or sprawling stems as often as necessary to keep them under control. Make cuts just above a set of leaves or side shoot to promote both bushiness and new buds. After the first round of blooms, especially if you haven't deadheaded, you can try giving plants an overall trimming to encourage a new round of blooms. So which annuals require serious pruning? You'll probably need to worry only about globe amaranthus, four o'clocks, felicia, and some types of petunia, especially cascading or trailing varieties that become very leggy.

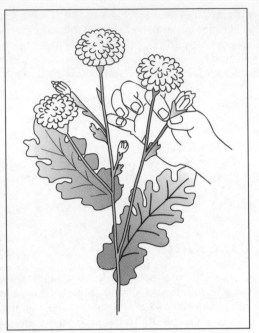

Figure 3-2:
Pinching or
pruning off
side shoots
promotes a
fuller, more
compact
plant.

Mulching miracles

A *mulch* is simply a soil cover. Mulching an annual garden cuts down on the amount of water needed and helps control weeds. The principle is simple: The soil is cooled and protected by the application of a top layer of some type of material. As long as the material is attractive, you'll have a neat-looking garden, to boot. A layer of mulch also helps hide drip irrigation tubes. (For more information on drip irrigation, turn to Chapter 4 in Book I.)

Your mulching schedule really depends on the type of annuals you grow and when you plant them:

- **Cool-season annuals planted in early spring:** Wait to mulch until after the soil starts to warm and the plants need regular water. As the days heat up, mulch keeps the plants cooler, helping them thrive and bloom longer into hot weather.

- **Cool-season annuals planted in late summer or early fall:** Spread the mulch right after planting. When the weather starts to cool, rake off or remove the mulch so that the soil can warm. Removing the mulch prolongs the bloom longer into the winter. If you really want to go all-out and try to get some of your hardier annuals through the winter so that they bloom very early the following spring, mulch again after the ground starts to freeze. This mulching schedule helps prevent the soil from repeated freezing and thawing, which can literally rip some plants right out of the ground.

✔ **Warm-season annuals planted in spring:** Keep the ground clear if you're planting really early — the more heat the better. Otherwise, mulch at planting time.

Try this trio of quick and easy steps for mulching the annuals in your garden:

1. **Select a mulch material.**

2. **Spread your mulch material around annuals, leaving a few inches of bare earth around the base of each plant.**

   This technique provides a little reservoir for water and keeps plant stems from rotting or becoming diseased. In general, annuals like a 2- to 3-inch layer of mulch; the thicker the mulch, the fewer weeds. Don't go beyond 3 inches, however; mulching too heavily could cause plants to suffocate. If you use a layer of newspapers or landscape fabric first, you'll need less mulch on top — just enough to cover.

3. **Make periodic inspections to see that mulch stays put.**

   This soil covering is easily displaced by any number of things. Keep extra mulch on hand so that you can always add mulch when and where you need it.

Acting as your garden's housekeeper

Here are a few more quick tasks to help you keep your annual garden looking its best.

✔ **Floral management:** For cut flowers, cut stems early in the morning and immediately immerse them in water.

✔ **Replanting:** You may have to replant two to three times during the seasons from spring into fall, especially if you live in a mild climate with a long growing period. If you start early with spring annuals, chances are that the garden will be on its way out by midsummer. At this point, remove tired plants and replant with fresh new annuals that will bloom into late summer and early fall. If you're lucky enough to have a long growing season (and have the energy for it), you may want to replant three times — in early spring, early summer, and fall. And in really warm regions, you can even enjoy a winter annual garden. Local nurseries usually carry plants appropriate for your seasons.

✔ **Wrapping up:** Tidy up your garden as the active growing season winds down. After you collect any seeds, pull up faded plants and then rake and clean up the bed. If anything looks diseased or shows pest damage, bag it and dispose of it properly — don't compost it. ***Note:*** Some plants grown as annuals, such as pansy and primrose, are actually tender perennials. If you leave such plants in place in a protected location, they may grow and flower for several seasons.

Outsmarting Pests and Diseases

Annuals are often called the racehorses of flowers. Few other plants grow so fast and provide so much color so quickly. But that speed can be both a blessing and a curse when dealing with insects and diseases:

- ✔ **The blessing:** Many annuals grow so fast that they can actually out-distance problems before the problems really get a chance to set in. Vigorous, healthy growth, the modus operandi of annuals, is in itself one of the best ways to fend off many pests. Healthy annuals are less susceptible to insects and diseases.

- ✔ **The curse:** The same fast growth that can outpace some pests is particularly attractive to others. Aphids, for example, are very fond of young, tender growth. Also, the fact that annuals are often grown in masses of just one kind creates an ideal breeding ground for pests drawn to that particular food source. And if the pests get out of hand, they can ruin the entire bed.

But fear not. If you choose adaptable annuals (those that can grow in a variety of conditions and climates), care for them properly, and observe them carefully, few problems will actually send you crying to your neighborhood nursery.

When bad bugs happen to nice gardens

Actually, bugs are neither bad nor good. They just do what they're programmed to do: eat, grow, and reproduce. The only problem comes in when bugs and gardeners want to enjoy the same flowers. A little conflict of interest, you might say! A bug becomes a pest only if it meets both these criteria:

- ✔ It wants to eat what you're trying to grow.
- ✔ The damage it causes makes the plant look unsightly and decline in health.

An errant grasshopper may not be cause for concern, but if that same grasshopper brings along his brothers, sisters, and cousins to join in on the zinnia feast at your expense, he becomes a pest. When you start seeing a number of the same type of insects in your garden, and you notice that their activity is focused on certain plants, you need to act quickly and decisively.

When insects snack on your annuals

Here are the most common insect pests that are likely to infest your annuals (Chapter 7 in Book I tells you how to control them):

- **Aphids:** These tiny, pear-shaped pests congregate on new growth and flower buds, sucking plant sap with their needlelike noses, and leaving a sticky sap behind that may turn black with sooty mold. Heavy infestations can cause distorted growth and weaken plants. Vinca and cosmos are two annuals that aphids commonly attack.

- **Geranium budworms:** These frustrating pests (shown in Figure 3-3) love geraniums, nicotiana, ageratum, and petunias. The small caterpillars bore into flower buds and eat the flowers before they open, or they simply feed on open blooms. The result is no flowers, only leaves. To confirm the presence of these heartless monsters, look for small holes in geranium blossoms or the tiny black droppings that the caterpillars leave behind. You may also see the worms on the flowers.

Figure 3-3:
Geranium budworms like to feast on petunias as well as geraniums.

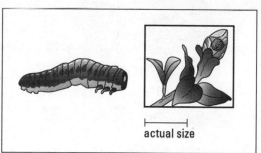

actual size

- **Japanese beetles:** Especially troublesome east of the Mississippi River, these ½-inch copper and metallic green pests feed on both flowers and foliage, often skeletonizing leaves. They particularly love zinnias and marigolds.

- **Cutworms:** These ½-inch-long, grayish caterpillars emerge during spring and early summer nights to eat young seedling stems, causing them to fall over like small timbers. They also move on to older plants and feed on leaves and flowers.

- **Snails and slugs:** These soft-bodied mollusks feed on tender leaves and flowers during the cool of the night or during rainy weather. Snails have shells; slugs don't. Both proliferate in damp areas, hiding under boards, mulch, and other garden debris.

- **Spider mites:** You can barely see these tiny arachnids without a magnifying glass, but if the population gets big enough, you can see their fine webbing beneath the leaves. As they suck plant juices, the leaves become yellowish, with silvery stippling or sheen. If things get really bad, the plant may start dropping leaves. Mites are most common in hot, dry summer climates and on dusty plants. Marigolds and columbines are commonly infested.

- **Thrips:** Another nearly invisible troublemaker (see Figure 3-4), thrips feed on flower petals, causing them to be discolored and the buds to be deformed as they open. Thrips also feed on leaves, giving the foliage a deformed and stippled look. (You can distinguish thrips from spider mites by the small fecal pellets that thrips leave behind.) Impatiens and many other annuals can become thrip targets.

✔ **Whiteflies:** Looking like small white gnats, whiteflies suck plant juices and can proliferate in warm climates and greenhouses. They tend to congregate on the undersides of leaves.

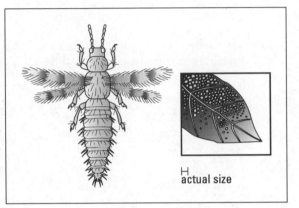

Figure 3-4:
Thrips
damage
flower
petals and
leaves.

actual size

When the flower bed becomes a sick bed

Only a few diseases are really troublesome for annual flowers, and you can prevent or at least reduce in severity most of them by observing good cultural practices, planting resistant varieties, or choosing another plant if you know that a certain disease is a problem in your area.

When summer oil lies dormant

Summer oil is a highly refined pesticide that works well for annuals. The words *highly refined,* in this case, mean that the sulfur and other components of the oil that damage the plant are removed. It is relatively nontoxic and short-lived. When you spray summer oil on a plant, it smothers insect pests and their eggs. Use it to control aphids, mites, thrips, and certain caterpillars.

Don't confuse summer oil with dormant oil. You apply *dormant oil* to leafless trees and shrubs during winter; using it on your annuals will fry them. Double-check the product label to make sure that you can use the oil on annual flowers during the growing season. Then follow the mixing instructions carefully. Water the plants before and after applying summer oil, and to avoid damaging plant leaves, don't spray if temperatures are likely to rise above 85°F (29°C).

Chemical warfare

Chemical fungicides are among the nastiest pesticides. They can contain some very toxic compounds that linger in the environment for a long time. If you can, try not to use them. If, however, a prized planting comes up with a really stubborn disease, you may feel that you have no other choice. Before you spray, make sure to identify the disease properly. Enlist the help of a local nursery or cooperative extension specialist. Then, use a product specifically labeled for that disease occurring on the plants that you're growing. Follow the label instructions exactly.

Following are some cultural practices that can help prevent plant diseases:

- ✔ **Remove infected plants.** After you notice a plant with a problem, give it the yank.

- ✔ **Avoid overhead watering.** Or at least water early in the morning so that plants have a chance to dry off before nightfall. Using drip irrigation or watering in furrows (as described in Chapter 4 in Book I) also helps keep foliage dry. Overhead watering can ruin many flowers — particularly petunias and geraniums — washing out their color or making them look like they've melted.

- ✔ **Space plants properly.** Planting annuals too close together reduces air circulation between plants, creating conditions that favor disease.

- ✔ **Prepare the soil.** Add organic matter to increase drainage and aeration, which helps sidestep many soilborne diseases.

- ✔ **Keep your garden clean and tidy.** Many diseases spread on plant debris, so rake up fallen leaves and remove dead plants. Simply removing diseased leaves can slow the spread of some organisms.

- ✔ **Rotate plants.** Putting the same annuals in the same beds year after year creates a breeding ground for disease. Plant something new.

Here are some tips on how to prevent, identify, and — if possible — treat some common diseases of annual flowers:

- ✔ **Botrytis blight:** Also called *gray mold,* this fungal disease *overwinters* (survives in the soil or on plant debris through the winter to reinfect the plant again in spring) on plant debris and is common on petunias and ageratum, among others. It's most notable as gray fuzz forming on old flowers, turning them to moldy mush, but it can also discolor or spot foliage. Botrytis blight is most troublesome on older plant parts and in cool, humid weather. To discourage this disease, make sure that plants are properly spaced and avoid overhead watering. Remove and destroy any infected plant parts, and give your garden a good cleaning at the end of each growing season.

✔ **Damping off:** This fungus attacks the base of seedling stems, causing them to wilt and fall over (see Figure 3-5). The best way to prevent the disease is to plant seeds in sterile potting soil and avoid overwatering. After the disease gets a foothold, it's hard to stop.

✔ **Powdery mildew:** This fungus coats leaves and flowers with a white powder. Most common when days are warm but nights are cool, it's particularly troublesome on zinnias, dahlias, begonias, and cosmos. Control is difficult, but resistant varieties of those flowers are available. The disease also becomes less of a problem as the weather changes, so if you keep young plants growing vigorously, they may grow out of it. Neem oil (see Chapter 7 in Book I) also may help.

✔ **Rust:** This fungal disease is easy to identify: It forms rust-colored pustules on the undersides of plant leaves. Gradually, the upper sides of the leaves turn yellow, and the whole plant begins to decline. Snapdragons and hollyhocks are common hosts. To avoid rust, plant resistant varieties. Also, space plants to allow good air circulation, keep the garden clean, and avoid overhead watering. Destroy infected plants.

✔ **Root rot:** Several soilborne fungi cause plants to suddenly wilt and die, regardless of whether the soil is moist. Vinca is notorious for checking out this way. The best way to prevent root rot is to prepare the soil properly before planting and make sure that you aren't overwatering. Otherwise, all you can do is remove the dead plants.

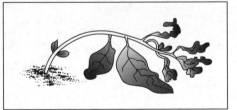

Figure 3-5:
Damping off can be hard to control.

Chapter 4

Singing the Annual Alphabet Song

· ·

How many different annuals are available? Add up all the basic kinds sold as nursery seedlings, all the new improved varieties and strains, all the rarities marketed by countless seed catalogs, and the total is . . . well, a lot. This chapter tells you about hundreds of annuals (taking into account the many varieties and strains). If you want to plant one of the top ten — at least, our arbitrary grouping of the top ten — most popular and reliable annuals, read the sidebars interspersed throughout this chapter.

African Daisy (Arctotis)

Plant African daisy seeds randomly, directly in the ground, and in full sun, for a multicolored spring or summer carpet of cheerful 3-inch-wide daisies in bright orange, red, yellow, white, pink, and bicolors. Arctotis hybrids, the most available types of this plant, grow up to 18 inches tall and produce beautiful cut flowers, although they last only a few days after cutting. In cold-winter climates, plant in the spring, after any danger of frost; in mild-winter climates, plant in the fall. African daisies don't withstand high heat and humidity. They bloom best in areas with cool nights, particularly in coastal climates. Remove faded flowers to prolong the bloom season.

African Daisy (Dimorphotheca Sinuata)

The *Dimorphotheca sinuata* African daisy, compared with the *Arctotis* African daisy, has smaller flowers and lower, more spreading plants — 12 inches tall and 18 inches wide. Bright, dark-centered flowers in shades of orange, pink, red, and white make a cheerful show in late winter in mild climates, and in summer elsewhere. Use the plants for a carpetlike effect, as a border, or to fill in between ground covers. Sow these seeds directly in the ground in full sun. Plant in early spring in cold-winter climates, or in fall in mild-winter climates. African daisies come back from year to year if conditions suit them.

Ageratum, or Floss Flower (Ageratum Houstonianum)

The appeal of ageratum is its blueness. The well-mannered plants are mostly 6 to 12 inches tall. In summer, the puffy flowers come in some of the garden's truest shades of blue. Use ageratum in containers (see Chapter 3 in Book II for more on container gardening) or as an edging for borders. Set out transplants in spring, when temperatures begin to warm up and the danger of frost has passed. Provide full sun unless you live in a hot-summer climate, where part shade is best. Nursery plants are often sold in bloom. After you plant them, pinch back the flowers to encourage bushy growth. Make a special effort to cut off faded flowers, especially the white ones, which turn an unsightly brown.

Aster, or China Aster (Callistephus Chinensis)

Though not easy to grow, asters are long-stemmed, long-lasting, and come in shades of purple, rose, and pink. Plant asters in full sun in the spring, after any danger of frost. Nursery transplants are widely sold but not easy to grow; you may do just as well sowing seeds directly in the ground and then thinning seedlings to 6 to 12 inches. You'll have better luck with asters if you improve the soil with plenty of additional organic matter. Stake tall varieties to keep flowers from flopping over. Asters are disease-prone; pull out stunted, wilted, or yellowed plants. To keep diseases from spreading, don't plant asters in the same spot two years in a row.

Baby Blue Eyes (Nemophila Menziesii)

These delicate plants have sky blue flowers with pale centers that look like little bells and trail low to the ground. Sow seeds directly in the ground in full sun or part shade. Plant in early spring in cold-winter climates; in fall in mild-winter areas. Baby blue eyes prefer a soil that's constantly moist. Under favorable conditions, the plants reseed themselves and come back yearly.

Baby's Breath (Gypsophila Elegans)

Tiny flowers in midsummer seem to form white, pink, or red clouds on upright plants up to 18 inches tall. Sow seeds directly in the ground in a sunny spot. Plant in spring, after any danger of frost. Keep the soil on the dry side. These plants live only six weeks or so; for a longer bloom season, stagger seed sowings over several months. To dry cut flowers, hang them upside down in a cool, dry place.

Bedding Begonia, or Wax Begonia (Begonia Semperflorens)

Crisp, glossy, and succulent, bedding begonias have small but profuse flowers, in shades of pink, red, and white, that last from late spring through summer. Begonia leaves can be colorful, too, with dark bronzy tones and bright greens. These easy-to-grow, very dependable plants grow 6 to 12 inches tall. Use them to edge borders, as mass plantings in beds, or in containers. Set out transplants in full sun in mild-summer climates, or in part shade in hot-summer climates. Plant in spring, after the danger of frost.

Bells of Ireland (Moluccella Laevis)

Spikes of pale green, bell-like blooms make this plant a standout in borders or bouquets. These Irish beauties grow 18 to 36 inches tall, and their cut flowers work well fresh or dried. Sow seeds directly in the ground in full sun or light shade. Plant in early spring in cold-winter climates, or in fall in mild-winter areas. Your chances for successful sprouting improve if you chill these seeds in the refrigerator for a week or two before sowing them.

Blanket Flower (Gaillardia Pulchella)

Blanket flower is another sun-loving, easy-to-grow, warm-hued daisy. Its summer flowers of orange, red, yellow, and bicolors are excellent for cutting. Growing up to 24 inches tall, these plants are at home in containers, borders, or mixed wildflower plantings. Sow seeds directly in the ground in full sun. Plant them in the spring after any danger of frost. Keep the soil on the dry side after germination and encourage a long bloom season by removing faded flowers.

Calendula, or Pot Marigold (Calendula Officinalis)

Reliable and easy-to-grow, these big (2 to 4 inches across) daisylike flowers, are typically orange or yellow but are also available in cream and white shades. Use these plants, which grow 12 to 30 inches tall, in containers, in borders, or massed in beds. Calendulas are among the stalwarts of winter-spring gardens in mild climates. In cold-winter climates, calendulas bloom best in the spring and early summer. Plant transplants in full sun, spaced about 12 inches apart. In cold-winter climates, plant in early spring; in mild-winter climates, plant in the fall. Calendulas thrive in cool weather. Watch for mildew under less than favorable conditions, and bait for snails and slugs. Remove flowers as soon as they start to fade.

California Poppy (Eschscholzia Californica)

These 8- to 24-inch, easygoing, sometimes unpredictable, and fun-to-grow plants work well in a natural-style border or as fill-in among ground covers. Seed companies offer varieties and strains in many colors. Sow seeds directly in the ground in full sun. In cold-winter climates, plant in early spring, as soon as the ground is soft enough for digging. In mild-winter climates, plant in fall. California poppies prefer soil that drains very well and may be on the dry side. Don't try transplanting seedlings; their deep, brittle taproots won't appreciate it. Poppies form unattractive dry mounds after they finish blooming. Be prepared to get rid of them. In mild climates, plants can reseed themselves and come back year after year. In colder regions, cut off the seedhead, and save the seeds in a cool, dry place until next year.

Calliopsis, or Annual Coreopsis (Coreopsis Tinctoria)

This scaled-down member of the sunflower family (up to 24 inches tall) has yellow, orange, and red flowers, 2 to 3 inches in diameter, that bloom freely. Plant calliopsis in masses in beds and borders, or combine them with wildflowers in naturalized settings. The flowers are also great for cutting. Check seed catalogs for dwarf and double-flowered varieties, as well. Sow seeds directly in the ground in full sun. Plant in early spring, as soon as you can dig the ground. Thin seedlings to stand 6 inches apart and keep the soil on the dry side after seedlings are up. Stake taller varieties.

Canary Creeper (Tropaeolum Peregrinum)

Canary creeper is a fast-growing, climbing vine that can reach 15 feet in one season. Plant this annual near a fence or trellis, or provide stakes for support. Sow seeds directly in the ground in full sun or part shade after any danger of frost. Canary creeper does best in cool summer climates. Keep roots cool with an insulating mulch of organic matter.

Candytuft (Iberis Umbellata)

Edging borders is candytuft's specialty. Its plants are compact and low to the ground, less than 12 inches tall. In summer, its white flowers resemble familiar sweet alyssum and perennial candytuft *(Iberis sempervirens)*. Look for varieties of annual candytuft in pink and other pastel shades, as well. Sow the seeds of this plant directly in the ground in full sun or, where summers are hot, in part shade. Plant in early spring in cold-winter climates, or in fall or early spring in mild-winter areas. If your candytuft plants become rangy, shear the top growth like a hedge and wait for new flowers.

Canterbury Bells (Campanula Medium)

Impressive enough to hold their own at the back of a border, these medium-sized plants (up to 30 inches tall) bear abundant bell-shaped flowers up to 2 inches long. The prized color for these flowers is deep blue, but you can also find mixes in pink, lavender, and white. The flowers are handsome when cut and brought indoors. Technically, Canterbury bells are biennials. But you can get blooms within a year by setting out nursery transplants in early spring if you live in a cold-winter climate, or in fall if your winters are mild. Plant seedlings in soil enriched with organic matter and in part shade in hot-summer areas, or in full sun where it's cool. Be sure to stake these plants.

Carnation (Dianthus)

Border carnations, bushier and more compact than the cut flowers you see at the florist's, are easy to grow and have a spicy, clovelike fragrance. The flowers of border carnations are typically about 2 inches wide and come mainly in red, pink, and white. Set out transplants in full sun in springtime, after any danger of frost. Stake taller varieties of this plant. Remove faded flowers to prolong blooming. Most carnations do better in cooler climates, although some varieties are developed for heat resistance.

Chinese Forget-Me-Not (Cynoglossum Amabile)

Think of the Chinese forget-me-not as an almost-wildflower. It resembles the familiar forget-me-not, but its flowers are a bit larger. The plant is easy to grow from seed, spreads and sprawls like a weed, and reseeds to return the next year if conditions suit it. The tiny but abundant skyblue or deep blue flowers are striking in spring borders with bulbs. Plants grow up to 18 inches tall. In early spring (or fall, in mild-winter climates), sow this plant's seeds directly in the ground. Chinese forget-me-nots prefer to be in full sun. The seeds of this plant are sticky and can attach themselves to clothing and pets.

Chinese Lantern (Physalis Alkekengi)

Grow this plant to witness the bright orange, papery 2-inch "lanterns" (actually fruits) that appear in late summer. Use these Chinese lanterns to make striking arrangements all winter. Plants grow up to 2 feet tall. In spring, after the danger of frost passes, sow these seeds directly in the ground in full sun. To use this plant for dried arrangements, wait until the lanterns turn color and the plants start to dry up. Pull up the entire plant by its roots and hang it upside-down in a cool, dry spot.

Chrysanthemums, Annual (Chrysanthemum)

The chrysanthemums of football season are actually perennials, but you can find many attractive chrysanthemums that are true annuals and bloom earlier in the year, including feverfew, painted daisy or tricolor daisy, and miniature Marguerite (all mostly white and yellow). Sow chrysanthemum seeds directly in the ground in full sun as soon as you can work the ground. Thin seedlings to stand 12 inches apart. You also can set out transplants in spring, or in fall, if available, in mild-winter climates. These daisies do best in cooler climates. With luck, these plants may reseed themselves and come back yearly.

Cigar Plant, or Firecracker Plant (Cuphea Ignea)

This plant's flowers are tubular, about ¾-inch long, and bright red with a black ring (the "cigar's" ashes?) at one end. The plants themselves grow about a foot tall. Set out transplants in full sun or part shade in the spring, when the weather and soil have warmed and the danger of frost has passed. Grow this plant as a curiosity or conversation piece in a pot or hanging basket, or at the front of a border.

Clarkia, or Godetia (Clarkia)

Clarkia produces cheerful, abundant, good-for-cutting flowers in cool climates early in the season, when they're most welcome. Farewell-to-spring (Clarkia amoena) is a favorite type that comes in low- or tall-growing forms and has satiny, 2-inch blooms of mostly red, pink, and white. Sow clarkia seeds directly in the ground in full sun. Plant in early spring if you live in a cold-winter climate, or in fall if you live in a mild climate, such as its native California. Clarkia blooms in spring and early summer and doesn't tolerate hot weather. Plant it in a sunny mixed border or wildflower garden.

Coleus

Though the flowers are incidental, at best, this plant has very colorful leaves. Grow coleus for a tropical effect in pots and borders — indoors, too. These plants grow quickly, up to 24 inches. Set out transplants in spring, after any danger of frost. Plant in light shade. To encourage bushy growth, pinch back tips — and flowers if you notice them. At the end of the season, bring plants indoors before frost strikes, and keep them in a sunny window all winter.

Cornflower, or Bachelor's Button (Centaurea Cyanus)

These deep blue flowers are great in bouquets and boutonnieres. The plants, however, are on the homely side. Tall and gawky (up to 36 inches), cornflower is best planted at the back of a border, where lower-growing annuals camouflage it. Sow seeds in full sun. If you live in a cold-winter climate, plant in early spring. If your winters are mild, plant in fall or early spring. Stake tall varieties. Remove old flowers to prolong bloom, and when flowering slows down and growth looks ragged, pull out the whole plant.

Cosmos (Cosmos Bipinnatus)

Easy-to-grow, abundant, one- to two-inch daisylike flowers in pink, purple, and white appear from late spring through summer with a lacy elegance. Nice for cutting, cosmos grows quickly to 4 feet or more; dwarf types grow half as high. Use cosmos at the back of borders; dwarfs are good for edging or in containers. Set out transplants in full sun in spring, after any danger of frost, or sow seeds directly in the ground in full sun. Stake taller varieties and remove flowers as they fade.

Creeping Zinnia (Santvitalia Procumbens)

With its bright yellow or orange flowers, creeping zinnia — not actually a zinnia at all — is a fine plant to use as ground cover or in containers. It only grows 8 inches tall and may spread a foot and a half. Sow seeds in full sun directly in the ground after the soil and air have warmed up. These plants thrive in hot weather. Just make sure that the soil never dries out.

Dahlberg Daisy, or Golden Fleece (Dyssodia Tenuiloba)

This plant's small (½ inch) but profuse, bright daisies cover dark green, sprawling plants no taller than 12 inches. In bloom for most of summer and fall, Dahlberg daisy is a great choice for a pot or hanging basket, or as a ground cover. In cold-winter climates, set out seedlings in full sun in spring, after any danger of frost. In mild-winter climates, plant in the fall, late winter, or early spring. Remove dead flowers to encourage a long bloom season. In mild climates, these plants may live through winter like a perennial, but get rid of them if growth becomes scraggly.

Dusty Miller (Senecio Cineraria)

Several plants go by the name dusty miller. This particular one is the annual grown for its handsome silvery gray leaves — its yellow flowers are fairly worthless in comparison. These plants grow about a foot tall and become taller and almost permanent in mild-winter climates. Use them to edge borders or in containers as a contrast with bright flowers, such as geraniums and petunias. Plant transplants in spring, after any danger of frost, in full sun, 8 inches apart. Cut off flowers as soon as you see them.

If you can't find a dusty miller called *Senecio cineraria,* look for it as *Cineraria maritima.* Or look for *Centaurea cineraria,* a related annual that's also called dusty miller.

Felicia, or Blue Marguerite (Felicia Amelloides)

Another small but profuse producer of daisylike flowers, felicia's blooms are from 1 to 3 inches wide and bright blue with yellow centers. The plants form dense mounds 18 inches tall, up to 5 feet wide. Use these plants in borders or containers. Felicia is a perennial in mild climates. Kingfisher daisy *(Felicia bergeriana)* is smaller and more compact, only 6 to 8 inches tall. Set out transplants in spring in cold-winter climates, or in fall where winters are mild. Plant in full sun. Kingfisher daisy is easy to grow from seeds sown directly in the ground. Cut back felicia for bushier plants and more abundant blooms. Pinch off the tips of young plants to encourage branching, and cut off dead flowers to prolong the bloom season.

Dilly dahlias

Actually tender perennials, dwarf or bedding dahlias are sold as annuals. These plants grow about 12 to 15 inches tall, with flowers 2 or 3 inches across. Colors include orange, pink, purple, red, white, and yellow. They have a long bloom season (usually from early summer until frost), an abundance of bloom, and handsome, dark green foliage. And they're easy to grow.

Dwarf dahlias are sold as nursery transplants. Set them out in full sun or part shade in the spring after frost danger; space plants 12 inches apart. For vigorous growth, dwarf dahlias need lots of water and fertilizer. To encourage bushy growth, pinch stem tips of young plants. Watch for snails, earwigs, Japanese beetles, and spider mites.

Flax (Linum Grandiflorum)

Color as quick and easy as from a wildflower is what you can expect from flax. Spring and summer bring brilliant red flowers (white varieties, too) that are 1 to 2 inches wide. Plants grow up to 30 inches tall, but dwarf varieties are about half that size. Sow flax seeds directly in the ground in full sun. Plant in early spring in cold-winter climates; plant in fall if your winters are mild. Use flax to cover those bare spaces between spring bulbs.

Forget-Me-Not (Myosotis Sylvatica)

Forget-me-nots are prized for producing delicate blue springtime flowers in shady spots. The plants are low and spreading, about 6 to 12 inches tall. Grow them under trees and shrubs, combined with yellow tulips or daffodils, for a classic look. Set out transplants or sow seeds directly in the ground in spring in cold climates, or in fall where winters are mild. Provide cool, moist conditions and light shade. Incorporate plenty of organic matter into the planting bed. Hot, dry weather makes life tough for forget-me-nots; but under the right conditions, they may reseed and bloom again in fall. In particularly favorable situations, they can reseed themselves permanently.

Four O'Clock (Mirabilis Jalapa)

Easy to grow in a variety of situations, these fragrant, 2-inch-long flowers in shades of pink, red, white, and yellow are named for their propensity to open in midafternoon each day. The plants themselves are rangy, from 2 to 4 feet tall. Use four o'clocks as big accent plants in beds and border. Sow seeds directly in the soil in full sun. Plant them in spring, after any danger of frost. The plants may reseed and can live through winter, becoming a perennial in mild climates. From summer through fall, its flowers attract hummingbirds.

All parts of this plant are poisonous. Choose another annual if you have young children or curious pets.

Foxglove (Digitalis Purpurea)

Foxgloves are the towers of flowers you see at the back of old-fashioned borders. The plants grow up to 6 feet tall (although dwarf varieties are also available). Funnel-shaped flowers, like the fingers of a glove, come in many colors, including pink, purple, red, white, and yellow. Foxglove is a biennial, but nursery plants set out in spring bloom in spring and summer. For blooms the first year, set out transplants in a sunny or partly shady spot in spring (or fall, in mild-winter climates). You can also sow seeds directly in the ground in early spring; most varieties of foxglove will bloom the following spring. Make sure that the soil is always moist. Watch for insects, and put out bait in snail-prone areas. After the first bloom, cut off the main spike to encourage flowers from side shoots.

Foxglove seeds are poisonous if eaten.

Gilia

These easy-to-grow wildflowers have small, abundant blooms in the summer. Blue thimble flower *(Gilia capitata)*, with blooms resembling pincushions, grows 3 feet and taller. Bird's eyes *(Gilia tricolor)*, with pale purplish flowers, grow only to 2 feet. Use any type of gilia in a border or wildflower garden. In spring, after any danger of frost, sow gilia seeds directly in the ground in full sun. Cool-summer climates are best for gilia. Taller plants may need staking. Don't let the shallow roots dry out.

Globe Amaranth (Gomphrena)

The little, papery, round blossoms of globe amaranth are great for cutting and drying. The low, mounding varieties make a nice border edging. *Gomphrena globosa*, which produces white, red, or purplish flowers in summer and fall, grows from 6 to 24 inches tall, depending on the variety. Plant in full sun in spring, after any danger of frost. Set out transplants 6 to 12 inches apart or sow seeds directly in the ground. To dry the flowers, cut them when they're fully mature and hang them upside down in a shady spot; they retain their shape and color through winter.

Jumpin' geraniums

The annual flower that most people call a geranium is, botanically speaking, a *Pelargonium*. This information is important to know because a very different plant uses *Geranium* as its botanical name. Look for the word *Pelargonium* to be sure that the plant you're buying is the annual described here, and chalk the whole mess up to another case where botanical names create more confusion than they clear up. Geraniums flourish worldwide and are universal favorites.

They're great for beginners. Geraniums are actually perennials and can survive for years in mild climates. Set out geraniums in the spring. Provide full sun or part shade in hot climates. Try to plant in soil with fast drainage. Geraniums are very responsive to pinching. For bushy growth, pinch out tips of young growth to force side branching. Remove dead flowers. Watch for budworm, aphids, spider mites, and whiteflies.

Heliotrope (Heliotropium Arborescens)

This fragrant plant's appearance is distinctive: dark green leaves with prominent veins and regal, deep blue flowers (white varieties, too). Use these 8- to 24-inch tall plants as accents in borders, or plant them in containers so that you can move the fragrance near a sitting area. Set out heliotrope transplants in full sun or part shade in the spring, when warm temperatures have arrived and the danger of frost has passed. Provide well-drained soil enriched with plenty of organic matter.

Hollyhock (Alcea Rosea)

With its tall spikes of pink, red, and white blooms, hollyhocks seem able to grow anywhere, and they reseed themselves year after year. Newer varieties are more compact — 4 or 5 feet, compared to your grandma's 9-footers. Annual strains can bloom the first year from seed. (Original hollyhocks are biennials and don't bloom until their second year.) Set out transplants in full sun in spring after warm weather has arrived or sow seeds directly in the ground; they may not bloom until the following year. Make sure that plants get plenty of water. Stake tall plants that start to tip. Watch for Japanese beetles and rust.

Hyacinth Bean (Dolichos Lablab)

This attractive, fast-growing vine with purplish-green leaves and little purple or white flowers is useful for a quick screen or training up a wall or fence. Both the flowers and the bean pods (when young) are edible. Sow the seeds in full sun or part shade in spring, after any danger of frost.

Iceland Poppy (Papaver Nudicaule)

Iceland poppy is truly an outstanding late-winter and early-spring performer in mild climates. Glistening cup-shaped flowers, up to 3 or 4 inches wide, sit atop elegant, thin stems 1 to 2 feet long; color range is brilliant, including orange, pink, yellow, and white. In cold climates, Iceland poppy has a shorter bloom season but may live on as a perennial. In mild-winter climates, set out transplants in full sun in fall or late winter. In cold-winter climates, set out transplants in early spring as soon as the ground can be worked. Plants do best in cool weather. Make sure that soil stays moist. Diligently remove dead flowers. Rains may batter down long-stemmed flowers.

Something shady about being impatiens

Impatiens are easy to grow, bloom better than just about anything else in shady conditions, hardly ever run into problems, stay compact, and have attractive foliage. You can grow impatiens from seeds or cuttings, but nursery transplants are the easiest. Plant impatiens in spring, after frost danger, when the weather has begun to warm up. Plant in part shade, or even full shade if that's all you have. In cool coastal climates, impatiens can take a great deal of sun. Impatiens have a remarkable ability to bounce back from drying out. Withered plants often bounce back if you provide them with a good soaking. Don't worry about removing faded flowers, but if plants get leggy late in the season, cut stems back halfway to force new growth.

Kale, or Ornamental Cabbage (Brassica Oleracea)

Grow these plants for their striking multicolored foliage that emerges early in the season. A relative of common kale and cabbage, this ornamental annual is edible. Plants grow 12 to 18 inches tall and look great massed in a bed or edging a border. They're also striking in containers: Grow a single plant in an 8-inch pot or several in a larger pot. Set out transplants in early spring in cold-winter climates, or in fall or late winter where winters are mild. Plant in full sun, spacing the plants 12 to 18 inches apart. Ensure that the soil stays constantly moist and watch for caterpillars.

Kochia, or Burning Bush (Kochia Scoparia)

Like kale, kochia is another annual with incidental flowers and big-time foliage. Kochia looks like a little cypress tree (up to 36 inches tall) with bushy, light green leaves that turn bright red in the fall. Use it as a temporary hedge for a border, as an accent, or in containers with low-growing flowers. Set out transplants in full sun in spring, after any danger of frost. Space plants 18 to 24 inches apart (8 inches for a hedge) or sow seeds directly in the ground at the same intervals. You can shear these shaggy plants into almost any shape you want.

Larkspur (Consolida Ambigua)

Larkspur plants grow up to 2 feet tall and make wonderful, intense blue additions to beds and borders. Plant taller types in the back and dwarfs in front. Flowers also come in white and shades of purple and pink — all are great for cutting. Sow seeds directly in the ground in sun or part shade. Larkspurs definitely perform best where summers are cool. Make sure that the soil stays moist constantly. Stake taller varieties and remove dead flowers to prolong the bloom season.

Larkspur plants are poisonous if eaten.

Lavatera, or Tree Mallow (Lavatera Trimestris)

Often referred to as "tree mallow," lavatera isn't exactly tree size, but it can grow to 6 feet from seeds sown in spring. White, pink, and red flowers that bloom from midsummer into fall resemble hibiscus. Use tall lavatera as a background plant; dwarf varieties are available if you want to bring these lovely flowers to the fore. Sow seeds directly in the ground in full sun in early spring; sow in fall where winters are mild for blooms in winter and spring. Thin seedlings to stand 24 inches apart. Moist, cool summers are best for this plant. Remove dead flowers and stake tall varieties.

Linaria, or Toadflax (Linaria)

These easy-to-grow little plants don't amount to much individually, but sown close together, they put on quite a show. Red, pink, blue, purple, yellow, cream, and bicolor flowers look like miniature snapdragons. Bloom time is early summer to fall; in mild-winter climates, flowering can start in winter and continue through spring. Plants typically grow 6 to 12 inches tall — some varieties are twice that size. Sow seeds directly in the ground in sun or part shade. In cold-winter climates, plant in early spring, as soon as you can work the ground. In mild climates, sow seeds in fall for winter bloom. Thin seedlings to stand no more than 6 inches apart. Cool weather provides the best blooms. Sow seeds thickly for peak performance.

Lisianthus (Eustoma Grandiflorum)

Silky blue, pink, purple, or white flowers can reach 3 inches in diameter. The plants grow 18 to 24 inches tall. Use lisianthus in borders, pots, or cutting gardens. Set out transplants in full sun or light shade in spring after any danger of frost. Be sure to take some lisianthus indoors as long-lasting cut flowers, and conscientiously cut off faded flowers.

Lobelia (Lobelia)

Lobelia's petite but abundant flowers, blooming through most of the summer, come in a beautiful range of blue shades (as well as more or less incidental white and reddish). Trailing lobelias make terrific container plants, especially hanging baskets. The edgers look neat and tidy along a border. Set out transplants in full sun or part shade in spring, after any danger of frost. Space plants 6 inches apart. Lobelia prefers cool weather. Provide light shade in hot climates and ensure that the soil stays moist. Plants can reseed in favorable situations or live over winter in mild climates.

Love-in-a-Mist (Nigella Damascena)

Striking in borders and bouquets, the dainty flowers on this old-timer come fully loaded with fancy accoutrements — pastel colors, feathery foliage, and puffy seed capsules. Plants grow 18 to 24 inches tall. Sow seeds directly in the ground in full sun or part shade in spring, after any danger of frost, or sow seeds in fall in mild-winter climates. Hot summers end the season for love-in-a-mist. To dry the papery, balloon-like seed pods for arrangements, cut off branches with mature pods and hang them upside down in an airy, shady spot.

Love-Lies-Bleeding (Amaranthus Caudatus)

This big plant (4 feet and more) has large, coarse leaves and distinctive flowers — red ropy things drooping as long as 2 feet. Use this unusual annual at the back of a border. Sow seeds directly in the ground in full sun or part shade in spring or early summer, after the soil has warmed up. Plant 18 to 36 inches apart, depending on variety size. Watch for signs of chewing insects, and bait for snails and slugs if they threaten.

Mexican Sunflower (Tithonia Rotundifolia)

This rangy, easy-to-grow, trouble-free heat lover grows up to 6 feet tall and makes a great background plant for sunny spots. Flowers up to 3 inches across are a vivid orange and make great cut flowers in bouquets. Sow seeds directly in the ground in full sun in the spring, after any danger of frost. Space plants 2 feet apart.

Mexican Tulip Poppy (Hunnemannia Fumariifolia)

Mexican tulip poppy flowers are a bright, pure yellow and bloom mostly in summer on plants that grow up to 2 feet tall. Use them in mixed plantings and wildflower gardens. Sow seeds directly in the ground in full sun in spring, after any danger of frost. Thin seedlings to stand 12 inches apart. Make sure that soil is well drained and keep plants on the dry side.

Mignonette (Reseda Odorata)

Unless you're fond of sprawling, medium green, nondescript plants, you grow mignonette for its intensely sweet fragrance. The flowers are small and greenish yellow, and the plants grow 12 to 18 inches tall. Plant mignonette near walkways, under windows, in containers, or in other spots where you can appreciate the fragrance. Sow seeds directly in the ground in early spring; or, if you live in a mild-winter climate, sow seeds in the fall. Mignonettes prefer cool weather; plant them in full sun in cool climates, in part shade in hotter areas. Thin seedlings to stand 10 to 12 inches apart.

Monkey Flower (Mimulus)

If you have a shady border or garden pond, grow this plant at its edge. Plants grow 12 to 18 inches tall. Some people think the 2-inch-long, funnel-shaped flowers look like smiling monkeys. Colors are bright orange, red, and yellow, often with spots and blotches. Set out transplants in part to full shade in spring after frost. Monkey flower does best in cool, moist climates and needs lots of water. Remove flowers as they fade.

Morning Glory (Ipomoea Imperialis)

Also sold as *Ipomoea nil,* morning glory sets the standard for fast-growing, big-leafed, free-flowering summer vines. Varieties can climb as much as 15 feet in one season! Trumpet flowers up to 4 or 5 inches wide come in a rich range of blues, pinks, and purples. Newer varieties stay open for longer periods of time, not just the morning, as suggested by the name. Plant vines near a trellis, fence, or arbor and let them climb. The closely related moonflower (*Ipomoea Alba*) is a perennial that's usually treated as an annual. It's very fast-growing, to 20 feet. The beautiful, big white flowers of this plant open in the evening and close the next morning. *Ipomoea* seeds don't sprout easily and usually need help; notch the seeds with a knife or file, or soak them for a couple of hours in warm water before planting. Sow morning glory or moonflower seeds directly in the ground in full sun in spring, after any danger of frost. Space plants 12 inches apart. Don't water or feed this plant too much; doing so encourages leaf growth at the expense of flowers.

Mannerly marigolds

Marigolds *(Tagetes)* are fast and easy to grow — so famously unfussy that seed catalogs even advise planting in "ordinary" soil. Marigolds have a scent that may be a little too pungent (they're rumored to repel insects). And the colors may be too basic — too orange or yellow — for some people. Plant marigolds in the spring after frost danger, when the weather warms up. Nurseries offer dozens of varieties as transplants, or you can sow directly in the ground. Removing dead flowers greatly prolongs the bloom season and improves the plant's appearance. Marigolds attract no special pests, but watch for slugs and snails when plants are young.

Nasturtium (Tropaeolum Majus)

Flowers in bright orange, yellow, cream, red, or pink blooms are abundant through the summer (or winter and spring, in mild climates). The bright green, round leaves look like waterlilies and can make a thick, low carpet that's attractive in its own right. Use bushy dwarf varieties, up to 15 inches tall, to edge a border. You can train climbing varieties, which trail up to 6 feet, on a trellis or as a ground cover. Sow seeds directly in the ground in full sun or part shade. In cold-winter climates, plant seeds in the spring; in mild-winter climates, plant seeds in the fall. Nasturtiums are easy to grow in well-drained soil, and are quick about it. Best in cool-summer climates, they live through winter in mild climates and can reseed themselves. Both its flowers and young leaves are edible and can add color and peppery flavor to salad greens; wash thoroughly before serving. Cut long-stemmed flowers for use in arrangements. Watch for aphids (especially if you eat the plants).

Nicotiana, or Flowering Tobacco (Nicotiana)

The blooming season for the newer varieties of this old-fashioned favorite is quite long, lasting through spring and summer, with flowers including pink, purple, red, and white. Use dwarf types massed like petunias. Plant taller varieties at the back of a border. For delightful fragrance at night, choose varieties, such as 'Grandiflora' and 'Fragrant Cloud'. Or go with the leggy old-timer, *Nicotiana sylvestris,* which grows up to 5 feet tall and has magnificently scented white flowers. Set out transplants in full sun or light shade in spring, after any danger of frost. Watch for tobacco budworms and aphids.

Nierembergia, or Cupflower

Tidy growth and a thick coat of flowers make nierembergia ideal for pots, hanging baskets, or edging. The summertime flowers are tiny (about ¼ inch) but abundant and come in purple or white. Plants grow from 6 to 15 inches tall. Set out transplants in full sun or part shade in spring, after any danger of frost. Nierembergia prefers cool summers; provide part shade in hot climates. To encourage long and heavy bloom, conscientiously remove dead flowers.

Who's the pansy with the viola?

Tolerant of cold, pansies and violas (*Viola wittrockiana*) can stand a light snow cover and are among the first annuals to bloom. In mild climates, they can flower through winter. Technically, pansies are just big violas, having 2- to 4-inch flowers that come in a range of bright colors: blue, purple, rose, yellow, and white, often striped or dramatically blotched. Use them in mass plantings, in borders, mixed in with bulbs, in containers, and as an edging. Violas stay less than 6 or 8 inches tall. Colors are mostly solid, including blue, apricot, mahogany red, purple, white, and yellow. Johnny-jump-up *(viola tricolor)* looks like a miniature pansy with purple and yellow flowers. It stays low and fits right in nestled among spring bulbs, such as daffodils. In cold-winter climates, plant pansies and violas in early spring, several weeks before the last frost. In mild-winter climates, plant in the fall or late winter. More and more cold-climate gardeners are planting pansies in the fall for a bit of fall color.

Phlox, Annual (Phlox Drummondii)

Big clusters of 1-inch flowers cover husky plants from 6 to 20 inches tall. Colors include blue, lavender, pink, red, and white. Use for mass plantings in beds and borders. Long-stemmed varieties make great cut flowers. Sow seeds directly in the ground in full sun. In cold-winter climates, plant in the spring, after any danger of frost; in mild-winter climates, plant in the fall, or set out transplants in spring, after frost danger. Space plants 10 inches apart and remove faded flowers to extend the bloom.

Pincushion Flower, or Sweet Scabious (Scabiosa Atropurpurea)

Pincushion flower's puffy 2-inch blooms account for its odd name. The plants grow 24 to 36 inches tall and make good additions to mixed beds and cut-flower bouquets. Sow seeds directly in the ground in full sun in early spring, or in fall if you live in a mild-winter climate. This plant is an easy one to grow in mild climates with cool summers — it *naturalizes* (naturally self-sows and comes back each year like a perennial without any special care from you) under favorable conditions.

Pink (Dianthus Chinensis)

Members of the carnation clan, pinks offer reliability, ease of growing, compact growth, and a wide range of heavy-blooming flowers, mainly in shades of pink, red, and white. The blooms are often bicolored, and some are fragrant. Pinks can grow up to 30 inches tall, but most modern varieties are closer to 12 inches. Taller varieties make outstanding cut flowers. Use compact varieties in containers or to edge borders. Set out transplants in full sun in spring. Space plants 6 to 12 inches apart. The best bloom comes during cool weather. Shear off dead flowers to encourage more blooming.

Portulaca, or Moss Rose (Portulaca Grandiflora)

With fleshy, succulent-like leaves and brilliantly colored flowers, portulaca is well equipped for sunny conditions. Its summer flowers look like little roses, in single- or double-flowered strains; colors include intense red, yellow, pink, white, and orange. Plants are ground-huggers, no more than 6 inches tall. Use them as ground cover or allow them to spill from hanging baskets and other containers. Set out transplants in full sun in spring, after any danger of frost. One of the easiest summer annuals to grow — even in hot, dry places — these plants prefer their soil to be kept on the dry side.

Petunia Pig's namesake

With their increased vigor and predictability, the state-of-the-art petunias that you see today are the result of hybridization. The blooms, which come in yellow, deep purple, pink, red, white, light blue, and bicolors, can be imaginatively ruffled and frilled, but the typical funnel-shaped, single flower is still the most popular type. Petunias bloom from summer until frost. In the hottest climates of the Southwest and Southeast, summer is too hot; but in some of those climates with mild winters, such as Arizona, you can plant petunias in fall for winter and spring bloom.

Petunias come in single and double blooms and a variety of classes; pay attention to the two main petunia classes:

✔ **Grandifloras:** These boast the biggest flowers, usually up to 4½ inches wide, in single or ruffled forms. Plants grow up to 24 inches tall and 24 to 36 inches wide — sometimes on the rangy side.

✔ **Multifloras:** Compared to grandifloras, the plants are more compact, and the flowers are smaller (about 2 inches wide) but more abundant, either single or double. This type is used by the acre in public gardens — very colorful and very reliable.

You may also encounter *millifloras,* a newer type, with small flowers (about 1½ inches wide) and a dwarf habit of growth that's ideal for pots, baskets, and border edging.

Start with nursery transplants, setting them out in full sun in spring after frost danger. Soon after planting, begin pinching back tips to encourage bushier growth. Be sure to remove dead flowers. Late in the season, when growth becomes leggy, cut back plants by as much as a half to force a new spurt of growth. Petunia problems are rare, but watch for tobacco budworms, aphids, snails, and slugs.

Salvia (Salvia)

If you see brilliant red flowers used in extravagant midsummer beds, chances are they're scarlet sage *(Salvia splendens)* — one of the more colorful and dependable warm-season annuals. This relative of culinary sage is valued for its red spikes of blooms, but its colors also include lilac, purple, and white. The plants grow from 10 to 30 inches tall. Use scarlet sage in masses in beds, or as accent plants in mixed borders. Mealy-cup sage *(Salvia farinacea)* is another choice plant, but it mainly bears beautiful blue flowers. Set out seedlings in full sun in spring, after any danger of frost and warm weather arrives. Both types of sage thrive in hot weather (though not high humidity) if given plenty of water. In hottest climates, salvia may benefit from partial shade.

Scaevola

This plant, which hasn't been around long enough to pick up a quaint common name, is a real eye-catcher. Blue or purple flowers are tiny but very abundant on long trailing branches. Nurseries mostly sell plants already in bloom. Move them into a basket or along a wall where they can trail. Plant in full sun or part shade in spring, after any danger of frost.

Schizanthus, or Butterfly Flower

Breathtaking flowers in summer are enough reason to try growing these fussy annuals. They look like little orchids — in pink, purple, orange, white, and yellow — with contrasting yellow throats and many spots. The plants grow 12 to 24 inches tall. Use them for mass displays in beds, at the front of borders, or in containers. Set out seedlings in full sun or part shade in spring, after any danger of frost. Cool summers are best for this plant. Enrich the soil with plenty of organic matter and keep it moist.

Shirley Poppy (Papaver Rhoeas)

The American Legion poppy, also called Flanders poppy or Field poppy, recalls the long-stemmed red flowers fluttering in the fields of World War I France. Cultivars include today's Shirley poppies. Colors of modern varieties include pastels and bicolors, as well as brilliant red. Some blooms are as wide as 3 inches across. Plants grow 24 to 36 inches and look lovely planted in clusters in wildflower beds and borders. Sow seeds directly in the ground in full sun in early spring a few weeks before the date of the last frost. Remove seed pods to prolong blooming.

Snappy snapdragons

Gardeners usually consider snapdragons *(Antirrhinium majus)* difficult to grow. Keys to success: Choose varieties carefully, watch the calendar, and be on guard for rust. Rewards are fragrant, striking spikes of blooms in rich colors — purple, red, lavender, and bronze. Snapdragons make great cut flowers and can stand a light frost and still look great. Snapdragons come in three height ranges: tall (up to 3 feet — use for accents in beds and borders), intermediate (up to 18 inches), and dwarfs (below 12 inches — use for edgings or in containers).

Snapdragons bloom best in cool weather. In mild climates, plant in the fall or late winter; plant in early spring elsewhere. Start with nursery transplants; growing snapdragons from seeds takes too long. Plant in full sun, spacing taller types 15 inches apart and dwarfs 9 inches apart. Never let snapdragons dry out, but don't water them from overhead. Pinch the tips of this plant frequently to force bushy growth, and stake taller varieties. Remove faded flowers or cut flowers freely for indoor use; cut flowers when half the buds are open.

When cutting flowers for bouquets, seal the stem ends with a flame before immersing in water.

Snow-on-the-Mountain (Euphorbia Marginata)

A mounding mass of white and bright green leaves, snow-on-the-mountain makes a nice border backdrop for colorful annuals, such as low zinnias. The plant grows 18 to 24 inches tall, and its flowers are hardly noticeable. Sow seeds directly in the ground in full sun in spring.

Milky sap in stems can irritate skin and eyes; wash it off immediately if you come into contact with it.

Spider Flower (Cleome Hasslerana)

When you plant spider flower, expect a shrub in just a few months. Plants grow quickly to 4 to 6 feet. Big clusters of spidery pink or white flowers stand tall. Use spider plant in the back of a border or as a temporary screen. Sow seeds directly in the ground in full sun. Plant them when warm weather arrives, after any danger of frost. Stake these leggy plants if necessary and be prepared for them to reseed themselves like weeds.

Statice (Limonium Sinuatum)

You may recognize statice as those dainty, papery, purple or yellow flowers in dried arrangements. Statice is also useful in dry, sunny, summer borders. Plants grow up to 30 inches tall. Set out transplants in full sun in spring, after danger of frost. Or sow seeds directly in the ground. For dried arrangements, cut flowers after they open and before they start to fade. Hang bunches of flowers upside down in a dry, shady spot.

Stock (Matthiola Incana)

Throughout spring and summer, spikes of flowers bloom in double or single forms with a sweet and spicy fragrance. Colors include cream, lavender, pink, purple, red, and white. Plants grow 12 to 30 inches tall. Grow them along walks or in containers where you can enjoy the fragrance. Cut flowers freely for indoor bouquets. Set out transplants in full sun in spring in cold-winter climates, or in fall or early spring where winters are mild. Stocks strongly prefer cool weather — plant early to get blooms before summer heat. Provide plenty of water and well-drained soil.

Strawflower (Helichrysum and Helipterum)

Strawflowers are considered *everlastings,* meaning that they hold their shape and color when dried — terrific for permanent bouquets. At least two different types go by the name strawflower:

- *Helichrysum bracteatum:* Has 2-inch daisylike flowers in bright colors, including orange, pink, red, yellow, and white. Plants grow from 12 to 36 inches tall; Bikini mixes grow only to 15 inches and are more practical in most gardens.

- *Helipterum roseum:* Offers softer colors, mostly pastel pink, rose, white, and yellow; plants grow 12 to 24 inches tall.

Both kinds of strawflowers are easy to grow in dry, sunny spots. Sow seeds directly in the ground in full sun in spring, after any danger of frost. To dry these flowers, cut long stems when the flowers are fully open, and hang them upside down in a shady place.

Sunsational sunflowers

Spectacular new varieties of sunflowers (*Helianthus annuus*) seem to come out every year. Old and new, sunflowers are striking, easy to grow, and fun. Sunflowers bloom in a variety of shapes. Take a look at the main types of sunflowers:

✔ **Giants, monsters, and conversation pieces:** Fast-growing (a foot a week), gangly, and clumsy. Plants can grow 10 feet tall or more, with flower heads spanning 12 inches or more; you need to stake them.

✔ **Garden varieties:** These are more compact, less coarse looking, with smaller flowers. Use them at the back of borders, to form a temporary hedge, massed in beds, or in containers.

✔ **Varieties for cutting:** New hybrids have long, single stems that produce several big flowers per plant. These plants take a good deal of space. For a long bloom season, stagger plantings every two weeks. Also excellent for cut flowers are the sunflowers with multiple flower stems; they look better in the garden because of a longer bloom season and greater number of blooms.

Plant in the spring after frost danger and into the summer as long as you have enough growing season ahead. Choose a spot in full sun. The taller types, in particular, produce better in soil that's enriched with organic matter. Nursery transplants are available, but sunflowers are easy to grow from seeds, which take about a week and a half to sprout. Plant seeds an inch deep.

If you want to save the seeds of big flowers, cut off flower heads after the seeds are fully formed and starting to dry and hang them in a dry, shady place. Just get to them before the birds do!

Summer Forget-Me-Not (Anchusa Capensis)

Summer forget-me-nots produce nice blue flowers, just like common forget-me-nots, but this variety takes more sun. It's perfect in mixed summer borders. Plants grow 8 to 20 inches tall. Set out transplants in full sun in spring, after any danger of frost. Provide plenty of water.

Swan River Daisy (Brachycome Iridifolia)

Almost everything about Swan River daisy is small — flowers, foliage, plant, and the length of the bloom season. Peak bloom in summer is just a few weeks, but the flowers nearly smother the plant. Flowers are about an inch across and available in blue, pink, or white. Plants grow 9 to 18 inches tall, usually at the lower end of the range. Use them in containers, spilling over the sides of a raised bed, or edging a border. Sow seeds directly in the ground in full sun in spring, after any danger of frost. If available, set out transplants after frost danger. Pinch tips of young plants to encourage bushy growth.

Sweet Alyssum (Lobularia Maritima)

Low-spreading growth makes this plant ideal for edging a border, filling in between tall annuals or bulbs, and spilling out of containers and between stepping stones. Flowers can be pure white, rosy lavender, and multicolored. Bloom season for all varieties is long: from spring to frost, or year-round in mild climates. Set out transplants in full sun or light shade in spring or sow seeds directly in the ground in full sun or light shade in spring. In mild-winter climates, sow seeds in spring or fall. Space plants 8 to 10 inches apart. Sweet alyssum is easy and quick to grow and may reseed itself under favorable conditions. Best blooming comes during cool weather.

Sweetly-scented sweet peas

They seem to bloom for just minutes, they're picky about the weather, they practically demand that you dig a planting trench deep enough to bury an automobile — so why bother even trying to grow sweet peas (*Lathyrus odoratus*)? Three reasons: (1) unforgettable fragrance that can fill a room or a garden, (2) a beautiful range of soft, pastel colors, (3) sheer old-fashioned charm. Sweet peas are grouped into two main types:

✔ **Tall climbers:** These familiar sweet peas, available in blue, orange, pink, purple, red, and white, climb to 5 feet or so. You have to provide a support for this giant to climb.

✔ **Bush types:** These sweet peas clamber and sprawl to a height of only 30 inches or so. The stems may be short, but they can still provide cut flowers. They're also great for growing in pots. (Use a big pot, at least 14 inches deep.)

Sweet peas can't stand heat and do best in cool climates. Before attempting to grow sweet peas, consider whether your environment can support their special needs. If you live in a typical cold-winter/hot-summer climate, you need to plant early in the spring, as soon as you can

dig the soil, so that the plant will bloom while the weather is still cool. In mild-winter climates, plant in the fall for blooms in winter and early spring. Choose varieties labeled *early-flowering* or *spring-flowering*. In hot climates, be sure to choose varieties labeled as *heat-resistant*. But be aware that, in the hottest climates, even these varieties don't work.

Sweet peas perform best if you plant the seeds directly where you intend for the plant to grow. Choose a spot in full sun with a climbing surface. To hasten seed germination, soak the seeds in warm water for at least a few hours up to 24 hours before planting. Prepare the soil thoroughly, and plant in trenches 12 inches wide and 1 to 2 feet deep. Plant seeds 1 inch deep, 6 inches apart (closer, if you later thin to that distance). The seeds take two or three weeks to sprout. When seedlings are 4 to 6 inches tall, pinch the tips carefully to force branching. Never let the soil dry out, and fertilize the plants regularly. When flowers start blooming, cut them daily or every other day — as soon as the buds break open — and remove all seed pods that form to prolong the bloom season.

Sweet William (Dianthus Barbatus)

Sweet William has robust growth and big, bright flower clusters in pink, purple, red, white, and bicolors. Annual varieties grow 6 to 12 inches tall. Use them in mass plantings, in containers, or to edge borders. Most sweet Williams are biennials, but they can bloom the first summer if you start seeds early or set out transplants in time. Sow seeds directly in the ground in full sun several weeks before the last frost date. Or set out transplants in early summer. Space plants 6 inches apart. To be sure of bloom the first season, look for varieties labeled as annuals. Cut back plants after the first bloom in early summer to encourage a second bloom.

Thunbergia, or Black-Eyed Susan Vine (Thunbergia Alata)

Throughout summer until frost, this fast-growing tropical vine's 1- to 2-inch-wide tubular flowers bloom in orange, white, or yellow, with a dark eye in the center. Plant near a fence or trellis, and the vine will twine up to 10 feet. If transplants are available, set them out in full sun or part shade in spring, after any danger of frost and when warm weather has arrived. Seeds can be sown directly in the ground at the same time. Ensure that these plants get plenty of water through their whole season. Blooming is best in cool weather, before and after summer heat.

Verbena (Verbena)

Verbena's talent is staying low and spreading wide, covering itself with bright flower clusters 2 or 3 inches wide. Colors include blue, lavender, pink, purple, red, white, and bicolors; bloom season is long, all through the warm months. Plants grow 6 to 12 inches tall and spread as wide as 24 inches. Use them to edge a bed, as a low mass-planting, or in containers. Wide-spreading strains work especially well as a ground cover or in hanging baskets. *Verbena bonariensis,* a perennial in mild climates, has a much different look; it's lacy and tall (3 to 6 feet), with purple flowers that look terrific at the back or front of a border. Set out transplants in full sun in spring, after any danger of frost. Verbena thrives in hot weather. For bushy growth, pinch back tips of young plants; remove dead flowers.

Vinca rosea, or Madagascar Periwinkle (Catharanthus Roseus)

This easy-to-grow champion of hot-climate performers thrives in desert climates. Even in midsummer, an abundance of 1½-inch white or pink flowers looks crisp and fresh, and the foliage manages to stay shiny and deep green. Plants grow up to 20 inches tall; compact varieties reach half that size or less. Use vinca rosea as a low-growing mass planting, to edge a border, or to spill from a container. Choose from many improved varieties. Set out transplants in full sun in spring, when warm weather has arrived and the danger of frost has passed. Space plants 8 to 12 inches apart. For vigorous and lush growth, provide plenty of water — as long as soil drains quickly. Bloom season can extend until the first frost, or later in mild climates.

Wallflower (Erysimum or Cheiranthus)

The traditional spring combination of tulips and wallflowers blooming together is hard to beat. Clusters of small flowers come mainly in bright shades of orange and yellow but also in cream, purple, and red. Plants grow 12 to 24 inches tall. Use them for mass display in beds and borders. For spring bloom, set out transplants in full sun or part shade in early spring; space plants 12 inches apart. For bloom later in summer, sow seeds directly in the ground in full sun in early spring, or fall in mild-winter climates. Wallflowers thrive in cool, moist climates. Keep their soil moist.

Wishbone Flower (Torenia Fournieri)

Wishbone flower is an ideal low plant to edge a shady border. Small, mainly blue flowers bloom for a long season, through summer and fall. Plants grow 6 to 12 inches tall, with a lushness that looks like they belong around a pond or other water feature. Set out transplants in part shade in spring, after any danger of frost. Space plants 6 to 8 inches apart. Enrich soil with plenty of organic matter and keep it moist. For bushy growth, pinch the tips of the stems.

Zesty zinnias

Easy to grow, sun-loving, and long-blooming, zinnias *(Zinnia elegans)* seem to have the right colors for the season — red, yellow, orange, purple, white, salmon, pink, and rose. Zinnias come in several flower forms. You owe it to yourself to consider the cactus with its large, double blooms and quilled, pointed petals, and the dahlia-flowered zinnia, which is similar to cactus, but has flat, rounded petals. Dwarf types, from 6 to 12 inches, work well as border edgings, in containers, or massed in low plantings. Taller types do well at the back of a border or massed in beds. A relative of *Zinnia elegans, Zinnia angustifolia* is a perennial in mild climates that acts more or less as a 15- or 18-inch ground cover with bright 1-inch flowers.

Plant zinnias in your sunniest spot, preferably in well-drained soil. Wait to plant until late spring, well after frost danger, when the soil and air are definitely warm. Nursery transplants are widely sold but are on the touchy side; be careful not to disturb roots and don't buy overgrown seedlings. Zinnias are so easy to grow from seeds that sowing directly in the ground usually works best. Zinnias are highly responsive to pinching. Cut off faded flowers to encourage a long season of blooms. Zinnias are mildew prone, especially in foggy or humid climates. Reduce the likelihood of mildew by watering them with a ground-level irrigation system rather than overhead sprinklers. Also be on the lookout for snails and slugs.

Book VI
Bulbs

"Aside from a little beginner's confusion, I've done very well with my bulbs."

In this book . . .

See whether you can answer this gardening riddle:

When is a bulb not a bulb?
When it's a rhizome or tuber.

If you love bulbs but that riddle made no sense, you've come to the right book! Here, we take the mystery out of growing bulbs (and rhizomes and tubers, for that matter). We tell you how to select, plant, and care for your bulbs, and we even offer suggestions for specific seasons or types of soil. The book ends with an alphabetical discussion of popular bulbs.

Turn on your mental camera, and enjoy the flash of bulbs in this book!

Here are the contents of Book VI at a glance:

Chapter 1

A Bulb's Life

Think of bulbs as multipurpose plants, easy to plant, easy to grow, attractive, and useful in all sorts of ways. The majority of bulbs are grown for their lovely flowers, but a few have attractive foliage. Whether for flowers or foliage, bulbs are great for garden use, work well in pots (see Chapter 3 in Book II for more on container gardening), and make good cut flowers. Bulbs are nice lumpy things that are easier to handle than tiny seeds. Because they're dormant when you plant them, most tolerate small delays better than the actively growing perennials that have roots and leaves to maintain. And because bulbs come from many different places in the world, all gardeners, regardless of location, can find suitable bulbs. This chapter introduces you to bulb basics.

Unwrapping Bulbs

Bulbs are lumpy underground things — see Figure 1-1 — that grow differently than grasses (see Book II), perennials (see Book IV), and annuals (see Book V). The bulb portion that lies underground is a plant in a package, protecting itself against difficult weather conditions and using reserves of food and moisture to begin growing when conditions start to improve. Bulbs store food because they intend to come back year after year.

Gardeners are probably most familiar with bulbs planted in fall. These bulbs "rest" through a cold winter, and in early spring, they begin to grow rapidly and flower. That's the scenario for tulips, daffodils, and lots more bulbs. Some bulbs originate in places that don't get very cold. These bulbs don't hibernate through winter. Instead, in their climate of origin, they go dormant when it's dry. (Weather patterns may be different where you garden.)

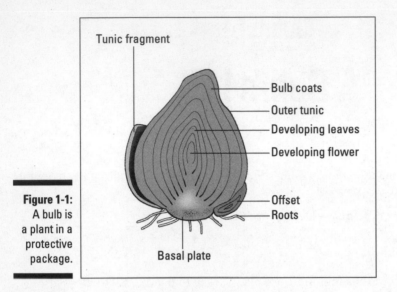

Figure 1-1:
A bulb is
a plant in a
protective
package.

Labels: Tunic fragment, Bulb coats, Outer tunic, Developing leaves, Developing flower, Offset, Roots, Basal plate

All bulbs aren't the same, and everything gardeners call a "bulb" isn't necessarily a bulb. Rather, *bulb* is a catch-all term for bulbous plants, which includes true bulbs, corms, tubers, and rhizomes. Why should you care? Because some of these differences have an effect on how you should grow the "bulbs" you plant. The following sections define some important terms.

Reviewing true bulbs, corms, and tubers

True bulbs, such as daffodils, tulips, hyacinths, and snowdrops, often have a papery skin or tunic on the outside, much like an onion. Bulbs with a papery covering are called *tunicate* bulbs. The tunic helps protect the bulb from drying out when it's resting or waiting to be planted. However, some true bulbs, such as lilies, don't have a tunic. These bulbs dry out faster and are more easily bruised. All true bulbs share the following characteristics:

✔ **They're more or less rounded, sort of ball-like, and narrow to a point on the top.** Leaves and flower stems appear from this point.

✔ **With or without a tunic, true bulbs have a flat part, called a *basal plate,* at the bottom.** That's where roots grow and also where shoots and scales are attached.

✔ **True bulbs have new bulbs, called *offsets,* that form from the basal plate (see Figure 1-2).** When they get big enough, these offsets, or daughter bulbs, produce flowers on their own.

✔ **True bulbs are made up of rings, called *scales,* which are modified leaves that store food.** Cut apart a true bulb, such as a hyacinth, at the right time of year, and you can find a miniature flower inside, just waiting to begin growing. Perennial true bulbs add new rings each year, from the inside. Old rings on the outside are used up, but the true bulb itself persists from year to year.

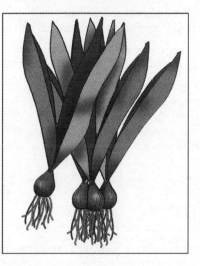

Figure 1-2:
True bulbs
form offsets.

If any of these characteristics are missing, the plant isn't a true bulb. Instead, it's a corm, tuber, tuberous root, or rhizome, as described in the following sections.

Corms, shown in Figure 1-3, have these traits:

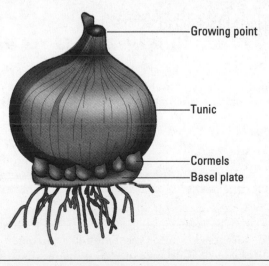

Figure 1-3:
Corms
resemble
true bulbs in
many ways;
this corm
has little
cormels at
its base.

Growing point

Tunic

Cormels
Basel plate

✔ **Corms have a tunic.** The tunic may be fibrous, what botanists call *netted* or *reticulate,* or the tunic may be smoother, with distinct rings, what botanists call *annulate.* Some crocuses have reticulate tunics, and others are annulate, which is one way you can tell crocus species apart.

✔ **Corms have a basal plate at the bottom and one or more growing points at the top.** Bulbs and corms both have a definite vertical orientation.

✔ **Corms are undifferentiated, uniform, and contain no rings when cut apart.** Corms are stem tissue, modified and developed to store food.

✔ **The corm you plant is used up growing the flower.** Before it withers away at the end of the growing season, however, a brand new corm (sometimes several new corms) forms and replaces the mother corm. The new corm contains the food reserve for the dormant crocus or gladiolus until it's time to grow again.

Tubers have these features:

✔ **Tubers have no tunic.**

✔ **Tubers lack a basal plate.** Most tubers root from the bottom.

✔ **Tubers have several growing points, called *eyes*.** More organized tubers, such as caladiums or tuberous begonias, have their eyes at the top. Some tubers, such as anemones, aren't so orderly. Distinguishing the top from the bottom of the tuber may be difficult. If you're not sure, plant it sideways and let the tuber figure out which direction to grow.

✔ **Tubers are made of modified, undifferentiated stem or enlarged hypocotyl tissue.** They have no highly specific internal structure.

✔ **Tubers don't make offsets or produce new tubers.** Tubers usually just get bigger each year, making more growing points.

Identifying other lumpy things as bulbs

Most of the "bulbs" that gardeners plant are true bulbs and corms, and a few are tubers. You can also find two other kinds of lumpy things at nurseries and garden centers along with the others that we discuss earlier in this chapter.

✔ **Tuberous roots:** These "bulbs" are modified, enlarged, specialized roots that store food, and are used up during the growing season to be replaced by new storage units (see Figure 1-4). The tuberous roots cluster together, joined to the bottom of a stem. The stem contains the new growing point for the next year — a piece of root alone won't grow.

✔ **Rhizomes:** Rhizomes are stems that grow sideways rather than up, running along the surface of the soil or just below it. Plants that use rhizomes for food storage have fatter, more bulblike rhizomes, covered with a dry base of leaves. Rhizomes branch out, and each new portion develops roots and a shoot of its own (see Figure 1-5).

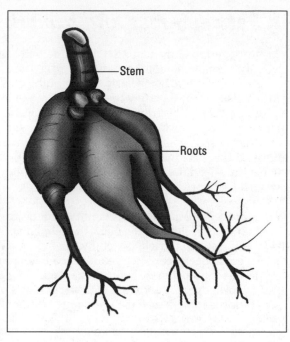

Figure 1-4:
You can plant other lumpy things, like this tuberous root.

Stem

Roots

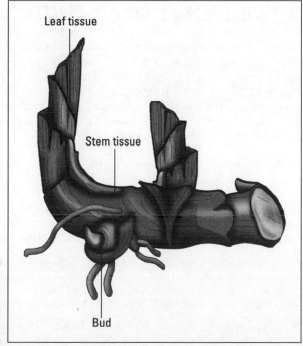

Leaf tissue

Stem tissue

Bud

Figure 1-5:
Rhizomes grow sideways.

Alternating between rest and growth

Most bulbs have a growing period and a resting time. Some bulbs grow for a short period of time, only a couple of months, before they go dormant. Others have a longer growing season. Some early spring bulbs grow early in the year when not much else is growing; they then rest while the majority of other plants are in bloom. Other bulbs grow later in the spring and summer, when all sorts of plants are busy growing. Some bulbs even flower in autumn when just about everything else is going dormant. All bulbs have a stored food reserve underground that gets them through tough times. Bulbs draw on these reserves when they need them as growth begins, and they replenish the depleted reserves before the resting phase begins.

What bulbs have going for the gardener is the certainty of good results the first time around. Start off with healthy bulbs, plant them in an appropriate place at the right time, and just stand back and enjoy the blooms. With little or no effort, many bulbs come back year after year. With a minimum of effort, results are even more assured. Sometimes, bulbs come back in increased numbers. Again, a little knowledge and effort on your part can help them along. The diversity of bulbs is remarkable, matched only by the pleasure they provide the gardener who grows them.

Planning a Garden That Uses Bulbs

Buying some bulbs helter-skelter and planting them any old way in whatever spot you're standing on doesn't do much to satisfy your longing for a beautiful garden. Beauty takes planning. Think of yourself as an artist who just happens to be working with plants rather than paint. Do you want a vivid picture with bright colors or something softer and romantic? If you can't visualize just what you want, visit a nearby botanical garden or public park and see what they're doing with bulbs. This book will give you plenty of ideas, too!

One major difference in gardens and paintings is that gardens undergo seasonal changes:

- ✔ **Bulbs grow, flower, and go dormant.** Think about what happens before and after the bulbs are in bloom, so you can team them up (called *companion planting*) with other kinds of plants to create the best effect.

- ✔ **Some bulbs increase and multiply over time.** Expansion is fine if you have the space and want an informal, cottage garden, or naturalistic look. In limited space or in a precise, formal kind of garden, a problem results if the bulbs crowd their neighbors and blur your design.

- ✔ **You can use some bulbs on a "here and gone" basis.** Treat them like annuals, enjoy them for one season's display, and then discard them.

After you decide what effect you want, sketch out the area you plan to use for your garden, indicating which flowers go where. (See Book II for tips on designing your garden.) Get a rough idea of how much space you have for your garden and how you want to use that space. Pay attention to flower heights, so you can place the tallest flowers at the back. Also check out spreading tendencies, so you can allow space for the spread.

Bulbs aren't all the same in their likes and dislikes. Some like it sunny, others shady. Just because many prefer soil with good drainage doesn't mean that they all do. Lots of bulbs actually prefer winter — or at least its edge — while others get frostbite if they freeze. Whatever your conditions, you can find bulbs that will work for you. Chapter 3 in Book VI offers suggestions for different situations, and we tell you each bulb's general likes and dislikes throughout Book VI.

Matching bulbs to climate

As you may expect from their protective layering, bulbs originate more frequently in places around the world with relatively harsh climates and conditions. But that doesn't mean that every bulb will grow in every place. They'll relocate, but they grow best in conditions similar to where they started. Gardeners, being brighter than their bulbs, can figure out how to get around potential limitations.

The bulbs you're probably most familiar with — tulips, daffodils, crocuses, and so on — are winter-hardy plants that thrive in temperate regions of the world. They accept cold winter conditions and a milder growing season. Other bulbs come from places where winters stay on the mild side, and a regular extended dry period occurs. Knowing where various bulbs originate gives you a better idea about which ones will grow best for you. Or, if you *really* want to grow a certain bulb, you'll know what you have to do to try to satisfy it.

Spacing your bulbs

You've probably seen public displays where the bed is just filled with tulips. If you come by at the right time, the display is fabulous. Come back a month later, and it's a different story. The tulips are finished (they've probably been yanked out), and the flower bed is full of annuals (Book V is all about annuals). That approach is fine for a public garden, but maintaining that kind of labor-intensive, materially expensive type of garden isn't really practical for homeowners. And what happens if the bulbs are daffodils, which you can't dig up and replant in the fall, as you can with tulips? Daffodils stay in place year-round, and you can't cut the leaves away until they turn yellow, so the space looks shabby and unattractive for the longest while.

In general, bulbs should occupy about 10 to 15 percent of the space in your flower beds and borders. That way, you won't break the bank when you buy them or wear yourself out planting them. If the bulbs are intended for seasonal color, you won't feel like a spendthrift when you discard them. And you can afford to replace them with annuals for another season's interest.

If the bulbs are permanent inhabitants of their piece of ground, nearby you can plant perennials (see Book IV for the scoop on perennials) that have spreading leaves to easily disguise the bulbs' aging foliage. Rather than the mainstay of the flower border, think of year-round bulbs as a permanent addition to the perennials you grow there, just as annuals and tender bulbs are temporary ones.

Creating a naturalistic garden

A naturalistic garden is more casual than flower beds and borders. Plants mingle together, giving the appearance of a setting that "just happened." The intention is to provide the look of a part of a meadow or forest. The design doesn't have to be grand and sweeping, either. For instance, you can transform a strip of lawn from turf grass to a grassland just by using ornamental grasses, bulbs, and perennials.

A naturalistic planting calls for bulbs that are especially good at taking care of themselves. Informal, naturalistic gardens are intended to be lower in maintenance — none of the staking, *deadheading* (nipping off dead flowers), or other miscellaneous chores that occupy time in the bed or border. Single flowers look more natural than double ones and need less support, which means that you won't have to stake the plants to keep them from keeling over. Rather than removing the spent flowers, you leave the bulb flowers alone, which is a good way for bulb flowers that go to seed (such as winter aconites and Siberian squills) to multiply themselves.

Bulbs that spread a little too well to be turned loose in a perennial border can be a good choice for naturalistic designs:

- **Grape hyacinths:** Their tendency to spread far and wide can be a nuisance in more formal plantings, but the same characteristic can be excellent if they're growing around shrubs.

- **Wood hyacinths:** These multiply by seeds and offsets, which is aggravating in a designed, precise planting. However, they become wonderfully luxuriant in a casual woodland.

Rock gardens are a very special kind of naturalistic garden. Not a collection of rocks, this kind of garden uses low-growing plants, usually sun-loving, that flourish among rocks in well-drained soils. Dwarf tulips and crocuses fit right in with herbs (see Book VII for more on herbs) and easy-to-grow carpeting perennial plants (such as moss pink, evergreen candytuft, or basket-of-gold alyssum).

Raising bulb flowers for cutting

Cutting flowers from the garden is fun, but every flower you cut is one less on display in your flower bed. You spoil the show if you cut too many. A better approach is to buy extra bulbs in the fall and plant them somewhere out of view, where you can cut to your heart's content. If you look around, you can easily find an out-of-the-way corner where you can plant a handful of bulbs to use for cut flowers.

Book VI

Bulbs

The best place to plant your extra bulbs is in the vegetable garden, if you have one. Rows of tulips or glads are just seasonal occupants, much like beets or carrots. Daffodils and lilies can be permanent plantings, just like the asparagus and rhubarb. (Book VII covers vegetables in detail.)

An established naturalistic planting can supply an occasional bouquet. Just make sure that you don't take all the flowers from one place.

Containing Bulbs in Pots

Certain bulbs are great when grown in pots. (Check out Chapter 3 in Book II for more on container gardening.) Pots of bulbs make ideal additions to your home's interior — and work well in the outdoor garden, too. Here are some tips for growing bulbs in containers:

- **Grow disposable bulbs in pots.** By "disposable," we mean those you grow as seasonal signs of spring or winter cheer. If you keep pots of hyacinths and daffodils green and growing after they flower, you can plant them outdoors when spring arrives.

- **Grow bulbs that don't like winter as houseplants.** Amaryllis is a good example.

- **Use potted bulbs as accents.** Place one pot (or several) of seasonal flowering bulbs on a patio or terrace at the same time these plants are flowering in the garden.

- **Jazz up shaded corners.** Summer containers in the shade can be kind of plain vanilla because most annuals are sun-lovers. However, a pot of caladiums thrives in low light and works perfectly in a shaded area.

- **Add a romantic touch.** For example, potted lilies are very elegant on a balcony or patio. Just remember to choose the lower-growing cultivars — a 7-foot-tall lily needs a big pot to anchor it!

Housing Bulbs Indoors

Houseplants are plants with staying power — plants that you choose to share your home with as more than a passing fancy. Some bulb species are widely known as good houseplants, while others are less familiar. Some of the popular bulbs may seem a little tricky to grow indoors; others — just waiting for you to discover them — grow easily. Here are a few bulbs that make great houseplants (we tell you about others that work well in Chapter 4 of Book VI):

- **Amaryllis:** The showy, trumpet-shaped blossoms are worth the wait, whether you grow the full-size or the miniature type. The flower bud is usually the first to emerge from the bulb, so if you get lots of leaves early in the growing season, then you may not get flowers.

- **Oxalis:** The purple-leaved kind with a hot violet-pink flare at the base of each leaflet grows from a small pink tuber. Keep this plant growing year-round if that's your fancy, or give it a dry winter resting period if you prefer.

- **Veltheimia:** This South African bulb likes a mild winter and a summer drought. Reliably, it flowers in February with a spike of small, drooping, dusty pink flowers in a dense cluster.

Chapter 2

Take Care, Little Bulb

*B*efore you plant bulbs, you have to buy them, and before you buy, you have to decide how you want to use them. Where you purchase bulbs and when you plant them is just as important as what you plant. The best bulbs in the world can be disappointing if you don't handle them correctly and don't plant them in a timely manner. However, with just a little attention on your part (which includes reading this chapter), buying, storing, planting, and caring for bulbs is a snap!

Buying Bulbs

If you've ever bought an onion at the grocery store, you already have an idea of which bulbs are good and which ones aren't. A good, healthy bulb is plump, firm, and heavy for its size. Reject any bulbs that are soft and mushy, or shriveled up. And make sure that no moldy patches are growing on them. If the bulb is supposed to have a *tunic* (refer to Chapter 1 in Book VI), make sure that the tunic is still on the bulb. Tulips that have been roughly handled, for example, easily lose their thin brown tunics. These bulbs dry out more quickly and bruise more easily than tulip bulbs that keep their tunics.

Size is relative when you're comparing different types of bulbs — for example, you'll never see a crocus's corm that's as big as a gladiolus's. But within a category, bigger is better. A large double-nose trumpet daffodil will have more flowers than a single-nosed "round" of the same *cultivar* (see Book I for an explanation of common gardening terms). It's something to consider if you have a choice of sizes.

Finding bulbs to buy

Coming home with bags of bulbs gives you a powerful sense of anticipation. The plain brown wrappers give no inkling of the colorful flowers that are waiting for spring. You can purchase bulbs in a number of ways:

- ✓ **A garden center or nursery:** Here you find knowledgeable gardeners who can help answer your questions. Some nurseries display their bulbs loose in bins, allowing you to carefully examine each bulb that you intend to buy. However, people may inadvertently mix bulbs up. You can easily spot a tulip that falls into a bin of daffodils, but recognizing a white flowering tulip from a red one is difficult in the bulb stage.

- ✓ **Home improvement stores:** Home improvement centers may or may not have qualified staff people, depending on the individual store. Home improvement stores offer packages and net bags of bulbs. Prepackaged bulbs aren't always available in the numbers that you need. Examining packaged bulbs to make sure that they're in good shape can be difficult, even if they're packaged in a mesh bag rather than a box.

- ✓ **Grocery stores:** Don't expect to receive any gardening advice from grocery store staff. Like home improvement centers, grocery stores offer packages and net bags of bulbs.

- ✓ **Catalogs:** Some bulb catalogs provide pictures, and some don't. Some promise fabulous displays from a preselected assortment of bulbs; others leave the choosing up to you. A specialty nursery can offer a wider selection of particular bulbs by mail than local nurseries can afford to stock. But because you're buying the bulbs sight unseen, you'll have to trust the dealer to be reputable and send you quality bulbs. On the downside, some (but not all) mail-order sources require you to pay for bulbs at the time that you place the order.

If prices in one catalog are significantly lower than in other catalogs or local sources, smaller bulb sizes may explain the difference. Undersized bulbs are less expensive, but their flowering display is correspondingly small. Also, be cautious about the truth of claims of fabulous displays that grow anywhere and everywhere. If the company's claim sounds too good to be true, it probably is.

Don't buy bulbs from any display set up near a heat vent or in a sunny window where it gets hot. Keep bulbs cool (50–65°F/10–18°C) and well ventilated before planting them.

You can propagate bulbs — from seed, by division, or some other means — just like other plants, so you can grow your own.

Leftover bulbs are no bargain

Buying leftover spring-flowering bulbs in the middle of winter just because they're cheap is a waste of money. Generally, all that bargain bulbs have going for them is a cheap price. Go for quality instead. Digging a hole for poor bulbs takes just as much effort as digging a hole for good ones, and the results are discouraging. Buy the best bulbs because they produce the best display.

Timing your purchase

You can't buy bulbs until they're available, and availability has much to do with when bulbs flower and go dormant:

✔ **Spring-flowering bulbs:** Nurseries get the bulk of their spring-flowering bulbs around Labor Day. Buy early, and buy everything you intend to get. If supplies of something popular sell out, the nursery may not replenish them. Catalogs come out *months* before planting time, allowing you the opportunity to buy early. If certain bulbs are in limited supply, an early order reserves them for you. Catalog orders are often shipped in rotation — early order, early shipping; later order, later shipping — so, specify a shipping date.

✔ **Summer-flowering bulbs:** Nurseries, home improvement stores, and supermarkets often have their supplies of tender-to-frost summer blooming bulbs while it's still winter. Catalogs for summer bulbs usually start arriving in your mailbox soon after New Year's. As with spring-flowering bulbs, buy dormant summer-blooming bulbs when you see them. If you go back later, they may be gone. You can pot bulbs for summer interest a month or more early — before frost-free weather arrives — if you have the appropriate indoor space to grow them. Early planting gives you a jump start on the season.

✔ **Potted bulbs:** After the weather becomes mild and settled, some tender bulbs may be available as potted growing plants — dahlias, cannas, and caladiums in particular. Although potted plants are more expensive, you can buy, plant, and enjoy all on the same day.

Stowing bulbs away until planting day

Buying bulbs, rushing home, and planting them all the same day is unusual. Generally you have some time in between buying and planting. For bulbs, staying underground is natural — they're *geophytes*. Although bulbs can tolerate the digging, shipping, and hanging around in stores, some tolerate the horticultural stresses better than others:

✔ **Spring-flowering bulbs:** Ideally, you want to plant spring-flowering blooming bulbs as soon as possible. But when immediate planting isn't feasible, keep the bulbs in suspended animation. Cool and on the dry side is the best environment for storing most spring-blooming bulbs. Don't put bulbs in the freezer — the freezing temperature turns them into mush. (However, a bulb can survive freezing conditions after it's planted and rooted in the ground.) Heat is also bad because it can harm the embryo flower bud inside true bulbs, such as tulips. A cool garage or tool shed is okay. A refrigerator temperature of 38–42°F (3–5°C) is excellent. Store most spring-blooming bulbs in open trays or paper bags, but not plastic bags. Even though the bulbs are sleeping, they're metabolizing at a very low rate and producing a little moisture. If the moisture collects in a plastic bag, the bulbs can get moldy. Spring-blooming bulbs that dry out really easily — dogtooth violets and guinea hen flowers, for example — store better if you pack them in wood shavings like those you use in a hamster cage.

If you do refrigerate your bulbs before planting them, keep them away from apples and other fruit. Apples give off ethylene gas, which damages the flower buds within the bulbs.

✔ **Summer-flowering bulbs:** Comfortably cool room temperatures for the holding period are best. If the temperature is too warm, the bulbs may awaken into growth before it's time to plant them outdoors. Temperatures that are too cold can damage the bulbs. Newly purchased dahlia tubers are sometimes coated with paraffin to keep them from shriveling up. If they aren't, pack them in dry peat moss or wood shavings. Holding dormant canna tubers in some packing material is also a good idea. Dormant gladiolus or peacock lily bulbs (they're really corms; see Chapter 1 in Book VI) are okay in a paper bag.

Digging Your Bulbs into a Hole

Before you dig, make sure you have the best digging tool — see Chapter 6 in Book I for details on garden tools — for your situation:

✔ **Trowel:** Trowels are fine for planting individual bulbs in good soil — that almost mythical "high organic, moist but well-drained loam" that books recommend. (See Chapter 3 in Book I for more on soil.) If you have ten crocuses or ten tulips and good soil, using a trowel may be okay. But if you have ten lilies, using a trowel is out of the question. A shovel moves more dirt than a trowel and requires less effort on your part.

✔ **Mattock:** A mattock is sort of like a pick, with one broad end and a pointy end on the digging head. This tool works really well if you have heavy clay soil laced with rocks.

- **Naturalizer tool:** If you have lots of bulbs to plant in a wooded area, look for the naturalizer tool, which looks sort of like a pogo stick without a spring. The tool has a T-handle, a shaft, a bar to step on near the bottom, and the working part is a V-shaped, fish-tailed piece of tool steel. Jab it into the ground, step on the lower bar to stab it further into the ground, wiggle it back and forth a bit, and you've made a nice hole in which to drop a bulb.

- **Bulb planters:** Avoid the silly things called bulb planters that look like an open-ended tin can on a shaft. They make a one-size-fits-all hole, but bulbs come in a variety of sizes. Unless you have perfect soil, they're difficult to get deep enough into the dirt for larger bulbs; either the soil stays in the columnar part in one solid chunk, or it all falls back into the hole as soon as you've made it — before you get the bulb in place.

If you prepare the entire planting area for that bag of daffodils, planting them will be a pleasure. But if you make individual spot holes, not only will planting be a chore, but the bulbs may not grow as well either. The general rule is to plant bulbs twice as deep as their height from top to bottom. Suppose that you have a big trumpet daffodil bulb, 2 inches (5 cm) from base to tip. Dig a 6-inch-deep (15 cm) hole and set the bulb; you should have 4 inches (10 cm) of dirt above the bulb. (The basic rule is 5 inches (12 cm) to base for small bulbs and 8 inches (20 cm) to base for large bulbs.)

Follow these tips for planting in special circumstances:

- **Light and sandy soil:** Plant a little deeper — 7 inches (17 cm) to base for small, and 10 inches (25 cm) to base for large.

- **Heavy, clay-loam soil:** Plant more shallowly — 3 inches (7 cm) to base for small, and 6 inches (15 cm) to base for large.

- **Rhizomes:** When you plant *rhizomes* (refer to Chapter 1 in Book VI for a definition), set them only a couple of inches deep.

One very important rule: Make sure that you plant the bulbs so that they make good contact with the soil at the bottom of the hole. If you casually drop the bulbs into place and create an air pocket below the bulb, roots can dry out.

Although you shouldn't just chuck bulbs around and scratch a little dirt over them, you needn't get uptight about planting correctly either. Bulbs do move in the soil. If they didn't move around, how could bulb seeds fall to the ground and the growing plants eventually have their bulb end up below ground? Many bulbs have contractile roots that can pull the bulb deeper if needed. Bulbs are really rather smart that way.

Looking up

Bulbs are so obliging. Even if you plant them upside down, they send their shoots up and their roots down. Sending up their shoots takes longer, and wastes some energy, but they manage. Eventually, the bulbs even reorient themselves in the ground. How about that! Still, planting bulbs right side up the first time gives your bulbs their best chance for healthy, hearty growth. Recognizing the upsides of bulbs and corms is easiest, because they have a *vertical orientation* (a definite up and down). If you look at them carefully, you see a flattened portion, called a *basal plate,* at the bottom. The roots emerge from here. When you plant, orient bulbs and corms so that the basal plate is at the bottom of the hole (see Figure 2-1).

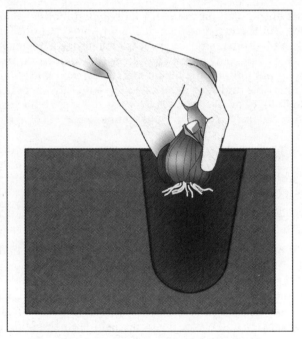

Figure 2-1: Securely place the basal plate against the bottom of the hole; for best growth, don't leave an air pocket between the bulb and the soil.

Some bulbs — such as lilies, crown imperials, naked ladies, and guinea hen flowers — have roots still attached to the basal plate when you buy them, so you can't miss knowing which end is up. Guinea hen flowers have dried-up, wiry roots, but the others still have fleshy, functional roots that you must handle carefully when planting.

The tuber is the problem child. Tubers are dried-up, shriveled, stick-like things, and even careful scrutiny may not be enough to reveal the top from the bottom. When in doubt, plant them sideways and let the plants figure it out. Cannas have fleshy rhizomes. New growth is revealed as pointed, ivory-colored shoots. These shoots go up. If any roots are still attached, try and get them down, but the shoot growth orientation is more important.

Preparing the soil for bulbs

Although bulbs store food very efficiently, you need to give them a good start at planting time for best results. Healthy soil allows the bulbs to make use of available food, and planting time is your only opportunity to get fertilizer down below the bulb.

Chapter 4 in Book I offers a great deal of information about fertilizing and amending your soil, but a few things are unique in relation to bulbs:

Book VI

Bulbs

✔ **Don't use bonemeal to fertilize bulbs.** Contrary to what some may think, modern-day bonemeal is *not* a good, complete fertilizer. Bonemeal used to be good back when bones were ground up fresh and had all sorts of little meat scraps and marrow attached. Now, bones are steamed, cleaned, and then ground up, so the nutritive value is less. Additionally, gardeners in suburban and rural areas quickly learn that skunks and raccoons persistently dig up the bulbs, looking for the bones that they think are there. They don't eat the bulbs, but you must make the additional effort of replanting the same bulb several times.

✔ **Use granular fertilizers when planting.** Fertilizers come in either granular or liquid form. Granular fertilizers, composed of tiny particles that don't dissolve quickly in water, remain in the soil longer than do liquid fertilizers — longer is better. To apply fertilizer, first mix granular fertilizers, organic or inorganic, with the soil at the bottom of the planting holes. Adding a thin layer of *unamended soil* (normal, ordinary soil — fresh from the ground, without any additives) is a good way to avoid any possibility of direct contact between the basal plate and fertilizer particles — especially important with inorganic fertilizers.

✔ **Use liquid fertilizers after bulbs are established.** In subsequent years, when doing so is necessary because flowering is decreasing (not because bulbs are overcrowded), fertilize spring-flowering, summer-dormant bulbs with a liquid fertilizer, which is absorbed by both a plant's leaves and roots. This process provides a readily available, but short in duration, source of nutrients. Use a fertilizer that's higher in phosphorus and potash, lower in nitrogen, and apply it at half-strength when the bulb leaves are well out of the ground. Fertilize a second time after the bulbs have finished flowering. If you have the time, give a third feeding, still at half-strength, two weeks after the second feeding.

✔ **Fertilize summer flowering bulbs just as you would any other perennial in the summer garden.** Book IV covers perennials.

Fertilizers are available to plants only when water is available to transport nutrients from the soil to the roots. If rainfall is lacking, water the bulbs as soon as you plant them.

Planting your spring-growing bulbs

Wait until the soil begins to cool off a bit to plant fall-planted, spring-blooming bulbs. After the bulbs are in the ground for a full cycle of growth, they adapt to the seasons, but planting too early can upset their natural pattern. Tulips are especially vulnerable — be sure that you wait until the soil cools down before planting; otherwise, tulips push up leaves right away and then freeze in the winter.

Fall-flowering bulbs — colchicums and fall crocuses, for example — move to the head of the autumn planting list simply because of their growth habits. They flower in autumn, and they're better off in the ground, with roots, when they do so. Smaller spring-blooming bulbs tend to dry out more quickly than bigger bulbs. So, plant crocuses and snowdrops before hyacinths. And any bulb without a tunic dries out more quickly than something that has that protection. So guinea hen flowers and wood hyacinths, for example, get priority planting over tulips and daffodils.

Some bulbs just don't like to wait — snowdrops have a tunic but are better off with as short an interval out of the ground as you can provide. Fritillaries all lack tunics and have an urge to grow roots right away. Plant all fritillaries ahead of other kinds of bulbs.

Tubers really shrivel up in storage. Winter aconites and Grecian windflowers get double preference — they're both tubers and small. Rehydrate winter aconites and Grecian windflowers before planting by placing them in a container of damp peat moss overnight.

Table 2-1 gives a brief overview of planting order.

Table 2-1	Bulb Planting Order
Type of Bulb	*Bulb Name*
Fall-flowering bulbs	Colchicums, fall crocuses, nerines
Tubers	Winter aconites, Grecian windflowers
Tuber-corms	Cyclamens
Little bulbs without tunics	Guinea hen flowers
Little bulbs with tunics	Crocuses and snowdrops

Type of Bulb	Bulb Name
Fritillaries	Persians, crown imperials
Big bulbs without tunics	Wood hyacinths
Big bulbs with tunics	Tulips and daffodils

Deciding when to plant spring-growing bulbs is really simple:

- **If you live someplace that has very cold winters, you can plant everything except tulips in autumn as soon as you have the bulbs.** Wait until the soil begins to cool off to plant tulips.

- **If you live in an area that has mild winters, hold off on just about everything until the soil begins to cool off.** Holding off also gives you time to precool tulips and daffodils in the refrigerator, if you didn't buy them already prepared.

Just remember to sequence your planting by the specific bulb's ability to wait, and store the bulbs in the most appropriate conditions.

Planting your summer-growing bulbs

Timing the planting of your summer-growing bulbs is simple:

- **If you live in a region with mild winters, you can plant summer-blooming bulbs when they're available in the stores, usually February.** They remain in the ground year-round.

- **If you live in an area with cold winters, wait until close to frost-free weather if you intend to plant directly in the ground.** You can plant two weeks before the last frost in spring; the weather will be frost-free by the time the bulbs send leaves above ground. Basically, if the weather is safe to plant tomatoes, you can plant tender bulbs also.

Space and place permitting, you can pot dahlias and cannas a month or more ahead and then plant outdoors during active growth. Caladiums need a longer head start, about three months.

For hardy bulbs in autumn, plant the little bulbs first, ones without tunics ahead of those with protection, along with a few odd-balls (such as autumn crocus, colchicum, and crown imperial) because they insist on jumping the queue. For spring-planted summer-flowering bulbs, wait until the weather is mild and settled.

Lilies, which are hardy bulbs often planted in spring, are the major exception to the "wait until it's warm" rule. Plant lilies as soon as you can find them in the stores. Lilies have fleshy bulbs, permanent roots, and no tunic — holding them out of the ground any longer than you must between purchase and planting will harm them. If you need to wait more than a few days but less than a week, keep the bulbs in barely damp peat moss in a cool place. Lilies will wait until the correct time to come up, and light frosts won't harm them.

Keeping the bloom in the bulb

Bulbs usually flower well the first season after they've been planted. Getting them to come back year after year *(perennialization)* can be more challenging. In Holland, the growers cut off the bulb flowers as soon as they're certain that the bulbs are *true to name* (meaning that the flower hasn't mutated in some form or that the wrong bulb wasn't planted) and have been inspected for carry-over diseases. They want the energy to go into the bulb, not into flower or seed production. You don't need to be that conservative, but unless you want bulb seeds for some reason, *deadheading* (cutting off) the flowers as they fade is more efficient (see Figure 2-2). Be reasonable, however. Cutting off dead blooms makes sense for tulips, hyacinths, daffodils, lilies, and such, but you'd go nuts trying to deadhead crocuses and snowdrops!

Figure 2-2: When you deadhead, make sure that you remove the little green swelling behind the withering flower — that's where the seeds will form.

Even when you don't see bulbs growing above ground, you can't assume that they're totally at rest. The spring blooming bulbs make autumn roots to help them get through winter. When you plant tulips, daffodils, hyacinths, crocuses, and snowdrops, make certain to give them ample water at that time. This careful watering encourages healthy root growth and gets the plants off to a good start.

Book VI

Bulbs

Avoid a factory shut-down

Leaves are the "factory" that manufactures a plant's food. When you cut lilies for bouquets, take as short a stem as is practical. The more leaves you remove, the less factory that remains to manufacture the food that the bulb stores for next year's display.

Good gardeners keep bulb leaves green and growing as long as possible — the greener the leaves and the longer they stay that way, the more food the bulbs will store. For the same reason, savvy gardeners don't fold, braid, bundle, or rubber-band bulb leaves if they want to grow good bulbs in subsequent years.

After bulbs have flowered, they still have work to do as they prepare for the next year. Bulbs need their leaves to produce food to store as reserves in their underground structures. Chopping the leaves away right after the flowers fade is a lousy gardening technique. It halts food production right then and there, when the bulb is at its most depleted stage. Particularly common with daffodils (whose long strap-like leaves are more obvious than the small grassy leaves of crocuses), gardeners bent on "tidying up" cut, fold, or twist the leaves into haystack bundles. Such neatnik techniques actually harm the bulbs. Keep the leaves growing as long as they're green and healthy looking. Don't remove them until they begin to yellow.

Don't forget to feed your bulbs, especially those that grow when conditions are tougher. Bulbs that grow early in spring when the soil is cool and nutrients less available need a ready source of fertilizer. Use liquid fertilizer that you can water on the leaves as well as the ground.

Storing Tender Bulbs in Cold Climates

By providing tender bulbs with a winter vacation, you can easily carry them over from year to year. Tender bulbs, such as cannas and dahlias, can survive light frosts that don't last for weeks on end. Even so, the first time the temperature dips much below 30°F (–1°C), dahlia and canna leaves turn to black mush. That's your signal to take the following steps:

1. **Carefully dig the bulbs out of the garden.**

2. **Gently shake off loose dirt and clip back the mushy leaves.**

3. **For the next few days, leave the roots out in a dry area.**

4. **Shake off any additional crumbly dry dirt that comes off easily.**

5. **Pack the roots in a cardboard box lined with a perforated plastic bag and fill with dry peat moss, wood shavings, buckwheat hulls, vermiculite, or any other similar material.**

   Make sure that individual root clumps don't touch — keep them separated with packing material. That way, if one clump does start to rot, the rot won't spread to all the stored plants.

6. **Punch a few holes in the plastic so excess moisture can escape, but not so many holes that the stored roots will dry up.**

   Keep the box (or boxes) in a cool, dry, place. For example, use the back wall (the one adjoining the house) of an attached, unheated garage.

Check every couple of months to see that the material isn't wet and that the roots aren't shriveling from dryness. Along about early to mid-March or April, depending on your location, you can unpack the tubers and rhizomes to pot them up. (Sometimes they will have already begun to grow, sort of insisting that you pot them or lose them.) Otherwise, wait until two weeks before your frost-free date to plant dormant cannas and dahlias in the garden.

Raising Hardy Bulbs in Mild Climates

Just as cold-climate gardeners manipulate dahlias and cannas to keep them from year to year, mild-climate gardeners need to finesse daffodils and tulips that insist on having a winter in order to flower. Hardy bulbs require several consecutive cold weeks *(chilling)* in order to send the correct signals to wake up the flower bud inside the bulb. You can always grow less demanding daffodil and tulip cultivars, such as tazetta and jonquilla daffodils and *Tulipa clusiana*. To have spring flowers in the winter house, use the same technique as when you pot these bulbs and chill them.

Vendors in mild-winter regions sell *precooled bulbs*. While still dormant, these bulbs have been carefully held at low temperatures to fool them into thinking that winter has come and gone. When you plant (using the same planting techniques you'd use anywhere), the bulbs grow and bloom as though they had gone through the winter. The trick is what happens next: After the bulbs go dormant, you have to dig and hold these bulbs through summer and then refrigerate for a couple of months before planting. This process is a little trickier than storing tender bulbs in cold climates. You may want to handle these bulbs as annuals, discarding them after they flower and planting new bulbs each year.

Making More of What You Have

Buying bulbs is a sure way to get more bulbs. But conveniently, many bulbs make more of themselves, providing an easy, less expensive way to have more bulbs.

Growing by offsets

Daffodils are an example of bulbs that are excellent at multiplying themselves. The bulb you originally planted makes some *offsets* (daughter bulbs) at the edge of the basal plate. The original mother bulb nourishes them as they grow. In due time (and it only takes a couple of years), the daughter bulbs become large enough to flower themselves. Then they start making daughter bulbs of their own. Eventually, the clump of bulbs becomes so crowded that heavy competition for nutrients can cause flowering to decline. At that point — or even sooner — you need to step in with a shovel and separate the bulbs.

The best time to separate bulbs is after the flower blooms have faded, but while the leaves are still green and growing vigorously.

Locating bulbs that still have leaves attached is much easier than searching for leafless bulbs lurking incognito beneath the soil.

Offsets are actively growing plants and thus need different handling than do dormant bulbs in autumn. Dig and divide a clump at a time to reduce the risk of roots drying out, and then follow these steps:

1. **Prepare the new soil if some bulbs are going into a different location.**

   Add organic matter — compost, leaf mold, or dry manure — and granular fertilizer. Have the same materials available to rejuvenate the original location.

2. **Dig the bulbs one clump at a time.**

   One clump of overcrowded daffodils may produce as much as 50 bulbs! Dig only what you can handle at one go.

3. **Have some wet burlap or wet newspaper to cover the bulbs as you work, and then quickly but carefully separate the bulbs.**

   Take a group and gently twist and rock the bulbs back and forth until they separate.

4. **Replant as many as you want at the appropriate depth.**

   You can choose to replant each and every division, down to the smallest, or only those big enough to flower in a year.

Book VI

Bulbs

5. **Water regularly.**

   Watering is important because you want the roots to re-establish quickly and nourish the leaves, enabling the bulbs to store more food and flower sooner.

6. **Mulch.**

7. **Move on to the next clump and start the process again.**

Unlike daffodils that make offsets, glads make little *cormels,* or baby corms. After you dig at the end of the growing season and find these cormels, store them separately from the large, flowering-size corms. Before replanting the next spring, soak the cormels in lukewarm water for a couple of hours — they have a very hard tunic, and can root more easily if the tunic is first softened by soaking. The new glads will probably flower the second year.

Reseeding

Offsets aren't the only means of propagation. A number of bulbs will reseed on their own, especially little ones, such as scilla, chionodoxa, crocus, and winter aconite. Seedlings of the first three look like grass blades, and young winter aconites look like miniatures of the mature plants.

Disturbing these immature seedlings their first year is risky — the nascent bulb is so tiny that it's easily damaged. Wait until the plants are a couple of years old and then dig and move them *in the green,* as the English phrase it — in other words, while they're still green and growing.

Minimizing Pests and Diseases

Okay. We have great news, good news and, well . . . *other* news. The great news is that flowering bulbs are tough plants and often provide years of outstanding garden service with truly a minimum of trouble from pests and diseases. The good news is that even if you do run into little problems, you can usually handle them easily with a variety of methods. That *other* news is that the garden, being a garden, will sooner or later run into some sort of difficulty. (For a complete discussion of pests and disease in the garden, see Chapter 7 in Book I.)

Practicing prevention first

Before getting to the nitty-gritty of diagnosing and solving disease and pest problems, we take a look at how to *avoid* the trouble in the first place. Some of the following are specific tips about bulbs, and others you'll recognize as good gardening practices that benefit all the plants you grow:

- ✓ **Start with high-quality, healthy bulbs.** Choose firm, plump bulbs. Avoid those showing any signs of molds, soft rots, or insect damage. Plant bulbs as soon as possible and at the proper time.

- ✓ **Store your bulbs properly.**

- ✓ **Give bulbs the conditions they need.** Bulbs need proper drainage, soil, light, air circulation, and nutrition. Match the right bulb with the right conditions. Do your homework before you buy.

- ✓ **Water carefully to avoid wetting the leaves.** Wet leaves may lead to mildew and other problems. Water early in the day or use a device such as a drip hose to wet the soil and not the foliage.

- ✓ **Keep your garden ship-shape.**

- ✓ **Be a detective.** By keeping an eye on your garden (the experts call this *scouting*), you can spot and correct problems early, before they get bad.

Arming your bulbs against bugs

When protecting your bulbs against pesky bugs, you have several options:

- ✓ **Enlist the good guys.** Lots of garden critters that hang around actually prey upon the bad bugs that harm plants. In a garden with a variety of plants and no pesticides, good and bad bugs co-exist in a natural balance. If the bad guys get a bit out of hand, you can bring in these reinforcements:

  - • **Green lacewings:** Buy lacewings eggs and larvae to spread throughout your garden. The larvae consume aphids voraciously, sometimes carrying the remains of their victims on their backs. The adult lacewings feed on nectar and pollen.

  - • **Lady beetles or lady bugs:** These familiar bugs feed on aphids, mites, and thrips. You can buy mesh bags with hundreds of lady beetles and release them with the hope that they stick around.

  - • **Parasitic nematodes:** These microscopic worms handle some soil pests, burrowing insects, and grubs.

  - • **Praying mantises:** These giants of the good bug army do serious damage to aphids, caterpillars, leaf hoppers, and the like. You can buy a cocoon-like sack with praying mantis eggs inside, but you have no guarantee that the mantises will remain in your garden.

- ✓ **Call up the organic cavalry.** If problems persist after prevention and signing on the good bug infantry, your next step is safe, organic, biodegradable controls. These methods include botanical insecticides (made from plants themselves), insecticidal soaps, and certain natural bacteria that are harmful only to the larvae of certain bugs.

✔ **Engage in chemical warfare.** If none of the previous methods work, your last line of defense is synthetic or chemical controls in the form of insecticides and fungicides. These poisons kill fastest and have the most impact on your garden's ecological balance. In all likelihood, you won't even need them. But if you do, follow the advice of a professional nursery staff person or agricultural extension agent to help you identify the problem and select the treatment. Follow instructions and safety precautions on product labels *exactly*.

Safety is a priority, and maintaining ecological balance is a worthy goal, so pest prevention and nontoxic controls are always your best bet. Use harsh chemical methods only as a last resort — sparingly, prudently, and carefully. (See Chapter 7 in Book I for more information on pest control in the garden.)

Sending pests packing

In this creature feature, we look at some common pests specific to bulbs.

Irritating insects

Here are some insects that may do their dirty work on bulbs (refer to Chapter 7 in Book I for more specifics on these pests):

✔ **Aphids:** They're fond of many bulbs, including crocuses, dahlias, tulips, daffodils, and glads.

✔ **Beetles:** Astilbe, begonia, cannas, cyclamen, and dahlias are susceptible, especially when grown in containers.

✔ **Mites:** They like crocus, cyclamen, begonia, hyacinth, lily, and freesia, among other bulbs.

✔ **Narcissus fly larvae or bulb maggots:** They bore in and eat bulb centers producing soft, mushy bulbs that don't grow well, if at all. They go for daffodils, amaryllis, rain lily, and others.

✔ **Snails and slugs:** Prime feeding targets are tulips, dahlias, and lilies.

✔ **Thrips:** They may hit daffodils, lilies, irises, glads, and others.

Annoying animals

Tasty treats that they are, your favorite bulbs may turn otherwise law-abiding animals into serious criminals. Beware the mice, rabbits, voles, woodchucks, and deer that unearth and munch bulbs or crunch foliage and flowers. Here's a tactic or two to try:

- ✔ **Use mothballs.** Sprinkle a few mothballs (not the flake type) around the base of plants and young trees and shrubs to repel rabbits.

- ✔ **Plant poisonous bulbs, such as daffodils, fritillarias, snowflakes, snowdrops, or colchicums.** Not only will animals leave them alone, but these bulbs may also protect neighboring bulbs.

- ✔ **Use repellents or scare tactics.** To stop deer from eating bulbs, some people place bars of deodorant soap (but not cocoa-based soap) around the garden, or sprinkle baby powder. Commercial deer repellent sprays are available. Dogs, if contained, can bark deer away, although neighbors may not appreciate the noise. Vigilant dogs (smaller breeds are easier on beds and borders) and cats can thwart rodents, including rats, mice, gophers, and voles.

- ✔ **Fence bulbs in, deer and rodents out.** You can stop these irritating and often hungry creatures by planting your bulbs in a wire mesh cage. Line the planting hole for a group of bulbs with chicken wire. To hinder mice, use hardware cloth over the bed and remove it when shoots poke out of the ground. Remember that deer don't seem to go in for calla lilies, daffodils, and irises.

- ✔ **Set traps.** Some people go for traps, baits, or electronic controls to foil rodents, but you have to consider how much the method will cost (in dollars, trouble, and toxins) to win the war.

Dismissing diseases

Your bulb-disease problems should be few because many bulbs seem to be naturally resistant to disease, but bulb rot, botrytis (or gray mold), powdery mildew, and viruses can strike bulbs. You can find information on prevention, control, and cure in Chapter 7 of Book I.

How many bulbs will a woodchuck crunch?

Woodchucks can be real bulb destroyers and are sometimes hard to combat. Try removing their favorite covers (weeds, woodpiles, and grass), planting a patch of clover or alfalfa to lure them away from the garden, or using repellent plants, such as alliums, onions, or garlic. A 3- to 4-foot (1- to 1.2-m) wire fence may do the trick, but don't secure it near the top (so that it's too flimsy for them to scale), and bury it 18 inches (46 cm) to stop burrowing.

Chapter 3

A Bulb for Every Garden

In This Chapter

▶ Choosing bulbs for spring and summer, beds and borders

▶ Selecting bulbs for the informal, shady garden

▶ Using bulbs for rock gardens and damp places

The world is filled with seemingly zillions of bulbs — each one as beautiful or more beautiful than the last, and all wonderfully versatile. Clearly, bulbs aren't interchangeable. You can't quite mix and match them because not all bulbs grow in the same places, and they don't all flower at the same time. But visiting a garden center just to buy a few bulbs to beautify your garden can be intimidating if you don't know what to buy or where to plant them. Even if you're quietly opening a catalog in the privacy of your own home, you may feel overwhelmed by the number and variety of bulbs available.

Bulbs are often multipurpose, as well. Tulips are great cut flowers. Some are excellent for coaxing into early bloom while it's still winter outdoors. Some are super for the rock garden. Some make a stunning display when massed together for a colorful tapestry of flowers. They also combine beautifully with other plants in a perennial border (see Book IV for details on perennials). Whatever your wants and needs, wherever you garden, whatever conditions your garden provides, bulbs are ready and willing to fulfill your wishes.

This chapter helps you sort things out. We don't tell you about specific plants — you have to turn to Chapter 4 in Book VI for that — but we do suggest plants that work best in a specific situation.

About Bedding and Borders

Before we get into what bulbs go well where, we need to define some simple terms:

✔ **Bedding:** *Bedding* is planting masses of whatever plant you're talking about for a really impressive display. The display is striking, no question about it, but you need to think about what happens next. The hyacinth flowers fade, the leaves turn yellow, and you're left with a large expanse of bare dirt — except that the hyacinth bulbs are asleep underground, so you can't really dig and delve too much. Annuals (see Book V) are the answer, but they can get expensive.

✔ **Bedding out:** Public settings, such as parks, botanic gardens, common areas of office buildings, and condominium associations, often practice *bedding out,* planting lots of the same thing in tight groups. You may decide to practice this technique in your own backyard.

✔ **Borders:** *Borders* are mixed plantings of perennials with some bulbs and annuals, and maybe even a few shrubs and small trees. If you mix and match in this fashion, allowing maybe 15 percent of the space for bulbs, the gaps that appear when bulbs go dormant aren't as obvious. In addition, the leafy growth of perennials, such as peonies and daylilies, also helps conceal the yellowing, aging bulb leaves.

For information on designing beds and borders, turn to Book II.

Bulbs for Spring Bedding

Hyacinths are ideal for bedding schemes. Their flowers are arranged in masses on stiff formal spikes that seem tailor-made for formal designs. With soft or deep blue, pale pink to deep red, cool white to creamy yellow to soft orange, you can create patterns or a design of geometric blocks, rhythmic curves, stripes, squares, or circles. The bulbs remain year after year, and while the spike of bloom may be somewhat smaller after the first year, it's still enough to satisfy all except the most critical gardener.

A jumbled combination of several different kinds of bulbs is going to look muddy and have a weaker effect than if you plant blocks of a single kind.

Daffodils are graceful enough for borders, emphatic enough for bedding. A host of golden daffodils is a sure sign of spring, even if you never memorized Wordsworth's poem in grade school! Choose larger, taller daffodils for bedding out; they make a more emphatic display than miniature daffodils. Although daffodils have a limited color range — yellow, white, and bicolors of yellow and white, yellow and orange, or white and orange — the difference is enough to be apparent.

Never buy mixtures, for any purpose. Sure, buy several different kinds of daffodils, but don't mix them within a single group. That way, you can control what's going where rather than leaving it to random chance. In a bedding scheme, the daffodils need to all flower at the same time. So, you want to make sure that early daffodils are grouped together, rather than having some early ones mixed with others that bloom later. If you mix them, some will be blooming while others are withering — not a pretty sight.

Daffodils stay in the ground year after year. Their bulbs generally increase into clumps. After several years, you need to dig them up, separate them, and then promptly replant. (We tell you when and how to do this task in Chapter 2 of Book VI.)

Tulips are simply fabulous for bedding out. With their riotous range of colors from soft pastels to jewel-tone bright, you can create a carpet of color. Generally, you plant bedding tulips in blocks or groups of a single color. The adjacent group can be a related color for a subtle effect, or strongly contrasting for a more dynamic result. Trickier is interplanting two different tulips for a color-blending effect, say a purple with a softer pink, or a yellow with a peachy apricot. The tulips can be somewhat different in height, but they absolutely must flower simultaneously. You can bed out any of the cultivated varieties *(cultivars)* of tulips. Avoid the original wild types, however; they just don't work well in beds.

Tulips flower best the first year you plant them. If you're striving for a lavish display of bedding tulips, you'll need to be extravagant. Discard the bulbs that have finished flowering and plant new bulbs each and every year. The method to this madness is that, every year, you get to change the colors and design to suit your fancy.

You don't usually see ornamental onions as bulbs for bedding out. The taller ones, such as *Allium aflatunense,* are really elegant for such use, however, with each bulb producing a soap bubble of purple flowers balanced on a slender stem. We saw them once in a public garden in England — the ornamental onions massed in a rectangular bed, with pink forget-me-nots carpeting the ground. The display was dynamite! Because ornamental onions flower from May to July, they help fill the gap between the more familiar spring bulbs, such as tulips, and summer bulbs, such as lilies.

Bulbs for Spring Borders

Hyacinths, daffodils, and tulips are also excellent in spring flower borders. Borders, no matter how formal, are less rigid than bedding out designs. In general, you plant a group of ten bulbs in a border rather than the many more used in a bedding scheme. You still keep to one kind within each group, say all white hyacinths rather than some pink, a couple of blue, one yellow, and the rest white. You can have several groups of hyacinths — all the same or a different color for each group — separated by other kinds of perennials (refer to Book IV for more about perennials), such as peonies, daylilies, or astilbes. Or, you can combine a group of hyacinths with some perennials, next to a group of tulips or daffodils.

Crown imperial *(Fritillaria imperialis)* is a stunning addition to the perennial border. At about 3 feet (91 cm) tall, crown imperials really stand out, and the wreath of good-sized orange flowers, topped with a pineapple-like tuft of

Book VI

Bulbs

leaves, is unusual enough to really command attention. Planted singly, crown imperial is like an exclamation point. Three to five of these big bulbs make a strong statement; more is really lavish.

Ornamental onions, *Allium* species and cultivars, make a great addition to the late spring border. Shorter ones, such as *Allium christophii* or *Allium karataviense* are charming with hardy geraniums. Taller ones, such as *Allium aflatunense* or the *Allium giganteum* cultivars, are stately with larger perennials and/or ornamental grasses. Because their flowers make such a good show (and the bulbs cost a bit more than tulips and daffodils), groups of three to five make quite a nice display.

Bulbs for Summer Beds

Gardeners don't do as much bedding out with summer bulbs. You find most summer bulbs in flower beds, combined with perennials and annuals.

Cannas are used for bedding, sometimes in those very Victorian bull's-eye schemes plopped into a lawn. Public parks often feature bedding schemes with blocks of cannas, probably because they're tall enough to stand out in a summer garden. Modern canna cultivars have showy flowers — fat tropical blooms in vivid colors. Don't overlook cannas as foliage plants, though. Their varieties of bold leaves may be plain green, rich copper-bronze, and even variegated.

Dahlias work as bedding plants when you choose moderately sized cultivars. Dinner-plate dahlias with huge flowers on tall plants that practically need scaffolding for support are rather awkward *en masse*. Mid- to modest-size cultivars — for example, mignon type — are more suitable. Dahlias bloom from late summer until frost, so they really extend the display season.

Caladiums are one of the major summer bulbs that work in the shade. Mass plantings create an attractive picture of tropical luxuriance, with large, broad, arrow-shaped leaves in various combinations of pink, red, or white with green.

Bulbs for Summer Borders

Both cannas and dahlias are suitable for summer borders, where these tender bulbs mingle with perennials and annuals in a sunny place.

If you think of cannas as foliage plants, you'll find it easier to discover combinations that work. Cannas are sometimes awkward as flowering plants because they can grow 5, 6, or even 7 feet tall. Place them at the back of the border where the cannas and their tall companions can hang out without concealing shorter plants. Dahlias continue flowering so late (right up to frost) that they team up well with other late season perennials. Consider fall asters, ornamental grasses, or shrubs. You can even mix and match cannas with dahlias. Try a copper/bronze-leafed canna with orange or scarlet flowered dahlias. That's hot!

Lilies are bulbs with real stage presence. They hold their flowers at the top of the stem, making a noticeable display. Because they like to grow with their heads in the sun and their bulbs in the shade, lilies are ideally suited for a mix-and-match planting with perennials.

Bulbs for the Informal Shady Garden

Even where trees are individual specimens plunked in a lawn, they still provide some shade. And the north side of a building isn't exactly sunny! What can you plant where the sun doesn't shine? Shade-loving bulbs, of course! And lots of 'em.

Spring bulbs

Many of these little bulbs flower so early in the year that, according to the calendar, it isn't even spring! Sensibly, they nestle close to the ground where they can find some protection from harsh winds. But size doesn't matter. Anything in bloom that early in the year is a welcome sight.

These bulbs are named in sequence by their Latin names, making it easier to look them up in a catalog index when you want to order some for your garden:

- **Grecian windflower *(Anemone blanda):*** Daisy-like flowers in blue, pink, or white. This bulb blooms at the same time that you'd put pansies and primroses in the garden. Additionally, the lower-growing Grecian windflower pairs nicely with smaller daffodils and the earlier-flowering, lower-growing tulips, adding a soft accent.

- **Glory of the snow *(Chionodoxa luciliae):*** This bulb blooms while the weather is still a little nippy. It has charming blue flowers, several along a stem that's only a few inches high. It's obliging about increasing — happily seeding about — so give it room to romp. Try it under early-flowering shrubs or shrubs with long-lingering fruits from last autumn.

- **Persian violet *(Cyclamen coum):*** The Persian violet is a treasure well worth the search. It flowers so early that snow often covers it, and yet it emerges unscathed. The vivid magenta flowers make a bright display. Nestle the tuber at the base of an oak tree or in some choice location where the ground-hugging plant won't be overrun by vigorous neighbors while dormant.

- **Winter aconite** *(Eranthis hyemalis):* Another harbinger of spring, this plant flowers before the snow is over. Yellow buttercup-like flowers on stems only a few inches high add early color to the woodland garden. Though sulky about having to be dried out for shipping and storage, those tubers that do survive the process are generous about seeding around and making more of themselves. This little treasure needs a place where it won't be disturbed when dormant.

- **Dogtooth violet** *(Erythronium species):* It looks like a miniature lily, with a nodding flower or two in white, yellow, or pink. The upswept petals give a graceful look to a plant that's less than 1 foot (30 cm) tall. When planting, handle the dormant corms gently because they bruise easily. Give the dogtooth violet a special place to be admired, near a path where you can easily pause to appreciate it.

- **Guinea hen flower** *(Fritillaria meleagris):* Each bulb has one or sometimes two nodding bell-like flowers clearly marked in purple and white, like a checker board. Either you like it or you don't, but no one's indifferent! Try this for something new and different because it's easier to grow than its uncommon appearance suggests.

- **Snowdrop** *(Galanthus nivalis):* This plant is arguably the most popular of the little, early blooming bulbs for shady places. Its fresh white flowers are a sure sign of winter's end. Sturdy and easy to grow, snowdrops come in more varieties than you may suspect.

- **Wood hyacinth** *(Hyacinthoides hispanica):* This vigorous plant is best suited to casual places where it has space to spread, or paired with shrubs that will stand up to its habit of extending its territory. It's not as fragrant as its namesake, but spikes of blue, bell-like flowers make it all worthwhile.

- **Siberian squill** *(Scilla siberica):* This excellent little bulb sports electric-blue flowers that follow hot on the heels of glory of the snow. The few little flower bells face downward on each stem. As bulbs multiply by seed and offset, they spread into pools of blue, irresistible in woodland, delightful in a lawn too thin and patchy to pass as a putting green.

- **Daffodils** *(Narcissus* **species and cultivars):** Daffodils are easy to grow, great in gardens and vases alike, and untouched by pests such as deer, rabbits, chipmunks, or voles. You have your choice of tall stately ones, small charming ones, singles or doubles, and even a few that are fragrant. Daffodils and narcissuses are the same thing.

Jonquil, what folks in the southeastern United States name every yellow narcissus, is more accurately used for a somewhat later-flowering group of usually fragrant daffodils that are mostly yellow (but earlier-flowering daffodils can also be yellow).

A shady summer bulb

Caladium is a real workhorse, accenting a shady place with colorful leaves. Caladium adds a special accent to a shady nook, perhaps in combination with annuals, such as impatiens, or perennials, such as ferns and hostas. Just remember that this tender tuber loathes frost and needs humid, hot weather and adequate moisture.

Bulbs for Rock and Herb Gardens

Book VI

Bulbs

A *rock garden* is a great place for small treasures. Generally, plants grown here are less than 1 foot (30 cm) tall. Rock gardens are usually places with relatively infertile, well-drained soil. *Herb gardens* aren't so different because most herbs are sun lovers that grow in well-drained sites and have the most intense flavor and fragrance when grown in infertile soil. (Find out more about herbs in Book VII.)

Crocus is one of the earliest, and best, little bulbs for these kinds of sites. Actually a toothsome corm popular for munchies with various pests, the gritty soil helps deter the underground vermin, and strong-scented herb foliage may provide a modicum of deer deterrence. Growing crocuses under a ground cover of thyme is one combination that's pretty and practical.

Tulips, not the big hybrids but the small species, are perfectly in scale for a rock garden and appreciate the sun and sharp drainage. Dainty and colorful, their early flowers pair nicely with moss pink, *Phlox subulata,* or evergreen candytuft, *Iberis sempervirens.*

Bulbs for Damp Places

In general, bulbs like good drainage, which is especially important when bulbs are resting. After all, a bulb is a plant's way of coping with stress, and stress often includes dry times. But every rule has exceptions, and a few bulbs do take constantly moist soil:

✔ **Guinea hen flowers (*Fritillaria meleagris*):** These plants hate to dry out. A sunny moist meadow (or a damp lawn) does just fine, and a damp woodland setting is even better. These smallish plants — flowering in early spring with unusual, purple-and-white checkered bell-like flowers, one or two to a stem — are ideally suited to your problem spot.

- ✔ **Spring snowflakes (*Leucojum vernum*) and their later-flowering cousin, the summer snowflake (*Leucojum aestivum*):** Both like moist soil in light shade. The spring version flowers as early as snowdrops do, with one or two green-tipped white bell-shaped flowers per stem. The summer version blooms with daffodils. Several somewhat larger flowers dangle jauntily from a taller stem.

- ✔ **Camassia (*Camassia* species and cultivars):** These plants flower along with the taller tulips. In fact, they combine nicely — the tall spikes of nicely spaced, soft blue, starry flowers look charming with yellow, white, pink, or purple tulips. This obliging bulb even thrives in wet clay, a struggle for many plants. So for your problem site, or just a wet one, try this native American bulb.

- ✔ **Cannas:** These bulbs love water so much that you can plant them in a pond! That's right, plunk their container right down in the water. Just remember that they don't like to freeze, so plan on storing the tubers indoors if winter is part of your yearly seasons. Think of cannas as bold and luxuriantly tropical foliage plants, colored of green, bronze, creamy yellow and green, blotched with white, or like a tropical sunset.

In general, don't expect lilies to like soggy sites. But every rule is said to have its exception, and *Lilium superbum* is a lily for that sunny damp (no standing water, please) spot in your yard. Summer blooming, a generous number of showy orange flowers, whose curled back petals clearly reveal their black-speckled insides, adorn the tall and stately stems. Mix and match lilies with other sun- and moisture-loving plants such as Joe Pye weed (*Eupatorium purpureum*) or tall astilbes such as 'Ostrich Plume'.

Bulbs for Summer Containers

Plants seem more important when displayed in a container, and the containers really dress up a patio or terrace. (Chapter 3 in Book II discusses container gardening in detail.) The following bulbs work very well in containers:

- ✔ **Cannas:** Cannas are suitable for big containers, half-whiskey-barrel size. More exciting than geraniums, these bold beauties work well with some trailing plants — for example, variegated vinca vine — to soften the container's edge. Because they're such large, moisture-loving plants, they need a great deal of water.

- ✔ **Caladiums:** They're not only great in shady gardens where they grow in the ground, but they're also super in containers on that shady patio or balcony. Their lush foliage adds a tropical look to your summer plantings.

✔ **Dahlias:** Dahlias are great container plants as long as you choose the lower-growing kinds. Some dahlias are even dainty enough for a window box.

✔ **Lilies:** These plants are nicely sized for container growing — especially the early summer-flowering mid-century hybrids. New, really dwarf lilies are just ideal for container use.

Bulbs for Spring Flowers in the Winter House

You can fool Mother Nature, and it's easy to boot! First, give potted spring-flowering bulbs several weeks at low temperature — a chilling period, so they think that it's winter. Then, bring them inside where the temperature is warmer, and the bulbs think that it's spring. So they bloom. Early. Following are some easy bulbs to force into bloom:

✔ **Tulips are easy to coax into early bloom.** The earlier they naturally flower in spring, the easier your job is. Conveniently, the very early tulips are lower growing.

✔ **Daffodils naturally flower earlier in spring than do tulips, so they're even easier to force.** Choose lower growing daffodils, so that you're not overwhelmed with very tall plants on your dinner table.

✔ **Hyacinths are not only easy to force, but they smell good, too.** With their prepackaged flowers inside the bulb, you don't even need soil. Hyacinths will bloom if you just add water.

Bulbs as Cut Flowers

Bulbs make great cut flowers. But you don't have to pay florist prices; you can grow bulbs for cut flowers yourself — and you can grow and cut bulbs that aren't often available.

Among cut flowers for early spring, consider snowdrops, grape hyacinths, daffodils, early tulips, and hyacinths. For midspring, try later blooming tulips and ornamental onions. Summer provides lilies, gladiolas, and the lovely leaves of caladiums. Later in summer, use crocosmia and the first dahlias for arrangements, continuing with dahlias right up to frost. Gardeners in mild winter regions can raise enough amaryllis, naked ladies, and nerines to have some to cut.

Chapter 4

A Bulb for All Seasons

• •

*B*ulbs (and corms and tubers and rhizomes) are versatile, enticing, and amazing little plant packages. Which bulbs you choose for your garden (or your containers or your houseplants) depends on many factors, including when you want them to bloom, what colors you want, how much effort you want to put into their care, and where you want to plant them. This chapter tells you about many different varieties of plants, which will either make your decision much easier, or send you househunting for a bigger yard!

Note: Refer to Chapter 2 in Book I and the color insert for an explanation of climate zones referred to throughout this chapter.

Amaryllis

Just to keep gardeners confused, what we in the United States call amaryllis, the taxonomists insist are *Hippeastrum*. (Technically, the naked ladies plants from South Africa are *Amaryllis*.) The U.S. amaryllis originated in South America. Popular in autumn, amaryllis are garden plants only in temperate, warm, subtropical climates, Zones 7 to 11.

Amaryllis cooks in pots

Sometimes, you can find an amaryllis already potted. All you need to do is take it out of the box, stand it on a window sill, and add water. A huge, rather phallic bud quickly emerges and grows to a top-heavy height. Four, sometimes six, huge, wide-open trumpet-like flowers appear. The biggest bulbs frequently send up a second, sometimes even a third, flowering stem. Then the long, strap-like leaves appear. You water, you feed the plant fertilizer, and then the leaves go dormant. Later, the bulb wakes up and starts making leaves, but no flower stem. This result causes frustration on your part and dogged determination on the part of the amaryllis — it needs to make seven leaves before it regains the strength to flower again. If it doesn't produce that many leaves at once, it does so sequentially.

Amaryllis (we're talking *Hippeastrum*, here) come in two forms: the familiar huge blooms from large bulbs, and daintier flowers from more moderately sized bulbs. The latter are quite easy to rebloom.

- **Full-size amaryllis:** Here are some excellent cultivars of amaryllis bulbs that produce large, impressive blooms:

  - **'Apple Blossom':** Stout, 12- to 20-inch (30- to 51-cm) stems hold two to six star-shaped flowers in creamy white with pink blush on the petal tips.

  - **'Lady Jane':** Double flowers in unique apricot rose with just a touch of white striping in the center of each petal create a lovely, layered effect on 18- to 24-inch (46- to 61-cm) stems.

  - **'Pasadena':** Double ring of regal red petals with white stripes offers festive beauty on stems that grow 18 to 24 inches (46 to 61 cm).

  - **'Sandra':** Warm, peachy rose flowers with darker veins, accented by a white brush stroke down the center of each petal. Multiple stems should reach 18 to 24 inches (46 to 61 cm).

- **Miniature amaryllis:** If you really want a show, try planting three to five bulbs of one variety of miniature amaryllis in a suitably sized pot:

  - **'Double Picotee':** Glistening white flowers edged with a pencil-thin band of red outlining every petal and a final brushstroke of pink at the petal tips. Stems reach 18 inches (46 cm) with multiple flowers.

  - **'Germa':** Soft yellow, starry blossoms with a hint of green in the heart have lily-like similarity on stems that reach 18 inches (46 cm).

  - **'Picotee':** Stunning white flowers edged delicately with a fine line of dark red and finished with pale green centers. One of the most popular cultivars, the tallest stems may reach 18 inches (46 cm).

  - **'Scarlet Baby':** Many brilliant red flowers with faint white dashes. Long-lasting color on compact 12- to 18-inch (30- to 46-cm) stems.

Caladiums

Caladiums are tubers that positively adore the dog days of August, when the weather's hot and humid and they can flaunt their large, flamboyant, arrow-shaped leaves in the shade. Who needs flowers when the leaves look this good! Caladiums work well in a shady window box or container, as well as in summer bouquets. Don't plant caladiums outside until the weather is consistently warm and soil temperature reaches 60°F (15°C). They get chilled very easily. Caladiums are only hardy in really subtropical regions (Zones 10 and 11) that replicate their tropical South American home. Elsewhere, you need to lift and store them dry and frost-free over winter. Bring containers indoors as is, and keep them in a dark closet until late winter or early spring when tubers need to awaken and begin growing again. Store caladiums at 70-75°F (21-24°C).

If you start the tubers just as you receive them, they'll produce fewer, but larger leaves. If you use a grapefruit spoon (or your thumbnail) to scoop away the growing points, you can grow shorter, bushier, leafier caladiums.

The following are just as attractive cut as they are in the garden, and they last pretty well, too:

✔ **'Blaze':** Outstanding, bright-red foliage is elegantly edged in deep green on 18-inch (46-cm) plants.

✔ **'Candidum':** Snowy-white leaves with medium green veins and borders on 18-inch (46-cm) plants. 'Candidum Jr.', mirrors the green and white beauty of 'Candidum', but it's shorter — 16 inches (41 cm) or less — with smaller leaves that show off more white.

✔ **'Miss Muffet':** Unusual and graceful lance-leafed caladium has smaller, narrower, and more pointed leaves that start out chartreuse and pale to a creamy white. Dappled red spots add zip to this 12- to 18-inch (30- to 46-cm) plant.

✔ **'Mrs. Arno Nehrling':** Low-growing (about 12 inches/30 cm or so) white, with arresting bright pink veins. Leaves also have occasional greenish markings.

Cannas

Either you love them or you don't, but not very many gardeners are indifferent to cannas. Rather than plopping a canna into the center of concentric rings of yellow marigolds and red salvia, think of cannas instead as bold, lush, tropical plants, and they become much more interesting. Cannas come in different sizes, different leaf colors, and many have lush flowers offering you a choice of colors:

✔ **Green-leafed cannas:** We recommend the following green-leafed cannas:

• **'Journey's End':** Striking flowers in creamy yellow splashed with glowing pink accents atop 3-foot-high (1 m) deep green foliage are reminiscent of a tropical sunset.

• **'Rose Futurity':** Unique blend of colors in flowers ranging from coral to rose on 3-foot (1-m) stems with dark burgundy leaves.

• **'Stadt Fellbach':** Vibrant, deep orange flowers on 3½-foot (3.1-m) stems are guaranteed to enliven the garden.

• **'The President':** Extra-large, extra-bright red flowers set against handsome deep green foliage on 3- to 4-feet (1- to 1.2-m) plants make this the most popular canna of all.

✔ **Red-leafed cannas:** The following are red-leafed cannas:

- **'Ambassador' (also known as 'Black Night'):** Regal red flowers with a velvet texture have attractive bronze foliage on 3½-foot (3.1-m) plants.

- **'Black Knight,':** Not to be confused with 'Black Night', also blooms in bright red and offers impressive deep mahogany to purple foliage on 3- to 5-foot (1- to 1.5-m) plants.

- **'Red King Humbert':** Scarlet flowers and dark leaves tinged with red on plants that range from 4 to 8 feet (1.2 to 2.4 m).

- **'Wyoming':** Tangerine flowers open above dark bronze leaves touched with purple. Plant reaches 4 to 7 feet (1.2 to 2 m).

✔ **Yellow-leafed cannas:** The following are yellow-leafed cannas:

- **'Bengal Tiger' (also known as 'Pretoria'):** Arresting variegated leaves striped with bold bands of cream, green, and gold on 4- to 5-foot (1.2- to 1.5-m) plants that also send up huge orange blossoms.

- **'Striped Beauty':** Leaves streaked with yellow are perfectly matched to bright canary-yellow flowers on 2- to 3-foot (0.6- to 1-m) stems.

✔ **Multicolored canna, 'Tropicana':** Striped leaves unfurl to reveal burgundy stripes and a greenish-yellow center vein that go quickly to red, pink, yellow, and gold — all against a dark green background. Impressive, bright orange flowers top the 2- to 4-foot (0.6- to 1.2-m) plants.

✔ **Water cannas:** These love to grow wet, in pools and ponds with water lilies. You may want to try them in large nondraining pots, which you can overwinter in a protected spot indoors. Try these cultivars:

- **'Erebus':** Graceful 4-foot-tall (1.2 m) plant with salmon-pink flowers.

- **'Ra':** Bright, cheerful yellow flowers are ideal against wide, bold leaves that reach 4 feet (1.2 m).

- **'Taney':** Radiant apricot-orange blossoms borne on 4-foot (1.2-m) plants.

✔ **White-blotched canna, 'Stuttgart':** Impressive 7-foot-tall (2-m) canna with medium green, narrow leaves attractively blotched with white and gray. It needs shade, especially at midday, or the leaves burn.

Crocosmia

When you first grow plants from winterless places, the tendency is to think that they're delicate, needing all sorts of pampering and protection. Sometimes, you'll be pleasantly surprised at how sturdy these plants can be, as is the case with crocosmia. Sometimes, crocosmia are called *crocosmiiflora* or *montbretia*.

Because the cultivars are hybrids, hardiness varies depending on which parent they most closely resemble. A gladiolus-like plant in leaf, crocosmia has a tall sheaf of sword-like leaves. The flowers are quite different, a spray of smaller blossoms in hot reds and oranges that really light up the late-summer garden. Consider them hardy in Zones 6 to 10 (use a winter mulch of pine boughs at the colder end of the range).

Plant crocosmias in spring, even in places where you're sure that they're hardy; wait until after the last frost, and then plant in a sunny, well-drained site. If the corms are showing signs of growth when you receive them, and the weather's still too chilly to plant them outdoors, pot them. It's important to let them begin growing if that's what they show you that they want to do. Then, you can just transplant them to the garden when the weather's mild and settled.

Try these varieties of crocosmias:

- ✔ **'Constance':** Dozens of funnel-shaped, showy, nasturtium-orange flowers in double rows on graceful, arching stems. Plants range from 2 to 3 feet (0.6 to 1 m) and bloom from August through September.

- ✔ **'James Coey':** Brilliant yellow flowers with vermilion accents on plants that grow 2 to 3 feet (0.6 to 1 m) tall and produce over a long bloom time.

- ✔ **'Lucifer':** Dozens of deep red blossoms on 3-foot (1-m) plants. Plant them in groups of 10 or more for a spectacular midsummer display. The hardiest of the lot, it can survive Zone-5 winters with protection. Provide a generous layer of mulch to ensure winter survival in coldest regions.

- ✔ *Crocosmia mansonorum:* Bright reddish-orange flowers with lighter orange-yellow flames set against pleated, deep green foliage.

Crocuses

All crocuses are technically corms (refer to Chapter 1 in Book VI). They have a definite up end and down end, are solid inside like a potato if you cut them open, and have a tunic. Crocuses like cold to moderate winter conditions — climate Zones 5 to 7. They fail to grow in hot climates. Regions where folks go to escape winter aren't suitable for crocuses.

Crocuses are small, so they dry out faster than large bulbs. Plant them early in autumn, as soon as you can buy them, and plant them in the open rather than the shade (unless you live in the South) because crocuses like sun. You can plant them in the lawn, but you can't cut the grass until their leaves turn yellow and disappear. And weed killers will harm them, especially if applied while the crocuses are still green and actively growing. Crocuses prefer a gritty, well-drained soil. A rock garden or herb garden (see Book VII for more on herb gardens) is a good site, and small perennials (Book IV covers perennials) that grow in such places make good crocus companions. Crocuses multiply by offsets. If you want to rearrange the extras, do so after the flowers fade but while the crocuses' leaves are still green.

Pests are a problem with crocuses — deer and rabbits eat the plants while mice and voles eat the corms. Planting in a gritty soil helps somewhat against tunneling pests. Deer and rabbit repellents are available at garden centers. Make sure to reapply repellents after it rains.

Here are a few crocuses worth investigating:

- ✔ **Snow crocus** *(Crocus chrysanthus)***:** Coax these little gems into the very earliest bloom by planting in a warm, sheltered microclimate. (Refer to Chapter 2 in Book I for an explanation of microclimates.) A site against a building on the sunny side of the structure is just the thing: A little warmth leaks through the foundation, the sun warms a masonry wall during the day, and both provide moderate conditions at night.

- ✔ **Dutch crocus** *(Crocus vernus)***:** This plant blossoms later in the spring. Yellow Dutch crocuses flower earlier than the purples, lavenders, striped, and white ones. And, as well as their golden yellow color, yellow Dutch crocuses inherited their early bloom time from their ancestor, *Crocus flavus.*

- ✔ **Woodland crocus** *(Crocus tommasinianus)***:** Attractive, easy, available, and tolerant of shady sites — what more could you want from this little treasure? This darling, soft-lavender crocus blooms in very early spring. This crocus reseeds freely and soon makes large colonies — sometimes a problem in formal gardens with precise plantings. But this free increase helps keep the price of most cultivars way down. (The white-flowered one does cost more.)

Crown Imperials

Crown imperials, *Fritillaria imperialis,* are big bulbs with a largish price — one crown imperial is about the price of five hyacinths or ten tulips. In spring, they grow into tall plants that you can't miss. And then there's their scent — sort of foxy, skunky, and pungent. Phew! Actually, the smell isn't bad at all outdoors in the garden, but the strong odor is overwhelming indoors. Perhaps the sharp odor protects crown imperials from animal pests, which leave both bulbs and growing plants alone. The stunning flowers are typically a brick orange-red color, very showy and conspicuous. One crown imperial makes an accent, three make a statement, and more are wonderfully lavish. Tulips in a softer orange make a nice companion plant.

Crown imperials have huge bulbs with no tunic, only two or three scales, and a gap in the middle from last year's flower stalk. Growth begins early and each bulb — usually offered for sale individually wrapped in tissue paper — often has roots starting into growth by late August. The size of a pencil lead, the new white roots are easily broken, setting back the bulb's growth. If the tissue-wrapped bulb is upside down in the box or bin where it awaits purchase, roots start growing in the wrong direction. Growth starts in mid-spring; crown imperial goes dormant in very early summer.

You may see recommendations to plant these big bulbs sideways, so water won't collect in the hole in the middle of the bulb. Ignore any such suggestion. If the site is that wet, the bulbs won't do well anyway.

Several cultivars are available (with the same or higher price tag):

- **'Aureomarginata':** Impressive stalks ringed with bright red flowers set above outstanding gold-edged leaves.
- **'Aurora':** Eye-catching, apricot-orange flowers on 2-foot (0.6-m) stems fairly glow above the dark foliage.
- **'Lutea':** Vivid yellow flowers with faint purple veins on stems that top out at about 2 feet (0.6 m).
- **'Rubra Maxima':** Very large flowers in an unusual burnt orange shade tinted with red and accented with light purple veins.

Book VI

Bulbs

Daffodils

If you're looking for a reliable spring bulb to add to a sunny perennial border, partially shaded woodland, or cutting garden, start right with daffodils. The great thing about daffodils is their easygoing nature. Just plant them in autumn and watch them flower the next spring, and come back year after year with almost no care.

Plant daffodils in groups of ten or more. Make a sort of circle with six or seven bulbs along the perimeter and three or four in the middle. For aesthetic reasons, don't mix different cultivars within each planting group — the effect will be stronger if you stay with one kind. Where space permits, you can plant in bigger blocks, 25 or even more. Daffodils in formal gardens look best in formal shapes, squares or circles. Informal plantings look good with tapered, fish-shaped drifts of daffodils. You may see photographs of great sweeps of lawn with daffodils in bloom. Remember, though, that you can't cut the grass until the daffodil leaves turn completely yellow. So the lawn's going to look shaggy and take awhile to recover after you cut the hay.

Don't use the cut grass mixed with daffodil leaves to feed your pet bunny or any other animal. Daffodils are poisonous — that's probably why deer, rabbits, woodchucks, and other pests leave them strictly alone.

Daffodils are classified in 13 divisions, based on the number of flowers to a stem, details of the flower's shape, and the wild species that was the parent of the modern hybrids. (Division 12 holds all the daffodils that don't fit the classifications in the other 11 — a miscellaneous division, so to speak. Division 13 includes wild variants, wild hybrids, and species.) All daffodils make great cut flowers, but some are better for one kind of garden use than another. As far as gardeners are concerned, Division 6, the cyclamineus hybrids of garden origin, and Division 9, poeticus hybrids of garden origin, are the absolutely most reliable about naturalizing and returning year after year (perennializing) with little care.

Division 1, trumpet daffodils

The plants that everyone thinks of when they think of daffodils. Impressive single-stemmed flowers feature a prominent trumpet that's as long as or longer than the petals. These familiar and popular plants also work well in beds, planted in drifts or naturalized, or used as cut flowers. They bloom from early to late spring and grow 8 to 18 inches (20 to 46 cm). Here a few recommendations:

- **"King Alfred" type:** Early yellow bloomer grows to 18 inches (46 cm). Perhaps the best-known daffodil, its large, deep yellow flower is ideal in mass plantings, beds, and borders.

- **'Primeur':** Long-lasting, abundant, richly colored golden-yellow flowers grow to 20 inches (51 cm) and bloom mid to late in the season, after almost all others.

- **'Spellbinder':** Early to midseason flowers fade from yellow to white on 1-inch (2.5-cm) stems. Unique, changing colors provide plenty of sparks in beds, borders, and mass plantings.

Division 2, large-cupped daffodils

This category includes popular bold flowers that have large central cups with ruffled edges, one blossom per stem. They're ideal for beds, borders, naturalizing, cutting, showing, and in some cases, forcing. Flowers bloom from early to midseason, ranging from 14 to 18 inches (36 to 46 cm). Try these cultivars:

- **'Camelot':** Sturdy, prolific, late bloomer with golden yellow flowers on 16-inch (41-cm) provides a long-lasting, late-season show.

- **'Delibes':** Early midseason bloomer with flowers that grow to 18 inches (46 cm). Long-lasting, showy flowers with gradually fading soft yellows and oranges set this cultivar apart.

- **'Ice Follies':** Early midseason flowers top 18-inch (46-cm) stems. Large flowers in creamy white and soft yellow highlight this ever-popular choice — the best large-cupped daffodil to start with!

Division 3, short-cupped daffodils

These early-to-late flowers feature a cup that is one-third or less than the length of the petals, with blossoms one to a stem. They work well naturalized, in beds or borders, and as cut flowers, growing 14 to 18 inches (36 to 46 m). Here are a couple of suggestions:

- ✔ **'Barrett Browning':** Early flowers top 16-inch (41-cm) stems. Striking pure white petals and red-orange cup are good naturalized and forced.
- ✔ **'Birma':** A deep red cup, ringed with dark yellow petals reaches 18 inches (46 cm). It adapts well to naturalize in the garden.

Division 4, double daffodils

Double daffodils are really fun, but some need more care than other daffodils. They have so many petals that when it rains, they soak up water like blotting paper, get heavy, and fall over. So you may need to stake or protect them. Showy, double, rose-like flowers in single and multiple blooms highlight this group. Many are fragrant. Check out these cultivars:

- ✔ **'Bridal Crown':** Soft, early midseason blooms in cream and pale yellow on 16-inch (41 cm) stems give this fragrant flower wide appeal. Excellent in beds, borders, containers, or forced.
- ✔ **'Ice King':** Early midseason flowers reach 18 inches (46 cm). Sports ruffled, pearly white petals with a fully double soft yellow cup.
- ✔ **'White Lion':** Midseason white and yellow flowers grow to 18 inches (46 cm). Delightful fragrance and large gardenia-shaped blossoms. Vigorous grower that adapts to tough conditions.

Division 5, triandrus daffodils

Small, nodding, fragrant flowers in this group offer an elegant display. Multiple flowers rise above slender foliage. Use them naturalized, in rock gardens, borders, containers, and as cut flowers. Bloom time is mid-to-late season, and the height range is 12 to 16 inches (30 to 41 cm). Try these cultivars:

- ✔ **'Ice Wings':** Early midseason, absolutely pure white flowers have two to three blooms per 14-inch (36-cm) stem. Long-lasting with a sweet scent.
- ✔ **'Liberty Bells':** Late midseason golden-yellow flowers sprout up to five blooms per 14-inch (36-cm) stem. Expect an abundance of these nearly perfect, bell-like flowers.

GARDEN JARGON

Daffodil bulbs are better bigger

Within each daffodil classification, you also find size grades:

✔ **Number 1, triple-nose:** Sometimes called *exhibition size* or *mother bulbs,* these bulbs have three "noses" or offsets, and you generally get a flower stem from each nose; pay for one bulb and get three flowers.

✔ **Number 2, double-nose:** Also called *top size* or *bedding size,* have two noses, and produce two flowers stems.

✔ **Number 3, round:** Also called *landscape* or *naturalizing* bulbs, have a single nose and produce a single flower stem.

When given a choice, spend the money to buy bigger bulbs. Keep in mind that actual bulb sizes (circumferences) vary from one classification to another. Trumpet, long-cup, and split trumpet daffodils are larger within each grade than a similar grade of short cup, *triandrus, cyclamineus, jonquilla, tazetta,* and *poeticus* daffodils. For example, *cyclamineus* daffodil 'Jack Snipe' bulbs are never as big as those of 'Dutch Master', a Trumpet daffodil.

✔ **'Tresamble':** Late midseason white flowers grow one to three blooms per 16-inch (41-cm) stem. Graceful, arching petals accent frilled cups on these large flowers. Another old-fashioned favorite.

Division 6, cyclamineus daffodils

These flowers feature a trumpet cup set above flared-back petals, much like cyclamen. Expect early blooms and reliable performance in rock gardens, borders, cutting gardens, containers, or naturalized in the landscape. They grow 7 to14 inches. Check out these varieties:

✔ **'Foundling':** Early or midseason flowers top 12-inch (30-cm) stems. Small flower with a dainty apricot cup and graceful white petals.

✔ **'Jetfire':** Midseason red-orange and yellow flowers top 14-inch (36-cm) stems. Abundant blooms in vivid, slightly varied colors.

✔ **'Peeping Tom':** Early midseason yellow flowers top 15-inch (38-cm) stems. A strong naturalizer with healthy, long-term garden performance.

Division 7, jonquilla

Jonquillas offer fragrant small flowers, several to a stem, and small, dark green, slender foliage. Bulbs naturalize very well but also shine in beds, borders, rock gardens, and arrangements. They bloom mid to late season and reach 8 to 18 inches (20 to 46 cm). Consider these:

- ✔ **'Bell Song':** Late bloomer with three to five cream and pink flowers per 14-inch (36-cm) stem. Sweet fragrance and classic good looks.

- ✔ **'Curlew':** Midseason flowers, two or three per 14-inch (36-cm) stem, have creamy petals with a longish white cup. Flowers offer classic beauty with subtle color changes.

- ✔ **'Quail':** Midseason, multiple sunny-yellow flowers top 18-inch (46-cm) stems. Abundant, long-lasting, and fragrant flowers.

Division 8, tazetta

Plants from 6 to18 inches (15 to 46 cm) tall have multiple, fragrant flowers of up to eight per stem that bloom from midseason to late spring. Ideal for forcing and useful in beds, borders, cutting gardens, or naturalized. Successful in warmer regions. Try these cultivars:

- ✔ **'Cragford':** Early midseason bloomer provides three to five white and orange flower clusters on 14-inch (36-cm) stems. Very fragrant, rounded flowers. Popular for forcing, but also effective in beds or borders.

- ✔ **'Geranium':** Growing in midseason, three to five white and orange flowers top each 17-inch (43-cm) stem. The long-lasting, fragrant flowers on this old-time favorite do well naturalized or forced late in the season. (This bulb is featured in the color insert.)

- ✔ **'Scarlet Gem':** Late midseason flowers in yellow and orange bloom three to five per 16-inch (41-cm) stem.

Division 9, poeticus

A good choice in cooler regions, dogwood-type flowers have white petals accented with yellow-orange cups. The spicy fragrance adds a lovely touch indoors, and the flowers perform well in beds, borders, or naturalized. Check out these cultivars:

- ✔ **'Actaea':** Late midseason bloomers top 17-inch (43-cm) stems. Flower has a strong yellow cup, banded in red, surrounded by perfect white petals.

- ✔ **'Cantabile':** Late flowers bloom on 14-inch (36-cm) stems. Fragrant flower has a green and yellow, red-edged cup against pure white petals.

- ✔ **'Milan':** Late flowers on this popular choice top 18-inch (46-cm) stems.

Division 10, species and wild forms

For an unusual but charming touch in the garden, select from this group of species and wild plants and their hybrids. Plants vary in size and shape but offer excellent results when naturalized or planted in many garden settings. Useful in woodland or rock gardens, these daffodils are often less available than the other kinds depending on which one(s) you choose:

- **Pheasant's eye** *(Narcissus poeticus recurvus):* This very late bloomer has white flowers with red/yellow cups atop 13-inch (33-cm) stems (33-cm). Spicy fragrance and good cold tolerance.

- **Tenby daffodil** *(Narcissus obvallaris):* Very early rich golden trumpets top 10-inch (25-cm) stems.

- **Van Sion** *(Narcissus telemonius plenus):* Early bloomer with double-flowered cup and yellow flowers reaches 14 inches (36-cm).

Division 11, split corona

With the *corona,* or cup, split by at least a third, having a flatter, full face gives these flowers the distinction of being among the showiest of daffodils. The funky split-corona daffodils of Division 11 look quite different from those traditional yellow trumpet daffodils. Try them if you're looking for something really different, but don't expect them to be as permanent as cyclamineus or poeticus daffodils. Use them naturalized in mass plantings, or in arrangements, beds, and borders. Plants range from 14 to 18 inches (36 to 46 cm). Consider these:

- **'Cum Laude':** Midseason white-and-yellow frilled flowers top 16-inch (41-cm) stems.

- **'Love Call':** Late midseason white, yellow, and orange flowers top 16-inch (41-cm) stems.

- **'Papillon Blanc':** Late flowers (yellow and greenish center surrounded by white) reach 18 inches (46-cm).

Dahlias

Dahlias are fabulous plants, as flamboyant in flower as you may expect from their colorful Mexican and Guatemalan origins. Dahlias come in all sizes, and all colors, too. You can find window-box dahlias under a foot tall on up to dinner-plate dahlias, which are 4 feet (1.2 m) tall or more. The shorter dahlias are great in the garden at the front of the border, in window-boxes, and in containers. Tall dahlias are stunning at the back of the border where their summer and early autumn flowers add fabulous color. All dahlias make great cut flowers. (Although the dinner-plate dahlias, with flowers a foot across, can be tricky to arrange!)

Dinner-plate dahlias

These dahlias reach 4 feet (1.2 m) tall or more and plants produce abundant flowers that are, yes, truly as big as a dinner plate. Expect a dozen or more 9- to 11-inch (23- to 28-cm) flowers per plant. Some catalogs refer to these as "Extra Large Decorative" dahlias. Space these giants 3 feet (1 m) apart. Try these varieties:

- ✔ **'Kelvin's Floodlight':** Glowing, deep yellow flowers have won awards in both the United States and Holland.

- ✔ **'Mistery Day' (sometimes spelled 'Mystery Day'):** Showy fuchsia-red flowers have white edges that create a stunning contrast.

- ✔ **'Mrs. Eileen':** This bold, bright display comes from huge flowers in as vivid and bright an orange as you can imagine.

- ✔ **'Rosella':** Bright and glowing pink hue looks as though it's lit from within.

Border decorative dahlias

Choose these 15-inch (38-cm) flowers when you want a burst of color near the front or in the middle of your bed or border. Flowers reach 3 to 4 inches (8 to 10 cm) across and are produced in great numbers — up to 40 per plant. The border decorative form and compact size make these ideal choices for containers, too. In the garden, space these cultivars 12 inches (30 cm) apart. Check out these varieties:

- ✔ **'Aspen':** Prolific plants sprout bright white flowers with slightly curved petals.

- ✔ **'Berliner Kleene':** Deep pink blossoms nearly cover plants.

- ✔ **'Claudette':** Very double, vivid flowers come in a purplish-pink hue.

- ✔ **'Zingaro':** Exquisite, long-blooming flowers start pale yellow in the center and unfold to a clear pale pink along the outer petals.

Border cactus dahlia

Cultivars in this category reach 2 feet (0.6 m) tall and display impressive double flowers with narrow, pointed petals that curve slightly inward, giving them a looser, more spiked look than other dahlias. The unusual form and vivid colors provide striking contrasts when combined with other dahlias in the garden or in arrangements. Blossoms are 4 to 5 inches (10 to 13 cm) across, and a single plant may produce 40 buds. Space tubers 12 inches (30 cm) apart. We recommend these cultivars:

- ✔ **'Park Princess':** A range of color from pale to dark pink is displayed on tightly rolled petals.

- ✔ **'Saba':** Arresting spiky red petals add drama and flair to the garden.

- ✔ **'Yellow Happiness':** Cheerful lemon-yellow flowers lend a bright but soothing look to the late-summer garden.

Decorative dahlias

Flowers under this heading are fully double with short, broad, pointed to rounded flat petals that curve slightly along the margins. Some have a very formal, tailored look, and others are slightly looser — almost fringed on the edges. Size can range from 15 inches to 4 feet (38 cm to 1.2 m). Expect a range of production, too, because some will produce as many as 25 flowers. Plant tubers 12 to 18 inches (30 to 46 cm) apart. Here are two beautiful decorative dahlias:

- ✔ **'Key West':** Five-inch flowers in a warm orange change to yellow at the base of each petal. Each 3-foot-tall (1 m) plant has up to 25 buds.

- ✔ **'Miami':** Strong white flowers have faint pink coloring at the petal tips, especially in the center of the flower. It grows 3 feet (1 m) and produces 5-inch (13-cm) flowers.

Spider dahlias

These unique cultivars have narrow curled petals that are almost tube-like as they radiate from the center of the flower. Similar to cactus dahlias, these are more spiked and slightly looser. They're ideal for an unusual accent. Plants produce about 25 flowers, each one 4 to 6 inches (10 to 15 cm) across. Set tubers 12 to 18 inches (30 to 46 cm) apart. Consider these two cultivars of spider dahlia:

- ✔ **'Alfred Grille':** Yellow center gives way to peach pink and pale pink petals along the flower's margins. It grows 2 to 4 feet (0.6 to 1.2 m) and produces an abundance of healthy blossoms.

- ✔ **'Yellow Star':** Layer upon layer of slender, vivid, long-blooming bright-yellow petals reach 30 inches (76 cm).

Mignon patio dahlias

Sweet and simple, these dahlias offer classic good looks from single flowers on compact, bushy 20-inch (51-cm) plants. Blossoms are 2 to 4 inches (5 to 10 cm) across with golden centers, and the flowers are flatter with fewer petals than other dahlia varieties. Prolific plants may give you as many as 40 blooms each. Try these for cheerful color along border fronts or in pots, planters, and window boxes. Plant these cultivars 8 to 12 inches (20 to 30 cm) apart. Following are some impressive mignon patio dahlias:

- ✔ **'Irene van der Zwet'**: Bright golden-yellow flowers combine well with other varieties.

- ✔ **'Murillo'**: Striking bright pink flowers have a dark pink ring around the golden center.

- ✔ **'Red Riding Hood'**: Bright red flowers nearly cover neat, tidy clumps of foliage.

Enjoy the dahlias in your garden and as cut flowers; the more you cut, the more they bloom. If you don't cut the flowers for bouquets, be sure to dead-head. Tall dahlias get top-heavy because they produce so many flowers, so they need staking. Placing the stakes at planting time is much better, because you can see where the tubers are, rather than running the risk of spearing through them later on.

Dogtooth Violet

Dogtooth violet, *Erythronium* species and cultivars, have a corm that really does look like a dog's canine tooth. You can see the dogtooth shape of the corm when you plant it, but it's hard to see afterward when it's concealed in the dirt. What makes this lumpy underground treasure special are its flowers. Dogtooth violets aren't anything like a violet; they're more like a miniature lily with curled-back petals in bright yellow, clean white, or soft rose-pink (see Figure 4-1). To successfully grow dogtooth violets, buy the corms early and plant them promptly. Ten is a generous number; five makes a nice start-up display.

Because the dogtooth violet corms dry out quickly, garden centers and nurseries often store them in wood shavings to retard moisture loss. Handle the fragile corms gently, and choose plump ones with no sign of bruising, such as soft flabby spots or mildew. Partway down one side of the corm, closer to the fatter end, you should find a tiny, almost stubbly tuft of old roots. If you can't find it, just plant with the tapered end pointed upward. Dogtooth violets like woodsy conditions: moist but well-drained soil high in organic matter, mulched with a nice layer of shredded leaves or wood chips.

GARDEN JARGON

Footloose and fancy fritillaries

Fritillaries are different in appearance from any other flower you may have grown. Their flowers — from few to many, depending on the type — are bell-shaped and dangle in a most interesting manner. That description sounds simple and straightforward, but the plants have rung in changes in size and color that result in remarkable diversity. All fritillaries are true bulbs, few-scaled, lacking a papery tunic or covering, and they dislike being out of the ground for any length of time. Purchase and plant all fritillaries as early in the autumn as they're available. They'll repay your efforts with an outstanding display in spring.

WARNING!

Deer like the leaves of dogtooth violets. Fences, large dogs, and repellents can help keep them at bay.

Figure 4-1: There's nothing hangdog about the dogtooth violet.

We recommend that you try these cultivars of dogtooth violet:

- ✔ *Erythronium dens-canis,* **'Purple King',:** Cyclamen-purple blossoms are accented attractively with white hearts. The open form and curled back petals are typical of dogtooth violets.

- ✔ *Erythronium dens-canis,* **'Rose Queen',:** Vivid rose-pink flowers combine well with cultivars in other shades.

- ✔ *Erythronium revolutum,* **'White Beauty',:** Rare, pure white, reflexed flowers accompany handsome spotted foliage for a very lily-like and impressive display. Large, graceful blossoms can reach 2 inches (5 cm) across.

✔ *Erythronium* **'Pagoda':** Bright, lemon-yellow flowers rise from glossy green foliage and are supported by vigorous, sturdy, 8-inch (20-cm) stems.

Fritillaria Michailovskyi

Very easily cultivated and readily propagated by bulb growers in Holland, the frit with the unpronounceable name is a moderately priced, easily grown addition to anybody's bulb repertoire. Michailovskyi has one or two boxy bells of flowers, with the petals somewhat curled outwards at their tips. For their small size, the flowers are very impressive. Near the stem, the flower is a rich, deep-purple maroon, and the last third is a vividly contrasting golden yellow. Sturdy stems stand only 4 to 6 inches (10 to 15 cm) tall. Recently, some plants are available with more flowers (up to seven on a stem). A little frit, michailovskyi has small, two-scaled bulbs that dry out quickly. Plant early in autumn in a gritty soil that drains well. A rock garden is most suitable.

This frit likes cold winters and cool, dryish summers. If conditions are too warm in winter — southeastern states along the coast, southern California, and mild southwestern states — the flowers often get stuck underground. If they appear at all, they're misshapen.

Gladiolus

Gladiolus is a great warm-weather corm with which to start your garden or flower bed. The 3- to 4-foot- (1- to 1.2-m) tall spikes of summer flowers are easy to produce in sequence, just by planting corms every couple of weeks. Flowers come in a rainbow array of colors, and are great as cut flowers. Gladiolus corms look like oversize crocus corms: They're covered in a fibrous brown wrapper with a small, flat place at the bottom, and they sometimes have pointy shoots already showing at the top. Some mail-order sources offer you a choice of sizes: the larger, top-size corms have somewhat longer flower spikes, which sometimes produce two flower spikes and bloom a bit earlier than the smaller ones. You can choose your glads by the color you want in the garden or for bouquets, as well as for their height and beauty. Glads are often sold by mixed colors, too.

You may want to try the following gladiolus cultivars:

✔ **'Home Coming':** Impressive two-toned creamy white flowers have a delicate purple throat on 3- to 4-foot (1- to 1.2-m) plants.

✔ **'Priscilla':** Stunning tricolored flowers feature a white background accented with bright pink along the wavy petal edges and finished with a soft yellow throat.

- ✔ **'Saphir':** Deep blue flowers accented with pure white throats bloom on plants that may reach 4 feet (1.2 m) tall.

- ✔ **'Victor Borge':** Dramatic, brilliant vermilion-orange flowers on 5-foot (1.5-m) stems. Blossoms open to reveal creamy white throat markings.

If you prefer shorter plants and smaller bouquets, try butterfly gladiolus. They grow only 2 to 3 feet (0.6 to 1 m) tall and are ideal tucked in among perennial plantings. You'll find them sold individually and as a mix with an array of colors including two-toned flowers. They're hardy in Zones 7 to 10 (refer to Chapter 2 in Book I for an explanation of climate zones). Following are a few butterfly gladiolus varieties:

- ✔ **'Green Bird':** Clean white flowers are flushed with green.

- ✔ **'Perky':** Robust, perfectly formed flowers are an arresting red, with white throats that provide a dramatic contrast.

- ✔ **'Perseus':** Glowing deep pink flowers are delicately dabbed with white in the center.

The "hardy gladiolus," *Gladiolus nanus,* is more cold-tolerant than the other gladiolus and can stay in the ground year-round in Zone 6 and warmer, Zone 5 with the added protection of a winter mulch. The following *Gladiolus nanus* cultivars make lovely additions to the garden:

- ✔ **'Albus':** Glistening crystal white flowers with yellow stripes and blue anthers are borne on 12- to 18-inch (30- to 46-cm) stems.

- ✔ **'Aranea':** Regal spikes — 15 to 20 inches (38 to 51 cm) — are gracefully decorated in rich purple flowers.

- ✔ **'Atom':** Vivid poppy-red flowers are accented boldly with a violet spot and white center. Plants reach 18 inches (46 cm).

- ✔ **'Nymph':** This strong grower has impressive white flowers, sporting cream to pale pink blotches edged in crimson.

You can dig the corms for storage four to six weeks after you pick the flowers, or four to six weeks after they fade.

Mice love gladiolus corms. Make sure that you store the corms in a vermin-proof place. If you live somewhere with cold winters where glads are planted fresh each year, don't replant them in the same place they were growing the year before. A new site gives better results. Cycle them around the garden, returning to a previous location in three to five years.

Glory of the Snow

Glory of the snow flowers earlier than scillas (occasionally, a brief overlap occurs as one finishes and the other starts — the result is several upward-facing, widely flaring bell-shaped flowers in an intense, almost glowing blue). A side benefit of small size is smaller leaves, which are less obvious and displeasing when they wither away. Glory of the snow is a true bulb, small in size, so plant early in the fall. Plant in shade or sun, but not where bulbs will bake in summer. Avoid soggy places.

Check out these glory of the snow varieties:

- ✔ ***Chionodoxa luciliae:*** Bright gentian-blue flowers are accented with a white eye. This most readily available glory of the snow also comes in white ('Alba') and pink ('Pink Giant').

- ✔ ***Chionodoxa forbesii:*** Soft blue-violet flowers accentuated by a white eye create an intense glowing effect.

- ✔ ***Chionodoxa sardensis:*** These very intense, deep gentian-blue flowers don't have the white eye. The 4- to 6-inch (10- to 15-cm) plant's flowers are smaller, but more plentiful.

Book VI

Bulbs

Golden Winter Aconite

The small golden flowers of the winter aconite *(Eranthis hyemalis)* make a bright, cheery welcome to the garden. Blooming from January in southeastern gardens and from March in the northeastern states, flowers appear when snow is still forecast (*hyemalis,* also spelled *hiemalis,* means "of winter").

Winter aconites grow only 3 or 4 inches (8 or 10 cm) tall, tiny enough to be covered with even a moderate snowfall. These durable messengers of spring reappear untouched as the snow melts, a frilly green leaf collar beneath their golden buttercup-like flowers. Sturdy and easy after they've begun growing, winter aconites can be a bit hard to establish at the start. Winter aconites grow from tubers that look like shriveled little sticks. Trying to get these tubers dry enough for storage and shipping to the store, but not letting them dry out too much so that they die, is a tricky task.

Buy tubers early and buy at least 25 tubers because only about 20 to 25 percent will grow and flower next spring. However, those tubers that do grow make lots of seeds and offsets and multiply rapidly.

Grape Hyacinths

Grape hyacinths do look sort of like a miniature hyacinth, if you squint a little bit. The plants are shorter, only 6 to 8 inches (15 to 20 cm) high. The flowers look like small beads strung closely together up and down the stem (see Figure 4-2). Grape hyacinths spread quickly; in fact, they can be invasive, so plant them where they'll be welcome to spread freely. Grape hyacinths are so eager to grow that they send their leaves up every fall after the first year of growing. The leaf tips get a little nipped and turn brown, but when spring rolls around, the bulbs flower right on schedule. Grape hyacinths need very little care after they flower. They seem to do fine with natural rainfall, and we don't bother to fertilize them — they multiply just fine without any kind of boost from us! You can find several varieties of grape hyacinth. Following are two of our favorites:

Figure 4-2:
The lovely little grape hyacinth.

- ✔ *Muscari armeniacum:* Bright cobalt-blue flowers are edged with a tiny, nearly imperceptible white edge in a densely flowered spike.

- ✔ *Muscari latifolium:* Two-tone flowers are hyacinth-blue on top and a nice violet on the bottom of the flower stalk. Plants grow only a single, rather large leaf, or, occasionally, a pair of leaves.

Grecian Windflower

This dainty daisy is so short that the flowers barely rise above the ground. Yellow-centered daisies in blue shades, pink shades, or white, greet the gardener provident enough to have planted them the autumn before. Blue shades create a wonderful carpet of color, ranging from pale to darker blue tones. These flowers are ideal for mixing with daffodils, where they provide a striking contrast. Pink shades give you soft to deep pink flowers that blend well with annuals and other spring bulbs. Plant this inexpensive tuber with a generous hand — we recommend at least 25 — in a bright, lightly shaded site; they happily come back year after year. Another bonus: Pests pretty much leave the Grecian windflower alone.

 A windflower's tuber is a shriveled little thing that looks like the trash that's left after you screen compost. You can improve the unpromising appearance of Grecian windflower tubers by giving them a quick soaking. The night before you plant them, cover the tubers with damp peat moss. The tubers absorb moisture and plump up, making them more ready to root as soon as you plant them. After you soak them, plant the tubers right away. If they sit too long after soaking, they start to mildew.

Book VI

Bulbs

Try these varieties of Grecian windflower:

- ✔ **'Charmer':** Radiant flowers feature deep rose-pink petals with a yellow center ringed in white.

- ✔ **'Violet Star':** Amethyst-violet flowers are borne in great profusion over many weeks.

- ✔ **'White Splendour,':** Long-lasting, bright blooms glisten in pure white. Plants form prolific, sturdy low mounds. Mix with early tulips in bold colors for a stunning effect.

Guinea Hen Flowers

Probably the easiest of the fritillaries (refer to the sidebar, "Footloose and fancy fritillaries," earlier in this chapter for a definition) to grow, Guinea hen flower *(Fritillaria meleagris)*, has one or two rather chunky bell-shaped flowers, marked like a checkerboard in somber purple and white (see Figure 4-3). Plant a bunch, and you may find the occasional white one, with faint green markings. Like most albino forms, these are a bit less vigorous and somewhat shorter. (You can buy them separately as *Fritillaria meleagris alba*.) The flowers dangle from a slender stem that's about 8 to 12 inches (20 to 30 cm) tall in midspring. The few leaves are also slender, and plants look so delicate that you wonder how they support the square-shouldered flowers.

The only variation you're likely to find available is 'Alba' with white and green checkered flowers. A few will even pop up in a bagful of plain Guinea hen flowers. Like so many other small bulbs, guinea hen flower is inexpensive, so you can afford to plant in quantity. Ten is a minimum number if the small plants are to make a display that you can see at a glance. And several groups of ten are even nicer.

The ivory-white bulbs of Guinea hen flower are just an inch or so wide, and have only two scales. Because these bulbs are both small and have no tunic, they dry out really quickly. If you have to keep them between the time of purchase and when you plant, store them in a paper bag mixed with a handful of wood shavings to reduce *desiccation* (drying). Make the waiting period until planting as brief as you can. Given conditions to their liking — light shade and nice, moist soil — Guinea hen flower will multiply by seed and offsets. Nothing seems to think of Guinea hen flower as salad, so this bulb is safe from deer, rabbits, squirrels, and other pests.

Figure 4-3:
The Guinea hen flower gets its name from the speckled feathers of the Guinea hen bird.

Hyacinths

Hyacinths look good and smell great — a floral perfume that's never cloying or heavy. The original wild hyacinths have pale-to-deep-violet-blue or pale-to-deep-pink flowers. You can now find hyacinths with white, soft yellow, salmon orange, or red flowers, as well as in their original colors. You can even find double- as well as single-flowered forms. (They're all suitable for growing in containers; but they're kind of top-heavy and fall over in rainy conditions or strong winds, so they may need support.)

Hyacinths are true bulbs. (Refer to Chapter 1 in Book VI for a definition of true bulb.) Here's a handy hint if you forget to label the bags of hyacinths you bought at the garden center. Those with pink, violet, or blue flowers have a deep reddish-violet tunic; white- and yellow-flowered forms have white tunics.

The tunics of dry hyacinth bulbs contain acid that can make your skin itch. We recommend that you wear gloves when handling hyacinth bulbs, and that you moisten the bulbs right before you plant them.

Because hyacinths have a full, fat spike of closely clustered flowers, they're more appropriate for traditional garden schemes than naturalistic planting designs. We find them better in somewhat orderly plantings — in small groups rather than scattered about. Hyacinths pair nicely with smaller bulbs, for a sort of jack-in-the-box design technique. Plant your hyacinths in early fall, so that they have enough time to grow a good mass of roots before winter. Choose a spot that has full sun in the north and light shade in the south with rich, moist, well-drained soil.

The following list recommends several choice cultivars that can be enjoyed along the edges of beds and borders or grouped in the landscape, and, of course, in pots placed indoors and out:

- ✔ **Single hyacinths:** Single flowered *inflorescences* (an arrangement of flowers along a single axis) make up the largest category of hyacinth, comprising a wide array of 8- to 12-inch (20- to 30-cm) flowers in a rainbow of colors. Each bulb sends up a single stalk covered in starry, fragrant florets. Consider the following single hyacinth cultivars:

  - • **'Anna Marie':** Soft, clear pink flowers top 12- to 15-inch (30- to 38-cm) stems.

  - • **'Blue Jacket':** Impressive, cool, deep-blue flowers lightly striped with purple reach 8 inches (20 cm) and make a bold statement.

  - • **'Carnegie':** Fragrant white flowers top 10-inch (25-cm) stalks. These are the brightest, purest white of all the hyacinths, and they have an early, densely flowered spike.

  - • **'Paul Hermann':** Amethyst-violet flowers with dark purple streaks stand on 10-inch (25-cm) bronze-brown stalks.

- ✔ **Double hyacinths:** These full, extra-fragrant flowers on compact but prolific spikes are striking. Each floret has a second floret blooming in its center. Use these bulbs in beds, borders, containers, or for forcing:

  - • **'Chestnut Flower':** Light pink and dark pink flowers grow on 8-inch (20-cm) stems. Blossoms resemble horse chestnut flowers.

  - • **'General Kohler':** Lavender flowers cover 8-inch (20-cm) spikes. This reliable hyacinth has been in cultivation since 1878.

  - • **'Hollyhock':** Crimson flowers top 8-inch (20-cm) stems. Arresting flowers and awesome fragrance give this popular double plenty of value.

  - • **'Madam Sophie':** Elegant white flowers top 8-inch (20-cm) stalks.

- ✔ **Multiflora hyacinths:** When you want a lighter, less formal hyacinth, try the cultivars in this category. Each bulb produces three to four loose spikes with up to a dozen fragrant flowers on each spike. Native to the south of France, these early bloomers come in white or blue and offer a soft, airy look. Try these in beds, borders, containers, and for forcing:

- **'Borah':** White flowers atop 8-inch (20-cm) stems add grace and charm to any border or indoor display.

- **'Blue Borah':** Soft blue flowers top 8-inch (20-cm) stems on this natural, fragrant, multiflowering bulb.

- **'Snow White':** Early, delicate, pure white flowers grow on 8-inch (20-cm) stems.

Iris

Iris flowers are different from most other blooms. The flowers consist of three upright petals, called *standards*. Think of them as "stand up" petals. Then, three more petals, called *falls,* kind of droop to the side. The *fleur de lis,* once a royal symbol of the French monarchy, is an idealized iris. In this section, we discuss the *bulbous iris,* the type with a lumpy underground structure much like a tulip. (Turn to Chapter 3 in Book IV for information on the bearded iris — the most colorful and, possibly, the best-known member of the genus. Although it has thickened, rhizomotous roots, it's usually classed as a perennial.)

✔ **Rock garden iris:** These small irises flower very early in the year, anywhere from January to April, depending on where you garden. You can grow them in Zones 3 to 7 (refer to Chapter 2 in Book I for information on climate zones). They do best in a sunny site with a somewhat heavy but freely draining soil. Plant in autumn, avoiding windy sites, and really dry, drought-stricken conditions. The leaves of these irises are narrow, bluish green, and sort of square in cross sections, stiff and upright. Each leaf has a little white horny-looking tip. The relatively inconspicuous leaves are nicely proportionate when the flowers appear; they continue to grow after the flowers fade. These plants are also easy to force. Check out these rock garden irises:

- *Iris danfordiae:* This iris, which has fragrant golden-yellow flowers about 1½ inches (4 cm) across with some brown freckles on the falls, is the earliest of the rock garden irises to bloom. The leaves are shorter than those of the other rock garden irises.

- *Iris histrioides:* Beautiful blue flowers with a yellow streak down the center of the falls vary in intensity between one cultivar and another. Leaves are just peeking up when the flowers are open.

- *Iris reticulata:* This iris flowers just a little later than *Iris histrioides,* and the leaves are more developed at flowering time, too. Although restricted to blues and violets (with a couple of stunning exceptions, including 'Natascha', which is ivory), this species has more cultivars from which to choose.

One problem with the rock garden iris, and most especially with *Iris danfordiae,* is that it flowers just fine the first year after planting, and then in subsequent years it just sends up leaves. Each original splits into little rice-grain-sized bulbs that don't have the food reserves to support flower production. Deeper planting helps, as does extra nourishment in the form of liquid fertilizer applied in very early spring while the leaves are actively growing. They're inexpensive bulbs, so you may just want to plant new ones each spring.

✔ **English iris *(Iris xiphioides [Iris latifolia]):*** They produce leaves in spring and are the hardiest of the irises. English irises have white, blue, violet, or purple flowers, all with a yellow streak on the center of the falls. Flowers are usually larger than those of Spanish or Dutch irises. They grow 18 to 30 inches (46 to 76 cm) tall. Often, catalogs offer only mixed colors. English iris cultivars include 'Isabella', rose-lilac flowers; 'Mont Blanc', white flowers very faintly tinted with lilac; and, 'Queen of the Blues', deep indigo standards with purple-blue falls.

✔ **Spanish iris *(Iris xiphium* or *Iris hispanica):*** They bring forth leaves in autumn when wintry weather can easily damage them. Spanish irises are somewhat daintier than English irises, with smaller flowers in a wider range of colors that appear earlier in summer. Flowers are light to deep blue or violet, and white. You can find other Spanish irises with yellow or bronze flowers, even bicolors with stands and falls of different colors. Plants grow 12 to 18 inches (30 to 46 cm) tall.

✔ **Dutch iris:** Hybrids between English and Spanish irises, Dutch irises also usually produce leaves in autumn. They all have two or three flowers per 16- to 24-inch (41- to 61-cm) stem. They flower earliest, usually in the first half of May, from bulbs planted in autumn. Sometimes, you can find bulbs for sale in spring — these will flower in late summer. Dutch irises are nice sturdy plants with lots of cultivars available. Although easy to grow, they're not very cold-hardy and need winter protection; plant them late in fall whenever possible. Try these:

- **'Casablanca':** This flower has white standards and falls, with a narrow yellow blotch on the falls.

- **'Golden Harvest':** Golden-yellow flowers shade to orange, with the standards lighter than the falls.

- **'Purple Sensation':** Violet-purple standards and falls, with yellow markings, are edged in gentian blue.

- **'Sky Beauty':** Soft blue standards veined in darker blue and French-blue falls with somewhat darker veining are accented with a lemon-yellow blotch.

Book VI

Bulbs

Vexed by grexes

Named lilies, which are cultivars and grexes, have some rather tricky classifications:

✔ A *grex* covers all lilies that came out of an individual seed capsule. They have the same parents, but look no more alike than you do to your siblings. The name of a grex — Dummies Delight, for example — is written in ordinary roman type rather than italics and has no quote marks around it.

✔ A particularly worthwhile individual plant may be selected and given *cultivar*

(cultivated variety) status. That means the cultivar — 'Dummies Wonder' for example — is an asexually propagated cultivated variety and, as a clone, everything with that name is identical. The name, also in ordinary roman type, always appears in single quotation marks.

Remember the difference between a grex and a cultivar, so that you won't be surprised when your grex lilies share only their name and not their looks.

Lilies

Lilies are wonderful winter-hardy bulbs that bloom in early to midsummer. Lilies once had a reputation as tricky plants to grow, but today, growers sell commercially propagated, healthy bulbs. Additionally, hybridizers have developed sensational colors that go beyond the original wild species. Not everything that's called "lily" really is one. Lilies grow from true bulbs, with many fleshy scales that have no papery covering or tunic. Scads of other plants masquerade as lilies, daylily being the one most commonly confused.

TIP

Lilies are easy to plant, but lily bulbs need prompt planting and gentle handling — no pinching, dropping, or throwing around — because the bulb always has some fleshy roots at its bottom, and no tunic covers the scales. Lilies go dormant late in the growing season — November and sometimes even December. Bulbs shipped in fall can arrive kind of late; any time after October in Zone 6 is considered late (see Chapter 2 in Book I for more on climate zones). If that's the case, prepare the area ahead of time, and then cover it with an unopened bag of mulch to protect the site. Even if the bag of mulch freezes, you can still pry it up and flip it out of the way, and then plant in the nice unfrozen soil beneath.

Lily bulbs are also available in spring. They need to be planted right away because they're primed to grow. If you leave a bulb in the bag for too long, the shoots are liable to begin growing. Also, the new shoot is very fragile, easily broken when you're planting. An even easier way to get lilies is to buy them as growing potted plants in spring. Just take them home from the garden center, pop them in the soil, and — *voilà!* — instant display.

Some lilies, such as most of the Asiatic and Oriental hybrids, are *stem-rooting* — they make seasonal roots along the portion of the stem that's underground. You need to plant these lilies deeper than nonstem-rooting lilies, which are generally planted to a depth of three times the bulb height.

Just as with tulips and daffodils, lilies have several classifications, which are based on parentage. Knowing the species of the parentage gives you an idea of what the flower shape, bloom time, height, and so on might be. The original wild parents of the modern hybrid lilies gave rise to seven divisions, the most interesting of which for gardeners are the Asiatic hybrids of Division 1, the Trumpet hybrids of Division 6, and the Oriental hybrids of Division 7. Some divisions have subsets, but we're not going to worry about that. The lilies in this book will give you a good start. Later, you may want to try your hand with other varieties.

Book VI

Bulbs

Asiatic hybrids

Asiatic hybrids flower in early summer, but some also spill into August with late color. Ranging in height from 2- to almost 4-feet (0.6- to 1.2-m) tall, they feature abundant, upward-facing, bowl-shaped flowers mostly in yellow through orange to red, with a few white and pink ones available. Flowers may be unspotted or else charmingly speckled with darker freckles. Although not fragrant, these wonderfully reliable garden plants reproduce freely. They also make eye-catching container plants (see Chapter 3 in Book II for more on container gardening) and perform beautifully as cut flowers. Try these:

- ✔ **'Connecticut King':** Vivid yellow petals turn to gold in the flower center. Blossoms reach 36 to 48 inches (91 to 122 cm) in June and July. Excellent reliability. Considered "the" yellow lily by many.

- ✔ **'Grand Paradiso':** Ruby-red blossoms atop 35- to 45-inch (89- to 114-cm) stems bloom in July and August and are intense and arresting flowers.

- ✔ **'Sterling Star':** White flowers atop 36- to 48-inch (91- to 122-cm) stems bloom in June and July. Stunning white blossoms with tiny dark spots over a glowing yellow center really do offer sterling results.

- ✔ **'Vivaldi':** Pink blossoms reach 24 to 36 inches (61 to 91 cm) in June and July. Clear color and showy star-shaped flowers make a strong statement.

Trumpet (Aurelian) hybrids

Tall and stately, Trumpet hybrids have tremendous stage presence. Midsummer blooms (July to August) are large and, well, trumpet-shaped. Their intense fragrance is most emphatic at dawn and dusk. Plants grow anywhere from 4 to 7 feet (1.2 to 2 m) tall. Flower color ranges from white through pinks to deep, almost purple-black hues, and from a range of yellows to apricot, peach, and orange. Some whites and yellows are flushed with brown on the outside; some yellows have an alluring touch of lime-green in the throat. Mass plantings make an astonishing display. Support the tall stalks and protect flowers by staking the stems. Try these:

- **African Queen:** These large, two-toned flowers are yellow-apricot inside, apricot-brown outside, and reach 36 to 48 inches (91 to 122 cm) in July and August. The have an alluring scent. This is a grex, so you'll find some variation from one individual to another.

- **'Black Dragon':** Extra-large, dramatic flowers reach 4 to 8 feet (1.2 to 2.4 m) in July and August. Bright white flower interior is accented with a vivid yellow throat, set off by a maroon reverse.

- **'Black Magic':** Wonderfully fragrant, creamy white-and-yellow interior and purplish-brown exterior on 4- to 6-foot (1.2- to 1.8-m) stems flowers in July and August.

- **Copper King Strain:** Golden-yellow flowers flushed with orange on top of 4- to 6-foot (1.2- to 1.8-m) stems. This grex is selected from the Golden Clarion Strain with fragrant, outstanding, trumpet-shaped flowers.

Oriental hybrids

Oriental hybrids flower in mid- to late-summer — late July into September. Each sturdy 2- to 4-foot (0.6- to 1.2-m) stem supports 6 to 12 outward facing or upright *recurved* (petals are curled back) flowers, as shown in Figure 4-4. Intensely fragrant, these lilies' flower colors range from white through rosy pinks to deeper red, ornamented with raised *papillae* (wart-like bumps) at the base of the petals. Good for cutting and containers, their perfume can be overwhelming at close quarters. Here are some other Oriental lilies:

Figure 4-4:
An Oriental hybrid lily.

✔ **'Emily' (or 'Emmely'):** Rosy to pink to white flowers crown 30- to 40-inch (76- to 101-cm) stems in July. Graceful, 7-inch (18-cm) flowers have deep pink centers and creamy edges. Each stem produces an abundance of buds, so plants massed in the garden make an impressive display.

✔ **'Gold Band':** Golden-yellow and white flowers top 30- to 40-inch (76- to 101-cm) stems in July and August. A central golden band accents huge, pure white petals. The band and sprinkle of freckles against a light background accentuate the flower's star shape and give it a glowing, radiant look.

✔ **'Le Reve':** Pink and yellow flowers bloom in July on 24- to 30-inch (61- to 76-cm) stems. Clear pink petals dashed with yellow deep in the center make it a popular and worthy choice.

✔ **'Marco Polo':** Very large, very unusual flowers reach 24 to 36 inches (61 to 91 cm) in July and August. Clear white flowers shade to a purplish-pink along the wavy edges of each petal. Expect as many as 20 fragrant blossoms per bulb.

Ornamental Onions

Onions? In the flower garden? You bet! Ornamental onions are easy-to-grow, true bulbs that have beautiful, unusual flowers that are different from anything you've ever grown. An ornamental onion looks like a splendid pale-to-deep purple soap bubble tethered on a sturdy stem. Ornamental onions can be the size of a small-to-large grapefruit or even larger. They don't smell oniony, so their long-lasting flowers are great for cutting, and the seed heads that follow the flowering have an elegant beauty of their own. Plant them in autumn, the same as tulips and daffodils. Flowering as they do after tulips and before lilies, you can use ornamental onions to fill this gap in your bulb display. Just remember to disguise their lack of leaves at blossom time. Deer, rabbits, voles, and chipmunks leave ornamental onions alone.

The onion bulbs can be costly. Try unusual bulbs in small numbers the first time that you grow them.

Following are a handful of ornamental onions you can grow:

✔ *Allium caeruleum* **(also known as** *Allium azureum***):** Charming plants bloom in May and have striking, 1- to 2-inch (2- to 5-cm) cornflower-blue flowers atop 12- to 20-inch (30- to 51-cm) stems. This versatile bulb naturalizes easily.

✔ *Allium flavum:* A loose, pendulous cluster of up to 30 small-but-radiant, bell-shaped, lemon-yellow florets top 12-inch (30-cm) stems This onion blooms late — in June or July — and will grow in light shade.

Seedy onions paint the town

Beyond flowers, ornamental onions have beautiful seed heads. Wait until the seed heads are fully developed and turn brown before you cut them. They're amazingly sturdy, and they last naturally. We prefer their natural color, but you can spray paint them any color you like. And don't worry about cutting the seed heads, the bulbs should flower just fine next year.

✔ *Allium giganteum:* Deep purple 4- to 6-inch (10- to 15-cm) flowers that bloom on 3- to 5-foot (1- to 1.5-m) stems make this the stateliest and tallest ornamental onion. The huge bulb, about as big as a crown imperial bulb, produces hundreds of richly colored florets that form a tight ball.

✔ **'Mount Everest':** Pure white, 6-inch (15-cm) flowers top straight, sturdy 3-foot (1-m) stems. Plants are especially vigorous, and flowers are long lasting.

Persian Fritillaria

The Persian fritillaria *(Fritillaria persica)* bulb is as big as a crown imperial's, but more egg-shaped than flattened. (See the earlier sidebar, "Footloose and fancy fritillaries," for more information on these plants.) The stout stem has gray-green leaves about two-thirds of the way up. The upper part of the stem has up to 30 small, dangling, somewhat conical bell-shaped flowers in a charming, dark-plum purple with a silvery gray-purple bloom. Big bulbs equal big price. Like the crown imperial, one plant is enough to catch attention, three are excellent, and more are lavish.

Eager to begin growing, Persian fritillary starts root growth in late summer, in the ground or out of it. The bulbs are covered by two fat fleshy scales and no protective covering, so they can wither pretty quickly. Buy early and plant promptly, providing the same sort of conditions as for the crown imperial. Growth begins in spring, with a sturdy stem quickly growing 3 feet (1 m) tall, or even a bit more. Unless it is in a site sheltered from wind, you may want to provide support with a stake and ties. Put the stake in place before filling the hole so the bulb is still visible. Be sure to push the stake in the ground far enough from the stem to avoid spearing the bulb, but close enough to provide secure support. Keep the leaves growing as long as you can, sending food back underground to nourish the bulb for next year's display. Only cut off the stem when leaves are yellowed and withering.

Don't mix crown imperials and Persian fritillaries. They're too different in appearance to look good together.

Scillas

As long as you understand that scillas will happily spread, making more and more year after year, you can't go wrong with these plants. Blues from skim-milk pale to azure, and flowers like little bells make these beauties a welcome addition to the spring garden.

Several varieties of scillas are available:

- ✔ *Scilla siberica:* This is the most familiar variety, with bright-blue dangling bells of flowers that bloom in March. 'Spring Beauty' is an even more desirable cultivar. It's larger overall than its parent species, with somewhat richer blue flowers. The 'Alba' cultivar is a pure white form of *scilla sibirica,* but it grows somewhat poorly.

- ✔ *Scilla mischtschenkoana:* This scilla flowers even earlier than the other types (in March in the mid-Atlantic region). It's so eager to display its nearly translucent bells of palest blue-white that flowers start to open as they poke through the ground. The exit-early blooming period means that not much else is available as a partner. Think about using ferns or hostas to cover the bare spots when this scilla is summer dormant.

Snowdrops

The name says it all — snowdrops *(Galanthus)*. Each little bulb sends up a few leaves and a single white flower, with three helicopter-like petals flaring out at the top of a green-tipped tube. The common snowdrop is inexpensive and grows 4 to 5 inches (10 to 13 cm) high.

Snowdrops are okay in cold-winter regions and fine with moderate winters, but they dislike warm winters. You'll have to pass up snowdrops if you live in Southern California, Florida, or other hot climates. Snowdrops are pest free — deer and rabbits don't eat the plants, and chipmunks and mice leave the bulbs alone.

Here are three popular snowdrops:

- ✔ **Common snowdrop *(Galanthus nivalis)*:** In double snowdrops, the inner tube is replaced with lots and lots of ruffled petals. The three flared petals of the green-tipped snowdrop each have a green dot. (This bulb is featured in the color insert.)

- ✔ **The giant snowdrop *(Galanthus elwesii)*:** At 8 to 10 inches (20 to 25 cm) tall, the giant snowdrop is twice the size of the common snowdrop, and it flowers two weeks earlier! The giant snowdrop has a second green band at the base of the tube; the common snowdrop has only one green band, at the opening.

✔ **'S. Arnott' (or 'Sam Arnott'):** This large and pricey snowdrop is quite robust and makes an attractive addition to a snowdrop collection.

Snowdrops have small bulbs that easily dry out, so they're not happy sitting around for several weeks waiting for you to plant them. Buy snowdrop bulbs and plant them immediately after you purchase them in autumn. Snowdrops like summer shade. Select a site with moist but well-drained soil under a tree or shrub, or on the shady side of your house, where you can easily see them.

Spring Cyclamens

If you've ever had a cyclamen as a house plant and wished that it was hardy enough to grow in the garden, the spring cyclamen (also called Persian violet), *Cyclamen coum,* is the plant for you. This sturdy little plant is astoundingly weatherproof — it sends its leaves up and makes flower buds in autumn to sit right through the winter and flower before spring arrives. Spring cyclamens know what they like and, given the right conditions, will thrive for years and years, getting bigger and fatter with more flowers, and even seeding to make new plants.

The spring cyclamen grows best in woodland shade, and, though it likes good drainage, it doesn't want drought. Dryness in summer when the plants are dormant is okay, but not when plants are growing in autumn and spring. Plant them in autumn just before the fat cookie-like tuber-corms start into growth. A *tuber-corm* is a little like a tuber, with several growing points, no interior structure, and no papery covering or tunic, and like a corm because it has a definite this-side-up orientation.

Making more cyclamens

Unlike most other bulbs, corms, and tubers, the cyclamen never makes offsets. The tuber-corm just gets bigger and fatter and makes more flowers. If you want more cyclamens, seed is the only way. Seed is ripe when the capsule holding the seed opens and spills out the sticky brown BB-sized seed. Ants like the seed and carry it away, so pay attention and collect seed before the ants do.

Soak the seed for a couple of hours or overnight in tepid water with a drop or two of dishwashing liquid. The detergent removes the sticky coat. Then, sow the seed right away. Grow them in pots, and then after the second growing season, transfer them to the regular garden. Fresh seed sprouts in about nine weeks; old seed can take nine months or longer, and fewer seeds will sprout. Mice like the tiny tubers and eat 'em up, so start them in pots, not open ground. Seedlings reach flowering size in their second or third year, and just get better and better.

Spring Snowflake

The spring snowflake *(Leucojum vernum)* flowers as early as the common snowdrop. It has richer green leaves, and the charming flowers, one or sometimes two to a stem, look like fat little bells with green-tipped petals. The spring snowflake is a small bulb, and plants grow only 6 inches (15 cm) tall. Spring snowflakes do best in light to medium shade. They prefer a site that won't dry out in summer, with soil that's high in organic matter. Plant spring snowflakes in regions where snowdrops thrive. Autumn planting is best.

Spring snowflakes make offsets at a modest rate. When the clumps become crowded, lift and separate them in spring (after flowering but before the leaves yellow and die back). Pests leave spring snowflakes alone — deer and rabbits, voles and mice seem to find them uninteresting.

Summer Snowflake

Summer snowflake, *Leucojum aestivum,* is a well-behaved bulb that flowers nicely in late spring, producing a few cool white bells of flowers, tipped with green and dangling from a 12- to 18-inch-tall (30- to 46-cm) stem. Summer snowflake likes moist sites and is excellent near a pond or slow-moving stream. Plant summer snowflake in autumn like most spring-flowering bulbs. Ten bulbs make a pleasant showing. This bulb is good for naturalizing; consider planting it in greater numbers to create large drifts.

Tulips

Wild tulips are native to arid regions of Central Asia. The original species have a limited color range — primarily reds and yellows — and tend to be smaller in flower than modern cultivars and hybrids, whose rainbow hues include strong bright colors and pastel shades, providing options and possibilities for any desired color scheme.

Choose tulips just like other bulbs — fat and firm is best. Avoid any that are soft, flabby, moldy, or whose papery brown tunic is missing. The bulbs you buy in fall already have an embryo flower tucked away inside, just waiting to begin growing in spring (see Figure 4-5). In fact, tulips are so eager to grow that if you plant them promptly in the fall, they'll send their leaves up right away, only to have them frozen in winter. So, buy tulip bulbs along with all your other bulbs in September, but wait to plant until October and November — even December if you live in mild winter areas. While you wait to plant them, store bulbs in paper bags, not plastic, and keep them in a cool place, away from heat ducts or furnaces, until you plant. Plant the bulbs in groups of ten in the perennial border, spacing them a couple of inches apart.

As with daffodils, tulips are classified by a variety of factors: number of flowers, shape of flowers, and time of bloom, among others. The following sections present the major *Tulipa* classifications.

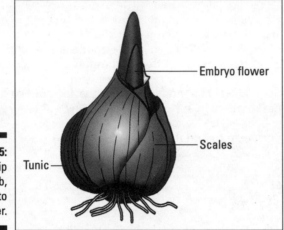

Figure 4-5:
Your tulip bulb, waiting to flower.

Embryo flower

Scales

Tunic

Single early tulips

These are early flowering, single-flowered cultivars, with strong 10- to 18-inch (25- to 46-cm) stems. Many are sweetly scented. Effective in beds, borders, and containers, these low-growing, early-blooming tulips are also good for cutting and forcing:

- ✔ **'Flair':** Excellent, showy, bright red flowers with a hint of yellow on strong 14-inch (36-cm) stems.

- ✔ **'Mickey Mouse':** Dramatic, fringed "Rembrandt" type red-on-yellow flowers with feathered and striped petals that reach 14 inches (36 cm).

- ✔ **'Purple Prince':** Large lilac-purple flowers that reach 14 inches (36 cm) make a strong statement next to other late spring bloomers.

Double early tulips

Among the best bedding tulips — these large, double-flowered, early-blooming, peony-like blossoms provide a blanket of color on 10- to 12-inch (25- to 30-cm) stems. Somewhat formal in appearance, they look best in the front of the perennial border. In addition to beds and borders, these are also good for forcing and as cut flowers:

- ✔ **'Abba':** Fragrant, flaming tomato-red blossoms on 12-inch (30-cm) stems.

- ✔ **'Monte Carlo':** Fragrant, bright yellow flowers top 12-inch (30-cm) stems.

- ✔ **'Peach Blossom':** Rosy-pink blossoms that reach 12 inches (30-cm) are known for honey scent and soft color.

Fringed tulips

Fringed tulips have one stem per bulb, a single flower per stem — but what an interesting flower. You'll want to reach out and touch the crystal-like petal fringes on these unique mid- to late-season beauties. Stem length varies from 16 to 26 inches (41 to 66 cm). Fringed tulips make a remarkable cut flower, or you can use them in beds, borders, or arrangements. Try these cultivars:

- ✔ **'Burgundy Lace':** Rich-looking, wine-red flowers reach 26 inches (66 cm). This cultivar is excellent for long-term plantings.

- ✔ **'Fringed Elegance':** Primrose-yellow-edged-in-red blossoms top 22-inch (56-cm) stems. This all-around favorite offers impressive repeat shows.

- ✔ **'Swan Wings':** Pure white flowers grow on 20-inch (51-cm) stems. The pristine feathery petals combine well with other tulips.

Double late tulips (or peony flowering tulips)

These double-flowered, late-blooming, long-stemmed tulips need some support in the form of staking, especially in wet weather when the extra petals soak up rain like blotting paper. They make an interesting cut flower and offer striking, full blossoms well into the season, and plants reach 16 to 20 inches (41 to 51 cm). With fragrance and long-lasting reliability, the following are useful in a variety of garden and indoor settings:

- ✔ **'Angelique':** Pale to dark rose double petals accented in white crown 18-inch (46-cm) stems. This is a most popular tulip for bedding.

- ✔ **'Carnaval de Nice':** Extra-large, showy white and red flowers on 20-inch (51-cm) stems make an excellent landscape or bedding choice.

- ✔ **'Mount Tacoma':** White blossoms top strong, 18-inch (46-cm) stems. Vigorous, full flowers have subtle green accents and long-lasting appeal in borders or clusters.

Darwin hybrid tulips

Huge, bright flowers on sturdy stems to 24 inches (61 cm) give this group much appeal. Plants bloom midseason and multiply in the garden, making them effective for use in beds and borders, and excellent as cut flowers. Consider these cultivars:

- ✔ **'Apeldoorn':** Unsurpassed in the garden and in bouquets, the brilliant red flowers on 24-inch (61-cm) stems are the classic red tulip.

- ✔ **'Beauty of Apeldoorn':** Striped, golden yellow and magenta flowers atop 22-inch (56-cm) stems offer a wonderful color range.

- ✔ **'Gudoshnik':** Yellow, pink, and red flowers sit atop 24-inch (61-cm) stems. No two of these multicolored beauties are the same.

Triumph tulips

These popular hybrids of early and late single tulips have a single flower on 16- to 20-inch (41- to 51-cm) stems, and they flower in midseason. This group produces large flowers that excel in containers and garden beds or when forced and cut:

- ✔ **'Attila':** Regal purple and violet flowers sit on substantial 18-inch (46-cm) stems. They're excellent for bedding and cutting.

- ✔ **'Beau Monde':** A striking, unbeatable combination of rosy flamed markings appears on a creamy ivory background. The flowers sit on 22-inch (56-cm) stems.

- ✔ **'Prinses Irene':** Unique apricot and purple blossoms (pale orange base, brushed with dark flaming strokes) top 14-inch (36-cm) stems.

- ✔ **'Striped Sail':** Atop 14-inch (36-cm) stems, impressive flowers turn from creamy yellow to white, accented with purple flame markings.

Single late tulips

Single late tulips boast an awesome late season show from strong, reliable 22- to 30-inch (56- to 76-cm) flowers in amazing colors. Use these in mass plantings, beds, borders, and for cutting:

- ✔ **'Bleu Aimable':** Lilac and blue blossoms top 24-inch (61-cm) stems. This unusual flower color is a cool and refreshing shade.

- ✔ **'Dillenburg':** Terra-cotta orange blossoms top 24-inch (61-cm) stems. Unusual and attractive color integrates easily into the garden.

- ✔ **'Esther':** Pale pink flowers top 18-inch (46-cm) stems. Wonderful pastel pink blossoms combine elegantly in beds and borders, and they can stand alone quite well, too.

- ✔ **'Queen of Night':** Velvety, deep maroon flowers bloom on 24-inch (61-cm) stems. This is one of the darkest tulips available.

Parrot tulips

With twisty, curled petals whose edges are snipped and clipped, the large, lush, late-blooming parrot tulips are sure show-stoppers in your garden. Use these showy, large flowers crowning 14- to 20-inch (36- to 51-cm) stems for accent in beds and borders. They're great as cut flowers, too. We recommend these cultivars:

- **'Apricot Parrot':** Fragrant, apricot, cream, and green flowers top 20-inch (51-cm) stems. The soft colors are ideal with green accents.

- **'Blue Parrot':** Cool and rich looking, the blue-violet flowers sit on 22-inch (56-cm) stems. They combine easily with other tulips.

- **'Estella Rijnveld':** Spectacular flowers in vivid red and bright white sit on 20-inch (51-cm) stems.

- **'White Parrot':** Fluffy white flowers are edged in feathery green and sit on 18-inch (46-cm) stems. They're great in gardens and with other cut flowers.

Book VI

Bulbs

Viridiflora tulips (or green tulips)

If they didn't flower in May, these tulips would be perfect for St. Patrick's Day! The plants have a single flower per 12- to 20-inch (30- to 51-cm) stem, with leaf-green edges or central streak on the petals, providing soft, feathery accents. These outstanding late-season pastel blossoms are long-lasting, making them ideal in borders. They also make interesting cut flower arrangements. Try these:

- **'Esperanto':** Dark pink and green flowers on 20-inch (51-cm) stems display an arresting two-toned combination.

- **'Groenland' ('Greenland'):** Pink and green flowers on 20-inch (51-cm) stems make an ideal combination of soft pink and feathery green stripes.

- **'Spring Green':** Elegant and long-lasting, these creamy white and green flowers top 20-inch (51-cm) stems.

Lily-flowered tulips

Distinctive, slender flowers in vivid colors with pointed petals gently curved outward give these mid- to late-season blossoms status in beds and borders. Stem length varies from 18 to 24 inches (46 to 61 cm), and each bulb provides one flower, with blooms appearing in mid- or late season. Lily-flowered tulips make a classy, elegant cut flower. We suggest these cultivars:

- **'Mariette':** Its white base flares into satiny, rose-pink color on a 22-inch (56-cm) stem, giving this cultivar elegance in the garden.

- ✔ **'Maytime':** This elegant, late-flowering tulip features reddish-purple flowers edged in cream and can reach 24 inches (61 cm) in height.

- ✔ **'Red Shine':** Perfectly formed, deep red flowers sit on 22-inch (56-cm) stems.

- ✔ **'West Point':** Sturdy and brilliant bright yellow flowers on 20-inch (51-cm) stems provide an accent in the garden or enliven an arrangement.

Kaufmanniana hybrid (waterlily) tulips

Very early flowering *Tulipa kaufmanniana* and all its offspring — cultivars and hybrids — are dwarf tulips under a foot tall. The star-like flowers in striking colors open wide on sunny days, giving rise to the common name of waterlily tulip. These charming gems are an excellent choice for the rock garden, and they're ideal for permanent plantings in beds and borders:

- ✔ **'Ancilla':** Soft pink, red, and white flowers sit on 6-inch (15-cm) stems. Large flowers offer a stunning blend of color and fine form.

- ✔ **'Johann Straus':** Rosy red and sulfur blossoms on 8-inch (20-cm) stems make an impressive two-toned flower with spotted foliage.

- ✔ **'Stresa':** Vivid, eye-catching, golden-yellow and carmine-red flowers top 8-inch (20-cm) stems.

Greigii hybrid tulips

Tulipa greigii has given rise to an assortment of very early flowering charming cultivars, varieties, and hybrids that flower just a tad later than *T. kaufmanniana*. The dwarf plants, 8 to 14 inches (20 to 36 cm) tall, have leaves flat on the ground, often with wavy edges and chocolate-maroon mottled or striped markings reminiscent of supermarket bar-code price tags. The vivid flowers are good for forcing, great in the rock garden, and perfect for borders, containers, and cutting gardens. Reliably perennial in northern climate zones, this is a great group of tulips:

- ✔ **'Corsage':** Deep salmon pink and yellow flowers on 12-inch (30-cm) stems are unusual and appealing in their subtle colors.

- ✔ **'Oriental Splendor':** Carmine-red, yellow, and purple flowers on 10-inch (25-cm) stems make another unbeatable color combination.

- ✔ **'Red Riding Hood':** Bright red flowers top 8-inch (20-cm) stems. Expect early, dazzling results from this flower with a black base.

Fosteriana hybrid tulips

Early fireworks are the payoff with these large, bright flowers offering impressive displays in mass plantings, borders, rock gardens, cutting gardens, and forcing jars. *Tulipa fosteriana* is parent to a number of early flowering cultivars, varieties, and hybrids noted for their large, long flowers on medium to long (8 to 18 inches/20 to 46 cm) stems. Flowers open wide in sunshine. Their flowering period overlaps with late-season daffodils. Try these:

- **'Orange Emperor':** Orange flowers bloom on 16-inch (41-cm) stems. A deep orange center gives way to soft, satin exterior petals.

- **'Princeps':** Vivid, show-stopping scarlet flowers top 8-inch (20-cm) stems. These little guys are tiny but mighty.

- **'White Emperor' (Purissima):** Glistening, pure white, fragrant flowers bloom on 18-inch (46-cm) stems.

- **'Yellow Empress':** Large, golden-yellow flowers atop 16-inch (41-cm) stems add early sunny cheer indoors and out.

Book VI

Bulbs

Bunch-flowering (multiflowered) tulips

If you like more bang for your buck, you should probably consider growing multiflowered tulips, where each bulb produces a single stem with four to six full-sized flowers. These varieties create a spectacular, long-lasting display in beds, borders, and bouquets. They bloom mid- to late season on 8- to 20-inch (20- to 51-cm) stems. Because bunch-flowering can occur in triumph, single late, and even greigii tulips, height and bloom time will vary from cultivar to cultivar. Try these varieties:

- **'Candy Club':** This single late tulip has ivory white flowers atop 20-inch (51-cm) stems. Subtle pink or purple accents appear on a white background.

- **'Georgette':** This single late tulip sports clear yellow flowers with red highlights on 20-inch (51-cm) stems.

- **'Toronto':** Salmon-colored flowers sit atop 12-inch (30-cm) stems. This greigii-type tulip sports mottled foliage and glowing flowers.

- *Tulipa praestans* **'Unicum':** Red-orange and white blossoms sit on 8-inch (20-cm) stems. This tulip has bright flowers and white-edged leaves.

Species tulips

These "wild" cultivars offer compact plants (6 to 8 inches/15 to 20 cm) that star in rock gardens, along border fronts, in containers, in heirloom plantings, and when naturalized in the landscape. Try the following:

- *Tulipa bakeri* **'Lilac Wonder':** Stunning, cupped, star-like, lilac and yellow flowers bloom on 7-inch (18-cm) stems. Excellent in the South.

- *Tulipa fosteriana:* Red and yellow-black centered flowers reach 20 inches (51 cm). Flowers offer interesting colors and markings.

- *Tulipa hageri* **'Spendens':** Bell-shaped flowers in rich coppery and bronze tones sprout three to five blooms per 8-inch (20-cm) stem.

- *Tulipa tarda:* Easy-to-grow, ground-cover-like selection with white, green, and yellow flowers sit atop 4-inch (10-cm) stems.

Wood Hyacinths

Also known as England's bluebells, these fat, fleshy bulbs delight in a woodland location. They grow happily beneath trees and shrubs, and they multiply in large numbers by offsets and seeds to carpet the ground in April and May. These bulbs are easy to grow, so you can create a little bit of England in your own garden. You may also want to consider trying the Spanish cousin to England's bluebells.

English bluebells are *Hyacinthoides non-scripta*. Bigger than a golf ball, but smaller than a tennis ball, the bulbs are fat and fleshy, without any papery tunic or covering. Plant promptly, so that they don't dry out. If you must store them — briefly — pack them in wood shavings. The spikes of pendant, bell-shaped, dark blue-violet, fragrant flowers grow about a foot tall and open in May. Leaves are rather conspicuous when they start to yellow.

Spanish bluebells are *Hyacinthoides hispanica*. The Spanish bulbs are about the same size as those of English bluebells, and they get the same treatment. Flowers open in April or May — bell-shaped and drooping, violet-blue — but they're no where near as fragrant as English bluebells. The wild type of Spanish bluebell has been in gardens since 1601. You may want to grow these colorful forms of lesser vintage, as well:

- **'Excelsior':** Fine dark blue-violet in color, this one is larger growing than the typical form.

- **'Rose Queen':** Deep rose-pink flowers cluster toward the top of the flowering stem.

- **'White Triumphator':** Clean, clear white flowers bloom on a robust, tall plant.

Book VII
Vegetables and Herbs

In this book . . .

A garden can be functional as well as beautiful. In fact, for some gardeners, the function makes the beauty. As forms of food, and in some cases, medicine, vegetables and herbs go hand-in-hand.

This book tells you how to select, plant, grow, and care for your vegetable and herb gardens. We show you how to plan each type of garden or how to create a garden that holds both. We discuss harvesting your plants and getting the most out of your growing season. And we devote two full chapters to the various types of vegetables and herbs that you may want to grow. These chapters are especially useful in helping you choose varieties and colors. The chapter devoted to various herbs also tells you which ones can be dangerous.

Nothing tastes quite as good or is quite as satisfying as food that you grow with your own hands in your own soil. Read on as we help you digest the information that can make that experience possible for you.

Here are the contents of Book VII at a glance:

Chapter 1

Visualizing Veggie Vineyards

In This Chapter

▶ Going from plot (or pot) to plant — planning your vegetable garden

▶ Sprouting vegetables in containers

So you've decided to plant a vegetable garden. You're in for a rewarding and healthy treat as you grow and serve your own food. Before you can "dig" in to your garden, though, you need to consider several things. And that's just what this chapter helps you do.

Choosing Your Vegetables

Part of the fun of planning a vegetable garden is deciding which varieties of a particular vegetable you want to grow. Selecting your veggies before you design your garden helps you ensure that you have the right amount of room and the best growing conditions.

Theme vegetable gardens

You can get creative and group vegetables by their special uses. Theme gardens don't have to take over your entire garden; they only need a corner or one raised bed. Just remember the spacing requirements for vegetables. Following are several popular garden themes:

✔ **Greens garden:** Grow a colorful salad greens garden filled with different colors and textures of lettuce, endive, spinach, Swiss chard, and parsley.

✔ **Mexican salsa garden:** Create a special nook for your own salsa garden, complete with different varieties of tomatoes, tomatillos, cilantro, peppers, and onions.

✔ **Asian stir fry garden:** Grow all the ingredients you need for a stir fry by planting pac choi, Chinese cabbage, snow peas, garlic, and scallions.

✔ **Pizza garden:** Design a circular garden, and in triangular sections (like pizza slices), grow favorite pizza toppings such as peppers, onions, and tomatoes.

A *variety* is a selection of a particular type of vegetable that has certain predictable, desirable traits. These traits may include the following:

- **Adaptation:** Some varieties are particularly well adapted to certain areas.

- **Appearance:** You can find common vegetables in a kaleidoscope of colors. The more beautiful the vegetables, the more beautiful the vegetable garden — and the more stunning the food.

- **Cooking and storage characteristics:** Certain varieties of beans and peas, for example, freeze better than others. Some squash varieties may be stored for months, but others need to be eaten immediately.

- **Days to maturity (or days to harvest):** *Days to maturity* refers to the number of days it will take (under normal conditions) for a vegetable planted from seed (or from transplants) to mature and produce a crop. This number is important for vegetable gardeners who live in short-summer climates. (Turn to Chapter 2 in Book I for more about climate.)

- **Extended harvest season:** By mixing varieties that ripen at different times, you can start harvesting as early as 60 days after seeding and continue for five or six weeks. Seed catalogs and packages often describe varieties as early season, midseason, or late season in relationship to other varieties of the same vegetable.

- **Pest resistance:** Many varieties are resistant to specific diseases or pests — a very important trait in many areas. Tomatoes in particular have outstanding pest resistance, with varieties labeled as resistant to *verticillium* wilt (V), *fusarium* wilt (F), and nematodes (N).

- **Plant size:** Many excellent, compact-growing vegetable varieties are ideal for small spaces or for growing in containers.

- **Taste:** You can find flavors for every taste bud.

The scope of your vegetable variety possibilities becomes apparent in Chapter 3 of Book VII.

As you begin to look at catalogs and seed packets, you'll come across some terms that may be new to you:

- **Hybrids:** As you look through seed catalogs or read seed packets, you may notice the phrase *F-1 hybrid* (or simply *hybrid*) before or after the names of some varieties. Generally, these seeds are more expensive than others. *Hybrid seeds* are the result of a *cross* (pollen from one flower fertilizing a flower from another similar plant, resulting in seed) of selected groups of plants of the same kind, called *inbred lines*. If you choose hybrid seeds, you need to buy a new batch every season. When hybrid plants cross with themselves and form seeds, these seeds lose the specific combination of genetic information that gave the hybrid its predictable qualities. If you plant seed from hybrids, you end up with a very mixed bag of plants.

✔ **Open pollination:** Open-pollinated varieties are basically inbred lines that are allowed to pollinate each other in open fields. The resulting seeds are pretty predictable, but they don't provide the consistency of F-1 hybrids. Open-pollinated varieties are subject to the whims of nature, and some plants may be a little different than you expect. However, if you want to save your own seeds as a seed collector, open-pollinated varieties are the only plants that you can replant from seed and have most of the plants turn out very similar to the parent.

✔ **Heirlooms:** Any open-pollinated variety that is at least 50 years old is generally considered an *heirloom*. Heirlooms are enjoying quite a revival because of the variety of fruit colors, tastes, and forms that are available. Heirloom vegetables are worth trying, but remember that some varieties may not have the disease resistance and wide adaptability that the hybrids generally have.

✔ **Altered genes:** *Genetically modified varieties* are plants that have a gene from a totally unrelated species inserted into the variety of vegetable so that the vegetable exhibits a certain trait. For example, geneticists may insert a gene of a harmless-to-humans pesticide into a seed to give the plant greater pest resistance. Genetically modified varieties of a number of vegetables are just now becoming available to home gardeners, but many unanswered questions remain about whether this new type of vegetable will be better or worse for people and the environment in the long run.

Book VII

Vegetables and Herbs

Spotting the Best Plot

Choosing a site is an important step in planning a vegetable garden. Much of your decision is based on common sense. You definitely want to locate your garden close to a water source, and if you plan to bring in truckloads of fertilizer, you want to put the garden where you can reach it by vehicle. You (and maybe your family) will spend more time in your garden if you can get to it easily. A bit of science is also involved in choosing the right spot. You need to be aware of your weather, climate, and microclimates, which we explain in detail in Chapter 2 of Book I. The following list offers some general considerations for deciding where to place your garden:

✔ **Location:** Locate your vegetable garden visibly and conveniently so that you can easily water, weed, feed, and harvest. (If your garden's out of sight, it's probably out of mind.) Take advantage of warm or cool spots in your yard to extend your harvest, and plant enough to feed your family.

✔ **Size:** Start small. The average vegetable garden is about 600 square feet (about 20 x 30 feet / 6 x 9 m). Consider the size of crop you want as well as how much time you have to devote to upkeep. If you're a first-timer,

600 square feet is plenty big enough. If you're a busy person, you may want a smaller garden that's approximately 200 square feet or even a small bed near your house that's 50 or 100 square feet. If your soil is in good condition (refer to Chapter 3 in Book I for more on soil), a novice gardener can keep up with a 400-square-foot garden by devoting about half an hour to it each day at the beginning of the season. In late spring through summer, half an hour of work every two to three days should keep the garden productive and looking good.

If space is limited, you can create a small-space block garden. Often called the "square-foot garden," this 3 x 3-foot square bed is divided into nine 1-foot (0.3 m) squares, each planted with a different vegetable. Space-saving vegetable varieties for smaller vegetables, such as lettuce and carrots work best. Containerized vegetable gardens are a good idea if all you have is a small patio or roof top. (Chapter 3 in Book II looks at container gardening more closely.)

✔ **Sun and shade:** Gardens do best if they get full sun — most vegetable plants (especially peppers, tomatoes, and beans) need a minimum of six hours of direct sunlight daily for optimum growth. Some crops, however — especially leafy ones, such as lettuce — produce reasonably well in a partially shaded location where the sun shines directly on the plants for four hours. Root crops, such as carrots and beets, need more light than leafy vegetables, but they may do well in a garden that gets only morning sun for four to six hours.

You don't have to plant all your vegetables in one plot. If your only sunny spot is in the front yard, plant a border of peppers and tomatoes along the front walk and set lettuce plants in a shadier spot out back. Or garden in one spot in summer and another in early spring or fall. If shade in your garden comes from nearby trees and shrubs, your vegetable plants will compete for water and nutrients as well as for light. Tree roots extend slightly beyond the *drip line,* the outer foliage reach of the tree. If possible, keep your garden out of the *root zones* (the areas that extend from the drip lines to the trunks) of surrounding trees and shrubs. Otherwise, give the vegetables more water and give fertilizer to compensate.

✔ **Drainage:** As we explain in Chapter 3 of Book I, soil needs good drainage for plants to thrive. Don't plant your garden near the leach lines of a septic system — we think you know why. And keep away from underground utilities. If you have questions, call your local utility company to locate underground lines.

✔ **Wind:** High winds can wreak havoc on tall crops, such as corn and pole beans, and can make any vegetable dry out rapidly. If wind is a problem in your area, protect your garden with a *windbreak* (a fence or several rows of taller plants). You provide maximum protection for your crops if you plant them downwind at a distance that's three to five times the height of the windbreak.

✔ **Slopes:** Ground with a gentle slope to the south makes for an ideal planting site, especially in cold climates. South-sloping soil warms up faster in the spring, diminishing the likelihood of frosts affecting plants. Because cold air is like water (it runs downhill and settles in low spots), frosty air moves past plants on slopes without doing damage. In hot climates, a north-facing slope may help keep plants cooler during midsummer heat. On any sloping ground, plant rows across rather than down the slope so that the plants catch water runoff. You may need to build terraces on very steep slopes to hold soil in place.

Mapping Out Your Garden

Designing a vegetable garden is both a practical and a creative process. Practically speaking, you must arrange plants so that they have room to grow and so that taller vegetables don't shade lower-growing types. Different planting techniques fit the growth habits of different kinds of vegetables. And you need to plan for easy access to the garden. On the other hand, creativity is important to the design process. After all, vegetables can be good-looking as well as practical. Consider mixing them with flowers or growing them in containers.

Before you sketch a garden plan, you need to decide how to arrange the plants. You can choose from three basic planting arrangements:

✔ **Rows:** You can plant any vegetable in rows, but this arrangement works best with types that need quite a bit of room, such as tomatoes, beans, cabbages, corn, potatoes, peppers, and summer squash.

✔ **Hills:** Hills are best for vining crops such as cucumbers, melons, and winter squash.

✔ **Raised beds:** Raised beds are best for smaller vegetables that can be planted close together, such as lettuce, carrots, onions, spinach, radishes, and turnips. You can plant vegetables in random patterns or in closely spaced rows. Raised beds have several advantages: They rise above soil problems and consolidate your work. They're also easy on your back, handicapped accessible, and attractive. Plus, raised beds warm early because more of the soil is exposed to the sun, which allows for early planting and extended harvest seasons. (Chapter 5 in Book IV tells you how to build a raised bed.)

In dry areas, such as the desert Southwest, the traditional bed is sunken, not raised. Dig into the soil about 6 inches (15 cm) and make a small wall of soil around the outside of the bed. This design allows the bed to catch any summer rains, protects young plants from drying winds, and concentrates water where the vegetables grow.

Book VII

Vegetables and Herbs

As you plan your garden, you need to pay attention to the following information in seed catalogs and on seed packets:

- **Seeds/Plants per 100 ft. of row:** How many plants and seed you need to purchase.

- **Spacing between rows:** The ideal distance you should leave between rows of different vegetables, usually a little more than the distance you should leave between plants.

- **Spacing between plants:** The ideal distance you should allow between individual vegetable plants within a row or planting bed.

- **Average yield per 10 ft. of row:** How much you can expect to harvest.

Vegetable spacings are just guidelines, most likely derived from agricultural recommendations for maximum yield per acre. With close attention to soil preparation, watering, and fertilizing, you can plant closer and still get a good harvest. However, if you plant so close that plants have to compete with each other for food, water, and light, you'll eventually get smaller harvests or lower quality vegetables.

Drawing a garden plan doesn't require any landscaping expertise. After you determine the location and dimensions of your garden, you just need a piece of graph paper and a pencil, a list of vegetables you want to grow, and maybe a seed catalog or two. Turn to Chapter 1 in Book II for information on designing your garden.

Growing Vegetables in Containers

You can grow almost any vegetable in a container; just fill a big pot with good soil, and water, and fertilize your plants regularly. (Chapter 3 in Book II discusses container gardening in detail.) Containers solve the problem of poor soil and garden pests, and they enable you to grow vegetables that you may not be able to grow in your garden. Some people grow vegetables in containers simply because they like having their crops nearby. With containers, you can bring your crops close to your house where you can enjoy them (and eat them at the peak of freshness!); and, you may not be able to move the sun, but you can certainly move your container to the sun!

Remember this one rule about soil: Don't fill your pot with soil from your garden even if your garden has the very best soil on the planet. It's too heavy and too dirty (you know, weed seeds, bugs, bacteria — stuff that you don't want in your pots), and it may not drain properly in a pot. Use potting soil instead.

Containers come in a wealth of shapes and sizes. When choosing a container for vegetables, keep the following in mind:

✔ **Size:** In most cases, pots that are bigger (in terms of width and volume) are better, especially for growing large plants like tomatoes. With some vegetables, the depth of a container is as important — if not more important — as its width. You can grow quite a few carrots or radishes in a narrow container, but the container must be deep enough to accommodate the length of the plant's mature roots.

✔ **Material:** If you want to use wood containers, choose root-resistant materials, such as cedar or redwood; otherwise, they won't last very long. You can build containers with lumber that's been pressure-treated with preservatives; however, even though there isn't strong proof that vegetable roots absorb these materials, we prefer not to use preservative-treated wood containers for growing edibles.

Remember that terra-cotta, no matter how attractive, tends to dry out quickly — a major problem for vegetables racing full steam ahead. You may be better off planting in plastic if you don't use wood.

✔ **Drainage:** If your pots don't come with drainage holes, drill your own (eight to ten evenly spaced, 1-inch / 2 cm holes should be fine).

✔ **Accessories:** When you buy containers, look for those that have a saucer to place underneath your pot. A saucer collects water that runs out of the holes in the bottom of a pot and prevents the pot from staining whatever it's sitting on. Something with wheels makes your life much easier. Most nurseries sell wheeled platforms that you place under pots to move them easily.

If you're persistent, you can grow any vegetable in a pot. However, some of the bigger plants, such as squash and watermelon, are pretty tricky to grow in containers and tend to get unruly. The following list looks at the most common vegetables to grow in containers:

✔ **Beans:** Bush varieties like 'Provider' and 'Derby' are best. You can grow pole types, but you have to attach some type of trellis.

✔ **Beets:** Any variety grows well in a pot, and smaller varieties like 'Action' and 'Kestrel' will grow in smaller pots.

✔ **Carrots:** Carrots are a perfect vegetable to grow in a pot. Start with baby varieties like 'Baby Spike', 'Short 'n Sweet', or 'Thumbelina'.

✔ **Cole crops — broccoli, cabbage, cauliflower, and so on:** All the cole crops grow well in containers as long as your pots are big enough.

✔ **Corn:** Plant 10 to 15 seeds per half barrel, and then fertilize and water like crazy. You may get only one ear per plant, but hey, it's fresh corn.

✔ **Cucumbers:** Grow small cucumber types, such as 'Bush Pickle'. Plants dangling over the edges of a hanging pot are something to behold.

✔ **Eggplant:** Eggplant is perfect for pots; any variety works as long the container is at least 5 gallons. Plant one eggplant per 5-gallon pot.

Book VII

Vegetables and Herbs

- **Lettuce and other greens:** These are the perfect container vegetables, and the size of your pot doesn't really matter.

- **Onions:** Green onions grow well in containers.

- **Peas:** Go with dwarf pea varieties like 'Green Arrow' and 'Maestro' English peas, 'Sugar Bon' snap peas, or 'Dwarf Grey Sugar'.

- **Peppers:** You can grow any pepper variety in a pot, but the bigger the pot the better.

- **Potatoes:** Potatoes are fun vegetables to grow in a container. Just place 8 to 10 inches (20 to 25 cm) of potting soil in a big pot (at least a 5-gallon size).

- **Radishes:** Growing radishes is quick and easy even in the smallest container.

- **Squash:** You're in business with space-saving winter squash varieties, such as 'Cream of the Crop', 'Green Magic II', or 'Table King'.

- **Tomatoes:** Anyone can grow tomatoes in pots.

Chapter 2

Vegetating the Day Away

• •

In This Chapter

▶ Getting your vegetable garden started

▶ Maintaining your garden

▶ Keeping plants pest-free and healthy

▶ Harvesting and storing your crop

• •

Are you ready to plant some vegetables? The fun really starts when you get your seeds (or transplants) in the ground. This chapter takes you through the whole veggie life cycle from planting to eating and everything in between.

Starting Your Veggies Off Right

Whether you choose to grow vegetables from seeds or transplants, each planting method has its advantages. Whichever planting method you choose, make sure that you time your planting for the most productive results. (You start vegetable seeds as you do perennials, and you look for the same things in starter plants. Refer to Chapter 3 in Book IV for instructions.)

You can start seeds indoors or outdoors. If you plant seeds indoors, you transplant them into your garden later. With *direct seeding,* you skip the indoor step and sow the seeds directly in your garden. If you're serious about growing vegetables, you'll probably end up using both options. Consider these points when making your choice:

✔ **You get a jump on the growing season when you start indoors.** If you start at the right time, you can have vigorous seedlings ready to go into the ground at the ideal time. In areas with short growing seasons, starting seedlings indoors really gives you a head start. The best candidates for an early start are plants that tolerate root disturbance and benefit from a jump on the season, including broccoli, Brussels sprouts, cabbage, cauliflower, celery, eggplant, leeks, onions, parsley, peppers, and tomatoes.

✔ **Seeds are easier to start indoors.** You can more easily provide the perfect conditions for hard-to-germinate or very small seeds, including the ideal temperature, moisture, and fertility.

✔ **Some vegetables don't like to be transplanted.** These vegetables include many of the root crops, such as carrots, beets, turnips, and parsnips. They're cold-hardy vegetables, so you can direct seed them pretty early anyway. Crops like corn, beans, and peas are also pretty finicky about transplanting and grow better when you direct seed them.

Planting roots in the ground

Harden off vegetable seedlings that have been grown indoors or purchased from a greenhouse before exposing them to the elements. Chapter 3 in Book IV explains hardening off in detail (you use the same method to harden off vegetables as you do perennials).

Don't overharden your plants. Certain crops, such as cabbage and broccoli, can *bolt* (flower before they're supposed to) quickly if seedlings over three weeks old are repeatedly exposed to temperatures lower than 40°F (4°C) for a couple of weeks.

Before transplanting your seedlings, you need to prepare your soil and sculpt beds or rows (as described in Books I and II), and your garden must be ready to plant. When setting out plants in biodegradable peat pots, make slits down the sides of the pots or gently tear the sides to enable the roots to push through. Also, tear off the lip (top) of the pot, so that it doesn't stick up above the soil surface and pull moisture out of the soil. With premade growing blocks encased in netting, cut off the netting before planting.

Peater, peater, pumpkin planter

For gardeners who put a premium on convenience and still want to start plants indoors, premade growing cubes are a good idea. But to be honest, we're not huge fans of peat pots or cubes. The idea behind a peat pot is that once planted (pot and all) in the garden, the plants' roots grow through the sides of the wet pot, and as the season progresses, the peat naturally breaks down and disappears. When we've used them, the peat didn't always break down. If you decide to use peat pots or cubes, gently tear the sides of the pots just before planting to create spaces for the roots to grow into the soil. Plant a peat pot with frayed sides into the garden.

The little cubes are flat, half-dollar-size peat cubes enclosed in nylon mesh that you place a seed in and then soak in water. As the cubes are soaking, the peat expands to cover the seed and grows into a small peat pot. They work okay, but they're hard to wet.

Choose a calm, cloudy day to transplant, if possible. Late afternoon is a good time because plants can recover from the shock of transplanting without sitting in the midday heat and sun. If you don't get an ideal transplanting day and the weather is hot and sunny, shade the plants until the sun goes down. Don't be alarmed if your plants look a little droopy after you set them out because they'll soon recover. Cabbage seedlings can droop and look almost dead, for example, and then be up and growing in a day or two.

Sowing seeds directly in your garden

Unless you live in an area where summers are really short, you're better off sowing some vegetables directly in a garden. Large-seeded, fast-growing vegetables, such as corn, melons, squash, beans, and peas, usually languish if they're grown in containers for even a day or two too long.

Before direct seeding, make sure that the soil has dried out sufficiently before you work it, and be sure that the soil is warm enough for the seeds that you want to plant. Pea seeds, for example, germinate in soil as cool as 40°F (4°C), and you can plant them as soon as you can work the soil in spring. Squash seeds, on the other hand, need warmth. If your soil temperature is much below 65°F (18°C), the seeds are likely to rot in the ground before they sprout. The best way to determine the temperature of your soil is to use a soil thermometer, which you can buy at a garden store.

Book VII

Vegetables and Herbs

You can plant seeds in a variety of patterns. The method that you choose depends on your climate, your tools, and your taste:

- **Row planting:** Mark the placement of a row within your garden, and then make a furrow at the correct depth along the row. Some seeds may not sprout, so sow seeds more thickly than you want the final spacing of the crops to be. Thinning rows is less of a chore if you space seeds as evenly as possible. Cover the seeds with fine soil and then firm them in with the back of a hoe to make sure that all the seeds are in contact with the soil. Water gently. If you plan to use furrow irrigation (refer to Chapter 4 in Book I), fill the furrows with water first and then push the large seeds into the top of raised beds.

- **Wide row planting:** This method allows you to plant more seeds in less space by concentrating watering, weeding, and fertilizing in a smaller area. Rows are generally 10 to 16 inches (25 to 41 cm) wide. Sprinkle seeds over the entire row — with most crops, try to land the seeds about ½ to 1 inch (1 to 2 cm) apart (for peas and beans, 1½ to 2 inches (4 to 5 cm)). Cover small seeds with a thin layer of potting soil. Pat the potting soil down again to bring the added soil into firm contact with the seeds.

- **Bed planting:** Planting beds is essentially the same as planting wide rows. Chapter 5 in Book IV provides information on planning and creating raised beds.

✔ **Hill planting:** Plant seeds for vining crops that spread out, such as squash, melons, or cucumbers, in hills or circular groups. Loosen the soil in a 1-foot-diameter (30 cm) area, level the area, and then plant five to six seeds close together. Thin out all but the two strongest seedlings. If your soil is heavy (refer to Chapter 3 in Book I for information on soil), you may want to plant in a raised hill, or *mound*. The raised soil warms up more quickly than the surrounding soil and drains better. Just don't let the mound dry out!

Soon after seedlings grow their second set of true leaves, you need to thin them out. When you thin plants, either discard the extra seedlings or move them to another part of your garden. Newly transplanted seedlings need extra attention until they get established. Shade them from the hot sun for a day or two and be sure to keep them well watered. Lettuce is one of the easiest vegetables to move when it's small. Root crops, such as beets and carrots, transplant poorly, as do beans and peas.

You can thin some crops in stages with delicious results. Carrots, lettuce, and beets are all good candidates for gradual thinning. If you've ever tasted beet greens cooked up with tender, marble-sized beets still attached, you know what a real treat they are. Start thinning carrot, lettuce, and beet seedlings when they're 1 to 2 inches (2 to 5 cm) apart. After the plants grow to 6 to 8 inches (15 to 20 cm) tall, pull up every other one and enjoy them. Leave a final 4- to 6-inch (10- to 15-cm) spacing for larger plants to develop.

Sing a song of succession planting

Succession planting is a method of extending the harvest of vegetables that ripen all at once and lose quality if left in the garden instead of being harvested. This technique ensures a constant supply of vegetables to take to your table. Basically, you make smaller plantings separated by a few weeks instead of planting everything at once. The length of your planting season determines how many successive plantings you can make and how successful the later plantings are. Depending on the weather, some of your later plantings may not yield well.

Succession planting is most successful with bush beans, beets, broccoli, cabbage, carrots, radishes, corn, lettuce and other greens, onions, and spinach. Here's how it works:

1. **Determine how much of a certain vegetable your family needs for a two- to three-week period, and how much room you need to grow it.**

2. **Break your planting beds into three or four appropriate-sized sections to grow that much of the vegetable.**

3. **Plant the first bed at the start of the planting season, wait about two weeks and plant the second bed, and then plant the third bed about two weeks later.**

When you just about finish harvesting the first bed, the second bed will be ready to harvest.

Planting by phases of the moon

This technique has been used for eons. Ancient farmers and gardeners noticed that certain vegetables perform better when planted during different moon phases. The planting seasons don't really change, but planting dates during those seasons become very important. Moon gardening divides the 28-day moon cycle (from the new moon to the full moon and back to the new moon) into quarters, as any calendar does. Certain quarters are thought to be better than others for planting specific vegetables. The following list gives you an idea of what to plant when, according to the moon cycle:

✔ **The first quarter, when the moon goes from new moon (invisible) to a quarter visible:** Plant asparagus, lettuce, broccoli, cabbage, cauliflower, and other vegetables that produce their seeds on parts of the plant that aren't eaten.

✔ **The second quarter, when the moon goes from half to full:** Plant vegetables in which the seeds are eaten, such as beans, tomatoes, peppers, and squash.

✔ **The third quarter, as the moon moves from full back to half again:** Plant root crops, such as beets, carrots, potatoes, radishes, and turnips.

✔ **The last quarter, when the moon goes from half to invisible:** Not a good planting time. Instead, prepare the soil and rid the garden of pests and weeds.

Meeting Your Garden's Needs

After you plant your vegetables, you need to keep them healthy and well-nourished throughout the growing season. If you let up just a bit on water or fertilizer, your harvest will be small or of poor quality.

Water

Different crops have different water needs. Some vegetables, such as celery, are real water lovers and prefer to have moist soil around their roots at all times. Shallow-rooted crops (such as onions and cabbage) need more careful watering during dry spells than deeper-rooted crops (such as tomatoes) that can pull water from greater depths. You also need to keep in mind a plant's growth stage when watering. Here are some general watering guidelines for different growth stages:

✔ **Watering seedlings and germinating seeds:** Water gently once a day to a few inches deep if it doesn't rain.

✔ **Watering transplants:** To help roots recover from transplant shock, water frequently for two weeks after putting transplants in the soil. After that, water every few days to 6 inches (15 cm) or so.

✔ **Watering established plants:** Water established plants deeply, to at least 6 inches (15 cm) deep. Give the soil a chance to dry out slightly before watering thoroughly again.

In general, most vegetables use about 1 inch (2 cm) of water per week (1 to 2 inches (2 to 5 cm) in hot, dry climates). If you don't get water from rainfall, you have to supply it. Each vegetable has a critical period when you need to be especially careful about watering, or your crop may be ruined. Table 2-1 shows the important watering periods for different types of vegetables.

Table 2-1	Critical Watering Periods for Vegetables
Vegetable	*Important Watering Stage*
Bean, lima	When flowering and forming pods
Bean, snap	When flowering and forming pods
Broccoli	When forming a head
Cabbage	When forming a head
Carrots	When forming roots
Cauliflower	When forming a head
Corn, sweet	When silking, tasseling, and forming ears
Cucumber	When flowering and developing fruit
Eggplant	Give uniform supply of water from flowering through harvest
Melon	During fruit set and early development
Onion, dry	During bulb enlargement
Pea	When flowering and during seed enlargement
Pepper	Give uniform supply of water from flowering through harvest
Potato	When tubers set and enlarge
Radish	When forming roots
Squash, summer	When forming buds and flowering
Tomato	Give uniform supply of water from flowering through harvest
Turnip	When forming roots

Mulch

Mulch is any material, organic or inorganic, that you place over the surface of soil, usually right over the root zone of growing plants. (Chapter 4 in Book I tells you all you need to know about mulch.) Choosing a mulch and deciding when to use it in your vegetable garden depends on the type of vegetables that you grow and when you plant them. Here are some mulching tips for different types of vegetables:

- **Cool-season vegetables planted in early spring:** Young plants get off to a fast start when they have a great deal of sun. Lay down organic mulch when the soil starts to warm and when the plants need regular water. If you mulch too early, the soil stays too cold and wet for proper root growth. In areas with short growing seasons, plant broccoli, cauliflower, and cool-season plants through plastic. Cover the plastic with organic matter when the weather warms.

- **Cool-season vegetables planted in late summer or early fall:** These vegetables need the cooling effect, so put down an organic mulch right after planting. When the weather starts to cool, rake off or remove the organic mulch so that the soil warms. You can plant through plastic late in the year, but cover it with an organic mulch immediately so that the soil doesn't get too hot. Remove the organic mulch when the weather cools and let the plastic warm the soil through harvest.

You can store many root crops in the ground well into winter by covering them with a thick organic mulch, such as straw. Applied before the ground freezes, the mulch keeps the soil loose and unfrozen so that you can dig the vegetables later into winter.

- **Warm-season vegetables planted in spring:** With these vegetables, keep the ground clear if you're planting really early — the more heat the better. Planting through plastic works in early spring. In hot climates, apply an organic mulch when the weather starts to heat up.

Fertilize

Even if you have the healthiest soil around, growing vegetables is an intensive process that takes many important nutrients from the soil. So you need to add some fertilizer to your soil to keep it in optimum shape to feed your plants. How much fertilizer you add depends on the soil and the plants you're growing. That's why it's hard to generalize across the board on what and how much fertilizer to use. Soil tests are a great way to know what to add. (Refer to Chapter 3 in Book I for more about soil tests.)

Depending on the type of fertilizer you use, the crops you grow, and the type of soil you have, you may need to add repeat doses of fertilizer throughout the growing season — a practice called *side-dressing*. You can use both chemical and natural fertilizers for side-dressing. A 5-10-10 fertilizer is a good choice for many crops. (Check out Chapter 4 in Book I for the scoop on fertilizer.) Depending on plant spacing, side-dress either in a narrow furrow down a row or around each individual plant (refer to Figure 2-1). In either case, spread granular fertilizer at least several inches away from the plant stem. Rake the fertilizer lightly into the soil and then water. Adding liquid fertilizers to your watering can and pouring the fertilizer around the bases of the plants is an easy way to side-dress.

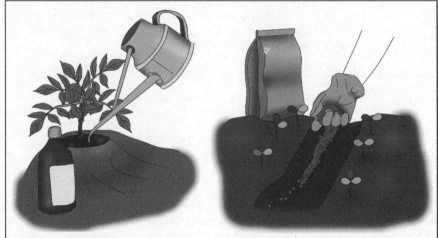

Figure 2-1: Ways to side-dress vegetable plants.

Too much fertilizer can be more harmful than too little. Excess fertilizer accumulates in the soil in the form of salts and damages plant roots. Be sure that growing conditions enable plants to use the fertilizer that you apply. For example, don't add fertilizer during a dry spell if you can't irrigate your garden because without adequate soil moisture, roots can't take up nutrients. And if cool weather causes your plants to grow slowly, go easy on the fertilizer until the temperature warms up.

The kind of plants that you grow makes a difference in how much you side-dress. Plants that take a long time to mature (such as tomatoes and egg-plants) and heavy feeders (such as corn) generally benefit more from side-dressing than quick-maturing crops, such as lettuce or legumes, that fix their own nitrogen. See Table 2-2 for some general side-dressing guidelines.

WARNING!

Using wood ashes to provide nutrients

Wood ashes are a source of potash and phosphate, although the exact amounts of these nutrients depend on the type of wood burned (hardwoods generally contain more nutrients than softwoods), the degree of combustion, and where the wood was stored (for example, dry storage prevents nutrient leaching). A general analysis is usually in the range of 0 percent nitrogen, 1 to 2 percent phosphate, and 4 to 10 percent potash. But the major benefit of wood ashes is as a liming agent to raise the pH of the soil. Naturally, if you live in an area where soils are alkaline, don't use wood ashes as a soil amendment; they raise the pH even higher.

Apply wood ashes to your soil in moderation (no more than 10 to 20 pounds per 1,000 square feet of garden) because they may contain small amounts of heavy metals, such as cadmium and copper. These metals build up in plants if you add too much wood ash to the soil *and can kill the plants or harm you if you eat several those plants.*

Table 2-2	Deciding When to Side-Dress Your Vegetables
Vegetable	*When to Side-Dress*
Beans, green	Not necessary.
Beet greens	Two weeks after leaves appear.
Beets	When tops are 4 to 5 inches (10 to 13 cm) high. Go light on nitrogen, which encourages leaf growth.
Broccoli	Three weeks after transplant. Go light on nitrogen.
Brussels sprouts	Three weeks after transplant; again when sprouts begin to appear.
Cabbage	Four to six weeks after planting.
Carrots	Three weeks after plants are well established and no longer seedlings.
Cauliflower	Four to six weeks after planting.
Celery	Three weeks after setting out; again six weeks later.
Corn, sweet	Three weeks after planting; again when plants are 8 to 10 inches (20 to 25 cm) high; again when tassels appear.

Book VII

Vegetables and Herbs

(continued)

Table 2-2 *(continued)*

Vegetable	When to Side-Dress
Cucumbers	When they first begin to *run* (form vines and sprawl); again when blossoms set.
Eggplant	Three weeks after planting.
Kale	When plants are 6 to 8 inches (15 to 20 cm) tall.
Lettuce, head	Three weeks after transplant; again when heads form.
Melons	When they begin to run; again a week after blossoms set; again three weeks later.
Onions	Three weeks after planting; again when tops are 6 to 8 inches (15 to 20 cm) tall; again when bulbs start to swell.
Peas, English	No need to side-dress.
Peppers, sweet	Three weeks after transplant; again after first fruit set.
Potatoes	When plants bloom.
Pumpkin	When plants start to run; again at blossom set.
Radishes	No need to side-dress.
Spinach	When plants are about 3 to 4 inches (8 to 10 cm) tall
Squash, summer	When plants are about 6 inches (15 cm) tall; again when they bloom.
Squash, winter	When plants start to run; again at blossom set.
Tomatoes	Two to three weeks after transplant; again before first picking; again two weeks after first picking. Go light on nitrogen.

Stake

Some vegetables, such as peas and beans, have climbing habits that require some type of support to grow on. Other vegetables — including tomatoes, cucumbers, and even melons — have sprawling habits that benefit from some type of staking or support. Staking plants, tying them to a trellis, or growing them inside wire cylinders keeps their fruits off the ground where they may be attacked by bugs or become sunburned (fruit skins get burned due to sudden exposure to strong sun, and these fruits eventually rot).

Supported plants are also easier to harvest and require less space to grow (they go *up* instead of *out*). Following are some suggestions for supporting different types of vegetables:

- **Cucumbers and melons:** Plant bush varieties inside small (2- to 3-foot or 0.6- to 1-m high) wire cylinders similar to those used for tomatoes. For more vigorous varieties, use a more sturdy version of the A-frame trellis that's used for peas and beans. Yes, you can grow melons on a trellis. Choose small-fruited varieties of watermelon or any variety of cantaloupe, and plant your seeds at the base of the trellis. Tie the vines to the trellis as they grow. After a fruit forms, slip the leg of an old nylon stocking over the fruit, tying the bottom of the stocking in a knot. Then, tie the other end of the stocking to the wire trellis so that the fruit is supported. As the melon grows, the stocking expands and supports the fruit, which may break off otherwise (see Figure 2-2).

- **Peas and beans:** These twining or clinging plants grow best when they're supported by some type of string trellis. An A-frame trellis allows you to grow plants on both sides, but single poles are fine, too.

- **Tomatoes:** You can support tomato plants by tying them to stakes, growing them inside wire cages, or constructing string or wire trellises. The type of support you choose depends on the tomato varieties that you grow. Smaller *determinate* varieties grow well in small cylinders or cages. Larger *indeterminate* varieties need supports that are a little sturdier and more firmly anchored. (See Chapter 3 in Book VII for info on tomato varieties.)

Book VII

Vegetables and Herbs

Figure 2-2: Support your trellised melons with a sling as soon as the fruits form.

Weed

A *weed* is any plant that's growing where you don't want it to. Weeds compete with vegetables for light, water, and nutrients. A large number of weeds creates weaker plants and a less substantial harvest. Chapter 7 in Book I tells you how to keep your garden weed-free.

Catching a Bug

Considering how tasty home-grown vegetables are, you shouldn't be too surprised to find that other creatures want to share in your harvest. The following sections help you identify insects, animals (sorry, we can't do much about your neighbors), and diseases to which your vegetable garden is particularly vulnerable. If you want more detailed information, turn to Chapter 7 in Book I.

In order to fight properly, you need to know your enemy, and insect pests command the largest army of invaders. The following list includes the most common insect pests that are likely to infest your vegetables:

- **Aphids:** Tiny, pear-shaped pests infest many vegetables, including cabbage, cucumbers, and broccoli.

- **Caterpillars and worms:** Moth and butterfly larvae, including tomato hornworms and cabbage loopers, are avid eaters and can cause substantial damage to a variety of plants.

- **Corn earworms (or fruitworms):** Found throughout the United States, these 1½-inch-long (4-cm) caterpillars attack a variety of plants, including tomatoes, beans, peas, peppers, potatoes, and squash. In spring, night-flying moths lay yellow eggs on the undersides of leaves. The resulting first-generation caterpillars feed on the leaves. You find the eggs of later generations on corn silks; the emerging caterpillars feed on the silks and the kernels at the tips of the corn ears, just inside the husks, as shown in Figure 2-3.

- **Cutworms:** Half-inch-long, grayish caterpillars eat the stems of young seedlings, causing them to fall over like small timbers.

- **Flea beetles:** Tiny 1/16-inch beetles feed on vegetable leaves, riddling them with small shot holes. Various species feed on just about any plant in a garden, including eggplant, tomatoes, broccoli, cabbage, corn, potatoes, spinach, peppers, and sweet potatoes. Adult beetles can spread diseases — wilt in sweet corn, for example — and larvae feed on roots. Adults overwinter in the soil and on garden debris, emerging in early spring, and they can destroy young plants quickly.

- **Japanese beetles:** These ½-inch-long (1-cm) beetles feed on the foliage of many vegetables, including corn, beans, and tomatoes.

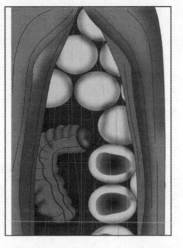

Figure 2-3: Corn infested with earworms is still fine to eat. Just break off the tip of the ear of corn and munch away.

✔ **Nematodes:** These microscopic wormlike pests infect soil, especially in warm climates. They feed on the roots of plants and attack many vegetables, including carrots, tomatoes, and potatoes.

✔ **Snails and slugs:** These soft-bodied mollusks feed on tender leaves and flowers during the cool of the night or during rainy weather.

✔ **Spider mites:** Barely visible arachnids often infest tomatoes and beans.

✔ **Thrips:** These almost-invisible troublemakers commonly feed on beans, cabbage, onions, and eggplants, often passing on diseases as they feed.

✔ **Whiteflies:** Looking like small white gnats, they congregate on the undersides of leaves, especially on tomatoes and beans.

Not all bugs are bad. Beneficial insects are the police of the garden, keeping the bad guys under control. We discuss the beneficials at length in Chapter 7 of Book I.

If you need to take further action, start with physical barriers that keep the bugs away from your plants. The next step is using pesticides that are effective against a certain pest, that are pretty safe to use, and that have a mild impact on the rest of your garden's life forms. For more on pesticides, refer to Chapter 7 in Book I.

The following list identifies methods for keeping common two- and four-footed pests out of your vegetable garden:

✔ **Bird tunnels or floating row covers:** As you may expect, these keep birds from eating seeds or pulling up newly sprouted plants.

✔ **Fences:** Fences deter cats, dogs, deer, neighbors, mice, rabbits, raccoons, and woodchucks. Lay chicken wire or hardware cloth over your seedbed

Book VII

Vegetables and Herbs

until plants sprout to encourage cats to dig elsewhere during the early part of the growing season. Use a slanted fence to keep deer out of your garden. Their instinct is to try to crawl under a fence before jumping it, and they're less likely to jump a wide fence. Keep raccoons out with a fence that's at least 4 feet high (1.2 m) (1 foot (30 cm) for mice, 2 feet (0.6 cm) for rabbits, and 3 feet (1 m) for woodchucks) with another 12 inches (30 cm) underground. Leave the top 18 inches (46 cm) of the fence unattached to support posts. As the woodchuck or raccoon attempts to climb over the fence, the fence will bend back down under the animal's weight.

✔ **Repellents:** The most effective way to control moles in your garden is to repel them by spraying a mole repellent that contains castor oil. Pepper spray may deter cats, dogs, and rabbits.

✔ **Traps:** Trapping is the most practical solution to rid your garden of gophers, and may be necessary to control moles.

Letting your family dog or cat prowl your grounds to ward off wild animals may sound like a good idea, but in reality, keeping your pets indoors or restrained is the best idea — especially when large animals are around. Rabies is a problem with many wild animals, such as raccoons and woodchucks, which are ferocious fighters.

Companion seeking bug for repulsive relationship

A *companion plant* provides some sort of benefit to other plants growing nearby. Some gardeners swear that certain companion plants, including many herbs, actually repel pests, although no hard evidence supports the theory. It is true that a variety of plants, herbs, and flowers will provide a diverse ecosystem so that predatory insects are more likely to hang around and take care of the bad guys. Following is a list of pests and the plants that repel them.

✔ **Aphids:** Catnip, mustard greens, and tansy

✔ **Colorado potato beetles:** Corn spurry, *Spergula arvensis,* marigolds, nasturtiums, and tansy

✔ **Gophers:** Gopher spurge, *Euphorbia lathyris*

✔ **Mexican bean beetles:** Marigolds

✔ **Nematodes:** Garlic (also good for other soil insects), marigolds (root nematode), and ryegrass (root-knot nematodes)

✔ **Moths:** Southernwood

✔ **Flea beetles:** Catnip, southernwood, and wormwood

✔ **Squash bugs:** Catnip and tansy

✔ **Cabbage root flies:** White clover

✔ **Cabbage worm:** Anise, when planted among members of the cabbage family

✔ **Cucumber beetles:** Catnip and radishes (striped-cucumber beetle)

You can interplant smaller companion plants, such as marigolds, with vegetables. Plant taller or more vigorous plants, such as ryegrass or wormwood, nearby, but not among the vegetables.

Practicing Preventative Medicine

After you see symptoms of disease, stopping the diseases from spreading is often difficult. However, you can prevent or at least reduce most vegetable diseases by using good growing practices or by planting resistant varieties.

Vegetables are prone to damping off, powdery mildew, root rot, and viruses, all of which we discuss in Chapter 7 of Book I. Southern blight, a rather nasty and hard-to-control disease that commonly affects corn in the southeastern United States, causes plants to rot at the base of their stems, wilt, turn yellow, and die. Your best bet is to rotate your crops each year, get rid of all infected plant material, and turn your soil in the fall.

Reaping Your Rewards

To get all the best flavor and highest nutritional value from your vegetables, you need to pick them at just the right time. Some vegetables taste terrible if you pick them too early; others are tough and stringy if you pick them too late. Properly stored, most vegetables will last a while without rotting or losing too much flavor. In fact, you can store some vegetables, like potatoes and winter squash, for months.

Book VII

Vegetables and Herbs

You harvest most vegetables when they're young and tender, which often means harvesting plants, roots, or fruits before they reach full size. A 15-inch (38-cm) zucchini is impressive, but it tastes better at 6 to 8 inches (15 to 20 cm). Carrots and beets get *woody* (tough textured) and bland the longer that they stay in the ground. You harvest other plants to keep them productive. If you keep harvesting vegetables like snap beans, summer squash, lima beans, snow and snap peas, broccoli, okra, spinach, and lettuce, they'll continue to produce pods, shoots, or leaves.

A good rule for many of your early crops is to start harvesting when you have enough of a vegetable for a one-meal serving. Spinach, Swiss chard, scallions, radishes, lettuce, and members of the cabbage family certainly fit the bill here. They don't grow as well in warm weather, so pick some of these crops in the spring when temperatures are cooler. After you start harvesting, visit your garden and pick something daily. Take along a good sharp knife and paper bags, buckets, or baskets. A wire or wood bucket works well because you can easily wash vegetables in it. Table 2-3 provides information on when to harvest.

Table 2-3	Harvesting Fresh Vegetables
Vegetable	*When to Harvest*
Asparagus	When spears are 6 to 9 inches (15 to 23 cm) long
Beans, snap	Start about two to three weeks after bloom, before seeds mature
Beets	When 1 to 3 inches (2 to 8 cm) wide
Broccoli	When flower heads are tight and green
Brussels sprouts	When sprouts reach 1 inch (2 cm) wide
Cabbage	When heads are compact and firm
Carrots	When tops are 1 inch (2 cm) wide
Cauliflower	While heads are still white but not ricey (the florets split apart)
Corn	When silks are dry and brown; kernels should be milky when cut with a thumbnail
Cucumbers	For slicing when 6 inches (15 cm) long; picklers at least 2 inches (5 cm) long
Eggplant	Before color dulls
Kohlrabi	When 2 to 3 inches (5 to 8 cm) wide
Lettuce and other greens	While leaves are tender
Muskmelons	When fruit slips off vine easily, while netting (raised area on skin) is even, fruit firm
Onions	When necks are tight, scales dry
Parsnips	When roots reach desired size, possibly after light frost
Peanuts	When leaves turn yellow
Peas	While pods are still tender
Peppers	When fruits reach desired size and color
Potatoes	When vines die back
Pumpkins	When shells harden, before frost
Radishes	When roots are up to 1¼ inches (3 cm) wide
Rutabagas	When roots reach desired size

Vegetable	When to Harvest
Spinach	When leaves are still tender
Squash, summer	When 6 to 8 inches (15 to 20 cm) long
Squash, winter	When shells harden, before frost
Sweet potatoes	When they reach adequate size
Tomatoes	When uniformly colored
Turnips	When 2 to 3 inches (5 to 8 cm) wide
Watermelons	When undersides turn yellow and produce dull sound when thumped

Gardening like a farmer

Over the years, farmers have tried almost anything to get a better or bigger harvest. The following techniques may work in your garden, too:

✔ **Cover crops and green manures:** A *cover crop* is any plant grown to prevent erosion, improve soil structure, and maintain soil fertility. *Green manures,* the most useful for gardeners, are cover crops that primarily add nutrients to the soil. You till them into the soil when they're still green. Cover crops can be annual or perennial; home gardeners do best sowing annual cover crops. Consider using annual ryegrass, berseem clover, buckwheat, fava beans, field peas, hairy vetch, or winter rye as a cover crop. Plant cover crops in late summer to early fall after your vegetables are done — otherwise, you have to sacrifice some garden space. In spring, work the crops into the ground just before they start to bloom, and then wait about two weeks before planting vegetables.

✔ **Intercropping:** A space-saving technique in which you grow fast-maturing crops among slower-growing, larger vegetables, *intercropping* makes one bed as productive as two. The best crops for intercropping include beets, carrots, lettuce, onions, radishes, spinach, and turnips. For instance, plant lettuce, carrots, or radishes among young tomatoes; plant turnips and other root crops among your cabbage; plant spinach or lettuce under your bean trellis; and plant green onions between rows of corn.

✔ **Crop rotation:** Growing the same vegetables in the same spot year after year depletes nutrients and attracts insects and disease that favor particular plants. Avoid these problems by planting entire vegetable families (tomatoes, peppers, eggplant, and potatoes, for example) in different beds, as far away as possible from where they were planted before. Keep a journal and make note of what was planted where, and then keep things out of the same beds for three years.

Book VII

Vegetables and Herbs

The harvesting information in Table 2-3 is based on picking mature vegetables. You can pick many vegetables — beets, broccoli, carrots, cauliflower, cucumbers, lettuce and other greens, onions, peas, potatoes, radishes, snap beans, summer squash, Swiss chard, and turnips — smaller and still have excellent flavor. Pick baby vegetables whenever they reach the size that you want.

Try to avoid harvesting when plants, especially beans, are wet. Many fungal diseases spread in moist conditions, and if you brush your tools or pant legs against diseased plants, you can transfer disease organisms to other plants down the row. Also avoid harvesting in the heat of the day if you can. For the freshest produce, harvest early in the day when vegetables' moisture levels are highest and the vegetables are at peak flavor. Then refrigerate the produce and prepare it later in the day.

In the fall, wait as long as you can to dig up root crops if you intend to store them in a root cellar or cold storage room. Root crops can withstand frosts, but harvest them before the ground freezes. They'll come out of the ground easiest if the soil is slightly moist. Don't wash crops that are going to the root cellar; instead, just gently brush away soil crumbs. Use any blemished or cut vegetables within a few days.

If you live in an area where the ground freezes in the winter, you can actually store some root crops — including carrots, leeks, rutabagas, and turnips — in the ground and harvest all winter long. After a good, hard frost, but before the ground freezes, cover your vegetable bed with a foot or more of dry hay. Cover the hay with heavy plastic (4 to 6 mil) and secure the edges with rocks, bricks, or heavy boards. The plastic keeps rain and snow from trickling down through the hay and rotting your vegetables yet keeps the soil from freezing solid. You can harvest periodically through winter, being careful to re-cover the opening after each harvest.

Store only the highest quality vegetables for long periods of time. Any vegetables that are damaged or scarred are likely to rot and spoil everything nearby. Make sure that your vegetables are well ventilated; you can store onions, potatoes, and other root crops in mesh bags. Shoot for a humidity level that is as high as you can get. To increase humidity, spread moist wood shavings or sawdust on the floor but keep the vegetables elevated on wooden boxes.

Chapter 3

Growing, Growing, Grown!

● ●

After you commit some soil and some energy to creating a vegetable garden, you need to decide which vegetables to plant. This chapter helps you decide what to grow (or it may convince you to get some more soil and some more energy for an even bigger garden!).

Asparagus

Asparagus has male and female plants. Female plants produce spears that eventually grow to produce flowers and seeds that not only take extra energy to produce, reducing spear production, but also create a jungle of little asparagus plants. Unfortunately, these young seedlings aren't productive and are mostly just weeds. Male plants don't have flowers and seeds, and are therefore more productive than the female plants.

Unlike most of the vegetables mentioned in this book, asparagus is a perennial plant (see Book IV for the lowdown on perennials). The *crown* (the short stem near the roots) actually expands with age, producing more spears each year. After the spring harvest, let the spears grow into towering ferns that feed the roots for next year's crop. Because asparagus is a perennial, you start harvesting in spring when the spears emerge and stop harvesting six to eight weeks later:

- **Year one:** Let all the spears grow into ferns.
- **Year two:** Harvest only those spears whose diameters are larger than a pencil; your harvest window is about three to four weeks in the spring. Snap off spears by hand at the soil line when they're 6 to 8 inches (15 to 20 cm) tall.
- **Year three:** Begin harvesting only the pencil-diameter-sized spears for six to eight weeks each spring. Stop after that and let the spears grow into ferns to replenish the crown and roots.

You can cut down the ferns after a hard frost in fall or winter. Weeds are the number one downfall of most asparagus beds, so keep the beds well weeded.

Ack! My bean is bald!

If your bean seedlings emerge from the soil without any leaves, they may have a condition called *bald heading*. Insects can cause this condition, but more likely, you've planted the seeds too deep in the ground or in gravel soil, which causes the leaves to rip off as they try to break through the soil. To prevent this condition, prepare the seed bed by removing rocks, sticks, and clods of soil before planting and don't plant too deep. If you see leafless beans, pull them out and replant. Leafless beans don't produce any crops.

Beans

For ensured success in your first garden, plant some bean seeds. They're large and easy to plant, they grow easily, and they don't require lots of extra fertilizer or care. Within 60 days, you're bound to have some beans to eat. The following list looks at bush and pole beans and suggests some varieties for you to try in your garden. (Bush and pole beans actually are the same type of bean, just with different growth habits.)

✔ **Bush beans:** These beans grow on a bush and tend to produce the earliest crops, maturing all at once (within a week or so). The plants generally are less than 2 feet (61 cm) tall and produce handfuls of beans at harvest. Depending on the variety, the beans are green, yellow, or purple. Most *pods* (the part of the bean that you eat) are 6 to 8 inches (15 to 20 cm) at maturity, but you can harvest beans that are flavorful sooner. Here are a few of the most reliable varieties:

  • **'Provider':** Green pods mature 50 days from seeding. Great disease resistance and can grow in adverse weather conditions.

  • **'Roc D'or Wax':** Long, slender, round, bright yellow pods are produced on sturdy plants in 53 days.

  • **'Sequoia Purple Pod':** Attractive purple-podded bean also has purple-colored stems, leaves, and flowers. Matures in 53 days, and it turns dark green when cooked.

✔ **Pole beans:** Pole beans need staking and usually grow on poles. They tend to mature their crops later than bush beans, but pole beans continue to produce all season (about a handful of beans per day) until frost or disease stops them. Here are two you may like to try:

  • **'Goldmarie':** Early yielding, wax pole bean variety produces 8-inch (20-cm) pods 54 days from seeding.

- **'Purple Pod':** Purple-colored variety grows on a 6-foot-tall (2 m) plant and matures 65 days from seeding. Color changes from purple to dark green when cooked.

✔ **Dried and shell beans:** Dried beans are actually varieties of bush or pole beans. You can eat them fresh, like bush or pole beans, but they're better if you allow them to dry and then just eat the bean seeds. Plant them, care for them, and harvest them when the pods are dried and the plants are almost dead. The seeds can range from white to red and can be striped and spotted. Consider the following for your garden:

  - **'Black Turtle':** Small black bean matures 85 days from seeding. Grows best in warmer climates. Each pod produces 7 to 8 beans.

  - **'French Horticultural':** An old-time favorite, tan-colored bean matures in 90 days.

  - **'Navy':** Small, semivining plant produces white, oval beans 85 days from seeding.

  - **'Vermont Cranberry':** Widely adapted, red, brown-speckled, New England classic matures 90 days from seeding.

Book VII

Vegetables and Herbs

Bean there, pick that

Beans harvested at different stages are called different names. A bean harvested when it's young, before seeds have formed, is called a *snap* bean. If the bean matures further and you harvest it when it's green in color and the bean seeds are fully formed, it's called a *shell* bean. Finally, if the pod dries on the plant and then you harvest it, it's called a *dried* bean. You can harvest some bean varieties at all stages. However, most bean varieties are best harvested at one particular stage — snap, shell, or dried — depending on their breeding.

Here's how to tell when the beans you've planted are ready for harvest:

✔ **Harvest snap beans when the pods are firm and crisp and the seeds inside the pods are undeveloped (the pod is smooth, not bumpy).** Carefully hold the bean stem with one hand to avoid breaking the plants and pull the individual beans off with your other hand. The more you pick, the more you'll get because the plant wants to produce mature seeds and you keep frustrating it by picking the pods.

✔ **Harvest shell beans when the pods are full, green, and firm but haven't dried out yet.** You can store the beans in a refrigerator for a few days before cooking them.

✔ **Harvest dried beans when the pods are dry on the plant and naturally beginning to split.** Break the bean seeds out of the pods by rubbing the pods in your hands. Store the beans in glass jars in a cool place; you can either eat them or save them to plant next year.

Beets

Beets *(Beta vulgaris)* are best known for their deep-red-colored roots and sweet flavor. However, you can use their very tasty leaves (called *greens*) as a Swiss chard or spinach substitute. Try slicing beet roots or greens in salads or cooking the roots in classic beet dishes such as borscht (beet soup). Like most root crops, beets' sweetness improves as the temperatures cool, so leave some in the garden for a late-season harvest. Beets tend to mature about 50 to 65 days from seeding. Some good varieties to try are 'Red Ace', 'Detroit Dark Red', and 'Lutz Green Leaf'. For a long, thin, red root, try 'Cylindra'. These varieties are consistent producers and widely adapted to various growing conditions. If you're interested in beets of different colors, try growing white-fleshed 'Albina Verduna', which is very sweet, and yellow-fleshed 'Golden' or red-and-white-striped 'Chioggia', which are sweet, too, but are mostly grown for their looks.

Broccoli

Broccoli is one of the easiest cole crops to grow. Modern broccoli varieties have been bred to form one large main head. This head is simply a tight cluster of flower buds. After the main head is cut off, multiple side branches and mini heads form along the plant. In most areas, the side branches and mini heads continue to form until the plant is killed by frost, insects, or disease, so from one plant, you can harvest right through summer, fall, and winter (if your climate is warm enough).

Choosing the right broccoli variety for your garden depends on a number of factors, including where you live and what you plan to do with the crop. Broccoli, like all cole crops, likes cool weather. Warm weather makes the heads flower too quickly, resulting in a bitter flavor. Gardeners in warm climates should choose varieties that withstand heat or mature early, before the heat of summer. If you plan to stock up for the winter by freezing broccoli heads, choose a variety with large heads that mature mostly at the same time. If you want a long, steady production of small but tender side shoots, choose an old-fashioned variety with good side-shoot production.

Here's a list of some of the best broccoli varieties to grow. The days to maturity number listed for each variety refers to the number of days from transplanting a seedling into the garden until the harvest of the main head. If you sow the seeds directly into the garden, add another 20 days to estimate the maturity date. Of course, the actual number of days will vary depending on weather and soil conditions. All plants listed reach about 1 to 2 feet (30 to 61 cm) tall:

- ✔ **'DeCicco':** Heirloom variety produces a 3-inch-diameter (8 cm) main head, multiple side shoots, and tender leaves and stems. Matures in 48 days.

- ✔ **'Early Dividend':** Hybrid that combines early maturity (43 days) with a large, 8-inch-diameter (20 cm) main head and lots of side shoots.

- ✔ **'Green Comet':** Early-maturing (58 days) hybrid produces a 6-inch-diameter (15 cm) head and is very tolerant of diseases and weather stress.

- ✔ **'Packman':** Hybrid that produces a 9-inch-diameter (23 cm) main head in 53 days. Excellent side-shoot production.

Harvest broccoli by cutting the main head when the flower buds are still tightly clustered together without any signs of blossoming — even if the head is smaller than you'd like it to be. After the yellow flowers open, the flavor turns bitter. If you leave a few inches of the main stem on the plant, many broccoli varieties respond by growing side branches that produce little heads.

Brussels Sprouts

Rows of Brussels sprouts stems standing tall in the garden loaded with sprouts are a sure sign of fall. Although the plants take a whole season for the sprouts to mature, they're relatively maintenance-free, and the sprouts turn a sweet, nutty flavor after they're touched by cold weather. The key to growing Brussels sprouts is having a long growing season and a cool fall to induce the best flavor. The flavor actually benefits from a light frost. The following varieties are widely adaptable and worth a try in any garden. The days to maturity are from setting out seedlings to first harvest:

- ✔ **'Jade Cross E':** Hybrid, 2½-foot-tall (76 cm) plants produce good-sized sprouts all the way up their stalks. Matures in 90 days.

- ✔ **'Oliver':** Early-maturing (90 days) hybrid is well adapted to many climates.

- ✔ **'Red Rubine':** Heirloom variety produces tasty and attractive red sprouts on a hardy, purplish-red-colored plant. (The red color remains even after cooking.) Matures in 95 days.

Brussels sprouts taste best after cool weather helps turn some of their carbohydrates into sugars. Following a frost, pick off the marble-sized sprouts from the bottom of the plant first, moving up the stalk. The more sprouts you pick from below, the larger the sprouts above will get. Pull off the lower leaves for easier picking. Brussels sprouts tolerate temperatures into the 20°Fs (around

–6°C), so you can harvest right into New Year's in some areas. To make the sprouts mature faster, snip off the top few inches of the plant after sprouts have formed on the bottom 12 inches (30 cm) of the stalk.

Cabbage

Cabbage-growing isn't as popular as it once was, but the sweet, tender flavor of freshly harvested cabbage makes it worthy of a spot in your garden. With so many varieties to choose from, you can have fresh and delicious cole slaw, sauerkraut, and boiled cabbage almost all season long. Cabbage requires the same conditions as other cole crops — cool weather, fertile soil, and proper watering — but the variety that you select is a bit more important to ensure a continuous harvest. You can easily get lost in the dizzying array of cabbage varieties. Growing two or three different varieties that mature at different times allows you to spread out the harvest over the growing season.

The following list introduces you to the cabbage universe. Cabbage plants can spread to 3 feet (1 m) in diameter, and all have green leaves and white centers unless otherwise noted. The late-maturing and fall-planted varieties are best for storage. The days to maturity for each variety are from setting out seedlings in the garden to first harvest. Add 20 days to the maturity date if you directly seed in the garden:

- ✔ **'Danish Ballhead':** Round heads (8-inch-diameter/20 cm) produce late in the season and are great for winter storage. Matures in 100 days. (Good variety for sauerkraut.)

- ✔ **'Ruby Perfection':** Midseason hybrid red variety produces attractive 5- to 6-inch-diameter (13- to 15-cm) reddish-purple heads. Matures in 80 days.

- ✔ **'Savoy Ace':** Early hybrid produces 6- to 8-inch-diameter (15- to 20-cm) heads that grow well in summer's heat. Matures in 76 days.

- ✔ **'Savoy Chieftain':** Midseason, savoy-leafed variety produces 6- to 8-inch-diameter (15- to 20- cm) heads and matures in 85 days. Best grown as a fall crop.

Harvest cabbage heads when they're firm when squeezed. Periodically squeeze your cabbages through the growing season, so you can tell when they're firm. To harvest, cut the head from the base of the plant with a sharp knife. When harvesting early maturing varieties in summer, don't dig up the plants. Cabbages have the ability to grow smaller side heads on the plant after the main head is harvested; harvest these side heads the same way.

GARDEN JARGON

My cabbage has a splitting headache

Sometimes, cabbage heads split before you can harvest them. *Splitting* occurs when the plant takes up too much fertilizer or water, especially around harvest time. This "overdose" causes the inner leaves to grow faster than the outer leaves, splitting the heads. Harvest splitting heads as soon as possible. To stop splitting after it starts, grab the head and give it a one-half turn to break some of the roots. You can also root prune the plant by digging in a circle about 1 foot (30 cm) from the base of the cabbage. Both of these methods slow the uptake of water and fertilizer to preserve the head.

Carrots

Carrot *(Daucus carota)* varieties are categorized by their shape. A few varieties are supercharged with vitamins, and some nonorange-colored varieties and many hybrids have added vigor and disease resistance. If you're trying to decide which carrot variety to grow, consider your type of soil as well as the use you plan for the carrots. Table 3-1 shows the common types of carrots and their characteristics. All the types listed, except Baby carrots and Imperators, range in size from 6 to 8 inches (15 to 20 cm). Baby carrots may be varieties that are naturally short or larger varieties harvested at an immature stage. All types are easy to grow and worth trying in your garden.

Book VII

Vegetables and Herbs

Table 3-1	Carrot Types	
Type	*Size and Uses*	*Best Soil Type*
Baby	Short (3 to 4 inches / 8 to 10 cm); early maturing; grows well in containers	Grows best in heavy, clay soil
Chantenay	Wide *shoulders* (the top of the carrot root), tapered to a point	Grows well in heavy soil
Danvers	Tapered to a point; thinner than Chantenay; good for storing	Grows best in sandy, loose soil
Imperator	Similar to Danvers, just longer (10 to 12 inches / 25 to 30 cm)	Grows best in sandy soil
Nantes	Cylindrical shape with blunt end; good for juicing	Grows well in sandy soil

Knowing a carrot's variety can help you decide which carrot to grow. The carrot varieties in the following list are flavorful, disease resistant, and easy to grow. All are good for baking. The days to maturity are from seeding in the ground until first harvest, although early season carrot varieties are flavorful even if you harvest them before they fully mature.

- ✔ **'Baby Spike':** Maturing in 50 days, this 3- to 4-inch (8- to 10-cm) Baby carrot *holds its shape* (stays sweet and small even if you forget to harvest it on time) well past maturity.

- ✔ **'Bolero':** Nantes-type carrot has extra disease resistance and stores well. Matures in 72 days.

- ✔ **'Healthmaster':** Danvers-type variety grows up to 10 inches (25 cm) long, matures in 110 days, and contains 30 percent more vitamin A than other carrot varieties.

- ✔ **'Imperator':** Imperator-type variety is long and narrow and has a deep orange color. Matures in 70 days.

- ✔ **'Short 'n Sweet':** Four-inch (10 cm) Chantenay-type carrot grows well in heavy clay soil. Matures in 68 days.

Cauliflower

Cauliflower requires similar growing conditions to broccoli's, but cauliflower plants produce only one head and no side shoots, and they have a reputation for being a bit tougher to grow. Cauliflower plants are finicky about weather conditions. Temperatures in the 70°F (20°C) range are ideal, so avoid growing cauliflower when it will mature in the heat of summer. Many gardeners prefer to grow cauliflower as a fall crop started in summer to mature in the cooler, autumn weather. With the right varieties, proper soil conditions, appropriate watering, and well-timed planting, cauliflower can be a joy to grow in the vegetable garden.

All the varieties in the following list produce 6- to 7-inch-diameter (15- to 18-cm) heads. The days to maturity number for each variety is from setting out seedlings in the garden until first harvest. Add 20 days to the maturity date for direct seeding in the garden:

- ✔ **'Fremont':** *Self-blanching* (the leaves naturally grow to cover the head and exclude light) hybrid variety known for dependable midseason production, even under adverse weather conditions. Matures in 70 days.

- ✔ **'Incline':** Hybrid Japanese variety produces dense, pure white heads late in the season. Self-blanching, vigorous grower. Matures in 76 days.

- ✔ **'Snow Crown':** Standard white hybrid variety is easy to grow, early, widely adaptable, and dependable. Matures in 60 days.

✔ **'Violet Queen':** Purple-colored heads on this easy-to-grow plant don't need blanching. The color fades when cooked. Matures in 64 days.

When heads are anywhere between 6 and 12 inches (15 to 30 cm) in diameter and blanched white (for white varieties), pull up the whole plant and cut off the head. Cauliflower, unlike cabbage and broccoli, won't form side heads after the main head is cut.

Celery

Home gardeners rarely grow celery *(Apium graveolens)* because the young plants can die easily, or the stems can get stringy. However, growing celery can be very rewarding. If you're growing celery for leaves and stalks, you usually won't get the seeds. Celery needs a long (120+ days) growing season. It grows best in areas with moderate summers or winters — it doesn't like extremes of heat or cold. For some widely adapted varieties of celery, try 'Ventura', 'Utah 52-70 Improved', and 'Giant Pascal'. For a unique, semiself-blanching type, try 'Golden Self-Blanching' or 'Stokes Golden Plume'. These varieties produce golden-yellow colored stalks that are naturally semiblanched. The flavor is milder than unblanched varieties, but it isn't as mild as fully blanched varieties. Harvest your celery stalks, either by pulling up the entire plant or just selecting outer stalks.

White stalks of celery are blanched. Home-grown, unblanched celery has a stronger flavor and better nutritional value than store-bought types, but if you like the white stalks, you can certainly blanch your celery. To blanch, place an empty metal can or milk carton with the ends removed over the stalks ten days before harvesting. You don't need to cover the leaves.

Book VII

Vegetables and Herbs

Collards

Collards *(Brassica oleracea),* unlike cabbages, don't form heads and can withstand heat and still grow well. You can eat the whole plant at any stage, and the large, smooth oval leaves, in particular, taste great steamed or mixed in soups. Healthwise, they're one of the best greens you can eat; they're high in vitamin A, iron, and calcium. Some good varieties for production and vigor include 'Champion', 'Georgia', and 'Vates'. Collards like cool weather and mature quickly within 60 to 80 days after seeding. Sow seeds directly in the garden four to six weeks before the last frost date for a spring harvest, and again in mid- to late summer for a fall harvest. Thin the seedlings to 10 inches (25 cm) apart. Use these thinnings in soups and casseroles. Fertilize, water, and mulch collards as you would cabbage.

Corn, Sweet

By selecting the right varieties to grow, you can have sweet corn maturing all summer long. And you don't need a 10-acre field to grow it. Five to six short rows are all you need to get plenty of ears for your family. Sweet corn kernels are actually seeds. Most sweet corn varieties come with white, yellow, or bicolor (yellow and white mixed) kernels. Some heirloom varieties that are mostly used for corn flour and roasting feature red and blue kernels. The color of corn that you choose depends on what flavor you like and what varieties grow well where you live. Varieties mature in 65 to 100 days, so choose a sampling that will mature over time in your garden. Gardeners in cold climates should stick with quick-maturing varieties.

Following are some varieties you may want to try. This list is the very tip of the iceberg, so don't be afraid to try others that grow well in your area:

- Standard heirloom yellow varieties include 'Golden Bantam' and 'Country Gentleman'. Some uniquely colored heirloom varieties include 'Black Mexican' (blue).

- A few "standard sugary" hybrids include 'Early Sunglow' (yellow), 'Sugar and Gold' (bicolor), and 'Silver Queen' (white).

Cucumbers

Cucumber varieties usually are categorized two ways: as slicers and picklers. Slicers are long, smooth-skinned cucumbers that tend to be larger, a darker shade of green, and have thicker skin with fewer bumps (spines) than pickling varieties, which are short and prickly. You can use picklers the same way as slicers, but if you do want to make pickles, the pickling varieties have better textures for it. Regular production of cucumbers is about 12 pounds per 10-foot row (about 10 cucmbers per plant). Choose varieties based on disease-resistance, size, productivity, and adaptability.

Take a look at a few varieties worth trying in your garden. Most of these varieties vine 4 to 5 feet (10 to 13 cm) unless otherwise noted. The days to maturity are from seeding in the ground until first harvest:

- **'Aria':** Hybrid parthenocarpic variety has good disease resistance and thin skin. Matures in 52 days.

- **'Marketmore 86':** Widely adapted slicing variety has good disease resistance and produces lots of fruits. Matures in 68 days.

✔ **'Suyo Long':** Unusual Oriental-type slicing cucumber is also *burpless* (which means this type of cucumber doesn't cause burping in people, a common reaction after eating cucumbers) and produces 15-inch fruits. Matures in 61 days.

✔ **'Wisconsin SMR-18':** Highly productive and disease resistant pickling cucumber. Matures in 56 days.

Cucumbers are best when harvested small: slicers when they're 6-inches (15-cm) long and picklers when they're 4-inches (10-cm) long. If they grow too large and begin to turn yellow, the seeds inside the cucumber are maturing, and the plant will stop producing flowers and fruits. Pick off and throw away any large fruits that you missed so that you can keep the young ones coming.

Eggplant

Eggplants come in a range of shapes, colors, and sizes. We arrange the varieties in the following list by shape so that you can choose the variety that's right for your tastes. (The days to maturity in the following descriptions represent the time from transplant to harvest.)

✔ **Large and oval:** These are the dark purple, teardrop-shaped fruits that you see in grocery stores. The plants grow 3 to 4 feet (1 to 1.2 m) tall, each producing an average of 8 to 10 fruits. Here are a few of our favorites:

- **'Black Beauty':** Classic, large, purple-skinned eggplants mature in 75 days and grow best in areas with long, hot growing seasons.

- **'Purple Rain' hybrid:** Beautiful, white-striped, lavender-skinned eggplants are early and productive, maturing in 66 days.

- **'Rosa Bianca':** Italian heirloom features white fruits with lavender streaks across them. They mature in 75 days.

- **'Violette Di Firenze':** Violet-skinned fruits have an unusual oval shape, are ribbed like squash, and take 80 days to mature.

✔ **Cylindrical:** Traditionally called Asian eggplants, these cylindrical fruits are long and thin (2 inches (5 cm) wide and up to 10 inches (25 cm) long). The plants are smaller than the oval-shaped varieties, reaching only 2- to 3-feet tall, and produce about 15 fruits. Try the following:

- **'Asian Bride' hybrid:** White with lavender streaks, these 6-inch-long (15 cm) fruits have tender skin and take 70 days to mature.

- **'Neon' hybrid:** Stunning deep-pink-skinned fruits are 6 inches (15 cm) long and take 65 days to mature.

- **'Ping Tung Long':** Long, lavender-skinned fruits grow on plants with good heat and disease resistance that take 65 days to mature.

Book VII

Vegetables and Herbs

Eggplant ripe for the pickin'

You can pick eggplants at almost any stage. The key is not to let them become overmature, or the texture will become soft and mushy. To check eggplant maturity, watch the fruit's skin. A dull-colored skin means it's over-mature. Double-check by cutting into the fruit and looking at the seeds. Brown-colored seeds are another sign of overmaturity. A simple test for maturity is to push the eggplant's skin with your finger nail. If the skin bounces back, then the fruits are ready to harvest. If your nail indents the skin, then the fruits are overmature. If your fruits are really mature and rotting on the vine, just pick them and throw them out; they won't taste very good. Some eggplant varieties have sharp spines on their stems, so wear gloves when harvesting. To harvest, cut eggplants with a sharp knife just above the top of the green cap on the fruit. The fruits will continue to ripen after you harvest them, so store them in a cool place.

Lettuce

The four basic types of lettuce (which we discuss in the following list) offer a number of tasty varieties to delight the palate. The most common are green-colored leaf varieties, but you can grown many red- and burgundy-colored leaf varieties, too. Some varieties form solid heads, others don't. As you look at days to maturity, remember that you can eat lettuce much younger, depending on your needs and appetite:

- ✔ **Crisphead:** Most widely known as the "iceberg" lettuces. This type forms a solid head when mature, with white, crunchy, densely packed inner leaves. Crispheads tend to take at least 70 days to mature from seeding in the garden. Following are popular varieties:

  - **'Iceberg':** Compact heads have tightly-packed leaves and white hearts. Best grown in cool conditions (below 70°F/20°C) to form solid heads.

  - **'Sierra' (or Batavian):** French crisphead lettuce with wavy, bright green-and-red tinged leaves. Good, heat-tolerant variety.

  - **'Summertime':** Able to form solid heads in the heat of summer, 'Summertime' has green leaves and a crisp texture.

- ✔ **Loose heads (Bibb, Boston, or Butterhead):** This lettuce type features dark or medium green leaves or red leaves and smooth, thick, outer leaves folded around a loosely-formed, yellow-to-white head. The head isn't solid like a crisphead type, but loose heads are easier to grow, especially during the summer heat. This type matures starting at 60 days from seeding:

- **'Buttercrunch':** Bolt-resistant, loose head type, 'Buttercrunch' has thick, juicy leaves. Best grown as a summer crop.

- **'Brune d'Hiver':** Very hardy, with bronzed, light green leaves. Good as a fall or winter lettuce.

- **'Deer Tongue':** Heirloom, loose head type lettuce with tongue-shaped green leaves. Slow to bolt.

✔ **Loose leaf:** Loose leaf lettuce doesn't form a solid head and is best harvested by picking off the mature outer leaves, allowing new leaves to continue growing. This type is often cut and allowed to "come again" to provide multiple crops of greens from one head. You can begin harvesting this type about 45 days from seeding:

- **'Black Seeded Simpson':** Heirloom lettuce with crinkled, light green leaves.

- **'Oak Leaf':** Green-leafed, this loose-leaf type features unusual, pointed, oak-shaped leaves.

- **'Red Sails':** Award-winning, red, loose-leaf lettuce. Fast-growing, heat-tolerant, and very attractive.

✔ **Romaine (Cos):** Romaine lettuce grows tall, upright heads and long, thick green or red leaves with solid *midribs* (the middle vein of the leaf). This type tends to take at least 70 days to mature from seeding and can withstand summer heat:

- **'Parris Island Cos':** Green-leafed romaine lettuce has 10-inch-tall (25 cm), thick, green leaves.

- **'Rosalita':** Red- to purple-colored lettuce is well-adapted to various growing regions and has yellow, blanched interior leaves.

- **'Winter Density':** Green, 8-inch (20-cm) tall romaine lettuce plant is a cross between a loose head and a romaine-type lettuce. Heat- and cold-tolerant.

Lettuce commence harvesting greens

Harvesting greens couldn't be easier. After all, you eat the leaves. Except for the crisphead lettuces, harvest greens while they're young and tender to avoid another common complaint of lettuce growers: bitter-tasting lettuce. Bitter taste usually develops in older plants, so start picking when the leaves are 4 inches (10 cm) long. You can also harvest crisphead or "iceberg" lettuce young, before heads form. However, to get the solid, blanched heads seen in grocery stores, wait until full maturity when heads are firm when squeezed. Harvest the outer leaves first to allow the inner leaves to continue to develop. Also, wait until you're almost ready to prepare your meal to harvest. That way, the greens will be fresh and crisp in your salad bowl.

Melons

Technically, melons are vegetables. Compared to cucumbers, melons are easy. They all have separate male and female flowers on each plant *(monoecious),* and they all need about 6 to 8 feet (1.8 to 2.4 m) of space to vine. Many different types of melons with many unique flavors are available. You can harvest a number of melons on the unripe side and mature them off the vine. Most gardeners are familiar with the two most popular types of melons: muskmelons (also known as cantaloupes) and watermelons. But more and more exotic melon types continue to show up in produce markets and seed catalogs. Melons tend to weigh between 2 and 5 pounds, but watermelons can run from 8 pounds to between 20 and 30 pounds.

Like all cucumber-family crops, melons need warmth, water, space, and sun. For those reasons, they grow well in the Southeast and the Southwest United States. But with the right variety selection and some growing tricks, cool-climate gardeners can also enjoy these sweet, juicy fruits The days to maturity are from seeding in the garden until first harvest. Here are some popular melons:

- ✔ **Muskmelon:** The round, netted, tan-colored, orange-fleshed fruits that you see in grocery stores usually are sold as "cantaloupes." However, true cantaloupes are tropical fruits that have green flesh and hard skin and are rarely seen in this country. What people from the United States refer to as cantaloupes technically are muskmelons. Here a few of them:

  - • **'Alaska':** Early hybrid muskmelon variety grows well in areas with short growing seasons, producing 4-pound (1.8-kg) fruits in 70 days.

  - • **'Earliqueen':** Hybrid 3- to 4-pound (1.3- to 1.8-kg) muskmelon variety has thick, orange flesh and matures in 70 days.

  - • **'French Orange':** Hybrid 2- to 4-pound (0.9- to 1.8-kg) melon has aromatic, deep orange flesh, good disease resistance, and matures in 75 days.

  - • **'Passport':** Widely adapted, hybrid Mediterranean-type, 5- to 6-pound (2.2- to 2.7-kg) melon has light green flesh, good disease resistance, and matures in 73 days.

- ✔ **Watermelon:** Seedless watermelon varieties may germinate more slowly than other varieties, especially in cool (below 65°F/18°C) soils. Following are popular watermelon varieties:

  - • **'Crimson Sweet':** Oval-shaped variety produces sweet, red-fleshed, 25-pound fruits, (11-kg) has good disease resistance, and matures in 90 days.

  - • **'King of Hearts':** Hybrid, seedless, oval-shaped variety produces 15-pound, (16-kg) oval-shaped fruits that mature in 82 days.

Taking melons from garden to table

Deciding when to harvest muskmelons and watermelons can be tricky. It's frustrating to grow a great crop of melons and then pick them either too soon or too late. With muskmelons, after their skin color turns from green to tan and the netting (the ribbing on the skin that's slightly raised) becomes more pronounced, gently lift the melons up. If they're ripe, the fruits will slip, or easily detach, from the vine. If you're not sure, harvesting early rather than late is better because most melons continue to ripen off the vine.

Two signs that it may be time to harvest watermelons are when the skin color turns from shiny to dull and when the color of the spot where the watermelon rests on the ground turns from white to yellow. Look at the watermelon's tendrils, the little curlicues coming off the stems that attach to whatever weeds and plants are around. Harvest when the tendril closest to the ripening watermelon turns brown.

- • **'Sugar Baby':** Round, compact variety produces icebox-size (8- to 10-pound or 3.6- to 4.5-kg) fruits that mature in 85 days.

- • **'Yellow Doll':** Hybrid, oval-shaped, yellow-fleshed watermelon produces 4- to 8-pound fruits that mature in 70 days.

- ✔ **Specialty melons:** Here's a description of some specialty melons:

  - • **Charentais:** Traditional French melon has modern varieties that look like muskmelons. It has deep orange flesh and a honeylike flavor.

  - • **Crenshaw:** Salmon-fleshed, oval-shaped melon with dark green skin that turns mottled yellow when ripe. Takes about four months to mature.

  - • **Honeydew:** Sweet, juicy melon has smooth tan skin and pale green flesh; unlike other melons, it doesn't continue to ripen off the vine. These melons store longer than muskmelons.

Book VII

Vegetables and Herbs

Mustard Greens

Another essential Asian green is mustard *(Brassica juncea)*. When full-sized, mustards have a strong, hot flavor, but if harvested young (6 inches/15 cm tall), the flavor is much milder. Mustard greens like growing in cool weather, and as with other greens, you can plant successive crops of them. They also regrow from cutting. The mature plants can get a couple feet tall, and some varieties have beautiful coloring on their leaves, making them attractive as well. Some of the most colorful varieties are 'Osaka Purple' and 'Red Giant'. 'Florida Broadleaf' is a standard variety grown in the Southeast. Direct sow seeds in spring or fall in cold-winter areas and late summer in mild-winter areas. Thin plants to 8 inches (20 cm) apart. Water, fertilize, and harvest as you would other greens.

Onions

The two most important factors to consider when choosing onion *(Allium cepa)* varieties are the onion's flavor and your garden's location. Onions are particular about how much sunlight they get, forming bulbs in response to the number of daylight hours. As a result, onion varieties are classified by day length — long day, short day, or intermediate day — as well as by taste — sweet (which are good for fresh eating only) or pungent (which are good for storing). In general, short-day onions grow well in the southern United States, long-day onions grow well in the northern United States, and intermediate-day onions grow well in the in-between regions.

Following is a list of our favorite onion varieties. The days to maturity are from either directly seeding in the garden or *setting out* (placing outdoors) sets or plants. You usually plant short-day onions in fall to grow through the winter, so they take longer to mature than other types. You plant long- and intermediate-day onions in spring. All the onions in the following list have yellow skin and white flesh unless otherwise noted.

- ✔ **'Candy':** Sweet, intermediate-day, widely adapted hybrid also available as a plant. Matures 85 days after seeding.

- ✔ **'Granex 33'** *(Vidalia):* Classic hybrid, sweet, short-day onion also available as a plant. Matures in spring 180 days after fall seeding.

- ✔ **'Red Burgermaster':** Hybrid, red-skinned, pink-fleshed, pungent, long-day onion stores well. Matures 110 days after seeding. (The classic onion that tastes so great in sandwiches.)

- ✔ **'White Bermuda' (Crystal Wax):** White skin and flesh matures 170 days after seeding this short-day onion. Available in a red version and as a plant.

Sulfur, not sugar, makes onions pungent or sweet. Sweet onions have less sulfur than pungent varieties, so they taste sweeter. Although the sulfur can make the onion more pungent, it also makes those varieties great storage onions. To keep your sweet onions as sweet as they can be, don't apply any sulfur fertilizers and keep the onion plants stress free by controlling weeds and making sure that the plants receive enough water and fertilizer.

Okra

Okra *(Abelmoschus esculentus)* is a classic southern vegetable that loves the heat. In fact, it's one of the few vegetables that keeps producing during the dog days of summer in the South. This tall (4 to 10 feet/1.2 to 3 m), stalky plant produces attractive, trumpetlike flowers along the main stem that mature into okra pods. Each flower potentially produces one pod. The standard okra variety is 'Clemson Spineless', which matures in 60 days, but for gardeners with a short growing season, better choices are 'Annie Oakley II' and

'Cajun Delight', which mature about 50 days from seeding. For a beautiful and unusual-colored variety, try 'Burgundy'. It has red leaves and pods.

Okra needs heat! Don't direct seed or transplant okra until the soil temperature is at least 65°F (18°C). Direct seed in early summer. In cold-winter areas, choose quick-maturing varieties. Use a knife to harvest the pods just above the *cap* (where the base of the pod attaches to the stem) when pods are 2 to 3 inches (5 to 8 cm) long and still tender. Check the plants every few days. The more you harvest, the more the plants will produce. Okra seed doesn't save well, so buy fresh seed every year.

Okra stems and leaves have spines that can irritate your skin. Wear gloves and long-sleeved shirts when working and harvesting in the okra patch.

Peas

One vegetable that is truly a treat to grow yourself is the pea, *Pisum sativum*. Peas are in the same legume family as beans, have large seeds, and don't require much care. The only difference between peas and beans is that peas like cool weather to grow and mature, whereas beans like it warm. A pea is described by the type of pods it has. An *English,* or garden, pea has a tough pod with tender peas inside. A *snap* pea has tender peas inside but also has an edible, sweet pod. A *snow* pea is harvested flat (that is, harvested before the pea seeds inside the pod form) mainly for its tender pea pod. Mind your peas and take a look at some excellent varieties:

✔ **English peas:** In the following list, the days to maturity represent the time from seeding to harvest. Here are some of the most reliable performing varieties of English peas:

- **'Green Arrow':** High-yielding, 2-foot-tall (61 cm), widely adapted variety matures in 70 days.

- **'Maestro':** Prolific early variety reaches only 2-feet (61 cm) tall but produces 4- to 5-inch (10- to 13-cm) pods on powdery-mildew-resistant plants.

- **'Novella':** Unique 20-inch-tall (51 cm), leafless variety produces tendrils and lots of peas in 65 days.

- **'Wando':** Very productive, warm weather variety grows 3 feet (1 m) tall and produces peas in 68 days.

✔ **Snap peas:** Recent breeding has created a pea pod that *fills out* (the pea seed inside the pod forms) like an English pea but has a sweet, tender pod like a snow pea. Upon harvesting snap peas, cut off the cap (stem end) of the pod and take the string (along the seam) out of the pod. These are the only two parts of the pod that are chewy. Try these:

- **'Cascadia':** Two-foot-tall (61 cm) vines produce 3-inch (8-cm), dark green peas 58 days after planting.

- **'Sugar Bon':** Sweet, 1- to 2-foot-tall (30- to 61-cm) snap pea matures in 56 days and resists powdery mildew disease.

- **'Sugar Daddy':** Vines are 30 inches (76 cm) tall and produces stringless, podded snap peas 75 days after planting.

✔ **Snow peas:** Snow peas are the easiest peas to grow because you don't have to wait for the pea pods to fill out to harvest them. They're tender, stringless, and best when harvested before the peas inside begin to swell. Here are two of the best producing varieties to try:

- **'Dwarf Gray Sugar':** Viny, 2- to 3-foot-tall (0.6- to 1-m) plant needs support but produces 3-inch (8-cm), dark green pods 57 days after planting. The pink flowers are very ornamental.

- **'Oregon Giant':** Large 4- to 5-inch (10- to 13-cm) sweet pods grow on disease-resistant, 3-foot-tall (1 m) vines 60 days after planting.

Peppers, Hot

Trying to generalize about hot peppers is difficult because the flavor and heat level varies with each type of pepper. Hot pepper plants generally are easier to grow and produce more peppers than sweet pepper plants.

The active ingredient that causes all the fire in hot peppers is called *capsaicin* (tiny, blisterlike sacs on the fruit's inner wall). Fewer sacs are located at the tips of hot peppers, so you can bite off the tip of a hot pepper and be fooled into thinking it's not that hot. If you cut into the pepper or handle it roughly, however, you break the inner-wall lining, releasing capsaicin throughout the fruit — even to the tip. Some varieties, such as habañero, are so hot that you can get serious burns in your mouth, eyes, or skin. Always wear gloves when harvesting peppers. To counteract the hotness of hot peppers, try eating dairy products such as yogurt, ice cream, or milk with your hot dishes.

Here are some different hot pepper varieties that you can grow:

✔ **'Cherry Bomb' hybrid:** Mildly hot, 2-inch-round (5 cm), thick-walled fruits mature in 65 days to a bright red.

✔ **'Hungarian Hot Wax':** Medium-hot, 7- to 8-inch-long (18- to 20-cm), tapered, peppers mature from yellow to red in 70 days and are great for pickling.

✔ **'Serrano':** Candle-flame-shaped, 2½-inch-long (6 cm), fiery hot peppers mature in 77 days and are born abundantly on 3-foot-tall (1 m) plants.

✔ **'Super Chili' hybrid:** Produce an abundance of 2-inch-long (5 cm), cone-shaped, hot fruits in 75 days that you can dry or eat fresh.

Heats off to Wilbur Scoville

The Scoville Heat Scale rates pepper hotness. The scale ranges from 0 to 350,000 and measures pepper hotness in multiples of 100. The following table shows some of the most popular hot pepper types and their hotness ratings. The chart gives a range for each rating because weather, growing conditions, and pepper variety can all affect how hot a pepper is.

Pepper Types	Scoville Rating Range
Bell	0–100
Hot cherry	100–500
Jalapeño	400–2500
Anaheim	500–2500
Ancho/poblano	1,000–1,500
Serrano	10,000–25,000
Hot wax	10,000–40,000
Tabasco	30,000–50,000
Cayenne	30,000–50,000
Habañero	100,000–350,000

Peppers, Sweet

An abundance of pepper varieties are available to home gardeners. Most plants grow to 2 to 3 feet (0.6 to 1 m) tall. Variety descriptions for sweet peppers frequently use words such as "lobes" and "blocky." When you cut a pepper crosswise near the stem, you'll notice that the walls divide the pepper fruit into sections. Pepper experts call these sections *cells* or *lobes*. Well-defined lobes or cells make peppers *blocky*. Most bell peppers have 3 to 4 lobes. Blocky fruits are best for stuffing or slicing into pepper rings.

The following list considers various sweet peppers for your garden:

✔ **Sweet bell peppers:** Bell pepper fruits come in blocky, round, or elongated shapes. Most fruits start out green but mature through a variety of colors before ripening to their final color. The days to maturity given in the following descriptions represent the time from transplant in the garden to full size. Add two weeks to this number to know when they'll mature to their final color. Sweet bells have the sweetest flavor when harvested at the mature color stage. The thick-walled varieties are best for stuffed-pepper recipes. Consider these:

• **'Arianne':** These blocky, Dutch-bred peppers mature early (in 68 days) to a deep orange color.

• **'California Wonder':** These classic, thick-walled, great-for-stuffing, 4-inch x 4-inch (10-cm x 10-cm) blocky bells mature to red in 75 days.

Book VII

Vegetables and Herbs

- **'Chocolate Beauty' hybrid:** These 3- to 4-lobe bells mature in 70 days to a rich chocolate color.

- **'Lilac Bell' hybrid:** These 3- to 4-lobe bells have beautiful lilac-purple skin with ivory-white flesh. Harvest the fruits at the lilac stage or allow them to mature to red. They mature in 70 days.

✔ **Sweet nonbell peppers:** Sweet peppers are more than big, blocky bells. Great sweet peppers also come in round, cherry shapes and short, fat heart shapes. Most of these pepper plants mature to the color red, which is when they're the sweetest:

- **'Biscayne' hybrid:** These 6-inch-long (15 cm), 2-inch-wide (5 cm), Cubanelle-type (feature a blunt end) fruits mature in 65 days.

- **'Large Red Cherry':** Thick-walled, 1-inch-round (2 cm) sweet peppers grow on very productive, compact plants — 1½ feet (46 cm) tall. They mature in 80 days.

- **'Paprika Supreme' hybrid:** Flattened, 7-inch-long (18 cm), thin-walled fruits are perfect for drying and making paprika after they mature, which takes 100 days.

- **'Sweet Banana':** Tapered, 6-inch-long fruits are born on compact 1½-foot-tall (46 cm) plants and mature from yellow to red in 72 days.

TIP

Peppers love magnesium. To give your peppers a boost, mix 1 tablespoon of Epsom salts in 1 gallon of water and spray the pepper plants at flowering.

Sun-poisoned potatoes

Potatoes require a special technique called *hilling,* which is mounding up the soil around the plants as they grow. For potatoes, hill at least twice during the growing season — about one week after the leaves emerge from the soil and again two to three weeks later. Hilling promotes the production of bigger potatoes and more of them, kills weeds that are growing, and keeps the sun off the tubers. Any direct sun on potatoes causes chlorophyll to form, turning the potato skins green and giving them an off taste. Tubers actually are mildly poisonous at this stage, but you'd have to eat a truck load to really get sick. If you have a small green patch on your potato, just cut if off; the rest of the tuber is fine to eat.

Harvesting potatoes is like going on an archeological dig. After a potato plant dies, use a metal garden fork and dig up the area 1 foot (30 cm) away from the row so that you don't spear the tubers. You'll be amazed at the number of tubers you find — on average, 10 to 20 per plant. Dry the potatoes for an hour or so in the shade, and then store them in a dark, airy, 60°F (15°C) area for *curing* (the process of letting the skin toughen so the vegetables store better).

Potatoes

Potatoes are one of the most foolproof crops to grow. Start planting early, while the weather is still cool, by placing a piece of the tuber (called a *seed potato*) in a furrow, or trench. After the potatoes start growing, if you *hill* them (push soil around the plants), water them, and keep the bugs away, you're almost guaranteed some great tubers. Potato varieties usually are classified as early (65 days), mid- (75–80 days), and late (90+ days) maturing from the time you plant the seed potato to harvest. If you have a short growing season, grow early maturing plants. For a constant supply of potatoes all summer, grow a bit of each.

Here are a few of our favorite potato varieties in terms of flavor, color, and ease of growing:

- ✔ **'All Blue':** Midseason spud that has mealy texture and blue skin *and flesh*. Best as a mashed potato. Yes, purple mashed potatoes!

- ✔ **'Butte':** Late-season, classic Idaho baking type. Features 20 percent more protein and 58 percent more vitamin C than other varieties.

- ✔ **'Kennebec':** All-purpose, dependable midseason variety with white skin and flesh. Resists disease and is a good variety for almost any use.

- ✔ **'Red Norland':** Early variety with red skin and white flesh. Harvest early when plants are just flowering. Tastes best boiled or mashed.

Book VII

Vegetables and Herbs

What a sweet little potato!

Sweet potatoes *(Ipomoea batatas)* are easy to grow in any climate (so long as you choose the right variety), and they store well indoors in winter. Some of the best short-season varieties (90 days) to grow are 'Beauregard', 'Centennial', and 'Georgia Jet'. Other varieties that mature one to two weeks later are 'Bush Porto Rico', 'Jewel', and 'Vardaman'.

To grow sweet potatoes, you buy small plants called *slips*. Slips are available at local garden centers in spring or through the mail. Sweet potatoes love the heat, so wait until the soil temperature is at least 60°F (15°C) before planting. To plant, create raised beds at least 6 inches (15 cm) tall and amend the soil with compost. Plant the slips up to their bottom leaves, 1 foot (30 cm) apart in the raised beds. Side-dress the plants once, one month after planting, with a 5-10-10; keep the plants well weeded and watered and the soil slightly acidic. The vines will create a dense mat-like groundcover, making this an attractive, as well as edible, plant to grow.

Before frost, or about 100 days after planting, dig under the plants and check for roots. Pull plants that have formed good-sized roots and cure (dry) these in a warm (80°F/26°C) room for two weeks. The curing process not only helps the skin toughen, but also converts starches to sugars, giving sweet potatoes their characteristic taste. After curing, eat the tubers or store them in a humid 55°F (12°C) basement (or in a cool area of your house) all winter.

Pumpkins

Pumpkins are *the* quintessential fall crop in many areas, and most peoples' favorite winter squash. (Yes, pumpkins are squashes, too. Most pumpkin varieties are in the *Cucurbita pepo* species, directly related to acorn- and spaghetti-type winter squash.) You grow pumpkins similar to winter squash; they need plenty of space to vine. Here are a few popular pumpkin varieties:

- ✔ **'Baby Bear':** Award-winning, 2-pound, minipumpkin that matures in 105 days. They're great for cooking, and seeds taste great roasted.

- ✔ **'Connecticut Field':** Flat-bottomed, 20-pound, jack-o'-lantern pumpkin matures on large vines in 115 days. Great for carving and baking.

- ✔ **'Lumina':** White-skinned, orange-fleshed, 20-pound pumpkin can be made into a ghostly looking jack-o'-lantern. Matures in 95 days.

- ✔ **'Small Sugar':** Smooth-textured flesh and a small seed cavity on a 4- to 6-pound variety that matures in 95 days. *The* pumpkin for pies.

Radish

If you're looking for quick satisfaction, grow radishes *(Raphanus sativus)*. The seeds germinate within days of planting, and most varieties mature their tasty roots within a month. When grown in cool weather and not stressed, radishes will have a juicy, slightly hot flavor. If radishes *are* stressed by lack of water, too much heat, or competition from weeds or each other, you end up with a fire-breathing dragon that people won't tolerate. Most gardeners are familiar with the spring-planted red globes or white elongated roots found in grocery stores, but exotic-looking international radishes are showing up in specialty food stores and restaurants. These radishes require a longer season and are often planted to mature in fall or winter.

The following varieties work well for the beginning gardener:

- ✔ **For the classic red or white round radishes:** Try 'Cherry Belle', 'Easter Egg' (a mix of red and white), and 'Scarlet Globe'.

- ✔ **For the elongated white or red roots:** Try 'French Breakfast' (a mix of red and white), 'White Icicle', or 'D'Avignon' (the top of the root is red, and the bottom is white).

- ✔ **For daikons:** Try 'Summer Cross #3' and 'April Cross'.

Rhubarb

Rhubarb *(Rheum rhubarbarum),* like asparagus, is an exception in the vegetable world. It's a perennial plant, except in Zones 8 and warmer where it's treated as an annual, and once established, it comes back faithfully year after year. (See Book IV for more on perennials and Book V for information on annuals.) It will even spread, allowing you to dig, divide, and share plants with friends. Hopefully, you have many friends, because you'll only need a few healthy rhubarb plants to produce plenty for pies, jams, and jellies. Not usually eaten raw, rhubarb is best used as an ingredient in cooking. Can't you just smell that strawberry-rhubarb pie fresh from the oven?

Rhubarb is one of those "plant and forget" crops. If it has full sun, well-drained soil, lots of compost and manure mixed in, and water, it will grow like a weed. Rhubarb does best in cool climates, so gardeners in Florida and Arizona may have to rely on their northern friends for fresh rhubarb. For best quality, harvest the leaf stalks as soon as the leaves completely unfold to a flat surface. Always leave at least two leaf stalks per plant so the plant can rejuvenate itself. If a seed stalk forms (usually from the center of the plant), cut it off to extend the leaf-stalk harvesting season. The plants die back in fall, but they reemerge in spring from the roots.

The part of the rhubarb plant you eat is the leaf stalk that grows from the crown of the plant. Don't eat the leaf itself, unless you want an upset stomach. Depending on the variety, the stalks are green or red and taste sour. The most tender varieties have leaf stalks that are red all the way through, such as 'Chipman' and 'Valentine.'

Book VII

Vegetables and Herbs

Spinach

Spinach is one of the first crops many gardeners plant in spring. In fact, when the heat comes, spinach quickly bolts. If you want to eat spinach throughout the summer, grow warm-weather, spinachlike crops that produce all summer, such as New Zealand spinach *(Tetragonia tetragonioides)* and Malabar spinach *(Basella rubra).* Spinach comes in two different leaf types: smooth and savoy (crinkled). The smooth-leaf types are easier to clean, but the savoy-leaf types give you more leaf surface to hold salad dressing. Unless otherwise noted, the varieties in the following list mature in about 30 to 45 days from a spring planting. As with lettuce, you can always harvest the young, tender greens earlier if you just can't wait:

- ✔ **'Bloomsdale Long Standing':** Heirloom, savoy-type variety with thick leaves.

- ✔ **'Melody':** Award-winning hybrid features large, semisavoy leaves and good disease resistance.

- ✔ **'Space':** Hybrid, smooth-leafed variety is productive and slow to bolt.

Squash

Squash may not be as glamorous as their melon cousins, but boy can they produce. Whether you're growing summer squash or winter squash, they'll produce an abundance of fruit and flowers with seemingly little attention. One way to slow production is actually to eat the flowers. They taste great sautéed with olive oil and garlic, along with some Italian bread.

Keep your squash areas weeded and watered, and you'll be rewarded with super squash. Just remember to give these squash room to grow. Summer squash varieties tend to stay in a bush form, but they still need a few feet to spread out. And even though winter squash do come in bush forms, most of the best-flavored varieties have at least 6-foot (2-m) vines. Harvest summer squash as small as possible — even if the flower is still attached — to help avoid that midsummer glut of zucchinis. You can harvest winter squash (and pumpkins) after they change to the expected color of their variety and after their skin is thick enough that your thumbnail can't puncture the fruits when you press on them. If you want to store winter squash (and pumpkins) through the fall and winter, don't let them get nipped by frost, or they'll rot. Leave 2 inches (5 cm) of the stem attached for best storing.

Summer squash

Summer squash are bush-type plants whose fruits are harvested when they're tender and immature. Summer squash usually are separated into yellow, straight, or crookneck varieties; green zucchini varieties; or green-, white-, or yellow-skinned, scallop-shaped fruits. Summer squash usually mature within two months of planting and continue to produce all season long. Summer squash don't store well, however. Following are good summer squash varieties to try:

- ✔ **'Black Zucchini':** Standard zucchini-type variety produces tons of dark green, slender fruits on bush plants. Matures in 53 days.

- ✔ **'Butterbar':** Hybrid, straightneck, yellow summer squash produces tons of golden-yellow fruits that mature in 49 days.

- ✔ **'Cocozelle':** Italian heirloom zucchini has green and white stripes and a good flavor.

- ✔ **'Sunburst':** Hybrid, yellow-skinned, summer squash has tender, scallop-shaped fruits that take 50 days to mature.

Winter squash

Winter squash are mostly vining-type plants whose fruits are harvested when they're fully mature. They mature after three months or more of growing and are best harvested after the cool, fall weather sets in. You can store them for months in a cool basement. They're also good for baking. You can easily get lost in the maze of winter squash types, so here's a quick list of the most popular types:

- **Acorn** *(Cucurbita pepo):* Black, dark green, or white skin and an acorn-shaped, ribbed fruit. Pale yellow flesh.

- **Buttercup** *(Cucurbita maxima):* Green or orange, turban-shaped type has a "button" on the end of its fruits. Dry, orange flesh.

- **Delicata** *(Cucurbita pepo):* Small, green- and yellow-striped, zucchini-shaped squash has sweet, pale yellow flesh.

- **Hubbard** *(Cucurbita maxima):* Large, blue or green, oval-shaped squash has a long neck and dry yellow or orange flesh.

- **Spaghetti** *(Cucurbita pepo):* Oblong, tan-colored squash has yellow flesh with a stringy texture.

Good winter squash varieties include:

- **'Burgess Buttercup':** Produces sweet, fiberless (not stringy), orange flesh on 3- to 5-pound fruit that matures in 95 days.

- **'Cream of the Crop':** Hybrid acorn squash features 3-pound fruits with white skin and golden flesh on a bush-type plant. Matures in 85 days.

- **'Spaghetti':** Ivory-skinned, yellow-fleshed, 4- to 5-pound winter squash has stringy, spaghetti-like flesh. Matures in 88 days.

- **'Waltham Butternut':** Produces light tan, 5-pound fruits that have smooth-textured orange flesh. Matures in 105 days.

Swiss Chard

Swiss chard is so easy to grow: It doesn't bolt like spinach, it has a consistent flavor even in the hot summer, and it has leaves that keep producing until frost. The following varieties all mature between 50 and 60 days from direct seeding in the garden, but the baby greens can be harvested as early as one month after seeding:

- **'Dorat':** Yellow midrib variety has thick crinkled leaves and a mild flavor.

- **'Fordhook Giant':** Heavy producer that features a thick, celerylike midrib with large, dark green savoy leaves.

- **'Rhubarb':** Heirloom, burgundy-red midrib variety with dark green leaves. Tasty and attractive, but a bit smaller than other chards.

Tomatoes

Before deciding which tomato variety to grow, you need to know the growth habits of the plants. They can grow into huge monsters or tiny pot plants. Whether a cherry tomato, paste tomato, or red slicing tomato variety, tomatoes all fall into one of these categories:

✔ **Indeterminate:** These tomato plants just keep growing, stopped only by frost, insect, disease, or an ax. The side branches and shoots continue to grow even after fruit is *set* (after the flower has been pollinated and the young tomato fruits begin to grow). They produce a ton of fruit, but the tomatoes tend to mature later in the season than those borne by the shorter plant varieties.

✔ **Determinate:** Determinate varieties tend to stop growing once the shoots set fruit. Varieties vary in the degree that they're determinate, but these plants generally tend to be shorter and produce less fruit while maturing fruit earlier than indeterminates.

✔ **Dwarf:** These stronger determinate plants tend to reach only a few feet tall, produce all of their fruit at once, and then stop producing for the season. These plants are excellent as patio or container plants, producing cherry tomato-sized fruits. (Refer to Chapter 3 in Book II for more information on container gardening.)

✔ **Dwarf-indeterminate:** The best of both worlds, these plants stay dwarf, only reaching about 3 to 4 feet (1 to 1.2 m) tall, but they continue to produce full-sized tomatoes all season long. They grow well when planted in containers or in the garden.

The following list breaks tomatoes down by color, size, shape, or use:

✔ **Red, round tomatoes:** Red, round tomatoes are the classic, bright red, juicy, meaty tomatoes that everyone wants to grow. You can choose from hundreds of varieties, but here are a few we especially like:

  • **'Delicious':** Indeterminate heirloom with fruits weighing more than 2 pounds each 77 days after transplanting.

  • **'Heatwave II':** Determinate hybrid bred to grow and produce 7-ounce fruits in hot, humid conditions 68 days after transplanting.

  • **'Oregon Spring':** Determinate, open-pollinated variety produces 7- to 8-ounce fruits 58 days after transplanting.

  • **'Siberia':** Determinate variety that can set 2- to 3-ounce fruits 55 days after transplanting in temperatures as low as 38°F (3°C).

✔ **Other-than-red tomatoes:** The flavor of many of these varieties is comparable to the red varieties, but the colors can be outstanding in salads and casseroles, or just by themselves:

- **'Big Rainbow':** Indeterminate heirloom produces 2-pound tomatoes with yellow shoulders, orange centers, and red bottoms 95 days after transplanting.

- **'Caro Rich':** Determinate, open-pollinated variety produces 5- to 6-ounce, bright orange-colored fruits that have 10 times the amount of vitamin A as other tomatoes 80 days after transplanting.

- **'Cherokee Purple':** Indeterminate bears 10-ounce dusky rose/purple fruits with thin skins about 80 days after transplanting.

- **'White Beauty':** Open-pollinated indeterminate produces creamy white 8-ounce fruits 85 days after transplanting.

✔ **Saucy tomatoes:** If you're growing tomatoes to make tomato sauce, paste, salsa, and juice, these paste tomato varieties are bred to order. You can process any tomato variety, but these pear- or plum-shaped types are meatier and thicker-walled and usually have less juice. Prevent blossom-end rot in elongated tomatoes by keeping the plants well watered, and mulching with a 4- to 6-inch-deep (10- to 15-cm) layer of hay:

- **'Italian Gold':** Determinate, golden-fruited, Roma-type, pear-shaped tomato matures 70 days after transplanting.

- **'Roma':** Popular, open-pollinated determinate produces plum-shaped, 3-ounce fruits on compact vines 78 days after transplanting.

- **'Super Marzano':** Indeterminate has 4- to 5-ounce pear-shaped fruits that mature 70 days after transplanting.

- **'Viva Italia':** Determinate produces pear-shaped 3- to 4-ounce fruits with great disease resistance 80 days after transplanting.

✔ **Cherry tomatoes:** Cherry tomatoes can be very productive, so only one or two plants are often enough to keep your family happy all season. The dwarf tomatoes do best in containers. (See Chapter 3 in Book II for more on container gardening.) Cherry tomato fruits do tend to crack more easily than larger-sized tomatoes, so make sure that they have plenty of water and mulch. Try these varieties:

- **'Micro-Tom':** Dwarf plant reaches only 6 to 8 inches (15 to 20 cm) tall and produces pea-sized red fruits 88 days after transplanting.

- **'Sun Gold':** Indeterminate plant produces fruity tasting 1- to 2-inch-diameter (15 to 20 cm) orange colored fruits 57 days after transplanting.

- **'Tiny Tim':** Open-pollinated, dwarf, 18-inch-tall (46 cm) plants produce 1-inch-diameter red fruits 60 days after transplanting.

- **'Yellow Pear':** Indeterminate produces clear yellow, 2-inch-diameter, (5 cm) pear-shaped fruits on huge plants about 78 days after transplanting.

Book VII

Vegetables and Herbs

Chapped tomato skin

Excess or lack of water, too much fertilizer, cold temperatures, and varietal differences can all contribute to deformed fruits. Here are a few of the more common problems and some solutions:

✔ **Blossom drop:** Your tomatoes are flowering beautifully, but the blossoms all seem to drop without forming any fruit. Air temperatures above 90°F (32°C) or below 55°F (12°C) cause this condition. At these temperatures, most tomato flowers will not set fruits. The solution is to grow varieties adapted to the heat ('Heatwave II') or cold ('Siberia'), or to protect the plants during flowering with shade cloths or covers.

✔ **Blossom-end rot:** The bottom, or blossom end, of tomatoes turns brown and rots. Fluctuating moisture conditions in the soil cause the problem, so mulch the plants well, make sure that they're planted in well-drained soil, and keep them evenly watered.

✔ **Sunscald:** The top surface of the tomato skin has lightly colored patches caused by direct exposure to the sun. These patches eventually rot. To avoid sunscald, grow indeterminate varieties that have lots of foliage to shade the fruits, avoid pruning the leaves, or provide afternoon shade with shade cloths.

Turnip

Turnips are easy to grow, and you can eat the greens as well as the roots. If grown in cool weather, they have a slightly sweet flavor. Turnips mature quickly (in less than 50 days from seeding). The greens are great steamed, and they walk hand in hand with collard greens as the favorite Southern leafy crop. Some varieties to try are 'Purple Top White Globe', 'Shogoin', and 'Tokyo Cross'. The latter two produce excellent, mild-tasting greens.

Turnips love cool weather. In most areas, you can grow spring and fall crops. Start in spring a few weeks before your last frost date. In early fall, wait until the hot summer weather has passed before planting. Turnips are best direct seeded in the garden. Keep the plants well watered and mulched with hay or straw, which, in addition to holding in moisture and controlling weeds, helps prevent the roots from developing a strong flavor. Begin harvesting when the roots are 3 to 4 inches (8 to 10 cm) in diameter; then enjoy. Turnips can take a frost, so harvest right into winter until the ground freezes.

Chapter 4

Getting Down to the Herb of the Matter

In This Chapter

▶ Understanding basic herb anatomy

▶ Finding ways to use the herbs you grow

▶ Preventing herbs from taking over the garden

▶ Recognizing toxic herbs

Herbs are very similar to the other garden plants you can read about throughout this book. At the same time, they're different enough to deserve special coverage. If you're interested in growing an herb garden, or adding herbs to an existing garden, this chapter lays the "groundwork" for you to do so.

Herbs from Stem to Stern

Like all plants, herbs are either annuals (basil, borage, calendula, and summer savory, for example) or perennials (such as anise hyssop, mint, and sweet woodruff). Some are biennials, which means they live for two growing seasons. (Book IV covers perennials and Book V looks at annuals and biennials.) A basic understanding of botany helps you grow happier, healthier plants. Much of the information in the following sections applies to all plants, not just herbs. However, we look at each item specifically with herbs in mind.

The root of the matter

Herb roots are as important as the plant parts you see aboveground. Most herbs have either fibrous roots or a taproot:

✔ **Fibrous roots are fine and highly branched.** Herbs with fibrous roots are more susceptible to droughts because these roots grow closer to the soil surface. Plants with fibrous roots are easier to transplant and divide.

> ✓ **Taproots are long and tapering with a few small side roots, or hairs.**
> Usually thick and fleshy, taproots store moisture and stretch deep into
> the soil. Plants with taproots can withstand temporary droughts, but
> they're less easy to transplant and can't be divided.

Stem dandy

Stems hold up the leaves and flowers, carrying water and nutrients to them
from the roots. Only a few herbs — flax is one — are grown primarily for their
stems, although you use the stems of many species in cooking and medicines.

Sometimes you're told to cut below or above a *node,* the places along a stem
where leaves are attached. The clear spaces between nodes are called *internodes;* without enough light, the internodes stretch more than usual, producing tall, spindly, *leggy* plants. *Erect* plants grow upward. Some shoot straight
up, rigidly vertical and often with few side stems, such as bee balm. Others
with more branched stems tend to sprawl. Climbing (or *scandent*) plants want
to grow even farther upward.

Leaf it be

Anyone with an herb garden ends up being keen about leaves, as many of the
most popular herbs have only small flowers. Herb leaves come in all sorts of
sizes, colors, textures, and shapes. Each leaf variation (and there are scores)
has its own name, but you can grow bee balm successfully for 50 years without knowing that its leaves are "simple, usually serrate," or have great luck
with geraniums without calling their leaves "alternate, palmate or pinnate,
simple or compound, usually lobed."

Following are a few of the most general leaf terms:

> ✓ **Deciduous:** Plants with leaves that die in winter and are replaced by new
> leaves in spring
>
> ✓ **Evergreen:** An everyday term for plants that retain leaves throughout
> the year
>
> ✓ **Simple:** A single leaf, like mint's
>
> ✓ **Compound:** A leaf that's made of several leaves, or leaflets, such as
> chervil's
>
> ✓ **Blade:** The flat part of the leaf
>
> ✓ **Margin:** The leaf's edge
>
> ✓ **Lobed:** A leaf, like most geraniums', that has deep cuts
>
> ✓ **Serration:** Leaf margins that are jagged, like most mints' (A leaf without
> serration, such as that of orrisroot, has *entire* margins.)

Flower children

Gardeners describe flowers both in terms of the individual blooms and the way those blooms are arranged. Knowing the basic terms for these *inflorescences* (flower clusters) helps you to choose the flower shape you want. And when other gardeners start talking blossoms, it won't be all Greek to you.

- **Composite:** A daisylike flower, such as the sunflower, that looks like a *single* (one flower on one stalk), but actually consists of a center made up of scores of tiny, tightly packed disc flowers surrounded by a ring of *ray flowers* (the flower parts we pick off while reciting, "He loves me, He loves me not").

- **Panicle:** An open, loosely branched cluster of flowers on a branched stem. Southern-wood and sweet woodruff have panicled flowers.

- **Raceme:** A cluster of flowers attached to a single, upright stem with short, individual stalks, such as those of sage and comfrey.

- **Spike:** An upright stem of flowers like those of agrimony and hyssop, which have little or no stalk and attach directly or almost directly to the stem.

- **Umbel:** An umbrellalike structure, with each flower stalk emerging from the same place at the top of the stem. Dill and lovage have umbel inflorescences.

Book VII

Vegetables and Herbs

Are you an herb or not?

Many experts define an herb as an *herbaceous plant* (a plant that forms a soft, tender stem rather than a woody stem), but that definition leaves out many plants, including rosemary, a charter member of the culinary herb hall of fame. And it includes plants like daffodils, which aren't on anyone's herb list. Herbs are also defined as "useful plants," but hundreds of plants are useful, such as corn and oats, that few of us would call herbs. Others define herbs as "plants grown for medicinal qualities and for seasoning foods," but that definition leaves out dye plants, plants used in rituals, and for making cosmetics, crafts, and more.

The Herb Society of America follows the "big-tent" philosophy and defines herbs as plants valued for their "flavor, fragrance, medicinal and healthful qualities, economic and industrial uses, pesticidal properties, and coloring materials." If that definition's good enough for the HSA, it's good enough for us — and broad enough. So if you've planted something that tastes or smells good (or bad), cures what ails you, or can be used in some way, feel free to call it an herb.

Medicine Cabinets and Crock Pots

Plants and medicines have been partners as far back as history reaches, although different cultures have had different approaches to herbal remedies. Many Eastern cultures, for example, traditionally view illness as a sign of cosmic disharmony; herbal cures are calculated to restore balance, to create peace between the opposing principles of yin and yang, rather than treat specific problems. The European herbal medicine tradition has been less holistic. Astronomy, too, has played a role in herbal medicine, and old herbals (books about herbs and their medicinal powers) are filled with references to herbs "owned by Venus" or "under the dominion of the moon." Whether their approach was systematic or eclectic, people have prescribed herbs for every condition known to humankind.

Even if you're skeptical about the power of fennel to cure "every kind of poison in a man's body" — the claim in one thirteenth-century herbal — there's no question that plants are rich with substances that can ease and cure diseases, even prevent them. Early physicians called herbs *simples,* meaning that each herb was a simple, or single, medicine, not a compound. In fact, most herbs contain more than one chemical compound — nearly 1,500 have been isolated to date.

The best-known herbs today are those used in the kitchen to flavor and color food and drink. Many are good for you, too. According to the U.S. Department of Agriculture, a teaspoon of dill seed contains 32 mg calcium; a teaspoon of ground basil contains 6 mg magnesium. The healthful-herb champ is the chili pepper: One teaspoon of chili powder contains potassium, sodium, ascorbic acid (vitamin C), niacin, and vitamin A. If you substitute chili powder for your multivitamin, we recommend taking each teaspoon with a gallon of milk (to offset the chili's heat).

Spice is another name for a culinary herb. Purists use the word "herb" when they refer to plants grown for their leaves and stems; spice plants are those cultivated for their flowers, seeds, bark, wood, resin, and roots. You also may come across the word *potherb.* That's an old term that refers to vegetables and herbs used in salads, soups, and stews.

In addition to their ties to the pantry and medicine chest, herbs have an ancient connection to rites and myths. The lotus *(Nelumbo nucifera)* was sacred to Isis, the Egyptian goddess of fertility; white roses *(Rosa damascena)* and madonna lilies *(Lilium candidum)* represent the Virgin Mary; Greek athletes were awarded wreaths of bay *(Laurus nobilis).* Herbs are still used to dye, to create wreaths and bouquets, and to make perfumes, cosmetics, bug repellants, cleaning compounds, and more.

Invasion of the Garden Snatchers

All herbs aren't created equal, or equally nice, as you'll find out if you choose invasive herbs as companions for your genteel basil and ladylike rosemary. As the term suggests, an invasive plant is a botanical Attila the Hun. Draw a line in the sand, and these bullies hop over it. When a garden seed catalog says a plant is "carefree," "vigorous," and "grows anywhere," be prepared for something that can scale a telephone pole faster than you can get rid of a telephone solicitor.

Rue the day

Climbing and clambering plants are especially notorious for exterminating everything in their path. Kudzu *(Pueraria lobata)*, which the Chinese use to treat alcoholism, is known as "the vine that ate the South" for good reason. English ivy *(Hedera helix)* and wild grape *(Vitis* spp.) are two more vigorous vines that are used medicinally — ivy for controlling skin problems, grape as a diuretic — but both may be prescriptions for trouble in your garden.

Most nonvining herbs make congenial neighbors for the other occupants of your garden, but not all. Turn your back on spearmint, and it will overwhelm the lettuce and lay siege to the parsley. Set out a tidy clump of garlic chives, famous for pungent flavor and the power to ward off disease, and you'll discover that even two or three unpicked flower heads give birth to hundreds of new plants. Come spring, your well-tended garden will look like scruffy lawn. Hoe down the grasslike stalks and they reappear, as dependable as the swallows that arrive each year at the San Juan Capistrano mission.

Book VII

Vegetables and Herbs

TIP

The seed stops here

You can usually dig or pull invasive herbs that multiply by seeds more successfully than you can perennial climbers and crawlers. Just don't give the seeds time to get the upper hand:

✔ Lay down a thick layer of mulch to discourage seeds from sprouting and to smother young plants.

✔ Pour boiling water on seedlings.

✔ Deadhead (pick flowers as soon as they wilt) to stop invasive plants from reseeding.

Tilling is supposed to bury seeds, blocking the light they need to sprout. Not so! Churning the soil usually brings more seeds to the surface — where they will sprout — than it buries.

Like politics, all gardening is local. Although the master list of universally incorrigible herbs is short, a list for your region may be much longer. To avoid catastrophe — years of swearing at yourself for planting that ~#@*! thing — find out which herbs may turn traitor. If you yearn to make a concoction that calls for an unabashed bully, don't plant more of it. Do the world a favor and harvest some from a friend's lawn or help a native plant society tidy up a park. Remember, you can make spring tonics and harvest greens without introducing dandelions to your garden. Consult other gardeners, local nurseries, and the local extension service about invasives. And if your neighbor brings you kudzu seedlings, find a nice way to say, "In a pig's eye."

Underground travelers

Some herbs, such as mint, travel by sending out rootlike stems, or rhizomes, that scoot just under the soil surface, sprouting new plants as they go. Scratching mint off your plant list won't make your garden an invasive-free zone, however. Other herbs overrun their neighbors by scattering seeds that sprout in the most awful conditions — such as the spaces between your patio stones — and without any help from you. Toss 100 basil seeds on the ground and you'll be buying, not making, pesto. But let one dandelion flower go to seed and you'll have enough plants to make wine for the Bowery Boys.

Be prepared to arm yourself as an "herban" guerilla if you plant any of the following invasives:

- **Artemisia (*Artemisia* spp.):** Gardening books advise dividing this herb to create more. But artemisia, famous for thriving in poor soil, multiplies so rapidly on its own that you'll need a calculator to add them up.

- **Comfrey (*Symphytum officinale*):** Notice that *Symphytum* has the same root as the word sympathy. Trust us, you'll get neither sympathy nor comfort from comfrey when your plants multiply.

- **Costmary (*Chrysanthemum balsamita*):** Rarely found in the wild, but in the garden, it increases fast enough to supply an entire city.

- **Fennel (*Foeniculum vulgare*):** The seeds taste like anise, its leaves like dill. But watch out! Fennel has invaded farm fields in California and Virginia, where it's now officially *herbus non grata*.

- **German, or annual, chamomile (*Matricaria recutita*):** This herb self-sows almost anywhere. In Boulder, Colorado, chamomile sprouts in sidewalk cracks, a pleasant alternative to crab grass.

- **Herb-Robert (*Geranium robertianum*):** Long associated with snakes, this plant slithers through the garden with ease, popping up where you least expect — or want — it.

- **Horseradish** *(Armoracia rusticana):* You're likely to leave behind a few bits of root when you dig horseradish, and every bit will turn into a new plant. Once you have it, you have it.

- **St. John's wort** *(Hypericum perforatum):* St. John's wort is an herbal mood-lifter with a reputation for getting wildly out of hand in the garden. Keep an eye on it, or you may end up depressed.

- **Tansy** *(Tanacetum vulgare):* Tansy can repel flies, ants, and other insects, but it can also be a pest in its own right.

- **Violet** *(Viola odorata):* Shrinking violets? Don't believe it. One day you have a demure clump of violets, the next week you can open a flower shop.

- **Yarrow** *(Achillea* **spp.):** Multiplying without help may be okay for a plant that reputedly heals bruises, burns, wounds, and sores; conditions oily hair; and looks great in dried arrangements.

No self-respecting herb garden is complete without spearmint or yarrow, but pulling, digging, or tilling these ground-spreaders may mean more plants, not fewer. To keep them from crowding out the carrots and zinnias, grow them in containers, either aboveground or sunk in the garden. See Chapter 3 in Book II for more information on container gardening.

Snow White's Poison Herb

Herbs have been associated with curses every bit as long as they've been associated with cures. Be aware that a good number of herbs are toxic. Their effects range from irritating skin to causing death. When Socrates drank hemlock, he wasn't kidding around. Here are some of the more common herbs to be wary of, including a couple that can kill:

- **Aconite** *(Aconitum napellus):* This herb, also known as monkshood and wolfsbane, deserves a skull-and-crossbones; it's highly poisonous.

- **Aloe** *(Aloe barbadensis):* Juice from these stems is great for minor burns, but never use it internally.

- **Wormwood** *(Artemisia absinthium):* Absinthe, as a drink, has been banned worldwide.

- **Deadly nightshade** *(Atropa belladonna):* In folklore, this herb is a favorite ingredient of witches' brews. The common name says it all.

- **Hemlock** *(Contium maculatum):* Think nausea, paralysis, and death.

- **Foxglove** *(Digitalis purpurea):* The source of a powerful heart medication, foxglove can cause convulsions and even death if used improperly.

- **Pokeweed** *(Phytolacca* **spp.):** All parts of mature plants, including their pretty purple berries, are toxic.

✔ **Comfrey *(Symphytum officinale):*** Laboratory research indicates comfrey, even in low concentrations, is carcinogenic in rats.

✔ **Hellebore:** Both American false hellebore *(Veratrum viride)* and black hellebore *(Helleborus niger)* are dangerous characters; they're major-league skin irritants and can be fatal if ingested.

With herbs, it's downright stupid to imbibe first and ask questions later. Don't put any herb in your mouth without knowing what it is and what it does. If your skin is unusually sensitive, don't going rolling around in your herb garden. Above all, clearly label any dangerous herbs, and fence them to protect those who can't read.

The wild ones

Wildcrafting is the term for gathering herbs and other plants from the outdoors. This activity is so popular that many species are being threatened by overcollection. Irresponsible collectors who take plants for profit are only part of the problem. The other part is that familiar feeling that we all have when we see a stand of goldenseal or bloodroot: "Oh, it won't matter if I take just a few." Of course, everyone else has the same feeling, so multiply "take a few" by 100 or 1,000 collectors, and you see the problem.

You can collect some herbs, such as dandelion and plantain *(Plantago major),* without a second thought about survival of the species. Other plants are problematic. Native orchids and lilies now grow in such small numbers that you should never disturb them. Overcollection threatens goldenseal, *(Hydrastis canadensis),* ginseng *(Panax quinquefolius),* and several species of Echinacea, our native coneflowers. And that's only a partial list.

Here are some other rules of the plant-collecting road:

✔ **Get permission to harvest.** Most public lands have regulations that you must follow when collecting plant material. Collect plants away from trails and roads, and be careful not to damage the environment.

✔ **Be sure that you're collecting what you think you're collecting.** Hemlock is highly toxic and looks like a half-dozen other benign herbs. You need an expert by your side or an illustrated handbook of native plants.

✔ **Collect only from large, healthy stands of plants.**

✔ **Never dig more than 5 percent (5 in 100) of any stand of plants.**

✔ **Collect seeds and avoid digging.** You can grow nearly all herbs from seeds, so rather than dig entire plants, collect their seeds. Collect a bit from several plants, leaving behind at least three-fourths of the seeds.

✔ **Don't harvest more than you can replant, sow, or use.**

Nearly all threatened herbs are available for sale from nurseries. Make sure that the firm you patronize *propagates* its plants — grows them from seeds or cuttings — rather than digs them in the wild and puts them in pots. Seeds also are available for most endangered herbs.

Chapter 5

Taking Care of Herbness, Every Day

This chapter takes you on a step-by-step journey of an herb garden's life cycle, from design to harvest and back again.

Designing Your Herb Garden

You may think that you need one special place for your herbs, off in a corner of your landscape, because historically, herbs have been rounded up in beds like wheels or laid out like Persian carpets. Impressive as these designs can be, the notion that you can only grow herbs this way keeps you from using them as creatively as you can. Sure, you can shape your herb garden like a sixteenth-century lover's knot or Elvis's guitar. But a more important consideration than your bed's configuration is your soil's condition and exposure to sun (good) and wind (bad).

If you're already an avid gardener, you may not have room for a special herb bed. Not to worry! As you discover more of their charming ways, you'll find that herbs mingle merrily with existing plantings, accentuating their colors or clothing their bare feet. Most herbs are so amenable to growing in pots (see Chapter 3 in Book II for more on container gardening) that you can play musical plants, trying the rosemary in the perennial border for its visual pizzazz, then scooting the pot close to the barbecue for smoking bluefish, and finally whisking it inside when winter winds begin to blow.

Where you place your herb garden depends largely on how you plan to use the herbs:

- **As culinary seasoning:** If you plan to harvest oregano, dill, and rosemary daily to season gourmet meals, you want them just seconds away from your chopping block, right outside the kitchen door. A raised bed (Chapter 5 in Book IV tells you all about raised beds) may be in order so that you can snip your chives or pull your parsley without getting on your knees in the mud.

- **As medicine:** If you plan to whip up tinctures and tisanes, you may harvest the entire herb crop once a year to dry for the months ahead. No need to plant your echinacea or valerian next to the back stoop, but you'll still want your herb patch where you can reach it with the garden hose.

- **As a retreat:** If you want your garden to be a retreat, a place where you can escape workaday cares, put your herbs in the nether reaches of your property where you can relax amidst their textures, scents, and colors.

- **As history:** If you want to astound your friends with discourses on Dioscorides, or the mythical link between sweet marjoram and Aphrodite, you'll also want a historically appropriate place to grow your herbs, perhaps tying them in an elaborate knot or laying them out in monasterian squares.

- **As a little something extra:** If all you need is a sprig of sage for the Thanksgiving turkey or enough mint for a single julep on Derby day, that's fine. Herbs are famously agreeable to being tucked in among other pretty plants or keeping a low profile in out-of-the-way corners.

Design basics

Landscape designers use the word *hardscape* for the permanent, nonliving parts of your garden design, which includes natural elements, such as boulders, as well as all the things made of rock, concrete, wood, or plastic. (Refer to Chapter 1 in Book II for more on hardscape.) Winter is the best time to see whether your garden has structure, or what the experts call its *bones*. Even after annual herbs have given up the ghost and most of the perennial herbs are hibernating below ground, your eye should be able to discern rhythmic horizontal lines in your paths and the edges of your beds. You should see strong vertical lines — perhaps with the bonus of a snow-shrouded garden ornament, such as a statue.

Choose rue for blue

Many herbs have a preponderance of blue, purple, and pink flowers, although you can easily add yellow and orange to your palette. When it comes to flowers, though, the best-known culinary and medicinal herbs are somewhat limited. Basil, parsley, and mint all have tiny and relatively colorless flowers that, while capable of driving bees into passionate frenzies, should be removed if you want to keep the fresh flavor of the herb or avoid lessening its health-giving components.

You'll create a more lasting tapestry of color, however, by collecting herbs with an eye to their foliage:

- **Blue:** Color is often in the eye of the beholder, but to most, rue has the bluest foliage among herbs, especially the cultivar plant called 'Jackman's Blue'.

- **Bronze:** Like rue, bronze fennel is in a color class by itself with its distinctive, shimmery, reddish brown foliage.

- **Gray, white, and silver:** Herbs are famous for pale foliage that helps tone down or blend bright colors that might otherwise clash. Choose from catmint, curry plant, lamb's ear *(Stachys byzantina)*, virtually any lavender, sage, santolina, or woolly thyme.

- **Purple and red:** You can bring deep burgundy red into the garden if you plant perilla, purple sage ('Purpurea'), or the basil cultivars 'Rubin' and 'Osmin'.

- **Variegation:** You don't want to overdo *variegated* leaves — those that are tinged with white, yellow, pink, or some combination — but a few scattered here and there provide a lively counterpoint to solid green. Tri-colored sage, which has swirls of pink and white on the usual green, and variegated catmint *(Calamintha grandiflora* 'Variegata') are among the most popular.

- **Yellow:** Just look for some form of aureum, the Latin word for "gold," in a species or cultivar name. You can buy golden feverfew, golden pot marjoram, golden oregano, golden hop, golden sage, golden thyme, or golden valerian.

GARDEN JARGON

Book VII

Vegetables and Herbs

Fuzzy, frilly, shiny, lacy

As you grow and study herbs, you'll notice that the texture of their leaves is even more varied than their color. Deciding which plants contrast most strikingly when planted next to each other is one of the endless pleasures of herb gardening. Here are some of the herbal textures you can stare at or stroke:

- **Feathery:** Dill, fennel, southernwood, wormwood, and yarrow are among the herbs with leaves so finely divided as to approach hairlike. Anise has fine leaves at the top of the plant, while those near its base are more parsleylike.

- **Fernlike:** Leaves that are divided or toothed like fern leaves include chamomile, chervil, feverfew, parsley, and tansy. Those of valerian are deeply divided, too, but the effect is quite different on this five-footer.

- **Pleated:** The leaves of lady's mantle and nasturtium are round and puckery, while those of silver sage *(Salvia argentea)* add white fuzz to the garden mix.

- **Prickly:** What's the point? Spiny leaves give your domain a bit of drama. Try cardoon or its relative globe artichoke *(Cynara scolymys),* liver-rejuvenating milk thistle, or a thicket of the prickle-surfeited eglantine rose.

- **Rough:** For true grit, grow sage. Rub a leaf over your teeth to clean them after dinner — it's good for your gums, too!

- **Smooth 'n' shiny:** The slick, glossy leaves of bay, eucalyptus *(Eucalyptus* spp.), myrtle, and laurel add light to a garden.

- **Succulent:** These plants have their own botanical category because of the way their thick, fleshy leaves store water. Aloe is the most common herb among them. Purslane *(Portulaca oleracea),* a nutritious plant rich in anti-aging antioxidants, looks a bit like a jade plant that's been stomped on.

- **Tiny leaves:** When you visit a well-stocked herb nursery, you may think that the thyme breeders are having a contest to see who can produce the dinkiest leaves. Ground-huggers, such as 'Minus' thyme, have the smallest.

Developing good habits

You may not be able to distinguish the sandpapery look of sage leaves or the satiny sheen of basil from a distance. But your eye will enjoy the differing *habits,* the overall shape of plants. In an informal garden, you can add to visual interest by combining as many shapes as possible. Repeating a shape gives rhythm to your design. In a formal garden, plants are traditionally the same height, so you may also want them to have similar habits:

- **Big 'n' bushy:** Lovage, marsh mallow, meadowsweet *(Filipendula ulmaria),* and Jerusalem artichoke look less like the Washington Monument and more like the Capitol Building. Tall, yes, but also ground gobblers.

- **Grasslike:** The fanlike foliage of orrisroot, like that of all irises, is handsome long after the flowers are gone. For a similar grasslike shape, lusty lemongrass and chipper chives are the long and short of it, respectively.

- **Groundcovers:** Creepy crawly herbs, such as sweet woodruff, cover ground and suppress weeds between other plants. Tuck chamomile and the low-growing thymes between stepping stones, where they release their fragrance when you step on them.

- **Hanging:** Herbs with limp stems look lush dangling from a hanging basket or draped across the side of a raised bed or window box. A few good candidates are borage, catmint and other mints, lemon balm, rosemary, thyme, nasturtium, oregano (especially dittany of Crete, *Origanum dictamnus*), and some scented geraniums, or pelargoniums.

- **Monster leaves:** Grow cardoon or castor bean *(Ricinus communis)* for pure mass. Castor bean is a tropical plant that reaches 10 feet in a single year, with palm-shaped leaves that are more than a foot wide. Oil from its seeds is pressed to make the old-fashioned laxative, castor oil. The seeds are highly poisonous, though, and other parts of the plant can give people with sensitive skin a rash.

- **Mound:** Some herbs form such perfect mounds that you want to reach down and pet them like a sleeping cat. These make good edging plants, or you can use them for contrast with floppy or spiky plants. Good mounders include chamomile, feverfew, and many lavenders.

- **Tall spires:** Angelica, black cohosh *(Cimicifuga racemosa),* evening primrose, Joe-Pye weed *(Eupatorium* spp.), mullein, pokeweed *(Phytolacca americana)* and other vertical herbs have an air of stateliness and drama. These plants command attention, so use them sparingly.

- **Vines:** Use climbing herbs, such as hop, honeysuckle *(Lonicera* spp.), Carolina jasmine *(Gelsenium sempervirens),* climbing nasturtium, or passionflower, on a trellis for privacy or to give other herbs a windbreak.

Aroma wasn't built in a day

Fragrance so characterizes herbs that coming up with a list of herbs that *don't* smell wonderful may have been the easiest way to deal with this category. However, here are a few of our favorites that do smell great. Crush a few leaves of the following plants and see if you agree:

- **Catmint:** Said not to attract cats the way catnip does, *Nepeta mussinii* also has a stronger and more appealing scent for the human nose. Some compare it to mint jelly; we think it has undertones of pine or cedar.

- **Curry:** Ironically, *Helichrysum italicum* isn't a culinary herb, but the silvery 12- to 18-inch (30- to 46-cm) plants make a great edging. You can also pluck the leaves for potpourri.

- **Lavenders:** English lavender *(Lavandula angustifolia)* has the clean scent of lingerie drawers and lace handkerchiefs, while French lavender *(L. stoechas)* smells more like something used for treating sports injuries and battling bugs.

- **Mints:** You can find mints that smell of apple laced with menthol, or lime, chocolate, banana, ginger, grapefruit, orange, and more.

- **Pelargoniums:** Also known as scented geraniums, these olfactory superstars come in rose, apricot, almond, cinnamon, nutmeg, chocolate mint, coconut, eucalyptus, lemon, orange, camphor, pine, strawberry, and apple scents.

- **Thymes:** Go for straight for lemon thyme, which actually does smell like citrus. Then try orange, caraway, lavender, mint, nutmeg, and oregano.

Book VII

Vegetables and Herbs

The pretty magnificent seven

An herb garden is its own theme, but you can specialize by choosing only herbs from the Bible, herbs used by Native Americans, herbs for teas, or herbs for dyes. Or you can tuck herbs into other specialized gardens. Use the designs we present here as inspiration for your own garden, and feel free to mix and match, enlarge or shrink, or change the shape of the beds we offer here.

✔ **A beginner's garden:** Start your garden with a raised bed of basil, campanula, catmint, chives, cilantro, dianthus, dill, lavender, parsley, rosemary, sage, tarragon, and thyme. The sage will eventually get too big; transplant it and use the space for more parsley. If the dianthus rebels against your hot summers, experiment with licorice plant. Build this garden at least knee-high with landscape timbers. If you place a board atop one edge, you can sit and admire your lavender. Located just outside the kitchen door, this garden gives you quick access when tarragon chicken is on the menu.

✔ **A garden for bees and butterflies:** If you enjoy watching butterflies float and bees industriously wallow in pollen, consider planting a garden of their favorite herbs: boneset, borage, buddleia, catnip, chamomile, coneflower, dill, hyssop, lavender, monarda, oregano, and parsley. The flowers of nearly every herb attract bees, so ruthlessly lop off flower buds before they open if you react severely to stings. If you collect herbs on an overcast day, the bees will be more laid back. Many of the plants that attract butterflies also supply food for their larvae. (As with second marriages, attracting butterflies is a case of "love me, love my children.")

Some male butterflies congregate in mud puddles because, during mating season, they need the sodium and other minerals that leach from the soil. Here, poorly draining soil, otherwise cursed by gardeners, is ideal. (You'll need to make mud with the garden hose on days that it doesn't rain.) Set out a shallow dish of water for butterflies that don't patronize mud baths.

✔ **A Shakespearean conceit:** *Conceit* can mean an elaborate metaphor, or a fanciful idea, the likes of which herb gardeners are quite fond. To create a relaxing place for reading or meditation, choose plants that flower in restful shades of blue and pink, such as bay, chamomile, dianthus, honeysuckle, hyssop, lavender, myrtle, orris, rose, and rosemary. (Bay and rosemary aren't cold hardy in most of the country, so grow them in containers and bring them inside during the winter.) Shakespeare's plays and poems are full of more plants than anyone could cram into a single garden, so the list of substitutions is limited only to the time you have to spend perusing the "The Greatest Works of." A formal design is less distracting than an informal garden's random patterns.

✔ **A culinary garden:** If you love to cook, grow your herbs where you can snatch a handful easily in all kinds of weather. Consider including basil, caraway, chervil, chives, cilantro, dill, garlic, mint, nasturtiums, onions, parsley, rosemary, sage, thyme, and winter savory.

✔ **A patio garden:** Herbs are heavily scented, but most of them don't release their delectable fragrances into the air by themselves. They must be crushed or at least brushed against, so we urge you to plant them where you can finger them or even dance on them. Consider including dame's rocket, fennel, honeysuckle, jasmine, juniper, lamb's ear, lavender, rosemary, soapwort, sweet Cicely, sweet woodruff, thyme, and valerian. Plant fennel and soapwort in containers because both species are invasive in a friendly climate.

✔ **A knot garden:** Knot gardens were basically intended to show off the wealth (or leisure time) of their owners. Even if you have space and time to spare, you may want to put your garden to a more productive purpose. The relatively simple knot design shown in Figure 5-1 allows you an ample variety of herbs useful for medicine and tea. The traditional knot in the center, based on an equilateral triangle, is a *triquetra* (also known as a shamrock design). Consider how much you plan to harvest any of these herbs before you plant, since some sections are bigger than others. (If you harvest too much of a knot, you'll "untie" it!) You want the herbs to knit together quickly, so plant them — annuals in particular — close together. You can make your plants appear to grow under and over each other by pruning one plant on the underside of its growth and pulling the long top growth over the adjacent plant — exactly like a bald man doing a comb-over. Keep the whole design to 5 feet across or less if you want to have any hope of reaching plants near the center without treading on the bed.

✔ **A mixed garden:** Mixing herbs with vegetables or flowers isn't a radical technique. English cottage gardeners were doing it centuries ago. Consider mixing lovage, borage, and savories with bush beans and onions; southernwood, mint, and chives with eggplant, cabbage, carrots, and radishes; monarda with tomatoes and potatoes; and, basil, tansy, tarragon, and calendula with tomatoes squash, peppers, and asparagus.

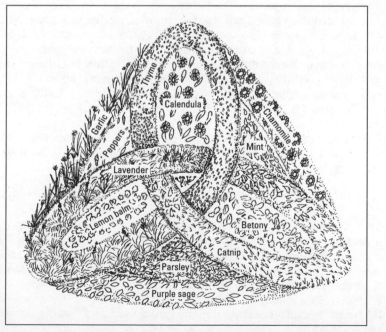

Figure 5-1: This knot design is easier than it looks.

A bed above the others

Raised beds are ideal for growing herbs. (Chapter 5 in Book IV discusses raised beds in detail and tells you how to create one for your garden.) Six inches (15 cm) is a good height for an herb bed (an inch or two lower in hot, dry climates where the soil dries out quickly); they can be any shape, but rectangular beds are the most practical.

If you must purchase topsoil to fill your bed, be aware that it usually contains little organic matter and few nutrients. Be sure to mix it with compost or some other organic matter (50:50 ratio).

Of herbal bondage: Growing in containers

Herbs adapt so well to containers (see Chapter 3 in Book II for a complete discussion of container gardening) that you can grow an impressive collection even if you have nowhere to garden but on a balcony or in a window box. Most annual herbs can thrive in pots for their brief span on earth, and many perennials (refer to Book IV) also cotton to these cozy confines.

Even if you have a sprawling estate, you should consider containerizing some of your herbs — for several good reasons. If you have heavy clay soil, pots can give herbs better drainage. You can readily move frost-shy plants (like rosemary) and tropicals (like ginger) indoors. If your herbs seem unhappy, you can instantly give them shadier, sunnier, wetter, or drier conditions. You can grow herbs with different soil and water needs next to each other if they're in pots. And if you simply don't like the way your herbs are arranged, you can create new combinations in minutes, rather than hours, weeks, or months. By setting potted herbs on pedestals, stairs, concrete blocks, or old milk crates, you can bring them closer to your nose for sniffing, to your fingers for stroking, and to your pruners for harvesting.

A pot that actually holds plants is a *growing pot*. An outer, decorative container is a *cachepot* (cash POE); you can slip a plain-Jane plastic growing pot into a cachepot for instant pizzazz.

Most plants that fail in containers that are placed outdoors do so for lack of water. Heavy spring rains can lure gardeners into complacency. This tendency is especially true with easy-going, low-water plants like herbs. Plan on watering outdoor containers every day from mid- to late-summer, more often and for a longer period of time if you live in an arid climate or if the weather is windy. (Gardeners in hot regions also should avoid planting in small containers, which dry out more quickly).

Herbs are by and large strict dieters, turning soft and vulnerable when overfed. But because most of the soilless mixes you use in containers are the equivalent of white bread and water, you need to give them some chicken and broccoli periodically. Give the potted plants the same healthy, organic stuff that you would give the herbs in your planting beds: seaweed or fish emulsion. For herbs growing in containers, use half the recommended amount in monthly doses.

A final reminder: Potting soil is like bath water. You need to toss it after it's been used (in this case, at the end of the growing season). If you're raising annual herbs, recycle the contents of your containers. As long as the plant wasn't diseased, add it and the soil mix to the compost pile. (If you're growing perennial herbs in containers, repot them, or at least refresh the potting mix they're growing in, every two or three years.)

Getting Down to Earth

We cover many of the factors that affect your herb garden, such as climate and soil, in Book I, and will only refer to those things that specifically affect herbs in this chapter. After you decide where to put your new herb garden and have developed a plan, you'll need to clear the site if it's never been a garden or if it hasn't been a garden in a long time. Clearing means removing everything, every last plant. Think scorched earth. After you clear your site, you need to ready the soil for planting, which we cover in Chapter 3 of Book I.

Digging a small garden by hand is altogether manageable, even for rookies, the out-of-shape, and the over-50 crowd. A spading fork is the best tool for this work, but a shovel or spade is nearly as good. Unless your soil is extremely heavy (clay) or extremely light (sand), you need to cultivate only one *spit* deep to grow herbs. (A spit is gardenese for the length of your fork or shovel's blade, about 1 foot (30 cm).) Work facing out so that when you move backward you don't tramp on the soil that you've just turned. If you're adding herbs to an existing bed or border, then single-digging a small area or just making a hole to slip in a clump of lavender or parsley may be all you need to do. Every time you dig, you also have an opportunity to add more organic matter to your soil. Don't pass it up!

If the soil in your garden lies at either end of the sand-clay soil continuum (see Chapter 4 in Book VII), if it drains poorly, or if it's badly compacted (that otherwise perfect site where your kids used to play basketball or your overweight St. Bernard once paced), single digging won't be enough. You need to double dig. (See Chapter 3 in Book I for instructions on double digging.)

Deciding what to grow and how to grow it

We're fans of starting plants from seed. The process is fun, interesting, and satisfying, and it's cheap. Moreover, you can get your hands on dozens and dozens of unusual herbs and herb cultivars only if you're willing to sow seeds. Starting from seed isn't required, however. Don't feel like a second-class gardener if you decide to begin with plants grown by someone else. Most garden centers offer the basic culinary herbs — basil, thyme, cilantro, chive, oregano, parsley, dill, mint, rosemary, sage, and tarragon — and perhaps a modest selection of less popular plants. We can't debate the fact that buying plants is simpler, and it saves you time.

Whether you're ordering packets of seeds or purchasing plants, let us sow one idea now: Start small. Remember that the work doesn't stop after you plant your garden — you have to take care of these herbs! You probably don't need four 20-foot rows of cilantro or 50 horseradish plants or a 20 x 20-foot bed of fenugreek. In fact, you may not need any of these herbs. Grow only what you'll enjoy and use, and only as much as you'll use and have time to care for. A weedy, out-of-control garden is more depressing than no garden at all.

Beginning seeds indoors takes lots of room. If you don't plant enough, there's always next year (with some herbs, there's even time for a second crop this year). Dying, drying, and craft projects require a hefty number of plants, but culinary herbs usually can be grown in smaller numbers unless you're planning to supply all your neighbors or to preserve your harvest. No one has time or room to grow everything, so ask yourself the following questions in order to rein in your purchases:

- ✔ **Will I use it?** You can grow herbs entirely for their own sake, but if you're the practical sort, be realistic about what herbs you'll use.

- ✔ **Will it grow in my garden?** Every herb has peculiar needs. Basil will be a bust if your garden is a large pot on a cool, shady patio; angelica won't survive in southern Florida's heat.

- ✔ **Is it too much trouble?** The majority of herbs are like good friends: cooperative, undemanding, tolerant, even forgiving. But all herbs require some care. Marsh mallow requires lots of moisture — do you have time for watering? Do you have time to start chive seeds in January so that you'll have plants in June?

- ✔ **How much should I grow?** Seed packets usually indicate how many seeds they contain — probably 50 times more than you need. Six basils aren't enough if want to freeze enough pesto to take you into spring, but six sage plants are probably more than the hautest gourmet cook can use.

Nonprofit organizations are another great source of herb seeds. If you belong to the Flower and Herb Exchange (http://www.seedsavers.com/wholepgs/Mainpgs/fhemembership.htm), a laudable nonprofit group that works to preserve heirloom, or older, cultivars of flowers and herbs, you'll also have access to hundreds of herb seeds, many available nowhere else.

ECO-SMART

For peat's sake

Adding peat is a recommendation that you find in any garden resource. It's a good way to add organic matter to your soil, but for all practical purposes, it's a finite resource. The peat you buy is sphagnum moss and other plants that have been decaying in bogs for millennia. Most scientists believe that peat bogs, once harvested, can be reclaimed but can't be regenerated. Drained bogs are unlikely to recover, to reestablish the conditions that produce peat. Even if they can recover, the time frame is 3,000 years and longer. As one scientist told us, "Harvesting peat is a euphemism for mining." Two renewable alternatives to peat are cocoa hulls and shredded coconut husks, products that are increasingly available at garden centers.

If you use peat, apply it sparingly as an additive to soil mixes or to amend planting holes when setting out individual herbs. Be aware that peat contains no nutrients and is devilishly difficult to wet. Spreading it on the soil surface is almost like laying down a layer of plastic: Water runs off rather than sinks in.

Buying peat can be confusing; you can choose from several products for sale:

✔ **Black peat, or peat humus (*terre noire* if it comes from Canada):** This peat looks like rich topsoil and is often sold in bulk. Sedge peat, like black peat, comes from sedge plants, but is less decomposed and reddish brown in color.

✔ **Sphagnum moss, or floral moss:** This peat consists of moss plants harvested from the tops of peat bogs; it's sold in small, packaged quantities for lining hanging baskets and other decorative purposes.

✔ **Peat, also known as sphagnum peat, brown peat, and peat moss:** This is the most common garden additive. Made of dried, partially decomposed sphagnum mosses, it's very acidic and can absorb 15 times its weight in water.

Book VII

Vegetables and Herbs

Planting seedlings indoors

You follow the same basic steps for planting herbs indoors as you do perennials, which we discuss in Chapter 3 of Book IV. The following list gives you some pointers about herbs in particular:

✔ **Sow annual herbs from four to eight weeks before your frost-free date.** Most perennial herbs grow more slowly than annuals, so you may need to sow them as many as 12 weeks before the last frost. (You can also find planting recommendation on the back of seed packets.)

✔ **Don't be tempted to half-fill a deep container when growing from seed.** Seedlings need fresh air, and they won't get it if the sides of a container surround them.

✔ **Don't sow different herbs in the same container.** Each herb has its own needs and timetable. Having the same seedlings in one flat or pot makes care easier.

- ✔ **Don't start seeds too early.** Seeds sown indoors sprout more quickly than those sown outdoors, and seedlings that have been grown too long indoors, especially without enough light, tend to be spindly and weak.

- ✔ **Stratify, if necessary.** A few herb seeds need special handling before they can germinate. Some species, such as sweet Cicely, must be *stratified,* or chilled for a period of time. (***Note:*** If you've purchased your seeds, any special treatments have been done for you.)

- ✔ **Sow seeds sparingly.** Most herbs have a high *germination rate* (the percentage of seeds that sprout — the number appears on the seed packet). You don't need 50 seeds to get 15 plants.

- ✔ **Label and date your seedling containers.** You may think that you'll remember what it is. You won't. When green sprouts shove their way through the soil's surface, you must be ready to give them the new conditions they require. If you can't provide seedlings with at least 14 hours of sun daily — or don't have artificial lights — you're better off buying plants at a local garden center or direct seeding.

Purchasing young herb plants is a great idea if you don't have the space, energy, or patience to start from seed. You also may not have the time to take care of seedlings. Perennial herbs, such as monarda (bee balm) and scented geranium, take a year or more before they're good-sized, so many gardeners purchase plants rather than grow them from seed.

Planting herbs outdoors

Direct seeding (sowing seed directly into your garden) outdoors is often a good idea with herbs. Seedlings with a *taproot* (a long single root with little side growth), such as borage and fennel, resent transplanting. You can start these herbs indoors, but grow them in individual containers so that you don't have to disturb their roots. Direct seeding (or direct sowing) also makes sense if you want to grow a huge quantity of herbs — few of us have space indoors for 200 calendula seedlings. In fact, many herbs simply don't need a head start. Sow most hardy annuals outdoors in spring, and they'll mature in plenty of time to provide you with a bountiful harvest.

Direct sowing is much less work if you heed two warnings: Don't sow seeds too early, and don't sow seeds too deep. Ignore our warnings and you'll be replanting. Most seeds rot if buried in cold, wet soil. Be patient. Wait until the soil warms up (70°F/21°C for most herbs). Also, don't bury your seeds so deeply that the sprouts can't make their way to the soil surface. The general rule for planting depth is to cover seeds two or three times their diameter — a little deeper if your soil is sandy and dries out quickly.

Space seeds as evenly apart as you can, but sow more densely than you would if you were indoors planting in a container. (The percentage of seeds that sprout will be lower outdoors, where you can't always provide ideal conditions.) Use a hoe or rake to cover the seeds; then *tamp*, or press down, the soil; water gently. Label.

Tending the Herb Garden

Much of the care that herbs need is identical to the care you give your other garden plants. Refer to Chapter 2 in Book VII, as well as Book I, Chapter 4 in Book IV, and Chapter 3 in Book V for more information. The following sections address issues specific to herbal care.

Wind protection

To keep your herbs — and yourself — from being annoyed, corrupted, choked, or dulled, keep your garden away from low spots, where air can pool. Cold air is heavier than warm air; that's why low areas are susceptible to frost. Pick a mountain town with "Hollow" in its name, and you've probably picked a place that holds some kind of record for a late spring frost. Poor air circulation also provides the stagnant conditions that plant diseases love, especially in humid climates. Do everything you can to ensure good air circulation. If you must fence your garden to ward off wildlife, four legged or two, don't make it a solid wall that will keep your herbs from getting the fresh air they need. At the same time, if your property is near the ocean — or regularly in the path of fierce winds — your herbs may need protection. Any garden site that regularly gets winds in the 15-mph range needs a windbreak, or wind barrier. Wind barriers also safeguard the soil from erosion and help keep it from drying out. A cold wind can annihilate a row of young basil plants in a matter of hours (or, if you're lucky, just slow their growth for weeks to come). In contrast, hot winds desiccate, or dehydrate, plants, and that, too, can be lethal.

If the wind that roars through your garden is constant, you'll probably want a permanent windbreak, such as trees, shrubs, vines, fences, and walls. Temporary barriers can tame winds that come and go — mostly in early spring, for example. You can choose from dozens of possibilities, including floating row covers (secured), wire cages wrapped with plastic, cloches, and more. Before you erect a permanent barrier, make absolutely sure that you know the direction of the prevailing winds. Put your windbreak on the wrong side and you could have cold winds pooling on your angelica and rosemary. By the way, you don't have to build the Great Wall of China. Semiopen structures do a better job than solid ones (plus they don't blow over in gales). Living windbreaks are one of the most attractive solutions, but they're also like kids' appetites: They get bigger and bigger. Plant them — especially trees — away from your garden at a distance of four times their mature height.

Book VII

Vegetables and Herbs

Dear Diary

A garden diary is fun, informative, and keeps you from relying on memory from season to season. Here are some things to include in yours:

✔ **What you're growing, when you planted it, how you grew it, and how successful you were (or weren't).**

✔ **Pertinent information for specific plants.** For instance, you may want to note that catnip took 11 days to germinate or that the chervil growing in partial shade did much better than the plants you set in full sun.

✔ **Weather and climate information.** Frost dates and rainfall amounts are important. Further, keeping a daily record of high and low temperatures and precipitation in your garden over several years will help you draw conclusions specific to *your* garden. You may find, for example, that the last frost of spring almost always comes in the second week of May. Being weather-savvy means making fewer mistakes in the garden. If you're just starting a weather diary and want to know how much rain fell last year, or when the first frost came, log on to the National Weather Service (www.nws.noaa.gov). For long-time climate records and trends, check your library for a copy of *Climates of the United States*. Scientists at the National Oceanic and Atmospheric Administration (NOAA) compiled this two-volume gold mine of facts from every state.

✔ **Yields.** Knowing that six dill plants weren't enough and six rosemary plants were too many is good information for planning next year's garden.

✔ **Notes on what's blooming in the wild.** Mother Nature may have already planted part of your garden for you.

If you leave your containers of herbs sitting outside in winter, the plants' roots aren't protected from the cold air. As a rule, you can leave perennial herbs outdoors in containers all winter if they're hardy to one zone farther north than your home. Gardeners in USDA Zone 6, for example, can leave out most thymes, which are hardy to Zone 5. (See Chapter 2 in Book I to find your climate zone.) You can give your potted herbs some insurance by burying them. In fall, dig holes for the containers of your perennial herbs and tuck them in for their winter sleep under soil and a comforter of leaves. A cold frame is handy for this, as is a nursery bed — a small tilled garden that you use in spring for starting seeds and in summer for heeling in, or temporarily planting, new perennials and other plants. One warning: If you live in the far North, you may be growing herbs that won't survive even with this coddling.

Water

Garden flowers, vegetables, and fruits require extra water when they're forming flowers or fruits. In contrast, herbs, most of which have small flowers and are grown primarily for their leaves, need even moisture throughout the garden season. Just as you need to water more in hot climates and less in cool ones, you need to water differently depending on the texture of your soil (refer to Chapter 3 in Book I). Install a rain gauge and keep track of rainfall, but don't be a slave to numbers: If there was an inch of rain in the past week but your plants clearly show that they're thirsty, water them. If you haven't had rain but your herbs look great, don't do a thing except feel grateful.

Some herbs practically qualify as *xeriscape* plants (the word comes from the Greek word xeros, for dry), camel-like species that can survive in an arid landscape. Among the herbs that get by on very little water are American pennyroyal, burdock, catnip, chicory, costmary, elecampane, hyssop, marjoram, oregano, rue, safflower, santolina, southernwood, thyme, winter savory, and wormwood.

Some herbs are willing to put up with ground that tends to stay damp — not soppy wet, or heavy, or packed. The soil should be rich in organic matter and drain well — but retain a bit more moisture than catnip or sage like. Herbs that do well in these conditions include bee balm, borage, cardamom, chervil, dill, elecampane, ginger, horseradish, lemon verbena, marsh mallow, sorrel, and valerian.

Pests and disease

Before you anticipate the horticultural version of Murphy's Law kicking in, remind yourself that herbs are among the garden plants least bothered by diseases and pests. With help from you, they'll grow vigorously, untroubled by plagues or pestilence.

Book VII

Vegetables and Herbs

Water by the numbers

To calculate how many gallons equals 1 inch (2 cm) of water, multiply the area of your garden by 0.083. Then multiply that product by 7.5. For example, if your garden is 10 feet by 10 feet (3 m by 3 m), then its area is 100 square feet (9 square meters).

$$100 \times 0.083 \times 7.5 = 62.25 \text{ gallons}$$

To know how long you need to water with your hose, first measure how long it takes to fill a 5-gallon bucket. Then divide the number of minutes by 5 to determine the gallon-per-minute rate. For example, if your hose filled the bucket in 1 minute, it runs at 5 gallons per minute, and you'll have to water for about 12 minutes to apply 1 inch (2 cm) of water (or 4 minutes of watering three times a week).

WARNING!

Can the sand

You may hear or read that you should add sand to clay soil to make it drain better. It's commonplace advice. Don't do it. If you combine the right amount of clay and sand, what you may get is a cementlike mix. Instead, add organic matter, which not only improves drainage but supplies nutrients to the soil at the same time.

Several ounces of prevention is the best and safest defense against pests and diseases — for you, your surroundings, and its wild inhabitants. The American landscape is already up to its knees in toxins — chemicals blended to combat weeds, diseases, and pests large and small. Don't add to the problem by bombing bugs and drenching diseases with more poisons. Take on some small battles for control with these and other foes, but don't engage in any all-out wars. Total extermination isn't your goal. In fact, killing everything except the herbs you want to grow makes it unlikely that you'll be able to grow healthy herbs — or anything else!

Many Americans have adopted the *integrated pest management* (IPM) approach to garden and landscape management. Refer to Chapter 7 in Book I for details on IPM. Also keep in mind that every caterpillar is a butterfly-in-waiting. Parsleyworms become swallowtail butterflies, so you should move rather than destroy them.

Good fellows

Biological controls are living organisms; using biological controls is based on the theory that every pest has a mortal enemy. It's a relatively new field of long-term pest control. The controls themselves, however, have been around forever — and many of them are already sharing your zip code. Following is a short list of beneficials that you want to keep around your herb garden. (Turn to Chapter 7 in Book I for more beneficial insects.)

- **Aphid midges:** The midge larvae — tiny orange maggots — commit "aphidcide."

- **Dragonflies:** You need water to attract these flyers, one of the garden's most beautiful do-gooders.

- **True bugs:** Believe it or not, "true bugs" is the scientific name for a group of insects, which includes predatory members that attack aphids, beetle larvae, caterpillars, and thrips.

- **Yellow jackets:** If yellow jackets nest far enough away not to sting you, leave them alone to gather caterpillars, flies, and assorted larvae for their offspring.

In addition to these small pest-control champs, some larger animals are worth having on garden patrol. We don't suggest that you import these helpers — they may be inappropriate for your location or sensibilities — but don't discount the good they can do:

- **Bats:** Forget all the scare stories about rabies — scientists say that the danger is remote — and remember that bats are champion insect-eaters.

- **Birds:** You can forgive birds a few transgressions, such as eating the cherries and blueberries, when you remember how many bugs they eat. One estimate is that aphid eggs make up half a chickadee's winter diet!

- **Skunks:** Although skunks are debatable as garden ornaments, they do love grubs. Moles are also great grub grubbers if you can put up with the lawn damage they cause.

- **Snakes:** We're sympathetic if you draw the line at encouraging snakes to dwell in your herb garden, but they're after rodents and insects, not you.

- **Toads:** Toads eat an almost exclusive diet of grubs, slugs, beetles, and other harmful insects. Encourage toads by chipping a doorway on the side of a terra-cotta pot and leaving it, turned upside down, in a shady spot in your garden.

We discuss the bad guys likely to plague your herbs in Chapter 7 of Book I. In the meantime, here are some tips for keeping the bad guys at bay in your herb garden:

- **Hot pepper spray:** Many repellents use hot peppers to discourage pests. A standard hot pepper spray consists of 1 cup of pureed hot peppers (be sure to include the seeds and membrane — that's where the fire burns) and 4 cups water. Strain the mixture, add 1 teaspoon dishwashing liquid, and mix. Keep your hands away from your face when you're working with hot peppers!

- **Wood ashes:** These discourage stem-attacking pests, such as root maggots. Spread them around but not on herb plants. Because wood ashes are alkaline and will raise your soil's pH, apply them sparingly.

- **Baking-soda repellent:** To help repel fungal diseases, such as powdery mildew and black spot, try this repellent: 1 tablespoon baking soda, 1 tablespoon horticultural oil, 1 gallon water. Mix and spray plants thoroughly.

- **Commercial antidesiccants, or antitranspirants:** These products, developed for helping plants retain moisture, also protect against a variety of plant diseases, including rust and powdery mildew. Follow label directions.

- **Compost tea:** Spraying herbs with compost tea (see Chapter 4 in Book I for brewing instructions) helps repel fungus diseases while providing nourishment.

Book VII

Vegetables and Herbs

In sickness and in sickness

The list of possible herb ailments is substantial. You can avoid most of them by following "avoidance therapy." (A 10-power hand lens is indispensable for seeing signs of diseases, as well as the small pests that can spread them.) Following are some diseases that plague herbs:

- **Bacterial wilt:** Bacterial wilts cause leaves, then entire plants, to droop and die, especially coriander, nasturtium, sage, and scented geranium.

- **Crown rot:** A fungus that attacks the base of plants, crown rot turns plants yellow, followed by wilting. Angelica, parsley, and violet are likely victims.

- **Damping-off:** Diagnosing this fungal disease is easy. Healthy seedlings — practically all herbs are susceptible, especially those sown indoors — suddenly fall over and die. You can help prevent this disease by spraying emerging seedlings with chamomile tea (steep 1 cup dried chamomile flowers in 1 quart water).

- **Downy mildew:** Most common when conditions are cool and humid, downy mildew is a particular foe of calendula, coriander, germander, tarragon, and violet. The fungi leave yellow spots on leaf tops, gray mold on their undersides.

- **Powdery mildew:** Another fungal disease, powdery mildew prefers warm, humid weather and is partial to agrimony, calendula, coriander, germander, lemon balm, monarda, sunflower, tarragon, and yarrow. You'll know it by the white, powdery splotches that it leaves on plant foliage.

- **Root rot:** Root rot occurs underground, but yellowing and slow growth are symptoms that your herb is infected with this fungal disease. Clary, fenugreek, lavender, mullein, myrtle, oregano, rosemary, sage, tarragon, thyme, and winter savory are most likely to be struck down.

- **Rusts:** All rust diseases are spread by wind-borne fungi that leave reddish brown marks on leaves. Affected plants, such as germander, mint, monarda, sunflower, and yarrow, often drop their leaves.

- **Verticillium wilt:** Common throughout North America, this fungal disease causes foliage to yellow and die, eventually killing the plant. Coriander, mint, nasturtium, and sage are common victims.

Curing plant diseases isn't easy for environmentally sensitive gardeners because only a few organic products are available to control diseases. Many fungal diseases — powdery mildew is one — spread so slowly that frost is more likely to end your plant's career than the disease is. Bacterial and viral diseases are more serious. After plants are infected, you can do little except remove and destroy them. Before you reach for disease-curing sprays and dusts, remember that the antibiotics produced in organically rich soil help your herbs ward off disease organisms; compost tea also appears to have some disease-fighting properties.

Reaping Your Herbwards

Unless you live in a very mild region, you have lots to do before winter has its nasty way with the calendula and cilantro. Foremost is harvesting. Fall is also the time to get ready for spring — to prepare tender plants for overwintering and propagate new ones, and to prepare the soil for next year. Hold on to your straw hat because the garden season isn't done yet!

Bringing in the sheaves

Just as you harvest different herbs at different times, you collect different parts of your herbs — leaves, stems, flowers, fruits, seeds, and roots — at different times. The timing of your harvest also depends on how you expect to use the herb: to make tea, for example, or to make a wreath or a nosegay. Annuals, biennials, and perennials (see Books IV and V for information on perennials and annuals) have their own quirks, but the rules for harvesting are pretty simple and straightforward.

Following are some general harvesting tips:

- **Don't get carried away on harvest day and pile your basket high.** Tightly packed, newly cut herbs generate heat. The effect is similar to what happens in a compost pile when you add a big load of fresh grass clippings.

- **Use labeled paper bags instead of a basket if you harvest more than one herb at a time.** Herbs can look alike once they start to dry.

- **Don't over-handle your harvest.** Many herbs bruise easily.

- **Don't rinse your herbs.** Dampness invites mold. Dust off dirt and dust specks with a soft brush; if plant leaves are muddy, rinse them off with a garden hose the day before you collect them.

- **Pop small amounts of unwashed leaves or sprigs in a plastic bag if you'll be using the herbs within the next day or two.** Leave the bag partly open to prevent mold or rot, and toss it into the refrigerator.

- **Keep leaves on their stems if you're going to dry your herbs.**

Leaves and stems

Don't be afraid to snap a few stems or pick a bouquet. Most of what you harvest is foliage, whether you're just grabbing a leaf or cutting armloads. Collect foliage when it's still tender. If you want herb leaves to use as greens in salads, harvest as soon as the leaves are large enough to be used. Harvest in late morning, after dew has dissipated, but before the day has started to heat up. The oils that make herbs taste and smell wonderful and work medicinally are at their most powerful then.

If you need large amounts of material for a family feast or a major craft project, you can generally harvest up to half of the tops of annual and biennial herbs. After perennials are established — at least a year old — you can take a half or a bit more of their top growth in late spring and another third in midsummer. Six weeks before your expected first frost, resist the urge to pinch more than a leaf or two off your perennial herbs. Perennials are a bit like bears and need time to collect extra "fat" in their roots to survive winter hibernation. In contrast, you can harvest annual herbs up until the moment frost kills them.

Seeds

Seeds are the real reason to grow some herbs, such as anise and caraway. With others, such as coriander/cilantro and dill, they're a bonus for the spice rack. In either case, you don't want to let seeds get away. Seeds begin forming when pollinated flowers drop away. The seeds are ripe and ready for collecting when they turn from green to brown or black. Watch, too, for seed pods to swell or change color. Shake the ripened flower head into a paper bag, and the seeds will fall into the bag. Be sure to label the bag with the name of the plant and the date you gathered the seed.

Some seeds are in a hurry to go forth and multiply and will shoot off the plant without notice. Others are hard to see within the drying flower head. A common trick is to tie a small paper bag around the flower head before the seeds drop. (Use a twist tie or rubber band to secure the bag.) In the case of herbs with only a few large seedheads, such as fennel, you can do this bagging while the plant is still in the garden. In other cases, you need to bag the head after you've cut and hung it upside down. The seeds of a few herbs — anise is one example — ripen over a period of time. Cut the entire head, shake the ripe seeds off, and let the rest ripen in a warm, dry, dark place.

If you've dried an entire seedhead, you may find you have nearly as many pieces of pod and other plant bits, or chaff, in your paper bag as you have seeds. In her infinite wisdom, Mother Nature made seeds heavier than chaff. To separate the two, pour the mixture in a shallow dish and use a hairdryer, small fan, or plain old pucker power to blow away the chaff.

Flowers

For most uses, harvest herb flowers just as they start to open. As with the rest of the plant, their freshness peaks and falls off quickly. Essential oils that provide flavor, fragrance, and healing qualities are all at their acme as the bud is swelling. Cut the flower off with a bit of stem (which helps keep flowers from falling apart) above the top set of leaves. For dry arrangements, wreaths, or crafts in which you use entire flowers, you achieve a more natural-looking result if you pick flowers at different stages — unopened, partially opened, completely opened. Harvest them with at least 6 inches (15 cm) of stem. Potpourri, too, has a more interesting texture if you include a few tight buds along with petals. If you're going to press flowers, let them open a bit more before you cut them — enough that you don't have to wrestle them to lay flat. After they've fully opened, don't leave them in the garden, where their color will fade, or where insects can damage them.

Deadheading goes only so far to retard the maturation of most herbs. Nature's urge to procreate is strong, and many plants will eventually send up so many flower stalks that you can't keep up. Moreover, in some cases, as with rosemary, catmint, nasturtium, and others, you'll want to enjoy or harvest the flowers. So if you plan to squirrel away enough herbs for several months of food or medicine, begin harvesting as early as you can.

Roots

The ideal time to harvest roots and rhizomes is in fall, after the foliage has died back. That's when roots are at their most potent. (If you forget, you can harvest the next spring before growth starts, but you may have a harder time finding the plant. In addition, the roots may be more full of moisture and take longer to dry.)

Here are a couple of rules for the underground harvester:

✔ **Be patient with roots.** Don't harvest perennials before the autumn of their second year. (A couple of exceptions among culinary roots are chicory, which you can harvest the first year before it goes to seed, and marsh mallow, which is better when harvested in the fall of its third year.) Biennials, such as angelica, begin wearing out and become woody in their second year, so harvest them in their first fall or second spring.

✔ **Dig roots when the earth is damp but not soppy wet.** Use a spading fork (which is less likely to damage the roots) and delve deep. Cut off the plant tops; if you can't use them, add them to the compost pile. Roots, unlike herb leaves, need washing after harvesting; if necessary, scrub them with a brush to remove dirt. In most cases, gardeners dig the entire plant when they harvest roots. But if you want that perennial in the same spot next year, remember to slice off a hefty section of root containing an eye, or bud, and replant it.

Book VII

Vegetables and Herbs

Be fruitful and multiply

Creating new plants from the ones already growing in your garden is called *propagating*. Like harvesting, propagating can take place throughout the garden season. Herb gardeners who want to collect seeds for next year's harvest leave several plants to do nothing but set seeds — botanical brood mares for next year's garden. Diversity is the key to a healthy gene pool, so save seeds from more than one plant. Some plants are genetically disposed to be more tolerant of drought, cold, heat, diseases, and pests, so designate your healthiest plants as "breeders."

You can easily start angelica, anise hyssop, basil, borage, burnet, calendula, catnip, caraway, chervil, coriander, dill, fennel, feverfew, German chamomile, lady's bedstraw, lemon balm, lovage, marjoram, nasturtium, oregano, parsley, summer savory, winter savory, and wormwood from seed. Some herbs — mints are the classic example — are nearly impossible to start from seed. Either the plants rarely flower or their seeds are sterile. Most variegated plants (cultivars with foliage marked with colors other than green, such as cream or white) can't be grown from seed, which is one reason that many variegated herbs are more expensive.

Collecting seeds is the same whether you're going to eat or plant your harvest. Storing is a slightly different matter. Keeping your seeds in a dormant, or inactive, state is essential. Those seeds may look dead, but the embryos inside are just napping. As with all babies, you want to keep them that way. Seeds saved for sowing need to be dry and clean, and stored in a cool, nonhumid location. Too hot or too cold, too wet or too dry and the embryo that each seed contains will either die or sprout prematurely. Your refrigerator is an ideal storage place. Use paper envelopes — don't forget to label and date them for each batch of seeds and then place all the envelopes in a sealed glass jar. You can add one tablespoon of dried milk (wrapped in unscented tissue) to each jar as a desiccant.

If you've saved seeds, you may need to apply some special treatments before they'll sprout — or sprout quickly:

- **Scarification:** Large seeds with very hard seedcoats germinate far faster if you scarify, or scratch, them. Nick them with a knife or rub them on sandpaper or emery board.

- **Soaking:** Some seeds, such as parsley and scented geranium, germinate far faster if you soak them in water overnight before you sow them.

- **Stratification:** The seeds of some perennial and biennial herbs, such as sweet Cicely, must be chilled, or stratified, in order for them to germinate. Storing seeds in the refrigerator for two months takes care of most seeds' chilling requirements.

Multiply by dividing

Dividing an established perennial herb is a quick way to turn one plant into several plants that are exactly the same as the one you're growing. Turn to Chapter 5 in Book I for instructions on dividing plants.

Common herbs that don't mind being divided include aloe, artemisia, betony, catnip, chamomile, chives, comfrey, costmary, elecampane, feverfew, garlic, germander, ginger, horehound, horseradish, hyssop, lady's bedstraw, lemongrass, lovage, madder, marjoram, marsh mallow, mint, monarda, oregano, orris, pennyroyal, roman chamomile, rue, sage, santolina, sorrel, southernwood, sweet Cicely, sweet woodruff, tarragon, valerian, violet, winter savory, wormwood, and yarrow. Be sure to get the divisions back into the ground quickly and give them plenty of moisture until they've taken hold in their new location.

A clip off the old block

Rooting cuttings is an ideal method for increasing your supply of plants, especially hybrids, cultivars whose names you lost long ago, and species that don't divide or grow from seed easily. You can take stem cuttings or tip cuttings (the green, succulent sections from the end of nonflowering stems) anytime your plant is growing actively (so don't wait until late fall, when plants are moving into dormancy). What you want is a cutting that's still growing, is firm and healthy, and is disease- and pest-free but not woody. A cutting is helpless and vulnerable once you separate it from the parent plant, so work quickly.

Many herbs, including basil, lavender, lemon verbena, and scented geraniums can root in water. Rooting in water is an easy process, just follow these steps:

1. **Use a sharp knife to take cuttings, 3–5 inches (8-13 cm) long, from the tips only of actively growing plants.**

2. **Remove the lower leaves so that no foliage is submerged; at least one or two nodes should be under water.**

3. **Place the cuttings in a glass jar filled with water and set it in bright light (but not direct sun).**

4. **Change the water every day so that bacteria doesn't form.**

5. **Transplant the cutting when roots are about ½-inch (1-cm) long, just as you would a seedling.**

If you don't root cuttings in water, you need a sterile, lightweight rooting-medium, something that retains moisture and drains well. Use a commercial potting soil mixed 50-50 with perlite, which lets more air and water reach the new roots. You also need shallow (no more than 3 inches (8 cm) deep), sterile containers and plastic bags to enclose them. (Garden-supply companies sell inexpensive plastic flats with clear dome lids designed for rooting cuttings.) Also, buy a small jar of powdered rooting hormone, a horticultural fairy dust that stimulates root production.

Here's the routine for rooting cuttings in a sterile rooting medium:

1. **Fill your containers with the rooting mixture; use a pointed stick — gardeners call it a *dibble* — or pencil to make holes for the cuttings.**

   Space the holes so that the leaves of each cutting don't bump into their neighbors.

2. **Use a sharp, clean knife to take cuttings 3 to 5 inches (8 to 13 cm) long from actively growing stems; sever just below a node.**

3. **Carefully remove the leaves from the bottom half of the cutting.**

4. **Dip the bottom portion of the stem into water and then into rooting hormone.**

5. **Stick the cuttings into the holes you made in the rooting medium and firm them in with your fingers; water gently but thoroughly.**

6. **Create a small greenhouse by enclosing the container in a plastic bag.**

   Use sticks or bent coat hangers to support the plastic and to keep it from touching the cuttings. Set the container in bright light but not in direct sun; or set under florescent lights, 14 hours on, 10 hours off. Mist your cuttings daily. Keep the bag closed during the day, but leave it open at night. If it becomes excessively wet inside the bag, leave it open for a couple of days. Check the soil daily, and water only if it's dry to the touch. Remove any cuttings with blackened leaves. Unlike Lazarus, cuttings won't rise from the dead.

7. **Pull gently on a couple of the cuttings after about two weeks.**

   If roots are forming, the cuttings will resist your tugging. When a cutting's roots are ½ inch (1 cm) long — uproot one to check — move the cutting from under the plastic, and transplant as you would any seedling.

Common herbs that are easily propagated from stem cuttings include bay, betony, catnip, comfrey, costmary, feverfew, germander, hop, horehound, hyssop, lavender, lemon balm, lemon verbena, marjoram, marsh mallow, monarda, mint, oregano, pennyroyal, rosemary, Roman chamomile, rue, sage, santolina, scented geranium, southernwood, sweet woodruff, tarragon, thyme, winter savory, and wormwood.

Pin your hopes on layering

Layering is rooting a cutting before you make the cut — rooting a stem before you remove it from its parent plant (see Figure 5-2). Not all herbs are suitable for layering. The best candidates are ground-hugging species, such as thyme, or plants like rosemary that branch close to the ground; the best time to layer is in late spring, after the soil warms. To try your hand at layering, follow these steps:

1. **Choose a long, healthy, flexible stem near the base of the plant, but don't detach it.**

2. **Starting from about 4 inches (10 cm) from the tip of the stem, strip the leaves from a 4- or 5-inch (10- or 13-cm) section of the stem.**

   You'll be burying this midportion.

3. **Use a knife to *just barely* scrape the bottom side of a 3-inch (8-cm) section, if the stem's diameter is greater than a straw's.**

4. **Make a shallow trench (about 2 inches (5 cm) deep), lay the stripped midportion of the stem in the trench, and cover that section only with soil that's rich in organic matter.**

   If necessary, use U-shaped pins fashioned from coat hangers to keep the stem parallel to the ground.

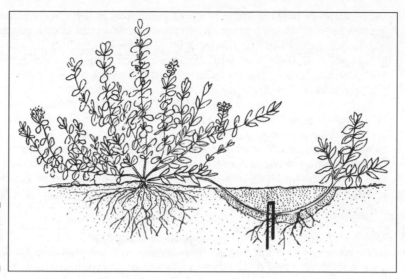

Figure 5-2:
Layering a
plant.

5. **Keep the soil moist (mulch, if necessary).**

6. **After the roots form — usually in five or six weeks — sever the stem from the parent plant.**

   You can tell whether the stem has rooted by gently pulling on it — a rooted stem resists your tugging.

7. **Let the plant grow where it is for an additional two or three weeks, and then move it to its new home.**

Mound layering is another way to increase the herbs in your garden. Choose species that have sprawling stems, such as santolina and winter savory. Mound soil over and around the base of the plant; after one or two months, the covered stems should have rooted. Use a sharp knife to detach them from the parent plant.

Some herbs, those with runners or rhizomes, are do-it-themselfers when it comes to layering. (Similar to a rhizome, a runner, or stolon, is a horizontal stem that snakes along the soil's surface.) When the nodes on the stem make good contact with the soil (especially if it's moist, organically rich soil), they root. All you have to do is to detach the new plants from the old.

Housing Herbs Inside

You can grow herbs indoors, but they're not philodendrons or even African violets. In other words, they aren't a snap to grow inside. Indoor gardening isn't harder than outdoor gardening; it's just different. You have to be vigilant: Herbs that are almost never troubled by insects and diseases in the garden are easy targets when grown indoors. As a bare-bones essential, you must offer indoor herbs artificial light. And even when you do, many of the plants will balk at confinement, like kids in a classroom. Some herbs are too tall to grow under lights; some have deep tap roots; some require a period of chilling or complete dormancy during the winter months.

With other herbs, it's a quality of life thing — for both of you. They'll survive, and you'll have enough parsley to garnish your lemon chicken but not enough to make tabbouleh. You'll have a sprig of basil to impart some personality to that grocery-store tomato, but pesto? Forget it. Forget, too, any herbs that you're growing for fruits or seeds, such as fennel or dill. Getting plants that far along indoors is impossible without a greenhouse . . . and darn hard even with one!

Many perennial herbs must come indoors during the cold months in most parts of North America. Leave them outside in December and January, and you're left with a few dead stems and a pot of soil to dump on the compost pile. Give these plenty of artificial light, and they'll struggle through winter. In their search for sunshine, many plants get leggy and impossibly tall, so prune stem tips frequently to keep them bushy. (Pinching off the ends tells the buds farther down on the branch to start growing.) Gardeners have moderately good luck with growing these herbs indoors:

✔ Artemisia	✔ Lemon balm
✔ Basil	✔ Marjoram
✔ Catnip	✔ Mint
✔ Chive	✔ Oregano
✔ Curry	✔ Parsley
✔ Costmary	✔ Rue
✔ Germander	✔ Santolina
✔ Ginger	✔ Winter savory

Moving day

Moving is a big change. When you take plants from outdoors to indoors, they adapt by producing a different type of foliage: leaves that can make sugars and carbohydrates efficiently in lower light. An abrupt move makes their current "outdoor" leaves turn yellow and drop off or become brown around the edges.

You can ease your herbs' transition by moving them under a tree, an over-hang, or a shelter of *shade cloth* (a mesh material available from garden shops or by mail order) for a few days. While the plants are in the transition area, check them carefully for any sign of insects.

You also need to reduce both fertilizer and water. Less fertilizer slows high-energy top growth (but the roots will keep growing). Drier soil "hardens off" the foliage, preparing it to cope with your home's drier environment. You can help plants adjust to the dry indoor air by enclosing them in a plastic bag for a few days — punch a few holes in the bag so that too much humidity doesn't build up.

Bright lights, big payoff

In providing light for your indoor plants, the goal is to mimic as closely as possible the light spectrum of the sun. The special bulbs and tubes sold as grow lights are supposed to do this, but they don't use electricity as efficiently as fluorescent lights. Gardeners who've tried both swear by fluorescents, which are inexpensive and available at the local hardware store.

For a full range of rays, you need two bulbs: a warm one to provide light from the red end of the sun's spectrum and a cool one to play the blues. Buy a standard workbench fixture that holds two bulbs under a hood so the light is directed down at your plants instead of out into the room. The bulbs should be no farther than 6 inches (15 cm) apart. Most of these fixtures hang from a chain or cable, which enables you to move them higher or lower. For seedlings and cuttings, the lights should be only a few inches away from the plants. Mature herbs should be about 10 or 12 inches (25 or 30 cm) away from the lights. Give your herbs 14 to 16 hours of light a day by plugging the light fixture into an inexpensive timer.

Book VII

Vegetables and Herbs

Air of superiority

Good air circulation is also essential to growing herbs indoors, where plants need air movement but not gale-force winds or even a cold draft. To encourage cross-ventilation, keep the door of the room where they're growing open. And don't crowd plants together — space them far enough from their neighbor so that their leaves don't touch. If your house or apartment is well-sealed, use a small tabletop fan to get the air moving.

Because the air in most homes is extremely dry, set your containers in trays lined with pebbles and filled with an inch or so of water. The herbs should sit over the water, not in it.

Some may like it hot, but most herbs like it cool, around 68°F (20°C) during the day. Nighttime temperatures should be 5° to 10°F (-15 to -12°C) lower. Make sure that the leaves of plants sitting on a windowsill don't touch the glass — if the windowpane freezes, so will the leaves!

Eating and drinking

Just as outdoor containers tend to suffer from too little water, indoor plants often get too much. Plants that are growing rapidly use more water, but many perennial herbs go semidormant or completely dormant in winter. These plants need much less water than they did in summer. Here are some watering tips:

- ✔ **Water most herbs only when the soil surface is dry.** Observation is key. Some plants are simply thirstier than others. Some, such as basil, even seem to need more water as indoor plants than as outdoor plants.

- ✔ **Water less often if your home is cool, your herbs are growing in plastic pots, or if plants seem to be ailing.** Rapid growth adds to their stress.

- ✔ **Don't let your plant sit in a saucer of water, and don't shock plants with cold tap water.** Water should be tepid — about room temperature.

Use less fertilizer indoors than you would outdoors because most plants are growing more slowly. Give the plants a monthly shot at one-fourth the recommended dose.

In sickness and in health

Dry heat, overwatering, and especially the proximity of their neighbors means that when pests strike indoor plants, the damage can spread like a plague. Vigilance is a must. Although the list of indoor pests is shorter than the list of outdoor foes, some of these foes are extremely difficult to control. Aphids, spider mites, and whiteflies are fond of herbs with succulent foliage and stems; bay and other woody plants are likely homes for scale. Mealybugs are equal opportunity enemies. To help keep pest and diseases away, follow these tips:

- ✔ **Keep things clean and spacious.** Remove dry leaves and other debris, use clean containers and potting soil, and clean the surfaces on which plants sit. Don't crowd plants.

- ✔ **Don't overfertilize.** Rapid growth weakens plants.

- ✔ **Isolate anything you bring indoors — cut flowers or new plants — for at least two weeks.** Isolate any herbs that become infested. If plants become badly infested, consider getting rid of them.

- ✔ **Use liquid measures.** At the first sign of pests, begin spraying the plant frequently with water, dab infested areas with a cotton swab dipped in rubbing alcohol, and try spraying with an insecticidal soap or horticultural oil for houseplants.

Chapter 6

Cataloging Herbs

· ·

*T*his chapter is the herbs' coming-out party. We take you around and introduce you to each herb one by one. After you size up their appearance, you can decide which herbs are worthy of adorning your garden. Don't let the fancy Latin names of these plants throw you off. Head to Book I, Chapter 1 for a close look at *gardenese*.

Note: Refer to Chapter 2 in Book I and the color insert for explanation of climate zones referred to throughout this chapter.

Agrimony (Agrimonia Eupatoria)

Agrimony (also known as church steeples, cockeburr, cocklebur, cockburr, and sticklewort) contain tannins, which are good for diarrhea, and mucilage that can take the scratch out of a sore throat in a gargle and soften skin in the bath. The fruity-scented leaves work well in a tea or as a garnish for fruit dishes. This 3- to 5-foot-tall (1- to 1.5-m)perennial has slightly hairy, deep green leaves that are heavily toothed with prominent veins. Each leaf is divided into six or eight pairs of leaflets and a terminal leaf, with tinier leaves in between. Beginning about midsummer and continuing for a couple months, it produces spikes of ⅝-inch, five-petalled, apricot-scented yellow flowers with blossoms that face out and up. When the flowers drop off, they leave a three-part calyx that develops into a little bur, which clings to pants and fur. Cold hardy through Zone 6, agrimony is happy in ordinary, well-drained soil, is unparticular about pH, and actually prefers a bit of shade. Its seeds can be hard to germinate, even though the plant readily seeds itself where you may not want it. Sow seeds outside in early spring and thin to 8 inches (20 cm), or start with a division.

Angelica (Angelica Archangelica)

Sometimes called wild parsnip, musky smelling Angelica has some antibacterial properties. Cooks candy this sweet plant and use it as a decoration. You can steam the stems and eat them like asparagus, or cook it with rhubarb to offset that vegetable's tart flavor. Angelica is used commercially to flavor alcoholic beverages, including gin, vermouth, Benedictine, and Chartreuse.

The plant grows up to 6 feet tall (2 m) and 4 feet (1.2 m) across. Each 2- to 3-foot (0.6- to 1-m), toothed leaf is divided into thirds, which again divides into thirds. The leafstalk has a puffy base; the thick ribbed stems are usually tinged purple. Softball-sized, off-white starburst flowers open early to mid-summer, usually in the plant's second year. Dramatic cluster-within-cluster seedheads follow; the ribbed seeds are ¼-inch long with papery wings. Biennial-like, angelica dies after it goes to seed in its second season. Harvest leaves the first fall, and roots the next spring or second fall. Roots rot quickly after seeds have ripened. Hardy through Zone 3, angelica is one of the few herbs that thrives in dank, dark, and cold. Deeply dug, loamy, acidic, and very moist (but still aerated) soil is best. You succeed best if you live north of Zone 7. Angelica self-seeds freely, but seeds need light to sprout and can take up to a month to germinate. Tamp the seeds into the soil and thin seedlings to 2 feet (61 cm) in all directions.

Angelica contains *furocoumarins,* which can make people highly sensitive to sunlight, and some evidence suggests that it contains carcinogens, so limit your consumption. Fresh roots are poisonous, so be sure to dry them thoroughly. Don't try to collect angelica in the wild. It looks all too much like the lethal water hemlock, *Cicuta maculata,* which also grows in wet places.

Anise (Pimpinella Anisum)

A member of the carrot family, anise tastes like licorice. In fact, licorice candy is likely to be flavored with anise. Use fresh anise leaves in salads, soups, and stocks, or as a garnish. Bake the seeds in breads, cookies, or cakes; stew them with apples and pears; or steam them with cabbages, onions, carrots, or turnips. Anise is a good breath freshener, used commercially in toothpaste and mouthwash. Lank and floppy, this 2-foot (61-cm) annual begins life with round, toothed leaves; but on a mature plant, the leaves are feathery and ferny. The mid-summer flowers are airy, flat, yellowish-white clusters about 2 inches (5 cm) across, followed by tiny gray-brown, comma-shaped, ribbed fruits. A bit touchy in the garden, anise won't set seed in climates with fewer than 120 frost-free days. Anise needs full sun but rebels against heat and humidity. Light, fast-draining soil of average fertility gives the best results. Shelter plants from wind and don't make them compete with weeds or other plants. Anise is hard to transplant, so start it outdoors after the soil and air have warmed. Sow seeds ¼ to ½ inch deep, and thin seedlings to 8 inches (20 cm) apart. If you live in a cold climate, try starting seeds in peat pots. In the Deep South, sow anise seeds in fall.

Anise hyssop (Agastache Foeniculum)

All anise hyssop varieties (like the one pictured in Figure 6-1) produce spikes covered with whorls of tubular, two-lipped flowers, similar to other members of the mint family. But unlike other mints, *Agastache* species are happy in a drought. This herb brings long-lasting texture and color to the garden and lends a minty-anise flavor to foods or honey. The flower spikes dry well for arrangements and wreaths, and the scent is potpourri worthy. Anise hyssop has relatively tiny, tightly packed flowers of a somewhat faded lavender that look like a mauve bottle brush. The toothed leaves look similar to those of lemon balm and some other mints, but they smell like anise when crushed. Hardy through Zone 4, anise hyssop is happy in dry, relatively poor, slightly alkaline soil and full sun (shade makes them floppy). Plants are easy to start from seed, will bloom in their first year, and tend to reseed.

Figure 6-1:
Agastache foeniculum

Basil (Ocimum Basilicum)

With more than 30 varieties, basil is a nice, friendly plant — sort of peppery and sort of sweet. In today's kitchens, basil is great in pesto and almost any pasta topping. Snip leaves into soups, stir fries, marinades, or over meat on the grill. Add the flowers to salads. The purple-leafed cultivars lend taste and color to vinegars. The most commonly grown type, sweet basil, grows 1 to 2 feet (30 to 61 cm) tall, 1 foot (30 cm) wide, and has bright green, oval, somewhat puckery leaves with serrated margins. The flowers are spikes of small, white tubular flowers, sometimes tinged with pink or purple, especially in the purple-leafed cultivars. Give basil plenty of sun and moderately rich, well-aerated soil that also retains moisture. Plants wilt easily in drought. You can sow seeds in your garden — it germinates easily — but we always start ours indoors, 4 to 6 weeks before the last frost date. Space plants about 1 foot (30 cm) apart. Plant basil among your flowers to help protect the herb from wind. A fine companion for tomatoes in the vegetable patch, basil's reputed to repel tomato hornworms. As soon as plants are 6 inches tall, begin pinching off stem tips and tops that are threatening to bloom to encourage more branching and leaf growth.

Bay (Laurus Nobilis)

A good addition to stews, soups, or bean dishes, bay is a must for Creole and Spanish cuisine. With the indoor-outdoor treatment most U. S. dwellers have to give bay, this shrub stays at around 5 feet (1.5 m) or less. Bay's narrow, pointy, oval leaves are leatherlike, glossy, and pungent. Mature plants may produce little pale yellow flowers in early summer, followed by dark purple berries. Bay requires good drainage, but doesn't mind fairly poor soil. Give your plant protection from wind and full sun, and don't let it thirst in a drought. Bay is an ideal container plant (refer to Chapter 3 in Book II for information on container gardening). You have to bring it inside during winter in Zones 6 and north because it won't survive outside. Gardeners in Zone 8 and south can leave it outdoors year-round, while those in borderline Zone 7 should sink its pot in the ground and mound soil and mulch around it to keep the roots from freezing. Bay seeds often turn moldy, so start with a small, purchased plant. Indoors, bay can tolerate temperatures from 45°F to 80°F (7°C to 26°C), but it needs a sunny window. Keep the soil barely moist, and don't feed it in winter.

Bee Balm (Monarda Didyma)

Members of this mint-family genus — all native to North America — go by a slew of common names, including bergamot and just plain monarda. Bees and hummingbirds love it, too. In addition to its charm in the garden, bee balm makes a tangy tea, more citrusy than minty. In cooking, use it with anything that benefits from a touch of citrus. Bee balm grows 2 to 4 (0.6 to 1.2 m) feet tall, has pointed oval leaves with fairly pronounced veins, and has tubular, two-lipped blooms; all a'whorl atop the stem, the flowers look like red daisies trimmed with pinking shears. You can find natural white forms; and cultivars and hybrids extend bloom colors into pink, lavender, and shades in between. Bee balm demands rich, moisture-retentive soil and does best in Zones 3 through 7. In the humid South, or when drought-stressed elsewhere, it's susceptible to powdery mildew, so buy mildew-resistant cultivars. Flowering starts in midsummer and continues for two months if you remove spent blooms. Bee balm may self-seed and spreads by underground stems, although at a more leisurely pace than other mints. Clumps die out in the center, so you need to divide it every couple of years. You can start it from seed, but division in spring is easier.

Betony (Stachys Officinalis)

Betony tea is bland, but the tannins in it are good for diarrhea. Nor will you waste your time gargling a betony infusion for a sore throat. The herb also contains some chemicals that may help headaches. Another member of the mint family, betony (or bishop's wort) is a 2-foot-tall (30 cm) European perennial (see Book IV for more on perennials). In late spring or early summer, it erupts into spikes of small neon violet, tubular blossoms that continue opening until early fall. Scalloped and hairy along the edges, the leaves are textured with veins, wrinkles, and oil glands. The lower leaves are roughly heart-shaped, while those near the top are narrow ovals without any stalks. Hardy in Zones 4 through 9, betony likes its soil deep, rich, and moist but well draining. If its feet get wet in winter, it turns up its toes and dies. Happy plants spread to form handsome mats that you need to divide every two or three years. Betony prefers full sun but can take some shade, especially in the South. You can start the species from seed or by division. Plant them at least a foot apart.

Borage (Borago Officinalis)

Borage has sky-blue blooms and cucumber-flavored leaves and stems. Freeze the flowers in ice cubes for your own cool tankard, candy them, or toss them in a salad. If the fuzz doesn't bother you, you can eat the leaves, too, steamed or raw (just be sure to peel the stems). Borage is difficult to dry and impossible to freeze. Use it fresh or preserve it in vinegar. Despite fears that borage may be toxic to the liver, trusted experts assure us that it's safe to drink and eat as long as you avoid "chronic consumption." Borage is a floppy annual (see Book V for more on annuals) that can reach 2 or 3 feet (0.6 or 1 m) high; it tends to sprawl in a laid-back mound. The leaves and hollow, succulent stems are clothed in tiny white hairs. Star-shaped, heavenly blue flowers open in humbly drooping clusters; five long stamens with black anthers heighten the drama. Borage is tough, but you still need to add well-rotted manure to your soil, provide good drainage and full sun, and prevent competition from weeds. With the right conditions, the plants will repay you by reseeding in perpetuity. Borage can be hard to transplant, so direct sow your first seeds. Space plants at least 1½ feet (46 cm) apart, and mingle it with plants of a similar devil-may-care habit.

Book VII

Vegetables and Herbs

Burdock (Arctium Lappa)

The fresh taproot has a celery/potato taste and contains some antibiotics, which some people use to treat dandruff and acne. You can dry the root to make a tea, which, as a diuretic, may lessen PMS symptoms. The herb also has a long-standing reputation as a liver tonic. You can eat every part of burdock (also known as beggar's buttons, love leaves, and pig's rhubarb), except the flowers and the bur, fresh or cooked. Scrub and peel root and stem like a potato, and use them in much the same way. If you're going to eat the stem and leaves, pick them while they're young. This 5-foot-tall (1.5 m) biennial with a root that grows up to 3 feet (1 m) has magenta, thistle-type flower heads and wavy, spade-shaped lower leaves (gray with down on the underside) that can be a foot long. Upper leaves are smaller and more oval. The flowers give way to round fruits bristling with hooks. Most people grow burdock as an annual. Give it rich, moisture-retentive, and deeply dug, loose soil. Some gardeners create a mound for it to make harvesting easier. You can dig the root at the end of the growing season, or wait until next spring, when you won't have to contend with the prickles.

Calendula (Calendula Officinalis)

Put calendula's antiviral and antifungal properties to work in oils and creams for treating wounds, skin problems, and bug bites. In the kitchen, it's known as the poor person's saffron. Use its petals in paella, polenta, and other dishes that call for that spice and you'll get a similar color, if not taste. Or just toss flowers in a salad to make it sizzle with summer color. In its natural state, this member of the daisy family calendula is a cheerful yellow-orange daisy, about 18 inches (46 cm) tall with numerous branches. The leaves are aromatic when crushed, and tiny hairs cover the plant all over. Start calendula (often called pot marigold) from fresh seeds in early spring; it germinates better in slightly cool conditions. You can sometimes sow it in the fall in the Deep South. Transplant seedlings into full sun or part shade in moderately fertile soil; space plants at least 10 inches (25 cm) apart. They're prone to powdery mildew. Calendula usually starts blooming about six weeks after germination, but it may peter out during summer's hottest days. Keep pinching off the flowers, and they'll oblige by making more.

Caraway (Carum Carvi)

Caraway is great in slaw and a must for sauerkraut and the pork that often accompanies it. The Germans still use it to make kummel, a liqueur. Try it in applesauce or apple pie, or a Waldorf-type salad with mayonnaise. You can make a caraway tea to combat flatulence, bloating, and other digestive miseries. Caraway's delicate, fernlike leaves have the same anise scent as the seeds do. When a plant reaches 18 to 24 inches (46 to 61 cm) tall — usually in the summer of its second year, but occasionally earlier — it produces white, umbrella flowers. Then come the seeds with five ribs and pointed ends. The long taproot looks and tastes like parsnip. Sow seeds ½ inch (1 cm) deep in spring (if you live in the South, in fall as well) in loose, fertile, moisture-retaining soil. Thin seedlings to 8 inches (20 cm). Caraway prefers full sun, although a bit of shade is your only hope in hot, rainless, humid summers. If you give it the right spot and don't collect all its seeds, it may make a return visit.

Catnip (Nepeta Cataria)

In about two-thirds of domestic cats, and also the big fierce ones like lions, volatile oils contained in catnip leaves induce utter ecstasy. Catnip tea makes most people tranquil or sleepy and may aid digestion. If you like the taste of the fresh leaves, include them in salads, or candy them. And if the smell appeals to you, toss a few in your potpourri. Just don't open the lid while Mitten is on the prowl. Catnip is a 2- to 3-foot (0.6- to 1-m) erect, branching perennial with downy gray-green toothed leaves shaped like stretched-out hearts, 1 to 3 inches (2 to 8 cm) long. Like other mints, it has square stems and spikes of tiny two-lipped flowers. In this plant, they're white with purple spots, blooming from mid- to late summer. Catnip likes fairly dry, even sandy, soil — good drainage is a must. It develops its pungent scent best in full sun, although some southern growers urge a little shade. Handling the plant is what releases its scent. Propagation from cuttings or root division is much easier than starting from seed. Plants tend to die out after about three years, so if you and your cat are addicted, take some insurance cuttings. Keep catnip well away from other valuable plants because they're likely to get flattened in any feline free-for-all.

Book VII

Vegetables and Herbs

Chamomile (Matricaria Recutita, Chamaemelum Nobile)

The Germans think that a 2-to-3-foot-tall (0.6- to 1-m) annual from Europe and western Asia (*Matricaria recutita*, or German chamomile) is the only true chamomile, while the English think that a 9-inch (23-cm) creeping perennial from western Europe and Ireland (*Chamaemelum nobile*, or Roman chamomile, featured in Figure 6-2) is the only true chamomile. Most people compare the scent of the chamomile flowers and foliage with apples. The Spanish call it "little apple" — *manzanilla* — and use it to flavor a sherry of the same name. Both plants look and smell a great deal alike and are used to make a relaxing tea. Chamomile does contain some sedative chemicals, and many herbalists are convinced that it's also good for heartburn. Antiseptic and anti-inflammatory compounds make a chamomile compress or ointment worth trying for rashes and other skin problems. Try an infusion in your bath if you have poison ivy.

Figure 6-2:
Chamaemel
um nobile

Both chamomiles have delicate, threadlike leaves and daisylike flowers with white rays and an endearing, cone-shaped button center. German chamomile is taller, more upright, and produces more flowers per plant. Roman chamomile has thicker and flatter leaves, but the acid test is to tear open the *receptacle* — the swelling behind the flower head — and see whether it's hollow (German) or solid (Roman). You can grow both chamomiles from seed, but the annual German chamomile is both easier to find on seed racks and to germinate. It prefers light, moisture retentive soil but is forgiving, and tolerates drought and alkaline soil. Sow in spring or fall; thin seedlings to 8 inches. Heat launches the flowering season, and you should be able to get about three good harvests every two weeks. When conditions are right, German chamomile reseeds into every nook and cranny. Fortunately, having chamomile as a companion is said to make every plant healthier. You won't get more than two or three cups of chamomile tea from a single plant, so cheer on all the volunteers. Roman chamomile, hardy through Zone 3, also grows almost anywhere. It doesn't like hot dry weather, though. In very hot regions, give plants some afternoon shade; elsewhere, full sun. Start Roman chamomile from seed, cuttings, or division, and space plants about 1 foot (30 cm) apart.

Chervil (Anthriscus Cerefolium)

Use chervil with spring vegetables for a subtle anise note. Later in summer, chervil is good with cold soups and salads. Preserve it in spreads, such as cream cheese, butter, or sour cream. High in protein and containing calcium and magnesium, chervil also goes well with eggs. Herbalists say that it may reduce high blood pressure. Dried chervil is delicate — expose leaves to high heat and they'll be as tasty as yesterday's newspaper. Chervil is an annual that has white umbrella flowers and somewhat ferny leaves. Growing 1 to 2 feet (30 to 61 cm) tall, with thin, branched stems, its divided leaves are easily mistaken for parsley's. And like parsley, it comes in both flat-leaf and curly varieties. In hot sun, chervil either goes to seed early or immediately shrivels. Plant it where it'll get some summer shade. You can begin harvesting this herb about eight weeks after germination; you can harvest continually if you sow seeds every couple of weeks in spring and again in late summer. Harvest leaves just before the flower clusters open. (Better still, remove flower stems to encourage new foliage.) Chervil seeds need light to germinate, so just press them into the soil with your hand and keep the soil moist. After the seeds sprout, thin plants to 10 inches. Chervil seeds don't age well, so don't keep them over winter.

Chicory (Cichorium Intybus)

Chicory has long been popular as a coffee substitute or additive. Some scientific evidence says that chicory is a mild sedative, so chicory-laced coffee smoothes out the coffee drinker. Chicory leaves look like a dandelion's, and have a similar taste and health benefits. Collect chicory's leaves in fall, but don't expect to freeze or dry them. If you don't enjoy the bitter edge of fresh chicory, cook them in several changes of water. This sunflower cousin can grow to 5 feet (1.5 m) or more. As it grows upward, it branches with sparse, smaller leaves, leaving its stem nearly naked. From late summer to early fall, it glows with 1½-inch-wide (4 cm), true blue flowers (ray petals with squarish, ragged tips) that often glow at dusk. Chicory's taproot can grow 2 feet (61 cm) down and 2 inches (5 cm) across. If you're going to dig its roots, double dig its bed (refer to Chapter 3 in Book I for instructions) and throw in lots of compost. It's cold hardy through Zone 3, but southern gardeners may struggle to grow it well. Sow seeds ¼ inch deep in early spring and thin the plants to about a foot apart. Plants usually flower in their second year. Some growers *blanch* the leaves — cover them with a newspaper or cloth — to reduce their bitterness.

Book VII

Vegetables and Herbs

Chives (Allium Schoenoprasum)

Closely related to onions and garlic, chives are the perfect beginner's herb. The hardy perennial is full of vitamins A and C, and they taste great. Even the flowers are edible. Use chives fresh; freezing turns them to mush; baking to crispy brown sprigs. Chives grow from bulbs (refer to Book VI for more on bulbs) in clumps of grasslike, onion-scented hollow leaves, pointed at the tip and usually about a foot tall. In midspring, on stems roughly the same height, the plants produce balls of tightly packed lavender blossoms. Hardy throughout the United States, chives can take sun or partial shade, and almost any soil, although they like good drainage. Chive seeds need temperatures of 75°F (23°C) or less to sprout, which takes two to three weeks. They're pretty sleepy the first season, so only take a snip or two. A better approach is to buy young plants or bulbs, or find a friend who'll dig you a clump or two. Set each clump (six to ten bulbs) 8 inches (20 cm) apart. To bring chives indoors for a short-lived winter crop, dig a small clump three or four weeks before your first expected frost. Pot it up but leave it outdoors for a couple of months in a protected location to go dormant (the tops should die back). When you bring it in, the bulbs will think that it's spring and send up shoots. You can harvest all the leaves from a clump at once as long as you leave about 3 inches (8 cm). Divide clumps every three or four years.

Don't let grasslike weeds get near them, or you may not be able to separate the good guys from the bad guys.

Cilantro or Coriander (Coriandrum Sativum)

Cilantro leaves taste musky and have a starring role in Asian and Latin American cookery, while the lemony-tasting seeds (known as *coriander*) are a key ingredient in Middle Eastern staples. The seeds' sweet citrusy tang adds a lively note to otherwise rather tame vegetables, such as cauliflower and parsnips. The root offers a crunchy variation on the foliage's flavor. This annual herb's divided leaves make it look very much like flat-leafed parsley. Its bottom leaves are rounded, while those near the top are smaller and ferny. Plants grow to about 20 inches (51 cm) — 8 inches (20 cm) wide — and bear flat clusters of small white or pale purple flowers followed by round, beige fruits. Give cilantro rich soil that drains readily and full sun (or light shade in very hot regions). After spring's last frost date, sow seeds directly in the garden. When they sprout in about two weeks, thin seedlings to 10 inches (25 cm). If you like, sow successive crops every three weeks into summer. Cilantro *bolts* (goes to seed) in heat, so Southerners usually plant seeds in fall and give their plants afternoon shade. Harvest plants for leaves when they're about 6 inches (15 cm) tall.

Clary (Salvia Sclarea)

Perfume-makers use clary, or clary sage, as a fixative to keep other odors on track, and aromatherapists claim that its scent (variously described as musky, balsam, fruity, and disgusting) can induce euphoria. Use it the same way you do common sage. Many people think that clary is far prettier than common sage, although they resemble each other. Its big, textured leaves turn heads at the same time that its long-lasting flower spikes draw butterflies and bees. Clary has square stems and spikes of two-lipped pale lavender-blue or white flowers. The flowers are made showy (even while still in bud) by surrounding bracts of white, lavender, or pink. The herb grows 2 to 3 feet (0.6 to 1 m) tall, bearing elongated-heart shaped, fuzzy, wrinkled leaves up to 9 inches (23 cm) long. Give clary sage average soil with very good drainage and full sun. It tolerates both drought and a wide pH range. Clary is easy to start from seed, indoors or out. Space seedlings 10 inches (25 cm) apart in the garden. After the first killing frost, cut back the plant tops. Hardy through Zone 5, northern gardeners should mulch plants to prevent plants from heaving out of the ground as soil contracts and expands during freezes and thaws. Plants may self-sow after they bloom in their second year, but collect a few seeds, just in case.

Comfrey (Symphytum Officinale)

For more than 2,000 years, comfrey, or knitbone, had a reputation as a healer of wounds, and broken bones (because its parts were so mucilaginous and sticky). More recently, we've learned that comfrey contains allantoin, a substance that causes cells to multiply — which should be good in healing wounds and knitting bones. But it also contains pyrrolizidine alkaloids, or PAs, and beginning in the late 1970s, researchers began to connect PA with a disease that causes major blood vessels from the liver to clot. Ever since, most herbalists advise never to use comfrey internally. Anyone with liver problems and pregnant and nursing women shouldn't use it externally, either. Others can use it as a compress or poultice for about any insult to the body's outer covering, from bruises to cuts and scrapes.

Erect and brawny, comfrey rises to at least 4 feet (1.2 m) tall and wide, is floppy in wind and rain, and bears 10-inch (25-cm) lower leaves covered in itch-producing hairs. The stems have pronounced "wings." Still, its forked tassels of bell-shaped flowers in blue-violet, pink, or pale yellow are hard to resist. It blooms from late spring to early summer, occasionally much longer. Large and made quite permanent by a taproot that can burrow as deep 6 feet (2 m), comfrey needs loose, deep soil, rich with organic matter. Comfrey doesn't produce many seeds, so start it from divisions or root cuttings. Hardy through Zone 3, comfrey can grow in partial shade, but full sun makes the stem stronger and less apt to fall over on blustery days.

Book VII

Vegetables and Herbs

Costmary (Tanacetum Balsamita)

Some people compare the smell and taste of costmary (or balsam herb) to wintergreen. Use its leaves in cooking as you would other mints, but with a lighter hand. Its camphor scent makes it a pleasant addition to a bath or facial steam. A perennial with handsome foliage, costmary is hardy through Zone 4, grows 3 feet (1 m) tall, is woody at its base, and forms mats with its rhizomes. Silvery hairs cover the serrated leaves, which are up to a foot long at the bottom of the plant, but less than half that at the top. The negligible yellow ray flowers bloom in late summer or early fall, and not at all in partial shade. Buy small plants, or start from divisions, setting them out in spring in the North, early fall in the South. Space plants a bare minimum of 18 inches (46 cm) apart. Average soil is fine as long as it drains well.

Dill (Anethum Graveolens)

Besides flavoring many foods, dill — packed with vitamin C, calcium, magnesium, iron, and potassium — is also a friend to the digestive system from stem (bad breath) to stern (gas). Toss it into your food at the last minute, because heat, like drying, steals its zip. The opposite is true of the tangy seeds; simmer them in soups, stews, and sauces to your heart's content. An annual that looks quite similar to fennel, dill gets 2 to 3 feet (0.6 to 1 m) tall. Plants have a single hollow stalk, feathery leaves that divide into hair-thin, blue-green leaflets, and tiny yellow flowers that appear in 6-inch (15-cm) compound clusters. The pods, filled with ribbed, aromatic seeds, explode readily when ripe. Dill doesn't like to be transplanted. Direct-sow its seeds, just barely covered, as soon as you can work the ground in spring, preferably in full sun and light, in sandy soil of average fertility. Thin 2-inch (5-cm) tall seedlings to 8 to 10 inches (20 to 25 cm). Sow more seed every three or four weeks to keep the dillweed coming. Protect dill from winds, or stake plants to keep them from snapping. You can cut about one-fifth of a plant's foliage as soon as the leaves are big enough to use. The foliage browns soon after the plant flowers (in hot weather, dill bolts quickly). Collect seeds as soon as they darken. A graceful foil for heavy leafed plants and a friendly companion for cabbage, dill is a favorite food for swallowtail butterfly larvae. Plant enough so that you and butterflies-in-waiting can both have your share.

Elecampane (Inula Helenium)

Modern research supports some of elecampane's longtime uses for respiratory distress — asthma and laryngitis — and as an expectorant. And, common names such as horseheal attest to its use by veterinarians. A perennial that reaches 6 feet (2 m), elecampane's bright yellow, 3- to 4-inch (8- to 10-cm) daisylike flowers have narrow petals, and while few at a time, they keep coming from late spring until frost. The leaves are rough on top with soft fuzz on the underside. Elecampane is at home in damp, partly shady places and is hardy through Zone 3. It's most easily propagated from 2-inch (5-cm) pieces of root — make sure that each piece has a bud, or eye — harvested in the fall of the plant's second year. Plant the pieces in containers of damp sand and overwinter them in a cool room, about 50°F (10°C); set the sprouted roots out in spring (after danger of frost) in organically rich, moist, well-draining soil. Space plants at least 2 feet (61 cm) apart, and don't let the soil dry out.

Fennel (Foeniculum Vulgare)

If anise speaks too loudly of licorice for you, try fennel, which is sweeter and lighter. Fennel is recommended for "crude" or oily fish. The stalks hold up better than leaves in cooked dishes. The seeds are popular in cabbage, sauerkraut, and potatoes. Recent research shows that fennel may actually stimulate the appetite. Fennel also helps soften skin and appears frequently in recipes for skin creams and lotions. Fennel has thread-thin, blue-green foliage on a 6- to 8-foot (2- to 2.4-m) plant, and like closely related dill, it has tiny yellow flowers in a flat umbrella, followed by ribbed seeds. Fennel is cold-hardy through Zone 5; northern gardeners grow it as an annual. In Virginia, California, and other warm areas, fennel self-seeds and is a pestiferous weed. Other than sun and humus-rich soil with good drainage, it needs little attention. Start it from seed where you want it to grow, ideally when the soil is around 60°F (15°C), and thin seedlings to at least a foot apart. Fennel may attract some swallowtail larvae, but this big plant has plenty for everyone.

Fenugreek (Trigonella Foenum-Graecum)

Walking a fine line between a bitter celerylike flavor and the sweetness of maple, fenugreek pops up as an ingredient in artificial maple flavoring, and it may have a valuable role to play in treating diabetes. Although popular in African, Middle Eastern, and East Indian dishes, cooking this herb is challenging. Fenugreek is a member of the bean family, grows up to 2 feet (61 cm) tall, and has three-part leaves that resemble clover. In midsummer, the plant begins producing fragrant, off-white flowers that can keep reappearing for several months. The seedpods look much like upward-pointing green beans. Fenugreek asks only for a sunny spot and well-drained, organically rich soil. Sow seeds in spring after the soil has warmed. Thin seedlings to 4 inches (10 cm) apart. Seeds ripen about four months after germination.

Book VII

Vegetables and Herbs

Feverfew (Tanacetum Parthenium)

Feverfew's camphorlike taste isn't necessarily a flavor you want in your salad dressing, but clinical trials have demonstrated feverfew's effectiveness against migraines. If you want to try feverfew to prevent migraines, chew three to four of the leaflets daily, but keep in mind that no good studies are available on the effects of long-term use. The leaves lose their medicinal punch when dried; freeze them instead. With divided leaves and daisylike flowers, this 2-foot (61-cm), somewhat short-lived perennial looks a bit like chamomile. However, feverfew's individual leaflets are rounded, with feathery edges, and the flower's central cone is flat. Woody at the base, feverfew at first forms a tidy mound, then sprawls when flowers begin blooming. Hardy through Zone 4, you won't have to baby it in your garden; give it full sun or partial shade, and ordinary, well-draining soil. In mild areas, direct sow seeds. In the North, start seeds indoors in March for planting out after the last-frost date. Feverfew is likely to self-seed. If not, you can propagate new plants by division or by taking cuttings (refer to Chapter 5 in Book VII). Space plants about a foot apart. Bees dislike feverfew, so don't plant it among plants that need pollinating.

Feverfew leaves cause mouth sores in a few people. Also, don't experiment with this herb if you're pregnant.

Flax (Linum Usitatissimum)

You can use flax (or linseed) seeds whole or grind them into a flour and use them in place of eggs as a thickener. Like other mucilaginous herbs, they can soothe the digestive tract and normalize diarrhea. Try sprouting the seeds for salads, or sprinkle them on cereal to add a nutty flavor. Crushed seeds are good in bread, and are used in tea to treat constipation, as are other fiber laxatives; follow your cup of linseed tea with a big glass of water. A constituent of linoleum, linseed oil is a drying agent in oil paints, varnishes, and inks. Flax is a wispy annual, 18 inches (46 cm) tall with an erect stem bearing narrow 1-inch (2-cm) leaves. The stem branches near the top, holding a 5-petal, sky-blue flower at the end of each branch. The flowers are only a ½ inch (1 cm) across, but they're numerous. Beginning in midsummer, flax blooms for more than two months. Seeds develop in round, brown capsules. Soil can't be too sandy, too heavy, too rich, or too lean, and of course, it must drain well. Add plenty of organic matter to whatever nature gave you, and give flax plenty of sun. Start flax from seed in either spring or fall, in warm-weather regions. Flax's shallow roots make cultivation difficult, so weed the bed well. Thin seedlings to 4 inches (10 cm) apart.

Be sure that flax seeds are brown before you use them — unripe seeds are toxic.

Garlic (Allium Sativum)

Among many potential health applications of garlic, the best-documented use is prevention and treatment of cardiovascular disorders. It appears to work by preventing blood coagulation. With the useful part hidden underground, garlic is unexciting in direct proportion to its value when harvested. The gray-green, bladelike leaves are solid and grow 1 to 2 feet (30 to 61 cm) tall; the tiny white or pinkish flowers, which pop out of a pointed, papery pouch in rounded clusters, are ho-hum even by allium standards. Many garlics developed for eating don't bloom at all. Provide full sun in a deeply worked bed of fluffy, generously amended, slightly acid soil that both retains moisture and drains well. Separating grass blades from garlic blades is tough, so get rid of the weeds before you plant bulbs. Buy cloves intended for planting from a garden center or mail-order supplier — don't plant supermarket garlic — and plant them, unpeeled, pointed end up, 2 inches (5 cm) deep and 5 inches (13 cm) apart. Side-dress the rows with compost and mulch to keep weeds at bay; mulch again after the ground is frozen. When growth begins in spring, pull the mulch back. Clip off any flower stalks that appear so that the plant's energy goes to the bulb. Dig garlic when the plants' leaves begin to turn brown; save the biggest, outer cloves for replanting.

Geranium (Pelargonium spp.)

Every scented geranium, more properly called *pelargonium,* is different, and not even subtly so. Some have leaves as big as the palm of your hand, sharply lobed and rough as a two-day beard. Leaves of others aren't much bigger than a quarter, scalloped, and downy as a peach. Many pelargoniums squat coyly at just about 6 inches (15 cm), while others shoot up quickly to a couple feet or more, and twice as wide. The differences in their scents can be subtle. They expect little in the way of water or fertilizer. Give them light soil amended with organic matter; a monthly diluted feed of organic fertilizer during the growing season; and enough water to keep them from wilting. They must have plenty of sun, so don't buy more than your south-facing windows or grow lights can accommodate in winter. Keeping them in pots that fit a bit tight helps restrain their growth. Don't be afraid to prune pelargoniums back — a little careful cutting will give you a bushier plant. Pelargonium cuttings can root in damp sand year-round, so you can give yourself some insurance plants or share with friends. Hardy only through Zone 10, pelargoniums do reasonably well indoors in winter. Stems of older plants become woody.

Book VII

Vegetables and Herbs

Ginger (Zingiber Officinale)

Ginger (shown in Figure 6-3) works so well against motion sickness that some cruise ships now make it available for passengers. It also seems to ease symptoms of morning sickness, and most herbalists consider it safe to use in pregnancy if you don't have a history of miscarriage. No relation to the cold-hardy ground cover called wild ginger in the *Asarum* genus, ginger has narrow, lance-shaped leaves, up to a foot long in a grasslike clump. The blooms are rather unexciting green cones with tiny dark red flowers, but both the leaves and flowers have a ginger scent. The knobby mature root has a tan skin covering a cream-colored, crunchy interior. Buy a plant or the root (called a *hand* because of the way it branches) from a nursery, or buy a root from the grocery store. Make sure that it's plump and smooth, not dry and wrinkled, and that it has several eyes like those you see on potatoes. You may have better luck with one of the green roots sold in Asian markets. Whether in the ground or a container, ginger needs loose, organically rich soil, warmth, and humidity. Set the hand two inches deep (about one foot apart, outdoors), keep the soil moist, and feed your plant monthly with compost tea. In eight to ten months, you can harvest the root. Save a plump piece to start your next crop.

If you need to keep fresh ginger longer than three weeks, peel and slice it into a bit of sherry, and store it in the refrigerator.

Figure 6-3:
Zingiber officinale

Horehound (Marrubium Vulgare)

Horehound has woolly looking stems and leaves, and a musky fragrance that disappears with drying. This perennial bears many mint family hallmarks, such as square stems and two-lipped flowers, which appear in the plant's second year. The white blooms, which appear in whorls along the stem in mid- to late summer, are followed by capsules containing four barbed seeds. Bushy and up to 2 feet (61 cm) tall, horehound is hardy through Zone 4. Growing in poor soil without much extra water, and in sun or partial shade, horehound can take over like neighbors who've heard about your new swimming pool. Plant the seeds with a light covering of soil in spring or fall; thin seedlings to 12 or 18 inches (30 or 46 cm). You can start new plants from division, but more likely, you'll need to weed out volunteers.

Many herbalists maintain that horehound is an effective expectorant. Buy or make some horehound candy the next time you're wheezing and hacking, make a tea with its leaves and flowers and put it to the test. You can disguise the bitter flavor with sugar or honey, and possibly some lemon. Don't consume too much, though, because this herb is also a laxative.

Horseradish (Armoracia Rusticana)

Horseradish is generally limited to the role of condiment, but you can eat spring leaves like spinach, or add a dab to mayonnaise-based salads, cream-based soups, and other sauces. Modern herbalists recommend it for blowing open clogged sinuses. Store harvested roots in a perforated bag in the refrigerator. Hardy through Zone 3 with roots that can extend 2 feet (61 cm) into the soil, this perennial's leaves are more than a foot long with wavy edges. As the plant reaches its mature height of 3 feet (1 m) or more, the leaves become smaller and more lance-shaped. Each tiny white flower, borne in clusters, has four petals. Start horseradish from roots in spring or fall, spaced at least a foot apart in full sun. If your growing season is shorter than 150 days, plant in fall or wait until the second year to harvest the root. Take cuttings from your harvested root and replant them for a new crop.

If you want good-sized roots, make sure that your soil is rich with organic matter, deeply dug, and welldraining. The root has brittle sideshoots, and any pieces left in the ground are likely to sprout. For that reason, you may want to consider planting it in a container sunk into the ground.

Hyssop (Hyssopus Officinalis)

Many cooks use hyssop — not to be confused with anise hyssop (*Agastache foeniculum*) — in tomato sauces in spite of its medicinal scent and taste. It marries especially well with cranberries, other fruits, and stuffing. When you have a cold, try inhaling hyssop in steam, or prepare it as tea or a gargle. For cleaning, add a strong hyssop infusion into a solution for scrubbing down your floors. Attractive to butterflies, hummingbirds, and bees, hyssop is hardy through Zone 3. Hyssop grows up to 2 feet (61 cm) tall and 3 feet (1 m) wide and bears 6-inch (15-cm) spikes of intense blue-violet flowers — brighter and larger than those of anise hyssop, up to a half-inch across with two upper lips and three lower lips — from midsummer to early fall. The leaves are smooth and lance-shaped. Hyssop needs plenty of sun to keep it from becoming leggy. Otherwise, it needs only light, well-drained soil, and a bit of deadheading and pruning now and then to stimulate growth and keep it tidy. Start it from seed (planted a week or two before the first frost date), cuttings, or divisions.

Lady's Bedstraw (Galium Verum)

This delicate perennial lends an airy note to the garden, with thin leaves that climb the stem in whorls, and clusters of tiny yellow flowers from spring to late summer. It averages about 2½ feet (76 cm) tall, although it tends to sprawl instead of grow upright, especially in a partly shady location. Start lady's bedstraw in spring, either from seed or by dividing an established clump. Space plants about 18 inches (46 cm) apart. Not particular about soil, the plants do well in sun or partial shade. The plants are hardy through Zone 3. Keep an eye open for slightly invasive behavior.

Lady's bedstraw makes a wonderful dye: the leaves for yellow and the roots for red.

Lavender (Lavandula spp.)

Use lavender in potpourris, sachets, sleep pillows, and virtually any cosmetic or cleaning agent that you want to scent. Classic companions to roses, helping to hide thorny or bare stems, lavenders play myriad roles in an ornamental garden and send bees into a frenzy. At least 25 species of lavenders are available. The plants are typically small (less than 3 feet/1 m), many-branched woody shrubs with gray-green or silvery 2-inch (5-cm) leaves, narrow and lance-shaped. In late spring to midsummer, lavenders produce lovely 6- to 8-inch (15- to 20-cm) spikes of tiny, two-lipped purple flowers. Lavenders require full sun and soil that has a neutral or slightly alkaline (sweet) pH, is rich with organic matter, and that drains in minutes. (Some growers believe that sandy, less fertile soil produces plants with more fragrance.) Buy plants not seeds (you can't count on species coming true, and seeds usually take forever to germinate), or start from cuttings or by layering (refer to Chapter 5 in Book VII for instructions). Space plants 2 to 4 feet (0.6 to 1.2 m) apart, depending on the species and how much pruning you want to do. Provide some shelter from wind to protect the flower stalks. Unfortunately, very few lavenders can survive a winter colder than winters in Zone 8.

Lemon Balm (Melissa Officinalis)

Use this delicately flavored herb fresh in salads or as a last-minute addition to foods that benefit from a hint of mint. Lemon balm's combination of relaxing and healing qualities make it a fine addition to bath water and facial washes. Despite the pretty names, this perennial is a scraggy little herb, usually only about a foot tall. Its leaves are somewhat heart shaped with toothed edges, making it look like a diminutive nettle. Sporadically through summer, it produces small clusters of yellow or white flowers that bees love. Let your fingers check for the signature scent of lemon and mint. Lemon balm is happy in any ordinary soil, although your plants will have bigger, plumper leaves if you add generous amounts of organic matter and water during a drought.

Cold hardy through Zone 4, this herb needs midday shade in the South. If hot weather beats it up, shear it back to the ground and it'll regrow. Balm doesn't spread rampantly like other mints, but it does self-sow. Remove the spent flowers if you don't want more lemon balm — or more bees. You can start lemon balm from seed, but taking stem cuttings or dividing an established plant (its shallow roots are thick and matted) is easier. Space plants about 18 inches (46 cm) apart.

Lemon Grass (Cymbopogon Citratus)

A key ingredient in Thai and Vietnamese cuisines, lemon grass's hollow stems also have medicinal properties. It contains a mild sedative and shows power against fungal infections, such as athlete's foot and ringworm, when taken in tea or applied as a compress. Lemon grass also has insect-repelling properties. This perennial forms a clump similar to many ornamental grasses. Its narrow, blue-green leaves shoot up to 3 feet (1 m) from the plant's onionlike base and are tough-textured with razor-sharp edges. The late-season flower panicles can add another 2 feet (61 cm), but only gardeners with subtropical conditions are likely to ever see them. Give lemon grass full sun and organically rich, moisture-retentive soil. Start by begging for or buying a division; plant it at the same depth it was growing. (If you're using a container, choose one that's at least 12 inches (30 cm) across.) In Zone 9 and south, well-watered lemon grass forms a clump 3 feet (1 m) wide. Yours is unlikely to be that large, but you can still divide clumps to obtain more plants. Divide during the growing season (cut the leaves of the new division down to 3 or 4 inches (8 or 10 cm) to reduce stress) or well before the first fall frost to overwinter indoors in pots. Harvest young lemon grass stalks while they're still tender.

Book VII

Vegetables and Herbs

Lemon Verbena (Aloysia Triphylla)

Use lemon verbena the same as any other lemon herb. An infusion of lemon verbena lends a squeaky clean, lemon-lime scent to cosmetics or cleaning agents. Lemon verbena is a deciduous shrub that grows to a dozen feet or more in Florida but stays under 5 feet (1.5 m) in most gardens. Its narrow, lance-shaped leaves appear in whorls along the stem and are a bit hairy. The flowers — tiny lavender tubes — appear in airy spikes but won't make the evening news. Lemon verbena prefers organically rich, well-draining soil that keeps its roots moist but never soggy. Plants rarely produce seed, so start with a purchased plant or stem cutting. Most gardeners grow this herb, hardy only through Zone 9, in a container, moving it outdoors in summer and back inside for winter. Feed plants with diluted fish emulsion while they're actively growing; be firm about pruning off small, weak branches. In winter, remember the word deciduous: Plants drop all their leaves and go dormant, which means no fertilizer and just an occasional dribble of water.

Lovage (Levisticum Officinale)

Lovage is celery to the max — both in stature and flavor. In the kitchen, use lovage stems, leaves, and seeds like celery, but more sparingly. Lovage makes an especially happy marriage with tomato. Snip it into spaghetti sauces, or use the hollow stem to sip tomato juice — or a Bloody Mary. Like celery, this perennial has the ribbed, U-shaped stems and compound, toothed leaves, dark green and shiny. The stout root is up to 6 inches (15 cm) long. The minuscule flowers are in umbels, about 3 inches (8 cm) across, and the small seeds are grooved. Plants are hardy through Zone 4. Unlike celery, lovage is easy to grow. Start it from seed, indoors or out. One plant is more than enough for the average family. Give that big root deeply worked soil that's preferably a bit a acidic and that has lots of organic matter. Site it in full sun (a bit of shade is fine in the South) where it can spread out, and top dress it with compost each fall. A floating row cover protects it from pests. Should you need more lovage, divide the clump in spring. Lovage seeds don't remain viable for long; if you collect your own, sow them in autumn, or store them in the refrigerator until spring. To produce large roots for medicine, hold back on manure (which promotes leaf growth) and keep flowers pinched off.

Marjoram, Sweet (Origanum Majorana)

A staple of Mediterranean cuisines, sweet marjoram (or knotted marjoram) is also great with squash, mushrooms, eggplant, and most root vegetables. Its clean, fresh scent makes it worth adding to homemade cleaning agents. In its native Mediterranean, sweet marjoram (pictured in Figure 6-4) is a shrubby, evergreen perennial, growing up to 2½ feet (76 cm) tall. It's hardy only through Zone 9, so most U.S. gardeners treat it as an annual. Sweet marjoram has many branching square stems; its oval leaves are gray-green and fuzzy. Marjoram's most distinguishing characteristic is the knotlike look of its buds before they open. The tiny white, lavender, or pink flowers have round, oily bracts and a one-lipped calyx with a slit down one side. Plants bloom from early to late summer. We recommend that you buy plants, because of the name confusion, because cultivars or hybrids won't come true from seed, and because wet conditions make seedlings susceptible to damping-off. Set plants in full sun, about 6 inches apart, in good garden soil amended with plenty of organic matter. After it's established, sweet marjoram grows quickly, although plants may sulk in the far South's humidity and clay soil. Begin harvesting in midsummer to supply your kitchen and to keep your plants shapely and productive. To overwinter marjoram indoors, pot up a division (cut the top back to 2 inches / 5 cm) in the fall, well before the first frost.

Figure 6-4:
Origanum majorana

Marsh Mallow (Althaea Officinalis)

Marsh mallow's ability to soothe the body inside and out has been touted for centuries. Make a decoction from dried, powdered marsh mallow root to drink for a sore throat, or make a thick gel to treat wounds, burns, or sunburns. For a face and body lotion, combine marsh mallow with rose water and lavender. Hardy through Zone 3, this perennial often grows more than 5 feet (1.5 m) tall and is covered from stem to stern with tiny hairs. Its velvety leaves are spade-shaped with teeth and several lobes. The lilac-pink flowers have brighter reddish-purple anthers and are up to 2 inches (5 cm) across with five notched petals. You get more mucilage from roots when they're growing in well-draining, but frequently watered, soil. If you start from seed, don't harvest roots until the third year; if you plant divisions in spring, you can collect some roots in the second fall. Save root pieces with buds (eyes) to replant. Set them 18 inches (46 cm) apart in a sunny location.

Milk Thistle (Silybum Marianum)

Every part of this herb is edible: young leaves in salads; mature leaves boiled like spinach; shoots peeled and steamed like asparagus; the root prepared like a parsnip. An annual or biennial, milk thistle shoots up from a basal rosette to 5, even 7, feet (1.5 to 2 m), stout and branching to 2 or 3 feet (0.6 or 1 m) across. The smooth, scalloped, shiny leaves, dramatically veined and marbled with white, clasp the stem. Thistlelike flowers are 2 inches (5 cm) across and flaming magenta. This herb actually grows too easily. It's a noxious weed in warm climates, and has naturalized in old fields and along roads in the eastern United States. This plant is happy in poor, dry soil (as long as drainage is good) and germinates from seed in one or two weeks.

Known as a liver protector since the first century A.D., the active ingredient in milk thistle seeds is silymarin. Modern laboratory and clinical studies have shown silymarin to protect the liver and help it recover from hepatitis, cirrhosis, and even the highly poisonous death's cap mushroom. If you want to help ensure a healthy liver, buy the readily available capsules.

Mints (Mentha spp.)

Mints are good for aiding digestion, and you can avail yourself of 20 species and more than 1,000 hybrids. For beginning herb gardeners, the choice usually comes down to spearmint *(Mentha spicata)* or peppermint *(M. X piperita)*, both hardy through Zone 3. Use mint anywhere that you want to feel clean and refreshed: in a steam tent or in facial lotions. Spearmint and peppermint are easier to tell apart by taste than appearance. Peppermint is stronger and has a "bite" to it. Both are perennials, growing between 2 and 3 feet (0.6 to 1 m) tall. Peppermint leaves tend to be more lance-shaped and less wrinkled; its stem is reddish, and it spreads along the top of the ground. Spearmint travels underground and may bloom a little earlier in summer than peppermint, with white flowers rather than the pink or lilac of peppermint blooms. Both have tiny, bell-shaped flowers held in whorls. Buy plants or beg some divisions in spring or fall. You can let them run amok as a groundcover, but most gardeners restrain them in above- or below-ground containers. Mints get bald in the middle, so divide them about every three years. Set mints just below the surface of moist, relatively rich, and slightly acidic soil. Keep them from drying out and prune or harvest them regularly for bushier plants and plumper leaves.

Mustard, Black (Brassica Nigra)

The basic mustard sauce recipe has been pretty much the same for centuries. Dijon types are made with black mustard seeds (the spiciest and most often grown for its seeds), milder yellow mustards with yellow or white mustard *(B. hirta),* or a middle-of-the-road brown mustard *(B. juncea).* You can also steam or cook the greens. All mustards are leafy annuals, ranging up to 6 feet tall in black mustard's case. Most have stout stalks and broad, dark green leaves, which are frequently puckered or wrinkled; lower leaves have lobes or teeth. Bright yellow flowers with four petals arranged in a cross shape appear on tall spikes. Mustard greens get hotter or more bitter when the plants are hot and dry, so they may need some midsummer shade. Otherwise, give them full sun and moisture-retentive, well-draining, slightly acidic soil.

Start seeds outdoors, a couple of weeks before the frost-free date; thin seedlings to 18 inches (46 cm) (for black mustard), less for other types. Top dress this nitrogen gobbler with compost. Plants mature in about 50 days, so depending on your climate, you may be able to plant two crops. Mustards bolt quickly in hot weather, so southern gardeners often plant them as a winter crop. (Of course, if you're growing mustard for seed, bolting is the goal.) Don't let this prolific plant's seeds fall on the ground unless you plan to start making mustard for the entire block.

Nasturtium (Tropaeolum Majus)

Although primarily used as food, all parts of vitamin C-packed nasturtium are antibiotic. Unopened flower buds pickled in wine are a substitute for capers; try the flowers and leaves to flavor and decorate vinegar. An annual vine growing to 10 feet (3 m), this herb has leaves that look like tiny, wavy-edged lily pads, each attached to its stem in the middle, like an umbrella. From summer to fall, 2-inch (5-cm) spurred flowers bloom, most often in hot orange, yellow, and red, although you can find more pastel shades. The species is a climber, but most of the cultivars form bushy mounds, perfect for containers (see Chapter 3 in Book II) or trailing over a ledge. Sow seeds (which germinate quickly and easily) outdoors in early spring, or in the South, in fall. In the far South, nasturtiums grow through winter, then fall apart when heat arrives. Provide full sun and quick-draining, poor to average soil. Too much fertilizer gets you more leaf than flower. Water well, and be greedy when pinching off leaves to munch — it makes plants bushier. Plant vining types about a foot apart, mounding types six inches apart. The climbers are lightweight enough to hang on thin wires, strings, netting, heavier vines, or to weave through shrubs.

Oregano (Origanum Vulgare)

Oregano, which contains vitamin A and niacin, is associated with the cuisines of many hot, sunny countries, and is reputed to help settle digestive problems. Medicinal plant expert Jim Duke includes it among herbs that may stop bacteria that cause body odor, although you may want to use a commercial product before your big job interview. Greek oregano is a perennial that's 2 feet (61 cm) high with round leaves less than an inch long and unexciting whorls of tiny white flowers. You can distinguish it from the wild oregano by tiny oil glands or hairs on the leaves, sepals, and stems. Wild oregano's flowers are usually pink. Out of flower, Greek oregano's most telling characteristic is its aroma. Always obtain oregano as a plant, so you can determine for yourself whether it has a pungent odor. Give the plants full sun in average, well-drained soil, spacing them about a foot apart, preferably among other perennial herbs. If volunteer seedlings pop up, pitch them on the compost unless you decide that they're as flavorful as the parent. Division is the best way to get new plants, which are hardy through Zone 5.

Parsley (Petroselinum Crispum)

Parsley is packed with vitamins A and C, plus calcium, iron, and magnesium. As a diuretic, it may help with menstrual or post-dinner bloating. Parsley is a biennial usually grown as an annual, about a foot tall and wide, with deep green, divided leaves. The leaves of the more flavorful flat, or Italian, parsley (*Petroselinum crispum* var. *neopolitanum*) look like they could have just come off the ironing board; those of curly parsley (*P. crispum* var. *crispum*) form crinkled little bunches. If you leave the plant in your garden for a second season, it puts up umbrellas of tiny yellow-green flowers. Parsley is content in a slightly shady garden. It likes cool weather, preferring full sun in the North; in the South, is needs a sunscreen. Parsley seeds are so slow to germinate, so soak the seeds overnight before sowing to help speed things up. Plant seeds directly in the garden in early spring (or in autumn, in mild climates), spacing plants about 8 inches (20 cm) apart in organically rich, slightly acid soil. Parsley is a favorite of swallowtail caterpillars; remove the caterpillars to a faraway plant or plan to sacrifice a few sprigs. Start harvesting leaves when the plant is about 8 inches tall, cutting off the outside leaves to stimulate new growth. Over-wintered leaves can be bitter, but in Zones 5 or warmer, plants survive and provide a second-season crop.

Parsley can stimulate uterine contractions, so pregnant women should avoid more than a nibble now and then.

Pennyroyal (Mentha Pulegium, Hedeoma Pulegioides)

Pennyroyal is used in some commercial product insect repellants. Try braiding some around your pet's neck or hanging a bag from his collar. Stuff some in Snowball's and Rover's beds — if nothing else, the beds will smell great. You can make an insect repellent for yourself by spritzing on an infusion, or making a lotion. If you have trouble with ants in your garden, try growing a plant near their hill. This creeper has stems up to 2 feet (61 cm) long; in mid-summer, it produces tiny lavender flowers in small whorls, 6 inches (15 cm) or more above the leaves. European pennyroyal is a perennial with half-inch leaves, while the American species is an annual, less sprawling with leaves up to twice as big. Pennyroyal needs rich, moisture-retentive, well-worked soil in either sun or shade. Start the European perennial from cuttings or divisions.

Although hardy through Zone 5, it needs winter mulch north of Zone 7. Plants spread by underground runners. It's no beauty (old nicknames include lurk-in-the-ditch), so confine it where it can hang over the edge of a raised bed or container, or tuck it between rocks. Launch the American species from seed; germination is iffy everywhere, so sow generously and then thin plants to 6 inches (15 cm) apart.

Although the herb and homemade pennyroyal products are safe for most people in small amounts, don't use them if you're pregnant. You should never take any essential oil internally, but ingesting even tiny amounts of penny-royal oil can cause convulsions, coma, or death.

Rose (Rosa spp.)

The *hips* (or fruits) of many rose species are especially high in vitamin C. Herbalists are most likely to grow the apothecary's rose (*R. gallica* var. *officinalis*), the dog rose *(R. canina),* the eglantine rose *(R. eglanteria),* or rugosa roses *(R. rugosa).* You can eat rose hips fresh, but some people are allergic to the *achenes* (the hairy seeds inside the hips), which can also cause diarrhea. You're better off using the cleaned hips in vinegar or to make tea, syrup, jelly, or topping for fruits and yogurt. Attar of roses, an expensive essential oil, is one of aromatherapy's favorite mood lifters. Use rose water in the bathtub, to splash on your face — it's soothing to irritated eyes — or mix with any other cosmetics. If you want roses for hips or fragrant petals, look to old species roses and their cultivars. Start by buying a potted or bare-root plant, and give these greedy feeders excellent drainage and plenty of soil amendments. In spite of roses' reputation as sun lovers, all of these roses — and especially the dog and eglantine roses — tolerate some shade, particularly during hot afternoons in warm regions. Give them a monthly topdressing with compost, regular mulching to keep the roots cool, and generous watering during droughts. (See Book III for more on roses.)

Rosemary (Rosmarinus Officinalis)

Medicinally, rosemary contains antioxidants that appear to put the brakes on free-radical molecules. Rosemary's signature flavor (and aroma) works best with substantial winter foods. Chop or crush the needlelike leaves before adding them to foods. This tender shrub's leaves are a shiny bluish-green on top and downy white or gray underneath. From late spring to midsummer, it produces small two-lipped flowers, ranging from soft lilac to bright blue. A typical plant holds its branches upright and can grow up to 6 feet (2 m) in warm climates, less than half that where it lives indoors all or part of the year.

Buy a plant and provide warmth, good drainage, and humidity. This combination is rare in gardens, so you may want to go with a deep container (at least a foot wide and deep for established plants). Use light potting soil that drains well, and feed your plant monthly (spring through midsummer) with compost tea. Rosemary has a long root and doesn't like to be moved, so give it a deep container — established plants need a pot at least a foot deep and wide. (Turn to Chapter 3 in Book II for information on container gardening.) Indoors, rosemary needs a sunny window with cool air and good circulation. Keep the soil damp enough that the foliage doesn't wilt, and mist the plant once or twice a week with room-temperature water. Prune off any limp new growth. In spring, harden it off again, just like a seedling, before it goes outdoors. If you've made it this far, congratulate yourself. Make more rosemary by layering or by taking cuttings when new growth has firmed up.

In Zone 8 and warmer, where you can grow rosemary in the ground, give your plant near-neutral soil, only slightly enriched but with excellent drainage. Wet feet mean sure death, but never let plants dry out completely. Rich soil makes its branches flabby and prey to insects and disease. Site it in full sun, or allow it a bit of afternoon shade if your region is extremely hot.

In summer, pick a whole branch of rosemary and lay it on your barbecue coals and/or on top of your food, so the flavored smoke permeates it. (You can try this with any herb, but rosemary's tough leaves stand up to the grill well, and you won't have to worry about the effect being too subtle.)

Rue (Ruta Graveolens)

Rue, an evergreen perennial featured in Figure 6-5, is somewhat woody near the bottom and grows up to 3 feet (1 m) tall and wide. The divided leaves are both fernlike and slightly succulent; each powdery-coated leaflet has a spoon or club shape. From late spring until fall, rue bears clusters of long-lasting bright yellow, five-petalled, half-inch-diameter flowers with a dimpled green center, followed by an ornamental five-lobed seed capsule. Rue's smell, to be charitable, is "interesting." Start rue seeds indoors in late winter. Transplant seedlings to a sunny spot with average, well-drained, neutral to slightly alkaline soil, spacing them about 18 inches (46 cm) apart. Rue is hardy through Zone 4.

You can propagate more rue from cuttings or division, but always wear gloves when you handle it. Some people react to the herb's touch as they would to poison ivy. Ingesting rue can cause powerful cramps, hallucinations, and twitching. More commonly, ingestion and even external contact can cause *phototoxicity* — ultrasensitivity to the sun — leading to severe burns and blisters.

Figure 6-5:
Ruta graveolens

Saffron (Crocus Sativus)

The "threads" of saffron are the stigmas from the heart of this fall-blooming crocus. Each flower has only three, so it takes some 60,000 blossoms to make a pound of this golden spice. Speaking of threads, saffron has been used as a dye since ancient times. Modern studies link its active ingredient, crocetin, to reduced risks of cardiovascular disease. The saffron crocus blooms in September. The 2-inch (5-cm), rich lilac-colored flowers have darker veins and throats. The long bright orange-red stigma may poke out of the blooms when they close at night. Give your crocuses light, gritty soil of average fertility. They prefer full sun, but will bloom with five hours of sun daily. Crocuses grow from *corms* (a modified bulb), which you should plant in spring or early summer. (Book V covers bulbs.) Set the corms 3 to 4 inches (8 to 10 cm) deep and 6 inches (15 cm) apart. You can provide a nutritional boost with a little rock phosphate, but put a layer of soil between corm and fertilizer so that your corm won't burn. Plants do best in Zones 5 to 8, disliking both cold, wet climates and hot, humid ones. If you collect the stigmas, handle them gingerly, dry with utmost care, and keep them in a stoppered glass vial in a cool place.

Book VII

Vegetables and Herbs

Sage (Salvia Officinalis)

Sage can act as an antiperspirant. Try applying an infusion externally or drinking some sage tea (if you can wait — it's not effective for two hours). Containing both astringents and antiseptics, it's often recommended for oral hygiene (just rub a fresh leaf over tooth and gum), as a mouthwash to prevent gum disease and bad breath, or as a gargle for sore throats. As for aromatic appeal, sage shouts "Thanksgiving." Sage is a hardy *subshrub* (woody at the bottom, with softer new growth above). Where happy, it grows 3 feet (1 m) tall and wide. The elongated oval leaves grow up to 3 inches (8 cm) long, pebbly in appearance and sandpapery to the touch; their hue is grayer in dry climates, greener in humid ones. Sage's late spring racemes of blue-violet flowers make this herb worth growing. Buy a plant or two, and give sage full sun and organically rich, slightly acidic, well-draining soil. Regular pruning keeps plants from becoming leggy (use stem cuttings to produce new plants). In winter, poor drainage is invariably fatal (with protection, common sage should survive winter as far north as Zone 5). Sages that are three or four years old are less vigorous, but even one old stalwart plant usually provides more than enough of this strong-flavored herb. Sage's high oil content makes it tricky to preserve. Make sure that it's completely dry before you store your harvest.

Santolina (Santolina Chamaecyparissus)

Santolina's knock-out camphor aroma ends any temptation to eat it, but you may find that it discourages moths. Try a sprig (or a bag of clippings) in your drawers and closets. A small, Mediterranean, evergreen shrub with silvery white leaves, santolina can grow up to 2 feet (61 cm) tall and up to twice as wide. It's crowned with little yellow button flowers from early to midsummer. Start with plants and provide slightly alkaline soil. Drainage is the crucial factor — santolina abhors dampness in the soil or the air. Prune in early spring and again after flowering so that plants, which are hardy through Zone 6, maintain their shape and don't become too woody.

Savory, Summer and Winter (Satureja Hortensis; S. Montana)

Winter savory has some mild antibacterial and gas-squelching properties, which works out well because this herb has a particular affinity for beans of all types. It combines the tastes of mint and thyme. Both of these herbs have needlelike leaves up to 1 inch (2 cm) long, erect stems, and whorls of blossoms summer through fall. Summer savory *(S. hortensis)*, which has the more delicate aroma and flavor of the two, is a rather slumping annual, growing to 18 inches (46 cm), with abundant, but tiny, pale pink flowers hunkering down in the leaf axils. The gray-green, downy leaves often turn purple in fall. Winter savory, *S. montana,* is a semievergreen perennial or subshrub, growing about a foot tall. The white to pale purple flowers often have purple spots on their lower lips, and bloom on spikes. The dark green, glossy leaves have a more peppery flavor than the annual species. It can be short-lived (although hardy through Zone 4), so take cuttings or make divisions during its second or third year so that you won't be without plants. You can start either type of savory from fresh seeds, sown indoors or out, but we recommend that you buy winter savory plants. Space either species about a foot apart in well-drained, neutral to slightly acid soil of average fertility. Summer savory wilts quickly in droughts — so be sure that its soil is rich in moisture-retaining organic matter — and bolts quickly in hot weather. Prune winter savory often to keep it producing new foliage.

Sorrel (Rumex spp.)

This genus has some 200 species, many of which are called either sorrel or dock, or in one instance, sorrel dock. Popular as a laxative, its tannins also prevent diarrhea. Oxalic acid gives sorrel a slightly sour taste, but the two species most commonly used for cooking are garden sorrel *(Rumex acetosa)* and French sorrel *(R. scutatus)*. You can cook the leaves (which are high in vitamin C, and contain vitamin A, calcium, phosphate, potassium, and magnesium) like spinach, or use them fresh in salads. Sorrel forms clumps of lance-shaped, wavy edged leaves that look a bit like spinach. In mid- to late summer, star-shaped flowers — first greenish and then flushed with purple or rust, followed by dark brown *achenes,* or fruits — whorl densely around spikes. The reddish-brown taproot, up to a foot long, is yellow inside. Garden, or common, sorrel has stems up to 3 feet (1 m) tall from clumps of 5- to 8-inch (13- to 20-cm) leaves, whereas French sorrel tends to form mats, 6 to 20 inches (15 to 51 cm) tall and twice as wide, with thick, broad leaves only 1 to 2 inches (2 to 5 cm) long. Sorrels are easy to start from seed, indoors or out. Space plants 8 inches (20 cm) apart in the garden in deeply dug, organically rich soil. Sorrels tolerate partial shade but not drought; most plants aren't long-lived but are root hardy through Zone 4. Pinch off flower heads to keep new foliage coming and to prevent self-sowing. Not only do plants seed generously, but their deep taproots can also be difficult to dislodge. Try it in a deep container.

Southernwood (Artemisia Abrotanum)

Southernwood repels moths and bees — a good thing to remember when choosing a spot for it in your garden. Southernwood also has antiseptic properties, so consider mixing it with oatmeal for a facial mask. Most species dry well for potpourri and crafts. Most artemisias have insignificant flowers and are grown for their aromatic, delicate, divided foliage. Southernwood is a woody perennial that grows to 3 to 4 feet (1 to 1.2 m) tall and about as wide, with finely divided gray-green leaves up to 2 inches (5 cm) long. You can barely discern individual leaves for all their threadlike lobes, which are gray underneath and somewhat hairy, especially on new growth. The almost invisible late summer flowers are dingy yellow on 4- to 12-inch (10- to 30-cm) long panicles. Start southernwood from a plant or a cutting — semihard stems root easily — spacing plants at least 2 feet (61 cm) apart. As long as they have good drainage, artemisias adapt well to any soil. They don't like wet winters or humid summers, but they tolerate light shade and drought. Prune southernwood — hardy through Zone 5 with winter protection — in spring to keep it from looking weedy.

Sweet Cicely (Myrrhis Odorata)

Sweet Cicely tastes like lovage combined with anise. Cook the root like other root vegetables, or eat the breath-freshening seeds out of hand. Add the seeds and/or chopped leaves to fruit salad or stewed fruits or baked goods. This perennial looks for all the world like a big, bright green fern, growing as tall as 4 feet (1.2 m). Its thick stems are hollow and slightly hairy; the leaves are white and downy underneath. Clusters of white flowers, similar to Queen-Anne's lace, appear in late spring or early summer. Sweet Cicely has a long taproot and thrives in woodland conditions, which means that plants need some shade and deep, humus-rich, moisture-retentive soil. It's rarely happy in the Deep South because it can't take the heat. If you saved your own seeds, refrigerate them for two or three months before sowing or sow them in the fall. Space plants 3 feet (1 m) apart. Don't let plants dry out, and remove flower heads to prevent self-sowing. Hardy through Zone 3, this herb is a great naturalizer.

Sweet Woodruff (Galium Odoratum)

This delicate herb's claim to fame is as the flavoring agent in May wine. The honey-and-vanilla-scented herb smooths the immature grapes' rough edges. The aroma is barely detectable until the foliage dries. Sweet woodruff's fragrance is produced by a chemical called coumarin, which is used in perfumery for its own sake as well as to "fix" other scents. This perennial's lance-shaped leaves march up its stem in whorls 1 to 2 inches (2 to 5 cm) across. A tough groundcover that creeps along the ground on horizontal stems, the plant rarely reaches more than 8 or 9 inches (20 or 23 cm) tall. From late spring to midsummer, it produces clouds of fragrant, white star-shaped flowers. Purchase plants and provide this woodland native, hardy through Zone 3, with a bit of shade and humus-rich soil that doesn't dry out. Divide plants in spring (make sure that each division has a piece of the crown with some root attached) or propagate from stem cuttings.

Sweet woodruff has been found to cause liver damage in laboratory animals, and large amounts can trigger dizziness and vomiting. You can employ it in a Maibowle, however, by steeping a couple sprigs in white wine for a day or two. (Most people use an inexpensive Rhine wine; it won't improve your best Pouilly-Fuisse one whit.)

Tansy (Tanacetum Vulgare)

Tansy has arching stems that form a mound of finely divided, fernlike leaves; plants reach 2 to 3 feet (0.6 to 1 m) tall, about 18 inches (46 cm) wide. Also called golden buttons for its 4-inch (10 cm), flat-topped clusters of ½-inch (1 cm) yellow knobs that appear from late summer through fall, this perennial looks much like feverfew. The entire plant smells of camphor. Spreading by underground rhizomes, this herb is easier to grow than to control. You should have no problem starting it from seed or from divisions from a neighbor who has way too much. Give tansy a home in a naturalized or contained area — plants are unparticular about soil but need good drainage and plenty of sun — where you can enjoy its graceful form and cheerful flowers.

Tansy is now considered far too strong and potentially toxic to be used in home remedies. If you're not pregnant, it's probably safe in small amounts as a seasoning. Remember that a little goes a long way.

Book VII

Vegetables and Herbs

Tarragon, French (Artemisia Dracunculus var. Sativa)

No Hollandaise, Béarnaise, or sauce tartare is complete without this herb, which is also a standard ingredient in the herb mix known as fines herbes and among the most popular herbs for herbal vinegar. This perennial doesn't look a thing like most other artemisias: Its 1- to 3-inch (2- to 8-cm), bluish green leaves aren't divided, but look more like blades of grass. Tarragon grows up to 2 feet (61 cm) tall with somewhat lax stems. Tiny yellow-green flowers rarely open and are almost always sterile. Always buy tarragon as a plant, either at a local market where you can do a scratch and sniff, or from a mail-order supplier you trust. One plant is enough. Give it full sun (perhaps a little afternoon shade in hot regions) and organically rich, well-worked soil that drains well. Lightly prune periodically, and provide a loose mulch during the winter months. Divide your plant every two or three years to keep its long fibrous roots from tangling and committing suicide. Tarragon is hardy through Zone 4.

Thyme (Thymus spp.)

Thyme contains a powerful antiseptic, *thymol,* that you can find in mouthwashes and other commercial products. The same properties make it a good face-lotion ingredient. Europeans use it for respiratory ailments; it seems to ease the spasms of coughs. Try sipping thyme tea, make a thyme syrup, or make a towel "tent" and inhale its steam. As an antispasmodic, it may relieve menstrual cramps or an upset stomach. Thyme has about 350 species — all evergreen perennials and subshrubs in the mint family — plus scores of subspecies and cultivars. Most cooks grow common or English thyme (*Thymus vulgaris*). As a rule, common thyme grows 12 to 18 inches (30 to 46 cm) tall, spreading as it ages. The base is woody and the branches upright with gray-green, oval or slightly lance-shaped leaves up to a half inch long. Bees love the small tubular pink or lilac flowers that cluster in early to midsummer. Common thyme's scrubby shape makes it good as a low hedge. Other thymes, known collectively as "creeping thymes," make ideal ground covers, are elegant in pots or window boxes, and are charming tucked between rocks or stepping stones. Thyme, which is hardy through Zone 4, is so easy to propagate from cuttings or divisions that few gardeners start from seed (although that's easy, too). Space plants 6 to 8 inches (15 to 20 cm) apart in light soil that has been enriched with organic matter. Harvesting with abandon to keep new growth coming. Divide, layer, or take cuttings every two to three years, when plants get sparse and woody in the center.

Valerian (Valeriana Officinalis)

Valerian's flowers smells sort of like sweet gym socks. Cats are said to like it as much as catnip; it's also irresistible to rats. The valium of the herb world, valerian — also known as all heal — calms the agitated and helps insomniacs nod off with no morning-after "hangover." It's been used to cure nervous disorders, cramps, and vertigo, to stop seizures, to reduce pain, to treat venomous bites, and to heal wounds. Almost never found in home kitchens, valerian extracts are used commercially to flavor ice cream, baked goods, condiments, soft drinks, liqueurs, and tobacco. This perennial, hardy to Zone 3, grows to 5 feet (1.5 m) tall. The tall stems, produced from a rosette of foliage in the second year, are hollow and grooved, branching with rows of toothed, dark green leaves set along the stems like ladder rungs. Both leaves and stems emit the signature aroma when touched. The herb's tiny white or pink flowers are arranged in flat clusters and appear from mid-spring until late summer. Start with plants spaced 18 inches (46 cm) apart and provide organically rich, moist, slightly acid soil, either in sun or partial shade. Plants sometimes self-sow, so you many want to remove spent blooms. Keep plants healthy by dividing them in spring every three years or so. Harvest valerian roots in their second fall. Their scent gets stronger as the root dries, and valerian tea is bitter. We prefer to admire the plant in the garden and buy stress-reducing valerian capsules if needed.

Violet (Viola Odorata)

You can toss violet flowers into salads and fruity drinks, candy them for desserts, or freeze them in ice cubes. Violet water, like rose water, adds subtle flavor to fruit salads and baked goods. Herb expert Jim Duke maintains that violet tea may help prevent varicose veins because it contains a compound called rutin that helps strengthen the walls of blood vessels. Some people believe that the scent of the flowers is so strong that the nose shuts down from sensory overload after a few seconds. The sweet violet (also known as the English violet, garden violet, and common violet) grows to 6 or 7 inches (15 or 18 cm) tall and a foot wide in a mound of kidney- or heart-shaped leaves that rise out of a tuft of roots. The ¾-inch flowers have five petals and are usually purple but occasionally pink or white. The perennial's runners root at their tips. Begin with divisions, either in fall or early spring. Space plants 18 inches (46 cm) apart, and give them organically rich soil and partial shade, especially in warm regions. Violets grow best in cool weather; red spider mites tend to plague plants where conditions are hot and dry.

Book VII

Vegetables and Herbs

Watercress (Nasturtium Officinale)

Watercress, a perennial member of the mustard family, contains vitamin C and has a slightly shocking flavor. Hardy through Zone 4, plants creep along for a way, then stick up 12-inch (30-cm) stems. The dark glossy leaves are compound, with oval or heart-shaped leaflets; the small, white, four-petalled flowers, which are borne in flat-topped clusters, bloom from late spring through summer. Watercress is unusual even among water plants for preferring moving rather than still water. It's at home in a cleared area along a natural streambank (be sure that the water isn't polluted). If you've built your own back-yard pond, grow it in a container placed where the pond's waterfall or fountain creates some gentle turbulence. Buy watercress at the supermarket, take cuttings, and root them in wet soil. (Chapter 5 in Book VII tells you how to take root cuttings.) You can also grow watercress by submerging clay pots in large tubs of water. To make the plants believe that they're in running water, run a hose into the tub for several hours at least four times a week.

Wormwood (Artemisia Absinthium)

Wormwood contains large amounts of thujone (also found in sage and tansy), which may work in the brain in the same manner as THC, the active substance in marijuana. Use it only externally, in a compress to relieve pain and kill germs. It contains antiseptics and also seems to act as an anesthetic and anti-inflammatory. The camphorous scent may help drive moths from your closet. Hardy through Zone 3, this Mediterranean perennial averages 3 feet (1 m) tall and 2 feet (61 cm) wide. It has a woody base and forms a sprawling mound of silver-green with deeply divided, pungent leaves that are covered with silky hairs. In summer, plants produce upright panicles of small yellow and gray flowers. Like other artemisias, wormwood looks delicate but grows tough. Start the seeds indoors and then transplant them, keeping in mind their slow but inevitable spread, or propagate new plants from divisions or cuttings.

You may want to site wormwood away from other plants, especially expensive specimens. Absinthin, one of the compounds that gives the herb its bitter taste, is toxic to some other plants, stunting them or killing them outright.

Yarrow (Achillea Millefolium)

The chemistry of yarrow plants varies immensely, but some scientific evidence that the herb contains blood-clotting and anti-inflammatory compounds — plus anecdotal accounts from friends — would prompt us to try a yarrow poultice if we had an accident in the garden. A perennial in the daisy family, yarrow grows upright to 3 feet (1 m) tall, and bears leaves up to 6 inches (15 cm) long that are so feathery they look like they belong in a hatband. The white flowers — occasionally pink — appear in 3-inch (8-cm) flat clusters in late summer. How to control may be a better question than how to grow. Yarrow has naturalized throughout North America — in old farm fields and along roadsides — and it may romp all over your garden if not there already. Impressively drought tolerant and hardy through Zone 3, yarrow will be happy and healthy if it has sun and enough soil in which to sink its roots. Seeds germinate quickly, or you can begin with divisions or purchased plants. To keep the flowers coming, deadhead your plants. If you really need more yarrow, divide. Dividing, which is the only way to propagate yarrow cultivars, also makes your plants more vigorous.

Index

• D •